The Good Skiin⌣
& Snowboarding
Guide **2001**

SKI CLUB OF GREAT BRITAIN
HALF-PRICE
MEMBERSHIP OFFER
(see page 11)

The Good Skiing & Snowboarding Guide **2001**

Edited by

Peter and Felice Hardy

in association with the
Ski Club of Great Britain

CONSUMERS' ASSOCIATION

Email address
You can now send your resort reports by email to:
goodskiandsnowguide@which.net

Introduction

The 1999–2000 season was a vintage one throughout much of Europe and North America. In Europe the snow fell in early December and, with frequent top-ups, lasted well beyond what was the latest Easter in many years. However, for the second successive year, Italy and a corner of France suffered from poor cover for most of the season with the Sella Ronda, the Milky Way and Serre Chevalier most affected. Unusually high winds buffeted the Alps on several occasions, most spectacularly at Christmas and New Year when a wind speed of 240kph (149mph) was recorded on La Solaise above Val d'Isère. Some parts of North America had a sparse start to the season, with resorts in Colorado and California struggling to provide sufficient open trails at Christmas; but they recovered well to finish the winter with an ample amount of snow.

Last season many skiers and snowboarders were deterred by the outrageous prices demanded by tour operators and hotels over the Millennium or by an Easter that fell so late that many resorts had already closed their lift systems.

In 2001 Easter falls one week earlier (15 April). Expect to pay the highest prices at New Year, during high-season February and at British half-term (the week beginning 17 February), which coincides with President's Weekend (17–19 February) in the United States. The French school holidays are staggered by zones but this does not eliminate overcrowding on the slopes. It is advisable to avoid the winter Paris holidays (10–26 February) and to a lesser extent the spring break (7–24 April). Visitors to the French Dauphiné (including Alpe d'Huez and Les Deux Alpes), resorts in the French Pyrenees (including Barèges) and Andorra should be aware of the Grenoble and Toulouse school dates (3–19 February and 31 March –17 April).

Awards and influence

Once again we have awarded the Golden Ski Award to those resorts, establishments and organisations that we feel have excelled themselves in the past season. At the same time we have given the infamous Broken Ski Award to those who have, in the opinion of our readers, contributors and reporters, failed to sharpen their edges.

Over the past 15 years *The Good Skiing & Snowboarding Guide* (originally *The Good Skiing Guide*) has established a reputation as the 'bible' of the ski industry. However, while readers appreciate our forthright and sometimes highly critical comments on resorts, the book is not always so well received by the resorts themselves. Tourist directors, who are used to the kind of promotional travel journalism that is prevalent in the rest of Europe and in the United States, angrily protest when we dare to question their stated number of runs or adversely comment on ancient lifts, poor hotels and ugly architecture.

7

It is therefore particularly satisfying for us and our reader-reporters when the Guide is instrumental in bringing about improvements. For years we have criticised Zermatt's Swiss Ski School (SSS),which is the subject of more letters of complaint than any other in the Alps. In the last edition of the Guide we awarded it a Broken Ski Award for the Most Outmoded Ski School for continuing to operate as 'a jobs-for-life co-operative with no true procedure for dismissal and no compulsory retirement age. As a result 10 per cent of teachers are over 65 – and one is 83'.

The consequent publicity for the award in the Swiss media has shamed Zermatt into allowing the school's monopoly to be broken. This season a rival, The Ski School, an offshoot of the resort's already successful Stoked snowboard school, is being established. Classes will be limited to 8 pupils and teachers will be no older than 40. Faced with such dynamic competition the SSS must pull up its ski socks or hang up its boots. If the Zermatt chapter in the 2002 edition sports a * for Beginners, it will be entirely thanks to our readers.

Peace on the piste

The Twenty Year War with France is officially over. Not only can British ski instructors now teach legally in Europe, but suddenly the BASI (British Association of Snowsports Instructors) qualification is the most sought-after in the world. Thanks to the dogged perseverance of a handful of Scottish skiers, top British teachers are set to earn up to £2,000 a week on the slopes of Courchevel and Val d'Isère, and expert skiers from other countries – including France – are clamouring to gain the British qualification that is the passport to potential piste riches. For British skiers and snowboarders the benefit of the agreement is inestimable: instruction in your own language from a native English speaker dramatically shortens the learning curve.

In the past, the bitter dispute over France's failure to recognise BASI's top qualification (because it did not include racing ability) led to the occasional British instructor being arrested in front of his or her ski class and even temporarily jailed as the French tried to enforce their position. A few Britons did pass the infamous *équivalence* test giving them equality with French instructors, but most holders of the top badge were left with an essentially Scottish qualification that had precious little application for a financially rewarding career outside the Highlands and Andorra.

Now the different systems have been harmonised and representatives from BASI sit beside those from France, Austria and Italy on the governing board of European ski instruction that decides who can and who cannot teach skiing and snowboarding in those countries. The price of victory was a retention of a milder form of race test for the joint qualification, but as one senior BASI instructor put it: 'with us on the judging panel the test is a fair one. No longer are the dice loaded against the British'. The net result is that anyone who passes the new BASI test for Alpine National Ski Teacher (it used to be called BASI I) is licensed to teach anywhere in Europe with the blessing of all national bodies.

However, peace between the opposing teams of professionals does not affect the parallel long-running dispute between British tour operators and the French authorities over the use of unqualified British ski 'guides' who lead their clients around the piste (see *Insurance*). But, for the moment at least, the issue has been brushed to the shadows in the light of this new *entente cordiale*. Hats off to BASI.

Children ski free

Saas-Fee is a smart, charming and essentially staid little Swiss resort that is not known for its spirit of innovation. Indeed, the five families who own and run just about every business in the town are positively resistant to change. During the 1999–2000 season they got cold feet and, at the eleventh hour, broke their contract with 1,500 British university students who had spent two years planning their ski and snowboard championships here. Perhaps the prospect of the inevitable inebriated behaviour was simply too much to stomach – although they should have thought of that before signing on the dotted line. Therefore, it is all the more remarkable that Saas-Fee should be breaking new ground this year with such a daring marketing move that other resorts may have little choice but to follow in its tracks. From 1 December 2000 children under the age of 16 can ski for free. This sensational offer represents a saving on lift passes of SF486 (about £186) for a family with three children. Of course, there is a catch: both parents must buy a minimum six-day lift pass or five-out-of-seven-day pass; it is not valid for groups or for season passes. But none of the restrictions is liable to affect families planning a one- or two-week holiday in a resort that will undoubtedly become a top destination.

Fresh air in the Alps

To the chagrin of most skiers and snowboarders, the Mont Blanc Tunnel is scheduled to re-open in March 2001 having been rebuilt at an estimated cost of £120 million. Chagrin? Since its closure after the tragic fire in March 1999 in which 39 people died, the beautiful Chamonix Valley has rediscovered its natural tranquillity, which disappeared when General de Gaulle opened the tunnel in 1965. The valley road is no longer choked day and night by international pantechnicons. The 619 inhabitants of the village of Servoz below the French mouth of the tunnel have – quite literally – been breathing a collective sigh of relief. The poisonous yellow layers of diesel pollution that hung over their homes have dissipated and they can again see the peak of Mont Blanc. Up on the mountain skiers, too, look forward this winter to a third season of inhaling sweet fresh air. In time, the pine forests on the lower slopes might recover from 35 years of acid rain.

Of course, there have been disadvantages for snow-users from the closure. Skiers and snowboarders in Chamonix and Courmayeur can no longer make use of their reciprocal lift passes. Courmayeur has been temporarily robbed of its cosmopolitan status and has returned to being the parochial and essentially Italian resort that it was before 1965.

However, this is tempered by the dramatic absence of traffic noise and air pollution. Anti-tunnel campaigners have been vociferous, but their voice is inevitably drowned by the roar of international commerce. Both the French and Italian governments have vowed to increase the amount of freight carried by the alternative Fréjus tunnel, and plans to build a new dedicated freight tunnel at a cost of £3.6 billion are on the EC drawing board. Nevertheless, the re-opening of the Mont Blanc Tunnel will be a sad day for skiers and snowboarders.

Cable-car blues

Cramming uncomfortably into cable-cars is an accepted part of a skier's day. Enjoyment (or lack of it) depends largely on which country you have chosen for your holiday. The Italians sing or shout cheerfully at their friends, while the Austrians and the Swiss talk quietly to each other. North Americans listen to the driver lecturing them on the terrain they are about to face, while the French stand in silence. However, a new hazard is not being taken into account by lift operators who are anxious to maximise uphill revenue. Backpacks, once the preserve of the mountain guide or serious off-piste skier, are now carried by up to 25 per cent of skiers. Tempers fray and ribs are bruised as the doors are squeezed closed on conditions that no animal would be allowed to endure. No doubt, the maximum safety weight of the car remains uncompromised, but children in particular are being put at risk by the crush. In winter, resorts must lower cable-car capacities to allow for this fashion trend.

How you can help

We need your help to update the Guide accurately each year. Together with our team of researchers, we try to visit as many resorts as possible, but it is not feasible to visit over 600 in a 20-week season. Lifts are constantly being upgraded, the standards and service of hotels and restaurants rise and fall, while the tuition given at ski and snowboard schools can vary from season to season. Please tell us about your ski holiday experiences – both the good and the bad – in as much detail as possible. Readers who send the best letters will receive a free copy of The Guide. Further details on how you can help can be found in *Reporting on the Resorts*. Remember, too, that you can email your report to: goodskiandsnowguide@which.net

The Ski Club of Great Britain and *The Good Skiing & Snowboarding Guide*

The Ski Club of Great Britain has enjoyed a strong association with *The Good Skiing Guide*, now *The Good Skiing & Snowboarding Guide*, for many years. Founded in 1903, it is the largest and most active club for British skiers and snowboarders in the UK. Catering for snow-users of all ages, it offers members services and benefits unavailable elsewhere.

Information and web site
The Club's information department provides members with impartial details and recommendations for over 300 resorts around the world. The Club's award-winning web site (www.skiclub.co.uk) contains information on Club matters as well as regular snow reports.

Reps in resorts
The Ski Club's reps – unpaid volunteers, trained and experienced in leading groups of skiers and snowboarders in search of the best snow – now operate in approximately 40 resorts in Europe and North America.

Holidays
The Ski Club's holiday programme covers 30 resorts in 8 countries. Holidays are organised by skiing standard and run by Ski Club reps/leaders. A wide range of ski instruction trips is offered, together with off-piste and advanced tours.

Events and other member benefits
The Ski Clubs keeps its members informed about their sports and enables them to meet at social events. Members receive four free copies per year of the Club magazine, *Ski and Board*, and details of the companies that offer Club members discounts on holidays, travel and accommodation, equipment and resort rental prices.

INTRODUCTORY HALF-PRICE MEMBERSHIP OFFER
Only £22.50 – Individual, £33 – family

This introductory offer, covering one year, is subject to production of the **corner flash** from the first page of this book, as proof of purchase, and signing a direct debit for your second and subsequent subscriptions. The offer expires on 30 April 2001 and may not be used in conjunction with any other offers.

To take advantage of this offer and for further information, call the Club's membership department on **020-8410 2015**.

This year's awards

The Golden Ski Awards are judged annually by the editors, contributors and reporters of *The Good Skiing & Snowboarding Guide*. These prestigious 'White Oscars' go to those resorts, establishments and facilities that we consider have provided an outstanding level of service to skiers and snowboarders during the 1999–2000 season. Two winners have been selected for each category: one in Europe and the other in North America (chalets are an exception). The not-so-enviable Broken Ski Awards go to establishments that – in the eyes of our judges – have failed to live up to their promise.

The Golden Ski Awards 2001

Resort of the Year
Winners: St Anton (Austria), Whistler (British Columbia)
Also nominated: Chamonix (France), Verbier (Switzerland), Aspen (Colorado), Telluride (Colorado)

Most Improved Resort of the Year
Winners: St Moritz (Switzerland), The Canyons (Utah)
Also nominated: Villars/Les Diablerets (Switzerland), Winter Park (Colorado)

Small Resort of the Year
Winners: La Tania (France), Red Mountain (British Columbia)
Also nominated: Sainte-Foy (France), Snowbasin (Utah), Grand Targhee (Wyoming)

Family Resort of the Year
Winners: Vaujany (France), Beaver Creek (Colorado)
Also nominated: Lech (Austria), Villars (Switzerland), Smugglers' Notch (Vermont), Whistler (British Columbia)

Hotel of the Year
Winners: Hameau Albert 1er (Chamonix), Amangani (Jackson Hole)
Also nominated: The Hostellerie Pas de l'Ours (Crans Montana), Hotel Eden (Arosa), The Chateau (Whistler)

Tour Operator Chalet of the Year
Winner: Chalet Saskia – Vaujany (Ski Peak)
Also nominated: Casa Rivas – Val d'Isère (Inghams),
Chalet Goodwood – Verbier (The Ski Company)

Resort Restaurant of the Year
Winners: Grande Ourse (Val d'Isère), Sushi Village (Whistler)
Also nominated: Chesa Verde (Zürs), Mariposa (Deer Valley)

Mountain Restaurant of the Year
Winners: L'Arbina (Tignes), The Lookout Cabin (The Canyons)

Also nominated: L'Ancolie (Peisey-Nancroix), La Fruitière (Val d'Isère), La Marmite (St Moritz)

Après-ski Venue of the Year
Winners: El Gringo (Villars), The Million Dollar Cowboy Bar (Jackson Hole)
Also nominated: The Vernissage (Zermatt), The Wobbly Barn (Killington)

Ski School of the Year
Winners: Evolution 2 (Tignes), Whistler/Blackcomb Ski and Snowboard School (Whistler) Also nominated: Le Ski School (Courchevel), Snow Fun (Val d'Isère), Oxygène (Plagne Centre)

Ski Shop of the Year
Winners: Precision Ski (Val d'Isère), Teton Sports (Jackson Hole)
Also nominated: Mountain Air (Verbier), Telluride Sports (Telluride)

Best Mountain Loo
Winner: Aeroplanstadl (Bad Hofgastein)
Also nominated: La Fruitière (Val d'Isère)

The Broken Ski Awards 2001

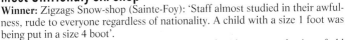

Most Unfriendly Ski Shop
Winner: Zigzags Snow-shop (Sainte-Foy): 'Staff almost studied in their awfulness, rude to everyone regardless of nationality. A child with a size 1 foot was being put in a size 4 boot'.
Also nominated: Breeze Ski Rentals (Park City) for 'the worst selection of old and clapped-out skis we have ever encountered'.

Most Unfriendly Hotel
Eurotel Victoria (Villars): 'The reception staff raised surliness to an art form'.

Most Unfriendly Mountain Restaurant
La Cabane du Poutat (Alpe d'Huez): 'Arrogant, hostile waiters made you feel that you were interrupting their day by being there to eat overpriced and mediocre food'.

Most Overpriced Mountain Restaurant
Le Cap Horn (Courchevel 1850): 'I passed on the £2,000 bottle of Burgundy and the Beluga caviar and settled for a glass of *plonk de Savoie* and a plate of pasta, but the bill was iniquitous even by London standards'.

Readers are invited to submit their nominations for *The Good Skiing & Snowboarding Guide 2002* Awards, together with a short explanation. Please send them to: Dept CD, Consumers' Association, FREEPOST, 2 Marylebone Road, London NW1 1YN. No stamp is needed. Alternatively, you can email them to us: goodskiandsnowguide@which.net

Using the Guide

Our research suggests that, when choosing a destination, most skiers and snowboarders first pick a country and then the resort that is best suited to their requirements. Major resorts are therefore listed in sections by country, in alphabetical order. Included within these resort chapters are smaller, linked villages or those sharing a lift pass. Additional, unconnected resorts within that country are to be found in the *Round-up* at the end of each section. *Offbeat resorts*, is devoted to destinations in the southern hemisphere and in Japan.

The ratings, with a maximum of three stars, at the start of each resort chapter indicate that resort's suitability for different categories of skiers and for snowboarders. For example, a resort with three stars for advanced skiing means that it has either steep slopes or exceptional off-piste terrain. A resort with no funpark but good freeriding might still receive stars for snowboarding.

The ticks and crosses in the box below the ratings record our verdicts on the strengths and weaknesses of the resorts we have covered in detail. A few of these headings may need further clarification. **Tree-level skiing** refers to locations that offer sheltered skiing on bad-weather days, with the correspondingly better visibility. Since there is no such thing as ugly mountain scenery, we have used the affirmative tick only for outstandingly **beautiful scenery**, such as in the Dolomites. **Alpine charm** applies to towns or villages that either have beautiful architecture or are rich in atmosphere. Aesthetically unappealing resorts and busy towns with particularly heavy traffic receive a cross.

Big vertical drop applies to resorts that have a difference of at least 1,300m in Europe, or 1,000m in North America, from the top to the bottom of the ski area. A cross against **skiing convenience** means that the skiing and accommodation are awkwardly linked. A tick for **low prices** indicates that the resort is cheaper than others in the same country.

A tick for **après-ski** refers not only to a lively nightlife but also to a large choice of good restaurants, as in Aspen and Whistler. **Family skiing** indicates resorts that are suitable for a family with a mixture of ages.

In *Simply the best*, on the following pages, you will find lists of what the editors consider to be the top ten resorts in Europe and North America in a variety of categories, from off-piste to après-ski.

The key on the right shows the types of lifts and grading of runs on the colour piste-maps.

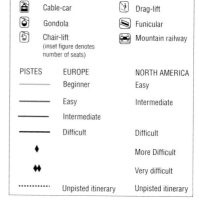

🚡	Cable-car	🚡	Drag-lift
🚡	Gondola	🚡	Funicular
🚡	Chair-lift (inset figure denotes number of seats)	🚞	Mountain railway

PISTES	EUROPE	NORTH AMERICA
———	Beginner	Easy
———	Easy	Intermediate
———	Intermediate	
———	Difficult	Difficult
◆		More Difficult
◆◆		Very difficult
··········	Unpisted itinerary	Unpisted itinerary

Simply the best

The resorts listed below are those considered by the editors and their contributors to be the best in a variety of categories. The ten entries in each one are listed in alphabetical order, rather than by ranking.

Beginners
Les Arcs
Courchevel
Flaine
Geilo
Mayrhofen
Niederau
La Plagne
Soldeu/El Tarter
Vail
Westendorf

Intermediates
Alpe d'Huez
Bad Gastein
Mayrhofen
Milky Way
La Plagne
Portes du Soleil
Selva/Val Gardena
Trois Vallées
Vail
Wengen

Advanced
Avoriaz
Chamonix
Jackson Hole
Red Mountain
St Anton
Snowbird
Val d'Isère
Verbier
Whistler
Zermatt

Moguls
Aspen
Avoriaz
Breckenridge
Davos/Klosters
Killington
Mürren
St Anton
Taos
Telluride
Verbier

Off-piste
Alagna
Alta
Chamonix
Fernie
La Grave
Sainte-Foy
Val d'Isère
Verbier
Whistler
Zermatt

Snowboarders
Avoriaz
Chamonix
Davos
Innsbruck
Red Mountain
Risoul
Serre Chevalier
St Anton
Tignes
Whistler

Families
Les Arcs
Beaver Creek
Lech
Obergurgl
Saalbach
Smugglers' Notch
Sunday River

Vaujany
Villars
Whistler

Non-skiers
Aspen
Bad Gastein
Cortina d'Ampezzo
Innsbruck
Kitzbühel
Lake Tahoe
Megève
Seefeld
St Moritz
Zermatt

Après-ski
Baqueira-Beret
Chamonix
Courmayeur
Ischgl
Kitzbühel
Sauze d'Oulx
Soldeu/El Tarter
St Anton
Val d'Isère
Zermatt

Eating out
Aspen
Cortina d'Ampezzo
Courchevel
Courmayeur
Kitzbühel
Megève
Park City
Tremblant
Whistler
Zermatt

Luxury accommodation
Aspen
Courchevel 1850
Crans Montana

Deer Valley
Gstaad
Lech/Zürs
Méribel
St Moritz
Vail/Beaver Creek
Zermatt

Airport convenience
Avoriaz
Chamonix
La Clusaz
Crans Montana
Innsbruck
Megève
Söll/SkiWelt
St Johann-im-Pongau
Verbier
Wildschönau

Value-for-money
Barèges
Big Sky
Livigno
Madesimo
Passo Tonale
Red Mountain
Schladming
Serre Chevalier
Söll/SkiWelt
Soldeu/El Tarter

Romantic/charming resorts
Alpbach
Courmayeur
Jackson Hole
Kitzbühel
Megève
Mürren
Saas-Fee
Stowe
Telluride
Zell am See

Austria

Austria no longer holds the title of premier destination for British skiers that it cherished throughout most of the second half of the twentieth century. But over the past four years, with increasingly favourable currency exchange rates, it has pulled back a sufficient percentage of lost ground to secure its number 2 spot behind France. However, for reasons beyond its control, it is unlikely to aspire to the premiership ever again. The immutable Austrian holiday formula is still synonymous with snow fun: rolling, tree-lined slopes above chocolate-box villages, jolly inns, foaming tankards of beer, lively bars and discos, and liberal sound-bites of accordion music. But the harsh reality is that its delightfully atmospheric resorts – with a couple of notable exceptions – are unable to satisfy the increasingly voracious demands of the accomplished snow-users of today.

Of course, Austrian destinations continue to provide excellent skiing and snowboarding for beginners and intermediates in an enjoyable environment (which no other country has ever managed to emulate successfully). But today's shortened learning-curve for skiers – and even more so for riders – has resulted in an increased number of more proficient holidaymakers. Those who absconded elsewhere in the late 1980s, when the sterling exchange rate dropped as low as ATS15, are not all keen to return – even though the rate is back up to over ATS21. They have come to demand steeper ski terrain than is typically found in the rolling pastureland of the Tyrol and Salzburgerland. Indeed, St Anton and its Arlberg neighbours stand almost alone as Austrian resorts that truly satisfy the needs of advanced skiers and freeriders.

Other negative factors have not helped Austria's cause. For the second successive season, two tragic avalanches captured international headlines. In December 1999 a group of 12 German ski-tourers died off-piste in the Silvretta region not far from the village of Galtür, where 40 people lost their lives in February 1999. In March 2000, 14 trainee ski instructors and their guides were killed at Kaprun. Neither of these accidents happened anywhere near prepared pistes. There is no reason to suggest that resort authorities were to blame for either incident but, after the tragedies of the preceding year, the publicity was unwelcome.

Similarly, Austria's pariah-status in the international community during the brief period of prominence of right-wing politician Jörg Haider did little to encourage tourism last winter.

However, the mainly benign quality of the skiing is tempered by the superlative standard of accommodation in Austrian resorts, which is higher than anywhere else in Europe. Reporters constantly express their surprise at finding spotless pensions as well as lavish hotels in the tiniest of villages, and one commented: 'all I want from a skiing holiday is plenty of easy piste-cruising and a first-class hotel that doesn't cost a fortune. That is why I return to Austria year after year'.

Alpbach

ALTITUDE 1,000m (3,280ft)

Beginners ✱ Intermediates ✱✱✱ Advanced ✱ Snowboarders ✱✱

If your Tyrolean holiday is incomplete without zither, harp and accordion music produced by rugged mountain lads in leather breeches, then Alpbach is the place for you. Tradition, combined with quality skiing and an intimate relationship with British skiers during the past 40 years, sets this resort apart from other Tyrolean destinations.

- ✔ Attractive village
- ✔ Alpine charm
- ✔ Lack of queues
- ✔ Ideal for non-skiers
- ✔ Long vertical drop
- ✔ Family skiing
- ✗ Lack of challenging slopes
- ✗ Poor access to slopes
- ✗ Limited number of pistes
- ✗ Unexciting nightlife

Alpbach is a small, sunny village set on a steep hillside. The compact centre is dominated by a pretty green-and-white church surrounded by old wooden chalets and the buttressed walls of the two medieval inns. It is a secluded and strikingly attractive resort, far removed from the overt commercial influences of mainstream Tyrol, and all the better for it. The hotels and restaurants are mainly owned and staffed by locals rather than seasonal employees, so they have a genuine interest in the welfare of their guests.

The ski area is limited in size but offers a variety of terrain, best suited to intermediates. The inconvenience of having to take a five-minute bus ride from the village to the main mountain, the Wiedersberger Horn, and back again each day is a drawback, particularly for families with small children confined to the village-centre nursery slope. However, a number of reporters have commented on the efficiency of the service – 'never have I done less walking in a ski resort'.

On the snow
top 2,025m (6,643ft) bottom 830m (2,722ft)

Apart from the nursery slopes next to the village and the Böglerlift, with its south-facing red (intermediate) run, all of Alpbach's skiing is on the Wiedersberger Horn. Mountain access from Alpbach is via the two-stage, six-seater Achenwirt gondola across the wooded, north-facing slopes to Hornboden at 1,850m. Queuing is not a problem, although the number of snow-users increases at weekends.

Alpbach has a large vertical drop and some long runs, but it is still stuck with the reputation of being a beginners' resort. Mountain access is also possible by chair-lift from **Inneralpbach** along the valley. Here

18

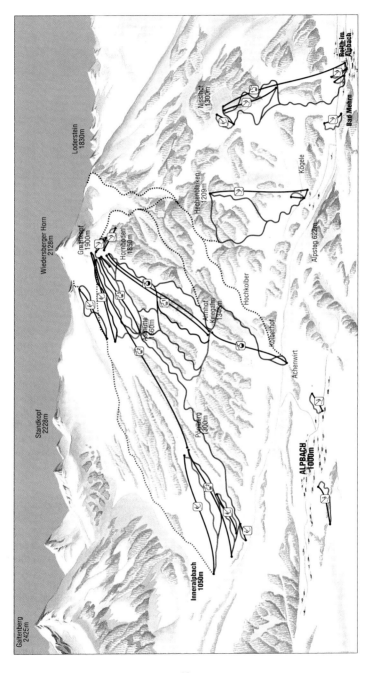

the lifts join up with the skiing above Hornboden. Snowmaking on the lower, rocky meadows beneath the first stage of the gondola has made it possible to ski down to the bottom for most of the season. The next-door village of **Reith** has five lifts, is not linked but shares a lift pass.

Beginners

Complete novices need not stray from the village. Easy nursery runs are served by a drag-lift in the centre beside the Böglerhof and the shorter Lukaslift. Once the basics have been mastered, skiers progress to the *Familienabfahrt* on the Hornboden via the gondola. This is a long path from Gmahbahn to Kriegalm, which reporters claim is often icy.

Intermediates

With the exception of a couple of moderately challenging black (difficult) runs, the whole mountain is given over to intermediate skiing. The small number of pistes (10) marked on the local lift map belies the actual size of the groomed area, and the pistes are extremely wide. The Hornbahn 2000 quad chair-lift, which opened last season (1999–2000), allows some challenging intermediate skiing on the piste marked 9 on the local lift map. The standard of piste preparation is high. The red piste number 8 is, according to reporters, 'a beautiful run down to Inneralpbach'.

WHAT'S NEW
Magic carpet lift at Frosty's Schneewelt

Advanced

From Hornboden, a couple of wide trails run back down to the Kriegalm mid-station, including an FIS (International Ski Federation) racecourse, which is one of the two black runs on the mountain; the other is Brandegg. From here a red run to the bottom creates a good, fast course of over 1,000m vertical, which is used by British racing clubs for their competitions. Piste 10 follows the fall-line beneath the Hornbahn 2000 chair.

Off-piste

Alpbach is ideal for 'lazy powder skiers'. According to one reporter you can lie in bed after a night of new snow until 10.30am and still cut fresh tracks. To the west of the main ski area is an interesting range of off-piste bowls. The long, red itinerary route from Gmahkopf down to Inneralpbach is not pisted, although it is usually well-skied. Some fairly challenging off-piste can be found around the Wiedersberger Horn.

Snowboarders

The undulating terrain is a topographical dream for riders and, along with having two funparks and a half-pipe, Alpbach regularly hosts international snowboarding events.

Skiing facts: Alpbach

TOURIST INFORMATION
Alpbach Conference Centre, A-6236, Alpbach 246
Tel 43 5336 600–0
Fax 43 5336 600 200
Email info@alpbach.at
Web site www.alpbach.at

THE RESORT
By road Calais 1,132km
By rail Brixlegg 10km
Airport transfer Innsbruck 1hr, Munich 2hrs
Visitor beds 2,000
Transport free ski bus

THE SKIING
Linked or nearby resorts Reith (n), Kramsach (n), Zillertal (n)
Number of lifts 19 in area
Total of trails/pistes 45km (20% easy, 70% intermediate, 10% difficult)
Nursery slopes 6 lifts

LIFT PASSES
Area pass (covers Alpbach and Reith) ATS1,390–1,560, Kitzbühler-Alpen-Skipass (covers Alpbach, Fieberbrunn, Kitzbühel, SkiWelt, St Johann in Tirol, Waidring, Wildschönau – 260 lifts) ATS2,200, both for 6 days
Beginners points tickets
Pensioners 15% reduction for 65yrs and over
Credit cards yes

TUITION
Adults Skischool Alpbach
tel: 5336 5515, Alpbach Skischool Aktiv
tel: 5336 5351, Skischool Reith
tel: 5337 62117
Snowboarding as ski schools
Other courses carving, cross-country, seniors, skiing for the disabled, ski-touring, teen skiing
Guiding through ski schools

CHILDREN
Lift pass (covers Alpbach and Reith), 5–13yrs, ATS780–900, 14–16yrs ATS1,060–1,130, Kitzbühler-Alpen-Skipass (area covered as adults) ATS1,100, both for 6 days
Ski & board school as adults
Kindergarten (ski) Frosty's Schneewelt ATS 1,300 for six days tel: as Skischool Alpbach, (non-ski) Alpbach Kindergarten tel: as Skischool Alpbach, or through tourist information

OTHER SPORTS
Curling, indoor tennis at Kramsach (12km away) parapente, skating, sleigh rides, snowshoeing, swimming, toboggan run at Reith (7km away)

FOOD AND DRINK
Coffee ATS25, glass of wine ATS28, small beer ATS28, soft drink ATS25, dish of the day ATS80–140

Tuition and guiding
Skischool Alpbach has a sound reputation. One reporter commented: 'the standard of instruction was about the best I have had anywhere'. Another described it as 'friendly and traditional, absolutely not *avant garde*'. We have positive reports of the Alpbach Skischool Aktiv.

Mountain restaurants

The Hornboden restaurant is situated 50m below the top stage of the gondola, which is fine for skiers but inconvenient for the many non-skiers, who have to walk down a steep stretch of piste to reach it. The lower section is self-service while upstairs is a restaurant serving Tyrolean food. The Gmahstuben is cheap and cheerful. The Böglalm is a farmhouse containing a self-service restaurant, but is criticised for being 'incredibly inefficient'. Gasthof Wiedersberger Horn at Inneralpbach is said to be one of the best restaurants in the region.

Accommodation

Most of Alpbach's accommodation is in hotels and guesthouses, ranging from basic bed-and-breakfasts to the very comfortable. Three of the most luxurious hotels are the Böglerhof ('superb facilities'), Alpbacherhof and the Alphof ('a 10-minute stroll from the centre but the cheapest four-star in Alpbach'). The village takes considerable pride in the fact that many of its hotels have remained in the same families for centuries.

Eating in and out

The restaurants do not offer much variety, although the recommended ones include the Gasthof Jakober, Alpbacher Taverne, the Reblaus for pizzas and the Gasthof Wiedersberger Horn. The restaurant in the Böglerhof is the most luxurious. The Rossmoos and Zottahof restaurants, both up the mountain, are popular in the evening.

Après-ski

If drinking and dancing until dawn are an integral component of your ski holiday, you should consider other, livelier resorts. Outside the main holiday weeks the resort is dead by 11pm, except at weekends when an influx of visitors gives it much needed cheer. Achenwirt, at the foot of the mountain, is 'good for a couple of beers on the way home'. The Siglu beside the nursery slopes attracts a busy crowd at the end of the day. The Jakober Bar is an early-evening rendezvous point. The Hornbeisl bar next to the lifts in Inneralpbach is recommended. The Waschkuch'l is good for a quiet drink, and the Birdy Pub in the village centre is recommended for a noisier one. The Alpbacher Weinstadl provides late-night music. Alpbach has half-a-dozen shops.

Childcare

The care of children at the ski school is more American-style than European: 'we were told not to worry about the children if we were late or the weather was bad. The instructors would take care of them, which they did. When the weather was bad the children were taken into a restaurant to get warm'. The ski-kindergarten, Frosty's Schneewelt, even has an American-style 'magic carpet' lift. The ski-kindergarten operates from a leisurely 10am to 3.15pm. Alpbach has a kindergarten that takes children from three years old, and baby-minders can be organised through the tourist board.

Bad Gastein

ALTITUDE 1,100m (3,608ft)

Intermediates ✱✱✱ Advanced ✱✱ Snowboarders ✱✱

The Gasteinertal, a long closed valley flanked by the Hohe Tauern mountains, offers a higher class of skiing than the lowland pastures of the Tyrol and an altogether more cosmopolitan atmosphere. Bad Gastein, the main resort in the valley, is a collection of once-grand hotels painted mostly in the imperial yellow of Vienna's Schönbrunn Palace and stacked dramatically up a steep hillside around a waterfall that plunges into the River Ache. The resort's elegant casino harks back to the days when this was one of the greatest spas of Europe. Franz Schubert and Johann Strauss both composed here, and the guest list never failed to include at least a couple of crowned heads. However, the year-round spa business is not what it was, although winter sports have given the region an injection of new life.

Five million gallons of hot water bubble up from 17 natural springs and is piped into all the main hotels. The public indoor and outdoor pools at the Felsenbad by the Bahnhof (railway station) are a popular rendezvous where you can wallow in the waters and, through a haze of steam, watch skiers in action just a few yards away. One million gallons of this hot water is also piped down the road to Bad Gastein's sister spa of **Bad Hofgastein**. This is a spacious and comfortable resort that is popular with families.

Dorf Gastein, at the entrance to the Gasteinertal, is a sleepy and unspoilt village with its own attractive ski area that extends over the 2,027-m Kreuzkogel to the resort of **Grossarl** in a neighbouring valley. **Sport Gastein**, at the head of the valley, is a separate ski area based around an abandoned gold-mining village. In the Middle Ages the area was responsible for 10 per cent of the world's gold and silver output.

> ✔ Large ski area
> ✔ Tree-level skiing
> ✔ Variety of après-ski
> ✔ Thermal baths
> ✔ Choice of mountain restaurants
> ✔ Easy rail access
> ✔ Reasonable prices
> ✘ Lack of skiing convenience
> ✘ Unconnected ski areas
> ✘ Heavy traffic
> ✘ Poor piste-marking
> ✘ Awkward for families with small children

On the snow
top 2,686m (8,810ft) bottom 850m (2,788ft)

The lift company is in the process of spending £20 million on upgrading its system, but first you have to get to the lift. If you are accustomed to clicking into your bindings outside your hotel door and skiing home at the end of the day, then Bad Gastein is not for you. It was built on a steep hillside as a spa, not a ski resort, and a considerable amount of walking is unavoidable. The main Stubnerkogel ski area is situated on the western side of the valley and is reached by a modern, two-stage gondola from the top of the town near the railway station. In theory, you can leave your equipment in the ski-and-boot store, which avoids the necessity to lug skis up tough gradients from the town centre. However, you may not finish here at the end of the day.

At the top of the Stubnerkogel a choice of beautifully manicured runs take you 1,100 vertical metres down to the floor of the Anger Valley. From here a new gondola whisks you up the Schlossalm above Bad Hofgastein. A funicular followed by the choice of cable-car or chair-lift provides alternative access to Schlossalm from Bad Hofgastein. However, the best piste skiing lies a few minutes by car further down the valley above the village of Dorf Gastein.

The ancient double chair-lift gives the initial impression that skiing is restricted to the benign rolling meadows immediately above. But the lift in turn gives access to a modern gondola that brings you swiftly up to the 2,000-m summit of the Fulseck. A series of demanding red (intermediate) and token black (advanced) runs take you either back down to Dorf Gastein or over the top to Grossarl.

Sport Gastein, at the head of the valley, is another separate ski area. It is an icy place when the weather closes in. However, on a fine day the piste-skiing is varied, and the off-piste can be quite exceptional. If snow conditions are poor elsewhere in the valley, Sport Gastein can become crowded. The small Graukogel area above Bad Gastein on the far side of the valley completes the skiing possibilities with a few satisfying descents that include a World Cup course.

An improved ski bus service links the separate resorts and ski areas, but is still oversubscribed in high-season weeks. Taxis are plentiful, but in order to explore the area fully, a car is a necessity. Reporters praise the lift map for its clarity and accuracy.

Beginners

The area has five nursery slopes served by drag-lifts, but overall it cannot be recommended for beginners. From Bad Gastein, the main novice slopes are a bus ride away at Angertal. Most blue (easy) runs are a pinkish-red in comparison with similar-sized Austrian resorts.

Intermediates

The entire valley is best suited to strong intermediates looking for a combination of mileage and challenge. Graukogel has superb tree-level

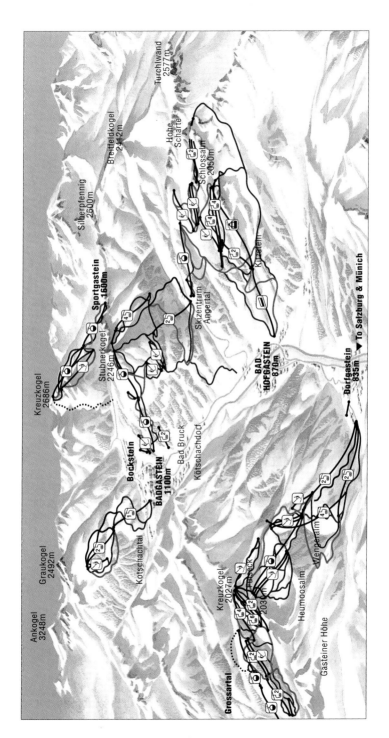

skiing and is the place where the locals go on a snowy day. Confident snow-users will be interested mainly in the long run around the back of the mountain, which is reached either from Hohe Scharte at 2,300m or from Kleine Scharte at 2,050m. In good snow conditions it is possible to ski 1,450m vertical over eight kilometres, all the way to the bottom of the railway. The fall-line run beneath the Gipfelbahn Fulseck at Dorf Gastein is also highly recommended.

Advanced
The north-facing runs down into the Angertal area provide some of the best skiing in the region. From Jungeralm, a long, undulating black (difficult) run drops directly through the woods. Laireiteralm at Grossarl is a long black run that provides considerable challenge. Schöneck at Sport Gastein is a short, but steep, bump run.

Off-piste
Untracked opportunities abound above the Schlossalm next to Hohe Scharte. Both the north and south faces of Sport Gastein can provide excellent powder runs after a new snowfall. In good conditions the aptly named 2.2-km Tiefschneeabfahrt (deep snow run) reached from the top of the Graukogelbahn, is just what it says, and most enjoyable.

Snowboarders
Bad Gastein, Bad Hofgastein and Sport Gastein all have commendable half-pipes, but most freestyle riders congregate in the funpark at Dorf Gastein. The nightlife at Bad Gastein is considered too staid by riders, with Bad Hofgastein a preferable lodging base.

Tuition and guiding
We have good reports of the Ski School Luigi in Bad Gastein. The size of classes seems to vary between 4 and 12 pupils, and the standard of the instructors' English is high. Ski School Bad Gastein and the Bad Hofgastein Ski and Racing School both have fine reputations. One reporter singled out the Bad Hofgastein school for praise: 'staff were especially friendly and the organisation was truly excellent'. Ski School Holleisn in Dorf Gastein is described as 'small and friendly with useful instruction'.

Mountain restaurants
The area is plentifully served with both pleasant huts on the slopes and self-service cafeterias at the lift stations. Prices are no higher than in the valley, where they are low by Austrian standards. Aeroplanstadl, on the home run to Bad Hofgastein, houses the finest WCs in the Alps. As one reporter commented: 'Both the Damen and the Herren bear witness to the fact that this whole valley is obsessed with waterworks. Together they form an underground ablutionary palace decorated with granite cattle troughs, giant boulders, and ancient cast-iron village pumps.'

The Jungerstube is praised for its Tirolergröstl ('a traditional dish of hash browns with bacon served in a giant copper pan'). Reporters recommend the Wengeralm above Dorf Gastein for its traditional fried potato pancakes. The Waldgasthof in the Angertal earns praise for its 'roaring log fire, cosy dining booths, and the best *Gulaschsuppe* we have ever tasted'.

Accommodation

Most of the accommodation is in hotels, of which there are quite literally hundreds in the valley. The position of your accommodation in Bad Gastein is crucial because of the steep layout of the resort. Bad Gastein has an annoyingly complicated one-way system; traffic is heavy, and parking can be difficult. The old hotels are flanked by smart boutiques and expensive jewellers, who set their sights on Bad Gastein's wealthy German visitors here for health treatments rather than the skiers and boarders.

The modern Elizabethpark beside the waterfall is said to be 'comfortable but a bit characterless and a long walk from the snow'. Villa Solitude, a magnificent town house next to the casino, has been lovingly restored as a designer hotel with six 1840s-style suites.

Hotel Wildbad, conveniently situated near the top of the town, is warmly recommended: 'Unbelievably good food for Austria, a true gastronomic treat'. Hotel Mozart is spacious and well-positioned. Hotel Grüner Baum, built in 1831 by Archduke Johann as a hunting lodge, is 5km out of town in a rural setting and has a justified reputation as one of the great hotels of Austria.

Eating in and out

The choice of restaurants is limited mainly to the hotels, but the Bahnhof restaurant is particularly recommended as good value for money. The Mozart is praised for its fondue. The Restaurant am Wasserfall is 'inexpensive and cheerful', as is the Felsenbad. The Chinarestaurant, according to one reporter, 'makes a pleasant change from *Wienerschnitzel*'. Hotel Rader and Gasthof Radhausberg in Böckstein are recommended. Villa Solitude's brasserie and the restaurant in the Grüner Baum have the best gourmet fare in town.

Après-ski

The Felsenbad, opposite the Bahnhof restaurant, has thermal indoor and outdoor pools as well as a bar, and attracts the crowds as they come off the slopes. The Austrians see nothing unhealthy in the marriage of beer and Bad, and a promotional video shows spa patrons happily imbibing. No visitor should miss the chance to improve his or her health by taking a train ride to the Healing Galleries, 2km inside the mountain near Böckstein. The combination of a 90°C temperature, relative humidity and low doses of rare radon gas can apparently cure respiratory and muscular ailments.

The Gatz Music Club and Hägblom's are the hot-spots at tea-time and again much later in the evening. Their late-night rival is the Central Park Entertainment near the waterfall. Eden's Pub is said to be usually crowded 'not least because a giant moose head takes up most of the room'. Ritz in the Salzburgerhof Hotel has live music and is more sophisticated. The casino is worth a visit, and the Manfreda and Kir Royal bars are ever popular. Other late bars to check out include Oslag, Hexn-Häusl, Weinfassl, Highlife, Pub am Wasserfall and the Zirbenstube. The bar at the British-owned Hotel Tannenburg has the cheapest drinks in town.

Childcare

As with all resorts with a disparate ski area, it is difficult to recommend Bad Gastein for children. All the villages have ski and non-ski kindergarten that take three- to five-year-olds. Hotel Grüner Baum runs a crèche for its small residents, which includes lunch.

Linked or nearby resorts

Bad Hofgastein
top 2,686m (8,810ft) bottom 870m (2,854ft)

Bad Hofgastein has neither the inconveniently steep, dark setting nor the faded grandeur of its neighbour. Although smaller it is still sizeable, with 50 hotels and guesthouses built around a pedestrianised centre and spread along the broadest part of the valley. The Kitzstein funicular is a hearty walk or a free bus-ride away. Bad Hofgastein is a good base for winter walking and cross-country skiing, and busy ice rinks complete the winter scene. There are indoor and outdoor thermal swimming-pools as well as a modern sports centre. Reporters complain that morning queues for the funicular can be annoying. It holds 100 people while the cable-car above it has a capacity for only 80. Wise people take the chair from the top of the train.

The ski-kindergarten takes children from three years old. The most convenient hotels are the more recently built ones lining the road from the centre to the river. The four-star Österreichischer Hof is described as 'delightful'. There are five discos and more than a dozen bars.

TOURIST INFORMATION
Tel 43 6432 7110–0
Fax 43 6432 7110–32
Email info@badhofgastein.com
Web site www.badhofgastein.com

Dorf Gastein
top 2,686m (8,810ft) bottom 835m (2,739ft)

Dorf Gastein is the first of the settlements you come to on entering the Gasteinertal. Too many visitors to the area drive through without stopping. What they miss is a delightful little village with a charming main street lined with arcades. It remains untouched by the slightly depressing health-conscious image of its bigger sisters. Horses and carts clatter along the narrow street past the old church, more often taking local folk

Skiing facts: Bad Gastein

TOURIST INFORMATION
Kaiser-Franz-Josef-Strasse 27, A–5640
Bad Gastein
Tel 43 6434 2531
Fax 43 6434 2531–37
Email fvv.badgastein@aon.at
Web site www.badgastein.at

THE RESORT
By road Calais 1,232km
By rail station in resort
Airport transfer Salzburg 1½hrs
Visitor beds 6,700
Transport free ski bus with lift pass

THE SKIING
Linked or nearby resorts Bad
Hofgastein (l), Dorf Gastein (n), Sport
Gastein (n), Grossarl (n)
Number of lifts 52
Total of trails/pistes 201km (30% easy,
58% intermediate, 12% difficult)
Nursery slopes 5 lifts and pistes

LIFT PASSES
Area pass Gastein Super Ski (covers
Schlossalm, Angertal–Stubnerkogel,
Graukogel, Grossarl and all Gastein
resorts), ATS2,050 for 6 days
Beginners points tickets
Pensioners ATS1,880 for women 60yrs
and over and men 65yrs and over
Credit cards yes

TUITION
Adults Ski School Bad Gastein
tel: 6434 2260,
Ski School Luigi tel: 6434 4440, Ski and
Racing School Bad Hofgastein tel: 6432
6339, Ski School Schossalm tel: 6432
3298, Ski School Fuchs tel: 6432 8485
Snowboarding as ski schools
Other courses carving, cross-country,
race camps, telemark
Guiding through ski schools and
L.Kravanja tel: 6434 2941, F. Sendlhofer
tel: 6434 2879, Hans Zlöbl
tel: 6434 5355

CHILDREN
Lift pass 6–14yrs, ATS1,230 for 6 days,
free for 5yrs and under
Ski & board school as adults
Kindergarten (non-ski) at Hotel Grüner
Baum tel: 6434 2516–0

OTHER SPORTS
Curling, indoor golf and tennis, parapente, riding, rifle shooting, skating,
sleigh rides, snowshoeing, squash,
swimming

FOOD AND DRINK PRICES
Coffee ATS27–35, glass of wine
ATS30–45, small beer ATS22–25, soft
drink ATS25–27, dish of the day
ATS100–170

about their business than taking tourists for joy rides. There are several friendly hotels in the centre. The Steindlwirt and Kirchenwirt are two of the larger ones. The skiing begins a good five-minute walk from the village. The Gasthof Schihäusl stands at the foot of the slopes. Evenings are said to be livelier than you might expect in a village of this size.

TOURIST INFORMATION
Tel 43 6433 7277
Fax 43 6433 727737

Innsbruck

ALTITUDE 575m (1,886ft)
RESORTS COVERED Axamer Lizum, Fulpmes, Igls, Neustift, Seefeld,
Stubai Glacier

Beginners ✱✱ Intermediates ✱✱✱ Advanced ✱✱ Snowboarders ✱✱✱

Innsbruck enjoys a reputation as a minor ski resort in its own right, but its true significance for the skier and snowboarder is as a jumping-off point for a host of big-name resorts in the Tyrol and even the Arlberg. These can be reached daily by bus, although a car adds both convenience and flexibility.

- ✔ Attractive town
- ✔ Short airport transfer
- ✔ Variety of skiing in area
- ✔ Summer skiing on Stubai Glacier
- ✔ Extensive cross-country
- ✔ Activities for non-skiers
- ✘ Small, separate ski areas
- ✘ Weekend lift queues

Austria's third most important city has twice hosted the Winter Olympics and has the advantage of having its own international airport, which is enclosed by dramatic towering mountain ranges on either side of the Inn Valley. Innsbruck is strategically positioned for road links in western Austria and is well-served by a network of motorways. The Ötztal and the snow-sure skiing of **Obergurgl** and **Sölden** can be reached in under 90 minutes by car. The journey to **Kitzbühel** and the **SkiWelt** takes an hour. As an additional incentive to stay in the city, a single ski pass called the Innsbruck Glacier Skipass covers the seven main local areas of **Igls, Axamer Lizum, Fulpmes, the Stubai Glacier, Tulfes, Hungerburg** and **Mutters**; it gives access to a total of 62 lifts serving 130km of piste and offers three days' skiing out of a total four or six days.

The two versions of the more expensive Innsbruck Super Skipass also allow you to ski or ride Kitzbühel and/or the Arlberg for a day as well as the Innsbruck area, thus providing 210 lifts and 520km of piste. It is as flexible as the Innsbruck Glacier Skipass, and bus travel is included in the price.

The cost of staying in the city is lower than in a conventional ski resort. The choice of restaurants is wide, and the nightlife is lively. The city's smartest hotel is the five-star Europa-Tyrol, which is attractively wood-panelled and boasts the well-respected Europastüberl restaurant. The 14 four-star hotels include the Goldener Adler and Romantikhotel Schwarzer Adler, both of which have recommended restaurants. At the lower end of the price scale are the many gasthofs and pensions. A colourful Christmas market is set up in the Old Town from the end of each November.

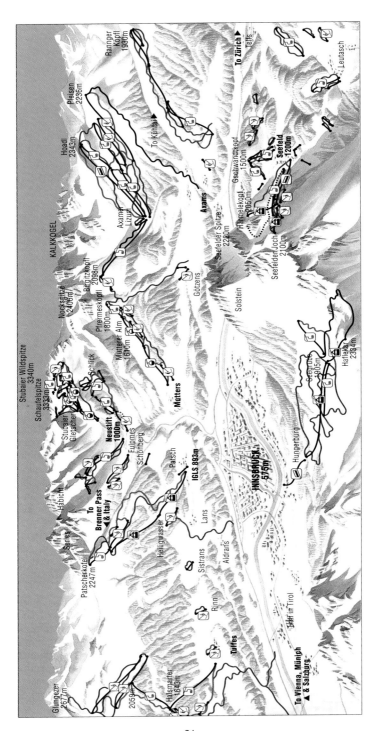

In recent years Innsbruck has become a snowboarding head-quarters, with the offices of both Burton, the board manufacturer, and the International Snowboard Federation in the city. This has proved to be a magnet for riders. Innsbruck's 'own' skiing is to be found just outside the city above Hungerburg on the south-facing slopes of the Hafelekar. The black (difficult) Karrine and the red (intermediate) Langes Tal runs are both challenging. The area above Tulfes on the other side of the valley consists of two blue (easy) runs and two reds.

Axamer Lizum
top 2,343m (7,687ft) bottom 874m (2,867ft)

This is a somewhat characterless ski station comprising four hotels and a huge car park at 1,553m beneath the peaks of the Hoadl and Pleisen mountains, but nevertheless it offers the best range of skiing and board-ing within immediate reach of Innsbruck. Weekend lift queues can be a problem owing to the proximity to Innsbruck, but the ten lifts provide extensive and varied pistes. This was the main Alpine venue for both the 1964 and 1976 Innsbruck Olympics, and the Olympic Museum is worth a visit. Axamer is one of the top snowboarding resorts in Austria, with freeriding a particular strength. Gullies form natural half-pipes, and riders can sometimes even outnumber skiers here. The 6.5-km Axamer run – graded black, but red by most resorts' standards – takes you all the way down to the quiet village of **Axams** at 874m.

The pick of the skiing is accessed by a fast quad chair-lift from the car park or by a funicular that climbs the ridge to the 2,340-m Hoadl, the high point of the area. From here the Olympic women's downhill course provides a demanding return route to the ski school meeting place. Across the narrow valley, a long chair-lift serves either a black run back to Axamer Lizum or gives access to a sunny, easy piste that takes you back down the valley to the little village of Götzens.

There is one mountain restaurant, the Gipfelhaus at Hoadl, which has panoramic views, home cooking and the names of the former Olympic medal winners (from the two Innsbruck Winter Olympics) engraved on the wall. The four-star Lizumerhof and Gasthaus Zsifkovits are both recommended hotels at the foot of the lifts. Gasthof Adelshof, situated on the approach road is 'clean, comfortable, and utterly Austrian'. Off Limits is the main bar, but most snowboarders will head for the brighter lights of Innsbruck.

Fulpmes
top 2,200m (7,218ft) bottom 937m (3,074ft)

Slightly further away, but still within easy reach by post-bus, the Stubai Valley offers a range of easy meadow skiing. **Mieders**, **Telfes**, Fulpmes and **Neustift** all share a lift pass. Above Fulpmes there is good skiing, branded as Schlick 2000, in a sheltered bowl on the 2,230-m Sennjoch. Some of the runs are tough and unpisted, but the majority are easy and confidence-building, and good for lower intermediates. The small, sunny nursery area receives favourable reports.

The Hotel Stubaierhof and the Hotel Alte Post are both recommended. Restaurants include the Leonardo Da Vinci ('popular and good value') and the Gasthaus Hofer, which serves 'simple, plain Austrian farmhouse fare'. The Café Corso, the Ossi-Keller, Platzwirt and Dorfalm discos make it a lively place by night.

Igls
top 2,247m (7,372ft) bottom 893m (2,930ft)

Igls, 5km from Innsbruck up towards the Europabrücke and the Italian border, is a fine example of a traditional Tyrolean village but with limited skiing. The four blue (easy) and red (intermediate) runs on the Patscherkofel have been greatly enhanced by the addition of a fast quad chair-lift to mid-mountain, and a second chair up to the Schutzhaus is planned for this winter. The top of the mountain is accessed by cable-car from above the village centre. The red Olympic downhill presents the biggest challenge. It was here in 1976 that Franz Klammer threw caution to the wind and hurled himself down the mountain to win the most memorable Winter Olympics gold of all time. Considerable snow-making allows skiing to continue through March. There are four mountain restaurants, most of them criticised for their high prices, although the one at the top of the cable-car receives substantial praise.

The resort supports two ski schools, Schigls and Igls 2000, both with instructors who speak good English. The two nursery slopes are covered by snow-cannon and are a five-minute walk from the village centre. Non-skiing children can attend Bobo's Children's Club from Monday to Friday, and there is a children's ski school.

The village is small and uncommercialised, with sedate hotels and coffee houses, excellent winter walks, and the Olympic bob-run, which is open to the public. The Sporthotel Igls is singled out for its cuisine, while the five-star Schlosshotel is warmly praised. Hotel Batzenhäusl is recommended for both comfort and cuisine. Nightlife is not the resort's strongest point, but the bars at the Bon Alpina and the Astoria are the livelier spots. The Sporthotel disco is open until late.

Neustift and the Stubai Glacier
top 3,200m (10,499ft) bottom 1,000m (3,281ft)

The main community of the broad and lush Stubaital (Stubai valley), Neustift is a large, sprawling village that has expanded greatly in recent years. Nevertheless, it remains very much the traditional Tyrolean village at heart, centred around a magnificent and ornately decorated church that is the landmark of the valley.

Recommended hotels include the Tirolerhof ('excellent food and a warm welcome') and the budget-priced and quaint Hotel Angelika in the centre of town. Nightlife is lively in the Romanastuben, and the Sumpflöchl in the Hotel Stubaierhof is popular. Neustift has its own gentle ski area on wooded north-facing slopes but it is also the main base for the Stubai Glacier, 20 minutes' drive away at the end of the valley.

The Stubai Glacier is one of the most extensive summer ski areas in Europe, with 21 trails. Twin gondolas take you up to the first stage at Fernau. From here you can either continue by gondola or chair-lift to a network of lifts. When snow is scarce elsewhere the slopes can become unbelievably crowded, and German bank holidays are to be avoided. The glacier is often closed in January. The Gamsgarten restaurant has a good choice of reasonably priced food.

Keen skiers and riders stay in the comfortable Alpensporthotel Mutterberg at the base of the lifts. It has its own swimming-pool and disco. Separate ski schools operate in both Neustift and on the glacier and each has a kindergarten. The Stubai Superskipass also covers a small area at **Milders** and the assorted lifts in the valley.

Seefeld
top 2,100m (6,890ft) bottom 1,200m (3,937ft)

Seefeld is a smaller version of Innsbruck, Kitzbühel and the other beautiful towns of Austria, with its frescoed medieval architecture. The resort is stylish and sophisticated and has seven luxury hotels, a casino, an extensive health centre and horse-drawn sleighs. The village centre is pedestrianised. Seefeld's main winter activity is cross-country skiing, but it also has three small, alpine ski areas: Geigenbühel for beginners, Gschwandtkopf, a low peak next to the cross-country loipe used mainly by the ski school, and Rosshütte, the more extensive area with steeper runs and a long off-piste trail. All three areas are reached from the village centre by the free bus service.

The town boasts some exotic hotels, including the five-star Klosterbräu, a former sixteenth-century monastery complete with indoor and outdoor swimming-pools and a Roman sauna with steam grotto. Others are the Creativhotel Viktoria and the less pricey Hotel Bergland. The four-star Karwendelhof is in the pedestrian precinct. The Kaltschmidt is 'handy for the nursery slope with a nice pool on the fourth floor'. The luxury Gartenhotel Tümmlerhof is set in its own park and offers daycare and a children's playground. The resort kindergarten is in the Olympia Sport and Congress Centre.

Gourmets can try the Alte Stube in the Hotel Karwendelhof. Café Nanni and Café Moccamühle are popular for après-ski. The Big Ben bar is as English as you would expect, and the Brittania Inn is another popular pub. Monroe's disco-bar attracts the late-night crowd along with the Miramare and the popular Postbar in the Hotel Post. The Kanne in the Hotel Klosterbräu, the centre of the village's social life, has live music. Reporters recommend the Lammkeller in Hotel Lamm. The bar Fledermaus has live jazz. Other activities include tubing down the bobsleigh run, a grotto 'saunarium' and indoor swimming-pool in the Olympia Sport and Congress Centre.

Snowboarding

Innsbruck is a popular base for riders, with a wide choice of resort destinations within easy reach. Axamer Lizum is the highlight, with a funpark and a half-pipe, but freestylers are even better served by the area's natural obstacles. Fulpmes, the Stubai Glacier and Hungerburg all have funparks.

Cross-country

Cross-country skiing started as a recreational sport in 1964 when Seefeld hosted the Winter Olympics Nordic events. The resort then went on to host the events in the 1976 Winter Olympics and in the 1985 Nordic World Championships. The excellent facilities include a team of specialist cross-country instructors at the Nordic Ski School in Seefeld's Olympia Sport and Congress Centre. The 200km of loipe are mechanically prepared, and a cross-country trail map is available from the tourist information office. The Innsbruck area has a total of 12 cross-country resorts covering 500km of loipe.

TOURIST INFORMATION
Innsbruck
Tel 43 5125 9850
Fax 43 5125 9850–7
Email info@innsbruck.tvb.co.at
Web site www.tiscover.com/innsbruck

Ischgl

ALTITUDE 1,400m (4,529ft)

Intermediates ✱✱✱ Advanced ✱ Snowboarders ✱✱✱

Ischgl is the focus of the Silvretta ski area on the Austrian–Swiss border, a long-established resort with some of the best skiing in Austria. It was painfully enshrined in the world's public consciousness in February 1999, when extraordinary snowfalls, coupled with hurricane-force winds, isolated Ischgl, while avalanches devastated neighbouring **Galtür** and nearby villages at the cost of 40 lives. As part of its attempt to overcome the resulting bad publicity Ischgl has introduced a compensation scheme for holiday-makers unable to get in or out of the resort as a result of road closures. After the first 24-hour period Ischgl will pay for the accommodation of snowed-in or snowed-out guests until the road reopens.

- ✔ Extensive intermediate cruising
- ✔ Large ski area
- ✔ Off-piste and ski-touring
- ✔ Biggest funpark in Europe
- ✔ Reliable snow record
- ✔ Wide choice of nightlife
- ✔ Beautiful scenery
- ✘ Lack of easy runs
- ✘ Crowded home pistes
- ✘ Poor choice of mountain restaurants

For most visitors, duty-free **Samnaun** (covered on the lift pass together with Galtür) on the Swiss side of the frontier, is the principal attraction of the Silvretta ski region. Alcohol at competitive prices, rucksacks for sale to transport it back over the mountain and the allure of a Swiss lunch make it an irresistible day trip. The return journey involves a ride on the Pendelbahn, the world's first double-decker cable-car, which is handsomely engineered and fitted with escalators for easy access. This is the spearhead of a general upgrading of the lift system to reduce the bottlenecks that haunted Ischgl and Samnaun during the early 1990s. The smart double-cable Funitel system is designed to allow operation even in high winds, with each car carrying up to 24 people.

Although Ischgl is only a few miles as the crow flies from St Anton, it remained largely unknown in Britain until the 1999 avalanches. The first lift was not installed in Ischgl until 1963. Since then, the resort has developed from a small farming village into a bustling community on a hillside to the south of the main road. It is compact, if somewhat overgrown, with some 9,300 beds. Wealthy young Germans still dominate what has always been an expensive resort, but the British are gradually discovering it. Many of the regulars consider Ischgl to be the second-best resort in Austria (after St Anton) – an assessment that takes both the skiing and the nightlife into account.

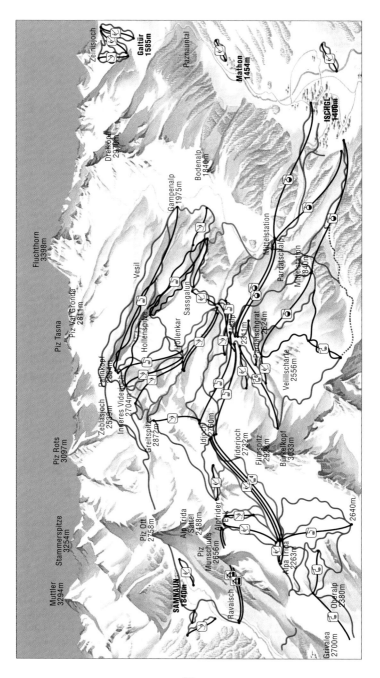

On the snow
top 2,864m (9,394ft) bottom 1,377m (4,517ft)

The spine of this ski area is the long ridge that forms the Austrian–Swiss border, with Ischgl's slopes facing northwest and west and Samnaun's facing southeast and east. The rapid Fimbabahn gondola, connected by a tunnel to the centre of town, and the Funitel Silvrettabahn provide comfortable and rapid access to Idalp, an open, mid-mountain plateau, while a third lift – the Pardatschgratbahn – ends 300m higher. From this focal point the pistes fan out over the upper slopes, with extensive and well-linked opportunities for fast cruising.

Two chair-lifts provide a choice of routes to the run down to Samnaun, with the much longer, covered chair from Gampenalp as a third alternative. After eating and shopping, snow-users can take a short roadside descent below the village to Ravaisch, the departure point for the 180-person double cable-car, which arrives at Alp Trida Sattel, a sun trap with spectacular views but no direct link back to Ischgl. Instead, snow-users must descend to Alp Trida, the starting point for parallel drag-lifts and a chair to Idjoch on the top of the ridge for the journey back to base. A new six-person chair-lift gives a speedy connection between Alp Trida and Alp Trida Sattel. Once back in the Ischgl area, there is a choice of two long paths through woods to the resort; in high season, however, both are dangerously crowded.

Beginners

With only one resort-level lift and no blue (easy) runs leading back to the resort, Ischgl is neither cheap nor particularly user-friendly for first-timers, who have no sensible choice but to return to the village by gondola. Idalp's sunny nursery slopes are inviting, although frequently crowded with ski school classes. The next stage in the learning curve is also tricky as blue runs are interrupted on occasion by short sharp red (intermediate) stretches. This is true of the adventurous blue descent from Inneres Viderjoch back to Idalp, though advanced beginners should have the skills to tackle it. The six-person Velilleckbahn chair-lift from Idalp is a better option for the less confident.

Intermediates

Ischgl has a number of long, challenging red runs, which makes it ideal for aspiring intermediates. On the extreme edge of the skiing, the descent from Palinkopf (the highest point in the lift system) to Gampenalp attracts relatively few skiers. On the other side of the ridge the lovely valley run to Samnaun is a real thigh-burner, especially as conditions are often more icy on the south-facing side. Those who complete it without stopping will have earned their lunch. The Palinkopfbahn chair, another relatively new addition to the lift system, takes skiers to the start of an equally testing red run all the way down to Bodenalp.

Advanced

Ischgl is short of genuine black (difficult) runs. The best ones are found between the Inneres Viderjoch and the Paznauner Taya. From the top of the Pardatschgrat there is a mild black descent to the bottom of the Velilleckbahn chair, at which point it turns into a challenging itinerary back to the resort. This is marked as a red dotted line but, as it is narrow and popular with advanced skiers and riders, it provides a stern and bumpy workout. The new six-person chair that has replaced the Schwarzwand and Palinkopf drag-lifts for the 2000–1 season gives access to a steep and challenging black run.

Off-piste

Although the Paznaun Valley is famous for its spring ski-touring, Ischgl itself is not known as a resort for advanced skiers and off-piste enthusiasts. In consequence, the powder is not skied out the moment the lifts open, as it would be in St Anton. The most favourable terrain is off the Gampenalp chair. Touring with a guide is a popular past-time but in an area that was blighted by tragic avalanches in both the 1998–9 and 1999–2000 seasons, the greatest care should be taken at all times.

Snowboarders

The Silvretta area has established itself as a major snowboard centre, with the Boarders Paradise Funpark at Idjoch, which is claimed to be the largest and one of the best in Europe and has a vertical drop of 350m. It is divided into separate areas for different disciplines such as freeride, mogul and new school (not just for riders but also for those on extreme carving skis and snowblades), and contains a good half-pipe and 30 obstacles. Samnaun has its own half-pipe.

Tuition and guiding

The Ischgl-Silvretta Ski and Snowboard School (SSS) offers tuition in English for groups of about 10 to 12 people. With 100 qualified instructors on its books, the school can arrange off-piste tours on demand.

Mountain restaurants

Why have an Austrian lunch when you can have a Swiss one? That is the question they trade on in Samnaun, but the reality is that it is quite difficult to find that great Swiss staple of *Rösti* with bacon, cheese and fried egg among the pizzerias and Austrian taverns that jostle for space among the duty-free shops in Samnaun. On the Swiss side, the Samnaunerhof and the Schmuggler Alm are recommended. The best options on the Austrian side include the restaurant in the hotel at Bodenalp and the Restaurant Idalp.

Skiing facts: Ischgl

TOURIST INFORMATION
Postfach 9, A–6561 Ischgl, Tyrol
Tel 43 5444 5266–0
Fax 43 5444 5636
Email tvb.ischgl@netway.at
Web site www.ischgl.com

THE RESORT
By road Calais 1,017km
By rail Landeck 30km, frequent buses
from station
By air Innsbruck 1½hrs
Visitor beds 9,300
Transport free bus service links Ischgl,
Kappl and Galtür

THE SKIING
Linked or nearby resorts Galtür (n),
Kappl (n), Samnaun (l)
Number of lifts 41 in Ischgl, 66 in
Silvretta area
Total of trails/pistes 200km in area
(27% easy, 63% intermediate,
10% difficult)
Nursery slopes 3 lifts

LIFT PASSES
Area pass Silvretta (covers Ischgl,
Samnaun, Galtür, Kappl and See)
ATS 2,195–2,560 for 6 days

Beginners no free tickets
Pensioners 60yrs and over,
ATS2,000 for 6 days
Credit cards no

TUITION
Adults Ischgl-Silvretta Ski and
Snowboard School tel: 5444 5257
Snowboarding as ski school
Other courses Big Foot, carving,
cross-country, telemark
Guiding Ski and Snowboard
School Ischgl

CHILDREN
Lift pass 7–16yrs, Silvretta
ATS1,450 for 6 days, family
passes available
Ski & board school as adults
Kindergarten as ski schools

OTHER SPORTS
Indoor climbing wall, indoor tennis,
parapente, skating, sleigh rides,
swimming

FOOD AND DRINK PRICES
Coffee ATS28, glass of wine ATS30,
small beer ATS35, soft drink ATS28,
dish of the day ATS140–180

Accommodation
Ischgl's popularity with German skiers and snowboarders has resulted in quality hotels in each category, many of them with a degree of solid alpine charm. One reporter considered Ischgl to be: 'the quintessential Alpine ski town'. However, the recent building boom has produced ugly extensions and overcrowding as the demand for more beds tempts hoteliers to outgrow their sites.

Negotiating the hilly terrain on foot can be hazardous, but progressive thinking has led to indoor public staircases linking the various resort levels. As you can walk through the village from end to end in 15 minutes, almost any hotel makes a convenient base for at least one of the three lifts up to the mid-station. The exception is the Hotel Antony, which is isolated near the Madlein drag-lift on the hillside opposite the village but is highly recommended in other respects. The curved bulk of the Hotel Elisabeth dominates the Pardatschgratbahn, while the Goldener Adler is close to the Silvrettabahn at the opposite end of the village. The family-run Hotel Solaria is central and comfortable, if somewhat quirky in its reception arrangements. Hotel Olympia is recommended for 'cost, location, accessible parking, as well as a small spa'.

Eating in and out

Hotel restaurants predominate, which means a wide choice of typically Austrian meals that lack individuality or merit. One reporter complained: 'there appeared to be few restaurants that were not part of a hotel'. The Goldener Adler is praised for its ambience and its fresh trout, and the Trofana Alm bar-restaurant for its pizza. The Buffalo Western Saloon provides a limited American alternative; the menu in the cocktail bar is impressive. The Heidelberger Hütte specialises in fondue evenings, with transport by snowcat or horse-drawn sleigh.

Après-ski

The international clientèle creates a real buzz when skiing finishes for the day, with the bars in the central area near the church overflowing into the streets when the weather is fine. In the early evening the crowds move on to the Kitzlock and Nicki's Stadl, *ancien régime* establishments that specialise in Austrian politesse and tea-dancing to the strains of Strauss. The Kuhstall by the Silvrettabahn attracts a young crowd in the early evening.

A rowdier scene is on offer at the Trofana Alm, where high spirits can lead to dancing on the tables but stop short of lager loutishness, which is not welcome in this upmarket resort. For clubbing, the best places are the Wunderbar in the Hotel Madlein and the bar in the Hotel Post. The Allegra Bar also has impromptu dancing, and the Hotel Elisabeth has dancing girls.

The Silvretta Centre has an adventure swimming-pool, bowling alley and pool tables. The farming museum in **Mathon** on the road to Galtür is also popular.

Childcare

Three-year-olds can learn the basics in the ski kindergarten then graduate to the children's ski school from four years of age, according to ability. The meeting point is beside the adventure garden, and lunch is served in the youth centre. There is also a kindergarten in the Silvretta cableway building on Idalp.

Linked or nearby resorts

Galtür
top 2,300m (7,546ft) bottom 1,585m (5,200ft)

In comparison with Ischgl, Galtür is an oasis of calm tucked away round a bend in the valley near the head of the Paznaun Valley. The resort is connected to neighbouring Ischgl by free shuttle buses during the day. Although it has more than 3,000 beds and a large modern sports centre, it has the genuine feel of an alpine village. It is easy to imagine Ernest Hemingway strolling into the local pub after climbing on skins from the neighbouring Montafon Valley in the spring of 1925. But sadly this image has been temporarily obscured by the avalanche tragedy of February 1999. Rebuilding has taken place, and any scars that remain are not physical.

Galtür's skiing is at **Wirl**, an outpost reached in five minutes by a free shuttle bus that runs frequently at peak times. There are several hotels here for those who prefer ski-in ski-out arrangements. The skiing is open, uncrowded and well-suited to beginners and families. Galtür is a notable centre for ski-touring, especially in spring, with a wide choice of climbs at all levels.

Unlike Ischgl, Galtür is quiet at night, but there are several bars where both locals and visitors meet. The most popular are La Tschuetta, just off the main square, and s'Platzli in the cellar of Hotel Rössle. Others include the Iglu in the village centre, along with Weiberhimmel and the Huber-Stadl at the ski area. The family-run Fluchthorn Hotel offers a warm welcome in a central location. The Post is also convenient. As in Ischgl, most dining takes place in hotel restaurants, with the Rössle and the Alpenrose recommended. Galtür has night-skiing and night-boarding, and a modern sports centre offering tennis, squash and swimming. The village also has a hang-gliding and parapente school, a toboggan run and a skating-rink with curling.

TOURIST INFORMATION
Tel 43 5443 8521
Fax 43 5443 852176
Email galtuer@netway.at
Web site www.galtuer.com

Samnaun
top 2,864m (9,394ft) bottom 1,840m (6,035ft)

Lost in an inaccessible pocket in the mountains on the Austrian–Swiss border, Samnaun lives off its duty-free status and its ski links with Ischgl. Although these are now very swift, it is hard to imagine anyone choosing to spend a holiday in a place that is as lacking in atmosphere as this resort. The Gästekindergarten takes potty-trained children all day Monday to Friday. Hotels include Chasa Montana, Hotel Post and Hotel Silvretta.

TOURIST INFORMATION
Tel 41 81 868 5858
Fax 41 81 868 5652
Email info@samnaun.ch
Web site www.samnaun.ch

Kitzbühel

ALTITUDE 760m (2,460ft)

Beginners ****** Intermediates ******* Advanced ***** Snowboarders ******

K itzbühel is a walled, medieval settlement of heavily buttressed buildings painted with delicate frescoes, which survives the relentless battering of a nine-month tourist season with measured aplomb. Throughout the season the town positively buzzes with excitement.

Wealthy fur-clad Germans mix with younger and often more financially challenged skiers from Britain, Holland and Italy to form an alpine social melting-pot with few equals. Serious shoppers will be disappointed, for Kitzbühel lacks the designer retailers you might expect in such an upmarket resort. The town centre is mercifully traffic-free, and a bus service ferries skiers to and from the Hahnenkamm and the Kitzbüheler Horn mountains.

> ✔ Large ski area
> ✔ Beautiful architecture
> ✔ Alpine charm
> ✔ Lively après-ski
> ✔ Wide range of activities for non-skiers
> ✔ Short airport transfer
> ✘ Low altitude and poor snow record
> ✘ Heavy traffic outside pedestrian centre
> ✘ Lack of skiing convenience

Kitzbühel's world renown as a ski centre is based largely around the annual Hahnenkamm downhill race, the Blue Riband event of the World Cup calendar. The race course is called the Streif, which when not prepared for racing is the benign red (intermediate) *Familienabfahrt* piste. Kitzbühel's skiing is largely intermediate, with few pisted challenges for experts. Apart from **Innsbruck**, this is the one destination in the Tyrol that is really appropriate for skiers and non-skiers alike.

On the snow
top 2,000m (6,562ft) bottom 760m (2,493ft)

The main skiing is divided between two mountains: the Kitzbüheler Horn and the more challenging Hahnenkamm, which is easily accessed from near the centre of town by a six-person gondola. From here an interesting network of mainly red and blue (easy) cruising runs spreads out down three faces of the mountain to form the largest and most challenging sector. Lift connections are not all that they should be, and a couple of notorious bottlenecks can result in annoying queues during high-season weeks. The new Pengelstein quad chair-lift should ease the congestion. Even though the area is confined, the variety of runs and scenery gives you the pleasant impression that you are going somewhere rather than skiing the same slopes over and over again.

Kitzbühel's second ski area, the Kitzbüheler Horn, is to the east of town, across the main road and the railway tracks. Towering above the resort, it is a distorted but beautiful pyramid of rock and ice. A cable-car takes you up to 1,996m, the highest point in the area, where the views are spectacular. The skiing is pleasant and gentle, but experienced skiers will quickly find the Horn a disappointment.

Aurach, a ten-minute ski-bus ride away from Kitzbühel, is a third separate area served by a single-chair and a couple of drag-lifts, which provide access to three gentle blue runs and a marginally steeper reddish alternative.

Kitzbühel's insuperable problem is its lack of altitude. In the past two seasons it has been blessed with superb snow-cover, but outside the middle winter weeks you must be prepared to contend with slushy conditions as the norm – at least at lower levels. Artifical snowmaking covers 30km of piste including the Streif, as well as the pistes down to the village of Kirchberg.

Beginners

Kitzbühel has four good nursery slopes near the town and plenty of easy skiing for second-weekers. The blue (easy) Pengelstein run, served by

WHAT'S NEW

Pengelstein II quad chair-lift

the new quad chair, takes you all the way down to Kirchberg and is one of the best in the resort. Over on the Kitzbüheler Horn, the long Hagstein blue run (number 3 on the piste map) is a gentle but interesting cruise from top to bottom. However, nervous skiers should beware of the Pletzerwald variation through the trees, which turns into a choice between an awkward red (intermediate) and the steep black (difficult) Horn Standard.

Intermediates

Kitzbühel is essentially for cruisers. Pengelstein-Süd is a long, flowing red that starts at the top of the Pengelstein chair and is the gateway into the Ski Safari (see below). It brings you down to the hamlet of **Trampelpfad**. The Hochsaukaser red at Pengelstein is a wide, fast piste with wonderful lips and rolls – one side is usually left unprepared and becomes a challenging mogul field.

The celebrated Ski Safari, marked by elephant signposts, is an enjoyable pisted itinerary that takes you from the Hahnenkamm up the Kitzbühel Valley to **Jochberg** and **Pass Thurn**. Anyone with a couple of weeks' ski experience can manage the outing, which consists of a series of blue and gentle red runs linked by lifts along the east-facing slopes of the valley. The wooded skiing on the Wurzhöhe above Jochberg is always uncrowded, and it is worth spending some time here before moving on up the valley. Pass Thurn is cold and isolated, but it holds the best snow in the region. The downside is that the Safari is no circuit – it

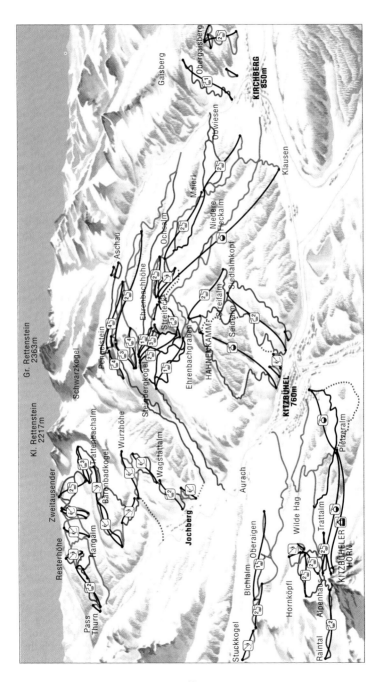

can only be fully skied in one direction. To return to Kitzbühel you have to queue for a bus for the 19-km road journey from Pass Thurn. Plans to build the crucial link lift from Jochberg back up the Hahnenkamm are unlikely to be realised in the near future, despite promises.

Advanced
The best of the steep skiing is reached via a network of lifts in the Ehrenbach sector of the Hahnenkamm. Try the Sedlboden and Ochsenboden. The black variation of Oxalm-Nord is part of the otherwise long intermediate run down to **Kirchberg**. Rettenstein at Pass Thurn is a short, sharp black, which ends up at the bottom of the Zweitausender double-chair.

Snowboarders
Riders tend to congregate on the Horn, which has a well-equipped funpark with a half-pipe and boardercross course. The area has many natural obstacles as well as some good off-piste for freeriders.

Off-piste
Those who are new to off-piste skiing can find plenty of easy powder skiing close to the pistes in the Hahnenkamm area after a fresh snowfall. Pass Thurn is particularly recommended. Bichlalm is another enjoyable area for powder. Kitzbühel's specialist off-piste ski school is called Ski Alpin.

Tuition and guiding
Kitzbühel has six separate ski schools including the famous Rote Teufel (Red Devils). All have a generally good reputation. However, we continue to receive mixed reports of the Rote Teufel. Oversized classes and instruction that amounts to little more than guiding, with no individual tuition, are just some of the complaints.

Mountain restaurants
The Hoch Kitzbühel restaurant at the top of the Hahnenkamm gondola is a welcome addition. It has a sun terrace as well as waiter- and self-service sections indoors. 'Wonderful Wienerschnitzel and a great atmosphere – don't miss the adjoining Hahnenkamm museum,' commented one reporter. The Alpenhaus at the top of the Kitzbüheler Horn is noted for its *Germknödl*. The Hagstein, also on the Horn, is 'small, reasonably priced and overflowing with charm'. The Ochsalm on the Hahnenkamm is renowned for its *Apfelstrudel*. Trattenbergalm between Jochberg and Pass Thurn has some of the best simple food in the region. Panorama-Alm above Pass Thurn has a glass-walled bar outside to keep out the wind, and a roaring log fire within. The Pengelstein restaurant has been expensively extended but still tends to be crowded.

Accommodation
For both comfort and service the Goldener Greif and the Jägerwirt head an impressive list of 16 four-star hotels. The Maria Theresia has under-

Skiing facts: Kitzbühel

TOURIST INFORMATION
PO Box 164, A-6370 Kitzbühel, Tyrol
Tel 43 5356 621550
Fax 43 5356 62307
Email info@kitzbuehel.com
Web site www.kitzbuehel.com

THE RESORT
By road Calais 1,130km
By rail station in resort
Airport transfer Salzburg 1½hrs,
Munich 2½hrs, Innsbruck 2hrs
Visitor beds 8,763 in Kitzbühel, Reith
and Aurach
Transport free ski bus

THE SKIING
Linked or nearby resorts Aurach (n),
Kirchberg (l), Jochberg (l), Pass Thurn (l),
St Johann in Tyrol (n)
Number of lifts 26 in Kitzbühel,
59 in linked area
Total of trails/pistes 164km in linked
area (39% easy, 46% intermediate,
15% difficult)
Nursery slopes 9 in linked area

LIFT PASSES
Area pass (covers Kitzbühel, Kirchberg,
Jochberg, Pass Thurn, includes ski bus,
swimming-pool and reduction for sauna)
ATS1,875–2,040 for 6 days
Beginners learn to ski pass
Pensioners ATS340 per day for women
60yrs and over and men 65yrs and over

Credit cards yes

TUITION
Adults Crystal tel: 5356 75277,
Hahnenkamm tel: 5356 71126,
Kitzbüheler Horn tel: 5356 64454,
Rote Teufel (Red Devils) tel: 5356 62500,
Ski Alpin tel: 5356 62767,
Total tel: 5356 72011
Snowboarding as ski schools
Other courses carving, cross-country,
skiing for the disabled, teen skiing, telemark
Guiding through Ski Alpin

CHILDREN
Lift pass 6–15yrs, ATS990 for 6 days,
free for 5yrs and under and for sized
1.20m (4ft) and under when
accompanied by an adult
Ski & board school as adults
Kindergarten (ski) through ski schools,
(non-ski) Anita Halder tel: 5356 75063

OTHER SPORTS
Bobsleigh, curling, floodlit tobogganing,
hang-gliding, horse-riding, hot-air
ballooning, indoor tennis and squash,
night skiing, parapente, shooting range,
skating, ski-jumping, sleigh rides,
snowshoeing, swimming

FOOD AND DRINK PRICES
Coffee ATS28, glass of wine ATS24,
small beer ATS30, soft drink ATS28,
dish of the day ATS120

gone refurbishment and improved the standard of its restaurant.
Sporthotel Bichlhof is centrally located and warmly recommended. The
converted hunting lodge of Schloss Lebensberg, on the outskirts, has a
medieval-style interior complete with four-poster beds, and offers a
hedonistic level of pampering. This includes a health centre with swimming-pool and free weekday babysitting. The Hotel zur Tenne in the
town centre is a comfortable designer hotel. The Weisses Rössl, once

the town's prominent coaching inn, is a picture of faded splendour and enormously popular. Schloss Münichau, in the village of **Reith** on the far side of the Schwarzsee, is a 500-year-old castle, which is said to be 'delightfully quiet, with reasonable prices and superb food'.

Eating in and out

Austrian alpine food wins few gastronomic prizes, but you can eat better and with more variety in Kitzbühel than in most resorts. The Goldener Greif is renowned for its *Salzburger Nockerl*, a kind of hot meringue soufflé. The Hotel zur Tenne specialises in fresh trout and is said to be 'outstanding, but expensive'. The Landeshäusl and Huberbräu are both reasonably priced and cheerful. Landgasthof Oberaigen at the Bichlalm mid-station offers 'an enjoyable evening out, with wholesome cooking and a mountain ambience'. Chinarestaurant Peking in the Kirchplatz rings the culinary changes. The existence of a McDonald's seems a shame in such beautiful surroundings, but thankfully its presence is muted.

Après-ski

Life after skiing centres almost entirely around the pedestrianised streets in the Vorderstadt. Two British-style pubs, The Londoner and Big Ben, attract the lion's share of business along with Highways, which offers live music. Seppi's is where Austria meets the Old Kent Road. The locals congregate in Stamperl and Fünferl while the Goldener Gams is a modest restaurant and bar with live music and a sophisticated Tyrolean atmosphere that attracts all ages. s'Lichtl, also in the Vorderstadt, is a bar with a warm atmosphere, which draws a more sophisticated crowd. Late-night revellers head for Royal Dancing, the most popular disco. K und K and Take Five are more expensive night-clubs. The Aquarena health centre is free with a ski pass.

Childcare

Although for skiing convenience Kitzbühel gets a heavy minus mark, beginner children are well catered for, with five lifts that make up the extensive nursery area on the golf course at the foot of the Hahnenkamm. All the ski schools accept children.

Linked or nearby resorts

Kirchberg
top 2,000m (6,562ft) bottom 850m (2,788ft)

Once upon a time Kirchberg was the no-frills dormitory village that gave you a back door into Kitzbühel's skiing at knockdown prices, but without its medieval charm. This once poor relation, only 6km around the shoulder of the Hahnenkamm at the head of the Brixen Valley, still gives alternative access to Kitzbühel's main ski area, but circumstances have changed and it now boasts 25 three- and four-star hotels. The resort has its own small beginner and intermediate lifts on the Gaisberg, and offers access to the Hahnenkamm by a two-stage chair and the Klausen gondola. It has a kindergarten, Miniclub Total, and two ski schools, Skischool Total and Skischool Kirchberg.

The town's layout is not designed for ski convenience; distances are considerable, and the ski bus service is seriously over-subscribed. Choose where you stay with care in relation to both price and where you want to ski. The Tiroler Adler Schlössl is neither particularly convenient nor cheap, but is one of the best hotels in town. The nightlife is just as busy as in Kitzbühel but less sophisticated. Charley's Club and Le Moustache are among the main centres of activity. The 3.5-km toboggan run on the Gaisberg is floodlit in the evenings.

TOURIST INFORMATION
Tel 43 5357 2309
Fax 43 5357 3732
Email info@kirchberg.at
Web site www.kirchberg.at

Lech/Zürs

ALTITUDE Lech 1,450m (4,756ft), Zürs 1,720m (5,642ft)

Beginners ✱✱ Intermediates ✱✱✱ Advanced ✱✱ Snowboarders ✱

Every skiing nation has at least one ultra-smart resort that lures the 'beautiful people' to its manicured slopes, and Lech and neighbouring Zürs are the most exclusive resorts in Austria. Not only do these villages attract the rich and famous to their portfolio of six five-star hotels but they quite literally exclude skiers from the slopes when they consider these to be full. As soon as 14,000 tickets have been sold the tills are closed, and electronic signs on approach motorways warn day-trippers to ski elsewhere. Priority is given to those skiers who are staying in the resort. The result is that even on the busiest weekends of the year queues are never longer than ten minutes.

✔ Alpine charm
✔ Beautiful scenery
✔ Long intermediate runs
✔ Efficient lift system
✔ Varied off-piste skiing
✔ Efficient piste signposting
✔ High standard of hotels
✔ Lack of queues
✔ Facilities for families
✘ Difficult road and rail access
✘ High prices

Lech was first inhabited by Swiss immigrants in the fourteenth century, and this corner of Austria still looks more towards Switzerland, its nearest neighbour, than to the main part of Austria. Despite the presence of luxury hotels, Lech is still a traditional village centred around an onion-domed church and a river. Over 100 hotels and businesses now receive their heating and hot water from a communal eco-friendly plant up the valley, and during construction work the opportunity was taken to improve the main street. Pavements and pedestrian zones have been widened, and three new bridges now give better access across the river. A new underground car park for short-stay visitors has also been built in the village centre.

Over the years, the biggest expansion has been in **Oberlech**, a satellite 200m up the mountain that was once the summer home of herdsmen and shepherds. The collection of hotels here is ideally placed for the skiing and provides a safe and car-free centre for families with small children. The network of underground tunnels beneath the top cable-car station and the hotels means that visitors arriving by cable-car do not have to lug suitcases across the piste.

Zürs is little more than a collection of mainly four- and five-star hotels in an isolated position astride the Flexen Pass. The village lacks much of the charm of Lech, although resort-level snow is guaranteed for most of a long season, which continues to the end of April.

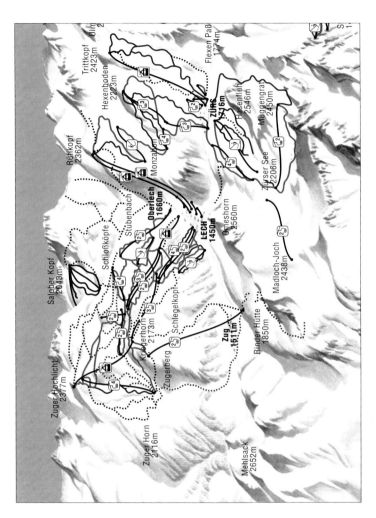

Zug, 3km by road through the woods from Lech and fully integrated into the lift system, also offers rural tranquillity. An evening journey from Lech through the star-lit woods by horse-drawn sleigh is delightful and romantic.

The resorts share a varied and extensive ski area, although advanced skiers might be more interested in the abundant off-piste and ski-touring opportunities. **St Anton**, with its larger choice of advanced piste terrain, is 40 minutes' drive away and is included in the same hands-free lift pass, along with the free bus service. Prices are high and as one reporter commented: 'Lech and Zürs are best suited to skiers who regard cost as secondary'.

The only access is via the Flexen Pass from **Stuben** which is liable to closure due to avalanche danger in extreme weather conditions. During the freak snowfalls of February 1999 both Lech and Zürs were repeatedly cut off for days at a time.

On the snow
top 2,450m (8,036ft) bottom 1,445m (4,741ft)

The Lech/Zürs circuit of 110km of prepared pistes, spread over three mountains and served by 32 lifts, provides mainly intermediate skiing of the highest quality. The circuit can be skied only in a clockwise direction, and pistes are particularly well signposted. The steady upgrading of the lifts and the limitation on the number of skiers have alleviated any queuing problems; most of the older chair-lifts have been speeded up and have 'moving carpet' conveyor belts to enable skiers to progress on to the lift more quickly.

WHAT'S NEW

Weekly mountain casino on the Rufikopf
New bridges and street improvements
Underground car park for
short-stay visitors
Filomena apartment-hotel

Mountain access to the circuit is via the twin Rüfikopf cable-cars, which scale an impressive wall from the centre of Lech. Long and challenging itineraries lead down off the shoulder in either direction through the woods to the road by Zürs, or back to Lech via a scenic itinerary through the Wöstertäli. Alternatively, you can enjoy the lengthy and benignly beautiful pistes towards Zürs.

Lech's main skiing area, on the other side of the valley, is contrastingly open and mostly gentle, although the slopes immediately above the village are of a more challenging gradient. Mountain access on this side is via an assortment of four lifts – including a detachable quad-chair – from different points in or near the village. Above Oberlech, lifts and pistes spread throughout a wide, fragmented basin below the peaks of the Kriegerhorn and the Mohnenfluh. The two are linked by a cable-car with spectacular views.

Beginners
First-timers can use a beginner's ticket and should not buy the expensive Arlberg Ski Pass. Lech has excellent nursery slopes behind the church as well as at Oberlech. Beginners should quickly progress to a whole range of blue (easy) runs on the Oberlech side of the valley. One of the attractions of the resort for second-week skiers is that they should be able to negotiate the blue Rüfikopf run from the top of the cable-car, which in turn links into the *Familienabfahrt* to bring them all the way to Zürs.

Intermediates
Confident skiers head up the Rüfikopf cable-car for the choice of red (intermediate) pistes down the Hexenboden and Trittkopf. Follow the local lift map with care: appropriately coloured circles indicate pisted runs, while ski-routes are marked by diamonds. It is easy to think that a

red-diamond with a thin black border is a hard intermediate run. In fact it is an extreme itinerary that is neither patrolled nor pisted, although some are so well skied that they become pistes. From Zürs you can either take the scenic Zürsertäli or choose more direct routes down to the Zürsersee and on via the Madloch towards Lech.

Advanced
Zürs has the steeper skiing of the two main resorts, including a couple of short, sharp black (difficult) pistes, notably the Hexenboden Direkte. Langerzug and Tannegg are two challenging runs down the shoulder of the Rüfikopf, and Kriegerhorn Südhang is another recommended piste. The ski-routes marked on the lift map offer a considerable challenge.

Off-piste
When fresh snow falls, both Lech and Zürs are a delight. Experts can try the various descents of the 2173-m Kriegerhorn and the Zuger Hochlicht beyond it. The long run down from the top to the village of Zug via the narrow Zuger Tobel can be spectacular in powder snow conditions. Langerzug and Tannegg around the shoulder of the Rüfikopf are dramatic in the extreme. For environmental reasons, it is strictly forbidden to ski off-piste through the trees – anyone caught doing so risks having their lift pass confiscated. Ski-touring and heli-skiing (see *Heli-skiing*) are popular.

Snowboarders
Lech's Boarderland funpark on the Schlegelkopf is 300m long, with a half-pipe, a quarter-pipe and a series of obstacles. Zug has myriad gullies and drops, as well as a natural half-pipe when snow conditions allow. However, the resort is too expensive to attract substantial numbers of young riders.

Tuition and guiding
The Austrian Ski School in Lech, Oberlech and Zürs has a particularly fine reputation. At the ski school meeting area, instructors' names are nailed to the class boards – the same instructors teach the same level all season. This means that classes do not suffer from a change of instructor mid-week or even daily, as is the case in many resorts. On the whole good English is spoken, because of the international clientèle. However, one reporter said that because the majority of guests are German, instructors have to be reminded to translate into English for their British pupils. Eighty per cent of ski teachers in Zürs and over 50 per cent in Lech are booked for private rather than group lessons each day – an indication of the spending power of the clientèle.

Mountain restaurants
Most of the hotels on the slopes in Oberlech and Zürs serve lunch, so there is no need for other restaurants. Two exceptions are the atmospheric Alte Goldener Berg above Oberlech and the simple Flexen Pass

on the piste near Zürs. Hotel Montana in Oberlech is owned by the family of former Olympic downhill champion Patrick Ortlieb and is recommended for its food. Hotel Burg, also in Oberlech, has a gourmet restaurant that needs to be booked in advance at weekends and during high season. The Mohnenfluh is criticised for its slow service. The Seekopf at Zürs is recommended. The Palmenalpe above Zug is one of the better self-service eating places, provided you avoid peak hours. The Sonnenburg is another reasonable self-service eatery.

Accommodation

Lodging is mostly in comfortable and expensive hotels, plus some spacious apartments. The village is fairly compact, and location is not particularly important. The smartest hotel, indeed one of the most celebrated five-stars in Austria, is the sumptuous Gasthof Post. It has only 38 rooms, including 10 suites with private steam baths, and you need to book a year in advance. Hotel Kristiania, set in a quiet position 500 metres from the centre, quietly competes with the Gasthof Post. Its bland-looking exterior hides a colourful interior decorated with 'delectable fabrics and modern paintings contrasting with flamboyant Baroque wall lights'.

The Arlberg, Gotthard, Krone and the Almhof Schneider are all warmly recommended by regulars. The Tannbergerhof is popular with the British and is the centre of Lech's social life. Hotel Elizabeth is said to be very comfortable. There are numerous less formal hotels and plenty of pensions, but nothing is cheap. It is worth noting that even the best hotels do not generally accept credit cards. The new Filomena apartment-hotel houses a food market.

In Oberlech, the Sporthotel Petersboden is known for its piste-side Red Umbrella bar. Zürs has three five-star hotels including Thurnhers Alpenhof, where all rooms have superb mountain views. The four-star Arlberghaus receives glowing reports and has a curling-rink on its roof. Zug's original inn, the Rote Wand, is now a four-star hotel.

Regular ski buses connect Lech, Zug, Zürs, Stuben and Rauz/St Anton, and post-buses run to the railhead at Langen.

Eating in and out

Good restaurants abound, as you might expect in resorts of this calibre, but most are in the hotels and none is cheap. Haus 8 in Lech, opposite the Post Hotel, needs to be booked at least three days in advance. The Brunnenhof is strongly recommended, together with Bistro s'Caserole, Rudi's Stamperl and the Dorf Stüberl. For a special evening, Gasthof Post and the Schneider Almhof are good bets. Don Enzo serves pizzas and pasta. In Oberlech, the Ilga Kellerstübli and the Goldener Berg are famous for fondues. In Zürs, the Chesa Verde is an award-winning restaurant, while in Zug the Klösterle is highly recommended.

Après-ski

The average age of the clientèle in Lech and Zürs is higher than that in other alpine resorts. Wherever you look you will see bronzed and fit

Skiing facts: Lech/Zürs

TOURIST INFORMATION
A-6764 Lech, A-6763 Zürs, Am Arlberg
Tel Lech: 43 5583 2161
Zürs: 43 5583 2245
Fax Lech: 43 5583 3155
Zürs: 43 5583 2982
Email Lech: lech-info@lech.at
Zürs: zuersinfo@zuers.at
Web sites www.lech.at www.zuers.at

THE RESORT
By road Calais 975km
By rail Langen 17km, frequent buses daily
Airport transfer Innsbruck 2hrs,
Zurich 2½hrs
Visitor beds 8,450 (with Zürs)
Transport free ski buses between Lech,
Zürs and Rauz. Shuttle bus at weekends,
Lech–Zurich Airport ATS800 return

THE SKIING
Linked or nearby resorts Zürs (l),
St Anton (n), Stuben (n), St Christoph (n),
Zug (l)
Number of lifts 34 in Lech/Zürs,
85 on Arlberg Ski Pass
Total of trails/pistes 110km in Lech/Zürs
(40% easy, 40% intermediate,
20% difficult). 260km on Arlberg Ski Pass
Nursery slopes 1 free lift

LIFT PASSES
Area pass Arlberg Ski Pass (covers Lech,
Oberlech, Zürs, Rauz, St Christoph,
St Anton, Stuben, Sonnenkopf–Klösterle)
ATS1,960–2,360 for 6 days
Beginners 1 free lift, points card available
Pensioners Senior ticket for women 60yrs

and over, and men 65yrs and over,
ATS1,710–1,900 for 6 days. 75yrs and
over, ATS100 for whole season
Credit cards no

TUITION
Adults Austrian Ski School:
Lech tel: 5583 2355,
Oberlech tel: 5583 200,
Zürs tel: 5582 2611
Snowboarding as ski schools
Other courses carving, cross-country,
heli-skiing, race training, snowshoeing,
telemark
Guiding through ski schools, Wucher
Heli-skiing tel: 5583 2950

CHILDREN
Lift pass (covers resorts and linked area)
6–15yrs, ATS1,180–1,420 for 6 days.
Free until 6th birthday
Ski & board school as adults
Kindergarten Lech: Miniclub
tel: 5583 2161–0,
Oberlech: Kindergarten tel: 5583 3236,
Zürs: Kinder & Skikindergarten
tel: 5582 2245–15,
Little Zürs Kindergarten tel: 5583 2245

FOOD AND DRINK PRICES
Coffee ATS35, glass of wine ATS45,
small beer ATS40, soft drink ATS38,
dish of the day ATS120–250

OTHER SPORTS
Curling, floodlit tobogganing, helicopter
rides, indoor golf, indoor squash and
tennis, paragliding, skating, sleigh rides

60-year-olds wearing the latest in designer ski suits, as well as thirty-somethings who might, perhaps, aspire to look like this in the autumn of their lives. Consequently, après-skiers at these resorts prefer to put their hair up, rather than let it down.

The ice-bar outside the Tannbergerhof in Lech is where, weather permitting, the evening begins in earnest as the slopes close. Guests filter inside to join in the tea-dancing, which swings into action as night falls. The hotel also hosts a disco with a good atmosphere later on in the evening. The Sidestep Bar in the Hotel Krone attracts the over-25s for dancing, and the Klausur Bar in the Schneider Almhof is popular. The s'Pfefferkörndl bar now has dancing. At 5.30pm each Thursday the Rüfikopf cable-car is transformed into a bar, and the restaurant at the top becomes the highest casino in the Alps. For ATS350 you are each given a free glass of champagne on the way up to the blackjack and roulette tables. Places must be reserved in advance for a minimum of 15 people.

The floodlit toboggan run is the quickest way to travel down from Oberlech to Lech at the start of the evening's entertainment. Sleigh rides to Zug for dinner are a treat, and you can take the cable-car up to Oberlech and toboggan down afterwards. Die Vernissage in Zürs is recommended, and the Zürserl in the Hotel Edelweiss is the biggest disco in town, while the Rote Wand and the Sennkessel in Zug are both lively.

Public transport comes to a halt in the early evening. Taxis are expensive, but a collective service until 4am called 'James' will return you to wherever you are staying in Lech, Zürs and Zug for a reasonable set fee of ATS30 per person one-way, or AT50 for the evening.

Childcare

The area lends itself well to family skiing, particularly at Oberlech, the site of the main nursery slopes. A number of hotels run their own crèches. We have positive reports of the Oberlech kindergarten. Children under six years old ski for ATS100 for the whole season. The ski school takes children all day and supervises lunch (parents must remember to provide lunch money each day). The Lech Miniclub is for children from three years of age. The Little Zürs kindergarten takes children from three years old and provides ski instruction for children from four years of age.

Mayrhofen

ALTITUDE 630m (2,066ft)

Beginners ✱✱ Intermediates ✱✱✱ Snowboarders ✱

Mayrhofen has taught generations of British skiers to love low-lying Tyrol. Many remain intensely loyal to a resort that does its best to take care of children, who ski for free under the age of five and receive a reduction up to the age of 15. The resort is only 75km from Innsbruck on fast, flat, snow-free roads; you arrive without having travelled perceptibly uphill. At the top of the broad Ziller Valley, Mayrhofen's own skiing on the Penken, Ahorn and **Finkenberg** slopes covers 102km of pistes with 29 lifts. Local passes are sold, but if you want to ski further afield, the regional Zillertal Superskipass allows access to a wider network of 148 lifts and 462km of piste – including the Hintertux Glacier as a supplementary option.

- ✔ Competent ski teaching
- ✔ High standard of accommodation
- ✔ Summer skiing on Hintertux Glacier
- ✔ Extensive ski pass region
- ✔ Focus on children's activities
- ✘ Low altitude skiing
- ✘ No skiing to village from main mountain
- ✘ Crowded slopes

Everybody loves to party in Mayrhofen, where clients are typically from the south of Germany or the north of England; British skiers total nine per cent of the market here. The resort has singles weeks, and music events attract bands such as the Four Tops and ELO. Regular live music takes place on the outdoor stage on Penken, and clowns perform in the village streets.

In Mayrhofen large green areas are preserved; cows are kept (and slaughtered) right across the street from the Penken lift station. You can stroll across town in 15 minutes. Buses are free only when you are wearing ski clothes and are equipped with a ski pass. At night buses are neither available nor necessary. All lift stations in the region have free parking, except for the Penkenbahn in the centre of Mayrhofen.

On the snow
top 2,250m (7,382ft) bottom 630m (2,066ft)

Mayrhofen's main mountain is the Penken, to which gondolas rise from the town centre as well as from the outlying hamlets of Finkenberg and **Schwendau**. There is no route whatsoever back down to Mayrhofen, and reporters complain of queues with 'up to 30 minutes' wait to get on the Penkenbahn out of Mayrhofen every morning and similar queues to get down to town at the end of the day'. Both the red (intermediate) piste back to Finkenberg and black (difficult) ski route to Schwendau usually suffer from a shortage of snow in March, although the 1998–9 and 1999–2000 seasons were exceptions. However, the new six-person Penken-Express quad chair has greatly alleviated congestion at the mid-mountain stage.

Mayrhofen's easiest mountain, the Ahorn, is accessed only by a limited-capacity cable-car, which is a 10-minute hike from town. The 5.5-km black Ebenwald piste on Ahorn – the only village-run in Mayrhofen – has snowmaking, but at this low altitude it is often too warm for the cannons to operate. Grooming is good, and electronic boards tell you which lifts have queues – always a problem on mountains with no runs down to the village at the end of the day, no matter how modern the lifts.

Beginners

Babies are better catered for than adult beginners. The former have their own play areas, whereas the latter are forced to ride awkward drag-lifts for all the blue (easy) runs on Ahorn and in most cases on Penken, which at least has one ultra-flat, long, beginner itinerary – the 'Horberg Baby Tour'. Reporters criticise the ski schools for teaching their beginner classes on the Penken instead of on the more suitable Ahorn: 'standing in the beginners area was like being in a football crowd, with different classes converging into each other and not enough room for any of them to learn properly'.

> **WHAT'S NEW**
>
> Penken-Express quad chair-lift
> Second stage of Glacier Bus gondola to top of Hintertux

Intermediates

Many Penken runs are graded red, not because they are steep but because they are narrow – often less than 20m wide. This creates diffi-culties for skiers and riders when descending together. Long fall-line cruises are conspicuous by their absence.

Advanced

As one reader put it: 'experts are better off in another resort'. Their greatest challenge is avoiding collisions with aimlessly wandering schools of neophyte skiers and boarders. The Tappental and Schafskopf ski itineraries on Gerent offer the odd hour's amusement before you take the bus to the Hintertux Glacier.

Off-piste

The ingenious will find short, steep descents through rocks and woods on Penken and Gerent. Peter Habeler, who climbed Everest without oxygen in 1978, has a school that also offers off-piste tours with overnight stops in a mountain hut.

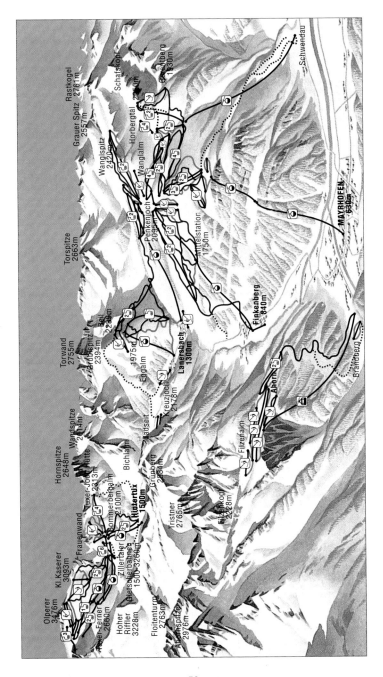

Snowboarders

The funpark on Horberg features two quarter-pipes, a range of obstacles and a sound system. The Ahorn is a good learning area, although there are still too many T-bars in the whole area for comfort. Hintertux has a large funpark open all year round, and the 120-m Olperer is Europe's highest half-pipe.

Tuition and guiding

Mayrhofen has more than 100 instructors from three competing schools. Despite typical classes of 12, most students give the teaching high marks, although crowded slopes are a problem. Manfred Gager's school offers carving courses. Max Rahm's SMT offers video analysis. Peter Habeler's Mount Everest school also offers instruction. All three schools teach snowboarding, although SMT is the only one to have a separate department for riders – the Mayrhofen Snowboard School.

Mountain restaurants

Numerous 'umbrella bars', some open-air and others weatherised, serve quick snacks, schnapps and beer – generally to the accompaniment of raucous accordion music, but without the ear-splitting drinking games of Hilde's (priciest in region) and Vroni's (al fresco barbecue chicken). Josef's Bio Hütte is where an old farmer serves his own potato and cheese dishes and a popular home-made schnapps.

Accommodation

In Mayrhofen every house is a *Gasthaus*, every home a *Gastheim*, and 406 such inns and pensions account for the vast majority of the resort's 8,680 beds. Chalet and self-catering accommodation are considered inimical to local employment prospects. The general standard of accommodation is superlative, with many hotels featuring swimming-pools, saunas or Turkish baths. Rooms are bigger and better than in Switzerland or France. Hotel Strass is next door to the Penken lift and home of both the Ice Bar and Sports Arena disco. Just up the road is the Waldheim, which has comfortable rooms with views. Most tour operators feature the Neuhaus along the main road ('excellent, with a high standard of food'), but the Elisabeth is more luxurious, and the impeccable Hotel Berghof has its own indoor tennis courts. The Alpenhotel Kramerwirt is recommended. Hotel Obermair is 'basic, but comfortable'.

Eating in and out

Most guests choose half-board, but several reporters complain that the portions in the hotels are inadequate. Mayrhofen has fewer independent dining venues than one might expect. Among them is the Wirthaus zum Griena, which is a listed 400-year-old building and includes a menu of 'poor people's food'. Singapore is an average Chinese restaurant, Mo's serves Cajun burgers, and Mamma Mia is a bright Italian. Grill Kuchl has a good, inexpensive menu. Café Dengg has the best pizza. The Sports Bar Grill in Hotel Strass serves Mexican food.

Après-ski

Reporters' accounts of nightlife vary: 'some bars were lively up to about 7pm, after which time the town seemed to go to bed. This is a dull, thirty-something family resort'. The yellow umbrella bars are numerous and right on the slopes, offering: 'lively but monotonous Euro-rock repeated every night in every bar'. However, the Ice Bar, with its dancing 'polar bear', claims to be Europe's biggest sales point for Grolsch beer and Mayrhofen's most popular meeting place. Virtually every hotel has an entertainer.

The Sports Arena is one of the most high-tech discos in the Alps. Rundum is a bar in green glass with a real tree upstairs but 'suffers from '80s Euro-rock'. The Scotland Yard Pub is a popular hang-out for riders and has darts, a working red telephone box and British beer. However, it is criticised for its slow service. There are no bargains along the winding high street, although the Mikesch toy shop is a treasure. The Aqua Adventure Pool, with its 101-m chute, is unique in the Alps.

Childcare

If you register your child at the tourist office, he or she will receive a birthday gift in the post. In town, childcare includes Wuppy's Kinderland, which minds children from three months to seven years of age. SMT and Gager both run ski- and non-ski kindergartens, while Peter Habeler takes children from five years of age.

Linked or nearby resorts

The Zillertal region covers 12 different local areas stretching down to the River Inn and the Germany–Innsbruck autobahn, and up the valley sides east as far as **Gerlos** and west as far as **Fügenberg**. **Hintertux**, **Lanersbach**, **Kramsach** and **Kaltenbach** are all included on the Zillertal Superskipass. Few of these Zillertal resorts are linked together by piste. Individually, none offers much more than a single day's interesting skiing. But bus transport is free and generally efficient, and a free train goes from Mayrhofen down the valley to **Zell am Ziller**, and on to **Fügen** and the mainline junction at **Jenbach**.

Finkenberg is the closest village to Mayrhofen on the road up towards Hintertux. But its previous appeal, quicker access to Penken, was eliminated by the construction of the Penken gondola from downtown Mayrhofen. Lanersbach is the best choice for price and nightlife, not to mention its own ski runs, for those focusing on daily skiing at Hintertux. With neighbouring **Vorderlanersbach**, Lanersbach boasts 13 lifts servicing the small areas of Eggalm and Rastkogel, with skiing up to 2,300m on 33km of pistes.

After Mayrhofen, Zell am Ziller is the second most substantial valley resort. The name should not be confused with Kaprun's twin resort near Salzburg, Zell am See. In fact, Zell am Ziller is the antithesis of a ski resort. Sitting in the Ziller river valley at 570m, Zell is a bustling, commercialised market town. Counting the lift systems of its

Skiing facts: Mayrhofen

TOURIST INFORMATION
Postfach 21, A-6290 Mayrhofen, Zillertal
Tel 43 5285 6760
Fax 43 5285 6760 33
Email mayrhofen@zillertal.tirol.at
Web site www.mayrhofen.com

THE RESORT
By road Calais 1,159km
By rail Jenbach station in resort
Airport transfer Innsbruck 1hr,
Munich 2hrs
Visitor beds 8,680
Transport free day-time bus service
around Zillertal included in lift pass

THE SKIING
Linked or nearby resorts Finkenberg (l),
Fügen (n), Fügenberg (n), Gerlos (n),
Hintertux (n), Hippach (n), Juns (n),
Kaltenbach (n), Kramsach (n),
Lanersbach (n), Madseit (n),
Ramsau-im-Ziller (n), Schwendau (n),
Vorderlanersbach (n), Zell am Ziller (n)
Number of lifts 29 in Mayrhofen,
148 in Zillertal
Total of trails/pistes 102km in Mayrhofen
(22% easy, 52% intermediate,
26% difficult), 462km in Zillertal
Nursery slopes 3 runs and lifts
Summer skiing 18km of piste on
Hintertux Glacier

LIFT PASSES
Area pass Zillertal Superskipass
(includes glacier), ATS2,130 for 6 days

Beginners no free lifts
Pensioners no reduction
Credit cards no

TUITION
Adults Manfred Gager tel: 5285 63800,
Peter Habeler tel: 5285 62829,
Max Rahm's SMT tel: 5285 63939
Snowboarding Mayrhofen Snowboard
School (SMT) tel: 5285 63939
Other courses carving, cross-country,
race training, ski-touring, teen skiing
Guiding Peter Habeler

CHILDREN
Lift pass Zillertal Superskipass
(includes glacier), 6–15yrs,
ATS1,300-1,720 for 6 days,
free for 5yrs and under
Ski & board school as adults
Kindergarten (ski) Peter Habeler,
(non-ski) Wuppy's Kinderland
tel: 5285 63612,
(ski/non-ski) Gager, Max Rahm's SMT

OTHER SPORTS
Curling, hang-gliding, horse-riding,
hot-air ballooning, ice-climbing,
indoor tennis and squash, night-skiing,
parapente, skating, sleigh rides,
snow-shoeing, swimming, tubing

FOOD AND DRINK PRICES
Coffee ATS25–30, glass of wine ATS30,
small beer ATS25, soft drink ATS25,
dish of the day ATS80–200

neighbours, **Ramsau-in-Ziller** and **Hippach**, Zell am Ziller claims a
regional area with 47km of pistes and 22 lifts. Neither of Zell's own
two areas, Kreuzjoch or Gerlosstein, is within walking distance of the
town. Kreuzjoch's centrepiece is a swift eight-person gondola, and
Gerlosstein has twin cable-cars – testimony to the crowds that flock in
from Germany each weekend.

Tux im Zillertal
top 3,250m (10,663ft) bottom 1,500m (4,920ft)

The Tux ski region consists of five small villages – Hintertux, **Madseit**, Juns, Lanersbach and Vorderlanersbach. Hintertux, or the Tuxer Glacier as the locals call it, boasts the steepest glacier skiing in Austria and, snow permitting, is open 365 days a year (18km of the piste is open all summer). It also offers the most advanced skiing on the otherwise strictly low-altitude Zillertal Superskipass. Skiing at this end of the Zillertal extends to 120km of piste served by 33 lifts.

Hintertux consists of a handful of modern four-star hotels. These are little frequented by British skiers, who find more life at less cost down the valley in Lanersbach. The Tuxer Valley winds steeply southwest for 17km from Mayrhofen, requiring a 45-minute free shuttle transfer from Mayrhofen to Hintertux. Buses run every 15 minutes during the morning peak hours.

The glacier attracts such vast numbers that, as a result, two-metre-high metal cattle pens welcome skiers and snowboarders at the Hintertux base-station. Hotel residents in Hintertux with six-day lift passes enjoy their own separate entrance. Lower glacier lifts and pistes are very crowded. Higher lifts are less crowded, with the more testing top runs often empty in less-than-ideal weather.

From Hintertux a four-person gondola and a double chair-lift take you up to the foot of the glacier at Sommerbergalm, site of a comfortable self-service cafeteria and an outdoor umbrella bar blaring schmaltzy folk tunes. From here, two drag-lifts and a covered quad-chair branch to the right towards the Tuxer Joch. Branching to the left and up to the Tuxerfernerhaus restaurant complex is the Gletscherbus Funitel gondola, carrying up to 24 skiers in sit-down comfort. In April 2000 the long-awaited second stage of the gondola was opened. It now provides direct and easy access all the way up to the top of the glacier at 3250m and Austria's highest privately owned mountain hut. The Funitel provides considerably greater stability and allows the lift to operate even in moderately high winds. For the present, the old chair-lifts that it has replaced remain open and can provide alternative access to the top of the mountain at peak times.

Nowhere on the glacier is the skiing overly challenging, with most runs groomed and free of bumps. However, the pistes are considered to be the best year-round downhill training ground in Europe, and national teams spend much of their summer here. The home run to Sommerbergalm is narrow and can be dangerously overcrowded in places. The only marked off-piste itinerary, the Schwarze Pfanne, goes all the way down to Hintertux but is frequently closed. Hintertux has its own ski and snowboard school. The regular pitch of the glacier is ideal for beginner riders.

TOURIST INFORMATION
Tel 43 5287 8506
Fax 43 5287 8508
Email info@tux.at
Web site www.tux.at

Obergurgl/Hochgurgl

ALTITUDE 1,930m (6,330ft)

Beginners ✱✱ Intermediates ✱✱✱ Advanced ✱✱ Snowboarders ✱✱

The charming village of Obergurgl has an entrenched reputation as Austria's leading skiing destination for families. Although serious skiers were previously deterred by its limited piste-skiing, this situation has now been rectified by the addition of an ambitious cross-mountain gondola. It has an hourly capacity of 1,200 snow-users and connects directly to neighbouring Hochgurgl, creating the sizeable linked ski area that the resort sorely lacked. Its high altitude means that snow is guaranteed from November until after Easter (even when late).

✔ Ideal for families
✔ Extensive ski-touring
✔ Late-season skiing
✔ Resort charm
✔ Magnificent scenery
✗ Lack of tough runs
✗ Limited facilities for non-skiers
✗ High prices

Obergurgl is situated at the head of the remote and beautiful Ötz Valley, which is a 90-minute drive from **Innsbruck**. Building in Obergurgl has reached capacity within the avalanche-safe area and despite the large number of luxury hotels, it remains a small village, set around the church and a handful of shops on the lower level and around an open-air ice-rink on the upper level. At the heart of it all is the Edelweiss und Gurgl Hotel, the focal four-star around which much of village life rotates.

The wealth of luxury hotels in the village attracts an upmarket clientèle, predominantly from Germany but traditionally bolstered by British families. However, prices are reasonable compared to larger resorts such as **Ischgl**. Guests confess to being bowled over by the natural, unspoilt beauty of the resort, which instils unfailing loyalty. As one reader put it: 'I almost didn't want to send in this report in case too many others discover this lovely resort'.

Cars are banned from the village between 11pm and 6am, and parking is not easy. Most Obergurgl visitors are more than content to remain in their elegant eyrie at the head of the valley: only limited **Vent** and mass-market **Sölden** are within easy reach for a day out from Obergurgl, but lift passes are not compatible.

Hochgurgl is little more than a collection of modern hotels perched by the side of the road leading up to the Timmelsjoch Pass, which is closed in winter. In the past Obergurgl and Hochgurgl were seen as entirely separate destinations – while Obergurgl drew families like a moth to a searchlight, Hochgurgl had a more serious skiing image.

However, the resort is now linked across the König and Verwall valleys by the eight-person gondola.

Obergurgl first made its mark on the European skiing map on 27 May 1931, when the Swiss aviation pioneer Professor Auguste Piccard made a forced landing in his hot-air balloon on the Gurgler-Ferner Glacier after achieving the world altitude record of 16,203m. A local mountain guide, Hans Falkner, spotted the balloon landing in the last light of the day. The following morning he carried out a triumphant rescue of the explorers, leading them between the crevasses to Obergurgl and glory for all concerned. World recognition followed for the village, then one of Austria's most exclusive ski resorts.

On the snow
top 3,080m (10,104ft) bottom 1,793m (5,881ft)

The slopes of both Obergurgl and Hochgurgl occupy a northwest-facing area at the southern end of the Ötztal on the Italian border. These are linked via the 3.6-km gondola, which runs from the bottom of the Wurmkogl lift at Hochgurgl to the bottom of the blue Run 3, halfway up the Festkoglbahn. Most of the skiing is above the tree-line, and runs are intermediate. Not all of the handful of black (difficult) runs justify their gradings, and advanced snow-users will soon tire of the limited pistes – unless they are interested in ski-touring, for which the area is outstanding. However, the truly magnificent surroundings offer plenty to keep less adventurous snow-users and families occupied.

The skiing takes place over three small areas naturally divided by the contours of the terrain. Hochgurgl offers the greatest vertical drop off the glacier but also the most severe weather conditions: even on a sunny day in February, extreme cold can be the price you pay for high-quality snow. The wide, wooded hillside leads down to **Untergurgl**, which is little more than a roadside lift station and car park.

Obergurgl's two sectors, properly linked in one direction only, generally comprise more interesting terrain, with the steeper runs at the top and some good off-piste alternatives. Easy access to the Festkogl area is provided via a four-seater enclosed chair, which starts from directly behind the Hotel Edelweiss und Gurgl. Alternative access is via a gondola on the outskirts of Obergurgl, while Gaisberg is reached by a chair-lift, which rises lazily over gentle slopes from the village centre. Reporters noted that the area's piste grooming and signposting is excellent.

Beginners

Complete novices start on nursery slopes set well away from the village near the cross-country track. While Obergurgl has easy skiing in both its main sectors, Hochgurgl has a far more comprehensive selection of blue (easy) pistes. The top of the long glacier is served by two chairs – one a high-speed covered quad which affords some protection against the elements, often quite severe at this altitude.

Intermediates

The Festkogl gondola rises steeply to a sunny plateau with a restaurant and a couple of drag-lifts. The area of mainly red (but not difficult) intermediate runs is served by a modern quad-chair, which takes you up to the highest point of Obergurgl's skiing at 3,035m. Less confident skiers and snowboarders will enjoy the blue run from the gondola station down to the bottom of the Rosskar double-chair.

While Hochgurgl's skiing is generally less challenging, the Schermer-Spitz chair, with conveyor-belt entry, gives access to a wide and easy red piste, which is the start of nearly 1,500m vertical all the way down to Untergurgl. A two-stage covered quad-chair takes you up to the summit of the Wurmkogl, which offers an exciting descent for strong intermediates. The drag-lift on the southern side of the ski area has a short, steep, second section. It serves a long and varied red run with moguls. One reporter describes the bottom half as 'much more difficult than any other red run in the resort'.

Advanced

The pistes offer little serious challenge or scope. In the Gaisberg sector a long, antique single-chair goes up to the Hohe Mut at 2,670m. The first part of the only official run down is a ski route, which in turn becomes a black piste, but the 1.8-km descent is not difficult when

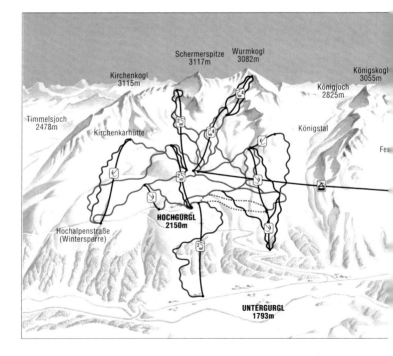

snow cover is deep, and one suspects that the grading is designed to reduce traffic and avoid bottlenecks at the outdated lift.

Accomplished snow-users will enjoy the black itinerary down the Ferwalltal from the top of the Festkogl gondola. However, the run is prone to avalanche danger, and great care should be taken.

Off-piste
Obergurgl, with its 21 glaciers, is one of the great ski-touring centres of Europe. More limited opportunities also exist for those who prefer to take their powder by lift rather than on skins. An off-piste run in good powder conditions off the back of the Hohe Mut takes you on a glorious descent that ends up near the Schönwieshütte.

Snowboarders
This is a good place for riders of all levels, with some excellent carving opportunities on the gentle slopes. Wurmkogl has a half-pipe and a funpark with a small range of obstacles in the Festkogl ski area.

Tuition and guiding
Obergurgl is one of the homes of the Austrian Instructors' Ski School, and the standard of teaching and organisation here should therefore be among the highest in Austria. However, we have received considerable

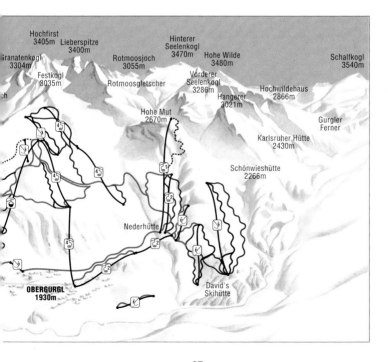

criticism of both the Obergurgl and Hochgurgl schools, with lack of motivation being the main complaint. One reporter said that his teacher 'was simply not interested in improving the standard of the class. You got the impression that he was only going through the motions in return for his meal ticket. It may have been a long season for him, but for us it was our precious one-week holiday'.

Other reporters complained of as many as 15 pupils per class, and criticised division into language groups (not always well organised): 'the ski school seemed to allocate children mainly by height'). Gripes include a lack of English-speaking instructors, poor group selection and 'almost non-existent tuition skills'.

Mountain restaurants

'Lunch in Obergurgl is a treat', says one reporter. The Hohe Mut Hütte, at the top of the single-chair at Gaisberg, provides magnificent views of the Ötztal and the Dolomites. Although you can make the return journey by chair-lift, the alternative post-prandial prospect of the black ski route down acts as a deterrent to those wanting lunch and means that the old wooden chalet is the least crowded restaurant in the area. On fine days there is an ice-bar and barbecue on the terrace. The Schönwieshütte, a 15-minute walk from the Sattellift piste, is a touring refuge, which serves simple meals ('best *Gulaschsuppe* and *Kaiserschmarren* ever').

David's Schihütte at the bottom of the Steinmannlift is recommended for its *Tirolergröstl* (potato with bacon), although the service can be 'so slow as to be non-existent, with Serbian waiters who speak no English or German'. The Festkogl mountain restaurant is described by a number of reporters as 'indifferent'. The Nederhütte is warmly recommended for 'good food and an excellent atmosphere'.

In Hochgurgl, the Wurmkogl (by the top of the Wurmkogl quad-chair) is the best of the three altitude restaurants. Toni's Almhütte – a rustic wooden hut owned by the Sporthotel Olymp – is highly praised. The sun terrace of the Hotel Riml has great views 'back up the valley to Obergurgl and beyond'.

Accommodation

Most of the accommodation is in smart hotels and, to a lesser extent, in gasthofs and pensions. It is also possible to rent attractive and spacious apartments by contacting the resort direct. Hotel Crystal is a monster of a building, completely out of keeping with resort character, but extremely comfortable inside. The Deutschmann takes its name from the old Obergurgl family that owns it. The Bergwelt ('art-deco furniture and a great pool') and the Austria are both highly recommended. Hotel Gotthard is also warmly praised: 'the welcome matched the luxurious surroundings'.

In the centre, Hotel Edelweiss und Gurgl is highly thought of, although its bedrooms are not as large or as well-equipped as those in the new four-stars. The Jenewein is praised for its friendly service and

Skiing facts: Obergurgl

TOURIST INFORMATION
Hauptstrasse 108,
A-6456 Obergurgl, Ötztal
Tel 43 5256 6466
Fax 43 5256 6353
Email info@obergurgl.com
Web site www.obergurgl.com

THE RESORT
By road Calais 1,102km
By rail Ötztal 54km, regular buses
from station
Airport transfer Innsbruck 1½hrs
Visitor beds 4,000
Transport free ski bus

THE SKIING
Linked or nearby resorts Hochgurgl (l),
Sölden (n), Vent (n)
Number of lifts 23
Total of trails/pistes 110km (32% easy,
50% intermediate, 18% difficult)
Nursery slopes 4 runs and lifts

LIFT PASSES
Area pass Gurgl (covers
Obergurgl/Hochgurgl) ATS1,960–2,230
for 6 days

Beginners no free lifts
Pensioners 60yrs and over, as children
Credit cards no

TUITION
Adults Obergurgl tel: 5256 6305,
Hochgurgl tel: 5256 6265–99
Snowboarding as ski schools
Other courses carving, cross-country,
extreme skiing, monoski, seniors,
ski-touring, Skwal, snowblading, telemark
Guiding through Obergurgl ski school

CHILDREN
Lift pass 8–16yrs, ATS1,360 for 6 days
Ski & board as adults
Kindergarten Bobo's Kinderclub
tel: 5256 6305

OTHER SPORTS
Curling, night-skiing/night-riding,
shooting, skating, squash, sleigh rides,
snowshoeing, swimming

FOOD AND DRINK PRICES
Coffee ATS27–32, glass of wine ATS25,
small beer ATS35, soft drink ATS25–32,
dish of the day ATS100–130

'quite exceptional demi-pension food'. Hotel Alpina was described as 'outstanding, with wonderful hospitality'. The Schönblick has 'helpful owners, large rooms, and excellent buffet breakfasts'.

In Hochgurgl we have good reports of the Hotel Riml and the less expensive Hotel Ideal ('it is, as the name implies'). The three-star Alpenhotel Laurin is highly recommended for its excellent food ('superb farmers' buffet').

Eating in and out
Dining is largely confined to the main hotels, most of which have separate à la carte restaurants. Pizzeria Romantika in the Hotel Madeleine provides some respite from the ubiquitous rounds of Wienerschnitzel. The Edelweiss has a comfortable candlelit stübli with an atmosphere of 'relaxed elegance'.

The Bergwelt is recommended for its nouvelle cuisine. Pizzeria Belmonte in Haus Gurgl has 'the best pizzas in town'. Restaurant Pic-Nic is also recommended. A reporter spoke warmly of fondue evenings organised at the Nederhütte. One small supermarket in Obergurgl looks after the needs of self-caterers. Reporters warn that restaurants in Hochgurgl itself are nearly all attached to the smart hotels and are expensive.

Après-ski

Non-skiing activities are limited in this small resort, but Obergurgl is surprisingly active in the evenings. The Nederhütte at the top of the Gaisberg lift becomes crowded as the lifts close for the day. Dancing to the owner's three-piece band and copious measures of gluhwein prepare you for the gentle run down to the village at dusk. The outdoor bar of the Edelweiss at the foot of the Gaisberg lift continues to attract customers until dark. Its cellar disco is said by most reporters to be the best in town. The Joslkeller has a cosy atmosphere and good music, which gets louder with dancing as the evening progresses. You will find the odd person in ski suit and ski boots still here in the early hours. The Krump'n'Stadl is noisy, with yodelling on alternate nights. Hexenkuch'l has live music, as does Toni's Almhütte in Hochgurgl.

Childcare

In a move to attract more families, the resort allows children aged seven years and under to ski for free – a higher age limit than in many other resorts in the Alps. Bobo's Kinderclub takes non-skiing children from three years old. A number of hotels operate their own crèches, usually free of charge. These include the Alpina, Austria, Bellevue, Bergwelt, Crystal, Hochfirst, Hochgurgl and Olymp. The minimum age accepted varies from hotel to hotel. Obergurgl Ski School takes children from five years old, and Hochgurgl accepts children as young as three years old for lessons.

Obertauern

ALTITUDE 1,740m (5,707ft)

Beginners ✷✷ Intermediates ✷✷✷ Snowboarders ✷

Obertauern is Austria's best shot at a purpose-built resort and is as far removed as possible from the popular image of a cute Austrian ski resort centred around an onion-domed church and the village inn. Instead, it consists of a long straggle of roadside hotels and bars and looks more like a Wild West town. However, Obertauern is by no means devoid of charm, and any architectural liberties at variance with the usual perception of an Austrian ski resort are generally hidden under a reliable blanket of snow. Indeed, its renown is based largely on its reputation for guaranteed snow-cover, and if there is decent snow anywhere in Austria, you will find it here.

✔ Excellent snow record
✔ Reliable resort-level snow
✔ Superb piste-grooming
✔ Skiing convenience
✔ Interesting off-piste
✘ Late-season queues
✘ No bus system
✘ Lack of non-skiing activities
✘ Quiet après-ski
✘ Spread-out village

The resort lies on a high pass in the Niedere Tauern mountains, 90km (56 miles) south of Salzburg. The main cluster of buildings, which constitutes the centre, is around the village nursery slope and the tourist information office. Obertauern is one of Austria's top-five winter destinations, although it was only discovered by British skiers in the mid-1980s. The impressive peaks of the Niedere Tauern mountain range surround the road around the resort, allowing the construction of lifts from a central point to fan out into a natural ski circus. The ski area is not particularly extensive but provides an interesting variety of gradient and terrain.

On the snow
top 2,313m (7,587ft) bottom 1,640m (5,379ft)

The circus of 27 lifts covers 95km and can be skied in both directions, but the skiing is concentrated on the north side of the resort, spread around a broad, undulating and mainly treeless bowl ringed by rocky peaks. Four main lifts rise from around the bowl to points near the rim. Two of them ascend to approximately 2,000m from almost the same point as each other at Hochalm (1,940m); the Seekareckbahn quad chair-lift takes you up over a steep, east-facing slope, and the Panorama triple-chair takes you over a more varied south-facing one.

A clockwise circuit of this northern part of the area need not involve any of the higher, more difficult runs. The pistes of most

71

interest to timid skiers are the easy, open runs across the middle of the bowl, served by drag-lifts including the long Zentral lift from just below the village. On the south side of the resort the mountains rise more dramatically, keeping the village in shade for much of the day in mid-winter. The local lift map fails to show either piste names or numbers, but the signposting of the clockwise and anticlockwise circuits is generally sufficient.

Beginners

The nursery slopes are excellent, with a short, gentle drag-lift in the heart of the village, just north of the main road, and another longer one on the lower slopes at the eastern end. Another runs parallel to and just south of the road. The high Gamskarlift, at the top of the steep Schaidberg chair, also affords gentle skiing.

Intermediates

The entire circuit is geared towards intermediates, with some truly excellent long, but not over demanding, red (intermediate) descents from the lip of the bowl. Some of the best are accessed from the Panorama Sesselbahn and Hundskogel lifts. The top of the Plattenkarbahn quad-chair is the starting point for a challenging run of over 400m vertical.

Advanced

There is enough to keep advanced skiers happy here for a week, although the more adventurous will want to explore the other resorts in the region (such as St Johann im Pongau). Pistes can become heavily mogulled around the edge of the bowl.

Off-piste

In powder conditions the off-piste skiing is spectacular, with long runs both above and below the tree-line. To find the best and safest runs you need the services of a local guide. Vertical is the off-piste guiding company.

Snowboarders

The freeriding here is excellent, but not so the half-pipe, which is said to be 'unexciting'. Beginners have some good tame trails to learn on.

Tuition and guiding

Obertauern has six ski and snowboard schools, including the Krallinger Obertauern-Süd, which has a higher than average number of female instructors and is much favoured by tour operators. The others are CSA (known as Skischule Willi Grillitsch), Schischule Top and Schischule Frau Holle. Christian and Werner Schmidt run their dedicated Snowwave Snowboardschule from the Hotel Solaria, and Gerfried Schuller runs the Obertauern Snowboardschule. The Frau Holle school also gives snowboarding lessons.

Mountain restaurants

Because of the ski-in ski-out nature of Obertauern, it is quite easy to return to the village for lunch. Alternatively, the choice of mountain restaurants is more than adequate. The Dikt'nalm has table service. The Lurzeralm is 'piste-side, rustic, and pleasant'. The Seekarhaus at Kringsalm, which is a cosy spot with enjoyable food, can become crowded. It is being rebuilt for the 2000–1 season as a four-star hotel. The Sonnhof is equally busy, and one reporter warned that at weekends you need to lunch before noon to be sure of obtaining a table at all at the smaller mountain restaurants.

Accommodation

Nearly all the accommodation is in hotels and guesthouses, few of them cheap. Location is not particularly critical unless you have small children (choose a hotel within easy walking distance of one of the kindergartens). Hotel Krallinger is recommended as a good ski-in ski-out base with satellite television in the rooms. Haus Kärntnerland is said to be 'clean, comfortable and friendly, with exceptional food'. The Alpenrose apartments in the village centre are described as 'cosy and well-appointed'. The lavish Sporthotel Marietta remains a favourite with reporters.

Eating in and out

Most of the restaurants are in hotels. The Stüberl restaurant in the Hotel Regina is reported to be extremely good value ('quiet, candlelit, and serves enormous portions'). The Lurzeralm requires reservations and serves 'well-presented, good food'. The Latsch'n'Stüberl has friendly service and well-prepared food.

Après-ski

This is centred on the main hotel bars, of which more than 15 offer music and dancing. The Edelweisshütte is the place to go at the end of the day, along with the Gamsmilch Bar and the Achenrainhutte. Later on the action moves to La Bar and Premillos, next to the Hotel Steiner. The Gasthof Taverne reportedly has the liveliest disco later in the evening.

Childcare

Non-skiing children from two to six years of age are cared for all day in the Petzi-Bar crèche or in the CSA Mini Club. All the ski schools run ski kindergartens, with lunch provided on request.

TOURIST INFORMATION
Tel 43 6456 7252
Fax 43 6456 7515
Email info@ski-obertauern.com
Web site www.ski-obertauern.com

Saalbach-Hinterglemm

ALTITUDE 1,000m (3,280ft)

Beginners ✳✳✳ Intermediates ✳✳✳ Advanced ✳✳ Snowboarders ✳✳✳

Saalbach-Hinterglemm is the collective marketing name of two once separate villages in the pretty Glemmtal valley near **Zell am See**. The narrow valley, with uniform 2,000-m peaks on either side, lends itself to a natural ski circus, which can be skied as happily in one direction as in the other. It provides some of the best intermediate and advanced skiing in Austria, second only to that in the Arlberg region.

The two villages, a five-minute drive apart, have grown so much over the years that they now stretch along the valley and almost meet. Those looking for two cheap and cosy little Austrian villages will be disappointed; both are large and expensive.

The steep and thankfully pedestrianised main street of Saalbach, with its smart hotels and high-priced fashion boutiques, gives one the distinct feeling of having strayed on to the set of a Hollywood studio preparing to shoot a twenty-first-century sequel to *The Sound of Music*. The alpine charm is positively Disneyesque. Old it may appear, but most of the village dates from the 1980s. Hinterglemm is little more than a collection of stolid Austrian hotels, which acts as an alternative base at the far end of the ski system. A third village, **Leogang**, provides a back door into the ski area and is a quieter, more attractive alternative.

✔ Short airport transfer
✔ Reliable snow cover
✔ Traffic-free village centres
✔ Wide selection of accommodation
✔ Good child facilities
✔ Large choice of ski schools
✔ Extensive ski area
✘ Lift queues
✘ Sprawling villages
✘ High prices
✘ Noisy at night

On the snow
top 2,096m (6,877ft) bottom 1,000m (3,280ft)

Both sides of the valley are lined with a network of 52 lifts, which also links to neighbouring Leogang. Much of the system has been upgraded to provide an easy traffic flow around the 200-km circuit of prepared pistes. From the bottom of Saalbach, the Schattberg-Ost cable-car gives direct and easy access (in good snow conditions) to the southern half of the circuit. The 100-person lift is prone to serious queues when the sunny side of the valley opposite has scarce snow cover. A triple-chair at the top end of the village is the starting point for the northern half of

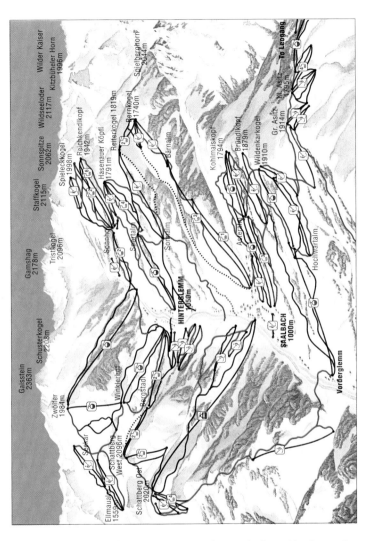

the ski area. From **Vorderglemm**, which is a ski-bus ride down the valley, the two-stage Schönleitenbahn gondola takes you up to Wildenkarkogel and into the Leogang ski area. You can also find your way here from Saalbach via a gondola, which feeds a network of gentle, south-facing runs. The picturesque Glemmtal offers considerable langlauf opportunities.

Beginners

Both villages have their own nursery slopes, and the north side of the valley is dotted with T-bars serving an unusual variety of beginner terrain. When you feel capable of graduating to the main circus, the gentler southern side offers a vast area of blue (easy) runs. When snow conditions are patchy, take either gondola to the 1,984-m Zwölfer; the long *Familienabfahrt* back to the valley usually holds the snow well. From Schattberg-Ost the 7-km *Jausernabfahrt* is a gentle cruise down to Vorderglemm, where you can take the Wildenkarkogel gondola up the other side of the valley for the easiest of cruises back to Saalbach.

Intermediates

Anyone who can ski parallel will enjoy the full circuit, although it is possible to shorten the outing by cutting across the valley at four separate points. Those seeking confidence-building slopes will have a field day here as most of the southern side of the valley is an easy blue playground. Challenging exceptions to this are the Schönleiten Talstation from beneath the Brundlkopf, the women's downhill from Kohlmaiskopf and a few shorter red (intermediate) runs above Hinterglemm. The Leogang sector has some usually uncrowded terrain which is well worth exploring at weekends when the main slopes are busy.

<aside>
WHAT'S NEW

Hochalm double chair-lift upgraded to six-person chair
Reiterkogel-Gifellift replaced by covered quad-chair
Additional snowmaking
</aside>

Advanced

Schattberg-Ost, Schattberg-West and Zwölferkogel make up the more challenging north-facing slopes. The north face of the Zwölfer is a classic, harsh black (difficult) run, which can be heavily mogulled. The home run from Schattberg-Ost can be extremely icy and crowded. A far more interesting route begins with the Westgipfel triple-chair to Schattberg-West, from where you can take a steep black to the bottom and, after another chair ride, follow the challenging itinerary to Bergstadl.

Off-piste

The north side of the valley offers some outstanding powder runs, but a local guide is necessary to discover which slopes are safe, and when. Sepp Mitterer, as well as all the regular ski and board schools, can arrange off-piste guiding.

Snowboarders

Saalbach has devoted 13km of slopes to riders of all levels and is now recognised as a major resort for snowboarders. The vast 12-km snowboard-only funpark includes a boardercross course. Both Saalbach and Hinterglem have separate half-pipes. Off-piste snowboarding opportunities can be wonderful, with good riding down to the main valley road, which is served by a regular, free shuttle bus. The large number of T-bars make Saalbach a tricky place for beginners to learn to snowboard.

Tuition and guiding

Since deregulation permitted the establishment of alternative ski schools in Austria, no less than nine now compete for the resort's big business. Schischule Wolf, based in Hinterglemm, attracts a disproportionate number of Anglo-Saxon guests. The smaller Mitterlengau (also known as Activ) in Hinterglemm, is praised for 'excellent instruction, with clear and precise analysis of bad habits and practical help in correcting them'. Schischule Fürstauer in Saalbach is particularly recommended for teaching children – 'all instructors were English-speaking, cheerful, professional and highly committed to teaching young people'. Snowboardschule Saalbach is the resorts' specialist school for riders.

Mountain restaurants

Saalbach-Hinterglemm has a wide selection of mountain eating establishments. As one reporter put it 'there are almost as many restaurants and delightful huts as there are runs. The Pfefferalm above Hinterglemm is the most picturesque old farmhouse we have ever encountered'.

The Goatssalm is equally rustic and is recommended for its glühwein. The good-value Rosswaldhütte, beside the Rosswald lift in the Hochalmspitze area, is an attractive chalet where the friendly staff wear traditional costume. The rather twee Wildenkarkogel Hütte at the top of the Vorderglemm gondola is also accessible for non-skiers.

Accommodation

The resort is brimming with four-star hotels; Saalbach has 15 and Hinterglemm 12. These include the comfortable Alpenhotel and the luxurious Hotel Ingonda, both in Saalbach. Hotel Hasenauer in Hinterglemm is convenient for the lifts, but one reporter commented: 'rooms, water and staff were all rather too cool for comfort'. Hotel Glemmtalerhof is described as 'pleasant enough, but German oriented'. However, the resort also has some more reasonably priced establishments. Three-star Hotel Sonnblick at Hinterglemm has 'excellent food and a friendly bar – it is difficult to see the need to pay more for one of the posher hotels'. Haus Wolf is said to be 'clean and very friendly'.

Eating in and out

Bäckstättstall is the most exclusive restaurant in Saalbach. The Hotel Bauer is said to be 'good value, with a much more varied menu than you expect in Austria'. Hotel Hasenauer in Hinterglemm is 'cheaper than anywhere else'. The Bärenbachhof is 'not as expensive and better than most'. Two reporters spoke warmly of Hotel Gollingerhof's restaurant in Saalbach.

Skiing facts: Saalbach-Hinterglemm

TOURIST INFORMATION
Glemmtaler Landesstrasse 550, A-5753 Saalbach
Tel 43 6541 680068
Fax 43 6541 680069
Email contact@saalbach.com
Web site www.saalbach.com

THE RESORT
By road Calais 1,193km
By rail Zell am See 19km
Airport transfer Salzburg 1½hrs
Visitor beds 16,360
Transport free ski bus with lift pass

THE SKIING
Linked or nearby resorts Bad Gastein (n), Bad Hofgastein (n), Grossarl (n), Kaprun (n), Leogang (l), Zell am See (n)
Number of lifts 52
Total of trails/pistes 200km (45% easy, 47% intermediate, 8% difficult)
Nursery slopes 5 lifts

LIFT PASSES
Area pass (covers Saalbach-Hinterglemm and Leogang) ATS1,790–2,010 for 6 days
Beginners points tickets
Pensioners reductions for women 60yrs and over, men 65yrs and over
Credit cards yes

TUITION
Adults Saalbach: Aamadall tel: 6541 6246, Fürstauer tel: 6541 8444,

Hinterholzer tel: 6541 7607, Heugenhauser tel: 663 860790, Zinc tel: 6541 8420. Hinterglemm: Gensbichler tel: 6541 7511, Lechner tel: 6541 7328, Mitterlengau (or Activ) tel: 6541 7255, Wolf tel: 6541 6346–0,
Snowboarding as ski schools and Snowboardschule Saalbach tel: 6541 20047
Other courses cross-country, race-training, telemark
Guiding Sepp Mitterer tel: 6541 7008, or through ski schools

CHILDREN
Lift pass 7–15yrs ATS1,075–1,215, 16–19yrs ATS1,810–1,785, both for 6 days, free for 6yrs and under
Ski & board school as adults
Kindergarten (ski) Wolf, Fürstauer, (non-ski) Gartenhotel Theresia tel: 6541 7415–40, Hotel Glemmtalerhof tel: 6541 7135, Hotel Lengauerhof tel: 6541 7255, Partnerhotels tel: 6541 74080

OTHER SPORTS
Curling, hang-gliding, ice-hockey, indoor tennis and squash, parapente, skating, sleigh rides, swimming

FOOD AND DRINK PRICES
Coffee ATS26–30, glass of wine ATS25–60, small beer ATS32–38, soft drink ATS26–30, dish of the day ATS110–120

Après-ski

The endearing feature of Saalbach is the immutable, jolly Austrian formula. True, the folk dancers now save their thigh-slapping and yodels for the more appreciative lakes-and-mountains clientèle in the summer, but the waitresses still wear their *Dirndl* dresses and genuine smiles of welcome as they pocket your money. Après-ski starts with a drink at the Bäckstättstall Umbrella Bar with 'a disco/band and striking views over Saalbach; they also do a potent glühwein to add some challenge to the very short run down to the street'. The Schirmbar is also recommended. Hinterhagalm has a huge copper pot of glühwein on the bar, and it is on draft at Bauer's Schialm by the church in Saalbach. The Classic bustles, and the snow-bar at Hotel Glemmtalerhof is always crowded. Lumpi's Bla Bla in Hinterglemm has a good atmosphere. The Pfeiffenmuseum Café in the Glemmtalerhof houses a quite enormous collection of pipes and smoking paraphernalia. Later on, the village's 15 discos come to life: King's is popular with teenagers, and the London Pub is Hinterglemm's hot-spot for noisy skiers and snowboarders. A regular bus service for night-owls now runs up and down the valley from 8pm to 3am.

Childcare

Schischule Wolf and Fürstauer both operate their own ski kindergartens every day except Sunday for children from four years of age. Hotels including Gartenhotel Theresia, Hotel Glemmtalerhof, Partnerhotels and Hotel Lengauerhof care for non-skiing children from two-and-a-half or three years of age.

Linked or nearby resorts

Leogang
top 2,096m (6,875ft) bottom 800m (2,625ft)

Leogang is a spread-out farming community, which claims the title of the longest village in Europe. A smart, modern gondola takes skiers and snowboarders up to Sitzhütte at 1,758m. A short run down followed by a quad-chair and three subsequent T-bars brings you into the ski circus. Accommodation is in a mixture of hotels and chalets. We have excellent reports of the Chalet Thurnhaus, which is an eight-minute walk from the gondola. Readers recommend both the Gerhard Altenberger and Franz Deisenberger ski schools. Five cross-country trails total more than 40km, and snow-rafting is also available. The kindergarten in Hotel Krallerhof takes children from two years of age.

TOURIST INFORMATION
Tel 43 6583 8234
Fax 43 6583 7302

Schladming

ALTITUDE 745m (2,224ft)

Beginners ✱✱✱ Intermediates ✱✱✱ Snowboarders ✱✱

Schladming is essentially an ordinary Austrian town that derives much of its income from outside skiing. Not much happens here. Indeed, during its entire 680-year history , unless you count a little bloodshed in the sixteenth century and the birth of Arnold Schwarzenegger – you would be hard pushed to find any single event of international significance. Day-to-day life in this attractive provincial town, with its onion-domed church and magnificent eighteenth-century town square, continues at a rhythm that is not dictated solely by tourism. The resort also has the country's smallest brewery, and its lift pass covers a larger area than any other in Austria.

> ✔ Large ski area
> ✔ Lively après-ski
> ✔ Tree-level skiing
> ✔ Excellent for cross-country
> ✔ Short airport transfer
> ✔ Summer skiing on Dachstein Glacier
> ✔ Variety of mountain restaurants
> ✔ Recommended childcare
> ✘ Poor skiing convenience

All these contributory factors make Schladming an utterly charming and unspoilt base from which to explore huge tracts of mostly linked inter-mediate skiing and snowboarding that are entirely unknown to the majority of British snow-users. Anyone looking for Lederhosen-und-oompah *Gemütlichkeit* will discover that it still thrives here.

On the snow
top 2,015m (6,609ft) bottom 750m (2,460ft)

Schladming lies in the centre of a long and beautiful valley, with the main slopes spread disparately across the mountains on the southern side. Planai at 1,894m and Hochwurzen at 1,850m are the mountains closest to Schladming. The easiest access to Planai is via a two-stage gondola from the edge of Schladming, which is a comfortable walk from the centre. The Kessleralm mid-station of the gondola can also be reached by car. Planai is somewhat precariously linked at valley level to the next mountain, Hochwurzen, by a series of chair-lifts. It offers several long red (intermediate) runs, which are served by two steep drags, a jumbo gondola and a double-chair. A gondola from the village of **Pichl** to the bottom of the Hochwurzenbahn gives access to the Reiteralm, which offers a variety of red and blue (easy) tree-lined runs served by a double chair-lift and a gondola.

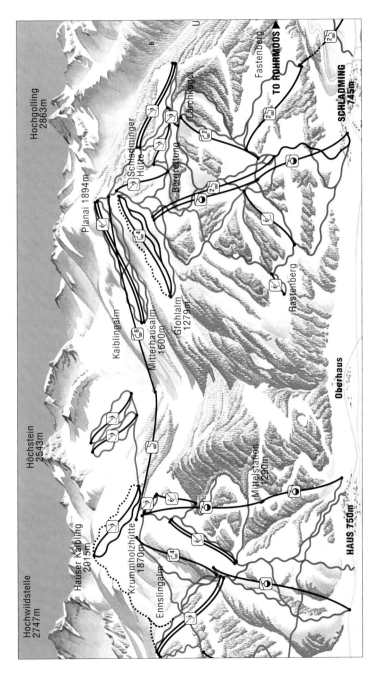

Hochwildstelle 2747m

Hochgolling 2863m

Höchstein 2543m

Hauser Kaibling 2015m

Krummholzhütte 1870m

Ennslingalm

Mittelstation 1290m

HAUS 750m

Oberhaus

Kaiblingalm

Mitterhausalm 1600m

Gfohlalm 1279m

Planai 1894m

Schladminger Hütte

Bergrettung

Lärchkogel

Rastenberg

Fastenberg

SCHLADMING 745m

TO ROHRMOOS

Above Schladming, on the eastern side of Planai, two chair-lifts link up with the Mitterhaus double drag-lift to provide a gateway to Hauser Kaibling, a 2,015-m peak that towers over the pretty village of **Haus-im-Emmstal**. A replacement eight-person gondola built in summer 2000 at the Pruggern end of the village should greatly improve mountain access and reduce queues for the other gondola at the Schladming end.

Still further to the east along the valley, the Galsterbergalm at 1,976m offers a few (mainly gentle) slopes reached by cable-car from the village of **Pruggern**. This in turn gives access to a couple of further lifts for skiing above the tree-line. The small, separate **Fageralm** area is also included in the local lift pass.

On the other side of the valley from Schladming, the commune of **Ramsau-Ort** at 1,200m has no less than 19 lifts scattered around the hills on either side of the village. All are short and easy slopes. **Turlwand**, outside Ramsau, is the starting point for the cable-car up to the **Dachstein Glacier**; the village is served by a chair-lift and three drag-lifts, and has limited year-round skiing that is too gentle to be of much more than scenic interest for alpine skiers.

The Schladming area has some of the best cross-country skiing in Austria, with 250km of trails against a dramatically scenic backdrop and plenty of small huts to call in at for refreshments.

Beginners

At this low altitude, the functioning of the 25 listed nursery slopes is heavily dependent on the weather. The gentle **Rohrmoos** meadows on the lower slopes of Hochwurzen provide the best arena for first turns when snow cover permits, with plenty of easy alternatives on the higher slopes of the main mountains.

Intermediates

Despite the lack of variety, the red and blue cruising terrain is plentiful enough to keep any skier busy for a week. The World Cup racecourses on both Planai and Hauser Kaibling should please fast intermediates, and the long downhill course on Hochwurzen is thigh-burning. The usually uncrowded Reiteralm piste also gives plenty of opportunity for high-speed cruising.

Advanced

Advanced piste-skiers will quickly tire of the limited terrain, where only one short run is graded black (advanced). However, Schladming is an attractive base from which to explore a huge range of skiing including **Obertauern** and the Sportwelt Amadé, which is centred on **St Johann im Pongau**. For a modest supplement you can buy the six-day Top-Tauern Skischeck lift pass, which gives access to 270 lifts serving 660km of prepared runs in this corner of Austria.

All the resorts covered on the lift pass are within an hour's drive of Schladming. These include **Flachau** and **Wagrain**.

Off-piste
Skiing outside the marked pistes is discouraged on the main mountains, except on the ski routes. In good snow conditions the north face of Hauser Kaibling offers great scope, and the runs through the trees from Bergstallalm on Planai are recommended.

Snowboarding
Schladming is great for beginner and intermediate riders, with the Planai and Dachstein Glacier having the best terrain. A funpark and two half-pipes add to the attractions. Snowboarding has been a commercial success in Schladming, not least because it is the home of former European champion Gerfried Schuller, who has his own school here. He also runs the Blue Tomato snowboard shop as well as Snowboardschule Dachstein-Tauern.

Tuition and guiding
The Hopl-Planai ski school, owned by the veteran Austrian team-trainer Charly Kahr, has an outstanding reputation and counts Arnold Schwarzenegger among its annual pupils. The Franz Tritscher Ski School is also recommended ('good English, good teaching, good fun'). Snowboardschule Dachstein-Tauern is the alternative for riders.

Mountain restaurants
'Never,' said one reporter, 'have I been to a resort with so many mountain restaurants. Food and service vary, but at their best they are excellent'. However, first you have to find them – 'they are not marked on the inadequate piste map, and signs are nothing short of bemusing'. The Krümmelholze at Haus receives particular recommendation. On Planai the Mitterhausalm and Schladmingerhütte are praised. Onkel Willy's Hütte ('buzzing with atmosphere') has live music and a sunny terrace. The Eiskarhütte on Reiteralm, and the Seiterhütte ('excellent food and service') on Hochwurzen are both praised.

Accommodation
Most guests stay in hotels and guesthouses around the Enns Valley. Without a car, location is of crucial importance, and many of our reporters found themselves staying too far away from the town centre or the lifts – or both.

The Sporthotel Royer receives rave reviews. The Neue Post is criticised for its 'small, cramped rooms'. In addition 'the reception is not permanently manned, and the half-board food was disappointing, to say the least'. The nearby Alte Post ('small bedroom, but good food with Strauss, Mozart and Haydn in the background') is recommended. Haus Stangl, a simple bed-and-breakfast, is also praised.

Eating in and out

The restaurants are mainly in the hotels. We have good reports of the Rôtisserie Royer Grill in the Sporthotel Royer. The Alte Post is recommended for 'excellent trout and other dishes in a pretentious but friendly atmosphere'. Its *Postreindl* (pork fillet with creamed mushrooms and gnocchi) is 'not to be missed'. The Neue Post has two recommended à la carte restaurants, the Jägerstüberl and the Poststüberl. Le Jardin is a warmly commended French restaurant. The Gasthof Kirchenwirt is 'unmatched for quality of food, price, atmosphere and service'. Charly Kahr's Restaurant is also praised for its outstanding Salzburg cuisine.

Après-ski

Après-ski starts early at Onkel Willy's Hütte on Planai before filtering down to the Siglu in the Hauptplatz. Later on the action moves to The Pub, La Porta, the Hanglbar and – still later – to the Sonderbar disco. The Schwalbenbrau brewery is worth a visit, although the intentionally cloudy beer it produces is not to everyone's taste and may explain why it is the smallest brewery in Austria. The Planaistub'n, also known as Charly's Treff, draws large crowds. Café-Konditorei Landgraf and Niederl are both praised. One reporter favoured Ferry's Pub in the Steirergasse, another the Hanglbar; the bowling alley behind the latter is said to offer a good night out. The Beisl bar is 'intimate and lively with good music'. La Porta is 'small, crowded, with a great atmosphere'.

The toboggan run from the top to the bottom of Hochwurzen down the hairpin road can be used only at night (when the road is closed) and is claimed to be the longest in Austria.

Childcare

Few resorts receive such resounding reviews for both their ski and non-ski kindergarten. 'Outstanding facilities for very young children', commented one reader. 'There were 40 small children in the ski kindergarten, and the facilities were brilliant; this is definitely the area to bring small children to be well looked after and to learn to ski,' said another. Frau Ladreiter and Ma Petite Ecole are the two non-ski kindergartens.

Linked or nearby resorts

Haus-im-Ennstal
top 2,015m (6,611ft) bottom 750m (2,460ft)

Haus is a quiet village with its farming origins still in evidence, although it has a considerable amount of holiday accommodation in guesthouses and apartments. There are cafés, one of which has jazz nights, and a couple of shops. The upmarket Hauser Kaibling hotel has a swimming-pool and is recommended for its cuisine. Dorfhotel Kirchenwirt is a traditional hotel in the village centre, the Gasthof Reiter is a fine old

Skiing facts: Schladming

TOURIST INFORMATION
Erzherzog-Johann-Strasse 213, A-8970 Schladming
Tel 43 3687 22268
Fax 43 3687 24138
Email touristoffice@schladming.com
Web site www.schladming.com

THE RESORT
By road Calais 1221km
By rail station in resort
Airport transfer Salzburg 1hr, Munich 2½hrs
Visitor beds 3,900
Transport free ski-bus with lift pass

THE SKIING
Linked or nearby resorts Haus-im-Ennstal (l), Obertauern (n), Rohrmoos (l), Ramsau/Dachstein (n), St Johann im Pongau (n)
Number of lifts 24 in Schladming, 88 in linked area
Total of trails/pistes 53km in Schladming,170km (29% easy, 59% intermediate, 9% difficult, 3% very difficult) in linked area
Nursery slopes 25 lifts in area
Summer skiing nearest on Dachstein Glacier

LIFT PASSES
Area pass Schladming ATS1,845–1,985 for 6 days
Beginners reductions available

Pensioners 20% reduction for women 60yrs and over and men 65yrs and over, free for both 75 years and over
Credit cards Amex and Diners only

TUITION
Adults Hoppl-Planai tel: 3687 61525, Franz Tritscher tel: 3687 61142
Snowboarding Snowboardschule Dachstein-Tauern tel: 3687 24223
Other courses carving, cross-country, moguls, race-training, seniors, snow-blading, telemark
Guiding through ski schools

CHILDREN
Lift pass Schladming 5–15yrs, ATS965 for 6 days
Ski & board school as adults
Kindergarten (ski) through ski schools (non-ski) Frau Ladreiter tel: 3687 61313, Ma Petite Ecole tel: 3687 24407

OTHER SPORTS
Climbing wall, curling, hang-gliding, horse-riding, hot-air ballooning, ice-climbing, indoor tennis and squash, night-skiing, 8-km night-tobogganing run, parapente, skating, snow-biking, snow-rafting, snow-shoeing, sleigh rides, swimming

FOOD AND DRINK PRICES
Coffee ATS26, glass of wine ATS18, small beer ATS27–30, soft drink ATS25, dish of the day ATS120–130

chalet much cheaper than most of the accommodation, and the Gürtl is a quiet family-run hotel well situated for the cable-car.

A gentle nursery slope lies between the village and the gondola station, and there is a half-pipe. Skischule Brandner, WM-Ski und Snowboardschule and Snowboardschule Dachstein-Tauern all offer tuition.

TOURIST INFORMATION
Tel 43 3686 2234–0
Fax 43 3686 2234–4
Email haus-ennstal@aon.at
Web site www.haus.at

Rohrmoos
top 1,850m (6,070ft) bottom 870m (2,854ft)

This diffuse satellite has easy skiing to and from many of its hotel doorsteps. Among the choice of good-value hotels and guesthouses is the Austria, which is well-placed at the point where the lower, gentle slopes of Rohrmoos meet the steeper slopes of Hochwurzen. The smarter Schwaigerhof has an excellent position on the edge of the pistes and is one of the few places with a swimming-pool. Après-ski is informal and centres around the hotel bars. The café at the Tannerhof is a tea-time favourite. Barbara's and the Alm Bar are busy later on. Franz Tritscher and Hopl-Planai are the two ski schools, while the Franz Tritscher and Snowboardschule Dachstein-Tauern offer snowboard lessons. Max and Moritz Club is the non-skiing kindergarten for children aged two to five years.

TOURIST INFORMATION
Tel 43 3687 61147
Fax 43 3687 6114713
Email info@rohrmoos-untertal.at
Web site www.rohrmoos-untertal.at

Söll and the SkiWelt

ALTITUDE 703m (2,306ft)

Beginners ✱✱✱ Intermediates ✱✱✱ Snowboarders ✱

Once the top package resort in Austria, with a reputation in the 1980s for excessive drinking, Söll is now focusing on family values. Anyone unimpressed by purpose-built, ski-in ski-out tower blocks at 2,000m, who wants a reasonable amount of easy skiing at modest cost, and who does not mind a bit of accordion music, should consider Söll as a destination. It is a quiet, modern town of family homes, set back from the highway in open fields, and has minimal claims to Tyrolean charm. At the same time it is the hub of one of Austria's largest networks of interconnected pistes. Söll was a summer resort for walkers until skiing offered its 3,000 inhabitants winter work, hosting some 4,300 guests per week. Söll's car-free main street runs for less than 100m and is largely devoid of the overly cute, wooden architecture that is typical of the Tyrol. Shopping is limited to supermarkets and ski and souvenir shops. A free bus runs every 30 minutes to the gondola station but not to other SkiWelt resorts.

> ✔ Short airport transfer
> ✔ Friendly, low-key atmosphere
> ✔ Value-for-money
> ✔ Westendorf recommended for families
> ✘ Low-altitude skiing
> ✘ Short season
> ✘ Bus-ride from town to lifts

Officially dubbed the SkiWelt Wilder Kaiser-Brixental, the region counts 91 lifts and 250km of pistes spread around a 150-square-kilometre oval of 9 resorts sandwiched between the Kitzbüheler Alps to the south and the craggy Wilder Kaiser peaks to the north. It is only 70km from Innsbruck and within easy reach of the German border. Although skiing began here as early as 1948, when Europe's longest chair-lift was built in **Hopfgarten**, Söll's own lifts were not seriously developed until the 1960s, and links to the SkiWelt were not finished before the 1970s. All the skiing in the region is well below 2,000m but an extensive range of 240 snow cannons cover most of the lower slopes, allowing skiing into April when temperatures permit.

The British make up 20 per cent of what is a youngish clientèle, in which influxes of Scandinavians and Dutch outnumber the Germans. Nightlife at weekends is hectic, but with only one serious disco, Söll cannot begin to compare in this respect with **Kitzbühel**, a few kilometres down the road, or with St Anton.

Children under 7 ski free, and those 16 and under receive discounts of more than 40 per cent, as do women of any age on Wednesdays from January onwards each season.

On the snow
top 1,892m (6,207ft) bottom 622m (2,040ft)

Söll's skiing starts with a free, 15-minute bus ride across the resort to a modern eight-person gondola. The ancient single chair above this is scheduled to be replaced in the 2000–1 season by another eight-person gondola that will give speedy, direct access to Hohe Salve, which at 1,829m is the highest point in the entire SkiWelt.

Thanks to a lift capacity of over 120,000 skiers per hour, SkiWelt queues seldom exceed 20 minutes. Additional snowmaking now covers the run down to the village. Grooming standards are ensured by 45 snowcats, which run all night. Pistenhilfe security patrols were introduced with the aim of eliminating 'piste rowdies' and aiding lost tourists.

From Hohe Salve it is possible to ski to seven of the SkiWelt resorts; **Westendorf** requires a short bus transfer from **Brixen**, and **Kelchsau** a less frequent and longer bus trip from **Hopfgarten**. Advanced terrain is often limited by a lack of respectable snow depth. The SkiWelt is primarily suited to beginners and undemanding intermediates who do not mind short runs and uphill traverses. There is no ski bus itinerary connecting the resorts, so care must be taken when skiing far afield.

Beginners
The SkiWelt has more than 100km of blue (easy) runs. Most beginner areas are at the base of the ski area, where the snow often melts away. **Scheffau** is the only resort with a top-to-bottom blue piste. Söll has a simple, wooded run from mid-mountain. Zinsberg and Brandstadl offer ample easy terrain.

Intermediates
Almost half the pistes in the SkiWelt are graded intermediate, but short runs down to lifts, rather than long itineraries from village to village, are the rule. The red (intermediate) trail in the sun down to Hopfgarten, and the less exposed run down to Söll from Hohe Salve, are good cruisers, as is the 7.5-km Kraftalm run to **Itter**.

Advanced
From Hohe Salve the Lärchenhang is one of the unmarked local runs on the north side, where a bowl region called Mulde (not marked on the piste map) presents some challenge and a reasonable pitch.

Off-piste
Short, steep sections that require ducking under warning ropes do appear in Westendorf and are regularly skied by locals. The SkiWelt

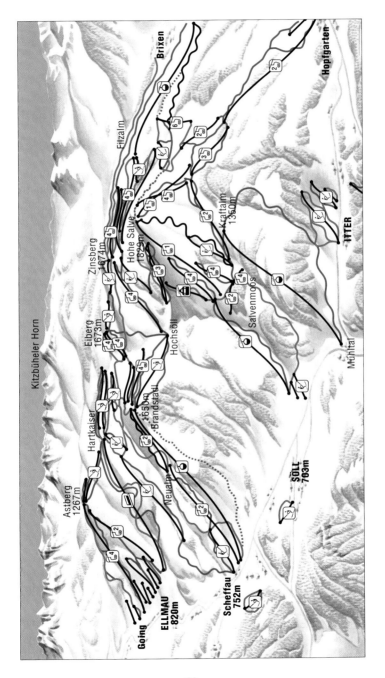

offers a wealth of guided ski-tours, for example Brechhorn, which demands little uphill effort when there is enough snow to make powder skiing possible.

Snowboarders
Brixen, Westendorf and Scheffau have official freestyle pistes, while Söll has a well-maintained funpark above Salvenmoos with a half-pipe and some jumps. The mainly gentle and undulating terrain of the SkiWelt is ideal for first-timers.

Tuition and guiding
More than 450 ski teachers in 16 SkiWelt ski schools specialise in making skiing fun for beginners. The standard of English is high. Söll's three schools promise – but do not guarantee – that by the end of their first week, pupils will make it all the way from the very top to the very bottom of the area.

Mountain restaurants
The SkiWelt lists a total of 63 mountain eateries, six of which are above Söll, and most suffer from peak-season lunchtime crowds. Schernthannstuberl (number 18) is praised for its 'fairly large choice, big portions and hot food'. Self-service and simple meals abound. Stöcklalm, Kraftalm and Gründalm are typical, unexceptional inns, all with terraces and wide panoramas. Hochschwendt (number 52) is said to be the cheapest. The glass-walled Siglu Bar at **Hochsöll** is popular with children.

Accommodation
Four of Söll's 70 hotels are rated four-star and the remainder are reasonably priced inns and guesthouses. The main hotel is the four-star Postwirt with its distinctive stuccoed exterior and an outdoor heated swimming-pool. The Alpenschlössl is even more luxurious, with an indoor waterfall, but it is a 30-minute walk from the centre. Tour-operator brochures feature the charming Tenne and the lively Christophorus, as well as the old-fashioned, out-of-town Agerhof.

Eating in and out
Most visitors are on hotel half-board packages. For Austrian coffee-and-cakes it is worth making the hike to Panorama for the view (and the food), and the modest Söller Stube on the main street merits a visit. Schindlhaus is advertised as a gourmet restaurant. Venezia and Don Giovanni ('pizzas the size of car wheels') serve cheap Italian fare.

Après-ski
At the Whisky Mühle, scantily clad go-go girls (and boys) kick away each Friday night until 3am. The Dorfstadl in the Hotel Tyrol comes a poor second. Salvenstadl is a new bar with live music. Buffaloes has a Wild West theme.

Childcare

The Söll-Hochsöll Ski School has the most extensive programmes for children of all ages. Bobo's Children's Club is part of this school and accepts children from 5 to 14 years of age. Bobo the Penguin is the symbol of an Austrian association that guarantees English-speaking, certified teachers with a training in psychology. However, reporters commented that not all staff are English-speakers.

Linked or nearby resorts

Brixen im Thale
top 1,892m (6,207ft) bottom 800m (2,624ft)

At the far end of the SkiWelt is the last fully connected resort of the area. The resort boasts 2,700 beds but as yet no British tour operators come here. A six-person gondola and covered high-speed chair lead up to Hohe Salve. The Parade Pub next to the lift station is unique in the SkiWelt, if not in the Alps: a computer monitors demand for specific drinks, then raises or lowers prices to provide the ultimate in 'demand economy' drinking. Gustl's Treff is a favourite hangout for snowboarders.

TOURIST INFORMATION
Tel 43 5334 8433
Fax 43 5334 8332
Email brixen.info@brixen.netwing.at
Web site www.netwing.at/tirol/brixen/rts

Ellmau
top 1,892m (6,207ft) bottom 820m (2,690ft)

With 4,900 beds, Ellmau is the biggest SkiWelt resort. Its 18 lifts include what is advertised as the fastest, most modern funicular in Austria. In addition, a new six-seater chair-lift now replaces the Kögl T-bar. Toboggan runs are floodlit at night. Hotel Christoph, a five-minute walk from the funicular, is described as 'excellent, with helpful staff and good food'. Ellmau's nightlife rivals that of Söll, with Pub Memory, Ellmauer Alm, Heldenbar and the Tenne all lively destinations. For children there are the Kaiserbad water chutes and adventure swimming-park. Adult activities include hanggliding, ice-climbing, the indoor climbing wall and parapente.

The three ski and board schools are Ellmauer Skischule, Skischule Ellmau-Hartkaiser, and Top-Skischule. All three also teach carving, cross-country and telemark. Alexandra Sollerer offers daycare for non-skiing children.

TOURIST INFORMATION
Tel 43 5358 2301
Fax 43 5358 3443
Email ellmau@netway.at
Web site www.ellmau.com

Going
top 1,892m (6,207ft) bottom 800m (2,624ft)

Fully linked into the SkiWelt, with the best views of the Wilder Kaiser and a large nursery slope, Going is beginning to be noticed by the British, not least because of the exceptional five-star Hotel Stanglewirt, which has indoor swimming, tennis and a Lipizzaner riding school. Going has its own ski and snowboard school.

TOURIST INFORMATION
Tel 43 5358 2438
Fax 43 5358 3501
Email going@netway.at
Web site www.going.at

Hopfgarten
top 1,829m (6,001ft) bottom 622m (2,040ft)

Few British skiers take advantage of the 2,000 beds in Hopfgarten, which has become a favourite with young Australian package tourists. Access to the top of Hohe Salve requires three chair-lift rides. The old Foisching T-bar has been replaced by a new six-seater chair. There is floodlit tobogganing, and the quiet chalet-style village is dominated by the twin yellow towers of the impressive local church. Spirited nightlife and dancing can be found at the 02 disco and the Cin-Cin. A backpacking reporter praises Haus Lukas as 'a cosy hotel with a great atmosphere'.

TOURIST INFORMATION
Tel 43 5335 2322
Fax 43 5335 2630
Email info@hopfgarten.tirol.at
Web site www.tiscover.com/hopfgarten-tirol

Itter
top 1,892m (6,207ft) bottom 703m (2,306ft)

Itter has only 800 visitor beds, but a fast gondola with no queues for the uphill journey, plus the longest run in the SkiWelt (8km), make it a quieter, cheaper alternative to Söll. The Schidisco in the Schusterhof Hotel and the Dorfpub are perhaps not up to the decibel level of Söll but sufficient for most.

TOURIST INFORMATION
Tel 43 5335 2670
Fax 43 5335 3028

Kelchsau
top 1,700m (5,576ft) bottom 800m (2,624ft)

Kelchsau is the odd man out of the SkiWelt, not connected by piste in any way and served by infrequent buses from Hopfgarten. It is primarily a cross-country centre, despite its four lifts.

Skiing facts: Söll

TOURIST INFORMATION
Postfach 21, A-6306 Söll, Tyrol
Tel 43 5333 5216
Fax 43 5333 6180
Email info@soell.com
Web site www.soell.com

THE RESORT
By road Calais 1,108km
By rail Kufstein 15km, St Johann 25km, Wörgl 15km
Airport transfer Munich 2hrs, Salzburg 1hr, Innsbruck 45mins
Visitor beds 4,000
Transport free bus between village and ski area

THE SKIING
Linked or nearby resorts Brixen (I), Ellmau (I), Going (I), Hopfgarten (I), Itter (I), Kelchsau (n), Kirchberg (n), Kitzbühel (n), Scheffau (I), Westendorf (n)
Number of lifts 12 in Söll, 91 in SkiWelt
Total of trails/pistes 34km in Söll, 250km in SkiWelt (43% easy, 51% intermediate, 6% difficult)
Nursery slopes 8 lifts and runs (22 in area)

LIFT PASSES
Area pass SkiWelt (covers all lifts in area) ATS1,620–1,890, Kitzbühler-Alpen-Skipass (covers Alpbach, Kitzbühel, SkiWelt, St Johann in Tirol, Waldring, Wildschönau – 260 lifts) ATS 2,200, both for 6 days

Beginners points tickets
Pensioners 10% reduction for 60yrs
Credit cards no

TUITION
Adults Söll-Hochsöll tel: 5333 5454, Austria Söll tel: 5333 5005, Ski & Snowboard School Pro Söll tel: 5332 72610
Snowboarding Freaks on Snow tel: 664 341 8409, and as ski schools
Other courses carving, cross-country, extreme skiing, freestyle, moguls, race-training, skiing for the disabled, ski safari, ski-touring, snowblading, telemark
Guiding through ski schools

CHILDREN
Lift pass 7–16yrs, Söll ATS760–890, SkiWelt ATS920–1,070, both free for under 7yrs
Ski & board school as adults
Kindergarten (ski) Bobo's Children's Club, (non-ski) Mini-Club Söll-Hochsöll tel for both: 5333 5454

OTHER SPORTS
Curling, floodlit toboggan run, hang-gliding, horse-riding, night-skiing, parapente, skating, squash, sleigh rides, swimming

FOOD AND DRINK PRICES
Coffee ATS25–30, glass of wine ATS25–40, small beer ATS26–35, soft drink ATS20–30, dish of the day ATS100–120

TOURIST INFORMATION
Tel 43 5335 8105
Fax 43 5335 8156

Scheffau
top 1,892m (6,207ft) bottom 752m (2,467ft)

Scheffau has only 2,200 beds and 15 lifts serving 23km of pistes, which begin at a gondola situated awkwardly across the main road from the sprawling village. Scheffau's hotel guests have their own queue-free VIP lift access. The Brandstadl bowl keeps its snow cover better than the sunnier slopes across in Söll, and Scheffau has more than its share of the SkiWelt's snowmaking. CC-Pub, Conny's Corner and the Pub Royal are the only nightspots.

TOURIST INFORMATION
Tel 43 5358 7373
Fax 43 5358 73737

Westendorf
top 1,892m (6,207ft) bottom 800m (2,624ft)

Westendorf's broad shoulder of open pistes looks steep from the valley floor. It is more snowsure than elsewhere in the SkiWelt, and skiing on the 45km of pistes can be more challenging. However, flat roads between lifts are an irritating feature, as is the 1-km distance between the modern gondola and the town.

Westendorf is one of the most attractive of all the SkiWelt villages and has a genuine Tyrolean atmosphere coupled with a vigour lacking in some of the others. Westendorf's substantial accommodation base of 4,100 beds, almost equal to Söll's, makes for lively entertainment, with 'acid house' at Gerry's Inn, 'techno' at the Wunderbar, and 'jello' shots at the Mosquito Bar. Hotel Jakobwirt is praised for its 'friendly staff, good food, good facilities and a central location'. Hotel Post is recommended as a family hotel and described as: 'well located, the staff were friendly, and the atmosphere at the bar was terrific. The owner, George, kept giving the youngsters lollipops and chocolates.' The Schermerhof apartments are 'modern, well-equipped, clean and fairly spacious'.

Pistes in the Brechhorn area are said to be 'an absolute dream, anyone could negotiate them'. The resort boasts three ski and board schools. Reporters recommend Ski School Top for its more personal service. Ski School Westendorf is warmly praised: 'we were a group of three families all in different classes and all of us were satisfied. The instructors spoke great English.' We have no reports on Skischule und Snowboardschule Ideal. Courses on offer include carving, cross-country, snowblading and telemark. The other activities in the resort are hang-gliding, horse-riding, curling and skating, sleigh rides and snowshoeing.

TOURIST INFORMATION
Tel 43 5334 6230
Fax 43 5334 2390
Email westendorf@netway.at
Web site www.westendorf.com

St Anton

ALTITUDE 1,304m (4,278ft)

Intermediates ✱✱✱ Advanced ✱✱✱ Snowboarders ✱✱✱

St Anton is to skiing what St Andrews is to golf. The Arlberg region, of which St Anton is the capital, is the birthplace of modern technique and in part responsible for the way in which we ski today. The awesome quality of the mountains means that St Anton's star has never faded. Other resorts have since risen to dominate the world stage, but St Anton still ranks among the top five for truly challenging skiing and high living. The 2000–1 season sees St Anton as the venue for the World Ski Championships and considerable improvements have been made to both the town and the lifts. The resort's hands-free 'smart card' lift pass works efficiently.

> ✔ Extensive off-piste
> ✔ Large ski area
> ✔ Ski-touring opportunities
> ✔ Efficient lift system
> ✔ Lively après-ski
> ✘ Few activities for non-skiers
> ✘ Crowded pistes

The percentage of snowboarders here is lower than in most European resorts, largely because the steep and usually heavily-mogulled main pistes are suitable only for the extremely proficient rider. However, the freeriding in the powder and among the trees is quite sensational. St Anton is twinned with the ski resort of **Mount Buller** in southern Australia, and the large number of Australians who work here may be either the cause or the result of this.

Skiing came to the Arlberg in the late nineteenth century. St Anton became accessible to the outside world in 1884 when the railway tunnel under the Arlberg Pass was completed. As early as 1895 the pastor of Lech visited his parishioners on skis. In 1921 Hannes Schneider opened the Arlberg Ski School. Generations of Europeans grew up with the distinctive Arlberg technique – skis clamped together, shoulders facing down the hill – a contrived yet elegant style that dominated the sport until the French, and Jean-Claude Killy, declared stylistic war during the 1960s.

St Anton is as easy to get to from Zurich as from Munich or Innsbruck. One major drawback has been that the village was bisected by the railway line. To reach the main ski area you first had to cross the tracks. However, in preparation for World Ski Championships the railway line has been shifted 200m to the south side of the valley and a giant sports hall is being built on its former site.

The undistinguished village architecture is a blend of old and new that owes little to planning and much to those who recognised an opportunity and seized it before the current strict zoning regulations came into force. A fierce policy of no outside ownership, no holiday homes and no expansion in the number of guest beds has saved St Anton from otherwise inevitable blight.

The centre is a relatively peaceful pedestrian zone lined with shops, cafés and St Anton's most handsome traditional hotels: the Post, the Alte Post and the Schwarzer Adler. The rest of the town straggles along the road in both directions, towards Mooserkreuz at the top of the resort to the west, and towards the satellite villages of **Nasserein** and **St Jakob** to the east. Nasserein is now fully accessible from St Anton, with a new chair-lift from the village to Gampen. But it is an isolated place in which to stay.

WHAT'S NEW

Nasserein–Gampen gondola for 2000–1 season
Relocation of the railway station to south side of village
Nassereinbahn chair-lift from Nasserein to Gampen

The shuttle bus does not run in the evening and the nightlife is limited to local bars unless you are prepared for a 20-minute walk.

On the snow
top 2,811m (9,222ft) bottom 1,304m (4,278ft)

The Arlberg Ski Pass covers the linked area of St Anton, **St Christoph** and **Stuben**, as well as **Klösterle** and the more famous villages of **Lech** and **Zürs**. A free ski bus links the ski areas.

St Anton's skiing takes place on both sides of the valley, but the most challenging area is on the northern slopes dominated by the 2,811-m Valluga. The old lifts on the Galzig and in St Christoph have been systematically replaced by covered quad-chairs, which have done much to improve mountain access.

The high-speed quad-chair to Gampen takes the morning strain off the Kandahar funicular and the Galzig cable-car. The new Nasserein chair is also a major improvement. However, the predictable result is that the volume of people has not been reduced but simply moved from the lift queue to the piste. The large number of snow-users – even in January – can be frightening ('terrifyingly busy – they should install traffic lights at the top!'). In the afternoon skiers and boarders jostle for position on the home run like Parisian taxi drivers. Anyone lacking in courage or technique feels wholly intimidated. However, a new blue (easy) run down from Galzig has gone some way towards alleviating the problem.

At mid-mountain level, the ski area splits into two, separated by a valley. Gampen, at 1,850m, is a sunny plateau with a six-person chair-lift rising to the higher slopes of Kapall at 2,333m. Galzig is the focal point of the serious skiing and riding.

From Galzig you can ski down to St Christoph at 1,800m, a small hamlet crowned by the Hotel Arlberg-Hospiz. Above Galzig lie the more sublime challenges of the Valluga and the Schindlergrat at 2,605m.

The Valluga is reached by a second and oversubscribed cable-car from Galzig, which has a confusing and unsatisfactory numbered-ticket system. You take a ticket and ask the lift attendant to translate it into a

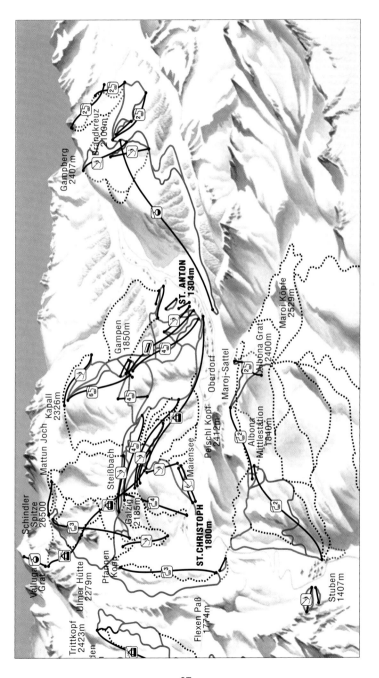

time so that you know when to return. The alternative is to ski down into the valley behind Galzig and take the quad up to the Schindlergrat. The skiing from here is some of the best in St Anton.

The Rendl at 2,100m is a separate ski area on the other side of the St Anton valley and is reached by the Rendlbahn gondola, a short ski-bus ride from town. It offers interesting and often uncrowded skiing and catches so much sun that its local nickname is Rendl Beach.

An 'Info Team' of five multilingual men or women can be found at the top of the lifts or on the pistes to give help and advice ('they cut the time spent looking at piste maps').

Beginners

St Anton is not a beginner's resort, and anyone less than a confident intermediate would be well-advised to avoid it. The few blue (easy) slopes that do exist would nearly all be classified as intermediate elsewhere ('some of the blues would be enough to put beginners off for life'). Even the crowded main run back into the village is seen as a challenging red (intermediate) by most skiers.

Three learner pistes with their own T-bars are spread between Nasserein and the funicular railway. The Gampen has a children's ski area and the gentle Gampenlift T-bar. St Christoph has its own Maiensee beginner piste and lift. Those with a little experience may also find some of the runs on the Rendl negotiable.

Intermediates

Confident intermediates head for Galzig. The sunny slopes below are served by the Ostbahn high-speed quad, and the main runs are sufficiently self-contained to encourage confidence but vary considerably in degree of difficulty. A delightful and easy blue run takes you down into St Christoph, and a quad-chair has been built to replace the old cable-car for the return journey. The Osthang, a fearsome bump run with a hostile camber, takes you back down towards St Anton, but there are other, less extreme, options. Timid skiers should note that St Anton has dispensed with black (difficult) runs in favour of unpisted ski-routes, in what some critics see as a negation of responsibility. These appear on the map as either plain red or black-bordered diamonds. For red read black, for black-bordered read double-black.

Advanced

Depending on the snow conditions, almost all of St Anton's skiing can be considered advanced. From the Vallugagrat, three of St Anton's finest long runs lead back to the broad flat valley of the Steissbachtal, a corridor between the Valluga runs and those on the adjoining Kapall.

The toughest of the three is the Schindlerkar, a wide 30-degree mogul marathon that seems to go on forever. Strong skiers can repeat it continually by riding the Schindlergratbahn high-speed quad, but its south-facing aspect makes it vulnerable to early-morning ice and late-afternoon slush. The Mattun is a series of mogulled bowls linked by a traverse; it is less steep in pitch but more interesting because of the variety of its challenges. The third, much easier, option – the long dog-leg via the Ulmerhütte – opens up the Valluga to confident intermediates. It is also the starting point for the run to Stuben.

Off-piste

The off-piste possibilities are limitless, and a guide can find fresh powder a week after the last fall. An experienced skier wanting to enjoy St Anton to the full should view the services of a local guide as part of the basic cost of the holiday, along with accommodation and food.

The patio-sized top of the Valluga is accessed by a final six-person cable-car confined to sightseers, or skiers accompanied by a qualified guide. From the top it is possible to ski down the Pazieltal into Zürs and Lech. The valley itself is not difficult to ski, but the first few metres of the north face of the Valluga are terrifying, with a cliff ready to take away anyone who falls. The Malfon Valley over the back of the Rendl is a wide, enjoyable off-piste run which, when there is sufficient snow, ends on a road at the base of the lift. Above Stuben, a 20-minute walk up the Maroi Kopfe gives entry to the Maroital Valley.

St Anton's mainly south-facing slopes have a good snow record but also harbour an extremely high avalanche risk.

Snowboarders

St Anton has some of the best snowboarding terrain in the whole of Austria, with a seemingly endless choice of natural obstacles and gullies, as well as steep powder fields and drop-offs. Gampen, Kapall and Rendl are particularly good areas to ride. Beginners will find the area steep, although Nasserein has some easier slopes. The Rendl has a funpark with an obstacle course and a half-pipe.

Tuition and guiding

The Arlberg Ski School has 180 instructors, half of whom teach group ski-school classes at any one time while the other half are hired out as private guides. The rival St Anton Ski School, run by Franz Klimmer, has 30 instructors. Competition between the two is fierce, which helps to maintain standards, with class sizes usually restricted to 10.

We have encouraging reports of both schools: 'our patient instructor spoke good English because he was English' (St Anton), and 'excellent instruction' (Arlberg). Alpine Faszination is a small, off-piste guiding service, which is strongly recommended by reporters. The rather pretentious-sounding St Anton am Arlberg Snowboard Academy is run under the banner of the Arlberg Ski School.

Mountain restaurants

According to reporters, most restaurants in the area offer reasonable fare at high-altitude prices. The Albonagrat only seats about 25 but is highly rated ('superb, great atmosphere, cheap food'). The bleak self-service at Galzig has panoramic views over the slopes and inevitably gets overcrowded, but it does have an adjoining table-service restaurant. The Sennhütte, Kaminstube and the Rodelhütte are all recommended. Stoppl's at St Christoph is popular. The terrace of the Arlberg-Hospiz-Alm is a particular favourite ('absolutely fabulous'), with attentive service from traditionally dressed waiters. Lunchtime prices match those in other mountain restaurants but by night it is transformed into a centre for gourmet dining. The Hotel Post in Stuben and the Maiensee Stube in St Christoph are both praised for 'warm, wood-panelled atmosphere and good food'.

Accommodation

The area has two five-star hotels: the historic and expensive Arlberg-Hospiz at St Christoph and the modern St Antoner Hof near the bypass. The four-star options are headed by the Post ('accommodation excellent'), the Hotel Alte Post and the Schwarzer Adler ('comfortable and convenient'), all much richer in tradition and much closer to the lifts. St Anton has an abundance of chalets, as well as a large number of pensions and apartments.

One reporter strongly recommends Haus Ludwig Strolz ('friendly, comfortable, and convenient'). Another has high praise for the Haus Lina ('fabulous breakfasts, en-suite bathrooms, Austrian décor and few Brits'). The Karl Schranz, owned by the former world champion, is said to be 'a very comfortable four-star with good food but quite far from the centre'. Hotel Arlberg has 'excellent food and rooms, and friendly, helpful, English-speaking staff'. Those who find themselves uncomfortably far away from the slopes can leave their skis and boots overnight in the storage at the bottom of the Galzig lift.

Eating in and out

With the exception of the restaurant in the Arlberg-Hospiz and its sister restaurant, the Arlberg Hospiz-Alm, where a magnum of Château Lafite-Rothschild 1959 will set you back £1,875, dining out is not a strong feature of St Anton. The family-run Floriani is warmly recommended. The Funky Chicken and Australian-run Pomodoro are both snowboarders' haunts, the latter offering 'fine pizzas and idiosyncratic Eastern Pacific music'. Sportcafé Schneider and the 60s-style Café Aquila are both praised. The Brunnenhof in St Jakob has 'some of the best food in the region'.

Après-ski

St Anton's undeniably vibrant après-ski scene starts to warm up from lunch-time in the Sennhütte before snow-users make their way down to the Mooserwirt and, just above the final descent to the resort, the Australian-inspired Krazy Kanguruh where a 4.5-m high yellow inflatable marsupial perched on the roof beckons thirsty skiers as they make their way home. Long before the lifts close for the day the bar is packed tighter than Bondi Beach. However, not all reports were favourable: 'We loathed the Krazy Kanguruh – I think we were too old.'

In the après-ski world of twenty-first century St Anton, the sedate tea-dancing of old has become 'beer-dancing' – with a pretty waitress administering Red Bull and vodka at £1.50 a shot. Most guests, after dancing in their ski boots and consuming copious amounts of alcohol, still manage to negotiate on skis the final 800 metres home in the dark. Down in the resort the action continues until sundown on the terrace of the Hotel Alte Post before switching to the Postkeller or to the Underground, which has good live music. The St Antoner Hof bar is recommended for 'a quiet, sophisticated drink'. Scottie's Bar in the Hotel Rosanna is a rendezvous for Brits. Late-evening entertainment is centred on The Piccadilly, Drop-In, and Kartouche. Riders frequent the pool tables at Amadeus, eat at the Funky Chicken and party at the Platz'l bar and Postkeller.

Childcare

St Anton has done much to improve its previously inadequate facilities for small children. The Arlberg Ski School runs Kinderwelt, a kindergarten with four 'campuses': at the ski school meeting place, on the Gampen, in Nasserein and in St Christoph. Small skiers are accepted from two-and-a-half years of age as long as they are out of nappies. Kiki Club, run by the St Anton ski school, runs ski classes for children.

Linked or nearby resorts

Stuben
top 2,811m (9,222ft) bottom 1,407m (4,616ft)

The village was named after the warm parlour – or Stube – of a solitary house on the Arlberg Pass where pilgrims used to shelter in the eighteenth century. Only 32 houses have been added since then, and Stuben has a mere 104 residents and 650 guest beds. The Post Inn, now a four-star hotel, was where mail-coach drivers changed horses for the steep journey up the pass. With its small collection of hotels and restaurants, Stuben is an ideal base for the Arlberg. Stuben Ski School has a pedigree that goes back to the beginning of alpine skiing.

TOURIST INFORMATION
Tel 43 5582 399
Fax 43 5582 3994
Email info@stuben.at
Web site www.stuben.com

St Christoph
top 2,811m (9,222ft) bottom 1,800m (5,906ft)

Further up the Arlberg Pass, St Christoph was the last dwelling place for the pilgrim making his way into the mountains. In 1386 a shepherd

Skiing facts: St Anton

TOURIST INFORMATION
A-6580 St Anton am Arlberg
Tel 43 5446 22690
Fax 43 5446 2532
Email st.anton@netway.at
Web site www.stantonamarlberg.com

THE RESORT
By road Calais 1,092km
By rail station in resort
Airport transfer Innsbruck 1hr,
Zurich 2–3hrs, Munich 3–4hrs
Visitor beds 8,500
Transport free ski bus

THE SKIING
Linked or nearby resorts St Christoph
(l), Klösterle (n), Lech (n), Pettneu (n),
Stuben (l), Zürs (n)
Number of lifts 41 (85 on Arlberg
Ski Pass)
Total of trails/pistes 260km of prepared
pistes (25% easy, 40% intermediate,
25% difficult, 10% very difficult)
Nursery slopes 8 lifts

LIFT PASSES
Area pass Arlberg Ski Pass (covers
St Anton, St Christoph, Stuben, Lech, Zürs,
Klösterle) ATS1,960–2,180 for 6 days
Beginners no free lifts, points cards
available
Pensioners ATS1,710–1,900 for 6 days

for women 60yrs and over and men
65yrs and over. Over 75yrs ATS100 for
whole season
Credit cards no

TUITION
Adults Arlberg Ski School tel: 5446 3411,
St Anton Ski School tel: 5446 3563,
Stuben Ski School tel: 6682 217
Snowboarding as ski schools
Other courses cross-country,
heli-skiing, off-piste, ski-touring, telemark
Guiding Alpine Faszination
tel: 5447 5682, and through ski schools

CHILDREN
Lift pass Arlberg Ski Pass, 7–15yrs,
ATS1,180–1,310 for 6 days. 6yrs and
under, ATS100 for whole season
Ski & board school as adults
Kindergarten (ski/non-ski) Kinderwelt
tel: 5446 2526, Kiki Club
tel: 5446 3563

OTHER SPORTS
Curling, floodlit tobogganing,
indoor tennis and squash, paragliding,
sleigh rides, swimming

FOOD AND DRINK PRICES
Coffee ATS28, glass of wine ATS20–35,
small beer ATS34, soft drink ATS28, dish
of the day ATS130–250

called Heinrich Findelkind von Kempten built a hospice on the pass with his own savings and manned it in the winter with two servants. The Brotherhood of St Christoph (a charitable foundation of locals inspired by von Kempten) still exists, but the hospice burned down in 1957. The five-star Arlberg-Hospiz hotel was built on the site. St Christoph has five other hotels and the Bundessportheim Ski Academy.

TOURIST INFORMATION
Tel/fax as St Anton

Wildschönau

ALTITUDE 830m (2,722ft)

Beginners ✳ Intermediates ✳

The Wildschönau, its name dating from the twelfth century and roughly translated as 'wild beauty', is a quiet corner of the Tyrol within sight of the ski slopes of both **Alpbach** and **Söll**, about 70km from Innsbruck on the edge of the Kitzbüheler Alps. The region is made up of four resorts – **Niederau**, **Oberau**, **Auffach** and **Thierbach**, which sprawl for kilometres along the highway, each with its own small centre. Niederau is the best known but it has neither the best skiing nor is it the biggest village in the Wildschönau. However, it is the most popular with British skiers, who make up a significant proportion of an otherwise predominantly German market (the border is only 20km away).

The appeal of Wildschönau, with its 28 lifts and 45km of low-altitude pistes, seems to be the fact that the slopes are so benign. Skiing began here in 1947, with the first chair-lift built in the Tyrol. Oberau (3km from Niederau) is the Wildschönau's regional centre and has an impressive Benedictine church and a year-round population of 1,850. Aside from a kitsch woodcutter's chalet, Auffach is a village of nondescript modern buildings.

Niederau, Auffach and Oberau are linked by 13 free buses per day. The old silver-mining village of Thierbach has only two drag-lifts on offer and 500 beds among a local population of 200, but boasts an elevation of 1,150m.

✔ High standard of accommodation
✔ Short airport transfer
✔ Reasonable prices
✘ Lack of long runs (Niederau)
✘ Exceptionally limited skiing network
✘ Low altitude
✘ Short ski season

On the snow
top 1,900m (6,232ft) bottom 830m (2,722ft)

From Niederau's gondola station, it is only seven minutes to the top at Markbachjoch (1,500m), where traversing uphill left or right leads to a total of three pisted runs back to the bottom. Niederau has 10 lifts, 8 of which are drags, and Oberau has a further 7 short drag-lifts. Auffach has the region's best skiing, with slopes rising to 1,900m (6,232ft) but is not featured in any British tour operator's brochure. The resort's modern four-person gondola rises in two stages through woods to a series of five parallel drag-lifts that are all high (between 1,500 and 1,900m).

Beginners
Despite being touted by tour operators as a resort for beginners, the Wildschönau is exceptionally limited even in relatively snow-sure beginner terrain, and Niederau demands tiresome pushing with ski poles to get anywhere at all. It has three drag-lifts serving nursery slopes near the gondola and two more drags which are a 15- to 20-minute hike away. There is no blue (easy) route down to Niederau from the mountain top, and only three very short blues at the top for those who do commute up and down from the village.

WHAT'S NEW

Hotel Panorama

Intermediates
An experienced intermediate who happens to find him- or herself in the Wildschönau will enjoy the Lanerköpfl International Ski Federation (FIS) downhill course. Auffach's four drag-lifts to the skier's left of the gondola serve exclusively red (intermediate) pistes, with some areas left unpisted. Auffach has the longest, most satisfying intermediate run in the region, with 1,000 vertical metres of enjoyable cruising.

Advanced
Niederau has two ski routes down the fall-line to the skier's right of the gondola, and the black (difficult) racecourse Lanerköpfl, which would challenge any advanced skier provided it is taken in a tuck from top to bottom.

Off-piste
The Wildschönau's rounded, low-lying hills make for easy ski-tours when snow conditions allow for powder skiing.

Snowboarders
There is nothing much to recommend the resort to riders, although Auffach does have a rather basic funpark and a half-pipe.

Tuition and guiding
Niederau has two schools, Activ and Wildschönau, with the former the better prepared of the two for ski-touring. Both have ample experience with beginners, and English is widely spoken. Oberau and Auffach each have their own ski schools.

Mountain restaurants
The Wildschönau region has a total of seven mountain restaurants. At the top of Niederau, Rudi's Markbachjoch is cosy with its blue curtains and sanded pine tables, and is celebrated for its plum pancakes. Auffach's Schatbergalm and Koglmoos are large self-service inns. The Anton Graf Hütte in Niederau is an authentic touring hut.

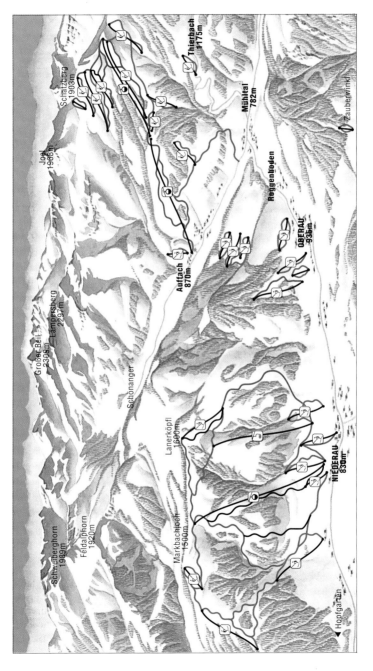

Skiing facts: Wildschönau

TOURIST INFORMATION
A-6311 Wildschönau, Tirol
Tel 43 5339 8255–0
Fax 43 5339 2433
Email info@wildschoenau.tirol.at
Web site www.wildschoenau.com

THE RESORT
By road Calais 1,114km
By rail Wörgl 10km
Airport transfer Innsbruck 45mins,
Salzburg 1½hrs
Visitor beds 7,790 in area
Transport free ski bus between centres

THE SKIING
Linked or nearby resorts Mühltal (n),
Roggenboden (n)
Number of lifts 28 in area
Total of trails/pistes 45km (6% beginner,
56% easy, 32% intermediate,
6% difficult)
Nursery slopes 5 lifts in area

LIFT PASSES
Area pass Wildschönau (covers
Niederau, Auffach, Oberau,Thierbach)
ATS1,435–1,595 for 6 days
Beginners package including lessons
Pensioners 27% discount

Credit cards yes

TUITION
Adults Niederau: Aktiv tel: 5339 2701,
Wildschönau tel: 5339 2200.
Auffach: Hochtal tel: 5339 2556.
Oberau: Happy Schischule
tel: 5339 2323
Snowboarding as ski schools
Other courses carving, cross-country,
moguls, race-training, seniors, ski-touring
Guiding through Activ or
Wildschönau ski schools

CHILDREN
Lift pass 6–16yrs, ATS860–955,
free for 6yrs and under
Ski & board school as adults
Kindergarten through ski schools

OTHER SPORTS
Hang-gliding, horse-riding, night-skiing,
parapente, skating, sleigh rides,
snowbiking, snowshoeing, swimming,
floodlit tobogganing

FOOD AND DRINK PRICES
Coffee ATS25, glass of wine ATS18–20,
small beer ATS24, soft drink ATS20–24,
dish of the day ATS70–120

Accommodation
Hotel Sonnschein in Niederau is 'in a class of its own: indoor pool, excellent half-board meals and sumptuous rooms'. The older Hotel Austria also has an indoor swimming-pool but is criticised for its standard of accommodation ('disappointing for four-star rating, with the half-board food rather plain and uninteresting'). The well-appointed Schneeberger boasts a popular disco. Auffach's traditional town/barn house Weissbacher is popular, as is the three-star modern Schatzberghaus. Oberau accommodates some 2,500 tourists in its central hotels, guesthouses and farms, including the Tirolerhof Hotel, which has a swimming-pool, and Gasthof Kellerwirt, an old monastery with elegant cuisine. Hotel Panorama is a new hotel situated on the piste at Markbachjoch at the top of the gondola.

Eating in and out

Most dining is done in hotels and guesthouses. In Niederau, Café Lois has extremely filling pizzas. Hotel Sonnschein provides 'good food in agreeable surroundings'. Sport Café-Pub has antique radios and TVs and serves cheap sausage and chips.

Après-ski

Zither and harp evenings, with Tyrolean costume, are regular hotel events. Sean plays the guitar at the Hotel Vicky, which now has a number of British and Irish brews on tap. Serious drinking takes place at the Cave Bar, while the Dorfstuben is more salubrious. Others include Bobo's, Sport Café Pub and Treff. Almbar has a disco. The Avalanche Pub in Auffach slides from afternoon to early morning (3pm to 3am), and Carlie's Pub is the other après-ski venue. Oberau's SnoBlau Pub is quite active.

Childcare

All four ski schools give lessons to children from four years of age, and the Wildschönau school minds children from two years of age indoors.

Zell am See

ALTITUDE 750m (2,460ft)

Beginners ✳✳ Intermediates ✳✳✳ Advanced ✳ Snowboarders ✳✳

Zell am See is an attractive medieval town at the gateway to Austria's highest mountain, the Grossglockner. It is just one hour by road from Salzburg and is bypassed by a 10-km tunnel which takes all the through-traffic underground from the satellite of **Schüttdorf** to the northern end of the lake. The town was first settled by a monastic order in the eighth century. Its medieval guesthouses and shops cluster around a smart pedestrianised centre with a tenth-century tower.

✔ Facilities for non-skiers
✔ Short airport transfer
✔ Extensive cross-country skiing
✔ Attractive pedestrian centre
✔ Lively nightlife
✔ Year-round skiing on Kitzsteinhorn Glacier
✘ Overcrowding at peak periods
✘ Skiing convenience

Zell am See's summer trade is even larger than its winter trade, and the resort's huge international popularity rests on its hard-to-beat geographical setting at the foot of the 2,000-m Schmittenhöhe.

The mountain provides an ample amount of easy intermediate skiing, and the towering presence of the Kitzsteinhorn above neighbouring **Kaprun** means that snow is guaranteed in winter. Kaprun has one of the best developed glaciers in Austria, which used to offer year-round skiing on the upper slopes. However, in recent years the glacier has shrunk alarmingly and its summer snow record is now by no means reliable. When winter cover is sparse elsewhere, its slopes become a daily point of pilgrimage for thousands of tourists from other resorts in Salzburgerland, and overcrowding here can be unacceptable.

Kaprun and Zell am See market themselves jointly as the Europa Sport Region. The shared ski pass provides a total of 130km of skiing and access to 55 lifts. Mountain facilities have improved, although Zell prides itself on its 'green' image and has vowed to replace old lifts but not to build any new ones. The focus on uphill transport has switched from the slow and overcrowded Schmittenhöhe cable-car at Schmittental to Schüttdorf. From here, the Areitbahn gondola has been extended so that the summit of the mountain can now be reached in just 20 minutes.

On the snow
top 1,965m (6,445ft) bottom 750m (2,460ft)

The Schmittenhöhe looks like a *Germknödl*, the rounded, sweet dumpling to be found in the nine mountain restaurants that are on it. Its moderate

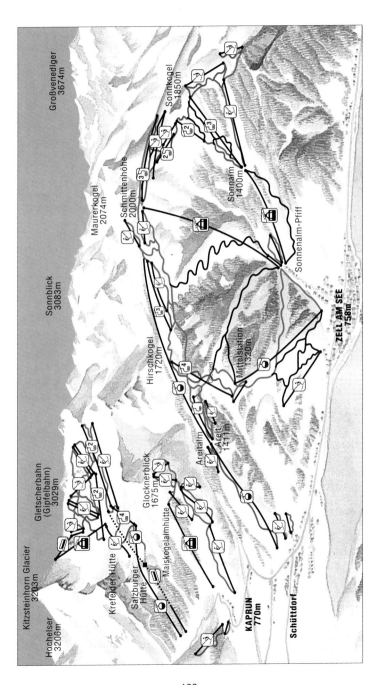

slopes provide long, gentle red (intermediate) runs both back down to the village and along the southern flank to Schüttdorf. Steeper slopes drop from a bowl and provide the most challenging skiing in the resort.

From Schmittental, 2km from the centre of Zell, the old Schmittenhöhe cable-car rises sedately to the summit, or a second cable-car takes you into the Sonnalm area on the sunny, south-facing side of the bowl, which is served by two more chairs and a drag-lift. A considerable number of skiers prefer to take the free bus and start the day on the Areitbahn gondola at Schüttdorf. The bus runs every 20 minutes.

The pretty village of Kaprun, a five-minute journey by road, also has its own ski area above the village comprising mainly blue (easy) runs. The edge of the area was struck by a giant avalanche in March 2000 which killed 14 off-piste skiers, but the village itself and the groomed slopes are not endangered, and potential visitors should not be deterred by the ensuing bad publicity.

The best of Kaprun's skiing is on the Kitzsteinhorn Glacier, 20 minutes by bus from Zell. A gondola followed by a quad-chair, or the original underground funicular, take you up to the Alpincenter at 2,450m, where lifts whisk you on up to the top of the ski area at 3,029m.

The Alpincenter includes a modest hotel, restaurants, ski shop and a ski school. The glacier offers good but exposed blue and red runs.

Beginners

The main novice slopes at Zell are on the top of the Schmittenhöhe, and you will need to take the lift down again at the end of the day. There are also nursery slopes at the bottom of the cable-car and at Schüttdorf. Kaprun has its own winter nursery slope on the edge of the village as well as extensive easy runs on the glacier.

Intermediates

On the south side of the Schmittenhöhe, a succession of gentle, broad and sunny pistes descend along the ridge and on down to Schüttdorf. A right fork takes you to Areitalm, which is the arrival point for the first stage of the gondola from Schüttdorf; the cruising piste down from here to the bottom does not keep its snow in warm weather. The left fork brings you down to the Zell am See mid-station. The Sonnalm area also provides plenty of easy cruising.

Advanced

The two black (advanced) runs that branch off over the southern lip of the bowl provide the best advanced terrain. These soon steepen into testing, but not intimidating, long runs with the occasional pitch of almost 30 degrees. The other two runs to the base-stations are less severe but receive more sun.

Off-piste

Zell's environmental policy means that off-piste skiing is restricted to the point of being almost forbidden. After a fresh fall, a number of tree-line runs look particularly enticing, but the protection of saplings is a priority, and you risk confiscation of your lift pass if you ski them.

Snowboarding

Zell am See is excellent for beginner riders and has a permanent half-pipe to satisfy freestylers. However, boarders should note that the small amount of off-piste on the Schmittenhöhe is not open to riders, and reporters noted that the area does not seem popular with snowboarders. Kaprun, with its glacier, is the more attractive destination, and its terrain is well suited to intermediate freeriders. The fun park has a half-pipe, which is in operation (snow permitting) all year round.

Tuition and guiding

Ski and snowboard schools in the valley seem to vary in quality, and we have mixed reports of the seven schools in the region. None of them has priority in the lift lines, so it is not worth taking lessons just to jump the queues. The Wallner-Prenner in Zell am See is the most highly recommended, with 'excellent instructors, all of whom speak good English'. The Schmittenhöhe receives considerable praise. The Kitzsteinhorn Ski School in Kaprun operates all-year-round and has a high standard of instruction, particularly for advanced skiers.

Mountain restaurants

Zell am See has a good choice of mountain eating-places, although these are crowded during busy weeks; prices are reasonable. The black run down from Sonnalm has a pleasant hut for those who can get to it. The Sonnenalm-Pfiff is praised for its 'delicious hot chocolate'. Schmiedhofalm has amazing views from its sunny terrace. The mid-station restaurant serves 'huge and excellent *Kaiserschmarren*' (chopped pancake with stewed plums). Glocknerhaus, on the way down to Schüttdorf, is also popular. Hans' Schnapps Bar on the summit has a live rock band two days a week and attracts dancing in ski boots, even on the bar.

Accommodation

The luxurious Grand Hotel, jutting out over the lake, and the five-star Salzburgerhof are the most comfortable hotels in town. The four-stars are the Alpin, Fischerwirt and the Alpenblick. The Alpenblick, two miles from the centre, is criticised as being: 'Not four-star standard. It has clean and plainly decorated bedrooms, but the furniture is rather battered 1980s MFI-lookalike. Meals uninspiring and the service at times inattentive'. Hotel Bellevue is a recommended three-star, and Hotel St Georg has smart, pine-panelled rooms and views of the lake. Hotel Berner, set above the town, has a heated outdoor swimming-pool and is popular with reporters ('decorated in a rather grand style, but the owners and staff are friendly').

Eating in and out

The Alpenkönig, Steinerwirt and Chataprunium are considered the best value for money along with the Kupferkessel and the Saustall.

Skiing facts: Zell am See

TOURIST INFORMATION
Brucker Bundesstr. 3,
A-5700 Zell am See
Tel 43 6542 770
Fax 43 6542 72032
Email zell@gold.at
Web site www.europa-sport-region.com

THE RESORT
By road Calais 1,184km
By rail station in resort
Airport transfer Salzburg 1hr
Visitor beds 13,800
Transport free ski bus

THE SKIING
Linked or nearby resorts Kaprun (l),
Maria Alm (n), Saalbach-Hinterglemm (n)
Number of lifts 28 in Zell am See, 27 in
Kaprun
Total of trails/pistes 75km in Zell am
See (38% easy, 50% intermediate, 12%
difficult), 130km in linked area
Nursery slopes 2 lifts in Zell am See, 2
lifts in Kaprun
Summer skiing 15 lifts on Kitzsteinhorn
Glacier

LIFT PASSES
Area pass Europa Sport Region (covers
Zell am See, Kaprun, Saalbach-
Hinterglemm) ATS1,860–2,020 for 6
days
Beginners ATS10–20 per ride for lower
drag-lifts
Pensioners ATS1,820 for women 60yrs
and over, men 65yrs and over
Credit cards yes

TUITION
Adults Zell am See: Schmittenhöhe tel:
6542 73207, Skischule Zell am See
Areitbahn tel: 6542 56020, Pro Alpin tel:
6542 72048, Thumersbach tel: 6542
73579, Wallner-Prenner tel: 6542
72324. Kaprun: Hartweger tel: 6547
7766, Kaprun tel: 6547 8070,
Professional tel: 6547 7562,
Oberschneider 6547 8232, Ski +
Rennschule Kitzsteinhorn tel: 6547
Snowboarding as ski schools, FOT
Snowboard Academy tel: 6547 7760
Other courses carving, cross-country,
moguls, race camps on Kitzsteinhorn,
skiing for the disabled, telemark
Guiding through ski schools

CHILDREN
Lift pass 6–15yrs, ATS1,180 for 6 days,
free for 5yrs and under
Ski school as adults
Kindergarten (ski/non-ski) Play & Fun
tel: 6542 56020

OTHER SPORTS
Climbing wall, curling, hang-gliding,
horse-riding, hot-air ballooning, ice-
climbing, ice-driving, ice-hockey, indoor
tennis and squash, luge, parapente,
shooting range, skating, ski jumping,
sleigh rides, snow-rafting, snowshoeing,
swimming, tubing

FOOD AND DRINK PRICES
Coffee ATS25–30, glass of wine
ATS20–30, small beer ATS28–32, soft
drink ATS25, dish of the day ATS80–150.

Hotel St Georg has a pleasant restaurant with good-quality food. The
Ampere, Landhotel Erlhof and the Salzburgerhof are also recommended for their high standard of cuisine. The Baum-Bar in Kaprun
has a large restaurant in a conservatory with stripped pine floor.

Après-ski

Zell am See is lively by any standards. Once the lifts have closed for the day the first stop is a choice of the Kellerbar of the Hotel Schwebebahn near the lifts, Café Feinschmeck, with its vast variety of pastries, and the Mösshammer in the main square, which also serves coffee and cakes. Tea-dancing still exists in Zell, and a number of reporters have enjoyed watching major-league ice-hockey matches. The Crazy Daisy bar is a focal point for Anglo-Saxon visitors, but is said by one reporter to be 'very expensive and unpleasantly crowded'. The Kellerbar of the Hotel zum Hirschen is bustling, and you can relax in the main bar of the Tirolerhof, and at the same time hear yourself think. Late-night action switches to the Viva nightclub, which swings on until dawn, Evergreens for the over 25s, and the Diele Bar, which attracts a young crowd until 2am.

Childcare

The children's facilities here are generally favourable, with a kindergarten taking children from 12 months and the ski kindergarten from two years. Ski lessons are given at all the ski schools from the age of four. One parent described his child's class as better than the adult class he attended. The Grand Hotel and the Feriendorf Hagleitner both run crèches.

Linked or nearby resorts

Kaprun
top 3,029m (9,938ft) bottom 770m (2,526ft)

This is a delightful, typical Austrian holiday village, set a few kilometres back into the mountains from the lakeside and connected to Zell am See by a free day-time bus service. Although this is a thriving resort with new hotel and apartment developments, Kaprun has managed to retain its essential village atmosphere.

The four-star Orgler hotel has comfortable accommodation and one of the best restaurants. The Sonnblick and the Kaprunserhof cater for families. We have good reports of the Pension Salzburgerhof ('spacious bedrooms'). The village has a handful of sports and gift shops, a tea-room or two, restaurants that include Mexican and Greek establishments, and several pizzerias.

A decent attempt has been made at providing nightlife for visitors, who range from holiday skiers to racers in training during the summer months. Kitsch and Bitter has a live band, the Baum-Bar has a late-night disco, while the Austrian Pub attracts snowboarders. The Optimum sports centre contains an indoor swimming-pool with a giant water-slide.

TOURIST INFORMATION
Tel 43 6547 8643–0
Fax 43 6547 8192
Email kaprun@kaprun.net
Web site www.europa-sport-region.com

Round-up

RESORTS COVERED Bad Kleinkirchheim, Fieberbrunn, Gargellen, Serfaus, Sölden, St Johann im Pongau, St Johann in Tirol, Tiroler Zugspitze (Lermoos/Ehrwald), Waidring

Bad Kleinkirchheim
top 2,000m (6,560ft) bottom 1,080m (3,543ft)

Bad Kleinkirchheim – or BKK as it is usually known – is the home resort of Austrian super-hero Franz Klammer. As one reporter put it, 'what is good enough for Franz is good enough for me'. These days the greatest of all Austrian downhill champions spends more time in Colorado than in Carinthia, but the old spa town and thriving summer resort continues to develop its skiing in his absence.

The ski area is linked to the neighbouring village of **St Oswald**, and together the two provide 85km of mainly intermediate pistes served by 32 lifts. Additions for the 2000–1 season include the new Brunnachalm chair-lift in St Oswald. BKK is quite spread out and has a wide choice of hotels, but après-ski is limited to a few bars, two discos and some good-value restaurants. The excellent spa facilities include indoor and outdoor thermal pools.

With the top lifts reaching 2,000m, the ski area is low; snow conditions are consequently unreliable both early and late in the season. However, some 50km of slopes are now covered by a battery of 350 snow-cannon. The World Cup downhill course was designed by Klammer himself and includes a sequence of jumps that, even when prepared as a recreational run, require considerable concentration. Most runs are wide and gentle, and queues are reported during high season. The lift pass also covers the neighbouring resorts of St Oswald and **Falkert**.

Both the BKK and St Oswald ski schools give group and private tuition in skiing, snowboarding and cross-country, the latter on its 42km of loipe. Three- to six-year-olds can attend the kindergarten for full or half days, where a mixture of games and skiing is offered. BKK actively encourages snowboarders, with a floodlit funpark and the Crazy Carving Company snowboard school. This school is part of Ski and Sportschool Krainer, which also offers the more unusual options of snowbiking, ice-tennis and ice-surfing.

TOURIST INFORMATION
Tel 43 4240 8212
Fax 43 4240 8537
Email bkaefer@bkk.at
Web site www.bkk.at

Fieberbrunn
top 2,020m (6,627ft) bottom 800m (2,625ft)

Ten kilometres up the road from **St Johann in Tirol** is the sprawling

114

village of Fieberbrunn. Its small but attractive ski area is north-facing and is known as a *Schneeloch*, or snowpocket. The main skiing is at tree level, with 13 lifts giving access to a small network of mainly long and easy runs totalling 35km. There are two rival ski schools, Rosenegg and Fieberbrunn, and we have favourable reports of both. The resort kindergarten takes children aged 12 months to 10 years from 9am to 3pm.

TOURIST INFORMATION
Tel 43 5354 56304
Fax 43 5354 52606
Email tvb.fieberbrunn@netway.at
Web site www.tiscover.com/fieberbrunn.at

Gargellen
top 2,300m (7,546ft) bottom 1,430m (4,692ft)

Gargellen is a chalet-style village in the Montafon area. A variety of hotels include the four-star Madrisa, which was built at the beginning of the twentieth century as a private home and opened as a hotel in the 1920s. It has 120 beds, a nightclub, swimming-pool and fitness centre. The resort itself boasts eight lifts, 36km of pistes and a total of 198km of skiing in an area that can be accessed by free ski buses. Ski and Snowboard Schule Gargellen offers all-day lessons as well as off-piste skiing and a children's ski school. The village kindergarten accepts children from two years old. Other activities in the resort include canyoning, curling and parapente. The further Montafon resorts of **Gaschurn** and **St Gallenkirch** are both within easy reach.

TOURIST INFORMATION
Tel 43 5557 6303
Fax 43 5557 6690
Email tourismus@gargellen.to
Web site www.gargellen.to

Serfaus
top 2,684m (8,806ft) bottom 1,427m (4,682ft)

The exclusive resort of Serfaus boasts many luxury modern hotels, which attract a mainly Austrian and German clientèle. The resort is car-free and has an unusual underground railway, which runs on air cushions rather like a hovercraft. This transports snow-users from the far end of the village to the ski lifts and contributes to the peaceful atmosphere in the resort. The Serfaus ski area is linked to the villages of **Fiss** and **Ladis**, making a total of 21 lifts serving some 80km of piste. The nursery slopes have three drag-lifts. The ski school offers daily lessons in skiing and snowboarding, with classes meeting in the Komperdell area at the top of the cable-car. Off-piste guiding and ski-touring are available, and there is also a ski kindergarten. Mini-Treff is the non-ski kindergarten. Other activities include cross-country on 60km of trails, bobsleigh, dogsledding and swimming.

TOURIST INFORMATION
Tel 43 5476 62390
Fax 43 5476 6813
Email info@serfaus.tirol.at
Web site www.serfaus.com

Sölden
top 3,250m (10,663ft) bottom 1,377m (4,517ft)

Sölden is a high-altitude, and therefore snow-sure, resort which is spread out along the main road in the upper reaches of the isolated Ötz Valley. The resort stretches over 2km on either side of the road and river along the valley floor. It is an unmemorable sprawl of hotels, restaurants and bars that lack charm. Nevertheless, it would be uncharitable to dismiss the whole as unattractive.

The skiing is suited mainly to intermediates. The two developed glaciers, Rettenbach and Tiefenbach, have now been linked into the main ski system, ensuring complete snow security. The glacial region has been made accessible by four new lifts – three four-seater chair-lifts and an eight-person Glacier Express gondola. Together with the revamped Giggijochbahn, these bring the total to 34 lifts in this vastly expanded area. The vertical drop is substantial by Austrian standards. The nightlife, at least in the high season weeks, is lively to the point of being raucous.

Sölden's ski area is in two sections linked by chairs up both walls of the narrow Rettenbachtal, which provides the toll road up to the glaciers. The Glacier Express gondola now forms the link between the two. Both sectors are reached by gondolas from either end of the village, which are in turn linked by a ski bus that runs efficiently every 10 minutes. **Hochsölden** is a collection of hotels set 700m up the mountainside on a shelf, giving dramatic views of the Ötztal and easy access to the slopes.

The area now boasts 108km of pistes, of which 42 per cent are graded blue (easy), 42 per cent red (intermediate) and 16 per cent black (difficult). Sölden is a popular spot for riders, with three ski schools offering lessons. The funpark at Giggijoch contains a half-pipe, boardercross course and a range of interesting obstacles and jumps. A second funpark is on the Rettenbach Glacier. This is a great resort for carvers, and freestylers will enjoy the natural gullies.

The choice of 17 mountain restaurants is large: Gampealm, Eugen's Obstlerhütte and Löple Alm are all authentic huts with plenty of Tyrolean atmosphere.

Position of accommodation is important, and a hotel near one of the two main lift stations is a must. The Hotel Regina, right by the Gaislachkoglbahn, is strongly recommended. Gasthof Sonnenheim, in the same area, is praised for being 'extremely cheap'. Hotel Stefan by the Giggijoch gondola station has a good restaurant. Gasthof Grüner continues to receive praise. Dominic is said to be the best eatery in the village. The Kupferpfanne in the Hotel Tirolerhof and the à la carte restaurants in the Alpina, Stefan and Hubertus hotels are also recommended. Hotel Liebe Sonne has a cosy stübli.

Café Philip at **Innerwald** has a lively atmosphere and is a gathering point for young people. The single-chair down from here runs until 6pm. The Hinterer, Dominic and Café Heiner are always crowded. Later in the evening, Jakob's Weinfassl attracts a 30-something clientèle. Discos includes the Alibi Bar in Hotel Central, which is the most sophisticated venue.

Apart from private babysitting, Sölden has no special facilities for non-skiing children. The Sölden/Hochsölden Ski School runs a ski kindergarten, with a play area for skiers aged three or more.

TOURIST INFORMATION
Tel 43 5254 5100
Fax 43 5254 510520
Email info@soelden.com
Web site www.soelden.com

St Johann im Pongau
top 2,188m (7,177ft) bottom 650m (2,132ft)

The four valleys of **Flachau**, **St Johann**, **Wagrain** and **Zauchensee** lie only 45 minutes from Salzburg and provide a playground for intermediates. The statistics are impressive: a dozen resorts with 350km of linked (albeit not always on the mountain) skiing, served by 130 lifts all covered by one ski pass. St Johann itself (not to be confused with St Johann in Tirol) is a cathedral town that was all but devastated by a disastrous fire in 1852; as a consequence it lacks the medieval charm of Austria's other county towns and larger resorts.

The ski area, which is known as the Sportwelt Amadé, has one of the best-value lift passes in Austria. This area is popular with almost every nationality apart from the British; this is partly because few tour operators come here as they cannot contract enough hotel beds to make the area's inclusion in their brochures a commercial viability. Wagrain and Flachau are the most convenient and attractive bases from which to explore the circuit. St Johann has its own small, separate ski area, and the link into the Sportwelt Amadé is via the hamlet of **Alpendorf**, a 3-km ski-bus ride away. The pistes in the area are well serviced with eating places, from small huts to larger self-services.

Each of the resorts has at least one ski school, and St Johann has three. We have good reports of all three as well as of those in Flachau. St Johann has a funpark. Vitamin B and Board Unlimited are two specialist boarding schools in Alpendorf. Cross-country skiers are well served by 160km of trails along the valleys.

Accommodation in St Johann includes the luxurious Sporthotel Alpenland, the three-star Hotel Brückenwirt-Tennerhof and Gasthof-Pension Taxenbacher. The resort's nightlife is limited to a few bars. The inconvenient bus journey to Alpendorf means that St Johann is not ideal for families.

The small village of Wagrain has fortunately been able to develop away from the minor road from St Johann to Flachau and **Radstadt**. Hotel Grafenwirt is discreetly upmarket; Hotel Enzian and the Wagrainerhof are both recommended. The ski kindergarten here takes children from three years old.

Neighbouring Flachau has undergone considerable expansion in recent years. The main accommodation is in large chalet-style hotels and inns, as well as apartment blocks. Beginners learn to ski on a gentle piste in the village. There is a non-ski kindergarten, and the Griessenkar Ski School takes children from three years old. Hotel Reslwirt is central and medium-priced, along with Gasthof Salzburgerhof. Flachau boasts two four-star hotels, Hotel Vierjahreszeiten and the luxurious Hotel Tauernhof.

The market town of **Altenmarkt** is a centre for the local sportswear and ski equipment industries, where, among others, Atomic skis and Steffner sweaters are manufactured. A modest ski area is linked to neighbouring Radstadt, but the main skiing is a bus ride away at **Zauchensee** or Flachau. British-run Fun Ski is based in Zauchensee and offers specialist skiing courses, and the cross-country opportunities, as in the rest of the area, are extensive. The kindergarten cares for children from three years old. The pleasant village has 22 hotels, including six of a luxury standard.

Filzmoos is another small village in the Sportwelt Amadé, dating from Edwardian times, when it was a popular holiday destination for the wealthy Viennese. Today it has a ski area served by 17 lifts, shared with neighbouring Neuberg. The **Dachstein Glacier** is only 18km away, and the rest of the Sportwelt Amadé is reached by bus via Flachau. The kindergarten takes children from three years old and has English-speaking staff. The choice of accommodation in 25 hotels and a selection of apartments is large in relation to the size of the village, which is famed as the hot-air ballooning capital of Austria.

TOURIST INFORMATION
Tel 43 6412 60360
Fax 43 6412 603674
Email info@stjohann.co.at
Web site www.stjohann.co.at

St Johann in Tirol
top 1,700m (5,576ft) bottom 680m (2,230ft)

St Johann in Tirol is a large, busy town with a ski area of 17 lifts. Its expansion from a pretty Tyrolean village to a sprawling light-industrial centre has done little for its charm. However, the centre, with its ornately frescoed buildings and fine old coaching inns, remains largely unspoilt, and the heavy traffic is confined to the outskirts. St Johann offers a pleasant setting for a lively and quite varied winter holiday at prices that are reasonable by Austrian standards. Queues are usually not a problem but are increased by weekend visitors from Innsbruck and Munich when conditions are good. In spite of this the northward orientation of the slopes and competent grooming generally keep the slopes in fine condition.

The resort is particularly geared towards beginners, with six nursery-slope lifts scattered between the town and the hamlet of **Eichenhof**, which is served by ski bus. The rolling lower pastures are ideal novice terrain, with a choice of blue (easy) runs higher up, to which beginners can progress after a few days. Practically all the skiing on the top half of the mountain is graded red (intermediate), but the area is limited in size and lacks any real challenge. Another major drawback is the distance across town to the lifts – the skiing can be accessed from five different points, but all are a long walk or a bus ride away from the centre.

Both of the two ski schools offer snowboard tuition, and the resort has a funpark with a 60m half-pipe. Non-ski Miniclub St Johann cares for children under four years every day except Saturday. The Ski Kinderclub takes children from four years. The choice of 18 mountain restaurants is way above average for a resort of this size – almost every piste has a welcoming mountain hut at the top, bottom or part-way down. The cross-country skiing is extensive and covers 210km of prepared tracks from St Johann to **Erpfendorf**, **Going**, **Kirchdorf**, **Oberndorf** and **Waidring**.

The central feature of St Johann is the three-star Hotel Gasthof Post, which dates from 1225 and is beautifully frescoed. Hotel Park, near the gondola, is recommended, and we have favourable reports of Hotel Fischer. Hotel Goldener Löwe is strongly endorsed for families. St Johann's nightlife is young and vibrant: popular bars include Buny's, Max's and Café Rainer, which has a regular Tyrolean evening each Monday. The restaurants in the Gasthof Post and in the Hotel Bären are both recommended. Lange Mauer is a rare Austrian Chinese restaurant. Masianco serves pizzas and Mexican food. Other activities include hot-air ballooning, indoor tennis, skating and swimming.

TOURIST INFORMATION
Tel 43 5352 63355
Fax 43 5352 65200
Email info@st.johann.tirol.at
Web site www.st.johann.tirol.at

Tiroler Zugspitze
top 2,964m (9,724ft) bottom 1,000m (3,280ft)

Lermoos and nearby **Ehrwald** are the principal villages of the Tiroler Zugspitze, a marketing consortium of small, separate ski areas, which share a lift pass, northwest of **Innsbruck** near the German border. The Zugspitze, at 2,964m (9,724ft), is the highest and is reached by cable-cars from both Austria and Germany. **Biberwier**, the third village, has installed a six-person chair-lift for the 2000–1 season that should transform mountain access. Lermoos has 9 lifts, Ehrwald 11, Biberwier 7, and **Zugspitze** 10.

Beginners can try the nursery slopes at the Lermoos base and graduate to a longer, gentle run by taking the gondola up Ehrwalder Alm. For intermediates, the Zugspitze Bowl offers wide pistes and easy red (intermediate) runs, which lead over the border into Germany. Advanced snow-users will find the area limited; there is one black (difficult) run on the Grubigstein above Lermoos. However, in good snow conditions you can ski down from the Zugspitze Glacier. This is an excellent area for cross-country skiing, with more than 100km of prepared tracks.

Lermooser Skischule, and Ehrwalder and Total in Ehrwald, are the three ski and snowboard schools, offering morning and afternoon tuition. Bergrettung is an off-piste guiding company based in Ehrwald. Bobo's is the ski kindergarten in Lermoos and Leo-Kinderhut is the crèche. Hotel Spielmann, on the edge of the village of Ehrwald, is a traditional, frescoed Tyrolean chalet. The owner and his son are both celebrated local climbers as well as being accomplished chefs who provide everything home-made. The hotel also has a health centre.

In Lermoos, the Hotel Lermooserhof is said to be 'friendly, but too far out of town'. Reporters were enthusiastic about Hotel Post in the centre. The Jux bar near the gondola base is the most popular meeting point at the end of the day. The post-dinner crowd move on to the Rustika Bar/Disco.

TOURIST INFORMATION
Tel (Lermoos) 43 5673 2401 /(Ehrwald) 43 5673 2395
Fax (Lermoos) 43 5673 2694 /(Ehrwald) 43 5673 3314
Email ehrwald@zugspitze.tirol.at
Web site www.tiscover.com/ehrwald

Waidring
top 1,860m (6,102ft) bottom 780m (2,558ft)
This unspoilt village is less than 20km from **St Johann in Tirol** and is situated in the same snowpocket as **Fieberbrunn**. The quiet resort is known for its family skiing, with convenient nursery slopes in the village centre. It boasts 25km of piste served by 10 lifts. The main skiing is at Steinplatte, 4km from the village, and is suited to beginners and intermediates.

There are five mountain restaurants on the slopes. The best hotel is the Waidringerhof, which has a swimming-pool and a pleasant dining-room. The central Hotel Tiroler Adler is also recommended. The nightlife in Waidring is relaxed and informal, and the Schniedermann Bar and the Alte Schmiede are both popular venues.

TOURIST INFORMATION
Tel 43 5353 5242
Fax 43 5353 52424
Email waidring@netway.at
Web site www.tiscover.com/waidring

France

France has the best skiing in the world. For anyone who has only skied elsewhere, the scale of the dozen top French destinations is truly stupefying. An American professional skier from Breckenridge described her introduction to Val d'Isère as 'feeling like a kid in a candy store. With 23 lifts I thought I lived in a world class resort, but 96 – that was almost beyond my comprehension'.

France offers the largest and most sophisticated lift systems in the world, which may explain why more British snow-users holiday here than in any other country. The mountains of Savoie, Haute-Savoie and Dauphiné offer more challenge than their counterparts in Austria. The Pyrenees have less demanding, but nevertheless attractive skiing and considerably lower prices. Myriad resorts – 319 to be exact – have been developed in France over the past 30 years, and those with international pretensions are far better equipped than their equivalents in Switzerland, Austria or Italy.

Since 1995 sterling has risen in value by 33 per cent against the franc and, as a consequence, ski holidays to France should be cheap – but they are not. While the basic price of package holidays may not have risen markedly, in-resort costs for such essentials as ski hire and mountain lunches are spiralling out of control. These figures are being inflated unacceptably by greedy locals, who are harvesting the tourist crop without thought for next year's seed.

Unlike their Alpine neighbours, the majority of French resorts are purpose-built *stations de ski*, which provide ski-in ski-out convenience often at a high cost to the ambience. The French have learned their lesson from the original architectural follies of the 1960s, such as Tignes, Flaine and the earlier villages of La Plagne. On the other hand, Valmorel, Risoul and other more recent developments have been constructed with consideration for their natural mountain environment. In all the French resorts there is more accommodation in apartments than in hotels, and the first concrete *résidences* were built with rooms that are now considered far too small for the demands of today's tourists.

Many reporters complain that French resorts lack the atmosphere of their Austrian cousins and that the staff and locals in France are not as welcoming as the Canadians. With a few notable exceptions, such as Chamonix, Megève and Les Deux Alpes, après-ski is muted. In many resorts visitors find themselves forced to prop up the neighbourhood bar or make their own entertainment in their chalets or apartments. The few discos are often grossly overpriced, underfrequented and play unrecognisable 'Euromusak'. However, none of these shortcomings seriously detracts from what the French resorts have to offer. The inescapable reason why more British now ski and snowboard in France than anywhere else is because, taking every factor into consideration, there is simply nowhere better.

Alpe d'Huez

ALTITUDE 1,860m (6,100ft)

Beginners ✳✳✳ Intermediates ✳✳✳ Advanced ✳✳✳ Snowboarders ✳✳

Alpe d'Huez first opened as a resort in 1936 with a handful of tourist beds. At the time of the 1968 Olympics it was little more than a one-street alpine village dominated by a futuristic modern church. The massive, apparently uncontrolled, building surge that followed led to the resort spreading out in all directions in a plethora of architectural styles. 'One of the worst blots on the landscape anywhere, but fortunately you only have to lift your eyes to the superb surroundings,' said one reporter. Traffic remains a problem, although it must be pointed out that as there is no through-road from the resort to anywhere else, it is more a question of overcrowded parking than busy main roads. Shops are limited to a few boutiques and tacky T-shirt and souvenir establishments.

✔ Extensive ski area
✔ Sunny position
✔ Beautiful scenery
✔ Variety of mountain restaurants
✔ Widespread artificial snow
✔ Ideal for families
✔ Varied off-piste
✘ Lack of alpine charm
✘ Limited tree-skiing
✘ Weekend crowds
✘ Uninspiring nightlife

A bucket lift acts as the primary people-mover. A shuttle bus takes skiers up to the slopes from the lower reaches of what is a steep resort for pedestrians, although several reporters say there was no sign of a bus during their entire stay. Alpe d'Huez is one of the few resorts that can be reached directly by aircraft as it has its own altiport. Les Deux Alpes is several minutes away by helicopter or 45 minutes by road.

The 3,330-m summit of Pic Blanc dominates Les Grandes-Rousses, the fifth largest ski area in France and one of increasing importance to the British market. Alpe d'Huez is its capital and the hub of 220km of linked skiing served by 85 lifts. Though not a purpose-built resort, so great are the additions to the original village that it has all the convenience of one. The lower satellites of **Auris-en-Oisans**, **Oz Station**, **Vaujany** and **Villard-Reculas** have emerged as resorts in their own right, and to some extent eclipse their grizzled old master.

Alpe d'Huez was chosen as one of the venues for the Killy Winter Olympics in 1968. For a while the village fathers toyed with the notion of cultivating the *exclusif* tag, which is attached to Megève and Courchevel 1850. In the end, the need to pay for what was then one of the most modern lift systems in the world pointed them in the direction of the mass-market. Sadly, lift upgrading has not continued at a

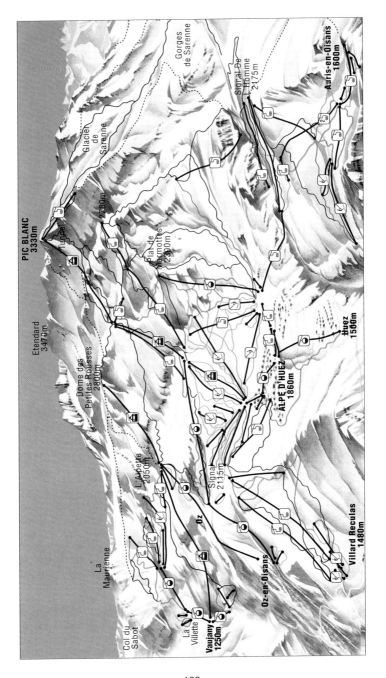

seasonal pace, and although the gondolas and cable-cars are modern there are still a number of slow old chair-lifts. The clientèle remains predominantly French, but Alpe d'Huez works hard at maintaining its international image.

On the snow
top 3,330m (10,922ft) bottom 1,100m (3,608ft)

Alpe d'Huez is a genuine all-round ski resort with excellent nursery slopes, good red (intermediate) runs, long black (difficult) trails and extremely serious off-piste opportunities. Mountain access is multiple: two main modern gondolas feed traffic out of the village into the Pic Blanc sector, and there are alternative routes at peak times. High-season queues for the first and particularly for the second stage of the main 25-person DMC gondola can develop into an unpleasant scrum. Feeding more skiers into such a high-capacity system has an obvious downside, and the pistes immediately above the village (Les Chamois, Le Signal and Le Lac Blanc) are prone to overcrowding.

First impressions can be deceptive, and none more so than here. The skiing as seen from Les Bergers lift station looks disarmingly mild: an open mountainside served by an array of gondolas, chair- and drag-lifts. However, skiers who have cut their teeth on the gentle pastures of the Tyrol will be shocked by the hidden severity of the skiing. Much of the Pic Blanc is concealed from sight by the lie of the land – from its 3,330-m summit it is possible to ski over 2000m vertical in good snow conditions down to well below Alpe d'Huez.

The area divides naturally into four main sectors: Pic Blanc, Signal de l'Homme/Auris, Signal/Villard-Reculas and Oz/Vaujany. The central part of the skiing takes place immediately northeast of the resort on sunny slopes and is reached via the two impressively efficient stages of the DMC gondola. Late in the season, some of the best skiing is to be found in Auris and in the Montfrais sector of Vaujany, which keep their snow well.

Beginners
The first stage of the DMC gondola serves an enormous area of green (beginner) runs close to the resort. The Rif Nel piste is the gentlest of the long pistes from the base of the gondola back down to Les Bergers. All the satellites have nursery slopes, some of them more novice-friendly than others. Vaujany's ski area starts at Montfrais, a sunny balcony above the resort that is reached by gondola. Two drag-lifts give access to green and blue (easy) runs, which are ideal beginners' terrain.

Intermediates
From the mid-station of the DMC gondola, the Lièvre Blanc chair provides access to a lot of challenging skiing. It serves its own red (intermediate) piste, which is more like a black (difficult) run in places, but also leads to the satisfyingly secluded red Balme, which takes you all

the way down to Alpe d'Huez. One reporter recommended Le Canyon, reached from the same chair, as 'a lot of fun'.

From the top of the DMC gondola try the long red Les Rousses (110 on the local piste map). Take the usually mogulled and crowded first 100m slowly so as not to miss the path that cuts northwest beneath the cableway into the Vaujany sector. From here you can ski all the way down to Oz or Vaujany. A wide and pleasant blue piste is L'Olympic from the top of Les Marmottes gondola.

Signal is a rounded, snow-covered peak adjacent to Alpe d'Huez. It is reached by a four-seater chair or alternative drag-lifts and provides some varied intermediate runs, which are easily accessible from the heart of the village. Behind Signal, longer runs drop down the open, west-facing slopes above the satellite village of Villard-Reculas. A quad-chair allows mountain access from the village, regardless of snow cover.

Advanced

A largely under-used piste takes you all the way down to the hamlet of L'Enversin d'Oz, which is linked to Vaujany by a cluster gondola. From the summit of Pic Blanc this represents a mighty vertical of 2,330m, claimed to be the longest in the Alps (with lifts to take you back up again). The top of the Clocher de Mâcle chair-lift is the starting point for some interesting black runs. These include the beautiful Combe Charbonnière past Europe's highest disused coal mine; from here pistes lead either down into the Sarenne Gorge or back to the resort. The short run down from Clocher de Mâcle to Lac Blanc is steep, but the snow is usually good. From the top of Pic Blanc two black pistes, the Sarenne and the Château Noir, take you all the way down into the Sarenne Gorge and are claimed, at 16km, to be the longest black runs in the Alps. However, it should be pointed out that they derive most of their length from the run-out along the bottom of the gorge. Only some pitches of the Sarenne are really difficult, but the run is long and tiring. Both pistes are narrow in places and can produce awkward bottlenecks.

The front face of Pic Blanc is accessed via a tunnel through the rock, 200m below the summit, with an awkward path at the end of it. The steep and usually icy Tunnel mogul field that awaits you can be extremely daunting when no snow has fallen for some weeks. However, in fresh powder the pitch is near perfect.

Off-piste

Opportunities for *ski sauvage* from the top of Pic Blanc are superb. Variations include the Grand Sablat, the Combe du Loup and a long and tricky descent via the Couloir de Fare. A 20-minute climb from the cable-car station takes you to the top of La Pyramide, the off-piste starting point for more than 2,000m of vertical, bringing you down through a range of gullies and open snowfields all the way to Vaujany or Oz. The top can be very icy, and ropes may be needed to negotiate the steeper couloirs in packed snow conditions. The off-piste variation from the ridge separating Oz from Alpe d'Huez is a gloriously steep powder field, which filters into the tree-studded gorge at the bottom. It is prone to avalanche and should be attempted only in the morning. There are seven itineraries in the area, all of which are marked on the piste map.

Snowboarders

The funpark on the Signal piste has a tunnel and a fairly dramatic half-pipe which, along with a boarder-cross course, are open both day and night. The area has a considerable number of natural drop-offs and the entire mountain is well-suited to freeriders.

Tuition and guiding

The French Ski School (ESF) has 300 instructors based in Alpe d'Huez, Auris, Oz and Vaujany. Reports of the ESF are improving, and separate classes are provided for English speakers. One reporter remarked that although the initial impression of the ski school in Alpe d'Huez was one of 'total chaos, with hundreds of instructors and students jostling together', the instructors were 'always cheerful and friendly with excellent English'.

The International Ski School (ESI) offers ski and snowboarding classes restricted to eight, with tuition in English. The third mainstream ski and snowboarding school is Fun Evasion, and British Masterclass courses are held in Alpe d'Huez for English-speaking clients.

Mountain restaurants

Chez Patou, a stone hut below the top of the Alpette gondola on the Oz piste, offers simple farmhouse fare at reasonable prices. Les Airelles is a restaurant built into the rock, with a sunny terrace, at the top of the nursery drag at Montfrais above Vaujany. La Cabane du Poutat, above Alpe d'Huez, is said to have 'overpriced and rather averagely prepared food with snooty service'.

La Bergerie, on the red run down to Villard-Reculas, is an alpine museum that doubles as a restaurant; the setting, complete with open fire and cow bells, is particularly attractive. The Chalet du Lac Besson, on the cross-country trail between the DMC gondola and Alpette, has a sunny terrace in a peaceful setting and has the best mountain cuisine in the region at a reasonable price.

Le Tetras in Auris serves fine pizzas and has a varied wine list. The Auberge Forêt de Maronne below Auris can usually only be reached in mid-winter via a choice of long blue or black runs through scenic alpine meadows. Combe Haute in the Sarenne Gorge has a welcoming atmosphere and is renowned for its salads.

Accommodation

The higher up the hill you are staying, the easier it is to get to and from the skiing. The hard core of one four-star (the Royal Ours Blanc) and eight three-star hotels is supported by numerous family-run hotels. Le Petit Prince is a small hotel which guests find relaxing but a little quiet ('an excellent standard of service'). The Christina is friendly and charming and one of the few attractive chalet-style buildings at the top of the resort. The Chamois d'Or is considered the best hotel, with a highly regarded restaurant. L'Ourson is a family-run hotel. The best apartments include those in the Rocher Soleil, which has its own outdoor heated swimming-pool and optional self-catering ('a little pokey but warm and comfortable'). Maeva's Les Bergers apartments are recommended by reporters.

Eating in and out

Dining is an important business in Alpe d'Huez, a legacy from its more exclusive days ('this is one of our favourite pastimes, and Alpe d'Huez is an excellent place to indulge it'). There are more than 50 restaurants in the resort itself. Au P'tit Creux ('intimate atmosphere and wonderful, but avoid it at weekends') is one of the best restaurants here. One reporter called it 'a restaurant to treasure'. Booking is essential. Le Chamois d'Or and L'Outa vie with it as the principal centres for haute cuisine in town. Le Colporteur has a strong following. La Pomme de Pin is praised for its 'enormous helpings – a meal like this would have cost quite a lot more in the Home Counties'. Another reporter commented: 'this restaurant certainly isn't cheap but the food is absolutely first class.' La Crémaillère, Caribou and Le Génépi ('a fine restaurant that can be recommended with confidence') all offer mountain specialities. La Taverne is praised: 'the atmosphere is lively without being rowdy and the food is both first-class and reasonably priced'. Pizza Origan is 'friendly with a good range of pizzas and pasta'. The restaurant in Vaujany's Hotel Rissiou is open to non-residents and has excellent cuisine and wines.

Supermarkets in Alpe d'Huez are adequate, and reporters recommend Les Bergers in the Centre Commercial. Serious food shoppers can drive down to the Rallye supermarket in Bourg d'Oisans.

Après-ski

The Cactus Bar offers a live band most nights; Le Petit Bar has live blues every night. The Pacific Pub and the Avalanche Bar are said to be 'lacking in atmosphere' with 'music and loud holidaymakers'. Le Sporting, which overlooks the skating rink, is 'a pleasant piano bar with an interesting and reasonably priced menu'. The Underground is 'noisy, crowded, and packed with Scandinavians'. Smithy's is 'more roomy than the Underground and also quieter'. Etoile des Neiges is a typical French café. Alpe d'Huez sports four discos, including the Igloo and Crystal. Snowboarders will find the resort eminently affordable.

Childcare

The ESF ski school guarantees class sizes of no more than ten. However, one reporter said that 'we regularly saw classes of 13 or more small children during April high season'. The ESI gives lessons to children from three and a half years and the ESF from four years. Les Eterlous, next to its Club Med building, takes skiing and non-skiing children from three to eleven years of age. Les Crapouilloux is a crèche for children from two years old.

Linked or nearby resorts

Auris-en-Oisans
top 3,330m (10,922ft) bottom 1,600m (5,249ft)

Auris consists mainly of apartment blocks and, though somewhat isolated from the bulk of the skiing in Les Grandes-Rousses, is well positioned for outings to **Les Deux Alpes**, **Briançon/Serre Chevalier** and **La Grave**. The Beau Site hotel attracts predominantly French guests. Down the hillside in the old village is the more traditional Auberge de Forêt de Maronne with its fine cuisine, as well as a variety of chalets and gîtes to rent.

TOURIST INFORMATION
Tel 33 476 80 13 52
Fax 33 476 80 20 16
Email Auris-en-oisans@wanadoo.fr

Oz Station
top 3,330m (10,922ft) bottom 1,350m (4,429ft)

This small, purpose-built village lies above the old village of Oz-en-Oisans. It is reached by a fast all-weather road from the valley in only 20 minutes and thereby provides an excellent back door into the lift system. Two gondolas branch upwards in different directions, one to L'Alpette above Vaujany and the other in two stages to the mid-station of the DMC gondola above Alpe d'Huez. The resort, which was built in the late 1980s, has unfortunately never fulfilled its early promise and still lacks a hotel. What shopping and nightlife there is remains extremely limited. The crèche takes children from six months to six years. More snow cannons and a new apartment block are planned for this season.

TOURIST INFORMATION
Tel 33 476 80 78 01
Fax 33 476 80 79
Email info@oz-en-oisans.com
Web site www.oz-en-oisans.com

Vaujany
top 3,330m (10,922ft) bottom 1,250m (4,101ft)

Vaujany is a sleepy farming community that would have slowly crumbled into agronomic oblivion but for a quirk of fate. Its fortunes took a turn for the better when compensation in the 1980s for a valley hydro-electric scheme made the village rich beyond its residents' wildest dreams. Oz benefited to a lesser extent from the scheme, and the two

Skiing facts: Alpe d'Huez

TOURIST INFORMATION
Place Paganon, F-38750 Alpe d'Huez
Tel 33 476 11 44 44
Fax 33 476 80 69 54
Email info@alpedhuez.com
Web site www.alpedhuez.com

THE RESORT
By road Calais 934km
By rail Grenoble 63km
Airport transfer Lyon 2hrs, Grenoble
1½hrs
Visitor beds 32,000
Transport free ski bus

THE SKIING
Linked or nearby resorts Auris-en-
Oisans (l), Les Deux Alpes (n), La Grave
(n), Oz Station (l), Vaujany (l),
Villard-Reculas (l)
Number of lifts 85
Total of trails/pistes 220km (36%
beginner, 28% easy, 24% intermediate,
12% difficult)
Nursery slopes 11
Summer skiing Sarenne Glacier
(July–August)

LIFT PASSES
Area pass (covers linked resorts and 1
day in Les Deux Alpes, La Grave, Milky
Way, Puy-St-Vincent) 1,030FF
for 6 days
Beginners 1 free lift at Alpe d'Huez.
Beginner pass 354FF for 6 days
Pensioners 60yrs and over 721FF for
6 days, free for 70yrs and over
Credit cards yes

TUITION
Adults ESF tel: 476 80 31 69, ESI
tel: 476 80 42 77, Fun Evasion
tel: 476 80 69 94, British Masterclass
tel: 01237 451099 (UK)
Snowboarding as ski schools
Other courses cross-country, freestyle,
moguls, monoski, race-training, ski
extreme, ski and snowboard touring,
skiing for the disabled, slalom,
snowblading, teen skiing, telemark
Guiding Bureau de Guides
tel: 476 80 42 55, Stages Vallençant
tel: 476 80 98 40

CHILDREN
Lift pass 5–15yrs 721FF for 6 days
Ski & board school as adults
Kindergarten (ski) La Garderie des
Neiges tel: as ESF, (ski/non-ski)
Le Baby Club (ESI) tel: 476 80 42 77,
Les Eterlous tel: 476 80 43 27,
Les Crapouilloux tel: 476 11 39 23

OTHER SPORTS
Aeroclub, curling, frozen-waterfall-
climbing, hang-gliding, helicopter rides,
ice-climbing, ice-driving, indoor
climbing wall, indoor archery and golf,
indoor squash and tennis, luge,
microlight, night-skiing, parapente,
skating, snowcat trips, snowshoeing,
swimming

FOOD AND DRINK
Coffee 10–16FF, glass of wine 15FF,
small beer 15FF, soft drink 15FF, dish of
the day 60–80FF

villages plunged their millions into the winter sports industry. This
explains why Vaujany, an apparently impoverished mountain village,
manages to own a state-of-the-art 160-person cable-car that still ranks
among the top half-dozen in the world. No one has yet seen a queue

here. A separate gondola provides slower alternative access to the main mountain via Vaujany's own attractive ski area of Montfrais.

Considerable, but considered, development is taking place, and a number of new chalets and apartments have been built. However, the community retains its rural atmosphere. There are four simple hotels in the village centre, with L'Etendard closest to the lift station, and the après-ski hub. The Rissiou is under British management in winter and offers a good standard of accommodation. Nightlife centres around the bars of L'Etendard and the Rissiou. Two discos provide late-night entertainment.

Vaujany has what we consider to be one of the best-equipped crèches in the French Alps and, if you have small children, this is almost a reason in itself for choosing the resort. The age range here is from six months to six years old. In the summer of 1999 a large indoor swimming-pool and health centre were built below the cable-car station.

TOURIST INFORMATION
Tel 33 476 80 72 37
Fax 33 476 79 82 49
Email info@vaujany.com
Web site www.vaujany.com

Villard-Reculas
top 3,330m (10,922ft) bottom 1,500m (4,921ft)

This rustic old village is linked into the ski area by a new quad-chair-lift. Much has been done in recent years to renovate the village; a number of apartments now supplement the single hotel and the converted cowsheds and barns. Sustenance is provided by one small supermarket and a couple of bars and restaurants, including the popular Bergerie. A blue (easy) piste from the bottom of the Petit Prince runs to the village, offering an alternative route to the steeper runs. The road to Allemont on the valley floor is wide and easily accessible in winter, but the one-track road to Huez is normally closed during the season.

TOURIST INFORMATION
Tel 33 476 80 45 69
Fax 33 476 80 45 69
Web site none

Les Arcs

ALTITUDE 1,600–2,000m (5,248–6,560ft)

Beginners ✱✱✱ Intermediates ✱✱✱ Advanced ✱✱✱ Snowboarders ✱✱✱

In the early 1960s, during the boom years of skiing, a mountain guide called Robert Blanc had a vision of a new type of ski resort to be built above his local market town of **Bourg-St-Maurice**. In time he managed to create not one but three ski villages at different altitudes, all of them sharing one ski area. From the 2001–2 season that ski area is to become one of the biggest in Europe when Les Arcs is joined to neighbouring La Plagne by a 200-person cable-car at a cost of £10 million. For the present Les Arcs has 200km of groomed runs served by 78 lifts.

✔ **Large ski area**
✔ **Modern lift system**
✔ **Excellent children's facilities**
✔ **Traffic-free villages**
✔ **Skiing convenience**
✔ **Extensive off-piste**
✔ **Beautiful scenery**
✘ **Lack of alpine charm**
✘ **Limited après-ski**

The first village, **Arc 1600**, opened in the winter of 1968. It consisted of one hotel and a few shops constructed on a plateau above Bourg. According to enthusiastic reporters Arc 1600 is the most compact and friendly place to stay.

Arc 1800, the largest and most cosmopolitan of the three villages, came on stream in 1974. Again it centred on one hotel and a collection of architecturally appealing apartment blocks. It has grown dramatically since it was first built and is now divided into three sub-villages of **Le Charvet**, **Villards** and **Charmettoger**. Arc 1800 is the heart of the three main villages and houses most of the accommodation, shops and après-ski.

The highest and bleakest centre is **Arc 2000**, which sits in its own secluded bowl at the foot of the main mountain, the Aiguille Rouge (3,226m), and is close to some of the best skiing. One reporter says: 'it is to be avoided unless you want snow-sure skiing at the end of the season'.

All three villages are served by a road from Bourg-St-Maurice; however, the Arc en Ciel (rainbow) funicular takes just seven minutes to reach Arc 1600 from there. Although Les Arcs is largely car-free and the resorts are linked by bus, a car is useful to reach the other resorts available on the same lift pass.

Throughout the first half of the 1980s, Les Arcs led the way with a range of snow sports known as *les nouvelles glisses* – alternative ways of sliding down a mountain. The monoski was first seen here, and the snowboard made its European debut in the resort. *Ski évolutif*, a revolutionary method of learning to ski, was introduced here when it crossed the Atlantic.

However, with worldwide recession in the late 1980s, Robert Blanc's dream began to fade. Skiers turned away from Les Arcs, and the resort was forced to the financial wall; for a while it looked as if it would be the first major ski resort in Europe to descend into receivership but it was saved from this fate by state intervention. Some of the properties that had fallen into disrepair were sold off to independent companies, which were offered considerable incentives to refurbish them.

Les Arcs is now facing a considerably brighter future and is continuing to try hard after its decade out in the cold. Both the resort and the lift system are steadily being upgraded. The piste marking is praised by reporters: 'every junction had signposts that would do any motorway proud, yet these signs were not obtrusive and did not detract from the natural beauty of the area'.

The undulating contours of its slopes make Les Arcs ideal for snow-boarding, and ever since the sport was introduced to Europe from America the resort has played an important role in establishing its popularity.

On the snow
top 3,226m (10,581ft) bottom 850m (2,788ft)

According to visitor surveys, the snow-users of Les Arcs want bump-free pistes – and that is what they get. Considerable time and money is spent ironing out moguls, and the result is a wealth of unusually long and smooth runs that start way above the tree-line and progress down through the woods to unspoilt villages like **Le Pré** and **Villaroger**. Intermediates can cruise forever, and beginners are especially well looked after.

WHAT'S NEW
Luxury MGM apartments above Arc 1800
Chalet des Neiges apartments in Arc 2000

The greatest concentration of lifts, slopes and therefore skiers is above Arc 1800, where sunny and gentle pistes attract intermediates and families. The skiing above Arc 1600 is steeper and more wooded, with some rewarding off-piste opportunities. Another claim to fame of Les Arcs is its Olympic speed-skiing track on the face of the Aiguille Rouge, which can be tested by members of the public. With typical Les Arcs panache, the course has also been used to establish records for motorbikes and even mountain bikes.

Lift queues are not generally a problem, although there are a few exceptions. At Carreley 20 and Chantel 21 reporters came across 'huge queues until 10am and again at the end of the day'. Some found mid-afternoon crowds for the Vallandry 74 lift.

Beginners
One of Robert Blanc's legacies was *ski évolutif*, an easy means of learning that originated in America as GLM (graduated length method).

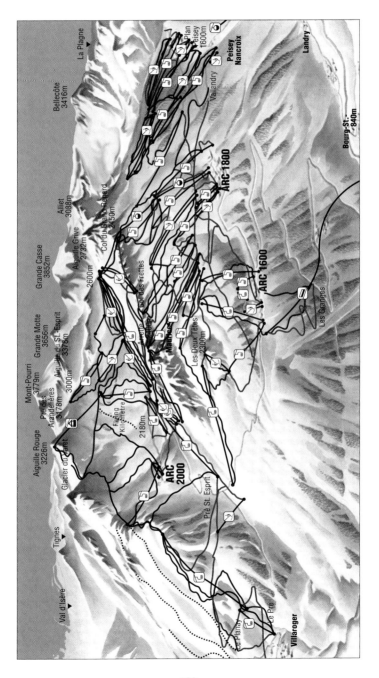

As the name implies, you start on skis as short as 100cm and progress to longer skis as your technique and confidence improve. The advantage is that by learning to ski parallel from day one, you can become a competent intermediate skier by day six. To reach that stage, skiers have a choice of 13 green (beginner) runs. Each of the three villages has user-friendly nursery slopes close by, with the most extensive just above Arc 1800 around the altiport and Le Chantel area, and in the bowl above Arc 2000. Above Arc 1600, strong beginners and timid intermediates can enjoy the long blue (easy) run from Les Deux Têtes.

Intermediates

As a rule, the bigger the ski area the more scope there is for inter-mediates, and Les Arcs is certainly no exception. Of the resort's 117 runs, more than half are divided between blue and red (intermediate) trails, and many of the reds are not difficult. The slopes above Arc 1800 are packed with relatively easy intermediate slopes. Good cruising runs are found between the Grand Col, Aiguille Grive and Arpette. Above **Peisey-Nancroix** and **Vallandry** there is much classic intermediate terrain. The Aigle and L'Ours reds are particularly recommended by reporters as 'nice, not too testing runs down through the trees'.

Advanced

The black (difficult) run down Comborcières to Pré-St-Esprit is one of the places where those who want to can still find testing moguls ('mogulled from head to foot'). But the classic run in Les Arcs is the 7-km descent from the top of the Aiguille Rouge all the way down to Le Pré and Villaroger, with a vertical drop of more than 2,000m. Among the 18 black runs, the Piste de L'Ours from Arpette is one of the most exciting descents.

Varet is a long, steep piste from the top of the Aiguille Rouge, which is a real challenge, especially in deep snow. The Robert Blanc piste is an excellent descent off the north face of the mountain. Drosets, down to Pré-St-Esprit, is another testing run from the Aiguille Rouge. The new Varet eight-person gondola, which replaced the Dou de L'Homme chair-lift for the 1999–2000 season, gives easy access to a number of long black trails.

Off-piste

With so many off-piste opportunities in Les Arcs it really does pay, both in terms of safety and finding the best terrain, to hire a guide. In fresh snow conditions the most exhilarating and steepest powder skiing is below the Aiguille Rouge. Steep bowl-skiing is found beneath the Crête de L'Homme, accessed by a traverse to the right as you exit the Aiguille Rouge cable-car. Other decent off-piste is behind the Aiguille Grive and the Aiguille Rouge at the south-western edge of Arc 1800's ski area. Exciting off-piste descents start from the Grand Col to Villaroger, with the route continuing behind the Aiguille Rouge, and from the Aiguille Grive down to Peisey-Nancroix.

Snowboarders

The dedicated funpark between Arc 1600 and 1800 has now been enlarged to incorporate seven jumps, a half-pipe and a boardercross course. The park is served by a chair and a shorter drag-lift, and international competitions are regularly held here. Freestylers favour the naturally wavy terrain of Les Deux Têtes black run and the red La Cachette. Hard-boot fans will enjoy Froides Fontaines, which is excellent for a carving work-out. The red Grand Renard is a natural downhill course which is superb for big turns. The Peisey sector is well-suited to freeriders.

Tuition and guiding

Les Arcs has the French Ski School (ESF) in all three high-altitude villages ('the instructors spoke good English'), as well as Arc Aventures, Ecole de Ski Virages and He'enalu, which are all based in Arc 1800. All the ski schools run snowboarding courses. Tip Top is a small specialist snowboard school operating from Arc 1600, while In Extremis is in Arc 1800.

Mountain restaurants

Mountain eating-places are not a particular strength of Les Arcs, but we have some enthusiastic reports: 'in 13 years of skiing holidays we have never been at such a good mountain restaurant as Aiguille Grive. We had lunch there every day'. Some excellent rustic-style establishments exist in the lower hamlets, with Pré-St-Esprit, below Arc 2000, boasting two popular lunch spots. Of these, the rustic Bélliou La Fumée, a 500-year-old hunting lodge, is the more attractive and is recommended by reporters for its wild mushroom omelettes. The cosy Solliet restaurant on the way down to Villaroger receives good reports, and in nearby Le Pré the Aiguille Rouge and La Ferme attract lunchtime skiers when the long run down is open. In nearby **Le Planay**, Chez Léa is highly recommended for its wholesome food and attractive farmhouse setting; booking is recommended. L'Ancolie at Nancroix, reached by bus from the bottom of the lift system at Peisey-Nancroix, 'serves outstanding food in an intimate atmosphere'.

Accommodation

About two-thirds of the skiers visiting Les Arcs stay in apartments, and of these the majority find themselves in Arc 1800. Hotel du Golf Latitudes in Le Charvet district ('excellent, the food was of a high standard') is the largest and most central hotel in Arc 1800. Hotel Club Latitudes and Grand Hotel Mercure ('bedrooms large, clean, with huge cupboards and dinner was a tremendous experience. It was worth every franc'), both in the Charmettoger sector, are the other three-stars. The MGM apartments that have been built above Arc 1800 offer the smartest accommodation in the resort.

La Cachette at Arc 1600 has nurtured a reputation as one of the best family hotels in the Alps. It has been refurbished to a standard above its official three stars. L'Explorers and Hotel Beguin are both small hotels in 1600. Hotel 3 Arcs, also in 1600, is a friendly hotel with good views. At the time of going to press, the Mélèzes Hotel Club and the popular two-star Aiguille Rouge were the only hotels in Arc 2000. A new luxury apartment block, the Chalet des Neiges, opens here in winter 2000.

There is a Club Med and a Club Aquarius at Arc 2000. Les Lauziers apartments in 1800 are convenient for the slopes but have their drawbacks ('a functional building with strange sloping floors; we didn't like the cramped and spartan interiors'). For those preferring to stay in the valley town of Bourg-St-Maurice, which is linked directly into the lift system and convenient for visiting other resorts such as **Val d'Isère**, the good-value Hostellerie du Petit-St-Bernard is welcoming to families and serves appetising food.

Eating in and out

Self-catering rules in Les Arcs, but no one wants to cook every night of the week. The best choice of restaurants is at Arc 1800; L'Equipe is the biggest ('excellent for a posh meal, with Savoyard dishes and a fixed-price menu') but not necessarily the best. Casa Mia specialises in Italian food ('basically a pasta and pizza place, décor rustic – after a fashion – and the service was friendly and informal'). L'Onglet and the Marmite (Le Charvet) and Le Coq Hardy (Villards) are also recommended. For value-for-money family fare the Laurus is worth visiting.

At Arc 2000, Le Red Rock is popular and informal with live music, and Le St Jacques is more intimate with higher prices. Les Chabottes at Pont Baudin near Peisey-Nancroix serves 'excellent local specialities at prices lower than at Arc 1800'.

Self-caterers will find a wider selection and lower prices in Bourg-St-Maurice, with its two hypermarkets on the outskirts of town. In Arc 1800 there are 'some fine bakeries, an expensive butcher and a small supermarket with limited fresh supplies'.

Visitors considering an outing to the traditional restaurants in out-lying villages between Les Arcs and Bourg-St-Maurice should try the rustic Bois de Lune at Montvenix. Booking is recommended, and the restaurant will collect you and take you back. Chez Mimi at Vallandry and Chez Léa at Le Planay are other options.

Après-ski

Reporters are unanimous that Les Arcs suffers from a dearth of après-ski activity. 'The highlight of most evenings was drinking tequila slammers in the bedroom watching football on Sky TV'. When the lifts close in Arc 1800, skiers and instructors tend to divide themselves between two bars at Le Charvet (Le Gabotte and Le Thuria). At nearby Les Villards, much of the action is at the Pub Russel and the Saloon Bar, which features live music. At 2000 the Red Rock is the 'in' place for a *vin chaud*. The Hotel du Golf Latitudes has live jazz and Le Fairway disco in the basement. All three resorts have discos, including the

Skiing facts: Les Arcs

TOURIST INFORMATION
BP 45, F73706 Arc Cedex
Tel 33 479 07 12 57
Fax 33 479 07 45 96
Email lesarcs@lesarcs.com
Web site www.lesarcs.com

LONDON AGENT
Erna Low Consultants (see *Which tour operator?*)

THE RESORT
By road Calais 937km
By rail Bourg-St-Maurice 15km, buses and funicular to Arc 1600
Airport transfer Lyon 2½hrs, Chambéry 2hrs, Geneva 2½hrs
Visitor beds 28,000
Transport free shuttle bus between villages

THE SKIING
Linked or nearby resorts Bourg-St-Maurice (l), Peisey-Nancroix (l), La Plagne (n), Le Pré (l), Vallandry (l), Villaroger (l)
Number of lifts 76
Total of trails/pistes 200km (11% easy, 44% intermediate, 31% difficult, 14% very difficult)
Nursery slopes 8 lifts

LIFT PASSES
Area pass Grand Domaine 710–1,065FF for 6 days (covers Les Arcs, Villaroger, Peisey, Vallandry, La Plagne, and 1 day in La Rosière/Trois Vallées/Tignes and Val d'Isère), 5% loyalty discount
Beginners 1 free lift in each centre
Pensioners 60–74yrs, 865FF for 6 days, free for 75yrs and over
Credit cards yes

TUITION
Adults Arc Aventures (1800) tel: 479 07 41 28, ESF (all centres) tel: 479 07 40 31, He'enalu (1800) tel: 479 07 46 88, Optimum tel: 01992 561085 (UK), Virages (1800) tel: 479 07 78 82
Snowboarding as ski schools, also In Extremis (1800) 479 07 21 72, Tip Top (1600) tel: 479 07 28 00, **Other courses** carving, cross-country, extreme skiing, heli-skiing and -boarding, moguls, seniors, powder clinics, race-training, ski-évolutif, skiing for the disabled, ski orienteering, snowblading, speed skiing, teen skiing, telemark, women's clinics
Guiding Bureau des Guides tel: 479 07 71 19

CHILDREN
Lift pass 7–14yrs 905FF for 6 days
Ski & board school Arc Aventures, ESF, In Extremis, Tip Top, Virages
Kindergarten (ski/non-ski) La Cachette/ESF (1600) tel: 479 07 70 50, Pomme de Pin (1800) tel: 479 04 15 35, Les Marmottons (2000) 479 07 64 25, (non-ski) Pomme d'Api (Bourg-St-Maurice) tel: 479 07 59 31

OTHER SPORTS
Climbing wall, dog-sledding, hang-gliding, horse-riding, ice-driving, night skiing, parapente, skating, ski-joring, ski-jumping, sleigh rides, snowbiking, snowmobiling, snowshoeing, speed skiing, squash

FOOD AND DRINK PRICES
Coffee 8FF, glass of wine 12FF, small beer 12–18FF, soft drink 16FF, dish of the day 60–90FF

Arcelle in 1600 and Rock Hill in Le Charvet, while snowboarders prefer the Carré Blanc in Les Villards.

Apocalypse at 1800 is 'wildly expensive'. The music at KL 92 in Arc 2000 is said to be sufficiently sympa to allow conversation. Reporters found the shopping area at Arc 1800 to be 'tacky – and smelling of chips, pizza and doughnuts'. Among the non-skiing activities available at Les Arcs is ski-joring, where you are pulled along on skis behind a horse.

Childcare

Les Arcs has a three-kids grading, the highest of the Label Kid stamp of approval from the Ministry of Tourism, denoting that the resort offers children a safe environment with plenty of entertainment, toys and equipment. Babies aged four months and over are welcome in the day nurseries at La Cachette in Arc 1600 and at the Pomme d'Api in Bourg-St-Maurice. The nursery at Arc 1800 takes children from one year of age. Les Marmottons at Arc 2000 accepts children from two. The ESF organises courses for children aged three years and over in Le Pomme de Pin club. Children from three-star level (intermediate) can enrol in Ski Nature courses to explore the mountain environment, learn map reading and discover animal tracks in the snow. All the adult ski and snowboard schools offer tuition for children.

Linked or nearby resorts

Peisey-Nancroix/Vallandry
top 3,226m (10,581ft) bottom 1,350–1,600m (4,428–5,248ft)

Snow-users in Les Arcs tend to regard this cluster of villages at the southwestern end of the ski area as a useful tree-level bolt hole in bad weather. French families, who have been coming here since the Second World War, prefer to think of it as a peaceful, undemanding ski area of 14 lifts that is occasionally invaded by Johnny-come-latelys from Les Arcs. These villages offer a more rural setting and a cheaper accommodation base for the region, but that will inevitably change with the proposed link to La Plagne. Peisey is a traditional farming community, and Nancroix is the starting point for 39km of cross-country trails. The small ski resorts of **Plan Peisey** and Vallandry are linked by gondola to Peisey in the valley below. Three lifts serve the nursery slopes.

TOURIST INFORMATION
Tel 33 479 07 94 28
Fax 33 479 07 95 34
Email info@peisey-vallandry.com
Web site www.peisey-vallandry.com

Barèges/La Mongie

ALTITUDE Barèges 1,250–1,800m (4,092–5,904ft)

Beginners **✶✶** Intermediates **✶✶✶** Snowboarders **✶**

Barèges is one of the great skiing secrets of Europe. This unspoilt village in the Pyrenees forms the gateway to an unexpected network of 120km of pistes far superior in quality to most 'alternative' European resorts. Skiers who have tired of the characterless and overcrowded ski circuses of the French Alps, with their ever-rising prices, should look westwards to the Pyrenees. Here you will find that elusive combination of a timeless French country village with reasonable prices, a short transfer time (one hour) from Lourdes Airport and the varied runs of a large intermediate ski area. The major attraction of the resort (and indeed of the rest of the French Pyrenees) is the people, who seem to be genuinely friendly and welcoming – a rare occurrence in some of the more popular resorts in the Alps. The locals have managed to retain their traditional way of life and at the same time adapt to the needs of tourism without the compulsion to milk their visitors for every centime.

Barèges was one of the original ski resorts of the Pyrenees. At first sight, the little spa village is down-at-heel and grey in its position near the head of a narrow valley. However, its lack of size engenders a friendly atmosphere. Prices are low by French standards but there is little to do after skiing except soak up the sulphur waters of the thermal spa. The village consists of not much more than a single street climbing steeply beside a river, surrounded by tree-studded mountainside. This is not a natural site for a village, and none would have appeared had it not been for the sulphur springs that became famous in the seventeenth century. Parking is restricted, and the ski bus cannot cope when runs to the village are closed and too many skiers have ended up at Tournaboup.

The village also comes under the spotlight in July, when it becomes part of the Tour de France route. Its lift system follows the course of the road, which (in summer only) leads over the Col du Tourmalet to the more modern, and considerably less charming, resort of **La Mongie**. This village offers no more facilities than Barèges and is set in the

✔ Short airport transfer
✔ Sunny slopes
✔ Low prices
✔ Small and unspoilt village (Barèges)
✔ Facilities for cross-country skiing
✘ Weekend lift queues
✘ Unreliable resort-level snow
✘ Unsuitable for late-season holidays
✘ Lack of nightlife
✘ Few activities for non-skiers
✘ Bleak village (La Mongie)

blander half of the ski area. The lower, main section of the village is a bleak and charmless place with a crescent of restaurants, shops and hotels, and a car park in the middle. The upper village of **La Mongie-Tourmalet** is a long and jagged complex with a single hotel, a restaurant and apartments. La Mongie and Barèges are both linked by bus and a chair-lift to the Coume de Pourteilh gondola. The lifts linking the two resorts sometimes close in bad weather.

On the snow
top 2,350m (7,708ft) bottom 1,250m (4,100ft)

Snowfall in the Pyrenees is a subject that always causes disagreement. There is little to support the belief that the mountains receive less precipitation in winter than the Alps; the trouble is that it does not always fall as snow. Because the Pyrenees are further west and closer to the warm Atlantic, the winter is shorter, but the advantage is the high number of sunny days.

Barèges and La Mongie form the largest ski area in the Pyrenees, sharing 120km of wide, mainly easy-to-intermediate pistes served by 60 lifts. The area's upper slopes are open and sunny, while the lower ones above Barèges offer sheltered tree-level skiing. The slopes are reached from Barèges by two mountain access lifts. The track of the Ayré

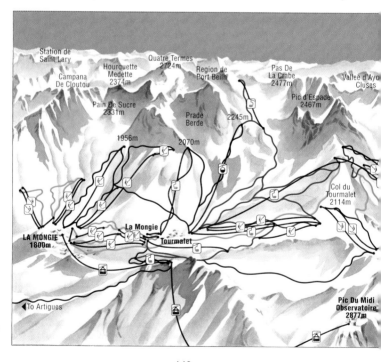

funicular climbs steeply from the village centre through the woods to serve red (intermediate) and black (difficult) runs down to a clearing at Lienz – this is some of the best skiing in the area when conditions are favourable.

The alternative access lift from the resort is La Laquette gondola, which provides the direct route towards La Mongie, as well as the way up to the ski-school meeting place. At Tournaboup, from the top of the lift, an easy link-run leads on to **Super Barèges**, actually little more than a restaurant. A development of ski terrain to the north of Super Barèges, below the Lac d'Oncet, recently added to the size of the whole area. Queues can be a serious problem at weekends; as Barèges cannot cope with many cars, the lifts from the top of the village and from Tournaboup become crowded, and the Col du Tourmalet can turn into a bottleneck in both directions.

Beginners

La Mongie is the better base for complete beginners, with easy slopes that keep their snow relatively well immediately around the resort. Barèges itself has no nursery slope; the main nursery slope is at the top of La Laquette gondola. Tournaboup, just outside Barèges, has a small nursery slope beside the car park, and there is also a baby lift at La Mongie-Tourmalet. At Barèges, second- and third-week skiers can

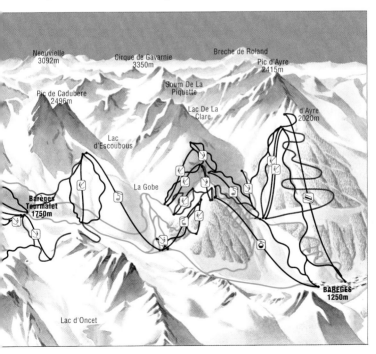

make their way across to Lienz from the mid-station of the Ayré funicular. Of the two runs from here down to the resort, the green (beginner) run is the path that begins with an uphill section.

Intermediates
A variety of short intermediate pistes cover the sides of the hill at the top of La Laquette gondola to Lienz on one side and to Tournaboup on the other. Above La Mongie the runs are mainly wide and easy. A gondola is the main lift on the north-facing side, serving a long and shaded blue (easy) gully.

The slopes beneath the Sud chair-lift are not particularly gentle, and the blue run contains a narrow section. On this sunny side of the mountain, the most interesting trails are reached from the top of the Coume Lounque drag- and chair-lift, where there are a couple of reds. One trail follows a valley down to La Mongie, the other leads down to Super Barèges; part of this run is steep enough to be graded black and can be icy in the morning.

Advanced
Ayré, at 2,020m, boasts some of the area's steepest skiing, and there is no easy way down from the top of the funicular. Some fairly sheer, west-facing slopes lie below the Col du Tourmalet, including a selection of short mogul fields. The rocky slopes bordering La Mongie and the road are steep, and although there are lifts, the terrain does not give much scope for pistes. The most challenging run around La Mongie is the black under the Prade Berde chair-lift.

Off-piste
The itinerary round to the Lac d'Oncet is a good place for spring snow even in mid-winter. At Tournaboup a long chair-lift rises over a wide and fairly steep west-facing mountainside, which is left unpisted although it is much skied in favourable conditions. At the top of the Coume de Pourteilh gondola above La Mongie, the Quatre Termes chair-lift has added to the overall length of the run. It gives access to an off-piste itinerary down the Aygues Cluses Valley, ending at Tournaboup. Both ski schools can provide off-piste guides.

Snowboarders
La Mongie has a boardercross course and three other dedicated snowboard spots at different points around the ski area.

Tuition and guiding
French Pyrenean resorts have made considerable efforts to improve ski school standards in recent years, and the number of fluent English-speaking instructors has risen. We have received disappointing reports of Ecoloski in Barèges: 'I was in much too difficult a group and when I asked to change I was told to have courage'. The French Ski School (ESF) in Barèges is said to be well-organised — 'our instructor was

patient, professional and spoke good English'. Courses include snow-blading and telemark. La Mongie and La Mongie-Tourmalet have their own ski schools.

Mountain restaurants

The mountain eating-places are inexpensive in comparison with those in the Alps but are few and far between. Chez Louisette is popular, and Auberge La Couquelle is small and friendly. Le Bastan is 'cheerful and cheap'. There is a restaurant at the Col du Tourmalet, and Le Yeti in La Mongie is recommended.

Accommodation

Those in search of luxury will be disappointed, as Barèges has nothing more superior than its four simple two-star hotels. Of these, the family-run Richelieu is 'clean and friendly' and is located just below the funic-ular station. Hotel Igloo is run by a former ski champion and is close to La Laquette gondola. Some reporters found the Hotel Central unfriendly. The one-star Poste and Modern hotels offer basic but clean bedrooms. The British-run Les Sorbiers is a popular small hotel ('simple, attractively furnished, clean accommodation. The bedrooms were warm but the public areas rather chilly. The vegetarian options were superb'). In Barèges there is a single supermarket for self-caterers.

La Mongie has a three-star hotel, Le Pourteilh, plus a handful of two-stars. The Lamandia, which has ski-in ski-out access, is the only three-star hotel in La Mongie-Tourmalet.

Eating in and out

The staple diet of the region is *magret de canard*, *confit de canard*, and *foie gras*. Le Pichounet serves a good brasserade. Auberge La Couquelle, with its welcoming fireplace, is close to Tournaboup and is open in the evening. La Rozelle is recommended for fondue and pizzas. La Bohème pizzeria in Barèges is warmly praised. The main event of the week is an evening at Chez Louisette, organised by the ESF, which culminates in a torch-lit descent. You can reach the restaurant by snowmobile or snowcat. La Mongie has 20 restaurants ranging from French and Italian to Creole.

Après-ski

Barèges is such a quiet resort that, as one reader put it, 'even the church was closed on Sunday'. Nightlife centres on a few bars, a handful of restaurants and two discos of which Le Club Jonathan is the most popu-lar. The liveliest places are Pub l'Oncet, L'Isba and the Café Richelieu.

Many visitors come to Barèges for the spa. They are treated in an austere building at the top of the high street. Facilities include whirlpools, thermal baths, an aqua-gym and aqua massage, all of which use the special healing waters – great for relaxing after a hard day on the slopes. La Mongie has a dozen shops, a few bars and a cinema.

Shops are confined to a chemist and the most basic of ski-hire and souvenir shops.

Childcare

The ESF and Ecoloski both have a ski kindergarten for children from four years of age. The two non-ski kindergartens take children from two to six years old. Hélios is an activity centre for three to twelve year olds, where creative play, igloo-building, snowshoeing, skating and dog-sleigh rides are organised. La Mongie has a ski and non-ski kindergarten.

TOURIST INFORMATION
Tel (Barèges) 33 562 92 16 00 (La Mongie) 33 562 91 94 15
Fax (Barèges) 33 562 92 69 13 (La Mongie) 33 562 95 33 13
Email station.bareges@wanadoo.fr
Web site www.pro.wanadoo.fr/barages

Linked or nearby resorts

Cauterets
top 2,350m (7,710ft) bottom 1,000m (3,280ft)

This attractive thermal spa became a ski station in 1962 and today it has more than 22,000 visitor beds in a large selection of hotels. The nearest airport is Lourdes, which is 40km away. The skiing is in the exposed Cirque du Lys bowl, accessed by a two-stage cable-car, which also brings skiers back to the resort at the end of the day. The terrain is best suited to beginners and intermediates. The 23 runs include two blacks, with the rest equally divided between red, blue and green. These are served by 18 lifts. Another small but developing ski area is nearby at **Pont d'Espagne**, which is renowned for its 36km of cross-country trails. Tuition at Cauterets is offered in freestyle skiing, alpine skiing and snowboarding. Les Marmottes non-ski kindergarten takes children from three months to six years of age. Children from four years old are taught in the ski school.

The extensive choice of accommodation includes gîtes, chalets and hotels, some of which date from the Belle Epoque. Hotel Bordeaux is a comfortable three-star with a good restaurant. The three-star Hotel Club Aladin has a fitness centre with a swimming-pool, squash courts and sauna. The Royalty pub is popular, as is the St Trop video-bar. Other resort facilities include a casino, two discos and ice-skating.

TOURIST INFORMATION
Tel 33 562 92 50 27
Fax 33 562 92 59 12
Email espace.cauterets@cauterets.com
Web site www.cauterets.com

Font-Romeu
top 2,204m (7,229ft) bottom 1,800m (5,906ft)

The resort, 19km from Perpignan and 200km from Toulouse, is set on a sunny plateau known for its mild climate, making it unreliable for snow at the beginning and end of the season. The skiing is 4km from the village and is linked by a bus service. The 52km of piste and 28 lifts suit beginners to intermediates and families. Weekend queues are a problem as the resort is popular with both French and Spanish skiers. 50 per cent of the total skiing terrain is covered by snow-cannon. There are two dozen hotels and pensions, over a dozen youth hostels and various self-catering apartments. Après-ski activities include a wide choice of shops and restaurants, a casino, cinemas, three discos and ten bars. Cross-country skiing is very important here, with two specialist schools. The resort also boasts a funpark.

TOURIST INFORMATION
Tel 33 468 30 68 30
Fax 33 468 30 29 70
Email office@font-romeu-station.com
Web site www.font-romeu-station.com

St-Lary
top 2,450m (8,038ft) bottom 850m (2,789ft)

St-Lary-Soulan, 80km from Lourdes, is a typically Pyrenean village of stone-built houses and one main, rather narrow street. The skiing is suitable for beginners to intermediates and it begins a four-minute walk from the village centre at the cable-car to **St-Lary 1700 (Pla d'Adet)**, a small but dull modern ski station with some accommodation. From here a bus runs to two other small centres, **St-Lary 1900 (Soum)** and **St-Lary 2400 (Espiaube)**. The ski area is served by a chain of 47 lifts but is mainly treeless and lacks variety. The funpark is in the Vallon du Portet sector.

There are six nursery slopes, and three ski schools take children from four years old as well as adults. Three mountain guiding companies arrange popular ski-tours, and three crèches care for small non-skiing children. Grand Hotel Mir is recommended, as well as the Mercure Coralia and Hotel La Terrasse Fleurie. The Andrédéna is in a quiet position. At Espiaube, Hotel La Sapinière provides reasonable accommodation at the bottom of the pistes. The resort boasts more than 30 restaurants, a range of shops, and activities such as cross-country, parapente and snowmobiling.

TOURIST INFORMATION
Tel 33 562 39 50 81
Fax 33 562 39 50 06
Email st-lary@wanadoo.fr

Chamonix

ALTITUDE 1,035m (3,396ft)

Intermediates ✱✱ Advanced ✱✱✱ Snowboarders ✱⁂✱

Chamonix is truly different from any other ski resort in the world. Anyone who has learned the basics on the rolling pastures of the Austrian Tyrol or in the purpose-built 'ski factories' of the French Tarentaise is in for a stupendous shock. This is high Alpine territory where misjudging the severity of a run or the sudden changes of weather above 3,000m can cost a life. After 48 hours here you discover that someone has gone up – or down – every slope, no matter how dangerous, in what is still acknowledged as the climbing and extreme skiing capital of the world. In the past, complacency was the biggest foe of this year-round holiday destination. However, new lifts have now been built in every ski area.

✔ Unsurpassed scenery
✔ Large vertical drop
✔ Extensive off-piste skiing
✔ Outstanding mountain guides
✔ Short airport transfer
✔ Wide choice of non-skiing activities
✔ Cosmopolitan atmosphere
✔ Vibrant nightlife
✘ Fragmented ski areas
✘ Lack of skiing convenience
✘ Unpredictable weather patterns
✘ Heavy traffic

Chamonix lies in the lee of Mont Blanc, the highest mountain in western Europe. It is home to the Compagnie des Guides de Chamonix, the oldest and most celebrated mountain guiding service in the world. As in many other parts of the Alps, the pioneering climbers were British. The celebrated explorer Richard Pococke and his 24-year-old companion, William Windham, arrived in the Chamonix Valley from Geneva in 1741. Their party of 13 had expected to meet 'savages' along the way and was consequently armed to the teeth. To further confuse the peaceful peasants they encountered, along what is now the Autoroute Blanche, Pococke was dressed as an Arab (for reasons best known to himself).

Forty-five years later, locally-born doctor Michel-Gabriel Paccard and his reclusive partner Jacques Balmat conquered Mont Blanc; this was the most famous of many first ascents that have made the town pre-eminent in climbing lore.

The tallest landmark is the Aiguille du Midi, a 3,842-m granite needle above Chamonix that acts as the starting point for some of the most beautiful off-piste skiing in the Alps. It is possibly the only mountain in the world that can claim two first ascents. In 1998 a few million tons of it suddenly sheared away through natural erosion, causing an

earthquake that registered 2.8 on the Richter scale. The new north face was deemed impossible, but within a couple of months a Russian, who had apparently only come to Chamonix for a business conference, shinned up it in a single day. From below, the Aiguille looks unassailable – a series of sheer granite pitches linked by ribbons of wind-blown snow – but not only has it been climbed, it has been skied by Yves Detry, a local guide.

Chamonix is not so much a single resort as a chain of unconnected ski areas set along both sides of the valley dominated by Mont Blanc. The success of a visit to Chamonix depends in part on the vagaries of the weather. On sunny days, it is glitteringly beautiful and deceptively tranquil. On stormy days, of which there are many, it is a brooding place, menaced by razor-sharp peaks and tumbling walls of ice.

The town itself is based around a core of hotels and villas built at the end of the nineteenth century and subsequently hemmed in by the neo-brutalist architecture of post-war tourism. Chamonix took shape before cars took over, and its current concerns are primarily to do with traffic management.

Most visitors to the valley rightly consider a car to be essential ('having a car around Chamonix can be truly liberating, as most of the ski areas are a few miles apart'), the alternative being a local bus service that links the base-stations with moderate efficiency.

The original village square is fully pedestrianised, and the main street is closed to traffic during daylight hours. This allows for the free flow of shoppers at the cost of considerable congestion on the outskirts, especially in the ever-expanding satellite township of **Chamonix Sud**. The shopping facilities in Chamonix are so comprehensive that one reporter commented: 'almost a range of shops that one would expect to find in any British town'.

In the course of February and March 1999 a fatal avalanche swept away houses in the hamlet of **Le Tour**, the worst fire since 1855 destroyed part of the town centre, and a further fire destroyed the Mont Blanc Tunnel. In other similarly affected resorts the tourist industry might have taken years to recover. But somehow resilience in the face of tragedy is so ingrained into the fabric of this climbing town that the local people – and indeed the mainly experienced skiers and snow-boarders who visit here each winter – seem to take such acts of *force majeure* in their stride.

The most enduring effect of the closure of the tunnel in the medium term has been the estrangement of Chamonix from neighbouring **Courmayeur** in Italy. At the time of writing, the French and Italian authorities are still arguing over the inquest into the inferno that has closed the major arterial truck route across Europe, and rebuilding has yet to begin.

However, the 619 inhabitants of the village of Servoz, below the French mouth of the tunnel, are breathing a collective sigh of relief at its long-term closure. For the first time since General de Gaulle opened it in 1965, the poisonous yellow layers of diesel pollution that hung over their homes have dissipated and they can once again see the peak of Mont Blanc. Skiers and snowboarders can also enjoy the purer air while it lasts.

On the snow
top 3,842m (12,605ft) bottom 1,035m (3,396ft)

The Chamonix Valley caters for all levels of skier and rider but not in the same place, making it difficult for mixed-ability groups to ski on the same mountain. With **Les Houches** (not included in the Cham'Ski lift pass), there are five main base-stations, most of which are a bus ride from the town centre. The closest mountain access point is the celebrated Aiguille du Midi cable-car, which takes skiers and snowboarders up on to the shoulder of Mont Blanc for the descent down the Vallée Blanche. The combined area of Le Brévent and La Flégère provides the bulk of the skiing, a sunny and often underrated circuit with excellent terrain for all levels of intermediate and advanced skiers and snowboarders. However, the toughest and easiest skiing lies further up the valley at **Argentière** and Le Tour respectively. A chair-lift off the back of Le Tour at Tête de Balme gives access to some delightful skiing down towards **Vallorcine** in Switzerland.

Les Houches has broken away from the Chamonix umbrella and to the chagrin of its former ally has established itself as a go-ahead resort in its own right, with modern lifts and a highly-rated FIS downhill course. It now seeks to align itself with its other big-name neighbour, **St-Gervais/Megève**. A much-discussed gondola would make it part of a separate 350-km linked ski circus centred on Megève, but this is still in the distant pipeline. In bad weather the best sheltered skiing in the valley can be found here.

The lift-pass situation is 'messy and confusing'. The main choice lies between no less than 12 permutations of the Cham'Ski pass and the Ski Pass Mont Blanc. You can also buy a whole range of half-day and one-day passes valid for certain areas only. The Ski Pass Mont Blanc is slightly more expensive but covers Les Houches and a number of other outlying resorts.

Beginners

Learn to ski in Chamonix if you must but do not expect to like it. The worst part is that the ski areas are so separate and spread out. The town has small training areas for absolute beginners at Les Planards and Le Savoy, but don't expect to link up before nightfall with more experienced family or friends.

Once you have mastered the basics, the best practice slopes are at Le Tour, the most far-flung of the valley's outposts. As Le Tour is tree-free, the light is often hostile, but on a clear day you can take the high-speed quad that has replaced the slow old gondola to access Charamillon and the wide, empty slopes that fan out across the Col de Balme above it. The best-protected area from bad weather is the small network of blue (easy) runs at the top of Prarion in Les Houches. The Brévent/Flégère area is south-facing, and therefore the sunniest place to learn, with Brévent boasting a green (beginner) run. Les Chosalets, located at the foot of the Grands Montets lift in Argentière, is another beginner area.

Intermediates

Such is the diversity of pistes that skiers and snowboarders with the skills to tackle a red (intermediate) run with confidence can spend a week in the valley without going to the same place twice. The most convenient starting point is Le Brévent, where the six-seater gondola to

Planpraz gives access to a choice of inviting blue runs down to the Col Cornu chair. This in turn opens up several moderately challenging reds, the longest of which goes to the bottom of La Charlanon drag-lift. Planpraz is also the launch point for the dramatic cable-car ride up to Le Brévent itself, a 2,525-m crag with unsurpassed views of Mont Blanc. From this point, the return to the mid-station is via a sweeping red piste or a bumpy black (difficult) trail. Only genuinely confident intermediates should attempt the return to Chamonix down the black run from the bottom of La Parsa chair.

La Flégère is reached from the suburb of **Les Praz**, a ten-minute bus-ride from the town centre. The terrain is similar to that of Le Brévent, to which it is linked by cable-car, with long red and blue runs from the top of L'Index to the mid-station and a black descent back to base.

No visit to Chamonix is complete without a ride up the two-stage Aiguille du Midi cable-car, the highest in Europe. This is the departure point for the 22-km glacier run down the Vallée Blanche, which, depending on the route your guide takes, is either a gentle cruise through some of the most grandiose mountain scenery in the world or a character-building encounter with ice-screws, karabiners and the other ironmongery of ski mountaineering. The easiest route can be attempted (and once you start, there is no alternative but to finish it) by any intermediate who can ski parallel – you can even ski it in the light of the full moon. The Vallée Blanche provides thousands of snow-users with their first unforgettable taste of high-mountain off-piste adventure. The trickiest part comes early on in the shape of the infamous steps cut into the spine of the ridge from the cable-car station and the skiing start-point. The only unnerving bit is the five-minute stroll down the ice steps at the top.

Chamonix guides now routinely rope up their clients and issue them with crampons. The kind guides carry your skis, and a fixed rope on the left gives added security against a slide into the 2,000-m abyss. To avoid yawning and hidden crevasses you must follow your guide's tracks, but the gradient is gentle enough for intermediates – so slight at times that freshly waxed skis are needed to cross the lower section of the glacier without continuous poling. Return to Chamonix is either by rack-and-pinion railway from Montenvers or via a short climb and a long (and at times inevitably uncontrolled) descent down a narrow path and short piste into the centre of Chamonix.

Advanced

When enthusiasts talk of Chamonix, they really mean the Grands Montets at Argentière. This is a truly magnificent mountain for expert skiers and riders – steep, complex and dramatic with seemingly unlimited possibilities. It is accessed either by the 80-person cable-car to Lognan or by the high-speed quad-chair to Plan Joran from the Argentière base-station. When the cognoscenti arrive at Lognan, they join the rush – and almost invariably the queue – for the Grands Montets cable-car.

The huge popularity of this lift is undiminished by both the 28FF supplement payable on top of the Mont Blanc lift pass and the 200 slippery metal steps leading from the top-station to the start of the skiing. This reveals itself to be a bumpy defile divided into two black runs, Les Pylones (under the cable-car) and the awkwardly cambered Point de Vue which, as its name suggests, provides stunning views of the glacier as it tracks down its edge. The Bochard gondola opens up another huge section of the mountain, including the 4.5-km Chamois descent to the Le Lavancher chair.

Off-piste

On powder mornings the rush for the Grands Montets is fierce, but the area is so enormous that skiing it out quickly is beyond even the powers of Europe's most dedicated first-track pack – they take at least a couple of hours to do this. Although open snowfields, bowls and gullies abound between the marked pistes, this is wild and dangerous terrain. The glacier is a web of crevasses and seracs that change position from season to season. Although the more macho of the temporary residents claim to know the mountain well enough to ski it alone, the truth is that to ski here without a qualified guide is to court death. From a skiing point of view, the most challenging descent is the Pas de Chèvre, a run from the top of Bochard via one of several extreme couloirs down the Mer de Glace to the bottom of the Vallée Blanche. Another classic is the Grand Envers route down the Vallée Blanche, reached from the top of the Aiguille du Midi cable-car, but far removed from the regular run in terms of degree of difficulty.

Snowboarders

Most riders here are out to shred some of the steepest and most demanding powder in the world ('a hot venue for boarders – unbelievably sheer faces, narrow chutes and huge cliffs have attracted a new breed of enthusiasts bent on pushing the sport to new horizons'). However, the Grands Montets also houses an impressive funpark that is managed by the Chamonix Snowboard Club. There is also a funpark at Charamillon, the mid-station at Le Tour and a half-pipe near the Kandahar chair in Les Houches.

Tuition and guiding

The Chamonix branch of the French Ski School (ESF) and the Compagnie des Guides share an office in the downtown area ('off-piste virgins should take a lesson as Chamonix contains extreme terrain suitable only for people with proper equipment and training'). The less traditional Sensation Ski takes a wilder approach to the learning curve, which is said to be popular with British clients. The ESF also has an office in Argentière, while Les Houches is served both by the ESF and the International Ski School (ESI).

Mountain restaurants

The Chamonix Valley is not generally recommended for those who like to lunch seriously on the mountain ('nondescript food served in small quantities at inflated prices'). However, the new Bergerie above the top of the Brévent cable-car is a welcome addition: 'excellent food in a warm atmosphere'. Plan Joran at Lognan is probably the best mountain restaurant in the valley. La Crèmerie du Glacier in the woods at the bottom of the Grands Montets is the only one that is independently owned and is warmly praised for its special menu of croûte fromage ('cheese and wild mushrooms – one of the best dishes I have ever eaten'). Those who ski the Vallée Blanche have little choice but to eat at the spectacularly-sited Requin refuge.

Accommodation

Chamonix offers the full spectrum, from dormitory-style youth hostels to four-star hotels (there are 70 hotels in all), plus a wide choice of chalets and apartments, many of them newly renovated. The most luxurious hotels are Le Hameau Albert 1er and Auberge du Bois Prin, owned by brothers Denis and Pierre Carrier. Hotel Mont-Blanc is the third four-star. Le Hameau Albert 1er includes a renovated complex called Les Fermes, which consists of two eighteen-century farmhouses containing 12 wood-panelled suites, a swimming-pool and health centre, and a rustic restaurant. In the three-star category, the Sapinière recalls the heyday of the British Empire, both in its furnishings and its clientèle. The pleasant Hotel Richemond also trades on the faded glories of yesteryear, but from a more central location. Hotels Alpina and Gustavia are both central, quality three-star hotels. Reporters staying at Hotel Le Chamonix complained of 'a bruisingly narrow bath, but the hotel location was ideal'.

Eating in and out

No one denies that the Michelin-rated Le Hameau Albert 1er has the best food in Chamonix, but prices have risen to such a level that even the seriously wealthy hesitate to visit the restaurant except on special occasions, when they can enjoy Chef Pierre Carrier's innovative cuisine and a cellar containing some 20,000 bottles of fine wine. The hotel's second restaurant, Les Fermes, is much more relaxed ('highly enjoyable mountain dishes in a convivial atmosphere'). L' Auberge du Bois Prin follows Le Hameau Albert 1er closely in both quality and price, and the food at the Hotel Eden in Les Praz is also recommended. La Bergerie serves Savoyard specialities, while the Bistro de la Gare is known for its cheap daily special. Le Sarpe in **Les Bois** is praised for quality combined with good value. L'Impossible, the ancient barn in Chamonix Sud converted by Sylvain Saudan, is a winner for atmosphere. Other recommendations include La Cantina for Mexican cuisine and Le Cafeteria, which is said to provide 'very reasonably priced, wholesome food'. Les Calèches ('possibly overdid the rustic beams a bit') is a typical Savoyard bistro, and La Flèche d'Or is an inexpensive brasserie. Self-caterers are well served by specialist food shops and supermarkets.

Skiing facts: Chamonix

TOURIST INFORMATION
85 Place du Triangle de L'Amitié,
F-74400 Chamonix Mont Blanc,
Haute Savoie
Tel 33 450 53 00 24
Fax 33 450 53 58 90
Email info@chamonix.com
Web site www.chamonix.com

THE RESORT
By road Calais 900km
By rail station in resort
Airport transfer Geneva 1½hrs
Visitor beds 63,000
Transport free ski bus included in lift pass

THE SKIING
Linked or nearby resorts
Argentière (n), Courmayeur (n), Les
Houches (n), Megève (n),
St-Gervais (n), Le Tour (n)
Number of lifts 49
Total of trails/pistes 140km (52%
easy, 36% intermediate, 12% difficult)
Nursery slopes 12 lifts

LIFT PASSES
Area pass Cham'Ski (covers valley
except Les Houches) 999FF, Mont Blanc
(covers Argentière, Chamonix,
Courmayeur, Les Houches, Megève)
1,180FF, both for 6 days
Beginners no free lifts
Pensioners 15% reduction for 60yrs
and over
Credit cards yes

TUITION
Adults ESF Chamonix tel: 450 53 22 57,
ESF Argentière tel: 450 54 00 12,
Ski Sensations tel: 450 53 56 46
Snowboarding as ski schools
Other courses cross-country,
heli-skiing, ski-touring
Guiding Compagnie des Guides de
Chamonix tel: 450 53 00 88,
Association Internationale des Guides
tel: 450 53 27 05, Stages Vallençant
tel: 450 54 05 11, Mont Blanc Ski Tours
tel: 450 53 82 16, Sensation Ski
International tel: 450 53 56 46, Stages
Muller tel: 450 55 94 26, Roland Stieger
tel: 450 54 43 53

CHILDREN
Lift pass Cham'Ski, 4–11yrs: 699FF,
12–15yrs: 849FF. Ski Pass Mont Blanc,
12yrs and under: 826FF, both for 6 days
Ski & board school as adults
Kindergarten (ski) Panda-Ski tel: 450
54 04 76, (ski/non-ski) Panda Club tel:
450 54 04 76. (non-ski), Halte Garderie
tel: 450 53 36 68

OTHER SPORTS
Curling, hang-gliding, helicopter rides,
ice-driving, indoor tennis and squash,
parapente, skating, snowshoeing,
swimming

FOOD AND DRINK
Coffee 15FF, glass of wine 20FF, small
beer 20FF, soft drink 20FF, dish of the
day 75FF

Après-ski
'Night-time activities are every bit as frenzied as the day-time skiing,'
noted one reporter. The ski- and board-mad early evening trade starts at
5pm at bars such as the Chambre Neuf. The video bars of Le Choucas
and Driver are fashionable, and there is no shortage of alternative

entertainment along the Rue du Docteur Paccard. The bars empty out at about 7.30pm when snow-users return to their chalets or apartments for dinner. From about 10.30pm the partying starts up again at Arbat, which has the best live music in town. Wild Wallabies, inspired by St Anton's Krazy Kanguruh, is a top choice for riders, as is Jekyll and Hyde, while real late-nighters end up at the Blue Night, which stays open until 5am.

The Bumble Bee, Bar du Moulin, La Cantina and the Mill Street Bar in Chamonix are all popular, as is The Office Bar in Argentière. Le Pub and The Ice Rock Café in Chamonix Sud are well-frequented; the latter is a large basement bar incorporating half a truck and various motorbikes and is packed until the early hours. Dick's Tea Bar, of Val d'Isère fame, is here.

Childcare

The ESF schools in Chamonix and Argentière have classes for children aged between four and twelve years. They also have a crèche with full daycare. The Panda Club in Argentière provides care for children aged six months to three years every day of the week. For three- and four-year-olds, Panda-Ski offers daily sessions in the Jardin des Neiges near the Lognan lift station. In addition, a municipal crèche provides entertainment for children aged between 18 months and 6 years, but this is available only through tour operators.

Linked or nearby resorts

Argentière
top 3,842m (12,605ft) bottom 1,240m (4,067ft)

In winter, Argentière's main street becomes 'Ski Bum Alley', with a large proportion of its rooms let out cheaply for the season. After dark, the bars hum with macho talk of the day's achievements. The Office Bar is the favoured British watering-hole. The Stone Bar is popular; the Rusticana more cosmopolitan. The Dahu Hotel, a prominent landmark on the congested road from Chamonix to Martigny, is recommended both for comfort and food.

TOURIST INFORMATION
Tel 33 450 54 02 14
Fax 33 450 54 06 39

Les Deux Alpes

ALTITUDE 1,650m (5,412ft)

Beginners ✳ Intermediates ✳✳✳ Advanced ✳✳ Snowboarders ✳✳✳

This efficient and only partly purpose-built resort lies between Grenoble and Briançon within easy reach of Alpe d'Huez in one direction and Serre Chevalier in the other. Its primary asset is the height of the skiing (3,600m), which means that snow is assured at any stage of the season, and the glacier is also open during the French summer holidays. Les Deux Alpes began as a ski resort shortly before the outbreak of the Second World War. Pride of place was a Heath-Robinson-style rope-tow, which fell down 15 minutes after the opening ceremony. It was not until the late 1950s that a new gondola and one of France's first ski passes – costing 2.50FF per day – paved the way for Les Deux Alpes to develop into a proper ski area. Today it resembles a large ski factory, but with fresh air and impressive scenery.

✔ Snow-sure slopes
✔ Modern lift system
✔ Long vertical drop
✔ Excellent child facilities
✔ Beautiful scenery
✔ Lively après-ski
✔ Summer skiing
✘ Large and spread-out village
✘ Disjointed bus system
✘ Crowded home runs
✘ Heavy traffic

Although the town itself is visually unappealing ('does not exude alpine charm'), it is by no means the worst example of modern French architecture. The shuttle-bus is said to be a disaster: 'the two distinct circuits (Petit Plan/Clos des Fonds area and the village centre/Venosc) are in no way timetabled to coincide, so you can easily be left waiting for some considerable time if you wish to go from one area to the next. There appeared to be only one rather beaten up bus on each circuit'.

Both village and ski area are long and narrow, and there is less skiing terrain than one would imagine for such a long vertical drop. However, the skiing links with **La Grave**, which is one of the most dramatic off-piste ski areas in Europe.

A quieter, alternative base is the quaint old hamlet of **Venosc** in the Véneon Valley below Les Deux Alpes. Its ancient cobbled streets are lined with craft shops and studios. More than half-a-dozen craft shops sell a range of high-quality goods with local mountain gems their speciality. It has three extremely pleasant and inexpensive restaurants: 'the crêperie has wonderful food at realistic prices in an idyllic rustic setting'. The village is linked by an efficient, modern gondola that you have to take down again at the end of the day as you cannot ski back to the resort.

On the snow
top 3,600m (11,808ft) bottom 1,600m (5,249ft)

The chamois hunters and shepherds who once roamed what are now the ski slopes would scarcely recognise their traditional haunts today. Indeed, it is easy for skiers to be confused by such a multitude of lifts and 200km of piste within a relatively confined area. Apart from a smaller, uncrowded sector to the west of the village, between Pied Moutet at 2,100m and the Alpe du Mont de Lans, the bulk of the skiing is between the village and La Toura (2,600m) to the east. Reporters criticise the 'sameness' of the pistes ('a huge array of blue (easy) and green (beginner) runs, all of which are rather dull').

The principal lift is the Jandri Express jumbo gondola, which deposits skiers on the glacier in 20 minutes. It is prone to rush-hour queues, and the alternative Jandri 1 or the Diable gondola from the other end of the village followed by the Jandri 2 cable car may provide less irksome, but not necessarily quicker, mountain access. Above the 2,600-m mid-station the terrain narrows down to a bottleneck, and Le Jandri pistes have 'too many skiers of too many ability levels thrown together'. The broad glacier plateau offers easy slopes and even a sub-glacial funicular for novice skiers, who find wind-blown drag-lifts daunting. La Fée chair-lift opens up some blue pistes.

Beginners

The most extensive nursery slopes are at the top of the ski area on the Glacier du Mont de Lans. A compensation is the excitement of being able to experience your first slither on skis high up the mountain with magnificent views of the Oisans mountain range. The slopes immediately above the village are steep, and learners can either download by gondola or take a green path, Chemin Demoiselles, from 2,200m to return to the village. However, this is 'only a narrow track, very crowded, icy in places, tiring and not at all enjoyable'. Another reporter pointed out: 'there is no getting away from that awful green run to the resort or queuing for the gondolas down'.

Intermediates

Competent cruisers can enjoy themselves on most of the upper slopes at Les Deux Alpes, although less experienced skiers may find themselves somewhat overwhelmed by the steep homeward-bound runs, which can become crowded at the end of the day (see 'Beginners'). One way to escape from the mainstream skiing is to try one of the rare runs through the trees. There is an enjoyable piste down to the village of Bons at 1,300m, while Mont de Lans can be reached from both ski areas. Les Gours is an easy red (intermediate) run.

Advanced

Experienced skiers inevitably gravitate towards the Tête Moute area, which provides some of the steepest terrain on the mountain. They will be tempted to go straight from the Venosc end of the village by gondola

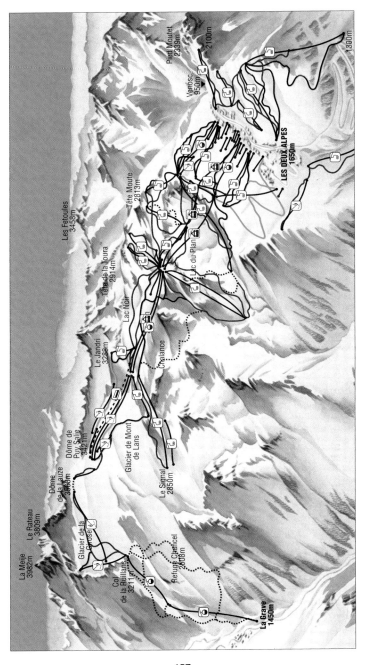

La Meije
3982m

Le Rateau
3809m

Les Fetoules
3458m

Pied Moutet
2339m

Ventosc
950m

2100m

1300m

LES DEUX ALPES
1650m

Tête Moute
2813m

Tête de la Toura
2914m

Dôme de
la Lauze
3568m

Dôme de Puy Salié
3421m

Glacier de la
Grotte

Glacier de Mont
de Lans

Le Jandri
3288m

Lac Noir

Lac du Plan

Chalance

Le Signal
2850m

Col
de la Rulllans
3211m

Refuge Chancel
2018m

La Grave
1450m

to Le Diable at 2,400m. From here, the Grand Diable chair reaches the Tête Moute itself, where steep, north-facing runs lead to Lac du Plan and onwards towards the Thuit chair. Le Diable ('a fearsome looking piste') offers a challenging and often mogulled 1,200-m descent to the village. A reporter noted that 'the last section just drops away into icy, inky blackness'. There are seven other black (difficult) runs.

Off-piste

Les Deux Alpes has enclosed bowl-skiing, which is ideal for those wanting to try off-piste for the first time. For seasoned deep-snow skiers there are a number of easily accessible (but not so easily skiable) couloirs. La Grave, one of the most exciting and scenic off-piste ski areas in the Alps, is on the doorstep – the 'over-the-top' link from Les Deux Alpes via the Glacier du Mont de Lans involves a 20-minute walk. Alternatively, you can take a bus between the two villages. A wonderful descent takes you 'off the back' towards the unspoilt climbing village of **St-Christophe-en-Oisans**.

Snowboarders

Riding takes pride of place in Les Deux Alpes each October as an apéritif to the winter ski season. The resort is the venue for the World Snowboard Meeting, which claims to be 'the highest and biggest exhibition of snowboarding on the planet'. Due to the layout of the pistes, riders need never take a drag-lift, which is a huge advantage. The funpark is on La Toura piste in winter and moves to the glacier in the summer. The park includes boardercross, a half-pipe, plus a barbecue and sound system.

Tuition and guiding

The main ski schools are the French Ski School (ESF) and the rival International Ski School St-Christophe (ESI). The British-run European Ski School offers tuition (in English) to classes of up to four pupils ('I cannot speak highly enough of the teachers, who explained everything fully and taught with a high degree of understanding and patience', said one reporter). Courses are for two hours each day and include video analysis and computerised ski simulators. Primitive Snowboard School is the specialist for wannabe riders.

Mountain restaurants

Les Deux Alpes receives few bouquets for its eight mountain restaurants, and if it were not so inconvenient, more skiers might consider lunching in town or downloading by gondola to Venosc. 'Uninviting' and 'over-priced' were two comments from reporters. The Panoramic ('we never had problems getting a table, service was quick and the loos excellent') is a convenient meeting point. The highest restaurant, Les Glaciers, is as its name suggests on the glacier and 'left us cold'. Chalet de La Toura over the back of the mountain is 'a useful find in an area otherwise bereft of gastronomic comforts'. La Fée Refuge is 'attractive and friendly but the menu choices are pedestrian'. La Meije offers a 'friendly, efficient service of local specialities at very reasonable prices'. La Patache and La Petite Marmite are both recommended.

Accommodation

Most of the accommodation is in apartments, with the remainder in the resort's 40 hotels and pensions. The top end of the market boasts two four-star hotels, of which the Bérangère is particularly praised. There are nine three-star hotels and 21 two-stars. The Edelweiss is warmly recommended for its 'wonderful gourmet dinners, with local produce properly cooked and well presented; the staff were patient and helpful and the bedrooms large, if a little spartan'. Hotel Les Marmottes is 'superb, with a five-course dinner, and large bedrooms'. Hotel Souleil'Or has 'friendly owners and decent accommodation'. Ten rental agencies deal with self-catering apartments. However, several reporters complained of the standard of the budget accommodation: 'we spent the first evening and night cleaning it and complaining about the lack of facilities such as light bulbs, beds and chairs'.

Eating in and out

L'Abri and La Spaghetteria are warmly recommended for pizza and pasta. Blue Salmon Farm specialises in fish dishes and Il Caminetto is a much-praised Italian restaurant. Le P'tit Polyte is 'smart, expensive, and worth every centime'. Le Four à Bois is renowned for its regional specialities while Le Saxo serves Tex-Mex cuisine, and La Papate is said to have 'a good atmosphere'. Les Deux Alpes appears to have a higher turnover of restaurants than any other major resort. As one reporter said: 'We marvelled at the value of more than one restaurant – only to find it had closed down by next season'. The restaurants cater well to those on a budget. A wide range of food shops makes life easy for the many self-caterers.

Après-ski

Les Deux Alpes scores highly for après-ski among those who like lively, noisy bars and discos and do not mind bumping into lots of other British people (more than 25 per cent of non-French visitors are British). However, resort transport is a deterrent: 'the poor bus facilities discouraged us from leaving our cosy chalet once we had returned there each night'. Pub Windsor is an enduringly popular haunt. Rodéo Saloon, at the Venosc end of town, has a bizarre mechanical bull which inevitably attracts the wilder element of après-skiers. The Asterix Bar, in the hotel of the same name, is 'not very pretty, but has friendly service'. Le Pressoir and Le Tonic are described as 'useful watering-holes'. Le Tanking Center, provides a therapeutic sensory-deprivation experience whereby you float in warm water in total darkness. Sensory-deprivation is far from absent at the four discos of La Casa, Le Club 92, L'Avalanche and L'Opéra Music Temple. The ice grotto is well worth a visit.

Skiing facts: Les Deux Alpes

TOURIST INFORMATION
BP 7, F-38860 Les Deux Alpes,
Dauphiné
Tel 33 476 79 22 00
Fax 33 476 79 01 38
Email Les2alp@icor.fr
Web site www.les2alpes.com

THE RESORT
By road Calais 953km
By rail Grenoble 70km
Airport transfer Grenoble 1½ hrs,
Lyon 2hrs
Visitor beds 35,000
Transport free ski bus

THE SKIING
Linked or nearby resorts La Grave (l),
Alpe d'Huez (n), Serre
Chevalier/Briançon (n), St-Christophe-
en-Oisans (l), Venosc (l)
Number of lifts 59 including La Grave
Total of trails/pistes 220km with La
Grave (24% easy, 44% intermediate,
16% difficult, 16% very difficult)
Nursery slopes 4 free lifts and 2 runs
Summer skiing mid-June–Sept, 16 lifts

LIFT PASSES
Area pass 851–945FF for 6 days
(includes 1 free day in Alpe d'Huez,
Serre Chevalier, Puy-St-Vincent or the
Milky Way)
Beginners 4 free lifts
Pensioners reduction for 60yrs and
over, free for 75yrs and over
Credit cards yes

TUITION
Adults ESF tel: 476 79 21 21, ESI

tel: 476 79 04 21, European Ski School
tel: 476 79 74 55, Ski Privilège
tel: 476 79 23 44, Stage Nano Pourtier
tel: 476 79 50 38
Snowboarding ESF, ESI, European Ski
School, Primitive Snowboard School
tel: 476 79 09 32
Other courses carving, cross-country,
extreme skiing, moguls, monoski,
powder clinics, race camps, skiing for
the disabled, ski-jumping, ski-touring,
slalom, snowblading, teen skiing,
telemark
Guiding Bureau des Guides
tel: 476 80 52 72,
Comptoir des Guides tel: 611 32 71 88,
ESF, ESI, Vénéon 2 Alpes
tel: 476 80 52 72

CHILDREN
Lift pass 5–12yrs, 638–709FF
for 6 days
Ski & board school ESF and ESI
Kindergarten (ski) ESF, ESI, (non-ski)
La Crèche du Village tel: 476 79 02 62,
Garderie Bonhomme de Neige
tel: 476 79 06 77

OTHER SPORTS
Bungee-jumping, climbing wall,
curling, helicopter rides, ice-climbing,
ice-diving, night-skiing, parapente,
quad-karting on ice, skating,
snowmobiling, snowshoeing, squash,
swimming

FOOD AND DRINK PRICES
Coffee 9–12FF, glass of wine 15–18FF,
small beer 15–18FF, soft drink 12FF,
dish of the day 80FF

Childcare

Among the bridges, tunnels and animal characters at the Espace Loisirs playground are a trampoline, a small slalom course, toboggan run, ski-biking, tubing and an inflatable bob run, with organised races most days. Bookings can be made through the tourist information office. Qualified staff welcome children from six months to two years old at the slope-side La Crèche du Village, and Garderie Bonhomme de Neige caters for two- to six-year-olds.

The ESF operates a kindergarten slope in the centre of town close to the Jandri Express, and the ESI has its own kindergarten. Both ski schools offer half- or full-day courses for children over four years of age who wish to ski, snowboard or monoski. We have mixed reports of the ESF children's ski school: 'the French instructors spoke adequate English and even in the worst of the weather they took the wee souls out for at least part of the three-hour lesson. When they got cold, wet and fed up they returned to the ESF chalet to dry out and watch videos'. However, another reporter said: 'Frankly, we were not impressed with the ESF ski kindergarten. On the first day we found our four-year-old son alone in the kindergarten hut, crying'.

Linked or nearby resorts

La Grave
top 3,550m (11,647ft) bottom 1,450m (4,757ft)

A 20-minute hike over the back of Les Deux Alpes brings you into the ski area of La Grave. The ancient, rugged village straggling the road up to the Col du Lauteret has in the past earned its reputation as a climbing centre rather than as a ski resort. It crouches in the shadow of the 3,983-m La Meije, which in 1876 was one of the last great European peaks to be conquered. Its reputation is founded on the fact that it has just one short piste and two lifts. This may sound insignificant until you realise that one of those lifts takes you up over 2,000m vertical. It does not normally open until late January, although the ski area can be reached from Les Deux Alpes. The steep, unpisted routes down provide some of the most challenging advanced skiing and riding in Europe. As the glacial area is heavily crevassed and the couloirs are steep, skiers are strongly advised to use the services of a local guide at all times. La Grave has a three-star and couple of simple hotels but little to offer anyone who does not climb or ski off-piste.

TOURIST INFORMATION
Tel 33 476 79 92 46
Fax 33 476 79 91 24
Email dominique.ferrero@wanadoo.fr
Web site www.la_grave.com

Flaine

ALTITUDE 1,600m (5,248ft)

Beginners ✱✱✱ Intermediates ✱✱✱ Advanced ✱✱✱ Snowboarders ✱✱✱

Flaine, a purpose-built resort much loved by the British in general, and the Scots in particular, is the focal point of the Grand Massif, France's fourth biggest ski area. Its proximity to Mont Blanc gives it a favourable micro-climate and in the winter of 1999–2000 this resort attracted more snow than any other in Europe.

✔ Large ski area
✔ Excellent family facilities
✔ Skiing convenience
✔ Short airport transfer
✔ Car-free resort
✔ Reliable resort-level snow
✔ Lack of queues
✔ Variety of off-piste skiing
✘ Old, slow lifts
✘ Tired apartments
✘ Lack of alpine charm
✘ Limited nightlife

The first view down into the village is an unexpected one; Flaine sits ostentatiously in an isolated bowl where you would not expect to find any habitation at all. The grey concrete of the resort matches the grey rock formation. Reporters' opinions of Flaine vary from 'no soul' and 'a ski ghetto, which does not give one the feeling of being in France,' to 'a pleasant atmosphere'. Two enclosed people-mover lifts operate day and night between the higher and lower villages, Forêt and Forum. Le Hameau de Flaine area is served by a free bus, which runs from the chalets to the nursery slopes every 15 minutes (from 8.30am until midnight). Flaine connects with the three lower and more traditional resorts of **Samoëns**, **Morillon** and **Les Carroz**, and a piste takes you down to the charming village of **Sixt**.

When Flaine opened in 1968 it was hailed as the showpiece of the French Alps – a unique resort where culture and skiing combined to produce what was described as a leisure environment. The celebrated American architect, Marcel Breuer, was commissioned to design the original buildings to blend in with the rocky surroundings of this extraordinarily beautiful valley. Depending on your viewpoint, his use of unpainted concrete is either a supreme example of the application of light and shade in the true spirit of the Bauhaus school of design, or an uncannily accurate portrayal of a 1960s GLC housing estate.

Works of art by Picasso, Vasarely and Dubuffet adorn the resort's museum and open spaces. The former world champion Emile Allais, the grandmaster of ski resort design, laid out the pistes, and winter tourists arrived in their thousands. Low-cost ski-in, ski-out rental apartments attracted budget skiers from all over the world. Les Lindars, one of the three modest hotels, won an international reputation as the best place in the Alps for families with young children. But in the 1980s the

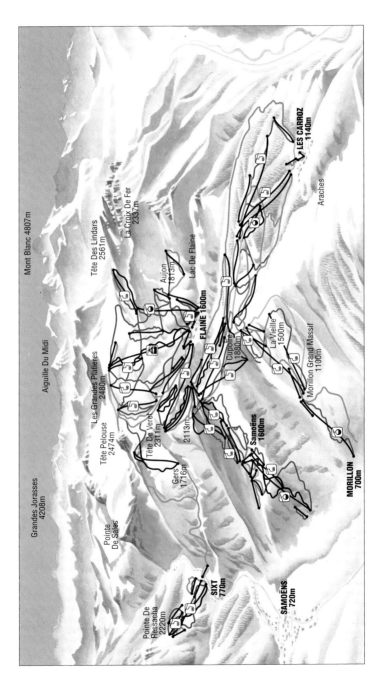

slide from grace began, and, like a ruptured slab avalanche, its only path was an accelerating downhill decline. As recession began to bite the French economy, Flaine became a victim of its own success. Its popularity was dependent on its then excellent lift system linked to the neighbouring communities of Les Carroz, Samoëns, Morillon and Sixt.

Seventy-four lifts serving 265km of piste made up this vast area, but the prohibitive daily costs of running even the Flaine sector depended on filling all 9,500 of its rental beds throughout the season. When it failed to do so the resort was broken up and sold off piecemeal along with most of its art collection. A French bank intervened when the resort was on the brink of insolvency and for 10 years acted as caretaker. Gradually Flaine withered from lack of investment. No new lifts were built and some of the old drag-lifts have passed their sell-by date. Many of the rental apartments, held on a long lease by the French property giant, Pierre & Vacances, are no longer just tired, but plain exhausted. Only 4,500 of the 9,500 beds appear to be in rental use.

WHAT'S NEW

Replacement eight-person chair-lift at Les Grands Vans
New cabins for the Grandes Platières gondola

However, all that is about to change. Almost the entire lift system (Les Carroz remains independent) and much of the resort itself has been bought by the Anglo-French company Méribel Alpina, which in turn is part of the empire of Compagnie des Alpes which also has its own 23 per cent stake in Flaine. The Compagnie des Alpes is a partner of Intrawest, the giant Canadian resort builder whose portfolio includes Whistler, Mont Tremblant and Copper Mountain. The company is poised to make a major assault on Europe, and Flaine has been earmarked for its first serious venture – a makeover that is expected to push the resort up to the premier league of European ski destinations. If the current plans to increase the size of the resort by a third get the go-ahead we can expect to see the rapid development of the first North American-style resort in Europe.

The new owners have started on a £20-million five-year investment plan. During the 1999–2000 season £6 million was spent on three new chair-lifts to take skiers up to the highest point of the ski area. Future plans include the gradual replacement of all obsolete lifts and huge improvements to the pistes, as well as an ambitious programme of snow-cannons that will give cover to a quarter of the entire area.

On the snow
top 2,480m (8,134ft) bottom 700m (2,296ft)

The area divides naturally into separate segments. Flaine's own skiing is ranged around the north-facing part of its home bowl, with lifts soaring to nearly 2,500m around the rim. Most of the skiing is open and unsheltered. The main mountain access from the village centre is by gondola up to Grandes Platières, a high, wide plateau with panoramic views. New cabins this season should greatly ease mountain access at peak times. A large number of runs go from here down to the resort; most are graded red (intermediate) or blue (easy). In general, the skiing in the enclosed Flaine bowl is somewhat limited, and its real attraction lies in its link with the remainder of the Grand Massif area; this is via the Grands Vans chair-lift, which used to attract large queues but is being upgraded to an eight-person detachable – the first of its kind in France – for the 2000–1 season.

The Tête du Pré des Saix is the central point of the entire Grand Massif system. From here, north-facing runs drop down steep mogul slopes towards Samoëns. The Aigle Noir run is reported to have 'an alarming jump-off start. Unfortunately, there is no easy way out'. Halfway down into Samoëns the descent is broken by the lifts that go up to Samoëns 1600. On the other side of the valley, the parallel easier pistes towards Morillon comprise long and gentle trails in the tree-line.

The runs to Les Carroz are short but offer a wide variety of trails, including more difficult sections at the top of the red runs and some good off-piste. Sixt, along the road from Samoëns, has its own small ski area. The resort is directly linked into the Grand Massif via a piste, but ski buses provide the only return.

Beginners

Flaine has extensive novice slopes in the middle of the village. Improvers can try wide, snaking blues on the bowl's west-facing slopes. Crystal and Serpentine are long, sweeping runs around the shoulder of the mountain that beginners will be able to tackle by the end of their first week.

Intermediates

The whole area is essentially designed for intermediates. Day-long forays into the far corners of the Grand Massif are well within the capabilities of most snow-users with a few weeks' experience. However, it is important to allow plenty of time for the return journey. The Tourmaline blue from the Grands Vans down to Le Forêt is usually well-groomed and is one of the classic runs of the resort.

Advanced

The more difficult skiing sections of the Flaine bowl are in the middle, graded black under the gondola and red to each side. The black Diamant Noir is an enjoyable mogul slope with 'a narrow gully to nego-tiate under the scrutiny of those going up the chair'. The Agate piste from the Tête des Lindars is 'an interesting black with a couple of awkward bits that get the adrenaline going a little'. Unlike some other large linked areas, there are plenty of steep runs and a good variety of terrain, making Flaine a suitable destination for advanced snow-users.

Off-piste

Flaine and the Grand Massif area offer outstanding off-piste possibili-ties. The rocky terrain means that powder hunts can all too easily end on a cliff, and the services of a local guide who really knows the region are essential. Mont Blanc Helicopters can be booked to pick you up from the end of an off-piste trip and return you to the resort.

Snowboarders

Flaine is home to one of the best funparks in Europe. The 3km-long section offers enough jumps and obstacles of all varieties to keep even the most hardcore freestyler happy. Fantasurf has a designated kids' half-pipe. At the bottom of the park is a well-prepared half-pipe. Combe des Gers bowl is popular with freeriders, and heli-boarding is available near the resort. Flaine is also popular with Alpine riders, or carvers, because of the large number of wide, easy pistes.

Tuition and guiding

Flaine now has five ski schools. We have mixed reports of the French Ski School (ESF): 'large classes, but our instructor was extremely helpful,' and 'we found our instructor typically volatile and he twice committed the cardinal sin of skiing on without waiting for all the class to catch up'. We continue to receive damning criticism of the International Ski School (ESI): 'little or no teaching – little more than 2 pieces of advice in 12 hours of tuition might be described as frugal'.

Flaine Superski offers half-day improvement courses. Ski Action-Ski Passion was set up by two former members of the French ski team and has a growing reputation. ESF Instructors at Fantasurf, the dedicated funpark, provide equipment and two hours of lessons per day for kids.

Mountain restaurants

Those in the immediate Flaine vicinity are limited, especially in the Aujon area, but there is a wide choice further afield. Close to the resort the Blanchot is recommended, and Chalet Bissac is 'busy, but has quick hot food'. Bar L'Eloge, by the Flaine gondola, has a simple choice of food and friendly service. La Combe, in the Morillon area, has 'terrific ambience'. The Oréade, at the top of the Kédeuse gondola, is praised for its food and large, sunny terrace. The restaurant on the Chariande piste at Samoëns has reasonable prices and an excellent view from the terrace. Le Pativerdans at Vercland is reported to be good value.

Accommodation

The heart of the resort is Flaine Forum, where the few shops and restaurants and the ski school meeting-place are located. The Totem, with Picasso's statue of the same name standing outside, is the main piste-side hotel. Reporters' views range alarmingly from 'expensive with clinical, modern décor,' to 'a truly grand establishment'. The food is praised by most of them. Les Lindars, Flaine's most famous, family-oriented hotel, is now a Club Med. The other family hotel is Le Flaine, which contains a kid's club. The two-star Aujon is a popular alternative: 'adequate, if a little like a factory. The standard of the evening meal was fair and breakfast was very good. But it did seem a little like a battery-hen place'.

Flaine Forêt, on a shelf above Flaine Forum, has mainly self-catering accommodation and its own shops and bars. Most of the rental apartments in the resort have been refurbished. The apartments are small, even by French standards ('thank goodness we had booked an apartment for eight for the six of us'), but cheap compared to the more fashionable French resorts. Le Hameau de Flaine, on the mountain at 1,800m, is a later development of attractive Scandinavian-style chalets inconveniently situated for the ski area.

Eating in and out

Chez La Jeanne is 'small and friendly with excellent pizzas and good house wine'. Also in Flaine Forum, the White Grouse Pub serves snacks, pizzas and fondues. La Perdrix Noire in Flaine Forêt serves regional specialities and is voted best restaurant by a number of reporters. La Pizzeria in the Forum is 'excellent and reasonably priced,' and La Trattoria has a 'pleasant, almost Italian atmosphere and good wine'. There are well-stocked supermarkets on both Forum and Forêt levels. L'Auroch in the Forum shopping centre serves traditional French cuisine.

Après-ski

People do not come to Flaine for the nightlife and many tend to opt for quiet evenings in, especially those with small children. The Cîmes Rock Café in Flaine Forum has karaoke. The White Grouse Pub, that little piece of France that is forever Scotland, has raised its standards and is reported to have fought its way back to being one of the principal meeting places of the resort. The Chaintre is the main disco.

Childcare

All five ski schools give lessons for children. The Green Mouse Club (Souris Verte) at the ESI takes children all day, as does the ESF Rabbit Club, which is the more French-oriented of the two. Both collect children from their accommodation each morning and return them at the end of the day. Non-skiing children are cared for at Les Petits Loups kindergarten, but priority is given to the families of resort workers and you need to book at least two months in advance. Both Hotel Le Flaine and Club Med have kindergarten for their residents.

Linked or nearby resorts

Les Carroz
top 2,480m (8,134ft) bottom 700m (2,296ft)

Les Carroz is large, and, in the view of most correspondents, more pleasing to the eye than Flaine. Its drawback is its low altitude. The resort spreads across a broad, sunny slope on the road to Flaine and attracts many families and weekend visitors.

The gondola and chair-lift are a steep walk from the centre of the village, but within easy reach of some attractive, simple old hotels

Skiing facts: Flaine

TOURIST INFORMATION
Galerie des Marchands, F-74300 Flaine
Tel 33 450 90 80 01
Fax 33 450 90 86 26
Email welcome@flaine.com
Web site www.flaine.com

LONDON AGENT
Erna Low Consultants (see *Which tour operator?*)

THE RESORT
By road Calais 890km
By rail Cluses 25km, frequent bus service to resort
Airport transfer Geneva 1½hrs
Visitor beds 9,500
Transport free ski bus

THE SKIING
Linked or nearby resorts Les Carroz (l), Morillon (l), Samoëns (l), Sixt (n)
Number of lifts 26 in Flaine, 74 in Le Grand Massif
Total of trails/pistes 140km in Flaine (14% easy, 32% intermediate, 46% difficult, 8% very difficult), 265km in Le Grand Massif
Nursery slopes 7 runs

LIFT PASSES
Area pass Grand Massif (covers Flaine, Les Carroz, Morillon, Samoëns and Sixt) 970FF for 6 days
Beginners 6 free lifts in area
Pensioners 640FF for 6 days

Credit cards yes

TUITION
Adults ESF tel: 450 90 81 00,
ESI tel: 450 90 84 41,
Ski Action-Ski Passion tel: 450 90 80 97,
Flaine Superski tel: 450 90 82 88,
Ski Global tel: 450 90 42 26
Snowboarding as ski schools
Other courses carving, cross-country, extreme skiing, heli-skiing and heli-boarding, race camps, seniors, snowblading, teen skiing, telemark
Guiding Mont Blanc Helicopters tel: 450 90 80 01, and through ski schools

CHILDREN
Lift pass Grand Massif, 5–11yrs 679FF, 12–15yrs 728FF. Both for 6 days
Ski & board school as adults
Kindergarten (ski) Rabbit Club (ESF), Green Mouse Club (ESI), as adults. (non-ski) Les Petits Loups tel: 450 90 87 82

OTHER SPORTS
Climbing wall, dog-sledding, hang-gliding, helicopter rides, ice-driving, parapente, skating, snowmobiling, snow-shoeing, swimming

FOOD AND DRINK PRICES
Coffee 10–18FF, glass of wine 15FF, small beer 15–20FF, soft drink 18FF, dish of the day 50–75FF

including Les Airelles and the Croix de Savoie. Most of the self-catering accommodation is much less conveniently placed. The bus is not included in the lift pass and runs intermittently to Flaine; late-night taxis between the two resorts are hard to find.

The resort boasts two ski and snowboard schools for adults and children: the ESF and Nouvelle Dimension. Both offer carving, cross-country skiing, snowblading and telemark among their list of special courses. Heli-skiing (see *Heli-skiing*) is available through the local Bureau des Guides.

TOURIST INFORMATION
Tel 33 450 90 00 04
Fax 33 450 90 07 00
Email lescarroz@lescarroz.com
Web site www.lescarroz.com

Morillon
top 2,480m (8,134ft) bottom 700m (2,296ft)
This is an old village with some 10,000 visitor beds and is a popular second-home resort with the French. It has seven of its own lifts and is linked into the Grand Massif ski area. Morillon has its own ESF for adults and children, and the local Bureau des Guides takes clients off-piste. The children's village accepts little ones from six months up to ten years of age.

TOURIST INFORMATION
Tel 33 450 90 15 76
Fax 33 450 90 11 47
Email otmorill@at-morillon.fr
Web site www.skimorillon.com

Samoëns
top 2,480m (8,134ft) bottom 700m (2,296ft)
The beautiful old town of Samoëns in the Giffre Valley has been a ski resort since 1912 and is the only one in France to be listed as a historical monument. It was once a thriving stone-cutting centre, and twice a week the tourist information office organises guided tours. Traditional-style bars and restaurants abound in what is a resort largely undiscovered by other nationalities. The Neige et Roc and Les Sept Monts hotels are recommended, together with Les Drugères. One reporter spoke highly of Le Pierrot Gourmet restaurant.

Samoëns has an ESF with 95 instructors and eight mountain guides, a crèche for children from six months old and a ski kindergarten for children from three to six years of age. It also has 90km of loipe and a cross-country ski school. Dog-sledding, indoor climbing and ice driving are all offered in the resort, plus the more unusual activities of archery in the forest for adults and children over seven years of age (on snowshoes if necessary), caving, winter bivouac weekends, and snowshoeing rambles with accommodation in mountain refuges.

TOURIST INFORMATION
Tel 33 450 34 40 28
Fax 33 450 34 95 82
Email samoens@wanadoo.fr
Web site www.skisamoens.com

Megève

ALTITUDE 1,100m (3,608ft)

Beginners ✱✱✱ Intermediates ✱✱✱ Snowboarders ✱

In 1916, Baroness Noémie de Rothschild decided to find a resort in her home country to rival St Moritz. On advice from her Norwegian ski instructor she visited the tiny village of Megève. So impressed was she that five years later she built the Palace Hotel Mont d'Arbois, which helped transform Megève into an international resort. Later on in its history, Megève boasted that at the height of the season it was home to more crowned heads of state than any other ski resort in Europe. During the boom years of the 1960s a week-long visit to Megève was mandatory for anyone with international social aspirations. Then its reputation faded. The stars migrated to brighter galaxies that offered more certain snow and more challenging skiing.

But now Megève is back as a serious contender for the most stylish resort in the Alps. A combination of extensive gentle skiing, excellent child facilities, lavish hotels and superlative restaurants all set in a village that oozes ambience, acts as the lure for a new generation of snow-users. The hotels have more atmosphere, and resort prices are lower than the equivalent in Courchevel 1850, but Megève's exclusive image endures.

The village heart is built around a fine medieval church and carefully restored old buildings set in a traffic-free main square where you can hire brightly painted sleigh-taxis driven by local farmers. The four streets branching off it are lined with designer boutiques that attract many non-skiers. Free buses link the mid-town with the lifts, and coaches run to other nearby resorts covered on the extensive Evasion Mont Blanc lift pass.

- ✔ Large linked ski area
- ✔ Attractive medieval town centre
- ✔ Excellent child facilities
- ✔ High standard of restaurants
- ✔ Sophisticated après-ski
- ✔ Range of non-skiing activities
- ✔ Short airport transfer
- ✔ Tree-line skiing
- ✘ Unreliable resort-level snow
- ✘ Heavy traffic outside pedestrian area
- ✘ Lack of steep slopes

On the snow
top 2,350m (7,708ft) bottom 850m (2,788ft)

The skiing takes place on smooth and well-groomed pistes. Two of the three areas, Mont d'Arbois and Rochebrune, are connected at their bases by cable-car. Mont d'Arbois is the most extensive and in turn is

accessed by separate gondolas from La Princesse outside **Combloux**, **Le Bettex** above St-Gervais, and **St-Nicolas-de-Véroce**. The skiing around Mont d'Arbois is mainly gentle, although some more challenging runs are to be found higher up on Mont Joux.

The access to the Rochebrune area is by a swift modern gondola that starts from the town centre. Rochebrune offers arguably the most attractive runs in the area in delightful tree-lined settings and it is less crowded than from Mont d'Arbois.

Megève's third skiing area is Le Jaillet – self-contained and reached by gondola only after a lengthy walk or bus ride from the middle of town. Its runs are mainly gentle and do not hold their snow well.

Langlaufers have a choice of four circuits totalling 75km, including a long, tricky but wonderfully scenic track from the Mont d'Arbois cable-car to Le Bettex and St-Nicolas-de-Véroce. Another links with the resort of **Praz-sur-Arly**. Activities for cross-country skiers include guided day-tours between Val d'Arly and Beaufortain.

Beginners

The nursery slopes at Mont d'Arbois are easily accessible by cable-car or ski bus. The resort also abounds in green (beginner) slopes and gentle blues (easy). From Mont Joux, long easy runs descend to Les Communailles near Le Bettex, with drag-lifts back up to the ridge. The runs into Megève itself are mostly wide and easy and include a long green piste. There is a drag-lift in the trees at the top-station of Le Jaillet, and the runs in this area are both mild and pleasant.

Intermediates

The skiing at Mont d'Arbois rises to its highest point of the area at Mont Joly at 2,350m. A choice of long and fairly gentle red (intermediate) runs takes you down into the attractive little village of St-Nicolas-de-Véroce as well as to St-Gervais. The large ski area is well suited to intermediates, although the low altitude makes the season a short one.

Advanced

Provided you have a car, Megève is the most pleasant resort in the Mont Blanc area in which to base yourself to enjoy the 13 resorts (including **Chamonix** and **Argentière)** covered by the Evasion Mont Blanc ski pass. The pistes on the north-facing La Princesse side of the mountain are wooded and more challenging than much of the area, but the black (advanced) grading is not altogether justified. From the top of the gondola at Rochebrune, further lifts take you on up to Alpette. The highest point and the start of the downhill course is Côte 2000, which provides some of the toughest skiing in the area and the best snow.

Off-piste

The area through the trees towards La Princesse provides excellent powder skiing after a fresh snowfall, as does Côte 2000. The off-piste is far less skied than in most of the other Mont Blanc resorts and is therefore likely to remain untracked for longer. A 90-minute walk up Mont Joly takes you to a point where you can ski down to the village of Les Contamines. Mont Blanc Helicopters (based in Annemasse) will pick up skiers and riders from off-piste trips and return them to Megève.

Snowboarding

As Megève has such a vast area, riders will be able to find plenty of suitable terrain. The gentle slopes make the resort particularly good for novice riders. The funpark is at Mont Joux.

Tuition and guiding

Megève's ski schools have fine reputations, particularly for beginners, who progress speedily from the nursery areas to the long and flattering easy and intermediate slopes. 'I can't praise the ESI enough,' said one reporter, 'my father, who is in his 70s and not very fit, felt confident after three lessons'. Bureau des Guides is warmly recommended.

Mountain restaurants

Megève certainly has no shortage of lunch venues, adding to its gourmet attraction. The ski area is home to about 30, most of which are marked on a special walker/cross-country skier lift map. However, reporters note that eating on the mountain can be expensive. Particularly recommended is the Auberge du Côte 2000, owned by the Rothschild family and serving some of the finest food in a resort where you are spoilt for choice. A trip to the Alpette restaurant is a must; the restaurant runs a snowcat service from the lift station for nonskiers. Radaz Ferme Auberge has 'a great atmosphere but slow service, so go early'.

> **WHAT'S NEW**
>
> La Ferme de Mon Père gourmet restaurant

In the Mont d'Arbois sector, Le Rosay is a 'reasonable self-service with an excellent balcony'. Chalet Idéal Sport, another Rothschildowned eatery, is popular with the fur-coated. Les Mandarines has 'some of the most inventive and delicious puddings we have ever eaten'. L'Igloo ('pricey but excellent, particularly if you are a cheese addict') has a terrace with magnificent views of Mont Blanc. La Ferme de la Sasse is in a remote location where the owner keeps his buffalo and horses.

Accommodation

Megève has more than 40 hotels, as well as both sumptuous and more utilitarian private chalets. The standard of its six four-stars and some of its 10 three-stars is outstanding. Chalet Hotel Relais et Châteaux du Mont d'Arbois used to be the Rothschild family home and is located some distance from the town near the Mont d'Arbois cable-car. We also have good reports of Hotel Au Coin du Feu ('the hotel has an original style') and La Chauminé. Au Vieux Moulin is said to be 'warm, spacious and tastefully decorated, and the food was excellent'.

Jocelyn and Jean-Louis Sibuet own a collection of charming hotels in the resort. The Mont Blanc is in the centre of the pedestrian zone and is one of the finest hotels in Europe. Les Fermes de Marie, a 10-minute walk from the town centre, is based around a sixteenth-century cow shed with vaulted ceiling; a collection of farm buildings in the grounds has been converted into luxury suites. The hotel has a fitness and beauty centre which is one of the best in the Alps. Four-star Le Lodge Parc de Megève has recently been bought and restored by the Sibuets; it boasts 53 bedrooms and is decorated in eclectic big game hunting and fishing style, with the atmosphere of a private club.

Cheaper accommodation includes the three-star Hotel Sporting ('unimaginative rooms') and the Gollet and Richmond apartments.

Eating in and out

A reporter commented on the 'extensive quantity and variety of eating places to suit all budgets'. This is certainly true; Megève has more than 70 restaurants and is one of the gourmet dining centres of the Alps. At the top of the range, the Hotel Mont Blanc's Les Enfants Terribles has 'delicious but expensive food'. The Chalet Hotel Relais et Châteaux du Mont d'Arbois has a high-quality restaurant. Le Fer à Cheval serves a fine dinner but is also recommended for its English breakfast. At Jacques Megean fresh truffles are the speciality. Flocon de Sel has inventive cuisine prepared by Emmanuel Renaut, who previously worked in the Crillon restaurant in Paris. La Ferme de Mon Père is a new restaurant in the town centre. Le Bar du Chamois is a lively and less expensive bistro with local white wines and fondues.

Après-ski

This is taken almost more seriously here than the skiing, and the choice of venues is enormous, ranging from the simplest of bars to the most exotic of nightspots. Le Prieuré is recommended for tea and cakes.

Later on the après-ski evolves largely around Megève's piano bars and nine nightclubs. Club de Jazz Les Cinq Rues is one of the most popular evening venues, set in cosy surroundings complete with open fire; during the season it attracts some of the big international names in jazz. However, we have some poor recent reports: 'the staff were rude and the house wine undrinkable'. Bar St Paul is 'cheap and frequented by locals'. The casino, originally a 1930s bus station, also houses a restaurant. Rosie Crève Coeur is an unusual bar that looks like it has stepped out of a 1940s US airforce base. Le Palace Café is popular with a young crowd, while Le Cave de Megève attracts the forty-somethings.

The Palais des Sports contains an Olympic-size skating-rink and a vast swimming-pool. Electric-powered ice bumper-cars are an unusual sport available on the skating-rink. Shopping is a major past-time here ('a window-shopper's paradise'), headed by the original Aalard department store, antiques and jewellery shops, designer clothing boutiques, and some delightful household and interior decoration outlets.

Childcare

In keeping with its family values, Megève has some of the most extensive nursery slopes and comprehensive childcare facilities of any resort
in France. The non-ski kindergarten, Meg'Loisirs, is housed in a well-
equipped two-storey building next to the Palais des Sports. Creative
children who want to take a break from skiing can attend Megève
Matériaux on the outskirts of town. Here, six- to thirteen-year-olds can
try their hand at stencilling, fabric painting and lots more.

Linked or nearby resorts

Les Contamines-Montjoie
top 2,500m (8,202ft) bottom 1,164m (3,818ft)

This unspoilt village is near the head of the narrow Montjoie Valley just
over the hill from Megève. It has a keen following despite the fact that
the whole set-up is awkward. The long village is on one side of the river
while the ski area is on the other, and Le Lay base-station is a long, 1-
km uphill walk from the centre. However, a shuttle bus runs between
the village and the gondolas. Prices are below average for this area of
France, and accommodation is modest.

The east-facing bowl, which makes up the ski area, tends to hold its
snow well and offers a good alternative when neighbouring resorts such
as Megève have none. Off-piste enthusiasts can find virtually untouched
powder all over the area after a fresh snowfall. Two efficient gondolas,
Auberge du Télé and Le Pontet (reporters recommend the latter as it is
further down the valley and therefore less busy) take snow-users up to
a plateau at 1,470m, where a further gondola takes them on to Le
Signal and the start of the skiing. The small nursery lift at Le Signal at
1,900m can often be busy but the runs have more reliable snow-cover
than L'Etape nursery slopes at 1,500m.

Almost half of the 44 runs are intermediate, with the higher runs
towards Mont Joly steeper and more testing. The Col du Joly at 2,000m
separates the main bowl from a smaller but open area. A new cable-car
is opening for the 2000–1 season.

Ski and board lessons are given by the ESF, and both the Bureau des
Guides et Accompagnateurs and Ellipse are for off-piste guiding. Croc
Noisettes offers daycare and lessons for children aged four months to
seven years old. The Jardin des Neiges is open only in the mornings
during the French school holidays. Auberge de Colombaz is on an off-
piste itinerary towards the village. The six mountain restaurants include
a rather basic one at Le Signal.

The village runs along a single street with a Baroque church,
old-fashioned chalet-style hotels and a few shops and cafés. The best
location is on the east side of the river near the gondola. The Chemenaz
is the leading three-star hotel; the rest are two- and three-star.
A wide variety of self-catering apartments is available. The
restaurants include half-a-dozen crêperies and some pizzerias.

Skiing facts: Megève

TOURIST INFORMATION
BP 24, F-74120 Megève, Haute Savoie
Tel 33 450 21 27 28
Fax 33 450 93 03 09
Email megeve@megeve.com
Web site www.megeve.com

THE RESORT
By road Calais 890km
By rail Sallanches 12km, regular bus
service to resort
Airport transfer Geneva 1hr
Visitor beds 40,500
Transport free ski bus with lift pass
(links centre with access lifts)

THE SKIING
Linked or nearby resorts Argentière,
Chamonix (n), Combloux (l), Flumet (n),
Le Bettex (l), Les Contamines-
Montjoie(n), Les Houches, Les Saisies
(n), Notre-Dame-de-Bellecombe (n),
Praz-sur-Arly (n), St-Gervais (l),
St-Nicolas-de-Véroce (l)
Number of lifts 79 in resort, 117 in
linked area
Total of trails/pistes 300km in resort,
450km in linked area (30% easy, 45%
intermediate, 25% difficult), 729km in
Mont Blanc ski area
Nursery slopes 5 lifts

LIFT PASSES
Area pass Evasion Mont Blanc 880FF
(covers 121 lifts in region), Mont Blanc
Ski Pass 1,180FF (also covers all
Chamonix and Courmayeur lifts), both
for 6 days
Beginners points tickets

Pensioners 60yrs and over 490–792FF
Credit cards yes

TUITION
Adults ESF (5 centres) tel: 450 21 00
97, ESI tel: 450 58 78 88
Snowboarding as ski schools
Other courses carving, cross-country,
freestyle, heli-skiing and -boarding,
moguls, seniors, skiing for the disabled,
snowblading, Skwal, race training,
telemark
Guiding Bureau des Guides et
Accompagnateurs tel: 450 21 55 11,
Mont Blanc Helicopters tel: 450 92 78
21, and through ski schools

CHILDREN
Lift pass Evasion Mont Blanc 634FF,
Mont Blanc 452FF, both 4–12yrs
for 6 days
Ski & board school as adults
Kindergarten (ski/non-ski) Caboche tel:
450 58 97 65, Princesse tel: 450 93 00
86, Meg'Loisirs tel: 450 58 77 84

OTHER SPORTS
Climbing wall, curling, dog-sledding,
hang-gliding, ice-bumper cars,
Ice-climbing, ice-hockey, indoor tennis,
light-aircraft flights, night-skiing,
parapente, skating, sleigh rides,
snowmobiling, snow polo, snowshoeing,
swimming,

FOOD AND DRINK PRICES
Coffee 12–16FF, glass of wine
10–14FF, small beer 18–23FF, soft
drink 15FF, dish of the day 75–120FF

TOURIST INFORMATION
Tel 33 450 47 01 58
Fax 33 450 47 09 54
Email Les.contamines@wanadoo.fr
Web site www.lescontamines.com

St-Gervais
top 2,350m (7,708ft) bottom 860m (2,788ft)

As a spa, St-Gervais has attracted tourists since 1806 and today is popular with families wanting a cheaper alternative to Megève. Spa treatments are available in the resort's hot springs. Nearby Le Bettex at 1,400m is a quieter village with a few comfortable hotels and some cross-country skiing.

The main ski area of St-Gervais is on the slopes of Mont d'Arbois and is linked with that of Megève. It has a funpark with a half-pipe, and the area is accessed by a fast, 20-person jumbo gondola from the edge of the resort to Le Bettex. The second stage goes up to St-Gervais 1850. This is a popular and often crowded entrance to Megève's pistes. Skiing on the Mont Blanc side of St-Gervais is served by the Tramway, a funicular that climbs slowly to the Col de Voza at 1,653m, where it links to the skiing above **Les Houches**. The only run back to St-Gervais is off-piste and is sometimes unskiable. Hotel-Restaurant Igloo and the Terminus in **Le Fayet** area both have good reputations.

St-Gervais has three nursery-slope lifts and two kindergarten. The ESF at St-Gervais and the ESI at Le Bettex both teach carving, cross-country, slalom, snowblading, snowboarding and telemark. The two local mountain guiding companies are Compagnie des Guides de St-Gervais and Guides des Cimes and both can organise heli-skiing (see *Heli-skiing*).

Hotels here include the Carlina, the Val d'Este and the Edelweiss. A reporter recommends the Regina, with its reasonable prices and friendly staff. At Le Bettex, the quiet Arbois-Bettex has a heated outdoor swimming-pool, large bedrooms, and is 'right on the piste'. The Flèche d'Or is recommended. St-Gervais has a moderate range of restaurants, with 4 Epices and L'Eterle both good value. Le Four and Le Robinson serve a variety of local specialities, while La Tanière and La Chalette are traditional. Nightlife is said to be extremely limited, with La Nuit des Temps the only disco.

TOURIST INFORMATION
Tel 33 450 47 76 08
Fax 33 450 47 75 69
Email welcome@st-gervais.net
Web site www.st-gervais.net

La Plagne

ALTITUDE 1,250m–2,100m (4,100–6,889ft)

Beginners ✳✳✳ Intermediates ✳✳✳ Advanced ✳✳ Snowboarders ✳✳✳

In all probability, this winter will be the last when La Plagne stands alone as France's most popular resort for domestic skiers and snowboarders. From the 2001–2 season its ski area is to become one of the biggest in Europe, when La Plagne is joined to neighbouring **Les Arcs** by a 200-person cable-car at a cost of £10 million.

✔ Large integrated ski area
✔ Skiing convenience
✔ Beautiful scenery
✔ Extensive off-piste
✔ Geared to family skiing
✔ Summer skiing on the glacier
✘ Limited nightlife
✘ Some villages lacking in atmosphere

After a decade of debate, the two resorts have finally agreed to build the link that will create one of the largest winter playgrounds in the world – 190 lifts and over 400km of groomed pistes designed to suit every category of skier from complete beginner to expert.

The new link across the mile-wide gorge between the satellite villages of Montchavin (La Plagne) and **Peisey Vallandry** (Les Arcs), should open in time for Christmas 2001. But even the most optimistic figures suggest that less than 30 per cent of visitors to either resort will actually use it.

Some would argue that La Plagne is already too big. From the air you get the impression that you are descending on to the jotting pad of a trainee town planner. Its 10 separate villages, which are joined by lift pylons and ribbons of white, resemble a suburban sprawl of outstandingly dubious architectural merit. The resort's signature on the landscape is the giant battleship apartment block of **Aime-la-Plagne**, which, depending on your viewpoint, is either monstrous or magnificent.

Under the dynamic ownership of the Compagnie des Alpes, La Plagne has been undergoing a renaissance in recent years. In the past, its shoebox apartments, exhausted two-star hotels and dated lift infrastructure have detracted from the skiing, which is undeniably its strongest asset. The company, which already owns 11 resorts in France as well as **Courmayeur** in Italy and a significant interest in **Verbier** in Switzerland, is now systematically upgrading La Plagne's 110 lifts that serve 212km of groomed piste, of which 66 per cent is classified as easy.

The British make up 37 per cent of all foreign visitors, and all the mass-market tour operators offer holidays here in villages and accommodation of varying character, so it is vital to choose carefully.

La Plagne's six high-altitude villages lie in the central area at altitudes ranging from 1,800m to 2,100m. As far as modern architecture is

concerned, the later the better: imaginatively designed **Belle Plagne** is the firm favourite, with its attractive village centre and integrated arcs of apartment buildings, while the low-rise wood-clad complexes at **Plagne 1800** and **Plagne Villages/Plagne Soleil** are inspired by Savoyard tradition.

Aime's apartments have been redecorated. **Bellecôte's** semi-circle of high-rise reddish blocks is an acquired taste. Inevitably, the complexities of the area are confusing at first, which may explain why regulars prefer to book the same apartment in the same block from one year to the next, rather than take a chance on unknown territory.

The four lower villages, **Montchavin**, **Montalbert**, **Les Coches** and **Champagny-en-Vanoise**, lie on different access roads in far-flung parts of the mountain but all are connected with the central complex by lift. Although the farming village of Montchavin was adapted to become part of La Plagne in the early 1970s, a rural smell still lingers in the air. It has a gondola link to neighbouring Les Coches, which is a modern ski complex with its own wooded slopes.

Champagny-en-Vanoise, at the base of the south-facing back side of the mountain, consists of a series of hamlets in a quiet valley linked to the ski area by an efficient gondola. Montalbert and its satellite holiday centre have £4 million of new snow-cannons on their west-facing slopes.

All 10 villages are self-sufficient, with their own selection of shops, bars and restaurants. The six high villages are connected by bus or covered lifts from 8am to 1am. As its name suggests, Plagne Centre has the lion's share of essential services – banks, a post office, police and doctors – in the environs of its bleak, subterranean commercial precinct. Aesthetic it is not, but it scores highly for convenience, as does Bellecôte, which also has banks and a post office.

WHAT'S NEW

Grande Rochette lift replaced by a new £10-million Funitel gondola
Four-star MGM résidence in Aime-la-Plagne
Additional snow-cannon

On the snow
top 3,250m (10,660ft) bottom 1,250m (4,100ft)

La Plagne represents the ultimate in ski-in ski-out convenience. To point your skis in any direction from the nexus in Plagne Centre is to lock into the network of lifts on the shallow gradients of La Grande Rochette, Les Verdons and Le Biolley. The old Grande Rochette lift is being replaced for the 2000–1 season by a new £10 million Funitel gondola. The Bellecôte gondola provides the most efficient connection with Roche de Mio, a steeper mountain with more challenging terrain; from here you can take the lift up to the Bellecôte Glacier, which is the highest point in the resort.

The Montchavin/Les Coches area is connected to the high-altitude area through Arpette, a direct quad-chair ride from Bellecôte. The predominantly wooded Montalbert-Longefoy pistes lie on the other side of the resort below Aime-la-Plagne. Access to Champagny-en-Vanoise is via Les Verdons, the mid-way point on the rim of the main bowl, or Roche de Mio.

La Plagne has few queues in good weather, but the links to the outlying areas close down rapidly in stormy weather, causing congestion in the centre. Reporters praise the ski area: 'the signposting is good and the pistes are well groomed'. La Plagne has 100km of marked cross-country trails in the lower villages but only 11km spread between the high-altitude satellites.

Beginners

With the exception of Champagny-en-Vanoise, all parts of the mountain have extensive beginner slopes. Those staying in the other three low-altitude villages of Les Coches, Montchavin and Plagne Montalbert gain in visibility by being below the tree-line, but this advantage used to be balanced by less reliable snow conditions, especially in spring. However, the area's investment in new snow-cannon for the 2000–1 season should do much to improve this.

Aesthetics aside, there can be no more encouraging place to learn to ski than La Plagne's central area in fine weather. The pistes on either side of the Arpette ridge above Bellecôte offer gradients so gentle that even the most fearful novice should gain in confidence, while the web of blue (easy) runs between Belle Plagne and Plagne Centre make for a natural second-week progression. The gentle blue Les Inversens from Roche de Mio is another popular run for second-weekers.

Intermediates

As befits a state-of-the-art ski area, La Plagne offers most to those snow-users dedicated to racking up the kilometres. This can be done most readily on the red (intermediate) runs on the eastern side of the bowl above Aime-la-Plagne. However, Roche de Mio has more varied terrain, with the run back to Belle Plagne via a long tunnel particularly recommended. An adventurous alternative is the Crozats piste down to Les Bauches 1800, which has a link back to the main circus via two chair-lifts.

The summer ski drag-lifts at the top of the glacier are not usually open in winter, but La Combe and Le Chiaupe runs to the Bellecôte gondola base-station hold no terrors for committed motorway cruisers. Enterprising intermediates will enjoy the exhilarating Mont de la Guerre run from Les Verdons to Champagny-en-Vanoise, but check conditions first as the descent is extremely rocky when snow is sparse. The same applies to the more wooded route from the Roche de Mio, via Les Borseliers.

Advanced

The resort has a general lack of black (difficult) runs, with most pistes described as 'fairly intermediate'. One reporter commented: 'this is definitely a family resort – tough runs are scarce'. Although glaciers are not generally known for steep skiing, La Plagne's is one of the exceptions. The disadvantage is the 45-minute trek to the top from the centre of the resort, but once in place advanced skiers and snowboarders will find plenty to test them, especially the black Bellecôte and Le Rochu runs to the bottom of the Chalet de Bellecôte chair. The other steep area is off Le Biolley ridge above Aime-la-Plagne. When conditions are good, the Morbleu piste is a compellingly direct drop to Le Fornelet cross-country area; return is via the Coqs chair. On the east-facing side of the ridge, the Emile Allais descent to the bottom of the outlying Charmettes chair, at the side of the Olympic bob run, is the longest black run in the resort.

Off-piste

As with the advanced pistes, the best areas of off-piste are on the fringes of the resort, with the long, sweeping descent from the top of the glacier down to Les Bauches high on most experienced snow-users' list. From here, the choice lies between an easy blue piste to Montchavin, a return to Arpette via the Bauches chair or, more dramatically, an itinerary down to **Peisey-Nancroix** in the adjacent valley. The other prime off-piste area lies on the western slopes of Le Biolley; it is especially enjoyable towards the end of the season, when spring snow is at its best. The back of the Bellecôte Glacier offers the demanding Col du Nant run into the remote valley of Champagny-le-Haut, followed by a return to **Champagny-en-Vanoise** by shuttle bus. The woods above Montchavin and Les Coches provide exciting powder skiing in the trees, but access is often restricted, at least as far as downtown La Plagne is concerned, by the closure of the link through Arpette.

Snowboarders

If La Plagne is not a favourite among dedicated freeriders, it is because of its lack of ambience rather than lack of opportunity, since there is plenty of excellent off-piste. Riders congregate at the Col de Forcle funpark between Plagne Bellecôte and Plagne Villages. Montchavin also has a funpark. The wide pistes and the lift system are ideal for Alpine snowboarders or carvers.

Tuition and guiding

The French Ski School (ESF) is based in each of the villages of the resort. The numbers wanting to learn are so great that one reporter said the process of dividing up beginners into separate classes was 'reminiscent of a cattle market with up to 16 steers in each'. On the plus side the volume of business means that the ESF has been able to introduce teenage ski classes for greater peer-group pleasure. It also has guided off-piste courses in La Plagne and the surrounding outposts of the Tarentaise Valley.

We have good reports of Oxygène at Plagne Centre, where instructors are said to be 'friendly and professional'. Elpro, based in Belle Plagne, and Evolution 2 in Montchavin, are the alternative ski and snowboard schools. La Plagne has a ski school called Antenne Handicap, which offers private lessons for physically and mentally disabled pupils.

Mountain restaurants

In an area increasingly well known for its mountain restaurants, there are two outstanding choices. The Au Bon Vieux Temps, just below Aime-la-Plagne, is recommended for its sunny terrace, traditional Savoyard dishes and efficient service. The Petit Chaperon Rouge, on the edge of the nursery slope just above Plagne 1800 ('quiet, pleasant, with nice food for a reasonable price') is the wiser choice on a snowy day because of its open fires.

Good value is represented by the Dou du Praz above Plagne Villages and La Rossa at the top of the Champagny gondola. Reporters favour

Chez Pat du Sauget, an old summer farm on the pastures above Montchavin, which has recently been elevated to *auberge* status, with the addition of simple bedrooms. Polly's, next to the skating rink at Plagne Bellecôte, is said to have 'wonderful food – the Salad Blue is fantastic and it is reasonably priced in general'. Le Bec Fin in Plagne Centre is recommended by reporters for its omelettes and is described as 'value-for-money'. The Plan Bois, above Les Coches, has 'rustic charm and is a great spot for lunch'.

Accommodation

Two-thirds of La Plagne's 50,000 beds are in the high-altitude villages, and one-third are in the villages down the valley. The Centaur apartments at Belle Plagne have been refurbished, turning them into a well-equipped three-star *résidence*. Aime-la-Plagne has a new four-star MGM apartment complex built around a swimming-pool. Belle Plagne has the four-star Les Montagnettes and Les Balcons de Belle Plagne *résidences*. Until now Hotel Eldorador ('very good food and wine included in the net price') was the only high-altitude hotel in the resort with ski-in ski-out convenience. It was joined by a new three-star, the Terra Nova, in Plagne Centre in 1999–2000: 'very pleasant by La Plagne standards although service was erratic'. The hotel welcomes children as young as 18 months and runs its own crèche and mini club.

New to Champagny-en-Vanoise is the four-star *résidence*, Les Chalets du Bouquetin, which is said to be 'the most beautiful in La Plagne'. Club Alpina, also in Champagny-en-Vanoise, is a chalet-style building containing a restaurant, and a sports centre with a swimming-pool. Le Centre apartments, also in Champagny, were praised by reporters: 'very clean and well equipped, with direct lift access and a good-sized south-facing balcony'. Les Balcons de Belle Plagne is a *résidence*/hotel, which provides much-needed high-quality accommodation. The luxurious Chalet/Hotel Les Montagnettes in Belle Plagne represents a welcome wind of change with its chalets and apartments of varying sizes; they can be rented for self-catering or with full hotel services. Self-caterers in search of a taste of rural France can rent one of 200 *gîtes* on the lower slopes of La Plagne. They are rated as normal, comfortable or luxurious and cost about half the price of the higher, purpose-built accommodation.

Eating in and out

La Soupe aux Schuss in Aime-la-Plagne is an expensive restaurant serving specialities from the Périgord region. Le Matafan in Belle Plagne stays closer to home, with a range of medium-priced Savoyard dishes including raclette and fondue. Le Loup Garou, a short sleigh ride (or walk) down the path from Plagne Centre to Plagne 1800, serves similar dishes in a festive atmosphere. However, as one reporter put it: 'La Plagne is definitely not a gastronome's resort'. Les Coches and Montchavin have half-a-dozen restaurants each, while Champagny and Plagne Montalbert have more than 10 each. All the villages have supermarkets for the self-catering brigade.

Skiing facts: La Plagne

TOURIST INFORMATION
BP 62, 73211, Aime Cedex
Tel 33 479 09 79 79
Fax 33 479 09 70 10
Email ot.laplagne@wanadoo.fr
Web site www.la-plagne.com
UK Agent Erna Low (see *Which tour operator?*)

THE RESORT
By road Calais 930km
By rail Aime 18km
Airport transfer Lyon 2hrs, Geneva 3hrs
Visitor beds 50,000
Transport free bus service

THE SKIING
Linked or nearby resorts Les Arcs (n), Peisey (n), Tignes (n), Trois Vallées (n), Val d'Isère (n), Vallandry (n)
Number of lifts 110
Total of trails/pistes 212km (66% easy, 28% intermediate, 6% difficult)
Nursery slopes 1 lift in each centre
Summer skiing Bellecôte Glacier open July and August

LIFT PASSES
Area pass 1,045–1,159FF for 6 days (covers 10 centres, Les Arcs and 1 day in L'Espace Killy or Trois Vallées)
Beginners free drag-lift in each resort
Pensioners 60yrs and over, 870FF for 6 days, free for 72yrs and over
Credit cards yes

TUITION
Adults ESF in all centres
tel: 479 09 00 40, Elpro (Belle Plagne)
tel: 479 09 11 62, Evolution 2

(Montchavin) tel: 479 07 81 67, Oxygène (Plagne Centre) tel: 479 09 03 99, Antenne Handicap tel: 479 09 13 80
Snowboarding ESF, Elpro, Evolution 2, Oxygène
Other courses carving, cross-country, extreme skiing, freestyle, heli-skiing/heli-boarding, moguls, monoski, powder clinics, seniors, skiing for the disabled, ski-touring, snowblading, speed skiing, Skwal, teen skiing, telemark, women's clinics
Guiding ESF, Evolution 2

CHILDREN
Lift pass 5–13yrs, 805FF (covers 10 centres) for 6 days
Ski & board school ESF, Elpro, Evolution 2, Formule Ski (Montchavin/Les Coches) tel: 479 07 82 82, Oxygène
Kindergarten (ski) through ski schools, (non-ski) as ski kindergarten, and Crèche Municipal Plagne Centre
tel: 479 09 00 83,
Garderie Marie Christine (Plagne Centre)
tel: 479 09 11 81,
Club Garderie (Montchavin/Les Coches)
tel: 479 07 82 82

OTHER SPORTS
Bob-rafting, bobsleigh, climbing wall, hang-gliding, luge-ing, night-skiing, parapente, skating, sleigh rides, snowmobiling, snowshoeing, squash, swimming, taxi-bob, tubing

FOOD AND DRINK
Coffee 8–10FF, glass of wine 12–20FF, small beer 12–18FF, soft drink 15FF, dish of the day 50–90FF

Après-ski

By comparison with its Tarentaise neighbours, Val d'Isère and Courchevel, La Plagne's nightlife is decidedly quiet ('our pack of cards was quite well used'). Clubs are mainly in Plagne Centre and Bellecôte. The current favourites in Plagne Centre are Le Must disco and Le King Café, which has live music most nights and a weekly karaoke ('turns into a national competition of pride, usually started by loud Brits who eventually get overwhelmed by the French'). Le Mat's Pub is a faithful re-creation of a British pub, making it a winner among Brits staying in Belle Plagne ('popular with holidaymakers and workers alike. I have seen people in there at 1am still in ski gear and ski boots'). Le Saloon is also popular. The watering-hole of choice in Bellecôte is Le Show Time Café/Le Jet Discotheque, while the Lincoln is the winner in Plagne Soleil. Aime-la-Plagne has Totobrix, while Le Galaxy is the night-spot in Champagny, and Oxygène disco is in Montchavin.

The most exhilarating non-skiing activity in La Plagne is the Olympic bob-run, which is open to the public whenever conditions permit. The Taxi-Bob is the genuine experience, with two rookies sandwiched between a professional driver and a brake man for a breathtaking 50-second descent at speeds of up to 100kph. The softer option is the Bob-Raft, a four-man, foam-rubber cocoon that hurtles down in gravity-propelled mode at 80kph. Reporters complain about a shortage of non-skiing activities in Champagny: 'lack of things to do, especially for children, in the early evenings. It would not suit teenagers or young couples'.

Childcare

'An excellent ski area for our intermediate children, and very cheerful lift operators – especially towards the children' was the comment from one reporter. Certainly the villages each have their own nursery slopes and children's ski school. However, ski school classes in high season 'sometimes contained up to 15 children'. The ESF has learn-to-ski programmes for children aged two to seven in specially designed snow gardens in all of the villages. 'We found the Belle Plagne kindergarten to be both friendly and flexible. However, in practice the one at Bellecôte involves less walking for toddlers'. The Oxygène ski school at Plagne Centre is recommended: 'The instructors' English is excellent and they are always friendly and caring too. Other parents tell me they are far better than the ESF who appear to have no patience with children'. The Club Garderie Montchavin-Les Coches has a mixed programme of skiing and other learning activities for children aged three and upwards.

La Plagne has 10 nurseries for toddlers and upwards; those in Montchavin/Les Coches, Belle Plagne and Plagne Centre accept children as young as nine months old. The Eldorador Hotel has its Mini-Eldo children's club (four- to twelve-year-olds) from 9am to 5pm, plus a supervised children's table in the hotel restaurant and babysitting by arrangement in the evening. Garderie Marie Christine is for non-skiing children aged two to six.

Portes du Soleil

ALTITUDE Avoriaz 1,800m (5,904ft), Morzine 1,000m (3,280ft)

Beginners ✱✱✱ Intermediates ✱✱✱ Advanced ✱✱ Snowboarders ✱✱✱

The Portes du Soleil might be considered to be one of Europe's greatest overall ski areas were it not for one major fault: it is too low. With a top height of only 2,350m and the villages mostly below 1,200m, snow cover is by no means guaranteed and the links are liable to rupture at any time. That said, it has experienced phenomenally good cover for the past two seasons, and the proximity to Mont Blanc does to some extent confer its own micro-climate.

✔ Vast ski area
✔ Ideal cruising territory
✔ Extensive cross-country trails
✔ Good childcare facilities
✔ Car-free resort (Avoriaz)
✔ Short airport transfer
✔ Tree-level skiing (Châtel and Morgins)
✘ Low altitude (except Avoriaz)
✘ Overcrowded pistes (Avoriaz)

One of Europe's three most extensive circuits, Portes du Soleil straddles the French–Swiss border close to Geneva and is an uneasy marketing consortium of a dozen ski villages, ranging from large, internationally recognised resorts to the tiniest of unspoilt hamlets.

The published statistics refer to 650km of piste (although how this figure is arrived at is best not examined) served by 212 lifts (though 117 of them are drag-lifts) to create a well-linked circus covering vast tracts of land bordered by Lac Léman. In reality the Portes du Soleil consists of a series of naturally separate ski areas. Most are joined by awkward and often confusing mountain links, while a few, such as **St-Jean d'Aulps/La Grande Terche** and **Abondance**, are entirely independent.

While it is possible to complete a tour of the main resorts in one day, this actually involves limited enjoyable skiing and a considerable amount of time spent on lifts, although the new hands-free lift pass eases passage. To explore the region fully you need four weeks, at least two bases, a car and exceptional snow conditions such as the region has recently been enjoying.

Out of the 12 resorts, only **Avoriaz** can be recommended as a snow-sure base and, when cover is poor or non-existent elsewhere, the overcrowding here becomes a complete misery. However, keen skiers and snowboarders should base themselves at this end of the circuit, where the slopes are the most challenging.

Signposting has improved but is still desperately confusing, as is the overall Portes du Soleil piste map. The introduction of suggested itineraries, each illustrated by a different bird or animal for different standards of skiers, has not been voted a great success by reporters. As

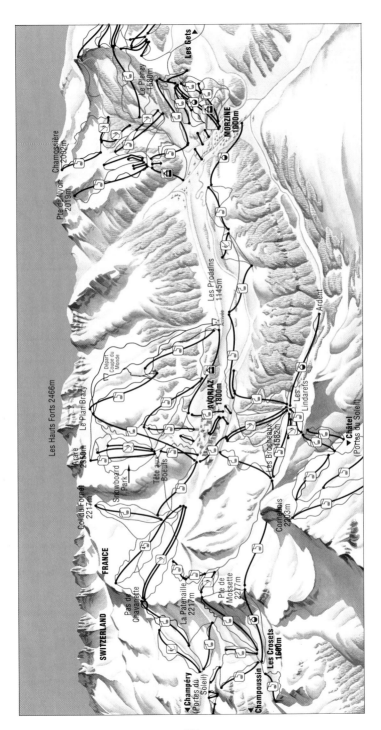

one commented: 'when trying to find my way back down to **Châtel** at the end of the day, a picture of a running rabbit is of little help'. Snow-users are advised to carry passports as well as two sets of currency; both countries accept both types of franc but not always at an advantageous rate to visitors.

Avoriaz is mainly a collection of apartment blocks perched on the edge of a cliff far above **Morzine** and built in what for the 1960s was a truly futuristic style. Unfortunately, many of the older blocks are showing their age, and no amount of face-lifts can improve the lack of space in their interiors. The resort is reached from the valley either by a narrow, winding road or by cable-car from Les Prodains. A vehicle has no useful purpose in car-free Avoriaz, and the charges in the car park are iniquitous. Transport to your apartment block or hotel is via horse-drawn sleigh, piste machine or on foot. When not on skis, moving around is made easier by public lifts within the apartment blocks to different levels of this steep resort. The busiest area is around the foot of the nursery slopes by the shops, bars and restaurants.

Morzine is a market town and long-established resort on the lower section of the road to Avoriaz. It has all the appeal of an old-style chalet resort set in charming, wooded surroundings. The biggest drawback is its lack of altitude (1,000m), which means that resort-level snow can be scarce. The town covers a large area on both sides of a river gorge and is on several levels. It has a serious traffic problem, but a high foot-bridge over the river makes getting around less tortuous for pedestrians than for motorists. The main congested shopping street climbs from the old village centre beside the river to more open ground at the foot of Le Pleney, where the resort has developed, with hotels and shops around the tourist information office.

WHAT'S NEW
Hands-free lift pass
Micro funpark for miniboarders (Avoriaz)
Extended avalanche control system

Such is the diffuse nature of the resort that the free buses and a miniature road train are an essential form of transport. Horse-drawn taxis are an alternative means of getting around. As Morzine is a proper working town, there is a better range of shops than in most ski resorts.

On the snow
top 2,350m (7,708ft) bottom 1,100m (3,608ft)

The skiing around Avoriaz is ideal for all standards of snow-users. Above the village is an extension of the main nursery slopes, with a variety of drag-lifts serving a series of confidence-building green (beginner) runs, which link with the lifts coming up from Morzine.

The best of the Avoriaz skiing is to be found in the Hauts Forts sector above the resort (from where you can descend 1,300m vertical to the cable-car station at Les Prodains) and on the Swiss border at Pas de Chavanette. From here the Chavanette black run – better known as The

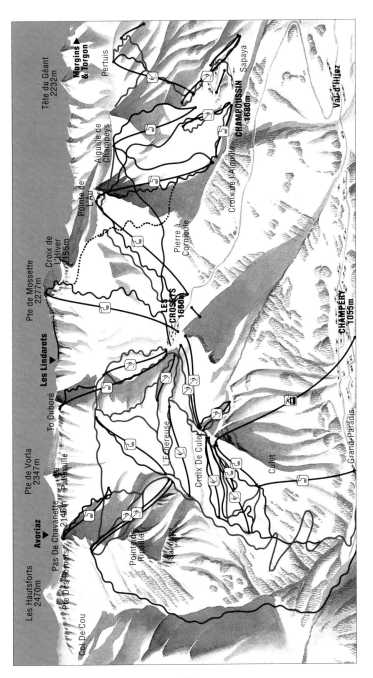

Wall – takes you down towards **Les Crosets**, **Champéry** and the rest of the Portes du Soleil.

Les Crosets sits above the tree-line surrounded by abundant wide pistes, some of them north-facing but most of them sunny. From here there are connections with **Champoussin** and **Morgins**. Morgins has little skiing on the approach side from Champoussin, but it includes an excellent north-facing intermediate run cut through the woods above the village. Those who wish to continue skiing the circuit must walk across the village or take a short bus ride to the nursery slopes and the lifts for **Super-Châtel** and France. In strong contrast to the sometimes bleak ski-fields of Avoriaz, the pistes here wind through the trees and are connected by a series of short drag-lifts.

The Morclan chair from Super-Châtel up to 1,970m serves the most challenging slope – a moderately difficult mogul field. The top of this chair is the departure point for **Torgon**, one of the further extremities of the Portes du Soleil, back across the border in Switzerland. The remainder of the skiing around Super-Châtel is mostly blue (easy) and red, on wide areas both above and below the lift-station. The valley runs catch the afternoon sun and can be tricky in poor snow conditions.

The Portes du Soleil circuit breaks down at Châtel and whichever way you are travelling, the link cannot be made on skis. You have to take a bus across the village to the gondola up to Linga; this is the first of a long chain of lifts and pistes towards Avoriaz and provides one of the best intermediate playgrounds in the region with a seemingly endless variation of terrain and gradients.

From Avoriaz you can also ski down to Les Prodains and Morzine, which has its own extensive ski area linking to **Les Gets**. Most queuing problems in the Portes du Soleil are in the Avoriaz sector.

Beginners

Given acceptable snow conditions, it does not really matter which end of the circus you choose. Châtel and Morgins both have easy nursery slopes and plenty of tree-level skiing to which novices can graduate after a few days. Morzine, and in particular the runs around **Super-Morzine**, are well-suited to first-timers.

Intermediates

The whole of the Portes du Soleil ski area is ideal cruising territory. Less confident snow-users will prefer the long, sweeping runs at the Châtel end of the circuit. Linga and Plaine Dranse have entertaining slopes that keep their snow well. Stronger skiers and boarders will look towards the greater challenges of Champéry and Avoriaz. Les Gets is also an ideal base from which to explore the intermediate skiing.

Advanced

Advanced snow-users should base themselves at the Avoriaz end of the circuit, although Champéry and Châtel are also delightful. Thanks to lift improvements, all are within easy reach of one another. It is perfectly

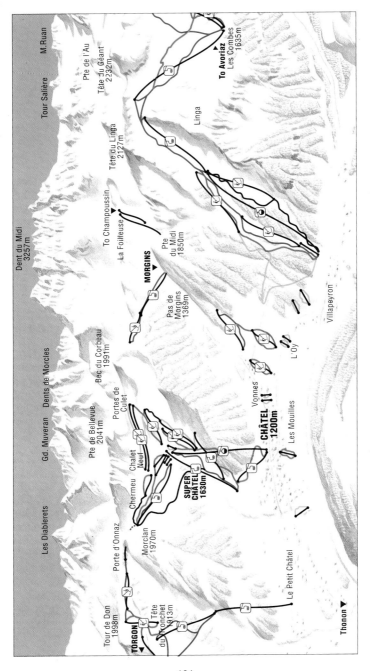

Dent du Midi 3257m

Tour Salière   M.Ruan

Gd Muveran   Dents de Morcles

Les Diablerets

Tour de Don 1998m

Tête du Tronchet 1913m

TORGON ▼

Porte d'Onnaz

Morclan 1970m

Pte de Bellevue 2041m

Bec du Corbeau 1991m

Portes de Culet

Chermeu

Chalet Neuf

SUPER CHÂTEL 1630m

Pas de Morgins 1369m

MORGINS

La Foilleuse

To Champoussin ▼

Pte du Midi 1850m

Tête du Linga 2127m

Linga

Pte de l'Au

Tête du Géant 2232m

To Avoriaz
Les Combes 1635m

Vonnes

CHÂTEL 1200m

Les Mouilles

L'Oy

Villapeyron

Le Petit Châtel

Thonon ▼

possible to make a leisurely start from Châtel, explore Avoriaz and Les Crosets, and return to Châtel within three hours. The Wall is the most notorious run in the area; a sign at the top warns that it is to be attempted only by experts, yet it is usually crowded with intermediates. Certainly the initial angle of descent is such that you cannot see what lies ahead. After the first 50m the run flattens out considerably, though the moguls tend to be poorly cut by the high intermediate traffic. However, there are plenty of other equally challenging pistes in the region, including the World Cup run from Le Plan Brazy above Avoriaz all the way down to Les Prodains.

Off-piste
The best powder runs are to be found within easy reach of the piste above Châtel and Avoriaz on both sides of the Swiss border. After a fresh snowfall various itineraries parallel to The Wall can be exhilarating. The area is prone to considerable avalanche danger, and the services of a qualified guide are essential. Other off-piste opportunities include the Crêtes, Le Fornet and La Suisse. Mont Blanc Helicopters can be booked to pick you up from the end of an off-piste trip and return you to Avoriaz (see *Heli-skiing*).

Snowboarders
Avoriaz was the first resort in Europe to appreciate the importance of snowboarding when the sport was in the early stages of development. It was also the first (in 1993) to build a half-pipe and is now recognised as one of the world's major snowboarding centres. The funpark has recently been improved with the addition of a permanent boardercross course and a separate section with gaps, tables and rails. The latest innovation is a micro-park for children with mini boardercross and smaller obstacles. For alpine riders, the Arare piste is hard to beat for high-speed carving. Les Crosets, Morgins, Super-Châtel, Torgon and Les Gets all have funparks.

Tuition and guiding
Avoriaz has the International Ski School (ESI) and the French Ski School (ESF). The ESF in Morzine is recommended for its 'friendly instructors'. However, some reporters observed that classes in Avoriaz had between 14 and 20 pupils each, many of them nearer the upper figure. Both the ESF and ESI also teach snowboarding, in healthy competition with Emery Snowboard School, Free Ride and the much-praised British Alpine Ski and Snowboarding School. The latter, in both Morzine and Avoriaz, was set up by a couple of BASI instructors, and was described by one reporter as 'everything the ESF is not – small classes and good technical advice in one's mother tongue'. You need to book well in advance, especially during school holidays. Ski Snowboard et Aventures is Morzine's specialist board school, while Bureau de la Montagne and Maison de la Montagne are the resort's mountain guiding companies.

Mountain restaurants

The Portes du Soleil has a mixed bag of eateries, ranging from over-crowded self-services to wonderful old huts off the beaten track. Prices are generally high on both sides of the border, and there are simply not enough restaurants. Coquoz at Planachaux has a circular open fire and offers wonderful local Swiss specialities. Les Lindarets, the hamlet just north of Avoriaz, has the best concentration of eating-places with competitive prices. La Chanterelle at the foot of the Chéry Nord chair is warmly recommended. La Cabushe near Le Ranfoilly is 'simple, but brilliant value'. Plan Dranse is said to be 'a great find – this is where the locals eat, so prices must be fair'.

Les Prodains, at the bottom of the Vuarnet run from Avoriaz, is much praised, not least for its reasonable prices. The two restaurants at the top of Le Pleney are said to be 'always busy, but the wait is worth it'. The one at the top of the Super-Morzine gondola receives compliments for its 'appetising food and prices, and spectacular view'. The Perdrix Blanche at Pré-la-Joux is good value and recommended for its warm atmosphere. Chez Gaby in Champoussin is highly praised. Le Corbeau above Morgins is said to be rustic, with reasonable prices.

Accommodation

The accommodation in Avoriaz is nearly all in apartment blocks, which vary in quality according to their age. The Alpage 1 apartments are said to be 'clean, but fairly cramped,' La Falaise units are similarly well-scrubbed but 'seriously short of storage space', and La Thuya apart-ments are 'rather dilapidated'. In general, it is prudent to halve the number of advertised bed spaces. The two hotels are Les Dromonts and La Falaise. Location within the resort is of no significance for skiing purposes, although some of the village streets, which are also pistes, may prove difficult for novices.

Morzine has a plentiful supply of hotels in each price bracket; most are chalet-style and none is luxurious. In the central area, Les Airelles is one of the more comfortable, while Hotel Fleur des Neiges is a reasonable two-star built in chalet style. Hotel Le Tremplin ('delightful family-run establishment') is on the edge of the piste with a grandstand view of the night-skiing and -snowboarding arena. We continue to receive rave reports of the Hotel Dahu ('excellent and friendly, with lovely rooms').

Eating in and out

Avoriaz has a choice of about 30 restaurants, most of which are rather overpriced. Les Intrets is a favourite with reporters for its raclette, fondue and pierrade. Le Petit Vatel serves rustic fare. The Bistro oppos-ite the Children's Village is 'good, but expensive'. Les Fontaines Blanches is 'reasonably priced, with a wide range of excellent food'. Le Savoyard has plenty of local flavour.

In Morzine, the Neige Roc at Les Prodains and Le Tremplin are also highly rated by reporters. L'Etale serves regional specialities in a 'wonderful, authentic mountain atmosphere'. La Chamade and La Grange are both highly rated for a special night out.

Après-ski

The Place in Avoriaz has live, non-French music and an 'excellent atmosphere'. Les Ruches and Le Choucas are hangouts for riders; the latter has live music and is usually not too crowded. Pub Le Tavaillon was described by one reporter as 'the nerve centre of Avoriaz'. The nightclubs are said to be generally overpriced and empty, except on striptease nights, when audience participation is invited. Le Festival and Midnight Express discos both have entrance fees. Midnight Express has a free 'bucking bronco'.

Morzine abounds with civilised tea-rooms and bars. Inside the Wallington complex are a bowling alley, pool hall, bar and disco. L'Opéra and Le Paradis de Laury's are the nightclubs.

Childcare

Le Village des Enfants/Le Village Snowboard in Avoriaz has a justified reputation as one of the better childcare establishments in France. Children from three years old are taught in the centre of the village, using methods developed by the celebrated French ski champion Annie Famose. Younger non-skiing children are looked after in Les P'tits Loups day nursery of which we have good reports.

Morzine's L'Outa crèche takes infants from two months to six years. Pingouins Malins is new for 2001 and provides daycare for children from four to twelve years with ski lessons.

Linked or nearby resorts

Abondance
top 1,800m (5,906ft) bottom 930m (3,050ft)

This tiny, historic village lies 7km from **La Chapelle d'Abondance** and is not linked into the main Portes du Soleil system. A bus service runs from Châtel and La Chapelle d'Abondance. It has its own small ski area on the slopes beneath the Col de l'Ecuelle, served by a gondola and a series of drags.

TOURIST INFORMATION
Tel 33 450 73 02 90
Fax 33 450 73 04 76
Email info@vald'abondance.com
Web site www.vald'abondance.com

Champéry
top 2,350m (7,708ft) bottom 1,053m (3,455ft)

This traditional Swiss village is set in dramatic surroundings at the foot of the Dents du Midi. The one-way main street is lined with attractive wooden chalets, hotels, shops and restaurants. The 125-person cable-car up to Planachaux is on the hill down to the valley road that skirts the village; the lift is served by a free minibus. Both Swiss Ski School and Freeride Company give snowboarding lessons.

Champéry's accommodation includes two long-established hotels, Hotel Suisse Golden Tulip and Hotel de Champéry, which are comfortable and welcoming. Auberge du Grand-Paradis and Hotel du Nord are also recommended. Hotel la Rose des Alpes offers value for money.

One of the best restaurants in the area, the Grand-Paradis, is 2km outside the village at the foot of the slopes and is reached by bus from Champéry. It has an atmospheric, wood-panelled interior with an open fire. Restaurant de Nord and Restaurant le Centre both offer traditional Swiss specialities, while Le Farinet serves Tex-Mex and Les Pervenches Asian specialities. Le Farinet has live music twice a week, and the other bars are Coquoz, Le Gueullhi and the Cantine des Rives. The comprehenive sports centre boasts indoor and outdoor ice-rinks, swimming-pools and a fitness centre.

Champéry has a gentle nursery slope with a simple rope-tow right in the middle of the village; snow permitting, this provides an ideal beginners' area for small children. The ESS mini-club takes children for the whole day.

TOURIST INFORMATION
Tel 41 24 479 20 20
Fax 41 24 479 20 21
Email champery-ch@portesdusoleil.com
Web site www.champery.ch

Champoussin
top 2,350m (7,708ft) bottom 1,580m (5,182ft)

Champoussin is a mini-resort of new, rustic-style buildings that are almost all apartments ('highly recommended'), and a main hotel, the Résidence Royal Alpage Club ('better value than it used to be'). The hotel has a sauna, swimming-pool, games room and disco, and runs its own kindergarten and mini-club. Après-ski is limited to the hotel and two restaurants: Le Poussin bar/restaurant and Chez Gaby, which runs a snowcat service from the village in the evening. Floodlit skiing takes place here on Wednesday evenings, and the thermal baths 10km away at **Val d'Iliez** are worth a visit.

The small ski school does not receive impressive ratings, and reporters have mixed views on the resort: 'great for family holidays, but singles, extreme skiers and snowboarders should look elsewhere,' and, 'Champoussin is so small and remote that just looking at it could give you cabin fever'.

TOURIST INFORMATION
Tel 41 24 476 83 00
Fax 41 24 476 83 01
Email hotel.royal.alpage@portesdusoleil.com

La Chapelle d'Abondance
top 1,700m (5,577ft) bottom 1,010m (3,313ft)

This old farming community, 6km down the valley from Châtel, straddles both sides of the road without any defined centre. On one side, two long chairs take you up to Crêt Béni at 1,650m, from where a series of drags serve a choice of mainly easy runs through the pine forest. On the other side of the road a gondola and a chair-lift link into Torgon and Châtel. Hotels Les Cornettes du Bis and the Alti Mille both have swimming-pools and fitness centres.

TOURIST INFORMATION
Tel 33 450 73 51 41
Fax 33 450 73 56 04
Email ot-chapelle@portesdusoleil.com
Web site www.portesdusoleil.com\station\chapelle

Châtel
top 2,350m (7,708ft) bottom 1,200m (3,936ft)

Châtel is still a pleasant farming village, but caring for livestock and tilling the fields takes a poor second place to the more lucrative business of tourism. Unfortunately, precious little planning has gone into the development of the village, which is a huge, ungainly straggle of buildings up towards the Morgins Pass and Switzerland, and down the hillside and along the valley towards the Linga lift and the connection with Avoriaz. The valley lifts are linked by free ski buses, which are crowded in the afternoon and have to fight their way through a village centre that is often choked with traffic. The diffuse nature of the resort makes a car an advantage for reaching the out-of-town lift stations and for travel to the other unlinked resorts on the circuit.

Châtel has a wide choice of hotels, most of them chalet-style and simple. Location is important and it is well worth checking out the distance from a main lift before booking. Hotel Fleur de Neige is praised for the quality of its food: 'more like a restaurant with rooms than a hotel'. The Flèche d'Or apartments are 'clean and comfortable, provided you halve the recommended occupancy figure'. Hotel Les Rhododendrons is 'perfectly located and typically French'.

Restaurants include Le Monchu on the Swiss border ('absolutely the best food and atmosphere in town'), La Bonne Ménagère, which is popular, and the Vieux Four ('slow service but food is good, basic French'). The resort has a bowling alley and an ice-rink, but otherwise the after-slopes entertainment is limited to a handful of bars including the popular Tunnel, L'Isba and Snowboard Café.

The ESF at Châtel has a solid reputation, although some reporters experienced classes of up to 20 pupils. Ecole de Ski Francis Sports is an alternative ski school, while Virages Snoways specialises in off-piste. Les Mouflets cares for children from ten months to six years. Le Village des Marmottons is for children from two to eight years old, with a mixture of games and skiing for the older ones. Ian and Jane

Skiing facts: Avoriaz

TOURIST INFORMATION
Place Central, F-74110 Avoriaz
Tel 33 450 74 02 11
Fax 33 450 74 18 25
Email info@avoriazski
Web site www.avoriazski.com

THE RESORT
By road Calais 902km
By rail Thonon les Bains 43km, Cluses 40km
Airport transfer Geneva 2hrs
Visitor beds 16,500
Transport traffic-free resort

THE SKIING
Linked or nearby resorts Abondance (n), Champéry (I), Champoussin (I), La Chapelle d'Abondance (I), Châtel (I), Les Crosets (I), Les Gets (I), Montriond (I), Morgins (I), Morzine (I), St-Jean d'Aulps/La Grande Terche (n), Torgon (I)
Number of lifts 39 in Avoriaz, 212 in Portes du Soleil
Total of trails/pistes Avoriaz 150km (8% beginner, 55% easy, 27% intermediate, 10% difficult), 650km in Portes du Soleil
Nursery slopes 4

LIFT PASSES
Area pass Portes du Soleil (covers 12 resorts) 998FF for 6 days
Beginners 485FF for 6 days

Pensioners 60yrs and over, 798FF for 6 days
Credit cards yes

TUITION
Adults British Alpine Ski/Snowboarding School tel: (01237) 451099 (UK), ESF tel: 450 74 05 65, ESI tel: 450 74 02 18
Snowboarding as ski schools, Emery Snowboard School tel: 450 74 12 64, Free Ride tel: 450 74 00 36
Other courses carving, cross-country, telemark
Guiding Mont Blanc Helicopters tel: 450 74 22 44

CHILDREN
Lift pass 5–16yrs, Portes du Soleil 669FF for 6 days
Ski & board school as adults, Le Village Snowboard tel: 450 74 04 46
Kindergarten (ski) Le Village des Enfants tel: 450 74 04 46, (non-ski) Les P'tits Loups tel: 450 74 00 38

OTHER SPORTS
Hang-gliding, parapente, skating, sleigh rides, snowmobiling, squash, swimming

FOOD AND DRINK PRICES
Coffee 8FF, glass of wine 20FF, small beer 12–16FF, soft drink 18FF, dish of the day 70FF

McGarry's ski courses (see *Skiing by numbers*) in the resort are highly rated by reporters.

TOURIST INFORMATION
Tel 33 450 73 22 44
Fax 33 450 73 22 87
Email touristoffice@chatel.com
Web site www.chatel.com

Les Crosets
top 2,350m (7,708ft) bottom 1,660m (5,445ft)

Les Crosets is a tiny ski station in the heart of the open slopes on the Swiss side of the Portes du Soleil. It is popular with riders and has its own snowboard school as well as a funpark. The hamlet is fairly functional and, apart from a visit to the Sundance Saloon disco, has no obvious appeal to anyone but serious snow-users who want an early night. However, four of the slopes are floodlit for skiing and riding until 11pm each Wednesday and Saturday. Hotel Télécabine is simple, British-run and serves excellent food. Half a dozen eateries on the piste are also open in the evening. The ESS has a branch here, and there is also a mini-club.

TOURIST INFORMATION
Tel 41 24 477 2077
Fax 41 24 477 3773
Email info@lescrosets.com
Web site www.lescrosets.com

Les Gets
top 2,350m (7,708ft) bottom 1,175m (3,854ft)

Les Gets is situated on a low mountain pass 6km from Morzine, with lifts and pistes on both sides and good nursery slopes on the edge of the village and higher up at Les Chavannes (1,490m), which is reached by road or gondola. This attractive village, an old farming community that has expanded almost out of recognition, has a large and under-used floodlit piste. Parts of the ski area and many of the mountain restaurants are accessible on foot. Les Gets is connected by ski-lifts to Morzine.

Les Gets has three ski schools, and we have generally favourable reports of them all. Ski Plus specialises in 'excellent private tuition in English'. The British Alpine Ski/Snowboarding School has a separate branch in Les Gets. The Ile des Enfants kindergarten ('quite Gallic but lots of fun, they don't take the skiing too seriously') receives better comments than the ESF. The non-ski Bébé Club takes children from three months old.

Much of the accommodation is in chalets. Hotel Ours Blanc is 'comfortable, with good service, and we would go back there again'. Hotel Régina is well placed in the quieter part of the village. The limited choice of restaurants include Le Tyrol for '*châteaubriand* cooked on an open fire' and pizzas. Most of the nightlife centres around hotel bars and the two discos. The English-run Pring's is popular.

TOURIST INFORMATION
Tel 33 450 75 80 80
Fax 33 450 79 76 90
Email lesgets@lesgets.com
Web site www.lesgets.com

Skiing facts: Morzine

TOURIST INFORMATION
BP 23 Place de la Crusaz, F-74110 Morzine
Tel 33 450 74 72 72
Fax 33 450 79 03 48
Email touristoffice@morzine.com
Web site www.morzine-avoriaz.com

THE RESORT
By road Calais 888km
By rail Cluses or Thonon les Bains 30km
Airport transfer Geneva 1½hrs
Visitor beds 16,000
Transport free bus service runs between Morzine and Les Prodains

THE SKIING
Linked or nearby resorts *as Avoriaz*
Number of lifts 39 in Morzine, 212 in Portes du Soleil
Total of trails/pistes Morzine 140km (10% beginner, 44% easy, 36% intermediate, 10% difficult), 650km in Portes du Soleil
Nursery slopes 6 lifts

LIFT PASSES
Area pass Portes du Soleil (covers 12 resorts) 998FF for 6 days
Beginners special prices for some lifts
Pensioners 798FF for six days
Credit cards yes

TUITION
Adults ESF tel: 450 79 13 13, British Alpine Ski/Snowboarding School Morzine tel: (014855) 72596 (UK)
Snowboarding as ski schools, Ski Snowboard et Aventures tel: 450 79 05 16
Other courses cross-country, race-training, Skwal, telemark
Guiding Bureau de la Montagne tel: 450 79 03 55, Maison de la Montagne tel: 450 75 96 65

CHILDREN
Lift pass 5–16yrs, Portes du Soleil 669FF for 6 days
Ski & board school as adults
Kindergarten (non-ski) L'Outa tel: 450 79 26 00, (ski/non-ski) Pingouins Malins tel: 450 79 13 13

OTHER SPORTS
Cascade climbing, climbing wall, curling, dog-sledding, hang-gliding, heli-skiing, ice-hockey, ice-snorkelling, night-skiing/night-riding, parapente, skating, ski-jumping, snowshoeing, swimming

FOOD AND DRINK PRICES
Coffee 7FF, glass of wine 15FF, small beer 14FF, soft drink 15FF, dish of the day 65FF

Montriond
top 2,350m (7,708ft) bottom 950m (3,116ft)
Montriond is little more than a suburb of Morzine, with no discernible centre and a number of simple, reasonably priced hotels. A bus links it to the resort's gondola, which provides direct access to the main lifts.

TOURIST INFORMATION
Tel 33 450 79 12 81
Fax 33 450 79 04 06
Email ot.montriond@valleedaulps.com

Morgins
top 2,000m (7,710ft) bottom 1,350m (4,428ft)

Morgins is a few kilometres from Châtel and is the border post with Switzerland. It is a relaxed, residential resort spread across a broad valley, but it lacks any real character and, as the best skiing is elsewhere, it is not the ideal base for keen snow-users. A car is useful for visiting other resorts in the region, but traffic is a problem.

Most of the accommodation is in chalets and apartments. Pension de Morgins is 'clean and comfortable'. The resort has a crèche, of which we have positive reports. The large nursery slope in the centre of the village is prone to overcrowding. Après-ski is limited to a skating-rink, indoor tennis and a few bars. Hotel Bellevue's disco provides lively late-night entertainment.

TOURIST INFORMATION
Tel 41 24 477 2361
Fax 41 24 477 3708
Email touristoffice@morgins.com
Web site www.morgins.ch

St-Jean d'Aulps/La Grande Terche
top 1,800m (5,906ft) bottom 900m (2,952ft)

St-Jean is the village, and La Grande Terche is the name given to a tiny development of apartments at the foot of the lifts, which are a 15-minute drive from Morzine. The skiing is not fully linked into the system but it is surprisingly good and well worth a visit if you are staying elsewhere in the area. It has a combined ski area with **Bellevaux**.

TOURIST INFORMATION
Tel 33 450 79 65 09
Fax 33 450 79 67 95
Email ot-saintjean@valleedaulps.com

Torgon
top 2,350m (7,708ft) bottom 1,100m (3,608ft)

Torgon is perched above the Rhône close to Lac Léman on the outer edge of the Portes du Soleil. Although it is in Switzerland, it is linked in one direction with La Chapelle d'Abondance and in the other with Châtel, both of which are in France. The distinctive and none-too-pleasing A-frame architecture contains comfortable apartments. There is little else to do here but ski. The Jardin des Neiges kindergarten takes children from three years of age.

TOURIST INFORMATION
Tel 41 24 481 3131
Fax 41 24 481 4620
Email tourisme@torgon.ch
Web site www.torgon.ch

Risoul 1850

ALTITUDE 1,850m (6,068ft)

Beginners ✱✱✱ Intermediates ✱✱ Snowboarders ✱✱✱

Although increasing in popularity, Risoul 1850 is still an underrated purpose-built resort. It has extensive and convenient family skiing and a reputation for reliable late-season snow. The main reason for its low-profile image is its remoteness from any international airport. It is situated at least three-and-a-half hours' drive from Turin, Lyon, Grenoble or Marseilles. It was first planned as a ski resort back in the 1930s but did not actually come into being until 1971. Its ski area of 56 lifts and 180km of pistes is shared with neighbouring **Vars 1850** and is known as the Domaine de la Forêt Blanche.

✔ Tree-level skiing
✔ Value-for-money
✔ Skiing convenience
✔ Suitable for families
✔ Lack of queues
✔ Good snow record
✔ Late-season skiing
✘ Long airport transfer
✘ Limited chalet and hotel accommodation
✘ Lack of restaurants
✘ No activities for non-skiers

Its difficult location means that the area is free of weekend over-crowding. The resort's clientèle is both family- and budget-oriented. Eastern European visitors are now arriving by the bus-load, supplanting the British among the 30 per cent of skiers who are not French. Risoul is the best snowboarding centre in France according to some riders.

Risoul has attractive wood-and-stone apartment complexes, but its small downtown section is blighted by illegally parked cars, a lack of proper pavements and a ghastly profusion of billboards. Reporters were impressed by the resort's convenience: 'the least amount of walking and the most amount of skiing we have ever done in the Alps'.

On the snow
top 2,750m (9,020ft) bottom 1,650m (5,412ft)

Risoul is primarily a beginner and intermediate resort, although there are also off-piste opportunities. Lifts fan out from the village base, but the lift system still has a predominance of drag-lifts and is in need of upgrading. The new Plate de la Nonne quad-chair makes the journey over to Vars 1850 much easier than it used to be. The skiing looks simple and most of it is, although experts can find some challenging terrain. Risoul offers three slalom race-training areas, a mogul-training course and a speed-skiing piste.

Beginners

It is possible to ski from Risoul to Vars 1850 and back on blue (easy) runs. The green (beginner) runs, with a children's park and snow-making at the bottom of Risoul, are some of the most attractive in Europe. The French Ski School (ESF) beginner area has its own bucket-lift. Two chair-lifts from Risoul give access to easy terrain.

Intermediates

A number of readers have complained that the resort has arbitrarily changed some of its blue runs to red (intermediate) runs. The official explanation is that these runs can be exactingly narrow for beginners. However, more cynical observers suggest that Risoul wants to upgrade its 'too easy' image. Most interesting are the ridge-line run from Risoul's high point, Crête de Chabrières, and the return to the village from the liaisons on Razis, which requires a hike back up from below the car park. Virtually unskied are the long, wide, mogul-free reds into **Vars-Sainte-Marie**.

Advanced

There are only eight black (difficult) runs, which readers say are graded thus more for their lack of grooming than their gradient.

Off-piste

Risoul has neither glaciers nor couloirs but it does have a lot of gladed powder skiing in fresh snow conditions. In the back bowl by Valbelle is a natural half-pipe shared by skiers and boarders. It is possible, given enough snow and the taxi fare home, to ski below the resort to the old village of Risoul. The area to the skier's left of the Chardon chair also offers reasonable challenges.

WHAT'S NEW
Plate de la Nonne quad-chair

Snowboarders

The Surfland funpark on L'Homme de Pierre is regularly used for boardercross competitions. It has a Renault 16 to jump over, several quarter-pipes, an excellent half-pipe, and numerous obstacles. Close to Surfland is a nursery slope that is ideal for beginner riders. Freeriders will be spoilt for choice with the resort's powder bowls.

Tuition and guiding

The ESF claims an average of 10 skiers per class, but reporters have spotted groups of 15 and complain that not enough instructors are available during peak holiday periods. The rival International Ski School (ESI) guarantees no more than eight pupils per class.

Mountain restaurants

If skiing with a sandwich is ever to make a comeback it may be in Risoul, where the eating places are cheap enough but seriously lacking

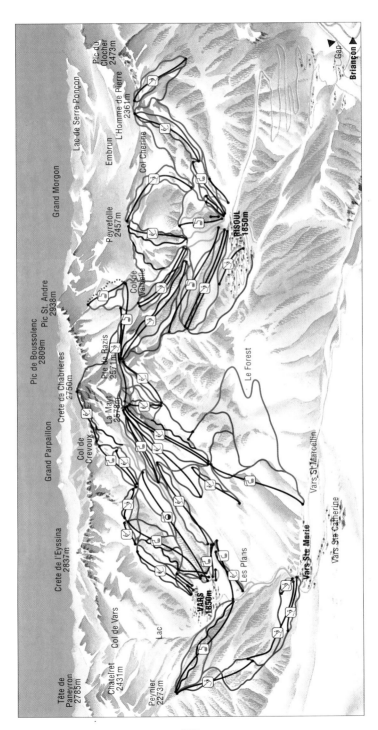

in both cuisine and character. Barjo at the bottom of the Mayt chair on the Vars 1850 side offers overnight accommodation and food. Vallon and Valbelle are small, spaghetti and *steak-frites* joints. Vars L'Horizon at the top of the Sainte-Marie chair-lift is 'typically French'. Le Tétras is new.

Accommodation
The two-star Le Chardon Bleu is the only hotel in Risoul 1850. Some chalet accommodation is available, but most visitors opt for self-catering apartments. Les Mélèzes is functional but seriously lacking in space. One reporter complained that: 'the corridors and stairs were filthy. The apartments have nice balconies but they overlook a communal area blowing with litter and contaminated by half-eaten pizzas'. Le Belvédère is bigger and better. There is no shuttle bus.

Eating in and out
Most of the eateries are unambitious in price as well as menu. Cheap and plentiful are the burgers and *frites* at Snack Attack and Chez Robert. La Dalle en Pente and Le Cesier Snowboard Café have low prices and frequent special offers. Le Phil Burger has fast food, a pool table and video games. L'Assiette Gourmande is the closest thing to gourmet cuisine. At La Cherine under the Mélèzes apartments 'you sit at long tables and muck in – very good value'.

Après-ski
The Grotte du Yeti is the young person's haunt for happy hour after the lifts close. La Dalle en Pente has live bands and is open until 2am. Readers commented that late-night noise in the resort is a serious problem: 'if you got to sleep before 2am you were woken up by revellers trying to find their way home. This contradicts the resort's family image'. Risoul has a two-screen cinema and a skating-rink but no swimming-pool. An unusual sport available here is 'ruissiling' – hiking with crampons and ice axes on frozen rivers.

Childcare
Les Pitchouns crèche is conveniently located above the ESF and takes children from six months to six years of age. A packed lunch must be provided if children are to be left all day. Both the ESF and ESI have children's learning areas.

Linked or nearby resorts
Vars 1850
top 2,750m (9,020ft) bottom 1,850m (6,068ft)
Vars 1850, with its 18,000 beds, is larger, less attractive and also less welcoming to the British than Risoul 1850. No tour operators currently come here. The old village is linked by drag-lift to the modern station,

Skiing facts: Risoul 1850

TOURIST INFORMATION
Risoul 1850, F-05600, Hautes-Alpes
Tel 33 492 46 02 60
Fax 33 492 46 01 23
Email o.t.risoul@wanadoo.fr
Web site www.risoul.com

THE RESORT
By road Calais 1,024km
By rail Montdauphin 30 mins,
bus connection with Risoul
Airport transfer Grenoble 3½hrs,
Marseilles 3½hrs
Visitor beds 17,300

THE SKIING
Linked or nearby resorts Vars 1850 (I),
Vars-Sainte-Marie (I)
Number of lifts 56 in the Forêt Blanche
area
Total of trails/pistes 180km (17% easy,
37% intermediate, 34% difficult,
12% very difficult)
Nursery slopes 10 lifts

LIFT PASSES
Area pass Forêt Blanche (covers Risoul
and Vars) 820FF for 6 days
Beginners 3 free lifts

Pensioners 65yrs and over, 700FF for 6
days. Free for 70yrs and over
Credit cards yes

TUITION
Adults ESF tel: 492 46 19 22,
ESI tel: 492 46 20 83
Snowboarding as ski schools
Other courses cross-country, monoski,
skwal, slalom, telemark
Guiding through ski schools

CHILDREN
Lift pass 5–11yrs, 700FF for 6 days,
free for 5yrs and under
Ski & board school as adults
Kindergarten (ski) ESF Mini-Club
tel: 492 46 19 22, ESI tel: 492 46 20 83,
(non-ski) Les Pitchouns Garderie
tel: 492 46 02 60

OTHER SPORTS
Motor neiges, parapente, ruissiling,
skating, snowmobiling, snowshoeing

FOOD AND DRINK PRICES
Coffee 7–8FF, glass of wine 10FF,
small beer 15–18FF, soft drink 15FF,
dish of the day 55–90FF

but you have to hike across town to access the Vars gondola and high-speed chair back to Risoul 1850. The local ESF offers alpine skiing and snowboarding courses, as well as carving, cross-country, race camps, snowblading and telemark. The baby club takes children from six months old and the ski school accepts children from four years of age. Other activities include dog-sledding, parapente, skating, snowshoeing, snowmobiling, and a museum of the history of speed skiing.

TOURIST INFORMATION
Tel 33 492 46 51 31
Fax 33 492 46 56 54
Email vars.ot@pacwan.fr
Web site www.vars-ski.com

Serre Chevalier/Briançon

ALTITUDE 1,200–1,500m (3,936–4,920ft)

Beginners ✱✱ Intermediates ✱✱✱ Advanced ✱✱ Snowboarders ✱✱✱

Serre Chevalier is not a resort in its own right, but the collective name for over a dozen villages and hamlets that line the main valley road between the Col du Lautaret and the ancient garrison town of **Briançon**. 'The most beautiful snow under the sun' is its current adver-tising slogan, but for the past two seasons the resort has been blighted by too much sun and a near-disastrous lack of natural snow cover that has led a number of tour operators seriously to consider their future here.

- ✔ Large linked ski area
- ✔ Good artificial snow cover
- ✔ Varied off-piste
- ✔ Tree-level skiing
- ✔ Recommended for families
- ✔ Value-for-money
- ✘ Heavy traffic along main highway
- ✘ Scattered resort
- ✘ Unreliable resort-level snow

Chantemerle (Serre Chevalier 1350) is the closest village to Briançon. **Villeneuve/Le Bez** (marketed as Serre Chevalier 1400) is the most central and lively, and **Monêtier-Les-Bains** (Serre Chevalier 1500) is a pretty spa village that attracts the fewest tourists. Briançon is a pleasant old garrison town in a beautiful setting with the added attraction of hilltop fortifications. The town is directly linked by gondola to the substantial ski area.

A car is a definite asset for taking advantage of the off-slope facilities in the various conurbations. The Grande Serre Chevalier lift pass covers five nearby resorts, including **Montgenèvre** in the extensive Milky Way area, 15 minutes down the road. The skiing is for all standards but is particularly well suited to the adept intermediate, who will enjoy the 250km of cruising and the well-linked, albeit rather old-fashioned, lift system.

On the snow
top 2,800m (9,184ft) bottom 1,200m (3,936ft)

The three main mountain access points are by gondola and cable-car from Villeneuve/Le Bez, Chantemerle and Briançon, with most of the lifts and pistes concentrated in the area above Villeneuve and Chantemerle. The Monêtier section also has its own lifts starting from the base and is the most appealing in the whole area, although the least accessible. There is a floodlit piste for night-skiing at Briançon. The bus system links all the villages but is 'hopelessly inadequate'. The area boasts efficient hands-free lift passes.

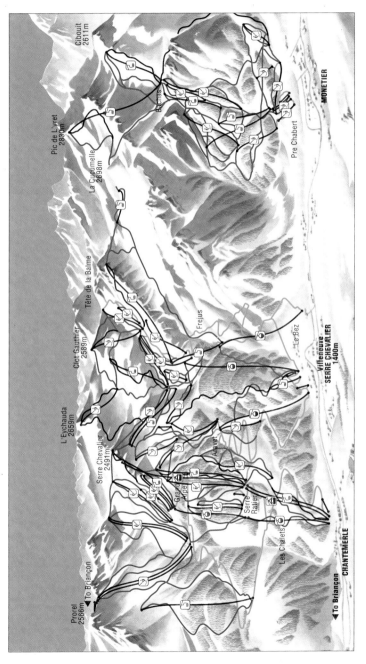

Cibouit 2611m
Pic de Lyret 2830m
La Cucumelle 2698m
Tête de la Balme
Clot Gauthier 2589m
L'Eychauda 2659m
Serre Chevalier 2491m
Prorel 2566m
Briançon
Fréjus
Aravet
Grand Alpe
Serre Ratier
Les Chalets
Pre Chabert
le Bez
MONETIER
Villeneuve
SERRE CHEVALIER 1400m
CHANTEMERLE
To Briançon

Beginners

Novice snow-users are well catered for with ski schools in all the main villages. The Grand Alpe section above Chantemerle has a decent but sometimes busy beginners' area, and Briançon has its own nursery slopes at the gondola mid-station. There are commendable starter slopes at Monêtier and Villeneuve with beginner lifts at their bases. A long green (beginner) run goes from Col Méa down to Villeneuve/Le Bez.

Intermediates

As one reporter noted, 'for an average skier there are few better places'. Monêtier has some enjoyable red (intermediate) pistes through the woods. The Vallon de la Cucumelle above Fréjus is a recommended red: 'varied from being wide and treeless at the top to narrow and mogulled in a few places'. From Bachas at 2,180m down to the valley at Monêtier there is a wide choice of intermediate runs through the woods. Le Bois is a short but fun red piste through the trees.

Advanced

Overall, Monêtier is the prime area of the mountain for advanced skiers, although the high and exposed link with Villeneuve can sometimes be closed. Isolée is an exciting black (difficult) run, which starts on the ridge from L'Eychauda at 2,659m and plunges down towards Echaillon. Tabuc is a long black run through the woods with a couple of steep and narrow pitches. The Casse du Boeuf, a sweeping ridge through the trees back to Villeneuve, is, according to one reporter, 'the best black run we have ever skied'.

> **WHAT'S NEW**
>
> Funpark at Villeneuve

Off-piste

The Fréjus–Echaillon section above Villeneuve provides some fine runs for experienced skiers, with short and unprepared trails beneath the mountain crest. The Yret chair gives easy access to some off-piste runs, including the testing face under the lift, which has a gradient of 35 degrees at its steepest point and often becomes mogulled.

Snowboarders

Many riders consider this to be the best resort in France. Freeriders benefit from the great terrain with its mixture of trees, gullies, bowls and natural jumps. The original funpark is at the bottom of the Yret chair-lift and a new one at Villeneuve contains half- and quarter-pipes. Snowboarders are also attracted by the resort's good-value accommodation and nightlife.

Tuition and guiding

We have generally favourable reports of the ESF in all the villages ('our instructor had good English and was very good humoured too') but currently no reports of the Evasion ESI school. In all, Serre Chevalier

Skiing facts: Serre Chevalier

TOURIST INFORMATION
BP 20, 05240 Serre Chevalier,
Hautes-Alpes
Tel 33 492 24 98 98
Fax 33 492 24 98 84
Email contact@ot-serrechevalier.fr
Web site www.serre-chevalier.com

THE RESORT
By road Calais 984km
By rail Briançon 6km, regular bus
service to resort
Airport Transfer Lyon 3hrs, Turin 2hrs,
Grenoble 2½hrs
Visitor beds 35,000
Transport free ski bus with lift pass

THE SKIING
Linked or nearby resorts Alpe d'Huez
(n), Briançon (l), Montgenèvre (n), La
Grave, Les Deux Alpes (n),
Puy-St-Vincent (n)
Number of lifts 74 in Grande Serre
Chevalier area
Total of trails/pistes 250km in linked
area (19% beginner, 69% intermediate,
12% difficult)
Nursery slopes 10 runs

LIFT PASSES
Area pass Grand Serre Chevalier
(covers all centres) 970FF for 6 days
including 1 day in each of Les Deux
Alpes, La Grave, Montgenèvre, Puy-St-
Vincent and Alpe d'Huez
Beginners 1 day lift pass 65FF
Pensioners 60–74yrs as children, free
for 75yrs and over
Credit cards yes

TUITION
Adults ESF (1350, 1400, 1500) tel: 492
24 17 41, Evasion ESI (1350, 1400) tel:
492 24 02 41, Montagne Aventure
(1350) tel: 492 24 05 51, Buissonnière
(1400) tel: 492 24 78 66, Mongtagne à
la Carte (1400) tel: 492 24 73 20,
Montagne et Ski (1500) tel:
492 24 46 81
Snowboarding ESF and ESI, Generation
Snow (1350) tel: 492 24 21 51
Other courses carving, cross-country,
extreme skiing, monoski, race training,
skiing for the disabled, Skwal,
snowblading, teen skiing, telemark
Guiding Compagnie des Guides de
L'Oisans tel: 492 24 75 90, Montagne à
la Carte tel: 492 24 73 20, Montagne et
Ski tel: 492 24 46 81

CHILDREN
Lift pass Grande Serre Chevalier,
5–12yrs, 690FF for 6 days
Ski & board school as adults
Kindergarten (ski/non-ski) 1350: Les
Poussins tel: 492 24 03 43, Jardin des
Neiges tel: 492 24 17 41 ,
1400: Schtroumpfs tel: 492 24 70 95,
Jardin des Neiges tel:
492 24 71 99, Kids de l'Aventure
tel: 492 24 93 10, 1500: Les Eterlous
tel: 492 24 45 75, Jardin des Neiges
492 24 42

OTHER SPORTS
Hang-gliding, horse riding, ice-climbing,
ice-driving, night-skiing, parapente,
skating, ski-joring, sleigh rides,
snowmobiling, snowshoeing

FOOD AND DRINK
Coffee 16FF, glass of wine 20FF, small
beer 15FF, soft drink 18FF, dish of the
day 45–80FF

has six ski schools, with three of them specialising in off-piste tours. First Tracks, which is run by the ESF, is a specialist snowboarding school in Villeneuve, and Generation Snow is in Chantemerle.

Mountain restaurants

The choice of eating places is small for an area of this size, and the quality is mixed. Café Soleil above Chantemerle is well-located and has 'very well-prepared food and a great atmosphere, the best *vin chaud*, and clean toilets, too'. Le Briance was also praised by one reporter. L'Echaillon is 'pretty and off the beaten track, with friendly staff', but is also said to be the 'poorest value for money'. Le Grand Alpe serves 'big portions'. Père et Noëlle has 'large, beautiful salads'.

Accommodation

Most of Serre Chevalier's accommodation is in apartments. The Altea, Vauban and Parc hotels are Briançon's three-stars, while the Pension des Ramparts is a small and simple hotel with a loyal following. Club Hotel Yeti in Briançon is said to have 'paper-thin walls, but the food is good'. The Grand Hotel at Chantemerle is 'a modest place despite its name, and excellently placed right opposite the lift station'. L'Auberge du Choucas, also in Monêtier, is known for its gourmet cuisine. Le Lièvre Blanc in Villeneuve, a British-owned two-star, is recommended.

Eating in and out

A car is useful for visiting the many restaurants along the valley. Le Petit Duc is a friendly crêperie beside the river in the lower part of Villeneuve/Le Bez. Le Petit Lard is 'rustic, French and fantastic value – but you have to book'. Pastelli in Le Bez has been criticised for its 'unimaginative food'. Le Bidule in Le Bez has a friendly ambience and specialises in fresh fish and seafood. Le Passé Simple in Briançon has a historic Vauban menu with dishes from the seventeenth century.

Après-ski

All three villages are quiet after dusk. Bars include Le Sous Sol in Villeneuve. Le Yeti and the Underground are the best late-night drinking places in Chantemerle; both have live bands and stay open until 2am. Le Frog and La Baita discos in Villeneuve come alive at weekends. Le Lièvre Blanc is a riders' hangout with weekly live music, and l'Iceberg is also rated cool by riders.

Childcare

Each village has its own crèche and children's ski school. In 1350, Les Poussins takes children from eight months, and the Jardin des Neiges from three years. In 1400, Les Schtroumpfs caters for children from six months, and the Jardin des Neiges from three years. Kids de l'Aventure, also in 1400, is for children from seven years; this includes activities such as dog-sledding. In 1500, Les Eterlous takes children aged eighteen months to six years, and the Jardin des Neiges from three years.

The Trois Vallées

ALTITUDE Méribel 1,450–1,700m (4,756–5,576ft), Courchevel 1,300–1,850m (4,264–6,068ft), La Tania 1,350m (4,429ft), Val Thorens 2,300m (7,544ft), Les Menuires 1,850m (6,068ft)

What puts the Trois Vallées ski-lengths ahead of its rivals in the super-circus league is the range and sophistication of the resorts it contains, coupled with the variety of skiing on offer. Ideal topography means that even the links between each valley are serious runs in their own right. Its critics claim that 90 per cent of the skiing is geared towards intermediates, but then 90 per cent of the skiers who visit the area are intermediate. However, the Trois Vallées still provides more than adequate scope for those of greater or lesser ability. This substantial chunk of the French Alps is covered by what is considered to be the most efficient overall lift system in the world.

Collectively, it is the most popular French ski destination for the British, and the French, who rarely venture beyond their own mountains, claim, with dubious justification, that it is also the largest ski area in the world. While the true winner in this category is almost certainly the Dolomiti Superski region of Italy, the Trois Vallées comes first on the international podium for best all-rounder.

MÉRIBEL
Beginners *
Intermediates *
Advanced *
Snowboarders **
✔ Superb mountain access
✔ Large ski area
✔ Choice of luxury chalets
✔ Resort-level snow (Mottaret)
✔ Off-piste skiing
✘ Fragmented resort layout
✘ Skiing inconveniently located
✘ High prices
✘ Heavy traffic, limited parking
✘ Poor reputation of ski school
✘ Crowded pistes at peak times

At one end of this ski area, above the Bozel Valley, sits chic **Courchevel 1850**, with its less smart satellites of **Courchevel 1650**, **Courchevel 1550**, and **Le Praz**, with pleasant budget-priced **La Tania** beneath it. At the other end, the pastoral Belleville Valley is dominated by functional **Val Thorens** and the bête noire, **Les Menuires**. In the middle is cosmopolitan **Méribel**, with its British bulldog overtones. The skiing in the Trois Vallées is reached by two winding mountain roads from Moûtiers or by an under-used gondola from **Brides-les-Bains**.

A fourth valley, the Maurienne, has no road access, but the skiing is linked by lift over the Cime de Caron above Val Thorens. The small town of **St-Michel de Maurienne**, previously known only for its carved choir stalls, acts as another tourist gateway into the Trois Vallées. The area can be reached by car in two hours from Turin via the Fréjus Tunnel.

The network of cable-cars, gondolas, detachable-chairs and tows is of gargantuan proportions and improves each year. Mammoth, the largest US resort, has 28 lifts; the Trois Vallées has 200, all of them linked by a mighty 600km of prepared slopes and uncounted hectares of off-piste terrain. Méribel alone has an extraordinary 16 gondolas. Given a single week's holiday, a competent skier will barely scratch the surface; it takes an entire 20-week season based in at least two different resorts to even begin to get to grips with it.

However, the area is not without faults. The mountains are managed by an uneasy alliance of five separate lift companies, each of which looks after itself extremely well and pays lip service to its agreement with the others. As a result ski passes are checked at almost every lift.

The French regard the Trois Vallées as their premier destination. At peak holiday times all beds will be taken, but even at New Year it passes the acid test of good ski resorts: when the whole area is operational you will struggle to find serious queues anywhere on the mountain, although the main motorway pistes will inevitably be overcrowded. As one reporter comments: 'the trouble is that the lift capacity is simply too high for the runs served'.

Each resort has its own character. So many British people holiday or work in Méribel during the winter months that any attempt to order a drink in French can be met with a look of blank incomprehension. It is an expensive resort, which offers more luxury-class chalets and apartments with en-suite bathrooms than any other ski destination in Europe.

Méribel was founded by an Englishman; Colonel Peter Lindsay, a dedicated pre-war skier, built the first lift here in 1938. Amazingly, the resort has stayed faithful to his original concept of a traditional chalet village: every building has been constructed in local stone and wood in harmony with the mountain setting. Today, it has stretched with little or no long-term planning into a hotch-potch of confusingly named hamlets at different altitudes. The convenience of these hamlets for skiing, shopping and nightlife varies considerably. 'The Heart of the Trois Vallées' is Méribel's marketing slogan, but because of its diffuse layout it is devoid of a single heart and its atmosphere is muted accordingly.

Méribel Centre (1,450m) is now known generally as Méribel and is the commercial core – a one-street village with the tourist information office 'square' as its focal point. It has a number of boutiques and souvenir shops beyond the usual sports shops, and one main supermarket. The bi-weekly street market provides colour and bargains.

Méribel Mottaret (1,700–1,800m), now 28 years old, is a ski-in, ski-out satellite situated further up the valley and is also now divided into individual hamlets. The higher altitude of Mottaret ensures good snowcover and is the starting point for the cream of the skiing. The different sectors of Méribel are all connected by a regular, free bus service that runs efficiently every 20 minutes until midnight. Traffic, parking and pollution from petrol fumes remain serious problems which are not adequately addressed by the local authorities. **Brides-les-Bains**, in the valley below Méribel, is connected by a 25-minute gondola ride and serves as a budget base and useful back door into the system.

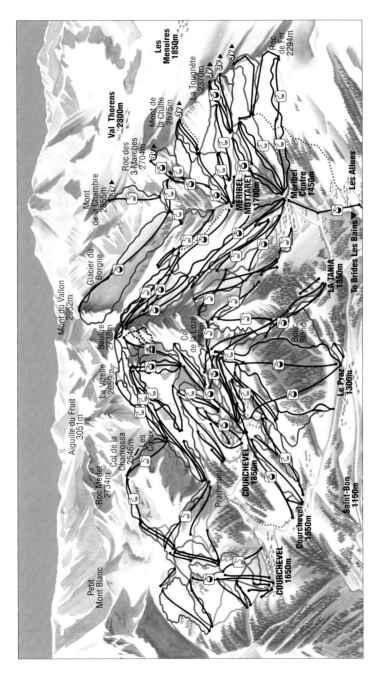

Courchevel is not one but four quite separate resorts at different altitudes, linked on piste but with nothing else in common. Before booking a holiday here it is crucial to ascertain exactly where you will be staying. **Courchevel 1850** is the international resort with the jet-set image, and most tour operators are happy for you to think their accommodation is here, even when it is in one of the lower villages. Like its stylistic rival, **Megève**, a high proportion of its designer-clad visitors come here to see and to be seen. The only exercise they take is to ferry gastronomic delights from plate to mouth at the resort's clutch of restaurants, which are among the finest in the Alps.

COURCHEVEL
Beginners ✱✱✱
Intermediates ✱✱✱
Advanced ✱✱✱
Snowboarders ✱✱
✔ Big vertical drop
✔ Long cruising runs
✔ Tree-level skiing
✔ Resort-level snow (1850)
✔ Gourmet restaurants
✔ Luxury accommodation (1850)
✔ Skiing convenience
✔ Large ski area
✔ Off-piste skiing
✘ Fragmented resort
✘ High prices (1850)
✘ Crowded pistes at peak times

A covered mall houses expensive boutiques, and a couple of supermarkets cater for the more mundane needs of self-caterers. Two chic boutiques are devoted entirely to the kind of lingerie that, in terms of money for weight, is matched only by rare postage stamps. The secluded Jardin Alpin sector is a Millionaire's Row of sumptuous chalets and shockingly expensive hotels tucked away in the trees that provide at least an illusion of privacy.

Courchevel 1650 is 200 vertical metres lower down both the mountain and the price scale. Many would argue that this is *le vrai* Courchevel, with its year-round population and atmosphere of the farming community it once was. One reporter commented: 'We are passionate about 1650 and would not go anywhere else. It is a completely separate resort and we have never felt we were missing out on the glitzier village above us'. The skiing here is both extensive and isolated from the main Trois Vallées thoroughfares; consequently, it remains wonderfully uncrowded.

Courchevel 1550 is off the beaten track and away from the heart of the skiing. It is little more than a cluster of apartment buildings and a few hotels and is popular with self-catering French families. **Le Praz** (sometimes known as **Courchevel 1300**) is a farming village at the foot of the lift system and a popular and cheap base for Courchevel's skiing ('if the road was re-routed and the snow a little more reliable, this would be a heavenly place'). Indeed, snow cover is by no means guaranteed in the hamlet, but two gondolas ('always free of queues') swiftly take you up towards the Col de la Loze or to 1850.

The modern but pleasing village of **La Tania** provides an alternative base for the price-conscious. It is a couple of kilometres by road from Le

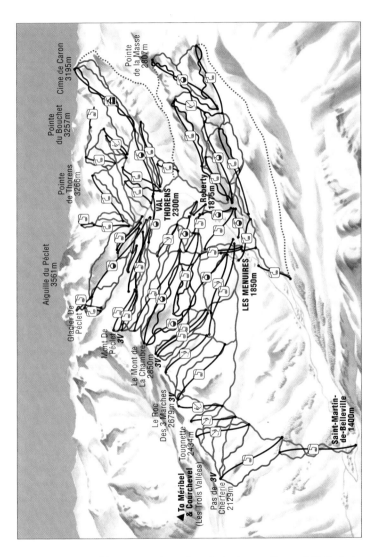

Praz and is linked by piste to Courchevel 1850 as well as to Méribel via the Col de la Loze. It was constructed as a dormitory satellite for the 1992 Albertville Olympics. The resort is served by a jumbo gondola and, despite its youth, has developed its own village atmosphere. An attractive new residential sector called Le Forêt is a collection of Scandinavian-style chalets set in the woods above the village.

At 2,300 metres, **Val Thorens** is the highest ski resort in Europe. Consequently, it is one of only a handful where you are virtually guaranteed snow at resort level over both Christmas and Easter. On a sunny day its functional, purpose-built architecture is positively attractive compared with neighbouring Les Menuires. You can ski into the centre of the car-free village, and the horseshoe of surrounding peaks is dramatic. In bad weather, this far above the tree-line, you may be forgiven for thinking you have been stranded amid the mountains of the moon; few places in the Alps are colder, and a white-out is just that ('good days, when they happen, are fantastic. But bad days don't come much worse').

Les Menuires, down the valley from Val Thorens at 1,850m, is a budget resort where the main evening entertainment for the bourgeois French, who make up its winter inhabitants, is watching the television set in their rented apartment.

It has a reputation, only partially justified, as the ugliest resort in the Alps. Certainly, the original centre, La Croisette, is a prime example of 1960s alpine architectural vandalism, but much has been done to smarten it up, and the more modern satellites of **Reberty** and **Les Bruyères** are far more appealing. You can holiday in comfort, hardly ever venturing into La Croisette. Both satellites are on the piste and have their own hotels and restaurants as well as all the shops you might need, apart from a chemist (there is one in La Croisette).

> **LA TANIA**
> Beginners ✳✳✳
> Intermediates ✳✳✳
> Advanced ✳✳✳
> Snowboarders ✳✳
> ✔ Skiing convenience
> ✔ Large ski area
> ✔ Large choice of chalet accommodation
> ✔ Reasonable prices for a Trois Vallées resort
> ✘ Uncertain resort snow cover

On the snow
top 3,300m (10,825ft) bottom 1,300m (4,264ft)

Each resort has its own large ski area, which is covered by a single-valley local pass. The links between the three valleys are liable to be suspended when snow-cover is insufficient or in storm conditions. You should also note that the Trois Vallées lift map is printed back to front; **Courchevel 1650**, which appears to be the most westerly resort in the complex, is in fact the most easterly. What appear to be south-facing slopes are therefore north-facing and consequently hold the snow well.

Les Allues Valley, dominated by **Méribel** and its higher satellite of **Mottaret**, lies in the middle and provides the ideal jumping-off point for exploring the whole area. However, it does not necessarily give the easiest access to the most rewarding skiing.

Both sides of the open valley are networked with modern lifts. The western side culminates in a long skiable ridge, which separates it from the beautiful Belleville Valley and the resorts of **Val Thorens**, **Les Menuires** and **St-Martin-de-Belleville**.

The eastern side rises to the rocky 2,738-m summit of Saulire and the Col de la Loze at 2,274m. Beyond lie the Bozel Valley and Courchevel. At the head of Les Allues Valley rises Mont du Vallon (2,952m) – the most easterly of the horseshoe of 3,300-m peaks accessed from Méribel and Val Thorens – which provides some of the most scenic and demanding off-piste in the region.

The ski area extends over the back, beyond **Val Thorens** and the Cime de Caron, into the Maurienne. The red (intermediate) run of 660m vertical takes you down to the Chalet Refuge de Plan Bouchet at 2,350m, from where a fast chair-lift takes you back up to the Col de Rosaël. A gondola carries skiers and riders from Orelle (880m) in the Maurienne up to Plan Bouchet.

Beginners

Facilities for beginners are good in all the major resorts, although the sheer volume of visitors here necessitates impersonal instruction, which is not conducive to the early-learning process. The runs surrounding the altiports at both **Courchevel** and **Méribel** are excellent beginner areas with enough length to help build confidence. Both **Val Thorens** and **Les Menuires** also have dedicated learning areas as does **La Tania**. Once the basics have been conquered, the area lends itself to easy exploration. Second-week skiers will quickly find that they can cover considerable distances on green (beginner) and blue (easy) runs, an experience that greatly adds to the feeling of achievement.

Intermediates

The Trois Vallées constitutes what many skiers rightly regard as the greatest intermediate playground in the world: a seemingly endless network of moderately graded runs that provide a challenge to all levels of skier. As one reader put it: 'we have been spoilt by the Trois Vallées and now look upon most other resorts with disdain'. The Combe de Vallon is a magnificent cruise of 1,100m vertical from the top of Mont Vallon all the way down to **Méribel-Mottaret**. The Cime de Caron above **Val Thorens** is more famous for its Combe du Caron black (difficult) descent, but there is also a red intermediate variation around the shoulder, as well as the scenic Itinéraire du Lou. The blue Arondiaz trail from the top of **Courchevel 1650** back down to the resort is a great last run of the day, and its north-facing aspect usually ensures excellent snow.

Advanced

With a maximum gradient of about 38°, the couloirs of Courchevel are among the most radical black runs marked on any piste map in the world. Take the 150-person cable-car up from the Courchevel side of Saulire and exercise special care on the entry route, which can be dangerously icy. In most conditions, the runs are not as difficult as they look from below, but as one reader put it: 'Actually getting to them is a life-threatening experience'.

The Courchevel side of Saulire is the starting point for a magnificent descent of 1,400m vertical to **Le Praz**. It is tiring rather than technically difficult, apart from the black Jockeys piste on the final section, which is shaded for most of the winter and consequently icy. La Masse above Les Menuires boasts Les Enverses and the usually icy La Dame Blanche.

Off-piste

The guided off-piste opportunities are outstanding, and one of the great charms of the Trois Vallées is that after a major snowfall the best powder runs are some of the most accessible. The long runs down to Les Menuires from the Méribel ridge are exhilarating. During a heavy snowfall, the tree-lined slopes above La Tania provide some of the most enjoyable powder skiing in the whole of the Trois Vallées, yet are always under-used.

The summit of La Masse on the far side of the Belleville Valley is also the starting point for long itineraries towards St-Martin. The powder possibilities from the summit of Cime de Caron include the Vallon du Lou. Roc Merlet above Courchevel 1650 is the jump-off point for a glorious descent around the shoulder into the Avals Valley, which brings you back, after a short walk, to 1650. Mont Vallon and the Col du Fruit offer further thrills.

Snowboarders

There is a funpark above Arpasson on the Tougnete side of Mottaret and a designated snowboard area below the second Plattières station above Mottaret. At Courchevel impossibly high moguls are interspersed with steep canyons on the Verdons piste for the use of skiers as well as snowboarders. Plantrey has a funpark with an obstacle course as well as a dedicated trick space and a giant half-pipe. A third funpark has been created at Biolley.

Tuition and guiding

The sheer volume of business during the main weeks of the season inevitably turns the various ski and snowboarding schools into sausage factories. Unless you feel you benefit from the 'follow-me' type of instruction, or decide that the lift priority given to a class warrants the cost, you might do better to save your money.

The French Ski School (ESF) is an organisation whose protectionist attitude to outside competition has earned it few friends in or outside the Trois Vallées. It has no less than 550 instructors in Courchevel alone, a proportion of whom spend the low-season weeks giving the evil eye to teachers from the smaller, less Gallic-oriented schools, who continue to find work when they do not.

Magic in Motion is generally considered to be the best school in **Méribel** and also the most expensive, 'but you get what you pay for'. All instructors are said to be 'full of enthusiasm and keen to teach'. Classes are restricted to seven skiers. Ian and Susan Saunders (BASI instructors who work for the ESF in Méribel) have their own company, Ski Principles, which provides 'great instruction by sympathetic teachers'.

Ski Cocktail, the Méribel school which also has a branch in **Courchevel 1850**, is back on form after some unfavourable reports last year ('only two of us in the class. The instruction and the support were outstanding'). Supreme in Courchevel 1850, an all-British school, has a long-standing reputation but comes in for some criticism: 'I don't rate them as highly as they seem to rate themselves. When the class failed to interpret or execute instructions, the teachers could not hide their exasperation. They need to sharpen their customer focus'.

Le Ski School, another all-British newcomer that is also known as New Generation, has already established a strong following in **Courchevel 1650** after only two seasons: 'the school has expanded but manages to maintain its high standard'. Another reporter commented: 'excellent teaching from a guy who was not only a natural English speaker but a good teacher as well'.

La Tania has its own branch of the ESF as well as three independent schools: Arthur Mac Lean, Magic in Motion and Snow Ball.

If British skiers do take lessons in either **Les Menuires** or **Val Thorens**, they don't tell us. We have no reports of the ski schools apart from the ESF in either resort. Val Thorens does, however, have a good choice of schools and courses including Pros-Neige and Ski Safari Pepi Prager, both

VAL THORENS
Beginners ✶✶
Intermediates ✶✶✶
Advanced ✶✶✶
Snowboarders ✶✶
✔ Resort-level snow
✔ Long season
✔ Large ski area
✔ Glacier skiing
✔ Ski-in ski-out convenience
✔ Off-piste skiing
✘ Lack of tree-level skiing
✘ Exposed and cold in mid-winter
✘ Limited for non-skiers
✘ Lack of nightlife

of which can organise heli-skiing trips (see *Heli-skiing*). Patrick and Eric Berthon offer specialist mogul skiing courses and Gilbert Smith's international race camps take place on the glacier. It is important to note that all ski lessons in the Trois Vallées must be booked in advance during high season.

Mountain restaurants

The majority of mountain restaurants in the Trois Vallées serve bland fast food at truly shocking prices. As one reporter commented: 'all food eaten out was ridiculously expensive, beyond the point where you got annoyed and just had to laugh. Most was of reasonable quality and occasionally of a high standard'. Regular visitors tend to head down into the resorts at lunchtime, where prices are not necessarily lower, but the standard is generally higher.

Bel-Air at the top of the **Courchevel 1650** gondola, has a 'great view and is one of the best-value waiter-served restaurants in the entire Trois Vallées, but booking is essential'. Le Petit Savoyard in Courchevel 1650 is also singled out for reasonable prices. La Soucoupe above Courchevel

1850 is also praised. Chalet de Pierres above **Courchevel 1850**, with liveried waiters hovering on the edge of the piste, is a gastronomic delight, but expensive. Cap Horn, just above the Courchevel altiport, has 'acceptable gastronomic fare at horrendous prices. The fact that the menu is in three languages – French, English and Russian – says it all. Romanée-Conti 1988 at £2,000 a bottle and Beluga caviar at £1,000 a kilo makes a hole in the holiday budget'.

Le Bouc Blanc at the top of **La Tania** gondola has 'good food at acceptable (by local standards) prices but the service is abysmal'. Pub Le Ski Lodge down in La Tania offers 'the cheapest lunches in the Trois Vallées'.

Les Castors, at the foot of the Truite run in **Méribel**, is a busy place, while Roc des Trois Marches offers consistently good value. Plein Soleil at Mottaret is 'perfect for a sunny day lunch'. Les Rhododendrons offers 'smashing burgers and chips', but the waiter-service section upstairs is 'nothing short of disastrous'.

L'Ours Blanc is the smartest hotel in **Les Menuires** and serves 'excellent-value lunches'. Chez Alfred is an old hut just off the piste above Les Menuires. Alfred doesn't always cook but, when the mood takes him, his are the finest and cheapest steak frites on the mountain. Quatres Vents at Les Bruyères 'maintains a consistent standard'. La Bouitte in St-Marcel near St-Martin-de-Belleville is a serious exercise in gastronomy.

LES MENUIRES
Beginners ✱✱
Intermediates ✱✱✱
Advanced ✱✱
Snowboarders ✱✱
✔ Large ski area
✔ Long cruising runs
✔ Sunny slopes
✔ Off-piste skiing
✔ Well-run children's village
✔ Budget prices
✔ Extensive snowmaking
✗ Ugly architecture in centre
✗ Heavy traffic
✗ Limited nightlife
✗ Lack of tree-level runs
✗ Few activities for non-skiers

Accommodation

Méribel began as a chalet resort and so it remains. In the short summer months the village rings to the sounds of saw and hammer as new luxury establishments sprout in response to demand. Those who don't like walking in their ski boots are strongly advised to check out the location of their chalet before booking. Of the hotels, the four-star Grand Coeur was one of the resort's first and remains its finest: 'the food and service are excellent; its understated luxury appeals equally to the Brits and the French'. The Marie Blanche and Le Yeti are also recommended. In **Mottaret**, La Tarentaise and the four-star Mont Vallon are praised.

Courchevel 1850 has a host of four-star de luxe hotels (there are no five-stars in France), which pamper their wealthy guests. The Byblos de Neige is the glitzy centrepiece. Les Airelles is more discreet. Hotel des Neiges is an established favourite, and the Trois Vallées is 'intimate and charming'. The family-run three-star La Sivolière provides four-star comfort and has a health centre. The more reasonably priced Courcheneige is situated on the edge of the piste near the altiport; during the school holidays the hotel is overrun with families from the Home Counties. Le Mélèzin, Les Ducs de Savoie, Le Dahu, Les Grandes-Alpes and L'Aiglon are singled out for praise. Le Lodge Nogentil is a smart chalet-hotel in a good location.

The quality of some of the luxury catered chalets here ranks alongside the smartest hotels. The Forum apartment complex is praised by reporters ('modern, with a perfect location'), although both the apartments themselves and the staircases are showing signs of wear and tear. **Courchevel 1650** consists mainly of chalets. However, the ski-in ski-out Hotel du Golf has 'pleasant rooms with balconies overlooking the piste'. **Le Praz** has the comfortable Hotel Les Peupliers ('a delightful base from which to ski Courchevel without paying through the nose').

La Tania has some delightful Scandinavian-style chalets set in the woods above the village, many of which are run by British tour operators. Hotel Montana in the centre is 'excellent, modern and clean with large rooms and a small swimming-pool'.

Accommodation in **Val Thorens** is divided between the standard French apartments and mainly unremarkable hotels. The four-star Fitz-Roy is the exception. Readers report that the apartments in the Naska block of the Temples du Soleil complex are 'surprisingly spacious, with enormous bathrooms'. Résidence Altineige is said to be 'extremely noisy thanks to the Ski Rock Café next to the reception area'. Le Bel Horizon and Le Sherpa ('the best hotel in town, very friendly') are reporters' favourites, along with Le Val Chavière where 'staff are actually pleased to see you'.

Les Menuires is mainly apartment territory: the older ones in La Croisette are cramped and to be avoided. Their more modern counterparts in **Les Bruyères** are beginning to show signs of exhaustion. Hotel Les Latitudes in Les Bruyères offers some of the best-value accommodation and five-course dinners in the region ('quite exceptional food, pleasant rooms and ideally situated on the edge of the piste. Don't tell anyone else'). Reporters praise the Necou apartments at Reberty 2000 ('a high-quality, well designed ski-in ski-out complex').

Eating in and out

Méribel has a surprisingly limited choice of recommended restaurants for a resort of its size, mainly because such a large proportion of its clientèle eat in their catered chalets. Les Enfants Terribles (formerly Le Jardin d'Hiver) is said to be 'worthy of a good night out'. La Cava is recommended for fondue, La Taverne offers pizzas and Savoyard dishes and has established itself as one of the resort's main rendezvous. Chez Kiki specialises in charcoal grills, and the surroundings are appealing. El Poncho is a friendly Tex-Mex at Méribel 1600 offering some of the best-value food in the resort.

In **Mottaret**, Ty Sable is strongly recommended. Hotel Tarentaise, on the edge of the piste, is British-managed and popular with the French for its food. The central Côte Brune is still a culinary mainstay. Pizzeria du Mottaret is 'the restaurant with the best ambience and prices'.

Courchevel 1850 abounds in fine restaurants at truly stratospheric prices. The Chabichou Hotel has two coveted Michelin stars, as does Le Bateau Ivre ('much better value than London and a real gastronomic treat for £120 for two, with lots of wine'). The seafood restaurant at the Byblos de Neige is a wonder to behold; however, few reporters found themselves in this envious price bracket. La Saulire (Jacques' Bar) in the square at 1850 offers haute cuisine at far wallet-friendlier prices and is without doubt the most welcoming and best-value restaurant in town: 'a resort institution with a passionate following'. Le Plancher des Vaches and La Chapelle are warmly praised.

Restaurants at **Courchevel 1650** are less Parisian in price. La Montagne is recommended for 'its outstanding, mouth-watering côte de boeuf'. L'Eterlou is 'family-run, welcoming and reasonably priced'. La Montagne is new and 'extremely popular on chalet staff night off'. In Courchevel 1550 the Oeil du Boeuf is 'good, but rather smart'. La Cortona and Le Caveau are warmly recommended: 'great atmosphere and food in both'. **Le Praz** is famed for the outrageously expensive but nevertheless compelling Bistrot du Praz and Charley, its *bon vivant* host. A *dégustation* of four different types of foie gras is the house speciality. However, even such venerable institutions do not last forever. Charley is planning to retire and has put the business up for sale at a suitably exorbitant price but so far has found no takers. Hotel Les Peupliers, the original village inn, is also worth a visit for lunch or dinner. So great was one reporter's enthusiasm that he described it as being 'a thoroughly pleasant and comfortable hotel with the finest food in the whole of Courchevel – at an acceptable price'. L'Orsonne Blanche is said to be a cheaper alternative 'with portions big enough to make your salopettes wince'.

La Tania has four reasonably priced restaurants including Pub Le Ski Lodge and La Taiga, which are described as 'welcoming and serve tasty, (relatively) inexpensive food'.

Val Thorens has 45 restaurants headed by the gourmet Chalet des Glaciers. Le Galoubet is recommended at lunch-time for its dish of the day. La Joyeuse Fondue, Le Vieux Chalet and Bloopers are all praised. El Gringo's Café in the Péclet shopping centre is among the most popular.

Les Menuires is no gastronomic haven, but the half-board food in Hotel Les Latitudes was described as 'much more exciting than we could have hoped for'. Better restaurants include La Bouitte in nearby St-Marcel, and La Mascotte and Chalet Nécou in Les Menuires.

Après-ski

In **Méribel** Jack's Bar close to the piste has a popular après-ski happy hour, 'lively, happy atmosphere, value for money' said one reporter, but 'full of sad, middle-aged English drinking lager and playing bar billiards to the strains of old Beach Boy tapes,' said another. Le Rond Point is equally busy as the lifts close. L'Artichaud, located above the ice-rink, has live music, a fun atmosphere and stays open late. Dick's Tea-Bar, a branch of the Val d'Isère original, is extremely popular.

Skiing facts: Courchevel

TOURIST INFORMATION
BP37, La Croisette, F-73122
Courchevel, Savoie
Tel 33 479 08 00 29
Fax 33 479 08 15 63
Email pro@courchevel.com
Web site www.courchevel.com

THE RESORT
By road Calais 968km
By rail TGV Moûtiers 25km, frequent
buses
Airport transfer Chambéry 2hrs,
Geneva 3hrs, Lyon 2½hrs
Visitor beds 32,000
Transport free ski bus

THE SKIING
Linked or nearby resorts Les Menuires
(l), Méribel (l), St-Martin-de-Belleville
(l), La Tania (l), Val Thorens (l)
Number of lifts 67 in Courchevel, 197
in Trois Vallées
Total of trails/pistes 180km in
Courchevel (26% beginner, 27% easy,
36% intermediate, 11% difficult),
600km in Trois Vallées
Nursery slopes 26 slopes

LIFT PASSES
Area pass Courchevel only 945FF, Trois
Vallées 1,160FF, both for 6 days
Beginners 11 free lifts
Pensioners 20% reduction for
60–69yrs, 50% reduction for 70–75yrs,
free for 76yrs and over
Credit cards yes

TUITION
Adults ESF 1850 tel: 479 08 07 72, ESF
1650 tel: 479 08 26 08, ESF 1550
tel: 479 08 21 07, Le Ski School (1650)
tel: 01484 548996 (UK),
Ski Académie (1850) tel: 479 08 11 99,
Ski Cocktail (1850) tel: 479 08 22 00,
Supreme (1850) tel: 479 08 27 87
Snowboarding as ski schools
Other courses carving, cross-country,
race-training, Skwal, telemark
Guiding Bureau des Guides
tel: 479 01 03 66

CHILDREN
Lift pass 5–10yrs Courchevel only
614FF, Trois Vallées 754FF, 10–16yrs
Courchevel only 710FF, Trois Vallées
870FF, all for 6 days.
Ski & board school as adults
Kindergarten (ski) ESF 1850 tel: 479
08 07 72, ESF 1650 tel: 479 08 26 08,
ESF 1550 tel: 479 08 21 07, (non-ski)
ESF Village des Enfants 1850 tel: 479
08 07 72, Les Pitchounets (1650) tel:
479 08 33 69

OTHER SPORTS
Climbing wall, ice-climbing, ice-driving,
ice hockey, lugeing, parapente, skating,
ski-jumping, snowmobiling,
snowshoeing, squash, swimming

FOOD AND DRINK PRICES
Coffee 13–15FF, glass of wine
20–25FF, small beer 28FF, soft drink
15FF, dish of the day 75FF

At Prends Ta Luge Et Tire-toi ('grab your toboggan and go') in the
Forum complex at **Courchevel 1850** you can surf the Web, buy a snowboard or get a tattoo. The 5 à 7 beneath the Hotel Albatross is popular.
L'Accord and Le Grenier are two usually crowded piano bars. La Grange
and Les Caves are the main late-night but prohibitively expensive venues

Skiing facts: La Tania

TOURIST INFORMATION
La Tania 73125, Courchevel Cedex
Tel 33 479 08 40 40
Fax 33 479 08 45 71
Email info@latania.com
Web site www.latania.com

THE RESORT
By road Calais 950km
By rail TGV Moûtiers 18km, bus service from Geneva and Lyon
Airport transfer Chambéry 2hrs, Geneva 3hrs, Lyon 2½hrs
Visitor beds 4,000
Transport free ski bus

THE SKIING
Linked or nearby resorts Courchevel (l), Les Menuires (l), Méribel (l), St-Martin-de-Belleville (l), Val Thorens (l)
Number of lifts 67 in Courchevel area, 197 in Trois Vallées
Total of trails/pistes 180km in Courchevel area (26% beginner, 27% easy, 36% intermediate, 11% difficult), 600km in Trois Vallées
Nursery slopes 11 lifts

LIFT PASSES
Area pass La Tania only 945FF, Trois Vallées 1,160FF, both for 6 days
Beginners points tickets
Pensioners 20% reduction for

60–69yrs, 50% reduction for 70–75yrs, free for 76yrs and over
Credit cards yes

TUITION
Adults ESF tel: 479 08 80 39, Arthur Mac Lean tel: 612 67 30 49, Magic in Motion tel: 479 01 07 17, Snow Ball tel: 479 08 24 21
Snowboarding ESF, Magic in Motion
Other courses carving, snowblading, teen skiing, telemark
Guiding through ESF, Olivier Houillot tel: 479 08 39 58

CHILDREN
Lift pass 5–10yrs La Tania only 614FF, Trois Vallées 754FF, 10-15yrs La Tania only 710FF, Trois Vallées 870FF, all for 6 days
Ski & board school as adults
Kindergarten (ski/non-ski) Jardin des Neiges, Maison des Enfants tel (both): 479 08 80 39

OTHER SPORTS
Dogsledding, snowshoeing, swimming

FOOD AND DRINK PRICES
Coffee 12FF, glass of wine 20FF, small beer 20FF, soft drink 13FF, dish of the day 65–75FF

('where the French glitterati buy vodka by the bottle while dancers gyrate to Euro anthems on podiums overlooking the dance floor'). Le Kalico is a much cheaper 2am alternative ('no entry fee and reminiscent of a student disco with Brits dancing ankle-deep in beer').

At **Courchevel 1650**, Le Signal is the bar-restaurant where the locals meet. Le Plouc is a small, smoky and busy bar. By night Le Green Club has a modest entry fee, a British DJ and 'the best music at any altitude in Courchevel'. Rocky's Bar is also always busy. At **Courchevel 1550** après-ski revolves around La Taverne ('very French, very friendly') and

Skiing facts: Méribel

TOURIST INFORMATION
BP1, F-73551 Méribel, Savoie
Tel 33 479 08 69 01
Fax 33 479 00 59 61
Email info@meribel.net
Web site www.meribel.net

THE RESORT
By road Calais 962km
By rail TGV Moûtiers 18km, regular bus
service to resort
Airport transfer Chambéry 2hrs,
Geneva 3hrs, Lyon 2½hrs
Visitor beds 31,000
Transport free ski bus

THE SKIING
Linked or nearby resorts Courchevel
(I), Les Menuires (I), St-Martin-de-
Belleville (I), La Tania (I), Val Thorens (I)
Number of lifts 75 in Méribel, 197 in
Trois Vallées
Total of trails/pistes 150km in Méribel
(15% easy, 71% intermediate, 14%
difficult), 600km in Trois Vallées
Nursery slopes 3 free lifts

LIFT PASSES
Area pass Méribel only 945FF, Trois
Vallées 1,160FF, both for 6 days
Beginners reduced lift pass available
with instruction
Pensioners 20% reduction for
60–69yrs, 50% reduction for 70–75yrs,
free for 76yrs and over
Credit cards yes

TUITION
Adults ESF tel: 479 08 60 31, Ski
Cocktail tel: 479 10 06 11, Magic in
Motion tel: 479 08 53 36, Ski Principles
tel: 01803 852185 (UK)
Snowboarding as ski schools
Other courses carving, cross-country,
moguls, race-training, telemark
Guiding Bureau des Guides tel:
479 00 30 38

CHILDREN
Lift pass 5—10yrs Méribel only 614FF,
Trois Vallées 754FF, 10-15yrs Méribel
only 710FF, Trois Vallées 870FF, all for 6
days
Ski & board school as adults
Kindergarten (ski) Les P'tits Loups
(Méribel and Mottaret)
tel: 479 08 60 31, (non-ski) Halte-
Garderie Club Saturnin tel: 479 08 66 90

OTHER SPORTS
Dog-sledding, ice-hockey, parapente,
skating, snowshoeing, snowbiking,
swimming

FOOD AND DRINK PRICES
Coffee 13—15FF, glass of wine
20—25FF, small beer 28FF, soft drink
15FF, dish of the day 75FF

the Glacier Bar ('full of British resort staff'). Chanrossa provides the
late-night action. Le Praz is not the place for raucous nightlife. The
crêperie has 'the best *vin chaud* in the business'. The Bar Brasserie (it
bears no other name) is 'the only place with any life'.

La Tania's nightlife has much improved in recent years. It has a handful
of bars with a relaxed atmosphere, and Pub Le Ski Lodge, which is a vibrant
place to be in the evenings.

Skiing facts: Val Thorens

TOURIST INFORMATION
F-73440 Val Thorens, Savoie
Tel 33 479 00 08 08
Fax 33 479 00 00 04
Email valtho@valthorens.com
Web site www.valthorens.com

THE RESORT
By road Calais 981km
By rail TGV Moûtiers 33km, frequent
buses to resort
Airport transfer Chambéry 2hrs,
Geneva 3hrs, Lyon 2½hrs
Visitor beds 23,500
Transport free ski bus

THE SKIING
Linked or nearby resorts Courchevel
(I), Les Menuires (I), Méribel (I), St-
Martin-de-Belleville (I), La Tania (I)
Number of lifts 30 in Val Thorens, 200
in Trois Vallées
Total of trails/pistes 140km in Val
Thorens (40% easy, 50% intermediate,
10% difficult), 600km in Trois Vallées
Nursery slopes 3 lifts
Summer skiing 3 lifts and 3 runs on
Péclet Glacier

LIFT PASSES
Area pass Val Thorens only 692–878FF,
Trois Vallées 1,160FF, both for 6 days
Beginners 4 free lifts
Pensioners 20% reduction for
60–69yrs, 50% reduction for 70–75yrs,
free 76yrs and over
Credit cards yes

TUITION
Adults ESF tel: 479 00 02 86, ESI Ski
Cool tel: 479 00 04 92, Gilbert Smith
International Race Camp tel: 479 00 04
24, Patrick and Eric Berthon tel: 479 00
06 16, Pros-Neige tel: 479 01 07 00, Ski
Surf Nature tel: 479 00 01 96
Snowboarding ESF, Pros-Neige, Ski
Cool, Ski Surf Nature
Other courses carving, cross-country,
extreme skiing, heli-skiing, moguls,
race-training, skiing for the disabled,
Skwal, telemark
Guiding Bureau des Guides tel: 479 00
08 08, Ski Safari Pepi Prager tel: 479 00
01 23, Ski The 12 Valleys
tel: 479 00 00 95

CHILDREN
Lift pass 5–10yrs Val Thorens only
614FF, Trois Vallées 754FF, 10–16yrs
Les Menuires only 710FF, Trois Vallées
870FF, all for 6 days
Ski & board school as adults, and
Marie Goitschel Village tel: 479 00 00 47
Kindergarten (ski/non-ski) ESF, Marie
Goitschel Village tel: as ski school

OTHER SPORTS
Climbing wall, indoor tennis and squash,
parapente, skating, snowmobiling,
snowshoeing, swimming

FOOD AND DRINK PRICES
Coffee 12FF, glass of wine 20FF, small
beer 20FF, soft drink 13FF, dish of the
day 65–75FF

Skiing facts: Les Menuires

TOURIST INFORMATION
BP22, Les Menuires, F-73440, Savoie
Tel 33 479 00 73 00
Fax 33 479 00 75 06
Email lesmenuires@lesmenuires.com
Web site www.lesmenuires.com

THE RESORT
By road Calais 972km
By rail TGV Moûtiers 28km
Airport transfer Chambéry 1½hrs,
Geneva 3hrs, Lyon 2hrs
Visitor beds 25,300
Transport free ski bus around resort

THE SKIING
Linked or nearby resorts Courchevel
(l), Méribel (l), St-Martin-de-Belleville
(l), La Tania (l), Val Thorens (l)
Number of lifts 45 in Les Menuires and
St-Martin, 200 in Trois Vallées
Total of trails/pistes 160km in Les
Menuires, (30% easy, 52%
intermediate, 18% difficult) 600km in
Trois Vallées
Nursery slopes 5 free lifts
Summer skiing in Val Thorens

LIFT PASSES
Area pass Les Menuires only 945FF,
Trois Vallées 1,160FF, both for 6 days
Beginners 5 free lifts
Pensioners 20% reduction for

60–69yrs, 50% reduction for 70–75yrs,
free for 76yrs and over
Credit cards yes

TUITION
Adults ESF tel: 479 00 61 43, ESI tel:
479 00 67 34
Snowboarding as ski school
Other courses carving, cross-country,
extreme skiing, moguls, race-training,
skiing for the disabled, teen skiing,
telemark
Guiding through ESF and ESI

CHILDREN
Lift pass 5–10yrs Les Menuires only
614FF, Trois Vallées 754FF, 10–16yrs
Les Menuires only 710FF, Trois Vallées
870FF, all for 6 days
Ski & board school as adults
Kindergarten (ski/non-ski) Village des
Schtroumpfs tel: 479 00 63 79, Village
des Marmottons tel: 479 00 69 50#

OTHER SPORTS
Hang-gliding, parapente, skating,
snowmobiling, snowshoeing,
swimming

FOOD AND DRINK PRICES
Coffee 12FF, glass of wine 20FF, small
beer 20FF, soft drink 13FF, dish of the
day 65–75FF

The popular watering holes at **Val Thorens** are Le Tango, the Ski Rock Café, the Viking Pub and the Frog and Roast Beef. The après-ski in **Les Menuires** is largely restricted to a handful of bars.

Childcare
All the main resorts are well-served with ESF ski and non-ski kinder-garten. However, it is important to note that the facilities offered may not be conducive to the enjoyment of your holiday. The Gallic approach to childcare may seem harsh by northern European standards, with a

serious emphasis on learning to ski without any accompanying element of fun. The number of children who tearfully refuse to return to these French establishments on day two of their holiday has led tour operators to set up more sympathetic crèches and even ski classes.

Reporters praise the **Méribel** ski school: 'although the classes were large, the teachers made the lessons fun. The Marie Goitschel Village in Val Thorens attracts predominantly French children. It has its own small ski area and accepts children from three years, Reporters say that the teaching is 'excellent'. The ESF in **Courchevel 1850** is criticised as being 'too serious' in its approach, and 'needs to be more organised'. Many parents staying here feel that **Le Praz** has a better ski school, and the instructors will come up to 1850 to collect children. However, at Le Praz kindergarten 'at least a third of the children were British, but the staff didn't make a big effort to speak English. Our three-year-old was not overly impressed, but enjoyed it enough to go back'. We have favourable reports of the ESF children's ski school in Courchevel 1650. The Maison des Enfants and the Jardin des Neiges non-ski and ski-kindergarten at **La Tania** take children from three to twelve years old. Children staying in **Les Menuires** are cared for at the Village des Schtroumpfs from three months and at the Village des Marmottons from two-and-a-half years of age.

Linked or nearby resorts

St-Martin-de-Belleville
top 3,300m (10,825ft) bottom 1,400m (4,593ft)

St-Martin-de-Belleville and La Tania are two contrastingly different villages that provide alternative bases for skiing the Trois Vallées while avoiding the hustle of the mainstream resorts and their high prices.

St-Martin, the 'capital' of the Belleville Valley, is a farming community at pastoral counterpoint to the high-tech world of the ski network above it. Reporters praise it as 'quiet and lived-in, unlike the larger towns in the area'. The old cheese-making village has considerable charm and a couple of fine restaurants: L'Etoile de Neige is a lunchtime favourite with ski guides, while Les Airelles offers 'delicious food'.

St-Martin is linked into the system by a slow triple-chair. However, the second stage has been upgraded to a high-speed quad chair that takes you directly to the top of Tougnette. Nevertheless, if you are staying in Méribel do not linger too long over lunch – allow a full 40 minutes to reach the ridge of the valley on your way home.

TOURIST INFORMATION
Tel 33 479 08 93 09
Fax 33 479 08 9171
Email lesmenuires@lesmenuires.com
Web site www.st-martin-belleville.com

Val d'Isère/Tignes

Val d'Isère 1,850m (6,068ft), Tignes 2,100m (6,888ft)

Beginners ✱✱ Intermediates ✱✱✱ Advanced ✱✱✱ Snowboarders ✱✱✱

Early in December Val d'Isère traditionally hosts the first European leg of the World Cup downhill or 'Super G'. Between then and the first week of May, more British skiers visit this remote and rather unprepossessing resort at the head of the Tarentaise Valley than anywhere else.

It is a destination for serious enthusiasts, which somehow manages to blend a cocktail of high ski-tech and mass-market tourism with a smooth topping of sophistication. The ski area is directly linked to neighbouring Tignes and is jointly marketed as L'Espace Killy, after its most revered son who swept the board of gold medals at the 1968 Winter Olympics. The fact that Jean-Claude Killy comes from lowland Alsace, and the clothing firm he founded now belongs to a Londoner, bothers no one at all.

- ✔ Large well-linked ski area
- ✔ Extensive off-piste
- ✔ Summer skiing (Tignes)
- ✔ Reliable snow record
- ✔ Excellent lift system
- ✔ Lively après-ski (Val d'Isère)
- ✔ Skiing convenience (Tignes)
- ✘ Few activities for non-skiers
- ✘ Lack of tree-level runs
- ✘ Unattractive village (Tignes)

The quality of the skiing in the area is so varied and demanding that it has raised a whole genre of international experts who never ski anywhere else. A vertical drop of 1,890m, coupled with 96 lifts, including two high-speed underground railways, six gondolas and four cable-cars, form the hardcore infrastructure. For the expert, however, the real joy lies in the unlimited off-piste opportunities to be found in this wild region on the edge of the Vanoise National Park. Apart from the eleventh-century church, precious little remains of the old village of Val d'Isère, which became a winter sports resort in 1932. Today, it has grown into a hotchpotch of a ski town, which sprawls from the apartment blocks of **La Daille** at one end to **Le Fornet** at the other.

Val Village, a cluster of 'old-style' stone buildings around the church, and housing smart boutiques, was created for the 1992 Olympics. It provided the village with an attractive focal point that it previously lacked. Much has since been done to improve the appearance of the rest of the town. Some of the original concrete apartment buildings have been resurfaced in wood and stone. New wide pavements dotted with mature trees have greatly enhanced its appeal for pedestrians.

The old village of Tignes disappeared beneath the waters of the Lac du Chevril when the valley was dammed in 1952. In May 2000 the remains of the original settlement re-emerged when the dam was drained for a maintenance inspection. Ironically, the dam is no longer part of France's frontline hydro-electric resources, but campaigners who want the village returned to them are unlikely to meet with short-term success. For the present, Tignes, which is synonymous with high-rise housing estates set at varying altitudes of about 2,000m, represents some of the most ghastly excesses of 1960s French Alpine architecture.

The hamlets of **Val Claret**, **Tignes-Le-Lac**, **Le Lavachet**, and even the much lower community of **Tignes-les-Boisses**, are visually unattractive. Only the valley farming community of **Tignes-les-Brévières** is more appealing. However, Tignes is in the process of spending £35 million in an effort to improve the resort's appearance. Many of the older buildings have been reclad, Tignes-le-Lac has a new *front de neige*, and a people-mover lift now links the car park at Val Claret with the funicular station. The lift company is also investing £35 million in lift improvements.

WHAT'S NEW

Tignes glacier now closed mid-May until mid-June and for second half of September

The glacier in Tignes is no longer open for 365 days of the year. In 2000 it closed from mid-May until mid-June and for the second half of September while the lifts were serviced. Permanent winter conditions on the Grande Motte Glacier allow dedicated snow-users to practise on its wide slopes even in July and August. In winter, at least, the ugliness of the resort is counterbalanced by the glory of the skiing.

Buses between Val d'Isère and Tignes are neither frequent nor cheap. If you have your own car and want a change of scenery, day-trips to **Les Arcs**, **La Plagne**, **La Rosière** and **Sainte-Foy** are all possible.

On the snow
top 3,456m (11,335ft) bottom 1,550m (5,084ft)

Val d'Isère alone has eight major points of mountain access including a high-speed underground train. The ski school rush hour (adults and children) must be avoided, and the French school holidays in February are inevitably crowded, but otherwise queuing is not a serious problem. The long valley floor is covered by an efficient ski-bus service known as Le Train Rouge, and with experience you can avoid the bottlenecks.

L'Espace Killy divides naturally into six separate ski sectors. On the Val d'Isère side are Col de l'Iseran/Pissaillas, Solaise and Bellevarde, which are strung in a row along the curving road between the satellites of Le Fornet and La Daille. The first two sectors are linked by lift at altitude, but Solaise and Bellevarde join only at valley level close to the resort centre. Bellevarde links with Tignes via the Tovière ridge/Col de Fresse. A long-running political/environmental dispute over the future development of the lifts on the Glacier de Pissaillas has greatly reduced access to this sector. One of the lifts is currently closed, and uphill transport takes the form of a tow behind a piste machine ('thoroughly unenjoyable. Not an experience that I will be repeating').

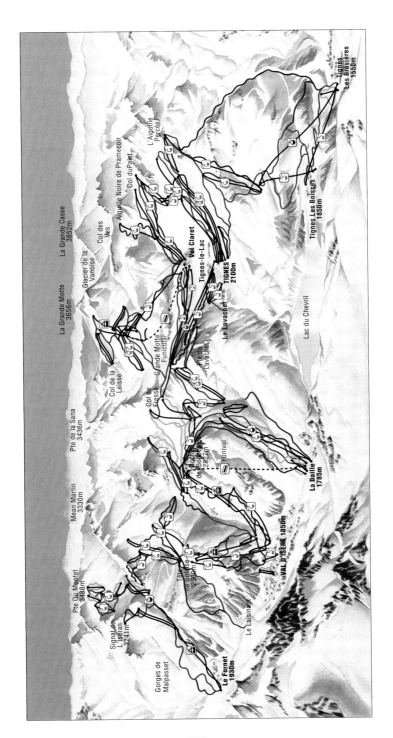

The skiing at Tignes is divided into three areas – Tovière, the Grande Motte Glacier and Palet/Aiguille Percée. Tignes also has a state-of-the-art underground railway. Passengers are whisked at high speed up through the rock and permafrost from Val Claret at 2,100m to the Panoramic restaurant at 3,030m in just six minutes.

An alternative lift network takes you from Tignes-Le-Lac towards the dramatic rock formation of L'Aiguille Percée, in one direction, or towards Val d'Isère's more demanding ski area in the other. For most of the season there is more skiing in Tignes down to the lower lying hamlets of Les Boisses at 1,850m and Les Brévières at 1,550m.

Piste-grooming in Val d'Isère is of an exceptionally high standard that is not always matched in Tignes. However, the severity of the terrain makes it greatly prone to avalanches. In bad weather those in the know take a day out to the protected pistes of Sainte-Foy. In moderately windy conditions, when chair-lifts cannot operate, both Val d'Isère and Tignes benefit enormously from their underground railways. The Funival at La Daille gives access to the Rocher de Bellevarde and some of the best runs in the resort.

Reporters have criticised the busy runs down to La Daille at the end of the day: 'I had to fight my way down every time and was terrified of being skied into or hit by a snowboarder'.

Beginners

Val d'Isère is unfairly denigrated for its facilities for beginners. In fact, it has acceptable – and free – nursery slopes right in the centre of the village and a wide choice of ski schools. The problem stems from the fact that there is nothing for the improving beginner. Do not trust the piste-map; some of the runs marked green (beginner) could frighten the daylights out of you. One solution is to ski on Solaise and take the chair-lift or cable-car back down. The Col de l'Iseran sector has some gentle runs, but here, as in other parts of the resort, it is too difficult to ski back to the valley. Tignes has a good choice of blue (easy) runs on the glacier but the usually chilly temperature is not conducive to learning.

Intermediates

Piste-grading is not Val's strongest point, and colour-coding is on the dark side – some blues would be red (intermediate) runs elsewhere, and you may find the odd red that is positively black (difficult) by Tyrolean standards. The Bellevarde sector provides plenty of variety. The L run (check to see if it is open) off the back of Solaise takes you down to the hamlet of **Le Laisinant** and is a superb cruise. The OK run around the shoulder of the Rocher de Bellevarde is the World Cup downhill course. The long descent to Val Claret from the Grande Motte glacier is a test for even the fittest thigh muscles when taken without stopping.

Advanced

The Face de Bellevarde, reached by the Funival funicular railway, was built as the men's downhill course for the 1992 Winter Olympics. The legacy is a superb black run, which leads you back to Val in rather more than the two minutes it took winner Patrick Ortlieb and his fellow competitors. Sache, a superb long black, starts from the blue Corniche run below L'Aiguille Percée and takes you down to Tignes-les-Brévières, where it merges with the red Pavot. The run through the trees from the top of Le Fornet can, at times, be the best in the resort. The steepest piste is the Epaule du Charvet ('when groomed, you can play at being a downhiller; otherwise, the bumps are legendary').

Off-piste

The starting points for some of the most challenging itineraries are marked on the piste-map. Once you begin, you are on your own and it is easy to get lost – or worse. It is imperative to have a local guide who can read the snow conditions and knows which routes are safe. In fresh powder the Charvet area is a particular favourite. One resident reporter commented: 'there is no greater thrill than cutting first tracks on the Face du Charvet or the Couloir Mont Blanc before skiing the Bec d'Aigle'. The Signal de l'Iseran/Glacier de Pissaillas sector provides some of the most dramatic runs, but the beauty of Val and Tignes is the accessibility of good off-piste throughout the region.

Snowboarders

Val's funpark is situated above La Daille on the upper slopes of Bellevarde. The Combe de Palafour funpark at Tignes has a half-pipe and assorted obstacles. A funpark operates on the Grande Motte Glacier throughout the summer. Both Val and Tignes offer some amazing freeriding as well as lots of natural cliffs and gullies.

Tuition and guiding

To get the best out of the ski area you need some expert help: the two resorts boast a clutch of rival ski and snowboarding schools. The ESF operates in both resorts, but Anglo-Saxons tend to favour the alternatives, which are more linguistically and emotionally geared towards the needs of the calibre of skier who wants to get the best out of the area. Pat Zimmer's Top Ski was the first independent ski school in France when founded in 1976. Its supporters would still argue that it is the best. The secret of its success is that it has remained small. Instructors take groups of six skiers off-piste in the mornings and give instruction on piste technique in the afternoons.

We have continuing good reports of Snow Fun: 'the instructors were personable, spoke fluent English and made the effort to learn the names of their pupils', and 'we were highly impressed by their organisation and emphasis on group grading', said another reporter. We have encouraging reports of Mountain Masters. One reporter described a guide from Alpine Experience as: 'the best I have ever come across anywhere'. Evolution 2, in both Val and Tignes, is widely praised for its expertise. The Tignes branch offers a range of non-skiing activities including ice-diving under the lake, and the school also owns a mountain restaurant and a hotel.

Hors-Limites Surf School in Val runs free introductory snowboard lessons, with equipment included, on the nursery slopes on Sunday afternoons. It takes riders from as young as five years old in small groups. We have no reports of Billabong and Misty Fly. In Tignes, Surf Feeling, Snocool and Kébra Surfing are the specialist board schools.

Mountain restaurants

Eating out at altitude is not Espace Killy's strongest point. The better establishments are on the Val side and include Trifollet ('good pizzas'), which is halfway down to La Daille, and La Folie Douce, at the top of La Daille gondola. Neighbouring La Fruitière is decorated as a Savoyard dairy, has some of the best food on the mountain as well as the best WCs, and should be booked in advance during high season.

The Ski d'Eté restaurant complex below the Grande Motte gondola was praised for its good value: 'a large attractive eating area with plenty of choices'. Le Panoramic, at the top of the Grande Motte funicular, has a self-service and separate waiter-service restaurant ('surprisingly good, with courteous staff').

At lunchtime many snow-users return to the valley, where restaurants are as busy as they are by night. The family-run Crech'Ouna, near the Funival station, used to be the prandial mainstay of the area but was sold in Spring 2000. Bananas is a favourite among reporters – for the ambience rather than the quality of the food. Clochetons is also praised for its 'reasonably priced *table d'hôte*'.

Upstairs at L'Arbina in Tignes-le-Lac is 'a serious gastronomic experience, but you must book, even at lunchtime'. The Bouida, by the gondola at Les Brévières, is said to be good value for money, although one reader waited an hour for a drink. The rebuilt restaurant at the Col du Palet is described as 'very welcoming'. La Taverne at Val Claret is 'better and cheaper than most restaurants in the region'.

Accommodation

In Val d'Isère a couple of four-stars heads a choice of 35 hotels. The Christiania is the most comfortable, while the four-star Blizzard, Savoyarde and the Tsanteleina have a strong British following. The piste-side Hotel Brussel's is praised by one reporter despite being 'stuck in a 70s time warp'. Most snow-users stay in chalets or in self-catering apartments. The Alpina Lodge is recommended for 'location, prices, reasonable accommodation and very helpful staff'. YSE is the largest specialist chalet operator here and runs Mountain Lodges, a seventeenth-century farmhouse divided into two units.

In Tignes, most accommodation is in self-catering apartments, which vary dramatically in quality in direct relation to their age. Hotels range from the comfortable four-star Le Ski d'Or in Val Claret ('bright, spacious rooms') to a clutch of two-stars including the well-positioned Hotel L'Arbina at Lac de Tignes, which has a health centre, and Hotel

Skiing facts: Val d'Isère

TOURIST INFORMATION
BP 228, F-73155 Val d'Isère, Savoie
Tel 33 479 06 06 60
Fax 33 479 06 04 56
Email info@valdisere.com
Web site www.valdisere.com

THE RESORT
By road Calais 1,003km
By rail Bourg-St-Maurice 30km
Airport transfer Chambéry 2hrs,
Geneva 2½hrs, Lyon 2½hrs
Visitor beds 26,500
Transport free ski bus between La
Daille and Le Fornet

THE SKIING
Linked or nearby resorts Tignes (l),
Sainte-Foy (n)
Number of lifts 50 in Val d'Isère, 96 in
L'Espace Killy
Total of trails/pistes 300km in
L'Espace Killy (15% easy, 47%
intermediate, 38% difficult)
Nursery slopes 7 free lifts
Summer skiing sometimes possible on
Glacier de Pissaillas

LIFT PASSES
Area pass L'Espace Killy, 1,047FF for
6 days
Beginners 6 lifts
Pensioners 60–69yrs 880FF for 6 days,
70–74yrs 597FF, free for 75yrs and over
Credit cards yes

TUITION
Adults Alpine Experience tel: 479 06 28
81, Atimanya tel: 479 06 25 38, ESF
tel: 479 06 02 34, Evolution 2
tel: 479 41 16 72,

Mountain Masters tel: 479 06 05 14,
Oxygene tel; 479 41 99 58, Ski
Adventure tel: 479 06 26 99, Ski
Cocktail tel: 479 06 08 14, Ski Prestige
tel: 479 06 62, Snow Fun tel: 479 06 19
79, Stages Val Gliss 479 06 00 72, Top
Ski tel: 479 06 14 80, Tetra Hors-piste
tel: 479 41 97 07
Snowboarding as ski schools, and
Billabong tel: 479 06 09 54, Hors-
Limites tel: 479 41 97 02, Misty Fly
tel: 479 41 95 77
Other courses carving, cross-country,
race-training, skiing for the disabled,
snowblading, telemark
Guiding through ski schools, and
Bureau des Guides tel: 479 06 94 03

CHILDREN
Lift pass 5–12yrs, 730FF for 6 days
Ski & board school ESF, Snow Fun,
Top Ski
Kindergarten ESF (ski/non-ski) Jardin
de Neige tel: 479 06 02 34, Le Petit
Poucet tel: 479 06 13 97, Village
d'Enfants tel 479 41 99 82,
Snow Fun Club Nounours tel: 479 06 16
79, Evolution 2 Yéti Courses tel: 479 41
16 72

OTHER SPORTS
Curling, dog-sledding, ice-climbing,
ice-driving, parapente, skating,
snowmobiling, snowshoeing,
swimming

FOOD AND DRINK
Coffee 10–15FF, glass of wine
12–16FF, small beer 15–25FF, soft
drink 16–24FF, dish of the day
80–110FF

de la Vanoise ('convenient, with an excellent breakfast and five-course dinner'). Hotel Les Résidences de Montana and The Alpaka Lodge are both said to be extremely comfortable.

Eating in and out

In Val d'Isère the Grand Ourse is 'in an attractive setting with delicious food'. Perdrix Blanche is unpretentious and renowned for its seafood. Chalet du Crêt is a 'wonderfully gastronomic' smart restaurant in a 300-year-old chalet. The restaurant in the Blizzard was praised: 'good atmosphere and excellent service'.

Les Clochetons in the Manchet valley provides a free minibus service as well as 'a great meal at a reasonable price in a lovely setting'. Pacific Pizzeria 'has good food, including fish at sensible prices'. Crêpe Val, close to the post office, is recommended for regional specialities as well as crêpes. L'Arolay in Le Fornet has 'fine food' but, according to one reporter, 'is a bun fight on the chalet girls' night off'. La Casserole is highly rated by reporters ('a charming chalet-style restaurant with reasonable prices)'. Victor's, above the Casino supermarket, 'offers quality food with a lively Scandinavian atmosphere'. Val d'Isère has three supermarkets and several specialist food shops.

Hotel L'Arbina in Tignes houses one of the best restaurants in the whole area. L'Osteria in Le Lavachet is recommended for raclette and pierrade. Le Ski d'Or is for fish. L'Arbina (upstairs restaurant) is 'outstanding, a *crêpe des escargots* to die for'. Daffy's Caffé in Val Claret serves Mexican food ('disappointingly bland with haphazard service'). Pizza 2000 at Val Claret is 'much more than just a pizzeria – great food, service, and ambience'. Le Bouf Mich in Val Claret is 'absolutely terrific, with great food and a jovial atmosphere'. The five supermarkets in Tignes sell a wide range of goods.

Après-ski

Val d'Isère buzzes with a fun-seeking après-ski crowd. 'Have An Affair in Val d'Isère' proclaimed the T-shirt of the 1980s as its owner gyrated sensually in the strobe-lighting of Dick's Tea-Bar. The Tea-Bar continues to be one of the most celebrated discos in the Alps, although reporters commented that it is less fun under its current corporate ownership. Café Face and Bananas are riding high. The Moris Pub and La Taverne have a lively, young following. L'Aventure is a popular club 'designed as a house, complete with double bed and bath'. Club 21 is the more sophisticated option.

The nightlife in Tignes is limited in comparison with that of its more cosmopolitan neighbour. Harry's Bar has a strong following, while Grizzly's Bar in Val Claret is warmly recommended ('one of the few drinking joints with character'). The Caves du Lac in Tignes-Le-Lac has a small dance floor and is much praised ('best nightclub in town'). Other discos are Jack's Club in Le Lac, Les Chandelles, and Blue Girl in Val Claret village.

Skiing facts: Tignes

TOURIST INFORMATION
BP 51, F-73321 Tignes, Savoie
Tel 33 479 40 04 40
Fax 33 479 40 03 15
Email information@tignes.net
Web site www.tignes.net

THE RESORT
By road Calais 1,001km
By rail Bourg-St-Maurice 26km
Airport transfer Chambéry 2hrs,
Geneva 2½hrs, Lyon 2½hrs
Visitor beds 28,000
Transport free ski bus

THE SKIING
Linked or nearby resorts Val d'Isère
(l), Sainte-Foy (n)
Number of lifts 46 in Tignes, 96 in
L'Espace Killy
Total of trails/pistes 300km in
L'Espace Killy (15 % easy, 46%
intermediate, 39 % difficult)
Nursery slopes 5
Summer skiing 7 pistes and 14 lifts on
Grande Motte Glacier

LIFT PASSES
Area pass L'Espace Killy 1,047FF
for 6 days
Beginners 5 free lifts
Pensioners 60–69yrs 880FF for 6 days,
70–74yrs 597FF, free for 75yrs and over

Credit cards yes

TUITION
Adults ESF tel: 479 06 30 28, ESI tel:
479 06 36 15, Evolution 2 tel: 479 06
43 78, Snow Fun tel: 479 06 46 10
Snowboarding as ski schools, and
Snocool tel: 479 40 08 58, Surf Feeling
tel: 479 06 53 63, Kébra Surfing tel:
479 06 43 37
Other courses carving, cross-country,
race-training, telemark
Guiding through ski schools, and
Bureau des Guides tel: 479 06 42 76

CHILDREN
Lift pass 5–12yrs, 730FF for 6 days
Ski & board school ESF, ESI, Evolution
2, Snow Fun
Kindergarten (ski/non-ski) Les
Marmottons tel: 479 06 51 67

OTHER SPORTS
Dog-sledding, hang-gliding, ice-
climbing, ice-diving, parapente, ski-
joring, skating, squash, snowshoeing,
indoor tennis

FOOD AND DRINK PRICES
Coffee 10–15FF, glass of wine
12–16FF, small beer 15–25FF, soft
drink 16––24FF, dish of the day
70–110FF

Childcare
The construction of a long-overdue children's village has greatly improved Val's attraction as a base for families, although the spread-out nature of the resort does not make it the most convenient. It caters for children aged three to thirteen years every day from 8.30am to 6.30pm, with ski lessons for older children. Le Petit Poucet kindergarten collects and delivers little ones aged three and over from your chalet or hotel.

Families with children at ski school should choose accommodation close to the Front de Neige to minimise the inconvenience of travelling backwards and forwards on the bus. ESF, Snow Fun and Evolution 2 all cater for young beginners from three to four years old. Hors-Limites give snowboard lessons from six years of age, and Billabong Snowboard School from seven years. Snow Fun is highly recommended by reporters: 'we wouldn't consider sending our children to any other ski school in the resort'.

In Tignes, Les Marmottons is for children from two years old. The ESF offers ski lessons from four years of age, and the International Ski School (ESI) from five.

Linked or nearby resorts

Sainte-Foy
top 2,620m (8,596ft) bottom 1,550m (5,084ft)

Sainte-Foy is an unremarkable old hamlet that you drive through on the road up from **Bourg-St-Maurice** to Tignes and Val d'Isère. But just above it, reached by a side road, is the ski resort of the same name. The lift ticket office, Zigzags ski hire shop ('the staff were rude and uninterested') and bar provide the main base facilities of this raw and exciting ski area.

The locals come to Sainte-Foy to enjoy untracked powder and to get away from the crowds at peak times. One reporter commented that over the Millennium New Year 'it wasn't busy by most resort standards, but you could see people ahead of you on the chairs – and that's a busy day for Sainte-Foy'. The resort is also an excellent location for freeriders looking for natural drops and walls. Another reporter remarked: 'the piste map is a complete smokescreen: it gives no indication of the hugeness of the off-piste terrain'. A guide is essential for enjoying the full off-piste potential. The resort is popular with experienced riders. The Local ESF has a sound reputation, and there is a Club Enfants crèche situated at the base area.

Three chair-lifts take you up to the Col de l'Aiguille and the starting point for 600 vertical metres of challenging piste and some dramatic powder descents. There are a few simple but atmospheric mountain eating-places. Les Brevettes, at the top of the first chair, is praised for its omelettes. Neighbouring Chez Leon 'has to be booked', and Maison à Colonnes at the base-station is 'very French and full of character'. The simple Hotel Le Monal is in the old village ('OK on price, dreadful service and staff'). Reporters praised the British-owned Auberge sur la Montagne in the neighbouring hamlet of La Thuile: 'this really is a gem of a place with heaps of mountain character. The food was gargantuan and utterly delicious'.

TOURIST INFORMATION
Tel 33 479 06 95 19
Fax 33 479 06 95 09
Web site www.sainte-foy-tarentaise.com

Valmorel

ALTITUDE 1,400m (4,592ft)

Beginners ✳✳✳ Intermediates ✳✳✳ Advanced ✳

Valmorel is an attractive family resort in the Tarentaise, which is reached by road from Moûtiers. It shares a network of 54 lifts and 151km of pistes with the popular French destination of **St François-Longchamp** in the Maurienne Valley and the beginner resort of **Doucy Combelouvière**. Together they market themselves as Le Grand Domaine and offer a wide range of skiing, mainly below advanced level. Unlike its purpose-built forerunners, the village is architecturally pleasing and fits so snugly into its mountain environment that it is hard to believe that it was only constructed in 1976. Central Valmorel is often referred to as Bourg-Morel to distinguish it from the satellite residential areas called *hameaux*, which lie some distance outside the small but charming car-free centre.

> ✔ Protected learning areas
> ✔ Sympathetic architecture
> ✔ Family atmosphere
> ✔ Central pedestrian area
> ✔ Value for money
> ✘ Few non-skiing activities
> ✘ No shuttle bus around residential satellites

It is important to note that the colour-coding of the local lift map flies in the face of all accepted procedure in Europe for reasons that are not at all clear. Green is listed as easy, blue as intermediate, red as difficult, and black as very difficult.

On the snow
top 2,550m (8,364ft) bottom 1,250m (4,100ft)

Valmorel is a planned family resort with exceptional nursery slopes (for adults and children), which are closed off to passing skiers and snowboarders. Its terrain is also sufficiently testing to keep competent skiers and snowboarders interested for a week. Mountain access is from various satellite hamlets at different altitudes. The Télébourg gondola runs from Bourg-Morel in two stages up to the hamlets of Crève-Coeur and Mottet, but is designed more as a people-carrier than a ski lift.

Le Grand Domaine network is divided into the bowl above Valmorel and a straight up-and-down system of lifts between Longchamp and St François across the Col de la Madeleine. All three sectors are accessible by blue (intermediate) pistes. The installation of La Grande Combe chair-lift has greatly eased queues returning from St François in the late afternoon.

Beginners

Valmorel is one of the best resorts in the Alps for beginners – both adults and children ('able to do most runs after two days'). The latter have a protected nursery area with a rope-tow at the Saperlipopette kindergarten down by the Télébourg tower, as well as a totally enclosed area with toys and a lift up the mountain in the Pierrafort area. Unusual, if not unique in the Alps, is a similarly enclosed adult training area by the Bois de la Croix drag-lift. It has hillocks and slalom snowplough runs specially designed to build confidence. The linked resort of Doucy Combelouvière has a network of the easiest of green (easy) runs.

> ### WHAT'S NEW
>
> Funpark with boardercross and half-pipe

Intermediates

This is a resort where you always feel you are going somewhere, rather than skiing the same runs or similar pistes in the same bowl over and over again. The long runs down into the Celliers Valley and the exciting descents off the Col de Gollet provide classic skiing. Bump bashers will want to hit the two red (difficult) runs under the Madeleine chair where the snow keeps cool and crisp. Reverdy off the Lauzière chair is a steeper option.

Advanced

There are not many black (very difficult) runs, nor are they especially ferocious, although the monster bumps under the Gollet chair have been used in championship competitions. The Mottet chair also leads to some testing bumps and is the setting-off point for the longest and most interesting black, unenterprisingly called the Noire du Mottet.

Off-piste

The beauty of Valmorel's off-piste is that even during the high-season weeks you can usually find whole stretches of untracked powder long after a snowfall. With its family image, the resort does not normally attract advanced skiers and snowboarders. Excellent powder-skiing after a snowfall can be found down the ridge between Mottet and Gollet.

Snowboarders

Valmorel has never been a great place for riders: far too many skier families and a dearth of cool bars to frequent in the evenings. However, the easy pistes will suit first-timers and the more experienced can try the funpark with its boardercross course and half-pipe. The Biollene piste is excellent for novice riders.

Tuition and guiding

Classes meet at the French Ski School (ESF) headquarters at the top of the Télébourg people-mover. Lessons given in English are held in the

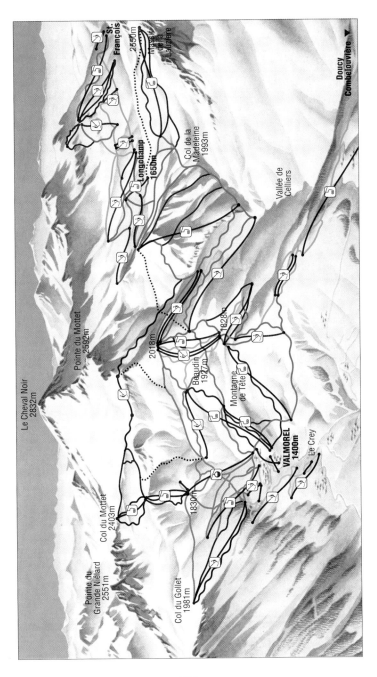

Skiing facts: Valmorel

TOURIST INFORMATION
La Maison de Valmorel, F-73260
Valmorel
Tel 33 479 09 85 55
Fax 33 479 09 85 29
Email valmorel.la.belle@wanadoo.fr
Web site www.valmorel-la-belle.com

THE RESORT
By road Calais 910km
By rail Moûtiers 15km, regular bus
service to resort
Airport transfer Geneva 3hrs,
Lyon 2½hrs
Visitor beds 8,700
Transport gondola between sectors

THE SKIING
Linked or nearby resorts
St François-Longchamp (l),
Doucy Combelouvière (l)
Number of lifts 37 in Valmorel,
55 in linked area
Total of trails/pistes 94km in Valmorel,
151km in linked area (34% easy,
41% intermediate, 15% difficult,
10% very difficult)
Nursery slopes 3 lifts

LIFT PASSES
Area pass Le Grand Domaine (covers
Valmorel, St François-Longchamp and
Doucy Combelouvière) 773–941FF for
6 days
Beginners no free lifts
Pensioners 60yrs and over,
15% reduction
Credit cards yes

TUITION
Adults ESF tel: 479 09 81 86
Snowboarding as ski school
Other courses carving, cross-country,
extreme skiing, seniors, powder clinics,
snowblading, teen skiing, telemark
Guiding ESF

CHILDREN
Lift pass Valmorel, 4–8yrs 603FF,
9–12yrs 648–788FF. Grand Domaine,
4–8yrs 640FF, 9–13yrs 683–836FF,
all for 6 days
Ski & board school ESF as adults
Kindergarten (ski/non-ski)
Saperlipopette tel: 479 09 84 45

OTHER SPORTS
Dog-sledding, hang-gliding, microlight,
parapente, sleigh rides, snowshoeing

FOOD AND DRINK PRICES
Coffee 8–10FF, glass of wine 15FF,
small beer 15FF, soft drink 15FF,
dish of the day 75FF

afternoons from Sunday to Friday; and in French in the mornings, from Monday to Saturday. The children's classes are criticised as being 'more like childminding, not sure how much instruction was given. English children were put together in a class with an instructor who spoke 'some' English'.

Mountain restaurants
These are mostly self-service and offer value for money rather than haute cuisine. The Alpage at the top of the Altispace chair-lift is recommended: 'a basic cafeteria with ample space and inspiring views'.

Altipiano on Pierrafort is smarter, while the Banquoise 2000 refuge on Col de la Madeleine is self-service but characterful, with rustic tables and a log fire. Les 2 Mazots has the best *croûte au fromage*, and Le Grenier, next to the ski school, is still extremely popular.

Accommodation

The resort has only three hotels, with the three-star Planchamp above the main village recommended by reporters. The two-star Hotel du Bourg is situated in the main village centre. Its rooms are unadorned boxes, and the beds are as narrow as coffins. The Hotel la Fontaine has bigger, better rooms. Self-catered apartments are generally larger and better-designed than their counterparts in other French purpose-built resorts, and most provide easy access to the pistes. There is no shuttle bus around the hamlets, and the Télébourg people-mover delivers residents either too high or too low for convenience.

Eating in and out

If proof were needed that the French now live off pizza and fast food, then Valmorel is it. This is not a resort renowned for fine dining, although reporters note La Grange has the ubiquitous range of Savoie specialities. Planchamp is 'cosy with a great atmosphere'. L'Aigle Blanche, just outside the village, is worth the visit. Ski-Roc is best for rabbit filet with garlic. Jumbo Lolo serves Tex-Mex, and La Marmite ('£43 for four') advertises couscous and paella, but you should stick with the steak frites. Chez Albert is best for pizza.

Après-ski

It is not that there isn't any, but it is all rather uninteresting. Jean's Club under the Télébourg tower is the only disco. Loud Top-20-type music is played in the Perce Neige, Café de la Gare and at La Cordée. The Shaker Bar in the Hotel la Fontaine has comfortable sofas and karaoke evenings.

Childcare

The only childminding service is the Saperlipopette nursery. The school has bedrooms and playrooms for infants from six months of age. Reservations should be made well in advance, as the school keeps to a strict ratio of five children per nanny. 'Good English, good care and exceptionally well-organised' was one of a number of positive comments about the nursery. Saperlipopette also has a ski kindergarten.

Round-up

RESORTS COVERED Chamrousse, La Clusaz, Isola 2000, Pra-Loup, Puy-St-Vincent, Valloire

Chamrousse
top 2,255m (7,398ft) bottom 1,400m (4,593ft)

Chamrousse offers some of the closest skiing to Grenoble (30 minutes from the city) in the Dauphiné region. The resort hosted the main alpine events in the 1968 Grenoble Winter Olympics.

Chamrousse is an unattractive, albeit reasonably convenient, collection of buildings on two levels – 1650 and 1750. The ski area has 77km of piste served by 26 lifts. Of the 36 pistes 10 per cent are difficult, 50 per cent intermediate and 40 per cent are easy. The French Ski School (ESF) teaches skiing and snowboarding to adults, and children from three years old. Les Marmots non-ski kindergarten cares for children aged three months to twelve years from 9am to 5pm. Les Oursons ski kindergarten gives lessons to children aged three to twelve years. The resort facilities include four hotels, 25 restaurants, shops and bars, an ice-rink and an outdoor heated swimming-pool. Snowmobiling and sleigh rides are the non-skiing activities on offer.

TOURIST INFORMATION
Tel 33 476 89 92 65
Fax 33 476 89 98 06
Email infos@chamrousse.com
Web site www.chamrousse.com

La Clusaz
top 2,600m (8,528ft) bottom 1,100m (3,608ft)

La Clusaz is a large, spread-out resort off the Autoroute Blanche on the way to Chamonix, less than two hours' drive from Geneva Airport. As a result, it is extremely attractive to skiers from Britain and Holland, some of whom have bought apartments here and visit for weekends. However, one drawback is its lack of altitude. The village itself lies at 1,100m, which is extremely low by Haute Savoie standards, and the ski area, with its 55 lifts, goes up to only 2,600m. The 40 lifts of nearby **Le Grand-Bornand** are included in the regional Aravis lift pass, as is the connecting ski bus.

La Clusaz has five ski areas spread around the sides of a number of neighbouring valleys. Mountain access to Beauregard and L'Aiguille is by lifts from the resort centre. The other three areas (Balme, L'Etale and Croix-Fry/Merdassier) are reached from various points along the valleys via a satisfactory ski-bus network. Despite roads and rivers all five are linked by lift or piste.

The best novice slopes are at Crêt du Merle in L'Aiguille sector and on the plateau top of Beauregard. The skiing is best suited to intermediates, and the pistes are of limited appeal to advanced skiers. A new gondola starting from the foot of the Balme Massif and going up to L'Aiguille area was installed for the 1999—2000 season, and the L'Aiguille drag lift is being replaced by a chair-lift for 2000–1.

The resort has two ski schools: the French Ski School (ESF) and Snow Académie. We have much improved reports of the ESF — 'the instruction was excellent. Our instructors spoke excellent English and quickly built confidence'. The ESF and Snow Académie both teach boarding, and there is a funpark with a half-pipe and quarter-pipe as well as such other delights as table-tops and fun boxes in the Etale sector. Le Club des Mouflets non-ski kindergarten cares for children aged eight months to four-and-a-half years, while Le Club des Champions provides daycare with optional ski lessons for children from three-and-a-half to six years old.

The village is built around a large church, with a stylish shopping precinct beside it and a fast-flowing stream below. Non-skiing activities include parapente, skating, sleigh rides, snowmobiling, snowshoeing and swimming. Accommodation is divided between tour-operator chalets and a varied selection of seven three-star and thirteen two-star hotels. We have glowing reports of the three-star Hotel Beauregard, ('extremely well-fitted, modern pine interior, the food is excellent and it really deserves a four-star rating'). Hotel Gai Soleil is described as 'excellent value'. The other three-stars include Chalet de la Serraz, Le Vieux Chalet and Hotel Alpenroc. The two-stars that receive favourable reports are hotels Christiania and Floralp. The skiing convenience here is one of the lowest we have found among French resorts, and location of accommodation is crucial.

La Clusaz has a much wider choice of restaurants than you would expect in a resort of this size. Le Foly is an attractive and expensive log-cabin in the Confins Valley serving regional specialities. The gastronomic Symphonie in the Hotel Beauregard offers 'excellent cuisine with cheerful service in a warm atmosphere'. Le Coin du Feu is recommended for its 'delicious *crêpe sucré*'. La Table du Berger specialises in fondue and raclette.

Après-ski centres around a few bars. Le Pressoir is the 'in' place for snowboarders, while resort workers meet in the Lion d'Or. Les Caves du Paccaly and Le Grenier are both popular meeting places. L'Ecluse is said to be the best of the discos, with a glass dance-floor over the river, while Le Club 18 has live bands and attracts the locals and an older clientèle. Nightlife is quiet during the week, some would say too quiet, but can become extremely lively during weekends. La Clusaz is rated as one of the best-equipped French resorts for children.

TOURIST INFORMATION
Tel 33 450 32 65 00
Fax 33 450 32 65 01
Email infos@laclusaz.com
Web site www.laclusaz.com

Isola 2000
top 2,610m (8,561ft) bottom 1,800m (5,904ft)

Isola is a purpose-built resort and the most southerly ski area in France. In reasonable weather conditions it is a 90-minute drive north of Nice along the dramatic road beside the Tinée Ravines. The resort was built by a British property company in the 1960s. Created with families in mind, it has a convenient complex of shops, bars, economically designed apartments and hotels, and a large, sunny nursery area. Isola is not accessible from the north, which in part accounts for why so few tour operators offer it in their brochures. However, British skiers make up a big slice of the winter business, and many of them own apartments in the resort.

Isola's original building, the ugly and soulless Front de Neige Centre, is right on the slopes. In an attempt to improve the resort's aesthetic appeal, the more attractive, wood-clad additions of Le Bristol, Le Hameau and Les Ardets apartment blocks were built behind it. These are less convenient but contain bigger and better apartments. They have greatly helped the overall look of Isola 2000, dissipating some of its claustrophobic atmosphere. Hotel Diva is the most comfortable hotel. The resort has 20 restaurants on and off the mountain, two discos and a cinema.

The ski area is limited, but varied enough for beginners, families with small children and intermediates. The 25 lifts serve 120km of pistes. The French Ski School (ESF) is the only ski school here. The non-ski Miniclub kindergarten takes children from two to five years old, and the ski kindergarten, Le Caribou, caters for little ones from four years of age. The resorts of **Auron** and **Valberg** are both within easy reach for a day's skiing.

TOURIST INFORMATION
Tel 33 493 23 15 15
Fax 33 493 23 14 25
Email isola@cote-dazur.com
Web site www.isola-2000.com

Pra-Loup
top 2,500m (8,202ft) bottom 1,600m (5,249ft)

This small resort in the Alpes de Haute-Provence was named after the wolves that once frequented these pine forests. It has a surprisingly extensive range of beginner and intermediate trails but few advanced. The 167km of piste is shared with neighbouring **La Foux d'Allos**. The skiing takes place on two main mountains, accessible by cable-car from the top of the village at 1600. Intermediates will find open-bowl skiing and good tree-line runs with spectacular scenery. The off-piste is extensive (you will need a guide), but there are only five black (difficult) runs. Weekend queues are said to be 'fearsome'. The ESF and ESI ski schools are rated as 'excellent', and heli-skiing (see *Heli-skiing*) is also available through the ESI. Les P'tits Loups kindergarten caters for children from six months to six years from 8.45am to 5.30pm every day.

The resort is split into the two villages of 1500 and 1600, which are linked by a chair-lift and consist of a collection of hotels and apartments built in the 1960s, along with some older chalets. Reporters recommend either staying close to the lifts at Pra-Loup 1500 or at the top of 1600. Prices at the restaurants and bars are lower than in better-known French resorts. On the mountain, La Costabelle is said to be 'busy', while Dalle en Pente is 'much nicer, more laid back and slightly cheaper'. Le Berger is recommended ('the nicest of hotels'). LouFoque and Mamas are the liveliest nightspots. A couple of discos, indoor tennis courts, a swimming-pool and night-skiing make up the rest of the activities on offer here.

TOURIST INFORMATION
Tel 33 492 84 10 04
Fax 33 492 84 02 93
Email info@praloup.com
Web site www.praloup.com

Puy-St-Vincent
top 2,750m (9,022ft) bottom 1,350m (4,429ft)

Puy-St-Vincent is an established resort that was extremely popular with British families in the 1970s and is now staging a major comeback. It is situated 20km from **Briançon**, three hours from Grenoble or Turin and on the edge of the Ecrins National Park. It has a microclimate that usually ensures secure late-season snow cover along with 300 days of sunshine per year.

Puy-St-Vincent 1400 is an unspoilt mountain village with three two-star hotels. It is connected by a double chair-lift and a drag-lift to the higher *station de ski* of **Puy-St-Vincent 1600**, which is dominated by a central apartment block that has seen better days. Newer *résidences* have been built on the edge of the piste. The ski area is small but challenging, with enough variety to suit all standards of skier. Queues are a rarity. Two chair-lifts and a gondola give easy access to the main skiing, which goes up to 2,750m. The ESF and the ESI both offer group lessons and a range of courses. The ESI runs classes for British children during the peak holiday weeks. Les P'tits Loups kindergarten at 1600 takes children aged 18 months to 6 years.

Accommodation is mainly in apartments, and nightlife is limited: 'Puy 1600 goes to bed at 9pm,' said one reporter. The St-Vincent and Cadran Solaire restaurants are both warmly recommended. There is a karaoke bar, a disco and night-skiing. As one reporter put it: 'Puy is a resort which visitors either love or hate. To some it is too small, with not enough to occupy avid skiers by day or après-skiers by night. To others it has great charm, character and intimacy. I have already booked again for next year'.

TOURIST INFORMATION
Tel 33 492 23 35 80
Fax 33 492 23 45 23
Email courrier@puysaintvincent.net
Web site www.puysaintvincent.com

Valloire
top 2,600m (8,528ft) bottom 1,430m (4,690ft)

Valloire is an attractive, reasonably large village set in an isolated bowl above the Maurienne Valley. It is still very much a traditional French farming community, and the odd whiff of manure mingling with the aroma of freshly baked bread is all part of the atmosphere.

This is a friendly, medium-priced resort, which is uncrowded except in high season, when its proximity to the Italian border means that it can be busy and very noisy. The 150km of skiing is served by 34 lifts and is divided between three areas – La Sétaz, Le Crey du Quart and **Valmeinier** – on adjacent mountains reached by lifts that start a few minutes' walk away from the village centre and rise to 2,600m. The terrain is varied, and some of the runs are as long as 1,000 vertical metres. The skiing is not difficult – even the black (difficult) runs would be red (intermediate) by many other resorts' standards.

Mountain access to La Sétaz is by a six-person gondola from the village up to Thimel, followed by a chair- and drag-lift to the summit. Served by artificial snow-cannon and groomed to a high standard, the area provides a good choice of runs from wide reds to gently meandering blue (easy) runs. Access to Le Crey du Quart is either by the Montissot and Colerieux chair-lifts, or directly from Valloire by an eight-person gondola. The skiing at Le Crey du Quart is mainly of the red motorway variety, with gentler slopes going down towards Valloire. Runs off the back of Le Crey du Quart lead down into the Valmeinier ski area which spans both sides of the adjacent valley.

Accommodation includes 12 hotels and a range of apartments and chalets. After skiing, a choice of 20 restaurants and 13 bars is available. The other activities here include a fitness centre, microlighting, skating, squash and snowmobiling.

TOURIST INFORMATION
Tel 33 479 59 03 96
Fax 33 479 59 09 66
Email info@valloire.net
Web site www.valloire.net

Italy

After a brief period of popularity, Italy has again lost its edge as a ski destination. In the the the closing years of the last century, it looked as if the country that gave us Alberto Tomba – possibly the finest technical skier of all time – would join France and Austria on a permanent basis as an equal rival for top piste billing. It is a position that Italy last achieved nearly 30 years ago, but despite a still favourable rate of exchange with Britain and its dominant German market, it has been unable to consolidate its position. In the international battle for beds North America and Andorra are now hot on Italy's heels, and France and Austria have streaked ahead.

The principal villain is the weather. While most of the Alps and the Pyrenees have enjoyed superb snowfalls over the past two seasons, cover in Italy has been at best adequate, and often sparse. The Dolomites had a generally poor winter in 1999–2000, and even in mid-season the Milky Way struggled to keep lifts open. This, coupled with an insufficient number of tourist beds, is to blame for snow-users turning away from its major regions once more.

This winter the pound in Italy is worth 33 per cent more than it was five years ago, a fact that might be expected to encourage more winter visitors. But snow-users are a discerning lot, and what they want are the best mountains and the best facilities. These happen to be in France and Austria, where currency exchange rates are also at their most favourable in 14 years.

Yet the Dolomites offer some of the most scenically charming and extensive skiing to be found anywhere. Gressoney and Champoluc provide excellent intermediate skiing in a beautiful environment, and neighbouring Alagna, also in the Monte Rosa area, has established itself as a point of pilgrimage for powderhounds.

The fragile fabric of Italian skiing remains largely unchanged. Lift systems have been improved, but enormous investment is needed to bring the main ski areas into line with the Trois Vallées or even the SkiWelt. Heavy investment in artificial snow-making can never fully compensate for the unreliability of the natural product in the country's key ski areas.

First-time visitors will be delighted by the Italian zest for enjoyment, both on and off the slopes, and as a nation Italy has raised the pastime of eating on the mountain to an art form. The Italian penchant for partying can be experienced in its nightlife, which starts early and carries on well into the morning.

Although the Italians are well-known for their love of children, the major resorts are mysteriously lacking in childcare facilities. This is possibly due to the fact that Italian families often travel as a whole – complete with granny to look after the *bambini*.

Bormio

ALTITUDE 1,225m (4,018ft)

Beginners ✱✱✱ Intermediates ✱✱✱ Advanced ✱

Bormio is one of Italy's most important ski towns, although the amount of skiing is limited in comparison with the larger and better-known circuits. A high top-lift altitude and a neighbouring glacier allow the season to last well into April. The resort shares a lift pass, but not a lift link, with the neighbouring village of **Santa Caterina** and with the small **San Colombano** ski area above the village of **Oga** on the opposite side of the valley. The lift pass is also valid for **Livigno**, which is an hour's drive away over a pass to the west. St Moritz, across the Swiss border, is another option for a day's excursion.

Bormio's history dates from Roman times, when its location at a crossroads in the Valtellina region in the mountains of Lombardy made it a natural staging post for trans-Alpine traffic. Attracted by hot springs and spectacular views over what is now the Stelvio National Park, the Romans built a town and thermal bath complex at the foot of the pass. The town prospered during the Middle Ages, and its ancient cobbled streets date from that time. In subsequent centuries it was sidelined by history, but the post-Second World War tourist boom has restored some of its former vitality. Today its rather ugly suburbs, with their modern hotels and high-rise apartment blocks, spread over the broad valley floor but do not tarnish the charm of the pedestrianised centre. As one reporter summed it up: 'Bormio is much nicer than the brochures suggest. It is upmarket, yet cheaper than the UK. It is authentically Italian and ideal for families and couples but not suitable for those looking for a rowdy nightlife.'

Bormio's nearest airports are Bergamo and Milan, both officially three-and-a-half hours away, although reporters have experienced transfer times of up to six-and-a-half hours from Bergamo. The drive from Milan includes a breathtakingly beautiful section along the shore of Lake Como.

- ✔ Lack of crowds on the slopes
- ✔ Late-season skiing
- ✔ Attractive medieval town centre
- ✔ High standard of restaurants
- ✔ Range of activities for non-skiers
- ✘ Long airport transfer
- ✘ Unattractive suburbs
- ✘ Lack of childcare facilities

On the snow
top 3,012m (9,879ft) bottom 1,225m (4,018ft)

Bormio's first lifts opened in the 1960s, but the resort came of age in 1985 when it hosted the World Alpine Skiing Championships. The

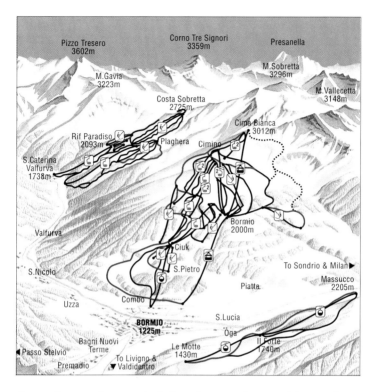

slopes rise steeply on a single broad mountain served by two base-stations, both within a few minutes' walk of the town centre. The main one is the starting point for the two-stage cable-car to the Cima Bianca via Bormio 2000, a substantial mid-station with a large family hotel and a small shopping mall. This can also be reached by car in most conditions. The alternative is the six-seater gondola to **Ciuk**, a lower mid-station, which also has accommodation and restaurants. The top third of the mountain is above the tree-line, with a network of chair-lifts providing a variety of choices. Lower down, the skiing takes place in glades cut from the forest, ensuring good visibility when the weather closes in.

Beginners
The only nursery slopes are at Bormio 2000; this is a mixed blessing as it means that everyone has to buy a lift pass from day one. On the positive side, the result is that everyone learns halfway up the mountain, which gives a better feeling of what skiing is all about. After a few days of mastering the basic manoeuvres, beginners will find plenty of easy pistes in the wooded area down to Ciuk. By the end of the week, many will be skiing the blue (easy) runs from the top of the cable-car.

Intermediates

For the two-week-plus brigade, Bormio's slopes are blissful – there are no particularly steep sections and lots of high-speed cruising. The 14-km descent from the Cima Bianca to the town is just one of many exhilarating options. The bottom section of the Bosco Basso piste below Cunk has been widened to provide an easy alternative route back to the gondola station.

Advanced

Strong piste-skiers may be frustrated by the lack of challenge on Bormio's slopes, as the two short runs that are graded black (difficult) might well be listed as red (intermediate) in a steeper resort. The Stelvio FIS course, which runs from just above La Rocca past Cink to the bottom of the gondola, is an annual choice for the World Cup circuit. In 2005 it will be the venue for the Alpine World Championships.

Off-piste

The powder opportunities off the Cima Bianca more than compensate for the shortage of black bump runs. To the west of the main piste a steep, open bowl leads down to some shallow-gradient, tree-level skiing. Those who plan to go below the right-hand turn-off to Bormio 2000 should check first that the Ornella drag-lift is running. To the east of the pistes, a wider choice of terrain gives access to a more heavily wooded area. A long trail leads back to the Praimont chair. Those who are prepared to hire a guide (Bormio has a choice of two mountain guiding companies) and climb on skins will find magnificent terrain in both winter and summer on the Stelvio Glacier.

Snowboarders

Although freeriders can have some fun in the powder and in the trees when conditions are good, snowboarders are otherwise completely ignored here. There is no pipe or funpark; the nearest is on the Stelvio Pass, 19km away.

Tuition and guiding

Of the six ski schools in Bormio, the Alta Valtellina, based near the nursery slopes at Bormio 2000, is highly recommended for its young, friendly, English-speaking instructors. The more traditional options include the Nazionale and Bormio 2000. The Anzi School is for hotel guests only. The Sertorelli and the Capitani organisations specialise in summer ski-touring, retaining only a skeleton winter staff for their valued clients.

Mountain restaurants

The favoured stopping-off point for lunch or refreshments is La Rocca, an old-fashioned hut on the main trail from the top of the mountain to Bormio 2000. It has two rooms, each with a wood-burning stove and friendly service. It also hosts dinner followed by a torchlit descent whenever there is sufficient demand. The Rhondendri near the top of La Rocca chair is also recommended ('quiet, small and pleasant, with a splendid viewing position at the top of a black mogul run'). The Girasole Hotel and the self-service cafeteria at Bormio 2000 are also convenient, though less traditional.

Accommodation

The modernised four-star Hotel Posta, on a pedestrianised street in the old town, offers luxurious accommodation, a swimming-pool and fitness centre. The other four-star recommendations include the Rezia and the Palace. Those who prefer to be near the lifts should consider one of the modern three-star options: the Derby, the Nevada or the Funivia. In the two-star category, the family-run Dante and the atmospheric Gufo offer exceptional value in central locations. Hotel Aurora is praised by reporters: 'the hotel was very clean and warm, the staff friendly and helpful, and the food excellent'.

As the town of Bormio is only ski-in ski-out when snow conditions are good in January and February, there is an excellent case to be made for staying in the three-star Girasole at Bormio 2000. This is especially true for holidays over the Easter period when the main resort begins to wind down. The hotel is run by the hospitable Alfredo Cantoni and his English wife, Elizabeth, with a strong emphasis on family entertainment.

Eating in and out

Although *pizzocheri*, a rather gritty indigenous pasta, is something of an acquired taste, the Valtellina also has an interesting range of specialities including charcuterie, mushrooms and locally produced wines. The best places to try them are the Rasiga (a beautifully converted saw mill), the Vecchia Combo, the Taulà and Osteria dei Magri. All four restaurants will prepare multi-course gourmet feasts at modest all-inclusive rates, provided they are booked in advance. Bormio also has five pizzerias and a spaghetteria. Self-catering is not the norm in a resort with a wide choice of cheap eating-places, but the specialist grocery shops on the Via Roma certainly stock all the necessary ingredients for home cooking on a magnificent scale.

Après-ski

Bormio is the most Italian of resorts, with a strong sense of style in its immaculate shops and restaurants. In the early evening, chattering crowds stroll down the narrow cobbled streets and fill the bars and cafés on the historic Via Roma, the centre of activity in the old town. The Bagni Vecchi, a few miles out of town in a cave in the hillside, comprises a natural sauna and curative hot baths. It includes an atmospheric turn-of-the-century spa complex offering a range of treatments for weary skiers. In town, the naturally heated water has been put to good use in the large public swimming-pool.

The Gorky on the Via Roma and the Vagabond in the church square are the pubs of choice, both after skiing and after dinner. Late nightlife

Skiing facts: Bormio

TOURIST INFORMATION
Via Roma 131B, I-23032 Bormio,
Sondrio
Tel 39 0342 903 300
Fax 39 0342 904 696
Email aptbormio@provincia.so.it
Web site
www.provinica.so.it/aptvaltellina

THE RESORT
By road Calais 1,205km
By rail Tirano 39km
Airport transfer Milan or Bergamo
3½hrs
Visitor beds 6,035
Transport free ski bus with lift pass

THE SKIING
Linked or nearby resorts Livigno (n),
Santa Caterina (n), San Colombano (n)
Number of lifts 17
Total of trails/pistes 50km in Bormio
(23% easy, 68% intermediate,
9% difficult)
Nursery slopes 4 on the mountain at
Ciuk and Bormio 2000
Summer skiing 20km on Stelvio Glacier
(May–November)

LIFT PASSES
Area pass Alta Valtellina (covers
Bormio, Livigno, Santa Caterina, San
Colombano) L225,000–265,000 for
6 days
Beginners points tickets
Pensioners 65yrs and over, as children

Credit cards yes

TUITION
Adults Alta Valtellina tel: 0342 911 010,
Anzi tel: 0342 904 381,
Bormio 2000 tel: 0342 903 135,
Capitani tel: 0342 910 130,
Nazionale tel: 0342 901 553,
Sertorelli tel: 0342 903 060
Snowboarding as ski schools
Other courses carving, cross-country,
seniors, race training, skiing for the
disabled, snowblading, teen skiing,
telemark
Guiding Scuola di Alpinismo Guide
Alpine Ortler Cevedale
tel: 0342 910 991, Associazione
Guide Alpine Alta Valtellina
tel: 0342 901 737

CHILDREN
Lift pass Alta Valtellina, 5–12yrs,
L158,000–185,000 for 6 days
Ski & board school as adults
Kindergarten (non-ski) through
Girasole Hotel tel: 0342 904 652

OTHER SPORTS
Climbing wall, indoor tennis and squash,
skating, snowmobiling, swimming,
thermal baths

FOOD AND DRINK PRICES
Coffee L1,500, glass of wine L1,500,
small beer L4,500, soft drink L3,500,
dish of the day L14,000–22,000

focuses on the King's Club disco, which is open until 3am, with the
piano bar at the Aurora Hotel a less frenetic option.

Childcare
The ski schools will take children from four years of age, provided there
are other children with whom to make up a class. Older children have

to fit in with the adult classes. There is no formal crèche service, but the Girasole Hotel can arrange local babysitters to care for children during the day and in the evening.

Linked or nearby resorts

Santa Caterina
top 3,296m (10,814ft) bottom 1,737m (5,697ft)

Santa Caterina (or 'San Cat', as it is known) is a quiet, attractive village with eight lifts and 40km of its own skiing. It is situated 30 minutes by bus from Bormio, up a mountain road that is a dead-end in winter when the Gavia Pass is closed. It shares a lift pass with its larger neighbour, Bormio, and it usually has better snow. Local skiing is on the northeast-facing slopes of the Sobretta. The higher slopes are fairly steep and graded black; some intermediate trails wind down between the trees.

The Santa Caterina Ski School receives mixed but generally favourable reviews. The Bimbi sulla Neve kindergarten cares for children from 10am to 1pm. Of the two cross-country trails, the 10-km Pista Valtellina is challenging, while the 8-km Pista La Fonte is classified as easy. There is also skating on a natural rink.

The San Matteo Hotel is recommended for comfort and food. Nightlife is limited, with one fairly large disco and a number of cosy bars that remain open until after midnight.

TOURIST INFORMATION
Tel 39 0342 935 598
Fax 39 0342 925 549
Email aptsanta.caterina@provincia.so.it
Web site www.provincia.so.it/aptvaltellina

Cervinia

ALTITUDE 2,050m (6,724ft)

Beginners ✱✱✱ Intermediates ✱✱✱ Snowboarders ✱

Cervinia is Italy's most snow-sure resort, set at 2,050m in the Aosta Valley within easy reach of Turin. It is dominated by Il Cervino, which is considerably better known under its Swiss name of the Matterhorn. The substantial ski area is linked with **Zermatt**, and for the past two seasons the adjacent resorts

✔ Excellent snow record
✔ Value for money
✔ Alpine scenery
✔ Sunny slopes
✔ Extensive skiing season
✔ Long runs
✘ Heavy traffic
✘ Inconvenient lift access
✘ Lift queues
✘ Unattractive village

have operated a joint lift pass covering all of Cervinia and the Klein Matterhorn sector of **Zermatt**, as well as their own separate lift passes. Subject to the outcome of protracted talks in summer 2000, Cervinia, at least, hopes to fully integrate the whole ski areas of both resorts this winter. Cervinia has a reputation as a resort best suited to beginners and intermediates, so the real advantage of this arrangement is that accomplished snow-users can enjoy some of the challenges offered on the Zermatt side of the mountain. Cervinia's skiing is linked to the nearby village of **Valtournenche** (1,524m), and the 12-person gondola greatly enhances this end of the ski area.

Mussolini, who was instrumental in the resort's construction in the 1930s, decreed the name should change from Breuil to the more Italian-sounding Cervinia. A nucleus of original buildings reflects the austere imperial style of the time. Post-war concrete edifices, thrown up without regard for the extraordinarily beautiful mountain environment, resemble 1960s council flats. More recent additions have façades of wood and natural stone but, despite some tarting up, the buildings have no authentic mountain charm nor do the shops have much class. Nevertheless, Cervinia's large bed-base has earned it the unassailable title of the most popular resort in Italy with the British; from December to April, about 1,000 British snow-users a week holiday here and not all of them can be wrong. The ambience remains overwhelmingly Italian, making weekends and school holiday periods hectic and prone to queues, though these are cheerful and unaggressive.

Parking at weekends is chaotic, since the influx from Milan and Turin insists on parking in the street instead of in the five free and one fee-paying parking areas. There is no free ski bus, but a municipal bus makes circuits every 20 minutes as far as **Cieloalto** until 8pm.

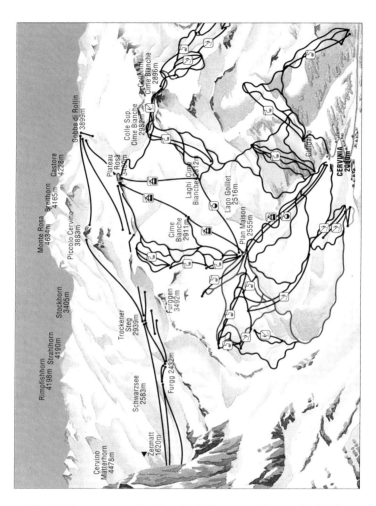

Cervinia is more expensive than the Italian resorts that are further from Switzerland and is not as chic as Cortina d'Ampezzo or even Courmayeur. However, it has a vibrant atmosphere and – although it is by no means anyone's image of a fairytale resort – Jack (of bean stalk fame) would appreciate the mysterious sign in English outside the Plan Maison gondola, which reads: 'Do not go on if you have not the ticket for going up plants'.

On the snow
top 3,490m (11,447ft) bottom 1,524m (4,999ft)

For years Italy's highest resort has been unfairly dismissed by competent snow-users as a playground for beginners and lower intermediates

– no match for its swanky Swiss neighbour. Certainly it is true that despite warnings of *solo per esperti* (only for experts), most of the handful of black (difficult) runs would be graded red (intermediate) on the Swiss side of the mountain.

Snow-users now have a choice of three lift passes. The first covers just Cervinia and Valtournenche, the second includes the Swiss Klein Matterhorn lifts, and the third includes all the Zermatt sectors. In practice, it is extremely difficult for anyone to explore the whole of Zermatt at leisure and return to the top of Klein Matterhorn for the long run home in one day. The majority of snow-users will be perfectly content with the wide, open motorway cruising that Cervinia has to offer. The length and quantity of Cervinia's flattering red and blue (easy) runs provide hours of effortless cruising, but readers criticise the lack of variety.

Mountain access is most direct from the queue-prone gondola and cable-car, which are an irritating hike uphill from the village. Access is also possible from drag-lifts in the nursery area to the left of the village, or from the satellite areas of Cieloalto and Valtournenche. Plan Maison is the mid-mountain station from which the main lifts fan out, with cable-cars rising to Plateau Rosa and the Swiss border.

When the resort opened in 1936 the lift system was considered state-of-the-art but it has since been updated only in parts, and considerable investment is now needed. In reality, some 34,000 snow-users per hour can be transported uphill, although not without annoying queues at weekends and during peak periods for some of the most essential links.

Beginners

If you learn to ski in this resort you will wonder what all the fuss is about. Beginners tend to spend no more than two days on the conveniently accessed nursery slopes at the village edge. Cervinia's excellent snow record means that novices have good conditions on the nursery slopes, before moving up to the network of green (beginner) and blue pistes at Plan Maison. There are few resorts where beginners can graduate so quickly and are able to ski runs as high as the top-to-bottom, wide and well-groomed blue piste from Plateau Rosa down to the village, which is a drop of nearly 1,500 vertical metres.

Intermediates

The 8-km Ventina (no. 7 on the piste map) from Plateau Rosa down to the resort is a classic alpine run. The series of runs from the Klein Matterhorn to the farming village of Valtournenche measures a total 22km and is long enough to transform even the toughest skier's knees to noodles. Many red runs in Cervinia would be graded blue in Switzerland. In fact, snow-users used to the intimidating steep slopes in Chamonix or Val d'Isère will find the gradual pitch of Cervinia's pistes both ego-boosting and useful for advancing technical skills.

Advanced

'Not even a hint of challenge,' said one reporter, 'even the blacks in Cieloalto are groomed flat'. The one true pisted challenge used to be the run down from Furggen, on the shoulder of the Matterhorn, from where you could see both resorts simultaneously. This was reached by an ancient cable-car and began from a cliff face after a walk down an internal staircase of nearly 300 steps. However, the piste became inaccessible when the cable-car was closed some years ago after failing a safety test. It now looks as if the closure is permanent. The marked black runs on Cieloalto and down from Plan Maison will not increase anyone's insurance premium. Zermatt's skiing is considerably more challenging.

Off-piste

On powder days, especially when the wind closes upper lifts, the skiing among the trees on the shoulder above Cieloalto is a good off-piste option. More ambitious routes require guides and mountaineering gear. Heli-skiing (see *Heli-skiing*) is available on the Zermatt side of the mountain and, in addition to ski-touring, provides access to a wealth of glacier runs.

Snowboarders

The Carosello area is now a funpark, with a half-pipe, boardercross course, and music played over loudspeakers to complete the atmosphere.

Tuition and guiding

The main Cervino School continues to receive some criticism but still appears to be more organised than the smaller school in Cieloalto. Reporters said of the Cervino: 'unsatisfactory instruction without much enthusiasm,' and 'having children and adults in the same class did not work'. Another reader noted that teachers at the Cervino seemed to do whatever they felt like, rather than following a strict and regimented method – 'the way they do in Austria'. We have no reports of the Breuil ski school. Valtournenche has its own ski school. Mountain guides from the local bureau in Cervinia charge considerably less than their Swiss counterparts but have equal expertise on the border peaks.

Mountain restaurants

The piste map shows where to stop for lunch. Cervinia's mountain meals are not cheap by Italian standards but are still much better value than on the other side of the Matterhorn. Bar Ventina on the eponymous run down from Plateau Rosa, Bar Bontadini on the slope of the same name and Chalet Etoile near the Rocce Nere chair-lift are among the best for polenta and fondue. Bar Le Pousset, just below Langi Cime Bianche, is also recommended. Baità Cretaz da Mario on the nursery slopes receives outstanding reviews for its cuisine, relaxed and attentive service and 'lovely linen table-cloths'. The Igloo – run by Pauline, an English exile – at the top of the Bardoney chair is praised for its tasty food and large portions. La Motta da Felice at the top of the Motta drag-lift is not to be missed.

Skiing facts: Cervinia

TOURIST INFORMATION
Via Carrel 29, I-11021 Breuil-Cervinia, AO
Tel 39 0166 949136
Fax 39 0166 949731
Email breuil-cervinia@netvallee.it
Web site www.cervinia.it

THE RESORT
By road Calais 1,000km
By rail Châtillon 27km, regular buses
to resort
Airport transfer Turin or Geneva 2hrs
Visitor beds 2,800
Transport no free bus service

THE SKIING
Linked or nearby resorts Zermatt (I),
Valtournenche (I)
Number of lifts 31 (70 including
Zermatt)
Total of trails/pistes 80km in Cervinia
(30% easy, 60% intermediate, 10%
difficult) 200km with Zermatt
Nursery slopes 2 lifts
Summer skiing on Plateau Rosa, 8 lifts

LIFT PASSES
Area pass (covers Cervinia and Swiss
Klein Matterhorn lifts) L212–264,000
for 6 days. Full area pass may be
available
Beginners points tickets

Pensioners 65yrs and over
L118,000–250,000 for 6 days
Credit cards yes

TUITION
Adults Breuil Tel: 0166 940960,
Cervino tel: 0166 949034,
Cieloalto tel: 0166 948451
Snowboarding as ski schools
Other courses carving, cross-country,
extreme skiing, heli-skiing, telemark
Guiding Guide del Cervino
tel: 0166 948169,
Heliski Cervinia tel: 0166 949267

CHILDREN
Lift pass under 12yrs L188,000–
250,000, free for under 8yrs with parent
Ski & board school as adults
Kindergarten (non-ski) Biancaneve
(at Valtournenche) tel: 0166 93123
Plan Maison tel: 0159 9155

OTHER SPORTS
Climbing wall, free-flying, horse-riding,
ice-climbing, parapente, skating,
swimming

FOOD AND DRINK PRICES
Coffee L1,500, glass of wine L2,500,
small beer L3,500, soft drink L3,000,
dish of the day L25,000

Accommodation
Cervinia has virtually no chalet or self-catering accommodation. Most
of its 40 hotels date from the 1930s and are seldom convenient for the
lifts. The Hermitage is in the super league of five-star alpine hotels, with
the highest standards of service, cuisine and price. The four-star Punta
Maquignaz is an attractive wood-clad hotel close to the drag-lifts. You
can ski back to the Petit Palais, which is close to the cable-car and a five-
minute walk from the village centre. The Cristallo is the oldest hotel, an
ugly arc of white concrete, though agreeably decorated inside and with
a swimming-pool. The Jumeau is 'pleasant, quiet and well-run'. The

Compagnoni on the main street is 'simple, convenient and welcoming'. Hotel Breuil is 'clean, spacious, and very acceptable'.

Eating in and out
The resort has a reasonable range of restaurants, which are priced rather highly compared with tourist expectations of Italy, but are mostly good value. The Hermitage has 'truly outstanding cuisine'. Il Capriccio is a close contender. Le Nicchia is similarly rich for pocket and paunch, while La Tana is recommended for wild boar, venison and everything with porcini mushrooms. The Copa Pan is a long-standing favourite – 'beautiful beamed room with a small bar centred around an open fire was the setting for probably the best meal I have had in my whole life'. La Maison de Sausure is the place to try the typical Valdostana specialities. It is hard to beat the pizzas at Al Solito Posto and the Matterhorn Pizzeria.

Après-ski
Lino's Bar beside the ice-rink is busy when the lifts close and just as popular later in the evening. Skating is a passionate pastime here, but reporters complain that the nightlife lacks lustre. 'Like the skiing,' said one reporter, 'it is all intermediate' – although another claims it is 'friendly and lively'. Yel Matrob cocktail bar is the liveliest, thanks to its animated patron, Renzo. The Copa Pan Irish bar is popular and serves Murphy's beer. La Chimera is still going after many a decade, but the Garage is the hippest disco ('loud and popular, it is still going strong well into the small hours'). The re-opened Dragon bar is as popular as ever.

Childcare
Italians appear to bring their grandmothers or nannies with them, as Cervinia still does not have a daycare centre for those too young for regular ski lessons. The Biancaneve non-ski kindergarten 9km away at Valtournenche is the only childcare centre. The tourist information office has a list of officially sanctioned babysitters but admits that few speak English.

Cortina d'Ampezzo

ALTITUDE 1,224m (4,015ft)

Beginners **✳✳✳** Intermediates **✳✳✳** Advanced **✳✳✳** Snowboarding **✳**

If we had to single out one ski resort in the world for the sheer beauty of its setting, combined with an attractive town and a truly all-round winter-sports resort, it would be Cortina d'Ampezzo in the craggy Dolomite mountains. Cortina sits in isolated splendour in the Ampezzo Valley, less than two hours' journey by road from Venice. Unlike its neighbours in the German-speaking Sud Tirol, Cortina is Italian to its voluptuous core and largely devoid of German and Austrian tourists. Some 90 per cent of its winter visitors are Italian.

- ✔ Extensive nursery slopes
- ✔ Variety of restaurants
- ✔ Long runs
- ✔ Activities for non-skiers
- ✔ Beautiful scenery
- ✔ Extensive cross-country
- ✔ Tree-level skiing
- ✔ Lively nightlife
- ✔ Resort ambience
- ✘ Spread-out ski areas
- ✘ Limited for late-season holidays
- ✘ Heavy traffic outside pedestrian area
- ✘ Oversubscribed ski bus system

The large, attractive town is centred around the main shopping street of Corso Italia and the Piazza Venezia with its green-and-white bell tower ('a lovely, lovely town, with loads of ambience'). The large, frescoed buildings have an air of faded grandeur, and the views of the pink rock-faces of Monte Cristallo are sensational. More recent architectural additions display a sympathetic Italian alpine style in keeping with the town's dramatic surroundings.

The centre is mercifully traffic-free, with cars confined to a busy one-way perimeter road. Parking is a problem in the centre, and reporters warn: 'if your hotel provides a private parking space at extra cost, pay up and don't complain'. Drivers should aim to avoid the huge Friday night/Saturday morning exodus, with queues that tail back all the way to the motorway exit.

However, Cortina's upmarket reputation can deter those skiers who see Italy as the destination for cheap and cheerful holidays, although by international standards it is not an exclusive or overtly expensive resort. There are plenty of charming, family-run hotels with reasonable prices as well as simple, welcoming bars. As one reporter put it: 'our holiday here cost no more than previous ones in Val d'Isère and Verbier. We were constantly surprised by the value for money that we experienced both on and off the slopes'. Cortina has some of the best nursery slopes anywhere, as

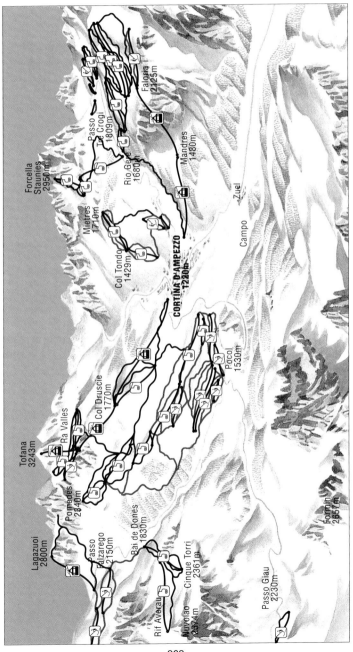

well as long, challenging runs for intermediate to accomplished skiers and snowboarders.

On the snow
top 3,243m (10,640ft) bottom 1,224m (4,015ft)
The skiing is divided between the main Tofana-Socrepes area to the west of town, which is reached via the Freccia nel Cielo (arrow in the sky) cable-car, and Staunies-Faloria on the other side of town, which consists of two sectors separated by a minor road. A scattering of smaller ski areas along the Passo Falzarego road still belong to individual farmers. One of these areas, Cinque Torri, reached by an isolated two-stage chair-lift, is small and uncrowded with reliable snow (it is north-facing), long runs and breathtaking scenery.

Passo Falzarego, further down the road and a 20-minute bus ride from the town centre, links in one direction only into the **Sella Ronda** circuit and shares the Dolomiti Superski lift pass. You need to start early in the day in order to achieve any distance on skis. At Passo Falzarego the dramatic cable-car soars 640 vertical metres up a cliff-face to Lagazuoi, followed by a beautiful 11-km red (intermediate) run past a shimmering turquoise ice-fall and several welcoming huts before reaching **Armentarola** and **San Cassiano** beyond. However, the whole day is a rush and can be stressful. To return to Cortina you take either a bus from Armentarola to Falzarego or one of the waiting taxis at Armentarola to Lagazuoi.

WHAT'S NEW
Chair-lift replaces Baby Socrepes lift
Reintroduction of ski and non-ski
kindergarten
Hotel Piccolo Pocol

If Cortina has one major flaw, it is the inefficient transport system. The buses linking the town with the various fragmented ski areas are both infrequent and hopelessly oversubscribed at peak hours. To enjoy the skiing to its full, you need your own car and a driver mentally equipped to cope with the stress of securing rare and much sought-after parking spaces against fearless Roman opposition in supercharged Alfa Romeos.

Both Tofana and Faloria can be reached on foot from most of the accommodation if you are prepared for a hearty hike in ski boots. Morning queues for the Tofana cable-car are not a problem owing to the late rising-time of the average Cortina visitor – the morning rush-hour never starts before 10.30am. The top section of Tofana is designated for sunbathers and sightseers only.

Beginners
A long serpentine blue (easy) piste takes you down from Tofana's mid-station to link with Socrepes, one of the best nursery slopes in Europe. Socrepes looks like a kind of sloping Kensington Gardens interspersed with easily negotiable lifts, including a new chair-lift for 2000–1. The more isolated Pierosà-Miétres is an equally gentle sector.

Intermediates

The majority of Cortina's skiing is of intermediate standard, with long runs in both the main ski areas. Between the resort and Col Drusciè the Tofana cable-car travels over gentle, tree-lined terrain and open fields with wide and easy trails, which cross rough roads without much warning to either skiers or drivers. Poor snow conditions often make these runs testing, which gives them their red and black (difficult) gradings. The second stage of the cable-car climbs the sheer, rocky mountainside to Ra Valles, in the middle of a pleasant bowl.

A day-trip into the Sella Ronda ski area should not be missed for anyone of intermediate standard and upwards. The good-value Dolomiti Superski lift pass covers both Cortina and the Sella Ronda.

Advanced

Higher up at Tofana, the Ra Valles sector at 2,700m offers the best snow in the resort. Near the bottom of the Tofana bowl, a gap in the rock gives access to an exhilarating black trail, which has a fairly steep south-facing stretch in the middle. The run ends up at the Pomedes chair-lifts, an area which itself offers some excellent runs including a couple of good blacks and the spectacular Canelone downhill racecourse.

The most dramatic skiing is found between Cristallo and Cresta Bianche, two soaring cathedrals of granite that dominate the landscape. From the foot of Monte Cristallo a four-stage chair climbs to Forcella Staunies, which starts with a steep black mogul field so sandwiched between the rock walls that it creates an illusion of narrowness. Halfway down, the bumps flatten out into a wide red race track ('each of us managed 150 linked turns on the deserted slope all the way down to the Padeon chair-lift').

Off-piste

After a fresh snowfall Forcella Staunies becomes an appealing off-piste area, as do the higher reaches of Tofana. Gruppo Guide Alpine Cortina, the resort's ski guiding organisation, arranges day ski-tours.

Snowboarders

The Tofana area is the most popular riders' area here, with plenty of powder opportunities and drop-offs. Cortina does not have a half-pipe or funpark but the terrain is well-suited to riders.

Cross-country

Cross-country skiing is popular in the Cortina area, with the Scuola Italiana Sci Fondo offering private lessons. Six trails in the valley north and east of the resort give a total 58km of loipe.

Tuition and guiding

The main Scuola Sci Cortina has meeting places at Socrepes, Pocol, Rio Gere and Pierosà-Miétres. The standards appear to be mixed, depending mainly on the level of English spoken by the instructor. Scuola Sci

Azzurra and Scuola Sci Cristallo-Cortina are smaller alternatives. Snowboarding lessons are available through the Scuola Sci Cortina and Scuola Sci Cristallo-Cortina.

Mountain restaurants

Eating is a memorable experience in Cortina, and the choice of restaurants is extensive in the main ski areas, as well as being good value for money: 'we found prices very reasonable: a hefty pizza or pasta dish was only about £4,' said one reporter. Rifugio Duca d'Aosta is recommended with its wood-panelled walls and heart-warming local dishes. Simple mountain fare can be eaten at Rifugio Son Forca, which is reached by a modern chair-lift from Rio Gere on the road separating the Cristallo and Faloria ski areas. Rifugio Berghaus Pomedes has hand-carved furniture and a varied menu. Reporters praise El Faral at the foot of Socrepes, and Col Taron in the same area, which serves delicious pasta.

The next stage down the mountain from the Duca d'Aosta is Baità Pie Tofana, a relaxed eating place with a sun terrace and attractive interior. Rifugio Averau at Cinque Torri has stunning views and was voted best restaurant in the ski area by one reporter. Rifugio Lagazuoi is situated a steep but worthwhile walk from the top of the Falzarego cable-car. Other recommended eating places are the Tondi restaurant, and Rifugio Scotoni on the long run down to **Armentarola** in the Sella Ronda.

Accommodation

Hotels range from the large international variety to simple, family-run establishments. A large number of private apartments and chalets are also available. The resort's smartest hotel, the Miramonti Majestic, is 2km out of town. The four-stars include the attractive Hotel de la Poste in the heart of Cortina, which is 'comfortable, if somewhat noisy', but the food was severely criticised by one reporter ('veal cooked to the consistency of a school blanket'). Also well-located is the charming Hotel Ancora on the Corso Italia, run by the indomitable Flavia Sartor, who uses the hotel to house her enormous collection of antiques and paintings. The Parc Victoria is advantageously placed and comfortably furnished by the Angeli family, who own the hotel. The three-star, family-run Aquila is highly recommended. The Italia is a popular two-star with wholesome food and a loyal following. Two-star Hotel Montana is highly recommended ('centrally located, cosy, comfortable and friendly'). The Olimpia is one of the cheapest and most central bed-and-breakfasts and is said to be comfortable with large rooms.

Eating in and out

Dining is taken seriously in Cortina. More than 80 restaurants cater for all tastes, from simple pizzas to gourmet dining. Michelin-starred Tivoli on the edge of town has a warm ambience with delicious and often unusual cooking. El Toula is a converted barn with a rustic atmosphere. The Croda Caffé, Il Ponte and the Cinque Torri are all good for pizzas. Leone e Anna specialises in Sardinian cuisine, while

Skiing facts: Cortina d'Ampezzo

TOURIST INFORMATION
Piazzetta San Francesco 8, I-32043
Cortina d'Ampezzo, Belluno
Tel 39 0436 3231
Fax 39 0436 3235
Email apt1@sunrise.it
Web site www.sunrise.it/dolomiti

THE RESORT
By road Calais 1,200km
By rail Calalzo–Pieve di Cadore 35km
Airport transfer Venice 2hrs
Visitor beds 22,800
Transport free bus connects town centre
with main lifts

THE SKIING
Linked or nearby resorts
Armentarola (I), San Cassiano (I),
San Vito di Cadore (n), Kronplatz (n)
Number of lifts 37 in Cortina, 52 in area
Total of trails/pistes 110km in area
(44% easy, 49% intermediate,
7% difficult)
Nursery slopes 5 runs, 3 lifts

LIFT PASSES
Area pass Dolomiti Superski
(covers 460 lifts)
L275,000–313,000 for 6 days
Beginners no special rates
Pensioners 15% reduction for over 60yrs
Credit cards yes

TUITION
Adults Scuola Sci Cortina tel: 0436 2911,
Scuola Sci Azzurra tel: 0436 2694,
Scuola Sci Cristallo-Cortina
tel: 0436 870073
Snowboarding Scuola Sci Cortina,
Scuola Sci Cristallo-Cortina
Other courses carving, cross-country,
race-training, skiing for the disabled,
ski-touring, telemark
Guiding Scuola Sci Cortina, Scuola Sci
Azzurra, Gruppo Guide Alpine Cortina
tel: 0436 868505

CHILDREN
Lift pass Dolomiti Superski
L193,000–219,000 for six days, free for
7yrs and under
Ski & board school as adults
Kindergarten tel: as Scuola Sci Cortina

OTHER SPORTS
Bobsleigh, curling, dog-sledding,
hang-gliding, horse-riding, ice-hockey,
ice-polo, indoor tennis, parapente, skating,
ski-joring, ski jumping, snowmobiling,
snow-rafting, snowshoeing, swimming

FOOD AND DRINK PRICES
Coffee L1,700, glass of wine
L1,500–2,500, small beer L3,000,
soft drink L3,000, dish of the day
L18,000–25,000

El Zoco has grilled meats. For self-caterers or those trying to save money, the Cooperativa department store has 'an outstanding wine selection at very reasonable prices'.

Après-ski
'In one week you can only scratch the surface of Cortina's après-ski,' commented one reporter. At about 5pm the early evening *passeggiata* along the pedestrianised Corso Italia heralds the start of the off-slope festivities. The street becomes alive with promenading, fur-clad Italians:

'Like a fashion show with mobile phones'. Cortina's shopping is absorbing and varied and includes antique and jewellery shops, sportswear and designer boutiques, interesting delicatessen and the six-storey Cooperativa department store, an Aladdin's Cave that seems to sell everything, with reasonable prices to match. As one reporter commented: 'it's the only town we know where the Co-op has marble floors and sells designer clothes'.

After dinner the action starts at the Enoteca wine bar, a serious drinking spot with a magnificent cellar. Jerry's Wine Bar is another popular meeting place. Later on, the Hyppo, Area and VIP discos are extremely lively. The entrance fee for the nightclubs does not subsidise the drink prices, as in some comparably smart resorts; partying is consequently an expensive occupation here.

Childcare

Cortina has some of the most extensive nursery slopes we have encountered in Europe, and the reintroduction of a ski and non-ski kindergarten for 2000–1 means that we can once again recommend it as a resort for families. The adult ski schools all offer children's tuition.

Linked or nearby resorts

Kronplatz
top 2,275m (7,464ft) bottom 900m (2,953ft)

This interesting ski area on the Italian–Austrian border is also known as Plan de Corones and is covered by the Dolomiti Superski lift pass. The region is little-known outside Italy and Germany, yet is an easy 60-km day-trip from Cortina. Eighty-five kilometres of piste are serviced by 32 lifts, of which an astonishing 12 are gondolas. The resort has a half-pipe served by a six-person chair-lift. The ski area can be reached from five different bases, most of which have car parks, while one – St Vigilio – has 3,534 tourist beds. Kronplatz has four ski schools, three kindergarten, five cross-country tracks and a half-pipe. Reporters comment on its excellent lifts, wide variety of intermediate runs and excellent snow-making ('it claims to have the most modern lift system in Europe and it may well be so').

TOURIST INFORMATION
Tel 39 0474 555 447
Fax 39 0474 530 018
Email info@kronplatz.com
Web site www.kronplatz.com

Courmayeur

ALTITUDE 1,230m (4,034ft)

Beginners ✶ Intermediates ✶✶✶ Advanced ✶✶ Snowboarders ✶✶

Courmayeur is a delightful old village, which established its reputation first as a climbing base for the forbidding granite peaks of Mont Blanc, Western Europe's highest massif, and second as a popular nineteenth-century spa with its curative, pungent-smelling waters. Its role as an internationally acclaimed ski resort only came about with the opening of the Mont Blanc Tunnel in 1962. At 11.31am on 14 August a delighted Italian miner thrust his fist through a hole in the rock-face five kilometres beneath Mont Blanc and swapped a bottle of Asti Spumante for a bottle of Veuve Clicquot with his French counterpart. The tunnel, then the longest underground road route in the world at 11.6km, ended Courmayeur's international isolation and linked it with **Chamonix**. Suddenly, Geneva Airport was only a 90-minute drive away. However, the closure of the tunnel after the tragic fire in March 1999 has, for the moment, returned Courmayeur to the Italians. Similarly, Courmayeur has temporarily lost some of its attraction for advanced skiers, who would usually spend part of the week on the more challenging slopes of Chamonix.

- ✔ Beautiful scenery
- ✔ Village atmosphere
- ✔ Easy resort access
- ✔ Excellent restaurants
- ✔ Lively nightlife
- ✔ Varied off-piste
- ✔ Long vertical drop
- ✔ Tree-level skiing
- ✔ Comprehensive snowmaking
- ✔ Extensive cross-country skiing
- ✘ Lack of skiing convenience
- ✘ Peak period queues

No longer can visitors to Chamonix or Megève pop over for lunch. Skiers from Britain must either fly to Turin or take the longer two-and-a-half hour transfer from Geneva through the Grand St Bernard Tunnel. The Mont Blanc tunnel is to be rebuilt but will not reopen before March 2001. The plus point is the almost complete absence of traffic on the main road that separates the village from the ski area, and the resulting purer air in the village. A joint lift pass with other resorts in the Aosta valley goes a long way towards compensating for the present loss of access to Chamonix and makes Courmayeur a good base from which to explore the substantial amount of skiing available in this corner of Italy.

The heart of the old village is a charming maze of cobbled alleys. It is largely traffic-free and lined with fashion boutiques, delicatessen and antique shops. There are more bars, cafés and restaurants than could ever seem necessary, with a lively clientèle. The atmosphere is, as one reader put it, 'completely compelling – this is real Italy, garnished with real skiing'. These days the suburbs stretch endlessly outwards, and for anyone interested in observing and therefore contributing to the prolonged après-ski *passeggiata* along Via Roma, it is important to find accommodation within easy walking distance of the pedestrian precinct. It is the favourite resort of the Milanese, a clientèle for whom lunch is frequently a greater priority than skiing, and as a result it proudly boasts some of the finest mountain restaurants in the Alps. Reporters consistently remark on the friendliness of the locals, in startling contrast to the dour Gallic attitude of those on the other side of the mountain.

On the snow
top 3,470m (11,381ft) bottom 1,370m (4,494ft)

The main mountain access is by a cable-car across the river gorge. This takes you up to Plan Chécrouit, a sunny plateau from where, annoyingly, you have to plod a further 75m to the foot of the lifts. You used to be faced with no alternative at the end of the day but to take the cable-car back down, with skis and boots left in lockers at Plan Chécrouit. However, the long-promised piste to the valley was finally open for the 1999–2000 season. The run brings you back down to Dolonne, where you have to take a ski bus back across the river to Courmayeur.

WHAT'S NEW

Arp lift open to the public without instructor

A new gondola is planned from Dolonne to the existing gondola station at Plan Chécrouit, and this will ease the cable-car congestion at peak times and eliminate the annoying mountain walk. However, the locals are divided on what they consider to be the best type of lift, and it is not expected to be operational until 2002. The mountain can also be reached by cable-car from **Val Veny**.

Extensive investment in snow-cannon has done much to improve skiing on the lower slopes down to Plan Chécrouit, Dolonne and to Val Veny. However, the skiing is not satisfactory for everyone; the pisted runs are mainly short and lack challenge. Advanced skiers will be more interested in the separate off-piste ski area shared with Chamonix, reached by the three-stage Mont Blanc cable-car at **La Palud**, near the village of **Entrèves** on the tunnel side of Courmayeur.

Opportunities for cross-country skiing are enormous here, with a major nordic centre at **Val Ferret**, a 15-minute drive away at the foot of the Grandes Jorasses. The centre offers four loipes totalling 30km, which wind through spectacular scenery. Cross-country tours can be arranged in the spring through the ski schools.

Beginners
The easiest slopes are somewhat hazardous, with those at Plan Chécrouit cramped by buildings and crowds of skiers descending from

Mont Maudit
4468m

Mont Blanc
Du Tacul

Aiguille Du Midi ▲
Chamonix ▲

Vallée
Blanche

Aiguille Noire
3778m

Aiguille Des Glaciers

Punta Helbronner
3470m

Rifugio Torino
3325m

Summer
Skiing

Ghiacciaio Del
Toula

Pavillon
2130m

Mont Blanc
Tunnel

Ghiacciaio
del Miage

Val Veny

Zerotta
1520m

Arp Vielle

Peindein

Pra de Pascal
1912m

Mt Chetif
2343m

Cresta D'Arp
2755m

M. Favre

Cresta Youla
2624m

Plan Checrouit
1706m

Lago
Checrouit
2256m

Dolonne

COURMAYEUR
1230m

the main pistes. The main nursery slope is situated at the top of the Maison Vieille chair-lift. The baby slopes at the top of Val Veny and Dolonne are quieter.

Intermediates

The east-facing Chécrouit bowl has many short intermediate runs served by a variety of lifts including a six-seater gondola. The pistes are often crowded, especially at the bottom where they merge. There are some surprisingly steep and narrow passages, even on some of the blue (easy) runs. The wooded, north-facing Val Veny side of the mountain is linked in a couple of places with the Chécrouit Bowl; the Val Veny side has longer and more varied pistes with two red (intermediate) runs and a black (difficult) trail following the fall-line through the trees. Queuing for the Plan Chécrouit and Mont Blanc areas is much worse at weekends, when the crowds arrive from Turin and Milan. Quad-chairs at La Gabba, Aretu and Zerotta have eased some of the other bottlenecks on the mountain, but the Youla cable-car can still be a problem.

Advanced

The pistes served by the Gabba quad-chair at the top of the ski area and to the west of Lago Chécrouit keep their snow well. The off-piste run underneath them is testing. The Youla cable-car above Lago Chécrouit opens up a deep and sheltered bowl, which serves a single, uncomplicated red run with plenty of space for short off-piste excursions. It is also possible to ski (with a guide) the long Arp itinerary runs off the back of Youla down into Val Veny or Dolonne.

Off-piste

The top of the two-stage cable-car at Cresta d'Arp is the starting point at 2,755m for a couple of long and demanding powder runs. One takes you down 1,500m vertical to the satellite village of Dolonne or to the river bank near **Pré-St-Didier**; the other brings you through the beautiful Vallon de Youla to La Balme, a few kilometres from **La Thuile**. The second stage of the cable-car runs only until 11.30am because of the high risk of avalanche later in the day, and you are strongly advised to use a local guide.

From the nearby hamlet of La Palud, the Mont Blanc cable-car rises over 3,000m to Punta Helbronner, giving easy access to the Vallée Blanche by avoiding the dreaded ice steps. For the present there is no easy way home from Chamonix. Instead, you can cruise the 10km back down the Toula Glacier to La Palud; it is steep at the top and involves a clamber along a fixed rope and the hair-raising negotiation of an exposed and awkward staircase – again, you are strongly advised to take a guide. The bottom stage of the cable-car from Pavillon has a long, uncomplicated red (but no longer marked) trail that is rarely skied. Heli-skiing (see *Heli-skiing*) on the Ruitor Glacier is also possible.

The Arp lift is now open to the public without an instructor. This opens up a huge north-facing off-piste area over the back of

Courmayeur that boasts three good runs: to Val Veny, to Dolonne and to La Balme near the resort of **La Thuile**.

Snowboarders

Beginner snowboarders need to go to Val Veny, and Plan Chécrouit has plenty of intermediate runs around the main ski area for riders. Courmayeur has neither funpark nor half-pipe, but the off-piste at Cresta d'Arp makes for some excellent freeriding.

Tuition and guiding

We continue to receive mixed reports of the Scuola di Sci Monte Bianco. The standard of spoken English has greatly improved in recent years, and the general verdict is that private instructors and guides are excellent value but that group instructors are often jaded: 'our instructor gave the impression that he wasn't interested in our skiing at all. He was never enthusiastic or encouraging'.

However, the strong presence of Interski, a British tour operator, which has been allowed to establish its own private British Association of Snowsport Instructors (BASI) ski school for a mixed clientèle of adults and schoolchildren, has served to raise standards dramatically (see *Which tour operator?*).

Mountain restaurants

Food in Courmayeur is taken just as seriously as skiing. In our experience there is nowhere you can eat better for less money in a greater variety of mountain restaurants than in Courmayeur. The prices are actually lower than in the resort itself. One reporter commented: 'it is hard to ski when you could be eating. The atmosphere in the huts scattered around the mountain is an integral part of our annual visit here'.

The Christiania at Plan Chécrouit is singled out for special praise – 'good meeting point for families, great pizzas' and 'the freshest seafood I have ever tasted; the owner comes from Elba and obviously pines for home'. The Chiecco, situated just above Plan Chécrouit, serves full meals and 'heavenly desserts'. La Grolla at Peindeint on the Val Veny side is worth a visit ('expensive, but worth it and difficult to find – thank goodness'). On the Mont Blanc side there are bars at each lift stage. The Rifugio Pavillon at the top of the first stage of the cable-car is reportedly excellent and has a sun terrace. Rifugio Torino, at the next stage, is also said to be good. Rifugio Maison Vieille at Col Chécrouit has a large wood-burning stove, serves pasta, polenta and sausages and has a good wine list.

Accommodation

The resort has six four-star hotels including the Gallia Gran Baità, which is described as 'worthy of its rating, but too far out of town unless you have a car'. Few of the hotels, apartments and chalets are well-situated for the main cable-car. However, the comfortable and expensive Hotel Pavillon ('the service was impressive') is well placed 150m from the cable-car and has a swimming-pool and sauna. Three-

Skiing facts: Courmayeur

TOURIST INFORMATION
Piazzale Monte Bianco 13, I-11013
Courmayeur (AO)
Tel 39 0165 842060
Fax 39 0165 842072
Email apt.montebianco@psw.it
Web site www.courmayeur.com

THE RESORT
By road Calais 968km
By rail Pré-St-Didier 5km, regular buses
from station
Airport transfer Turin 3hrs (Geneva
2½hrs through Grand St Bernard
Tunnel)
Visitor beds 5,856
Transport ski bus not included in
lift pass

THE SKIING
Linked or nearby resorts Cervinia (n),
Chamonix (n), Champoluc (n),
Gressoney-la-Trinité (n), Pila (n),
La Thuile (n)
Number of lifts 25
Total of trails/pistes 100km (44%
easy, 52% intermediate, 4% difficult)
Nursery slopes 3 free lifts

LIFT PASSES
Area pass (Courmayeur Mont Blanc)
L230,000–265,000 for 6 days
Beginners 3 free lifts
Pensioners no reductions

Credit cards yes

TUITION
Adults Scuola di Sci Monte Bianco
tel: 0165 842477
Snowboarding as ski school
Other courses cross-country,
race-training, ski-touring
Guiding Air Vallée tel: 0165 869814,
Società delle Guide di Courmayeur
tel: 0165 842064

CHILDREN
Lift pass (Courmayeur Mont Blanc)
L230,000–265,000 for 6 days, free for
children under 1.10m
Ski & board school as adults
Kindergarten (ski) Kinderheim at Plan
Chécrouit tel: 0165 842477, (non-ski)
Kinderheim at Sports Centre Crèche
tel: 0165 846545

OTHER SPORTS
Climbing wall, curling, dog sledding,
ice-climbing, indoor golf, indoor tennis
and squash, parapente, skating,
sleigh-rides, snowbiking, snowshoeing

FOOD AND DRINK PRICES
Coffee L1,500–1,800,
glass of wine L2,000–3,000,
small beer L3,000–4,000,
soft drink L2,600–3,500,
dish of the day L25,000–30,000

star Hotel Courmayeur is 'friendly, with a roaring log fire in the sitting area'. The family-run Bouton d'Or is 'conveniently located, quiet, comfortable, and has its own parking'. Auberge de la Maison in Entrèves is 'an outstandingly stylish three-star'.

Eating in and out
Restaurants are varied, plentiful and lively. Pierre Alexis rates as one of the best in town ('an extraordinary wine list to complement great

food'). Courmayeur also has plenty of pizzerias including Mont Frety ('wonderful for families'). Cadran Soliare is praised for both cuisine and ambience. La Maison de Filippo at Entrèves is an exercise in unparalleled gluttony; it offers a fixed-price menu of over 30 courses.

Après-ski
The evening begins with cocktails in the American Bar and evolves into a hanging-out situation, with certain times for certain bars, and often more than one in a night or a return visit after dinner. The Bar Roma, with its comfortable sofas and armchairs, fills up early. Ziggi's is a cyber-café, the Red Lion is frequented by snowboarders, and Cadran Solaire is where the sophisticated Milanese go. Bar Posta and Bar delle Guide both have a good atmosphere. Courmayeur has two discos. The swimming-pool is 5km away at Pré-St-Didier, and the floodlit skating-rink with disco music is open every evening until midnight.

Childcare
The Kinderheim up at Plan Chécrouit looks after children from six months old. Staff pick up children from the bottom of the cable-car in the village and return at the end of the day. A new Kinderheim at the sports centre now cares for children from nine months old and is particularly useful for parents wanting to ski on the Mont Blanc side. The Scuola di Sci Monte Bianco offers lessons, with lunch included. Tour operator Interski runs a ski school here for its own mainly young clients.

Livigno

ALTITUDE 1,820m (5,970ft)

Beginners ✱✱✱ Intermediates ✱✱ Snowboarders ✱

L ivigno – the cheapest of all Alpine resorts – is a duty-free village in one of the highest and remotest corners of Italy. It is user-friendly for skiers and revellers alike, but you have to suffer a three- to five-hour transfer from Bergamo, Milan or Zurich airports. What you get during your stay is a large, exposed ski area with a fine snow record, which is best suited to beginners and intermediate snow-users. The resort's main problem has always been access. The community developed near the Roman road from Milan to Innsbruck, a route that crossed the neighbouring Passo di San Giacomo. As frontiers moved back and forth, the Spol Valley became a distant border outpost in turn of Switzerland, Italy and the Austro-Hungarian Empire. Today it has slow road links with **Bormio** to the east, **St Moritz** to the west, and with **Davos** via the new Klösters–Engadine tunnel under the Flüela Pass.

- ✔ Ski-in ski-out convenience
- ✔ Reliable snow cover
- ✔ Low prices and duty free
- ✔ Choice of restaurants
- ✔ Recommended for telemark
- ✘ Long airport transfer
- ✘ Poor road links
- ✘ Bleak location
- ✘ No real resort centre
- ✘ Heavy traffic

Livigno's *raison d'être* is shopping, with stores dedicated to cheap alcohol, clothing and consumer durables ('Armani clothing a third of the price it is in the UK'). Anyone who is not perceived as Italian is addressed in German by over-eager assistants. With vodka selling in duty-free shops at less than £4 a litre, it can compete on price with Andorra. Livigno's fiscal privileges date from 1600 and were confirmed in 1805 when Napoleon, then the ruler of the Kingdom of Italy, granted 'customs benefits' that were validated by the Austro–Hungarian Empire in 1818, and by the European Community in 1960.

Although many of the individual buildings are attractive, Livigno's lack of town planning makes it unsympathetic overall. Its high, bleak location has earned it the nickname 'Piccolo Tibet' (Little Tibet), a description that is particularly apt in bad weather. An efficient free bus-service links the four hamlets of **Santa Maria**, **San Antonio**, **San Rocco** and **Trepalle**, which, stretched over 12km, make up the resort. A pedestrianised zone has been achieved by blocking off the centre section of the main road through San Antonio. It provides a rather tacky focus, crammed full of hotels, restaurants and noisy bars. Santa Maria is more distinguished architecturally but its charm is diluted by heavy traffic in its narrow streets.

On the snow
top 2,798m (9,180ft) bottom 1,820m (5,970ft)

International visitors began skiing in Livigno in 1964 when the Munt La Schera tunnel opened the resort up to northern Europe. In those days it had one lift; today there are 30, serving 110km of predominantly gentle slopes on both sides of the valley. The core of the skiing is the ski-in ski-out southeast-facing Carosello, which catches the morning sun. The two-stage Carosello 3000 gondola provides rapid access from the town to the highest point. The Carosello links with two supplementary areas, one served by the Federia drag-lift on the back side of the mountain, where the snow is better protected from the sun, and the other on Costaccia, where the high-speed Vetta quad-chair along the ridge gives various options.

The skiing is generally steeper on the west-facing side of the valley, where the setting sun attracts skiers late into the afternoon. The gondola station for Mottolino is at the suburb of **Teola**, a long walk or a short bus-ride from the town centre. There are notoriously chilly chair-lift connections with Monte della Neve, the departure point for the best skiing in the resort, and Trepalle, a windswept outpost on the road to Bormio.

Livigno has become the self-appointed telemark capital of the Alps, thanks to the annual Skieda International Festival.

Beginners
Livigno is justly proud of a lift system that provides blanket coverage of sun-soaked, resort-level nursery slopes within a stone's throw of the main street. The runs straggle along the flank of the mountain on the Carosello side, leaving beginners with no excuses for not practising when classes are over. The best graduation slopes for progressive novices are from Monte della Neve and Mottolino to Trepalle.

Intermediates
The heart of the skiing is Carosello and the linked area of Blesaccia, which together offer the widest choice of long descents. The toughest intermediate options in a generally flattering environment are on the slopes above Val Federia. On the other side of the valley, the rolling red (intermediate) runs from Mottolino, Monte Sponda and Monte della Neve back to Teola are rewarding, but those to Trepalle are rather short.

Advanced
The creators of the piste map have taken pains to include some statutory black (difficult) runs, but the grading is strictly complimentary. This is not a resort for advanced snow-users. Livigno's two main mogul fields are at the extremes of the resort, below Costaccia and on the descent from Carosello. A longer and much better black run winds down from Monte della Neve to the bottom of the Monte Sponda chair.

Off-piste
Very few visitors to Livigno have any intention of skiing off-piste, but extensive possibilities exist for those prepared to hire a guide and go exploring. The most accessible options are from Carosello 3000 and the ridge above Costaccia to Val Federia, or from Monte della Neve to Trepalle – but be prepared for long walk-outs.

Snowboarders
The wide pistes make Livigno a good place to learn, but that is where it ends. The half-pipe at Mottolino is unimpressive.

Tuition and guiding
Livigno has four ski schools. As far as British clients are concerned, Sci Livigno Italy is the major player. However, minority interests are better served by the Azzurra and Inverno-Estate schools, which offer telemark, ski-touring and snowboarding, and there is also a specialist nordic ski school.

Mountain restaurants
The main self-service restaurants at the top of the Mottolino and Carosello gondolas offer consistency at competitive prices, while the restaurant La Costaccia is known for its outdoor barbecue. More atmospheric mountain lunches can be found in the Teas, the mountain huts once used by herdsmen working the summer pastures. The Tea Borch, below Carosello, and the Tea del Plan, below Costaccia, specialise in *pizzoccheri*, the local brown pasta that is traditionally prepared with cabbage and cheese. Tea Bourk is warmly recommended.

Accommodation
The two four-star hotels, the Golf Parc and the Intermonti, are in Teola on the hillside overlooking the town – a suitable place to stay for the Mottolino lifts but not for the nightlife. In the pedestrian zone, the three-star Albergo Bivio has a swimming-pool and a terrace. Also convenient for both the nursery slopes and the après-ski are the Alpina, the Helvetia and the Victoria. In Santa Maria, the Livigno and the St Michael are two quiet and expertly-run family hotels. The Pedrana Rocco apartments are 'basic, but fairly big'.

Eating in and out
Livigno is not short of choice with the emphasis on quality local fare rather than haute cuisine. The Pesce d'Oro daringly advertises 'fresh fish every week' but still enjoys a sound reputation. The Camana Veglia has a notably good chef, while the Bellavista wins many friends with its pizzas. Reporters recommend Mario's as 'the best restaurant, both in quality and value'.

Après-ski
The après is cheap and cheerful, with lots of duty free alcohol. Tea del Vidal is a cheerful pit-stop on the Mottolino side. In town, the most

Skiing facts: Livigno

TOURIST INFORMATION
Via dala Gesa 65, I-23030 Livigno (SO)
Tel 39 0342 996 379
Fax 39 0342 996 881
Email info@aptlivigno.it
Web site www.aptlivigno.it

THE RESORT
By road Calais 1,072km
By rail Tirano 2½hrs
Airport transfer Milan 3½–5hrs,
Zurich 3–5hrs, Bergamo 4hrs
Visitor beds 8,500
Transport free ski bus

THE SKIING
Linked or nearby resorts Bormio (n),
Santa Caterina (n), St Moritz (n),
Valdidentro (n), Valdisotto (n)
Number of lifts 30 in Livigno
Total of trails/pistes 110km (40% easy,
45% intermediate, 15% difficult)
Nursery slopes 12 lifts, 5km of runs
Summer skiing Stelvio Pass

LIFT PASSES
Area pass (covers Bormio, Santa
Caterina, Valdidentro, Valdisotto and 1
day in St Moritz) L225,000–265,000 for
6 days
Beginners no free lifts
Pensioners 65yrs and over, as children
Credit cards yes

TUITION
Adults Scuola Sci Azzurra
tel: 0342 997 683,
Inverno-Estate tel: 0342 996 276,
Sci Livigno Italy tel: 0342 996 739,
Soc-Coop tel: 0342 970 300
Snowboarding as ski schools
Other courses carving, cross-country,
extreme skiing, monoski, race-training,
seniors, skiing for the disabled,
ski-touring, telemark
Guiding Matteo Galli tel: 0342 970 618,
Lodovico Sport tel: 0342 996 107,
Mario Mottini tel: 0335 43 20 57

CHILDREN
Lift pass 14yrs and under,
L158,000–185,000 for 6 days
Ski & board school as adults
Kindergarten (ski) Inverno-Estate,
(non-ski) Ali-Baba at Inverno-Estate
tel: 0342 996 276

OTHER SPORTS
Climbing wall, horse-riding, ice-climbing,
ice-driving, night-skiing, parapente,
skating, sleigh rides, snowmobiling,
snowshoeing, swimming

FOOD AND DRINK PRICES
Coffee L1,500, glass of wine L2,000,
small beer L3,000, soft drink L3,000,
dish of the day L18,000–20,000

popular watering holes are Foxi's Pub, with a slide for an entrance.
Noisy alternatives include the Underground and Galli's bar in San
Antonio ('lots of Brits singing silly songs'). Il Cielo, which sometimes
has live music, is rated as the smartest disco by the Italians, but the
Kokodi is generally preferred by British visitors.

Childcare
Skiing tuition is available at Livigno's four ski schools. Ski School
Inverno-Estate operates both a ski- and a non-ski kindergarten.

Madonna di Campiglio

ALTITUDE 1,550m (5,085ft)

Beginners ✱✱✱ Intermediates ✱✱✱ Advanced ✱ Snowboarding ✱✱✱

Madonna di Campiglio is one of Italy's two smartest resorts. Though pocket-sized in comparison with the equally expensive but more sophisticated **Cortina d'Ampezzo**, it is a definite rival in terms of social prestige. The town of Madonna stands on the site of a mountain hospice dating back 800 years, and its first cable-car was built in 1935. Today, it is compact and congenial with a predominantly modern architectural style and a high standard of accommodation.

Situated in a narrow valley in the Brenta Dolomites, Madonna is reached by a 60-km climb through galleried tunnels past spectacular drops from the *autostrada* and the valley town of Trento. The nearest airport is two-and-a-half hours' drive away at Verona.

- ✔ Beautiful scenery
- ✔ Extensive snowmaking
- ✔ Intensive piste-grooming
- ✔ Excellent nursery slopes
- ✔ Attractive cross-country
- ✗ High prices
- ✗ Skiing lacks challenge

The ski area is officially rated as Italy's premier for piste-grooming, and regularly hosts international winter sports events, including World Cup ski races and snowboarding championships. Long stays are the rule, with the better hotels booked out for the whole season. Ninety-five per cent of the resort's clientèle is Italian.

The village runs north–south, with the slopes coming right down to the town on either side. In the past the resort has been blighted by heavy traffic in high season and near-impossible parking. However, the long-awaited 1.8-km-long road bypass tunnel opened in December 1999 and has considerably reduced traffic. Four new underground car parks are being built for the 2000–1 season and there are plans to pedestrianise the village centre. The ski bus is not free but it covers the region well.

On the snow
top 2,505m (8,219ft) bottom 1,520m (4,987ft)

Although there are now some ultra-modern covered chair-lifts and swift gondolas, with more being upgraded every year, part of the lift system still dates from the 1950s. Today a modest 26 lifts cover 90km of pistes in the Madonna core area, although an additional 25 lifts and 60km of pistes can be accessed with the Superskirama lift pass, including the separate but linked resorts of **Folgarida** and **Marilleva**.

Madonna is a resort with flattering skiing and excellent nursery slopes, as well as a good range of far-flung intermediate terrain.

However, it has little to offer the expert or off-piste snow-user. What initially appear to be three entirely separate zones are cunningly interlinked at valley level by a snow-cannon-maintained piste that winds beneath a series of road bridges.

An ancient cable-car climbs slowly up to the first area, 5-Laghi, from the centre of town. The second is reached by a fast jumbo gondola north of the town centre, whisking you up to Pradalago at 2,100m, which is linked to Marilleva and Folgarida. The third area, Monte Spinale/Grosté, is dramatically positioned beneath the towering granite cliff faces of Petra Grande and is reached by high-speed gondola from the east of town.

The resort has accommodation for over 27,000 visitors, who in theory can be carried uphill in less than an hour. January and March are the best months in which to visit – you have the slopes largely to yourself. Overcrowding is the norm at Christmas and New Year, as well as during the February school holidays, particularly at the budget resorts of Marilleva and Folgarida.

When viewed from the village, the mountains appear steep; from above, they open into a civilised network of wide trails. Only the Grosté sector is entirely above the tree-line and is not covered by the exhaustive system of about 500 snow-cannon. Proficient skiers need to invest in the slightly more expensive regional Superskirama lift pass that covers Folgarida and Marilleva. Keycards can now be bought, providing a convenient hands-free entrance to all the lifts. A separate ticket is somewhat redundantly issued as soon as you cross into the neighbouring resort.

Beginners

Novices taking tuition should not buy a lift pass, as they will be taken by bus to the private Campo Carlo Magno nursery area five minutes' drive away. Beginners who are not enrolled at the ski or snowboard school pay a small fee for both the shuttle bus and the use of the nursery lifts. This is a superb learning area, serviced by its own drag-lifts and snow-making. Another private nursery area called Bambi is run by Des Alpes Ski School on the east side of Madonna.

All of Madonna's terrain is accessible to inexperienced snow-users, and blue (easy) runs make up more than half the slopes in the main Madonna area. The Zeledria blue continues for more than 3km all the way down to town from Pradalago, as does the Pozza Vecia on the other side of the mountain; this run can be combined with the Boch blue, providing a non-stop beginner cruise of 5km.

Intermediates

Madonna's ski area is ideal for intermediate skiers and boarders, with lots of long cruises on attractive tree-lined trails. Folgarida and Marilleva also provide a supply of flattering cruising pistes, including the long red (intermediate) Genziana. The two highest runs in the resort, reached by the Grosté chairs, are suitable for anyone who can ski parallel. The scenery in the form of awesome granite cliffs is truly spectacular. However, this is the most popular area of the resort with Italian visitors and should be avoided at peak holiday times. At the top of the Boch chair you can ski or ride Spinale Diretta, the resort's trickiest red piste.

Advanced
There is little challenge for mogul skiers in a resort where every bump is flattened nightly by a fleet of piste machines. None of the five runs listed as black (difficult) on the inadequate piste map is truly worthy of the grading. However, the Canelone Miramonti is a short, steep shock, and the FIS 3-Tre racecourse in the 5-Laghi area provides some challenge. Up on Grosté a dual slalom racecourse is open to the public.

Off-piste
The ski schools seldom break away from the prepared pistes, although snowboarders do. Tempting lines run through the trees but do not always bring you back to the piste. Above Spinale and towards the Cima Brenta is a wide couloir that requires a mountain guide and ski-touring equipment.

Snowboarders
Madonna is rated as one of the two best snowboarding resorts in Italy (the other is Selva). The Grosté funpark and boardercross course at 2,500m are being extended in preparation for the FIS snowboard world championships taking place here in January 2001. Madonna's terrain is well suited to beginner riders. An additional funpark has been created on the 2,100-m peak of Doss del Sabion where the views are sensational, a few kilometres away above the nearby resort of **Pinzolo**.

Tuition and guiding
Confusingly, Madonna has six ski and snowboard schools, all affiliated to the national Scuola Italiana Sci, and each changes its uniform colour every season. English is indifferently spoken. Group lessons may have between eight and twelve pupils and run for two hours in two shifts during the mornings.

Mountain restaurants
'All furs and no food' is how one reporter, expecting a truffles-and-caviar experience, responded to the self-service inns that are all you get in Madonna. For a resort of this stature, cosy mountain restaurants are sadly absent. Most of the converted *malga* (old wooden barns that once served as summer shelters for farmers and cows) have been transformed into high-volume self-service establishments. One exception is Cascina Zeledria, tucked away in the woods, which offers *Delizie alle Piastra* – steaks that you cook yourself on a hot stone. A free snowcat tows you back up to the piste after lunch. Malga Boch has a pine interior and

sometimes a DJ from the famous Zangola disco. La Grotte, in Albergo Fortini at the base of the Grosté gondola, is recommended by reporters. Agostini, on Pradalago, serves *picchiorosso*, a secret-recipe grappa.

Accommodation

Most guests stay in the resort's 18 four-star and 37 three-star hotels, which are booked for most of the season. Relais Club des Alpes (four-star) carries the most cachet and is the most central. The Savoia Palace is smart and well-positioned. The Lorenzetti is also four-star, though more rustic in setting and décor, and has its own free shuttle bus. The Diana is friendly, close to the lifts and furnished to a high standard. Arnica is a conveniently central, modern bed and breakfast. Equally central is the old-style Villa Principe, which has some of the cheapest rooms in town. There are also chalet-apartments and self-catering establishments, such as the Ambiez apartments, which have a swimming-pool and a fitness centre.

Eating in and out

A must in Madonna is piling into heated snowcats and jolting up to the mountain restaurants of Malga Montagnoli, Cascina Zeledria or Malga Boch, where the service and food are better by night. In town, Antico Focolare is the in-place to eat, serving typical Trentino food in atmospheric surroundings with open fires. Artini has good cuisine but lacks atmosphere. Papagallo has a generous set menu on Wednesdays. Cliffhanger serves fish platters. The Golden River has the only non-Italian menu Tex – Mex with influences – but even here Gorgonzola makes an appearance. Le Roi has the best pizzas until 2am. There are numerous supermarkets and delicatessen.

Après-ski

Immediately after skiing, the furs gather at Bar Suisse or the Franz-Josef Stube to flutter eyelashes behind dark glasses and make dates for later. Café Campiglio in the piazza is popular for coffee and cakes. However, although Madonna is often said to be lively, it doesn't really get into the groove until the early hours. The population then goes wild until 4 or sometimes even 8am in what has for 25 years been one of the most famous discos in the Italian Alps: the old cow barn, Zangola, 3km out of town but serviced by late-night buses. The disco features male strippers and dancing girls. Des Alpes has techno music as well as an upstairs piano bar. The Stork Club's clientèle is seriously under-age and the club itself closes when the school holidays end. Not to be confused with the bar of the same name, Cantina del Suisse has a live band and is a warm-up nightspot for Zangola. Cliffhanger disco is open until the early hours and shows heli-skiing videos. La Stalla has karaoke and live music. The billiard bar and two garish video-game centres are extremely popular with Italian boys.

The many elegant boutiques in the resort include Martini for Trentino-Tyrolean clothing and carved wooden artefacts, and Chalet Ferrari for designer clothing.

Skiing facts: Madonna di Campiglio

TOURIST INFORMATION
Via Pradolago 4, I-38084 Madonna di
Campiglio (TN)
Tel 39 0465 442000
Fax 39 0465 440404
Email info@campiglio.net
Web site www.campiglio.net

THE RESORT
By road Calais 1,200km
By rail Trento 72km
Airport transfer Verona 2½hrs
Visitor beds 27,055
Transport bus service L20,000
for 7 days

THE SKIING
Linked or nearby resorts Folgarida (I),
Marilleva (I), Monte Bondonne (n),
Pinzolo (n), Ponte di Legno-Tonale (n)
Number of lifts 26 in resort, 51 in
linked area
Total of trails/pistes 90km in Madonna
(44% easy, 40% intermediate, 16%
difficult), 150km in linked area
Nursery slopes 3 lifts

LIFT PASSES
Area pass Superskirama (covers Andalo,
Folgarida, Marilleva, Monte Bondone,
Pinzolo, Ponte di Legno-Tonale)
L288,000–320,000 for 6 days
Beginners points tickets
Pensioners 60yrs and over, as children

Credit cards yes

TUITION
Adults Campo Carlo Magno tel: 0465
443222, Des Alpes tel: 0465 442850,
5-Laghi tel: 0465 441650, Nazionale tel:
0465 443243, Rainalter tel: 0465 443300,
Fondo Malghette tel: 0465 441633
Snowboarding as ski schools,
Professional Snowboarding
tel: 0465 443251
Other courses carving, cross-country,
telemark
Guiding Elicampiglio tel: 0465 443222,
Guide Alpine-Sci tel: 0465 442634

CHILDREN
Lift pass 8–13yrs, L230,000–256,000
for 6 days. Free for 7yrs and under
Ski & board school as adults
Kindergarten (non-ski) Baby Parking tel:
0465 442222

OTHER SPORTS
Archery, curling, dog-sledding, horse-
riding, ice-climbing, night-skiing, parapente, skating, slalom, snowshoeing,
swimming

FOOD AND DRINK PRICES
Coffee L1,600–1,700, glass of wine
L2,000–2,500, small beer
L3,000–3,500, soft drink L3,000, dish of
the day L15,000–18,000

Childcare
Most Italians leave the little ones at home or bring nanny or granny.
Relais Club des Alpes has an informal childminding service for guests
and an outdoor playground by the skating rink. Hotel Spinale has a children's club for its small residents, and the new non-ski kindergarten is
Baby Parking. The ski schools accept children from five years old for
mornings only in large classes of 10 or more.

The Milky Way

ALTITUDE Montgenèvre 1,850m (6,068ft), Sauze d'Oulx 1,500m (4,920ft), Sestriere 2,035m (6,675ft)

Beginners ✱✱ Intermediates ✱✱✱ Advanced ✱✱

The Via Lattea, or Milky Way, straddles the Franco-Italian border and is reached more easily from Turin than from Grenoble. In past years its southerly location was compensated for by the height of the main resorts, and snow cover was usually sound. However, for the past two seasons snowfall has been conspicuous by its absence in this corner of Europe and at times the resorts have struggled to remain open, with most cover provided by artificial snow. That said, the Milky Way is one of the great and surprisingly undiscovered ski circuits of Europe, boasting 400km of groomed pistes served by 91 lifts. **Sestriere** successfully hosted the 1997 Alpine Skiing World Championships, and at the 11th hour snatched the rights to organise the 2006 Winter Olympics from Sion in Switzerland. Let us hope that there will be snow on the day.

> ✔ Large ski area
> ✔ Skiing convenience
> ✔ Extensive tree-line skiing
> ✔ Varied off-piste
> ✔ Value for money
> ✔ Lively après-ski (Sauze d'Oulx)
> ✘ Lack of non-skiing activities
> ✘ Limited mountain restaurants
> ✘ Poor trail-marking
> ✘ Lift queues

British skiers are perhaps more familiar with Sestriere's lively sister **Sauze d'Oulx** (pronounced Sow-Zee Doo) in the neighbouring valley, which, despite local efforts at rehabilitation, is still better known for its lager-oriented nightlife than for the quality of its slopes.

The third major resort (and the only French component) is Montgenèvre, an old stone village perched on the *col* separating France from Italy. It has been pleasantly developed for tourism and retains considerable charm. The first impression is of a higgledy-piggledy collection of bars, restaurants, shops and hotels lining an extremely busy main road where skiers joust with pantechnicons. The older part of the village is tucked away on the northern side and has plenty of atmosphere, despite the heavy traffic. Shopping facilities are limited, but the weekly open-air market adds colour and offers the occasional bargain. The Italian border is on the outskirts of town, and both currencies are in circulation here.

Sauze d'Oulx has tried to develop a more upmarket image – an attempt that cannot really succeed until more luxurious hotels are built to cater for a better class of clientèle. The main part of the village, adjacent to the slopes, is a largely uninspiring collection of modern

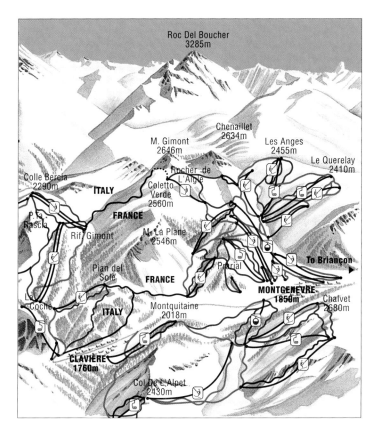

edifices constructed with budget rather than beauty in mind. In its past, raucous revellers, still in their ski boots and awash with cheap lager, would stagger homewards from the infamous Andy Capp Bar at 3am to the shabby two-star hotels for a few hours of further recreation before hitting the slopes again. To the young British skiers (50 per cent of the resort's customers) who flocked to this corner of Piedmont each winter in search of dissolute pleasures, it was known as 'Suzy does it'. Suzy, it seems, has matured beyond the gratifying excesses of her youth and is trying to cultivate a more sober image.

Sestriere, once one of the most fashionable wintering holes in Europe, was purpose-built in 1930 by Giovanni Agnelli, the founder of Fiat, who was frustrated by the fact that members of his family spent so much of their winter skiing abroad. Its location on a high, cold and barren pass is not enchanting, but high-quality snow cover is the norm rather than the exception. The skyline is dominated by the twin towers of the Albergo Duchi d'Aosta, once one of the smartest hotels in Europe but now a Club Med. The village is compact, but, despite being essentially Italian, appears to lack soul. As one reporter put it: 'there is no continuity, resulting in a confusion of styles, which seem to compete rather than harmonise'. Buses run to and from the satellites of **Borgata** and **Grangesises**.

The more shrewd Italians have now abandoned Sestriere for nearby **Sansicario**, which is a smaller, more sophisticated and modern development with its own ski area. It is linked to Sestriere and Sauze d'Oulx on one side and **Cesana Torinese** on the other.

On the snow
top 2,820m (9,250ft) bottom 1,350m (4,428ft)

Montgenèvre's slopes are on both sides of the Col de Montgenèvre. The south-facing side, Chalvet, is slightly higher, with runs going up to 2,600m, and is usually less crowded than the north-facing pistes, which create the main link with the Italian Milky Way resorts. Mountain access on the other side of the pass is by gondola from the **Briançon** end of the village, as well as by drag-lifts and a chair from the centre. These serve easy runs through woods, opening into wide nursery slopes above the road. From the top of the gondola there is a choice of three small ski areas. The wide, sheltered bowl of Le Querelay/Les Anges features ruined fortress buildings around the crest with some red (intermediate) and black (difficult) runs beneath them, but no challenging skiing.

WHAT'S NEW
Rocher de l'Aigle quad chair-lift
Quad-chair in Clavière for return towards France

The Milky Way link from Montgenèvre starts with a poorly sign-posted traverse around the mountain, which is easy to miss in bad light. Otherwise it is not difficult, and leads to a long run that starts as red and becomes blue (easy), past the Gimont drag-lifts and down to **Clavière**. The north-facing slopes of Monti della Luna above Clavière and Cesana Torinese offer plenty of challenge, including some vast trails through the woods and satisfying off-piste.

Reporters are unanimous in their opinion that the best skiing in the Milky Way is above Sestriere. This end of the lift system was upgraded for the 1997 Alpine World Championships and further improvements are now scheduled for the 2006 Olympics. The bulk of the skiing is on Sises and Banchetta mountains, which are separated by a deep valley.

The Sauze d'Oulx slopes face west and north, and the majority of them are below the tree-line. The lifts are old-fashioned in comparison with Sestriere's, even though they are run by the same company. A quad-chair takes you up to the centre of the skiing at **Sportinia**, a sunny woodland clearing with a few hotels, a small busy nursery area and a variety of restaurants. Above it is some wide, open intermediate skiing served by several chair- and drag-lifts. Below Sportinia are wide runs back through the woods, graded red and black; these are quite steep in

places, although never really demanding. There are also blue and black runs down to the hamlet of **Jouvenceaux**.

Queues in Montgenèvre are bad only at weekends. The main queue problems at the Italian end of the Milky Way are on the Sauze side of the mountain, described as 'horrendous' by a reporter who was there during an Italian bank holiday. The local lift map has improved, but it is still sometimes difficult to work out exactly where on the mountain you are. Reporters describe trail-marking as virtually non-existent to the point of being dangerous, which adds to the problems of orientation.

Beginners

A dozen nursery slopes are scattered around the different resorts of the Milky Way on both sides of the border, and the area is ideal learner territory. The main nursery slope for Sauze is at Sportinia; it is open and sunny but often very crowded. Nursery slopes are also available at Belvédère on the Genevris side, as well as in the village when there is snow. The Montgenèvre end of the circuit has the best blue runs.

Intermediates

The long red (intermediate) runs down to Sansicario from Monte Fraiteve are satisfyingly varied and some of the best on the circuit. Red run 29, back through the trees to Sauze, is the favourite of several reporters. Old hands say that high-season crowds are a problem throughout the Milky Way but particularly around Sestriere. One tip is to ski the remote Genevris/Moncrons/Bourget sector on Saturdays and Sundays ('a pleasure to ski and no queues at all').

Advanced

An assortment of black (difficult) runs scattered throughout the Milky Way makes this a much underrated playground for advanced skiers, who will find plenty of challenge. The Sauze sector quite wrongly has a novice label attached to it because of the predominance of beginner and early-intermediate skiers that it attracts. In fact, some of the reds here could easily be graded black, and a few of the blacks (notably 33 and 21) are seriously challenging in difficult snow conditions. The best of the skiing is found above Sansicario and Sestriere, although this may not be apparent from the local piste map.

The steep Motta drag- and chair-lifts serve the toughest of Sestriere's skiing and climb to the top point of the Milky Way. Here the mogulled slopes beside the drag can have gradients of up to 30°.

Off-piste

Monte Fraiteve is an exposed crest with impressive views of the French mountains, where the ski areas of Sauze d'Oulx, Sestriere and Sansicario meet. It is also the start of the famous Rio Nero off-piste run, which is a long descent that follows a river gully down to the Oulx–Cesana road, 1,600m below. An infrequent bus service takes you back to the lifts at Cesana. Rocher de l'Aigle is the starting point for an outstanding off-piste bowl and an alternative steep couloir. Anyone attempting the latter draws admiring glances from those on the piste below. Heli-skiing drops on the top of Valle d'Argentera and Val Thuras can now be arranged from all the resorts through either Guide Alpine Valsusa or Elisusa Heli-skiing (see *Heli-skiing*).

Snowboarders

First-timers are not particularly well served here, but freeriders can have some fun on the long Rio Nero off-piste route. There is no half-pipe anywhere in the area, but the natural obstacles should keep advanced freestylers happy.

Tuition and guiding

The French Ski School (ESF) at Montgenèvre receives sound reports ('first class – patient instructors all with good spoken English') for all grades of skier and for private lessons. Reports of the Sauze d'Oulx Ski School are much improved ('after Zermatt, the attitude of the instructors was like a breath of fresh air. Lessons were made to be fun'). The school has two rivals, Sauze Project and Sauze Sportinia. Sportinia has a high standard of teaching, but one reader complained that his instructor had only a few English phrases. Reports of the Sestriere ski school, which has in the past been the subject of criticism, are encouraging. As one reporter commented: 'clearly the publicity surrounding the Alpine Skiing World Championships has jolted improvements. Our instructor spoke excellent English and tuition was friendly and competent.' We have no reports of the Olimpionica ski school at Sestriere.

Mountain restaurants

'You can eat out in the mountain restaurants on the Italian side for the cost of a drink in Courchevel,' enthused one reporter. Montgenèvre is seriously short of mountain restaurants, with just the Altitude 2000 and Gondrands. The excellent and inexpensive bars and restaurants above Clavière (particularly La Coche) help make up for this shortfall. Ciao Pais in the Clotes sector is warmly praised.

The five busy restaurants at Sportinia maintain a high standard ('but eating in Piccadilly Circus is not my idea of a fun holiday'). Chalet Genevris in the area of the same name is renowned for its barbecue, where you can eat or drink for about £11 ('very friendly with an excellent atmosphere of camaraderie at lunchtime, which often stretched well into the afternoon').

Sestriere's Bar Chisonetto, halfway down Red 8 on Banchetta, is recommended for its hamburgers. Bar Conchinetto is a traditional wood-and-stone restaurant noted for its polenta, and atmospheric La Gargote is more expensive. Alpette is praised for its pasta.

Accommodation

Montgenèvre's accommodation is mostly in apartments scattered along the road, in the old village and on the lower south-facing slopes; there are also a few catered chalets. Access to the skiing is easy from most places, but the Italian end of the village is more convenient. The pick of Montgenèvre's half a dozen less-than-luxurious hotels are the Napoléon, which is convenient but basic, and the more attractive Valérie, near the church.

Accommodation in Sauze is mostly in cheap hotels, which reporters generally find adequate. The best location is around the bottom of Clotes, and the hotels in this area are the Hermitage ('very basic food'), Stella Alpina, and the Sauze ('clean and spacious'). The Gran Baita is recommended as 'excellent – very clean, the staff are pleasant and the hotel is five minutes' walk from everything'. San Giorgio is far from luxurious and badly placed, but friendly and inexpensive. The Chaberton is a basic bed-and-breakfast, and the Savoia is close to the lifts. Four-star La Torre is the biggest hotel in Sauze. Il Capricorno at Clotes is expensive and attractive. You can be first on the nursery slopes by staying at the Monte Triplex or the Capanna at Sportinia. The Ciao Pais above Clotes offers cheap accommodation.

Sestriere's accommodation is in hotels, modern apartments and at Club Med. The restored Principi de Piemonte Hotel is a couple of kilometres out of town but has its own access lift to the Sises ski area.

A third distinctive tower block in the style of the 1930s architect Vittorio Bottino was built to house competitors for the world championships and is now a hotel. Albergo Il Fraitevino is 'very simple for a four-star, but convenient'. The Hermitage and Banchetta are also recommended. The Biancaneve is just outside the town and provides its own minibus service to the slopes. Hotel du Col is said to be 'ugly but could not be better located with helpful and friendly staff'.

Eating in and out

Montgenèvre boasts more than a dozen eating-places, including the Ca del Sol for pizzas, Les Chalmettes, La Tourmente, L'Estable ('home-cooked cuisine'), Pizzeria Le Transalpin, Le Refuge, and smart Le Jamy.

In Sauze, La Griglia is strongly recommended. Del Falco is praised for its relaxed and friendly service ('food great and not expensive'). Albertino's is more of a café than a restaurant, with prices to match. Del Borgo has 'a pleasant buzz,' and is famed for its tiramisù.

Eating-places in Sestriere range from pizzerias to smart, international restaurants. Ristorante du Grandpère in the nearby hamlet of Champlas Janvier is praised for its wild boar stew and polenta. Antica Spelonca has 'a wonderful atmosphere and fine food'. Antica Osteria is an ancient chalet with considerable charm. L'Teit has 'the best pizzas we have ever eaten'. Jolly supermarket is said to be reasonably priced.

Après-ski

Off-slopes activity in Montgenèvre is limited, although a good choice of inexpensive bar-restaurants is on offer; three have nightclubs attached. The Ca del Sol and Le Graal are both popular bars. The Blue Night is the disco. The village has a good skating-rink.

In Sauze, the notorious Andy Capp and the New Scotch Bar (near the bottom of the home run) catch the early evening crowd and are awash with pints of Tartan long before dark. Later on, the action moves to the Cotton Club, Hotel Derby Bar and Moncrons. Max's Bar shows British sport on satellite TV. The Village Café and The Village Gossip both have live music six nights a week. The Bandito, Schuss and Rimini Nord discos 'keep you dancing as long as you want'. Entry to all clubs is free, which is in pleasant contrast to France.

Sestriere's nightlife is fairly lively and stylish when the Italians are in residence at weekends and in holiday periods, though at other times it

Skiing facts: Montegenèvre

TOURIST INFORMATION
F-05100 Montgenèvre, Hautes-Alpes
Tel 33 492 21 52 52
Fax 33 492 21 92 45
Email office.tourisme.montgenevre
@wanadoo.fr
Web site www.montgenevre.com

THE RESORT
By road Calais 978km
By rail TGV direct to Oulx 20km,
Briançon 10km
Airport transfer Turin 1hr 20mins,
Grenoble 3hrs
Visitor beds 8,000
Transport free bus service

THE SKIING
Linked or nearby resorts
Bardonecchia (n), Borgata (I),
Cesana Torinese (I), Clavière (I),
Grangesises (I), Jouvenceaux (I),
Sansicario (I), Sauze d'Oulx (I),
Sestriere (I), Sportinia (I)
Number of lifts 38 in
Montgenèvre–Monti della Luna, 91 in
Milky Way
Total of trails/pistes 100km in
Montgenèvre–Monti della Luna
(37% easy, 43% intermediate, 20%
difficult), 400km in Milky Way
Nursery slopes 1 free lift

LIFT PASSES
Area pass Milky Way, 770FF for 6 days
Beginners 1 free lift
Pensioners 60–69yrs 578FF, free for
70yrs and over
Credit cards yes

TUITION
Adults ESF tel: 492 21 90 46
Snowboarding as ski school
Other courses carving, cross-country,
freestyle, race-training
Guiding through ski school

CHILDREN
Lift pass 6–12yrs, Milky Way 616FF for
6 days. Beginners pass (covers 7 lifts)
70FF per day
Ski & board school as adults
Kindergarten (ski) ESF Jardin d'Enfants
tel: 492 21 90 46, (non-ski) Garderie
tel: 492 21 52 50

OTHER SPORTS
Heli-skiing and heli-boarding, horse-
riding, parapente, skating,
snowmobiling, snowshoeing

FOOD AND DRINK PRICES
Coffee 8FF, glass of wine 10FF, small
beer 15FF, soft drink 12FF, dish of the
day 60FF

is quiet. The Black Sun and Tabata discos are popular at weekends.
Brahms Pub is Irish and serves Guinness. Anno Zero, Pinky Bar,
Maialetto and People Pub are all popular.

Childcare
Montgenèvre's Garderie cares for children from one to four years of age.
The ESF takes three- to five-year-olds in its ski kindergarten. Although
Italy is not renowned for its childcare facilities, the Milky Way is a notable
exception. Sauze has Dumbo, which takes non-skiing children all day –
parents must provide their children's lunch, which staff will heat up. The

ski schools take children from four years old. Sestriere has no public crèche, but Club Med looks after its smallest members from four years old, as does the ski school, and there is a mini club at nearby Grangesises.

Linked or nearby resorts

Bardonecchia
top 2,750m (9,022ft) bottom 1,312m (4,303ft)

This is a large and traditional market town set in a sunny valley and surrounded by beautiful scenery. Although not part of the Milky Way circuit, it lies close to both Montgenèvre and Sestriere. The resort is popular with Italians, who flood in from Turin at weekends and on public holidays. The ski area is spread over three sectors, and these are linked by a free ski bus. The area boasts a total of 140km of piste, served by 24 lifts, and offers a surprising degree of challenge. The ski school has mixed classes for adults and children. One reporter complained that 'two children in my group whined every time the instructor stopped to explain techniques. They refused to go down one run because they didn't like it and wanted to go over the bumps on a lower slope'. Facilities for small children are non-existent.

The nightlife is limited to a couple of rather dull bars ('not enough après-ski'). La Gran Baita is a reasonably priced restaurant with a 'friendly, warm bar'. Filandra received mixed recommendations ('a fairly enjoyable evening with a chef on view making pizzas in a 'Ready, Steady, Cook' style, but it was a little disappointing to find the mushrooms on the pizza were tinned'). Hotels are quite spread out and include La Bettula, close to the shopping centre ('basic rooms, good food,'), Des Geneys ('very fine food'), set well back from the road, and Rosa Serenella ('although [our room] had a bath, the taps did not work. It looked as though it had been like that for some time').

TOURIST INFORMATION
Tel 39 0122 99032
Fax 39 0122 980612
Email bardonecchia@montagnedoc.it
Web site www.montagnedoc.it

Borgata
top 2,820m (9,250ft) bottom 1,840m (6,035ft)

This is a small resort five minutes by road from Sestriere, with an infrequent bus service between the two. Hotel Hermitage is recommended ('nice rooms, but the food was not up to much'). Reporters who stayed in the Nube d'Argenta self-catering apartments praised them as 'clean, modern and convenient for the lifts'.

There are complaints about the ski school ('very poor, with limited spoken English, but the teachers were pleasant enough'). Shopping is almost non-existent ('a poor selection of postcards and no stamps').

Skiing facts: Sauze d'Oulx

TOURIST INFORMATION
Piazza Assietta 18, I-10050 Sauze
d'Oulx, Piedmont
Tel 39 0122 858009
Fax 39 0122 85049700
Email sauze@montagnedoc.it
Web site www.montagnedoc.it

THE RESORT
By road Calais 998km
By rail Oulx 5km, frequent buses to
resort
Airport transfer Turin 1hr
Visitor beds 2009
Transport ski bus, L9,000 for 6 days

THE SKIING
Linked or nearby resorts
Bardonecchia (n), Borgata (l),
Cesana Torinese (l), Clavière (l),
Grangesises (l), Jouvenceaux (l),
Montgenèvre (l), Sansicario (l),
Sestriere (l), Sportinia (l)
Number of lifts 35 in Sauze d'Oulx,
91 in Milky Way
Total of trails/pistes 120km in Sauze
d'Oulx (27% easy, 61% intermediate,
12% difficult), 400km in Milky Way
Nursery slopes 2 lifts in Sauze d'Oulx

LIFT PASSES
Area pass Milky Way
L215,000–265,000 for 6 days
Beginners points tickets
Pensioners 60yrs and over,
L200,000–247,000 for 6 days
Credit cards yes

TUITION
Adults Sauze d'Oulx tel: 0122 858084,
Sauze Project tel: 0122 858942, Sauze
Sportinia tel: 0122 850218
Snowboarding as ski schools
Other courses carving, cross-country
Guiding Guide Alpine Valsusa tel:
0335 398984, Elisusa Heli-skiing tel:
0122 623162

CHILDREN
Lift pass 8–12yrs, L200,000–247,000
for 6 days
Ski & board school as adults
Kindergarten (ski) none, (non-ski)
Dumbo tel: 0347 6913531

FOOD AND DRINK PRICES
Coffee L1,500, glass of wine L2,000,
small beer L3,000, soft drink L3,500,
dish of the day L25,000–30,000

The nightlife is quiet ('a couple of sleepy bars'). As one reporter put it:
'when the sun goes down, it is time to eat and go to bed'.

TOURIST INFORMATION
Tel 39 0122 755449
Fax 39 0122 755171
Email borgata@montagnedoc.it
Web site www.montangedoc.it

Cesana Torinese
top 2,820m (9,250ft) bottom 1,350m (4,428ft)
This attractively shabby old village dates from the twelfth century and
is set on a busy road junction at the foot of the Italian approach to the

Montgenèvre Pass. It is rather confined and shaded, and accommodation is mainly in apartments and a few hotels. The chair-lifts up to the skiing above Clavière and Sansicario are a long walk from the centre, and the place can be safely recommended only to those with a car. The Chaberton is a three-star hotel and there are half a dozen small one-stars. Restaurant La Selvaggia specialises in regional dishes, La Noblerot is for French cuisine, and the smart Fraiteve serves truffles. Brusachoeur is a popular pizzeria. Nightspots include the Pussy-Cat pub and the Cremeria Rinaldo e Luciana bar.

TOURIST INFORMATION
Tel/Fax 39 0122 89202
Email cesana@montagnadoc.it
Web site www.montagnadoc.it

Clavière
top 2,820m (9,250ft) bottom 1,760m (5,773ft)

Clavière is a small village on the Franco-Italian border, which during the eighteenth century was part of Montgenèvre. The village consists of 10 hotels and a row of shops on the Italian side, specialising in food and cheap local alcohol. Reporters say Clavière has a pleasant, relaxed atmosphere; it is tightly enclosed by wooded slopes, and the nursery area is small and steep. Lifts give access to the skiing above Montgenèvre and Cesana, with easy runs back from both. Queuing is not a problem, although the resort does tend to become busier at weekends.

There is a 15km cross-country trail up to Montgenèvre and back, as well as a floodlit skating rink. The ski school has some English-speaking instructors and, outside high season, mainly English-speaking pupils. At weekends the village suffers from heavy through-traffic.

Along the road are 10 hotels: the two-star Hotel Roma, close to the main chair-lift, is recommended ('good value, plenty of food and comfortable rooms'). Others include the Clavière, Passero Pellegrino, Pian del Sole and the Savoia. Recommended restaurants include L'Gran Bouc, Gallo Cedrone, Pizzeria Kilt and La Montanina. Clavière is 'not a place for those interested in a hectic après-ski'.

TOURIST INFORMATION
Tel 39 0122 878856
Fax 39 0122 878888
Email claviere@montagnedoc.it
Web site www.montagnedoc.it

Sansicario
top 2,820m (9,250ft) bottom 1,710m (5,609ft)

The village is in a sunny position halfway up the west-facing mountainside and is well placed for exploring the Milky Way. It is purpose-built, consisting mainly of apartment buildings linked to a neat commercial precinct by shuttle lift. Facilities for beginners, especially children, are good. A ski- and

Skiing facts: Sestriere

TOURIST INFORMATION
Piazza Agnelli, I-10058 Sestriere, Piedmont
Tel 39 0122 799411
Fax 39 0122 799460
Email sestriere@montagnedoc.it
Web site www.montagnedoc.it

THE RESORT
By road Calais 1,020km
By rail Oulx 22km, buses to resort
Airport transfer Turin 1½hrs
Visitor beds 4,200
Transport ski bus L3,000 per day

THE SKIING
Linked or nearby resorts
Bardonecchia (n), Borgata (l),
Cesana Torinese (l), Clavière (l),
Grangesises (l), Jouvenceaux (l),
Montgenèvre (l), Sansicario (l),
Sauze d'Oulx (l), Sportinia (l)
Number of lifts 19 in Sestriere, 91
in Milky Way
Total of trails/pistes 120km in
Sestriere (39% easy, 42% intermediate,
19% difficult), 400km in Milky Way
Nursery slopes 12 in area

LIFT PASSES
Area pass Milky Way

L215,000–265,000 for 6 days
Beginners points tickets
Pensioners 60yrs and over,
L200,000–247,000 for 6 days
Credit cards yes

TUITION
Adults Sestriere Ski School tel: 0122
77060, Olimpionica tel: 0122 77116,
Borgata tel: 0122 77497
Snowboarding as ski schools
Other courses carving, cross-country,
heli-skiing
Guiding through ski schools and Elisusa
tel: 0122 623162

CHILDREN
Lift pass 8–12yrs L200,000–247,000
for 6 days
Ski & board school as adults
Kindergarten none (nearest is at
Grangesises)

OTHER SPORTS
Dog-sledding, parapente, snowmobiling

FOOD AND DRINK PRICES
Coffee L1,500, glass of wine L3,000,
small beer L3,500, soft drink L3,500,
dish of the day L20,000–30,000

non-ski kindergarten provides daycare for three- to eleven-year-olds.
Sansicario has its own ski school. The choice of après-ski facilities is limited.

Accommodation is of a generally high standard, mostly in apartments but with a few comfortable and expensive hotels. The most attractive is the Rio Envers, a short walk from the centre. Others include the Monti della Luna and the simpler Sansicario.

TOURIST INFORMATION
Tel/Fax 39 0122 89202
Web site www.montagnedoc.it

Monterosa Ski

Altitude Champoluc 1,568m (5,144ft), Gressoney-la-Trinité 1,624m
(5,327ft), Alagna 1,200m (3,936ft)

Beginners ✳✳ Intermediates ✳✳✳ Advanced ✳ Snowboarders ✳

Previously Monterosa Ski remained almost exclusively the domain of Italian holidaymakers despite the 10-year efforts of Crystal and other tour operators to lend an international tone to this unspoilt region at the eastern end of the Aosta Valley.

✔ Excellent off-piste
✔ Strong regional identity
✔ Rustic charm
✔ High-quality local cuisine
✔ No crowds or queues
✔ Low prices
✘ Shortage of non-skiing activities
✘ Limited nightlife

However, the introduction of a single ski pass covering the whole of Aosta has now encouraged British skiers and riders based in Courmayeur to sample its extensive terrain. The area comprises the resorts of **Champoluc, Gressoney**, and **Alagna** on the southern side of the border with Switzerland. While the Mont Blanc Tunnel remains closed, the area is no longer as easily accessible from Chamonix (see *Chamonix*).

The Matterhorn is more pimple than peak from this perspective, but this section of the Alps, with its crags and glaciers, provides spectacular views. The valleys were settled by the Walser people in the Middle Ages and their geographical isolation has resulted in a distinctive culture and a strong Germanic/French dialect that persist today. Although the three villages are close as the crow flies and well-connected by the lift system (at least in the case of Champoluc and Gressoney), it takes two to three hours to drive between any two of them.

Champoluc, at the top of the Ayas Valley, is reached by a long and winding road up from the Turin–Aosta *autostrada* and is set around a church and a fast-running mountain river. The old quarter was built in the fifteenth century, but the village has expanded in recent years to accommodate the requirements of a small ski resort. Gressoney-la-Trinité is on a similar scale, with a network of cobbled streets and wooden chalets surrounded by contemporary buildings. **Gressoney-St-Jean**, 5km down the valley, is larger and more attractive, while the outpost of **Stafal**, a modern hamlet above Gressoney-la-Trinité, tries to make up in convenience what it lacks in soul.

Given its remote location, Alagna is built on a puzzlingly large scale, with decaying buildings surrounding a church where bell-ringing rules. This is a genuine oddball of a place, which has unique wooden houses with built-in hay frames, and a charm all of its own. Work started in summer 2000 on an almost complete and long-overdue makeover of the lift system. Gressoney, in particular, has developed a strong following among British families in recent seasons, and the off-piste skiing of Alagna is no longer the best-kept secret of the Alps. The hopeless piste map resembles 'the footwork of a drunken spider'. However, on-piste signposts are plentiful and accurate.

On the snow
top 3,370m (11,056ft) bottom 1,200m (3,936ft)

The collection of slow chairs and ancient cable-cars is slowly being updated into a modern lift system, but main access lifts are susceptible to wind closure. All pistes eventually lead to Stafal, which is the central link in the chain of 42 lifts. Head up in the cable-car and chair-lift to the west and you reach the Colle Bettaforca, the departure point for the descents to Champoluc. Take the two-stage gondola to the east and you come to the Passo del Salati, the start of the Alagna connection. With slopes on both sides of the valley, Gressoney has the lion's share of the skiing in an area which totals 180km of pistes, and the fastest lifts.

There are two points of departure from Champoluc, one on the outskirts of the village and the other up the hill in **Frachey**, which provides much quicker access to the main area. Three small satellite areas – **Antagnod**, **Brusson** and **Gressoney-St-Jean** – are not connected to the central system. The ancient cable-car up from Alagna to Bocchetta delle Pisse is being replaced, and a high-speed chair is scheduled to open at the start of the 2000–1 season. Although its impressive vertical drop and its extensive powder fields attract rugged skiers, its links with Gressoney are unpisted in both directions, which at present makes it unsuitable for anyone else. However, there are plans to build more lifts and pistes in this sector.

WHAT'S NEW

Cable-car and high-speed chair-lift from Alagna to Nocchetta delle Pisse
Detachable chair-lift from Antagnod to Pian Pera

Beginners

The best place to learn is the sunny nursery slope at Crest, at the top of the first stage of the Champoluc gondola. In Gressoncy, beginners congregate around the Punta Jolanda lift, then progress via the 70-person cable-car to the wide plateau above Stafal on the Bettaforca side. Champoluc has its own sunny beginner area reached by gondola from the village centre.

Intermediates

Both Gressoney and Champoluc have plenty of interlinked inter-mediate cruising, rather more in fact than the piste map suggests; it is so badly printed that most of the blue (easy) runs appear to be black (difficult). Stadio dello Slalom above Champoluc is a challenging red (intermediate) used for local races. One reporter described the home run to Champoluc as 'one of the best-maintained runs I have ever seen'.

Advanced

The best black piste in the area is the 7-km descent from the top of the Punta Indren in Alagna, but even this would not be so severely rated in other resorts. The same could be said of the only mogul field, which is at Sarezza in Champoluc. The blue-ish red from Gabiet back to Stafal has been regraded into an undeserved black.

Off-piste

In the right conditions, all three resorts present challenges that are made all the more testing by bumpy terrain and narrow defiles between rock walls. The Mos and the Bettolina in Gressoney are excellent examples of this and they should not be attempted without a guide. The same is true of most of the skiing in Alagna, where the new cable-car should provide speedy access to huge snowfields that – inevitably in a predominantly south- and west-facing resort – are prone to avalanche.

The north-facing slopes in the Alta Valsesia National Park give a sense of extreme adventure, especially when accessed by the couloir at the top of the Malfatta. Alternatively, there is extensive heli-skiing (see *Heli-skiing*), with glacier drops at over 4,000m in the Monterosa range.

Snowboarders

Monterosa Ski has no special facilities for snowboarders, although the absence of drag-lifts is a bonus point. The off-piste challenge of the Alagna sector makes it extremely popular among the international hardcore of committed freeriders who might otherwise be found on the Grands Montets in **Chamonix**.

Tuition and guiding

In Gressoney, only 5 out of 30 ski instructors speak English, so you should request one of them when booking lessons in advance. The situation in Champoluc is similar ('delightful chap, enjoyed myself a lot, but didn't learn much because of his limited English'). Qualified alpine guides are available through the respective tourist information offices, but again language can be a problem. In Alagna, mountain guide Roberto Valzer arranges exciting off-piste adventures, as well as accommodation and evening meals in restaurants that are more like private homes.

Mountain restaurants

One reporter complained that 'some of the larger places were very functional and the service very slow indeed'. Bedemie, on the route down to Gressoney from Gabiet, has 'a beautiful terrace and nourishing soup'. Albergho del Ponte above Gabiet is praised for its cheap and excellent spaghetti carbonara. Rifugio Guglielmina, reached by a short off-piste route from Passo del Salati, is recommended for both its food and the view. Bettaforca has 'the biggest and best mixed grill in the business'. La Baita Refuge has superb mushroom pasta and friendly service.

Accommodation

In Champoluc the Hotel Castor is described by one reporter as 'an absolute gem, Italian-owned but managed by an Englishman who has married into the family'. The two-star Favre is small, well-managed and friendly. The four-star Monboso at Stafal earned mixed reviews from reporters but we understand it is now under new management.

The Scoiàttolo, in Gressoney-la-Trinité, is equally comfortable but with a better ambience. In the same resort, Hotel Residence is popular with reporters ('the rooms were comfortable, the food good, the staff helpful and the wine was reasonably priced'). In Alagna the Bar Mirella, a bed-and-breakfast with rooms over a cake shop, is 'a must if you can get in'. If not, try the Genzinella or the comfortable Cristallo.

Eating in and out

Le Sapin in Champoluc looks unpromising, not least for its multilingual tourist menus, but the food is something of a revelation. Otherwise, the Favre is consistently good, with a bias towards gargantuan feasts of local game. Cuisine at the Villa Anna Maria was described as 'variable, but the restaurant has an honest wine list'. In Alagna the Servan is surprisingly sophisticated and should not be missed. Capanna Carla in Gressoney-la-Trinité serves typical local cuisine at reasonable prices.

Après-ski

This is the kind of area where the nightlife is described by tour operators as 'informal and relaxed' – often a euphemism for dead in the winter. What there is takes place in the bars of family hotels, where locals and tourists drink and play cards. The Champoluc disco scene centres on the Gram Parsons in Frachey, while Gressoney-St-Jean offers Il Futuro. Gamblers with their own transport can visit the casino in St-Vincent (25km from Champoluc, 70km from Gressoney). The relaxed nightlife in Gressoney-la-Trinité consists of cafés such as the Hirsch Stube and the Petit Bar. Other activities include squash and skating.

Childcare

Daycare in the area is extremely limited, with no crèche or kindergarten facilities in Champoluc apart from the Hotel Castor. The ski school at Champoluc takes children from five years old. Hotel Monboso, above Gressoney at Stafal, has a mini-club for residents' children aged four to eight years. Those over six years old must join the adult classes.

TOURIST INFORMATION
Tel 39 0125 303111
Fax 39 0125 303145
Email kikesly@tin.it
Web site www.monterosa-ski.com

Sella Ronda

ALTITUDE 1,440–1,563m (4,724–5,128ft)

Beginners ✶✶✶ Intermediates ✶✶✶ Advanced ✶✶ Snowboarders ✶✶

The Dolomites are home to the largest and most beautiful ski area in the world. Others try to compete but nowhere else actually manages 1,180km of pistes served by 464 lifts in one region. Similarly, the backdrop of craggy peaks and dramatic cliff faces, which take on a distinctive and glorious shade of rose pink in the light of the setting sun, is without parallel. By no means are all of these runs and resorts linked by lift, but all are included in the Dolomiti Superski lift pass, which at less than £100 in high season represents the best-value lift pass in the northern hemisphere. The hands-free lift pass now operates in the region. At the core of it all lies the Sella Ronda, a celebrated circuit of four valleys involving 90 minutes of lifts, 120 minutes of downhill skiing and an always undetermined Joker factor of queuing time. It can be skied in both directions, but clockwise involves less poling and skating. Miss the crucial lift home because of deteriorating weather or volume of people and you are in for an expensive taxi ride.

✔ **Outstanding scenery**
✔ **Range of mountain restaurants**
✔ **Extensive ski-touring**
✔ **Good children's facilities (Selva)**
✔ **Excellent-value lift pass**
✗ **Unreliable snow record**
✗ **Skiing convenience**
✗ **Lift queues**
✗ **Heavy traffic**

Much has been done in recent years to improve the antiquated lifts that once blighted the Sella Ronda, but despite continuing innovations, queues can still become chronic at weekends and during the Italian school holidays ('it was the first time we have ever seen staff specifically employed to pack people into gondolas – we thought only the Tokyo underground needed these'). One reporter said the problem was exacerbated by 'the persistent Italian refusal either to queue sensibly or to share chair-lifts with strangers'. Snow-users are strongly advised to stray from the actual circuit, which anyway is less than enchanting, and explore and enjoy individual valleys for their own merits.

The best-known, but by no means the most important, of these valleys is **Val Gardena**. Selva Gardena, or Wolkenstein as it is also known in this bilingual border area of Italy, is the actual name of the resort. It is an unassuming village, which sprawls in suburban style up the Val Gardena. Traffic is heavy, and the weary are more at risk crossing the road than they ever are on piste. For all that, the village maintains a quiet, unsophisticated charm, which makes it popular with

families. Examples of the local woodcarving industry colourfully adorn houses and even lamp-posts.

The second most popular resort is **Canazei**, a large, attractive and lively village on a busy main road in the Italian-speaking Val di Fassa. It is the best place to stay for those in search of non-skiing activities and a lively nightlife. The village itself is a tangle of narrow streets with a mixture of old farm buildings, new hotels and some delightful shops. Such is the scramble for beds in the Val di Fassa that tour operators offer hotels in outlying villages as far away as **Pera**, **Pozza**, **Vigo di Fassa**, and even distant **Moena**.

On the periphery of the Sella Ronda circuit lies a whole range of resorts, from established international ski towns such as chic **Cortina d'Ampezzo** to sleepy and essentially Italian villages such as **San Martino di Castrozza**. You cannot hope to ski the whole area in a week, or even in a season.

Vastly improved services to the upgraded airports at Venice and Verona, coupled with two-and-a-half-hour motorway transfers to most Dolomite resorts, have reopened this unspoilt corner of the European ski map. The layout of the Sella Ronda and the whole Dolomiti Superski region is not as confusing as it sounds, and you will soon get your bearings, provided you invest in the Ordnance Survey-style map of the region, called *Sellaronda e Valli Ladine Carta Sciistica*, which can be bought at any newsagent in the resorts. It shows all the lifts and gives fairly accurate colour gradings. The different resorts now all produce much more accurate area maps than in the past, although the piste classifications are still suspect.

> **WHAT'S NEW**
>
> Sass Bece six-person chair-lift
> Belvedere chair-lift upgraded to quad

On the snow
top 2,950m (9,676ft) bottom 1,225m (4,018ft)

With its mainly blue (easy) and unproblematic red (intermediate) runs, the Sella Ronda is better for seeing some wonderful scenery than for really challenging skiing or snowboarding. Although the peaks of these mountains are high, virtually all the skiing takes place lower down; this is the main cause of the Dolomites' variable snow records. The whole region had poor seasons in both 1999 and 2000 in comparison with neighbouring Austria and the rest of the Alps. This climatic handicap has been offset by heavy investment in modern snowmaking techniques. Nevertheless, south-facing slopes, in particular, can become worn and unpleasant. One reporter recounted having to remove her skis and walk certain sections of the circuit during a mild spell, and indeed short walks between lifts are not uncommon, even when conditions are good.

The Sella Ronda can be skied in either direction with all kinds of variations. Clockwise mountain access from Selva Gardena is via the

Dantercëpies gondola to the start of a long and mainly red cruise through 730m vertical all the way to **Colfosco**. From here a chair-lift takes you to **Corvara**, and a 12-person gondola brings you to Boè and the Crep de Munt for a short red run down to **Campolungo**. You can take a drag-lift up to the Rifugio Bec de Roces, which is the start of a pleasant red and blue run with dramatic backdrops down into **Arabba**. Queues here can be unacceptable during busy weeks ('a 40-minute wait mid-morning for a four-minute uplift'). A chair-lift is the most direct, but not necessarily the quickest, onward route. The cable-car to Belvedere involves more skiing and a much more challenging piste that allows you to rejoin the blue route before Pont de Vauz. A desperately slow chair-lift, which is scheduled for replacement, is followed by a fast detachable quad-chair that brings you up to Sas Becè and the red run down to Lupo Bianco. Take a short red off the circuit into Canazei or continue via a gondola up to Col Salei. From here, a short red and a long blue cruise through 700m vertical return skiers and riders to Selva Gardena.

Beginners
The best of the novice skiing is found in the Alta Badia sector, bordered by **Armentarola** in the east, Corvara in the west and **La Villa** in the north. The wooded meadows here are reminiscent of the Austrian Tyrol. At the other end of the circuit, try the long blue that starts above the Passo Sella at 2,400m and takes you gently all the way down to Selva at 1,563m.

Intermediates
The whole of the Sella Ronda is ideally suited to cruisers who really want to put some mileage beneath their skis each day in this outstand-ing setting. Where to base yourself is a matter of personal choice. The Selva Gardena–Canazei end of the circuit has some of the better long runs, though fans of Corvara and Colfosco would strongly disagree. The favourite run among reporters is the Armentarola piste from Lagazuoi.

Advanced
Arabba is the Argentière of Italy and the place in which to base yourself for the toughest skiing in the area. Anyone who imagines that the Dolomites consist solely of scenic blue cruising runs is in for a wicked shock. From the edge of the village a two-stage jumbo gondola and a cable-car take you up nearly 900m over the granite cliffs off the Soura Sass to the start of what is, by any standard, some serious advanced skiing. The black (difficult) runs down the front face are testing in the extreme.

Alternatively, from the halfway stage of the gondola you can ski off the Sella Ronda on a wonderful 20-km journey down usually deserted pistes to the town of **Malga Ciapela**. From here you pay a daily L50,000 or six-day L200,000 supplement to your lift pass for the three cable-cars ('clearly ancient and one wonders about safety') to the top of the 3,269-m

Marmolada, revered by mountaineers in the same breath as the Matterhorn, the Eiger and Mont Blanc; the lifts open only in February. At the top of the second lift, the World War I museum depicting the deeds of the Alpine Brigade is worth a visit. From the summit, a long red run takes you to within a couple of slow lifts of the home run back down to Arabba.

Off-piste
Passo Pordoi, between Arabba and Canazei, is the base-station of the Sas Pordoi cable-car, which takes you up to the Rifugio Maria at 2,958m. Piste-grooming machines have never made it up here, and all the skiing is as nature intended. The long run down the Val de Mesdi is one of the most taxing in the Dolomites and should not be attempted without the services of a guide. The front face of Sas Pordoi is a shorter, difficult challenge, with a steep and usually icy entrance guaranteed to get anyone's adrenaline pumping; falling is not advised. Powderhounds can also enjoy moderately priced heli-skiing (see *Heli-skiing*) off the Marmolada peak.

Snowboarders
Riders of all standards from beginner to expert are well catered for here, with gentle runs as well as half-pipes in the Colfosco, Plan de Gralba-Piz Sella, Belvedere, Pordoi and Seceda areas. **Passo Pordoi** has the best freeriding terrain in the area. However, the number of difficult drag lifts and long, flat pistes, such as the blue run from Passo Pordoi towards Arabba may deter some riders.

Cross-country
For cross-country enthusiasts, the Dolomiti Superski area claims a mighty 1,033km of prepared loipe scattered throughout the region; some of the most scenic (98km) trails are situated in Selva Gardena.

Tuition and guiding
The Selva Gardena Ski School continues to generate excellent reports, and tuition appears to be of a high standard ('good teaching and no silly end-of-week races'). Reporters note that the standard of English spoken by instructors throughout the Sella Ronda appears to have improved dramatically in recent years. The other two ski schools in Val Gardena are at **Santa Cristina** and **Ortisei**. Organisation is said to be poor at the Canazei Marmolada Ski School: 'hardly any English spoken. Two different queues of different abilities led to a long, slow and totally confusing grading system with 16 in a class'.

Mountain restaurants
The Dolomites abound with mountain eateries, but the standard varies markedly between the Italian- and German-speaking regions, with the better food found in the former. Rifugio Lagazuoi is singled out as

'spectacular value with amazing views'. Rifugio Pralongia is praised for 'well-prepared meals at nice prices'. Rifugio Padon is popular with the ski patrol. Rifugio Porta Vescovo is 'modern, clean, bright, and has excellent food'.

Pizzeria El Table in Arabba comes strongly recommended. Rifugio Bec de Roces, reached by a chair-lift from Arabba, has a self-service downstairs and a waiter-service restaurant upstairs ('fantastic views and the most amazing lunch'). Plan Boè above the village is popular for traditional Austro-Italian fare. Trapper's Bar, on the Passo Campolungo between Corvara and Arabba, has a sun terrace and live music. Forcelles above Colfosco is warmly praised. Rifugio Crep de Munt, above Corvara, also has a terrace and a warm welcome. Try Mesules – its position on the edge of the road and the piste between Selva and Colfosco means it can be reached by skiers and non-skiers alike. Panorama (on the Selva side of the Dantercëpies piste) is 'a real sun-trap with good food'.

Rifugio Scotoni is a welcome wayside warming hut on the run down from Lagazuoi if you are unable to make it to the even cosier Alpina, 2km further on. Either way, you may need some refreshment before the next lift, which is one of the quaintest in the region – a horse-drawn tow (L2,000 supplement).

A more gastronomic lunch can be found at the Hotel Grand Angel on the edge of the Armentarola cross-country track. Baita del Gigio, on the nursery slopes above Malga Ciapela, is worth the long run down and is exceptionally good value. Chez Anna, on the run from Seceda to Ortisei, is said to be worth a visit for spectacular ham-and-eggs. Baita Fredarola, near Belvedere, is recommended for its pizzas. Way off the beaten track is the Ospizio di Santa Croce, reached by a ski bus from La Villa to **Pedraces** and two lifts up to the Abbey of the Holy Cross. Ristorante Lé, at the top of the chair, is renowned for the best *Gulaschsuppe* in the Sud Tyrol.

Accommodation

In Selva Gardena, accommodation is mainly in small, comfortable hotels. Hotel Gran Baita is the pick of the four-stars, together with the Aaritz and the Alpenroyal. Hotel Laurin is a favourite among visitors and is renowned for its food. We have good reports of the Hotel Solaia and, in particular, its buffet breakfast. The centrally situated Hotel Antares is praised, as is the simple Stella. Inexpensive bed-and-breakfasts include the Eden and the Somont. The more spacious Savoy also has a restaurant. Hotel Continental is well located for skiers beneath the Dantercëpies gondola, but 'non-skiers should note that the 10-minute walk into town can be steep and icy'.

The four-star Astoria and La Perla are the most luxurious hotels in town. The Croce Bianca, with hand-painted pine furniture in abundance, is also warmly recommended. The Dolomiti is built in grand hotel style, while Hotel Bellevue is well placed for the skiing, which is inconvenient from many of the village hotels. One reporter recommended the Stella Alpina ('good value bed-and-breakfast with friendly service').

Eating in and out

In Selva Gardena, reporters say one of the best restaurants is Pizzeria Rino. A wider selection of dishes can be found at the restaurant of the Hotel Laurin. Pizzeria Miravalle is praised for 'its high standard of cuisine with an excellent, varied menu'. Other eateries include Armin, Scoiàttolo, Freina, and the restaurant in the Hotel Gran Baita. In Santa Cristina, Plaza and Dosses are lauded.

Canazei boasts many modestly-priced restaurants. Rosticceria Meleser is singled out for praise ('you must book at weekends') as is La Stua dei Ladinos. Rosengarten has 'simple décor, but good food'. The Italia is popular with the locals and has live music. Try Al Vecchio Mulino for local Italian dishes. The Dolomiti is said to be 'pretentious and overpriced'.

Après-ski

At first sight, Selva Gardena does not appear to have much of a nightlife. Half-a-dozen cafés serve home-made cakes and pastries, but the resort is quiet in the evening, with few lights, seemingly little activity and none of the buzz of a serious party resort. In fact, behind the shutters is a thriving après-ski scene and a wide choice of nightspots, but light sleepers are unlikely to have their slumber disturbed. The Luisl is the most popular haunt after skiing ('the only place with any real life between skiing and dinner'). Bar La Stua has twice-weekly folk-music evenings. Also recommended are the Hotel Laurin Bar, Villa Frainela, the Monica and Mozart bars. The Dali disco throbs through the night. In nearby Santa Cristina, Yeti's Ombrella Bar is popular, and other bars include Calés and Tublà.

In Canazei The Montanara Bar is the place to meet for après-ski, as is the Frogs Pub, a few kilometres up the valley road in Alba. Peter's Bar by the Belvedere gondola is busy immediately after skiing. Popular nightspots include the Speck Keller, Husky Pub, La Teneta and El Binocol.

Childcare

A major plus point of the region is that children aged seven years and under ski free. Selva Gardena is an excellent area for children of all ages to learn to ski. The nursery slopes are based below the Dantercëpies gondola at the northern edge of the village. In the kindergarten at the bottom of the Biancaneve drag-lift, toddlers and small children are taught the rudiments of skiing among cartoon characters. Instructors are plentiful and patient, and there seems to be none of the 'here is an entire generation to be put off skiing' attitude that you encounter in some French resorts. The surrounding area is ideal for older children to learn or improve their skiing or snowboarding.

Skiing facts: Selva Gardena

TOURIST INFORMATION
Str. Dursan 78/bis, I-39047 S. Cristina
Tel 39 0471 7792277
Fax 39 0471 792235
Email info@val-gardena.com
Web site www.val-gardena.com

THE RESORT
By road Calais 1,226km
By rail bus service from Bressanone
35km, Bolzano 40km, Chiusa 27km
Airport transfer Munich and Milan
3–4hrs, Verona 2–3hrs, Innsbruck
1½hrs
Visitor beds 16,400 in Val Gardena
Transport free ski bus between Ortisei
and Selva Gardena

THE SKIING
Linked or nearby resorts Arabba (I),
Armentarola (I), Campitello (I), Canazei
(I), Colfosco (I), Cortina d'Ampezzo (I),
Corvara (I), La Villa (I), Ortisei (I),
Pedraces (I), San Cassiano (I),
Santa Cristina (I)
Number of lifts 82 in Val Gardena,
464 in region
Total of trails/pistes 175km in Val
Gardena/Alpe di Siusi, 1,180km in
region (30% easy, 60% intermediate,
10% difficult)
Nursery slopes 15 lifts

LIFT PASSES
Area pass Val Gardena only
238,000–272,000, Dolomiti Superski
(covers 464 lifts) L275,000–313,000 for

6 days
Beginners points tickets
Pensioners 20% discount for 60yrs
and over
Credit cards yes

TUITION
Adults Selva Gardena tel: 0471 795156,
Santa Cristina tel: 0471 792045, Ortisei
tel: 0471 796153
Snowboarding as ski schools
Other courses cross-country,
race-training, telemark
Guiding Val Gardena Guides tel: 0471
794133, Catores-Ortisei tel: 0471
798223

CHILDREN
Lift pass Val Gardena only
L167,000–191,000, Dolomiti Superski
L193,000–219,000, free for 7yrs
and under
Ski & board school as adults
Kindergarten (ski/non-ski) Selva
Gardena tel: 0471 795156, S. Cristina
tel: 0471 792045, Ortisei tel:
0471 796153

OTHER SPORTS
Indoor shooting range, indoor tennis
and squash, parapente, skating,
swimming

FOOD AND DRINK PRICES
Coffee L1,600-3,000, glass of wine
L3,000, small beer L3,500, soft drink
L3,500, dish of the day L18,000–25,000

In Canazei the Kinderland crèche and kindergarten, run by the Canazei Marmolada ski school, caters for children all day with a mixture of day care and lessons for older children.

Linked or nearby resorts

Arabba
top 2,950m (9,676ft) bottom 1,600m (3,808ft)

This small, unspoilt village with only 2,000 beds is tucked away in a fold of the landscape and is surrounded by the most challenging skiing in the area. The village itself is hopeless for non-skiers. We have excellent reports of the ski school: 'instructors spoke good English, classes were small and private lessons cost under £15 an hour'. However, the nursery slope suffers from through-traffic, and resort is not recommended for complete beginners. The crèche and ski kindergarten looks after children aged two years and over on weekdays from 9am to 4.30pm. The principal language here is Italian, although Arabba is only a couple of kilometres south of the Sud-Tyrol border.

The Grifone is a modern five-star hotel with an excellent reputation but it is outside the village in an isolated position up a steep road. The Sport is another smart hotel, but the three-star Portavescovo, which has a pool and fitness centre ('lovely hotel – highly recommended'), is more lively and houses the Stübe Bar. The nightlife is centred around Peter's Bar, the Stübe in the Portavescovo and the Sport Hotel Bar. There are plans to open a disco for the 2000–1 season ('but this is not the place for those who like to party until dawn'). The Rue de Mans is an excellent restaurant just outside the village. Public transport is limited to one daily bus to Corvara, and a hire car is strongly recommended.

TOURIST INFORMATION
Tel 39 0436 79130
Fax 39 0436 79300
Email arabba@rolmail.net
Web site www.arabba.org

Campitello
top 2,950m (9,676ft) bottom 1,440m (4,723ft)

A small collection of old buildings make up this quiet village set beside a stream, well back from the main road. The Col Rodella cable-car (45-minute queues reported) goes up to the ski area, and there is no piste back down again. The village is ideal for complete beginners as some of the area's best nursery slopes are right on its doorstep. Hotels include the Fedora, next to the lift station, and the Medil, which is a modern hotel built in traditional alpine style with the addition of a fitness centre and bar with music. Hotel Sella Ronda is an alpine-style hotel owned by a priest. Hotel Rubino has a swimming-pool and piano bar among its many facilities.

TOURIST INFORMATION
Tel 39 0462 750 525
Fax 39 0462 750 242

Skiing facts: Canazei

TOURIST INFORMATION
Via Costa 79, I-38032 Canazei
Tel 39 0462 6024 66
Fax 39 0462 602278
Email info@fassa.com
Web site www.fassa.com

THE RESORT
By road Calais 1,240km
By rail Bolzano 40km
Airport transfer Munich and Milan
3–4hrs, Verona 2–3hrs,
Innsbruck 1½hrs
Visitor beds 50,000
Transport free ski bus

THE SKIING
Linked or nearby resorts Arabba (I),
Armentarola (I), Campitello (I), Colfosco
(I), Cortina d'Ampezzo (I), Corvara (I),
La Villa (I), Ortisei (I), Pedraces (I), San
Cassiano (I), Santa Cristina (I),
Selva Gardena (I)
Number of lifts 59 in Val di Fassa, 464
in region
Total of trails/pistes 147km in Val di
Fassa, 1,180km in region (30% easy,
60% intermediate, 10% difficult)
Nursery slopes 10 lifts

LIFT PASSES
Area pass Dolomiti Superski (covers
464 lifts) L275,000–313,000 for 6 days

Beginners points tickets
Pensioners 20% discount for 60yrs
and over
Credit cards yes

TUITION
Adults Canazei Marmolada tel:
0462 601211
Snowboarding as ski schools
Other courses carving, cross-country,
extreme skiing, race-training, skiing for
the disabled, telemark, women's ski
clinics
Guiding through ski school

CHILDREN
Lift pass Dolomiti Superski
L193,000–219,000, free for 7yrs
and under
Ski & board school as adults
Kindergarten (ski/non-ski) Kinderland
tel: 0462 601211

OTHER SPORTS
Dog-sledding, hang-gliding, indoor
climbing wall, parapente, skating,
sleigh rides, snowshoeing, squash,
swimming

FOOD AND DRINK PRICES
Coffee L1,600–3,000, glass of wine
L3,000, small beer L3,500, soft drink
L3,500, dish of the day L18,000–25,000

Colfosco
top 2,950m (9,676ft) bottom 1,650m (5,412ft)
Colfosco has easy access to both Selva Gardena and Corvara's skiing,
although the village also has a small ski area of its own with good
nursery slopes. Recommended hotels are the Kolfuschgerhof and the
Centrale. Speckstube Peter, Mesoles, Stria, Matthiaskeller and Tabladel
are the most popular eating-places; the Capella is the smartest.
Restaurant Mesoles, situated just off the piste above the village, is
praised for its 'quite superb goulash soup'.

TOURIST INFORMATION
as Selva

Corvara
top 2,950m (9,676ft) bottom 1,550m (5,085ft)

This pleasant Sella Ronda resort fails to attract any British tour opera-tors, but it is strategically placed for some of the best skiing in the region. Hotel Posta-Zirm, the old post house at the bottom of the Col Alto chair-lift, is the place to stay. The building dates from 1808 and has been carefully renovated; the hotel also keeps alive the tradition of the tea dance ('it's good fun – when did you last see a man in a purple and silver one-piece suit with the zip pulled halfway down to reveal a giant gold medallion as he grooved away to hits from the 1970s?'). The Pensione Ladina nearby is a less expensive alternative and renowned for its home-made blueberry grappa. The resort has plenty of easy runs for beginners. Cross-country skiing is available, and the village boasts an outdoor skating-rink. The ski school has a kindergarten for children from three years of age, but English is not widely spoken. One reporter warmly recommends the Raetia Café on the main street for its wide selection of teas.

TOURIST INFORMATION
as Selva

San Cassiano
top 2,950m (9,676ft) bottom 1,537m (5,041ft)

A small, roadside village with mainly new Dolomite-style buildings, San Cassiano has some excellent skiing and snowboarding for beginners and early intermediates who want to avoid challenges. Long, easy runs go down to the village from Pralongia and Piz Sorega. Reporters mention the lack of spoken English in the resort, which attracts mainly wealthy Italians. The downside of this is being the sole English speaker in a ski class where lessons become 'laborious, with everything spoken in German and Italian'.

The Rosa Alpina is a large and comfortable hotel in the village centre and, with a live band, is also the focal point for nightlife. The Ski Bar is recommended for tasty, cheap pizzas, and the Capanna Alpina, Saré and Tirol are all busy restaurants. La Siriola, Rosa Alpina, Fanes and the restaurant in Hotel Diamant are more expensive. There is bowling at the Diamant, but otherwise the village tends to be on the quiet side. Armentarola, with its own hotels and restaurants, is a kilometre away.

TOURIST INFORMATION
as Selva

La Thuile/La Rosière

ALTITUDE La Thuile 1,441m (4,728ft), La Rosière 1,850m (6,070ft)

Beginners ✱✱✱ Intermediates ✱✱✱ Advanced ✱ Snowboarders ✱

The overriding attraction of this extensive but gentle ski area, which stretches in an uneasy *entente cordiale* across the Italian–French border, is the lack of crowds on its pistes – even at New Year. On the French side skiers tend to drive on up the Tarentaise past the turn-off at **Bourg-St-Maurice** to the more sophis-ticated charms of L'Espace Killy (Val d'Isère/Tignes), while remote road access in the Aosta Valley keeps the Italians in **Courmayeur**.

La Thuile is an old mining town clawing its way back to tourist-led prosperity, while La Rosière is a third-generation purpose-built resort content to rely on the rustic charm of its 1970s chalet-style architecture and the popularity of its low prices. Development at La Rosière on the

LA THUILE
✔ Lack of crowds
✔ Off-piste opportunities
✔ Choice of restaurants
✗ Little resort atmosphere
✗ Limited nightlife
✗ Few mountain restaurants
✗ Lack of childcare facilities

French side in recent years has been restricted to a single high-speed quad and one large block of apartments; this is a source of much irritation to its go-ahead Italian neighbour.

In summer the resorts are joined by road over the Petit-St-Bernard Pass – in winter the car journey via either the Mont Blanc Tunnel (which is currently closed) or the Grand St Bernard Tunnel takes four hours. It is widely held that Hannibal led 30,000 men, 8,000 horses and his 30 elephants over the pass in the course of his epic journey from Spain to Rome in 218BC. Under continuous attack from a murderous army of local Celts, who rained down rocks upon his column from every vantage point, it took him 15 days to cross from Bourg-St-Maurice.

The lift pass includes a day-out in **Les Arcs**, easily reached by funic-ular from Bourg-St-Maurice, and in **Sainte-Foy**, the best-kept secret of the Tarentaise. However, none of this is made easy. You first have to go to La Rosière's tourist information office to obtain a (free) special ticket for the day, which then has to be exchanged for yet another ticket at the main lift station of the resort you are visiting.

The heart of La Thuile is the Planibel, an integrated tourist unit with a hotel, apartments, a sports complex and a selection of shops and bars. The shops major on ski clothing and equipment, with no thought for the chic boutique factor that dominates in neighbouring Courmayeur. The efficient, but discouragingly clinical, complex contrasts sharply with the rest of the resort, which sprawls haphazardly through the surrounding woods.

La Rosière is situated at 1,850m on the French side of the *col* named after St Bernard of Clairvaux, patron saint of the Alps. The original hamlet was the home of Jean Arpin, one of France's first ski instructors, who earned his bronze badge in 1939 at the age of 18 shortly before he and the other inhabitants of the hamlet were forced to evacuate their houses at an hour's notice as Mussolini invaded over the pass.

> **LA ROSIÈRE**
> ✔ Ski-in ski-out convenience
> ✔ Facilities for children
> ✗ Unsuitable for non-skiers
> ✗ Limited nightlife
> ✗ Disappointing mountain restaurants

After the Second World War Arpin set about developing La Rosière as a ski resort, but the first drag-lifts were not built until 1961. The ski area was linked to that of La Thuile on the far side of the *col* in 1984. The village has slowly developed along the bends of the mountain road from Seez to the Petit-St-Bernard Pass. The result is an attractive, neo-Savoyard tiered village with low-rise accommodation built out of wood and local, roughly-hewn stone. In winter, the road ends in a bank of snow outside the Relais du Petit-St-Bernard hotel. Just beyond the hotel lies the kennels of the St Bernard dogs, which on and off have maintained a presence here as rescuers of snowbound travellers since the seventeenth century. The brandy-bearers are always willing to pose for snaps in exchange for scraps.

On the snow
top 2,652m (8,701ft) bottom 1,150m (3,773ft)

Both La Thuile and La Rosière have wide open slopes well suited to beginners and intermediates. In La Thuile these are supplemented by much tougher runs through the steeply wooded area just above the resort. In La Rosière, due to the greater height of the base, the slopes are predominantly above the tree-line. The highest point in the linked area is Bélvèdere, where lifts are often closed due to high winds.

La Thuile's main slopes face east, with a steeper north-facing area going down to the Petit-St-Bernard Pass. By taking the long, loopy alternative routes, it is possible for novices to cover the whole area. Most of the skiing in La Rosière faces south; these slopes are generally easier, with gentle blue (easy) pistes above the resort giving way to red (intermediate) ones on the higher part of the Col de la Traversette. As a result of being on different sides of an alpine divide, each resort has its own micro-climate; this often means that one is shrouded in cloud while the other is bathed in sunshine. By checking at the respective base-stations before deciding where to go, it may be possible to turn an unpromising day into a brilliant one. However, the infamous *Vent du St Bernard*, which cuts through even the most technical ski clothing – especially on the long slow lifts on the Italian side – must be borne throughout the winter.

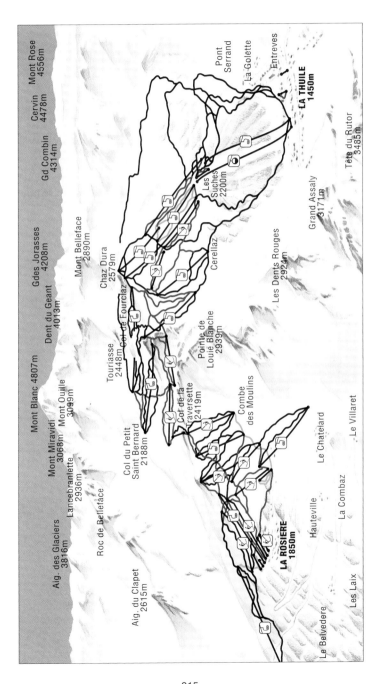

Mont Rose 4556m
Cervin 4478m
Gd Combin 4314m
Gdes Jorasses 4208m
Dent du Geant 4013m
Mont Blanc 4807m
Mont Miravidi 3068m
Mont Ouille 3099m
Lancebranlette 2936m
Aig. des Glaciers 3816m

Pont Serrand
La Golette
Entreves
LA THUILE 1450m
Tête du Rutor 3485m
Grand Assaly 3171m
Les Suches 2200m
Cerellaz
Les Dents Rouges 2924m
Mont Belleface 2890m
Chaz Dura 2579m
Col de Fourclaz
Touriasse 2448m
Pointe de Louie Blanche 2939m
Col de la Traversette 2419m
Combe des Moulins
Col du Petit Saint Bernard 2188m
Le Chatelard
Le Villaret
La Combaz
Hauteville
LA ROSIERE 1850m
Les Laix
Le Belvedere
Aig. du Clapet 2615m
Roc de Belleface

Beginners

Although there is a small nursery slope at resort level, the steepness of the lower mountain at La Thuile means that beginners soon take Les Suches gondola to the green (beginner) pistes served by La Combe lift. In La Rosière, there are several short nursery slopes near the resort, with more at the altiport nearby. Adventurous learners will soon move up the mountain to Les Eucherts, La Poletta and Roches Noires lifts, which serve a network of blue runs.

Intermediates

The linked area's 150km of mainly red pistes provide plenty of challenges for the average motorway cruiser. La Thuile offers a long run around the edges of the ski area from Chaz Dura and Bélvèdere, augmented by more aggressive terrain towards the road of the Petit-St-Bernard (a piste in winter), which usually holds the best snow. The main link with La Rosière has a tricky start, but the runs below the Col de la Traversette are mainly short reds with plenty of blue alternatives on the way down to lunch.

Advanced

The most testing black (difficult) runs are in the Touriasse sector from Bélvèdere or Chaz Dura to the Petit-St-Bernard Pass, between the San Bernardo and Fourclaz chair-lifts. In bad light, the Europa World Cup track through the woods from Les Suches to Golette is more user-friendly. The Ecureuil and Eterlou runs down to Les Ecudets below La Rosière do not deserve their black gradings, although their severity is frequently increased by indifferent snow conditions.

Off-piste

First-time visitors to the resort will be surprised by the variety and quality of La Thuile's off-piste possibilities. Wannabee powderhounds will find the regular pitch they need to gain confidence on the ungroomed sections under the chairs, while experts will enjoy the challenge of wooded, north-facing slopes between the pistes on the Touriasse. Better still is the heli-skiing (see *Heli-skiing*), which begins on the Italian side as it is forbidden in France.

The 20-km run from the Ruitor Glacier to La Rosière is suitable for intermediates and upwards, but the descent to La Thuile is a real adventure, complete with a short rope section across an ice gully and a long walk at the bottom. There are further extensive heli-skiing and heli-boarding options in **Valgrisenche**.

Snowboarders

La Rosière does not have a lot to offer riders, who would be better off in La Thuile, with its funpark and a good half-pipe as well as the best terrain for freeriders. La Combe, an encouragingly wide, flat area above Les Suches, is ideal learner riding territory. The transition to blue runs is best made in the catchment area of the Chalet Express, a chair-lift that is particularly easy to get on and off; board cred requires regular visits to the lively La Clotze Bar at the bottom of it.

Tuition and guiding

The choice used to be between La Thuile Ski School and the French Ski School (ESF) in La Rosière. However, Evolution 2 has opened a branch of its Tignes ski school in La Rosière, which receives favourable reports: 'a good mixture of encouragement and pushing'. We have conflicting reports of the Italian Ski School: 'the instructor's English was excellent and the standard of tuition high,' and 'our instructor's English was so limited she had problems understanding our questions'. We have no reports of the ESF.

Mountain restaurants

La Thuile is the exception to the rule that skiers invariably eat well on Italian mountain tops. This is not so much a question of quality as of availability. Les Suches self-service is undeniably soulless ('a motorway-style cafeteria, but the food was not bad'), while Le Foyer, higher up on the same hill, offers substantial but unsophisticated fare; both restaurants are criticised by reporters for their 'hole-in-the-ground style loos; it is not easy to balance in ski boots'.

At the top of the pass on the Italian side is an old fort that has been converted into an atmospheric restaurant specialising in grilled meats. The WCs are in the dungeons.

There are two fashionable Blues bars: the Roxi at the bottom of the Fourclaz chair and nautical Off Shore by the Belvédère chair. Both serve sandwiches and drinks to an aggressive backing track. The Bar du Lac at the bottom of the San Bernardo chair – the meeting-point for the weekly torchlight procession – serves a simple selection of Italian dishes at lunch-time.

The on-mountain options in La Rosière are Plan Repos, an adequate but crowded self-service restaurant with a large and sunny terrace, and L'Ancolie, a pleasant inn with home-made food above the cross-country track at the outlying hamlet of **Les Eucherts** (linked to La Rosière by a free bus-service while the lifts are open).

Accommodation

The four-star Planibel Hotel in La Thuile is the most convenient and luxurious place to stay, but reports suggest that the warmth of the reception can leave much to be desired. This is certainly not true of the Chalet Alpina, a 500-m walk away across a stream. Eddy Nico (South African-born but of Italian descent) and his British wife, Debbie, extend a warm welcome to their clients, who return year after year.

The Entrèves has a cheerful family atmosphere, while the Planibel Apartments have the advantages of the hotel with none of the disadvantages. Early booking is recommended for the bargain spacious two-, four- and six-person units.

Skiing facts: La Thuile

TOURIST INFORMATION
I-11016 La Thuile, Aosta
Tel/fax 39 0165 885179

THE RESORT
By road Calais 938km
By rail Pré-Saint-Didier 10km
Airport transfer Turin 3hrs
Visitor beds 2,400
Transport free bus service in the village

THE SKIING
Linked or nearby resorts La Rosière (l),
Courmayeur (n)
Number of lifts 16 in La Thuile,
35 in linked area
Total of trails/pistes 100km La Thuile,
150km in linked area (44% easy,
36% intermediate, 20% difficult)
Nursery slopes 1 free lift

LIFT PASSES
Area pass La Thuile/La Rosière
L224,000–252,000 for 6 days
Beginners 1 free baby-lift
Pensioners 65yrs and over,
L173,000–194,000 for 6 days

Credit cards yes

TUITION
Adults La Thuile Ski School
tel: 0165 884123
Snowboarding as ski school
Other courses carving, cross-country,
heli-skiing/heli-boarding, race-training,
telemark
Guiding Guide Alpine Ruitor La Thuile
tel: as ski school

CHILDREN
Lift pass L173,000–194,000 for six
days, free for 5yrs and under
Ski & board school as adults
Kindergarten (non-ski) Il Grande Albero
tel: 0165 884986, Miniclub La Thuile
tel: 0165 884541

OTHER SPORTS
Parapente, squash, swimming

FOOD AND DRINK PRICES
Coffee L1,800, glass of wine L1,800,
small beer L3,500, soft drink L3,000,
dish of the day L25,000–40,000

In La Rosière, the emphasis is on self-catering apartments. Hotel accommodation is limited, but the Relais du Petit-St-Bernard, the Roc Noir, the Vanoise and the Plein Soleil offer simple facilities in central locations. The family-run Solaret in Les Eucherts is also recommended.

Eating in and out

Valdostana cuisine, with its emphasis on game, polenta and mushrooms, is well represented in La Thuile. Le Rascard specialises in guinea-fowl stuffed with green peppers and spinach, while the long-running La Bricole, a converted barn, is known for its chamois, polenta and extensive wine list.

Fish lovers can enjoy lake perch at La Fordze. La Spaghetteria serves food that is 'cheap and tasty', while Pizza al Taglio 'is great for takeaways'. For ice-cream lovers the Cremeria in the Planibel complex is 'unmissable'. In the old village, La Grotta specialises in pizza.

Much of La Rosière's off-slope life focuses around two restaurants: Le Relais, the most popular bar in town, and the one at the Relais du Petit-St-Bernard, which serves local specialities, pizza and crêpes. Favoured alternatives include La Pitchounette, L'Ancolie and Le Plein Soleil. However, gourmets should make the 7-km trek to La Chaumière, a converted Savoyard farmhouse, which is full of atmosphere, in the village of **Montvalezan**.

Après-ski

Given their attraction for families, it is hardly surprising that neither La Thuile nor La Rosière is known for its riotous nightlife. In La Thuile, Planibel's Rendez-vous bar is 'decidedly laddish, especially late at night when the karaoke gets going'. Le Rascard is where riders hang out. Bar La Buvette near the gondola station attracts the later afternoon crowds. La Bricole video-disco has a genuine pub atmosphere, which appeals to British visitors, as well as live music at weekends. Night owls go to the Fantasia disco. The piano bar in the Hotel Planibel attracts a more sedate crowd.

La Rosière's entertainment starts at Bar Le Relais when the lifts close and continues at the Arpin, which has karaoke, and the Yeti. The resort has one disco.

Childcare

Il Grande Albero is the crèche for small children up to three years old, and Miniclub La Thuile is a free non-skiing kindergarten for children from four years old. In La Rosière, Le Village des Enfants takes care of children from 12 months to 8.30am to 7pm. The programme includes skiing, organised games and lunch. The new Evolution 2 ski school at la Rosière receives praise: 'For the first time our children really enjoyed their lessons with an English-speaking instructor'.

TOURIST INFORMATION
La Rosière
Tel 33 479 06 80 51
Fax 33 479 06 83 20
Email la.rosiere@wanadoo.fr
Web site www.skifrance.fr/~rosiere

Round-up

Cavalese
top 2,230m (7,316ft) bottom 980m (3,215ft)

Cavalese is the best-known resort of the Val di Fiemme, the collective name given to the 11 small towns and villages in the Trentino region in northern Italy to the south of the **Val di Fassa**. The other principal ski areas in the valley are Latemar above the villages of **Pampeago** and **Predazzo**, and Bellamonte-Alpe Lusia above the village of **Bellamonte**. **Passo Rolle** and **Passo Lavazè** are two other small resorts further along the valley. A sixth small area, **Ziano di Fiemme**, has night-skiing. The Fiemme-Obereggen area lift pass gives access to a total of 51 ski-lifts serving 140km of groomed pistes. All the areas are linked by free shuttle-bus.

As well as being the Val di Fiemme's principal town, Cavalese is also the resort base for **Alpe Cermis**, the area's main ski centre. This boasts 37 lifts of its own and is reached from the town by a cable-car giving magnificent views across the valley, with pistes for all standards of skier. The area has a total of seven ski and snowboard schools and two off-piste guiding companies. Courses include ski-jumping and race-training. Alpe Cermis, Bellamonte and Predazzo all have kindergartens.

Cavalese is the headquarters of Italian cross-country skiing and boasts 150km of trails. The Marcialonga di Fiemme e Fassa is a 75-km international cross-country marathon held every January. The race attracts over 6,000 athletes and starts at Moena in the Val di Fassa and finishes at Cavalese.

Hotels in Cavalese include the Park Hotel Bella Costa and the Bella Vista, and restaurants to suit every budget abound. The region offers four ski schools and three ski-kindergarten and crèches. Other activities available in the valley include dog-sledding, indoor tennis and ski-orienteering. A sixteenth-century local event, *The Trial of the Witches*, is staged in Cavalese town centre each January.

TOURIST INFORMATION
Tel 39 0462 241111
Fax 39 0462 241199
Email info@aptfiemme.tn.it
Web site www.aptfiemme.tn.it

Macugnaga
top 2,984m (9,790ft) bottom 1,327m (4,353ft)

The resort of Macugnaga is made up of five villages: **Staffa**, **Pecetto**, **Pestarena**, **Borca** and **Isella**. They lie on the opposite side of the Monte Rosa mountain to **Gressoney**, close to the Swiss border and two hours' drive from Turin. Macugnaga's proximity to the border has resulted in a style of architecture more in keeping with Switzerland than with Italy.

Staffa and Pecetto have their own small ski areas, which are linked by ski bus. One reporter summed up the area as 'a marvellous introduction to skiing'. Reporters praised the 'short queues, if any at all; often you can finish your run and ski right back on to an empty chairlift'. Staffa has better skiing for beginners ('only ten people on the nursery slopes at the very busiest'), a cable-car rising to the summit and a number of longer runs. We have encouraging reports of Scuola Sci Macugnaga: 'excellent value for money'. Off-piste enthusiasts can hire a local mountain guide to ski over the back of Monte Moro to **Saas-Fee** in Switzerland or book heli-skiing (see *Heli-skiing*) trips through Giana Helicopter.

Hotel du Four in Staffa's main square is 'clean and friendly, with plentiful and delicious food'. Hotel Zumstein is close to the resort centre and the cable-car. Recommended restaurants include the Miramonti at the Mt Belvedere base ('good lunchtime pizzas and great fondue nights'), and the Glacier ('you must book at weekends'). There are various other bars and restaurants in town, as well as a few small shops, but on the whole the nightlife is limited. The Big Ben disco 'appears to be in a 1960s time warp'. Skating and night-skiing are two of the other activities on offer.

TOURIST INFORMATION
Tel 39 0324 65119
Fax 39 0324 65775
Email suiua@libero.it
Web site www.infosquare.it/serviei/macugnaga

Madesimo
top 2,984m (9,790ft) bottom 1,530m (5,018ft)

This small, attractive resort, centred around an old church, is a two-hour drive north of Bergamo. It is right on the Swiss border and close enough for a shopping spree in **St Moritz**. The old village has narrow streets with a few shops and some old converted farm houses, as well as some less pleasing concrete buildings. Madesimo's appeal is that it is cheaper than other, better-known resorts and offers excellent value for money.

The skiing is mostly intermediate and is concentrated on the usually uncrowded slopes of the 2,984-m Pizzo Groppera, with long runs leading down into the neighbouring Valle di Lei. The high altitude normally ensures reasonable snow conditions. Sixteen lifts serve 50km of mostly red (intermediate) pistes and some challenging black (difficult) trails, including the famous Canalone run. There are two funparks and a halfpipe. The nursery slopes are pleasant and served by a quad chair-lift, and the Madesimo Ski School has a reputation for small classes ('excellent, with plenty of English-speaking instructors').

Hotels include the central Emet and the family-run Andossi, which has a fitness room and a lively bar. The Arlecchino has 'small rooms, but a brilliant location and delicious hot chocolate in the hotel bar'. Hotel Cascata e Cristallo has excellent facilities including a swimming-pool, piano bar and a mini-club for four- to twelve-year-olds. You can ski back to most of the accommodation.

TOURIST INFORMATION
Tel 39 0343 53015
Fax 39 0343 53782
Email aptmadesimo@provincia.so.it
Web site www.madesimo.com

Passo Tonale
top 3,069m (10,069ft) bottom 1,883m (6,178ft)

Passo Tonale is one of a group of Italian resorts which, with the lure of good snow and low prices, are dramatically increasing in popularity. The resort is situated 100km (62 miles) from Bolzano and shares its skiing with the charming village of **Ponte di Legno**, 600m along the pass to the west. Together they offer 28 lifts with the capacity to carry 33,000 snow-users per hour to 70km of pistes.

The resort is a thin line of three 12-storey tower blocks and rows of condominiums that resemble army barracks. Hotels hug the single roadway, but fortunately there is little through-traffic by night. You can walk across the village in 10 minutes. The only bus runs seven times daily to Ponte di Legno. The clientèle is a combination of families, ski clubs and school groups, who all appreciate the easy, affordable skiing. The area has become popular with British, Belgian, French, German and eastern European snow-users.

Passo Tonale is a resort with exceptional snow quality, ideal beginner and easy intermediate terrain, as well as extensive ski-touring and off-piste. As one reporter commented: 'of all the resorts we have visited this is probably one of the best for beginners, although high-altitude and exposed pistes can make it very cold'.

Mountain access is on either side of the main road, with most of the chair- and drag-lifts starting from the south-facing snowfields. The only cable-car is a 1-km walk west from the village; at the top is a chair-lift that leads to two drags on the Presena Glacier, which has summer skiing. Ponte di Legno is a separate sector, normally accessible on skis or by bus, with a handful of lifts starting at the edge of the forest. The Contrabbandieri and Valbiolo chair-lifts together serve a 4.5-km red run and access an ungroomed area.

Passo Tonale has a choice of four schools. Instructors at both Tonale-Presena and Ponte di Legno-Tonale are described as 'unspoilt, simple and sympathetic'. We have also received a favourable report for the third school, Il Castellaccio. G & G is the specialist snowboard school. The Miniclub in the Hotel Miramonti cares for small non-skiers, while Fantaski is the ski kindergarten.

Negritella, up the mountain, serves 'very good local dishes in a friendly and efficient environment'. Malga Valbiolo is 'lacking in atmosphere and serves poorer-quality food than elsewhere'. Hotel Redivalle is the resort's oldest hotel. Orchidea is one of the most attractive hotels, along with the historic Mirandola Hospice, where resident guests must rely on snowmobile transport, which is available until 2am. For fine dining, the snowmobile ride up to the hospice is mandatory. Bianca Neve features bright orange décor in a 12-storey, white tower block but has good food. Sporthotel Vittoria has a pub with live music and is often used by school parties.

In town, intimate décor and delicious gorgonzola *Spätzle* are found at Il Focolare ('impressive but not cheap'). La Torretta is praised for 'the best thin, crispy-base pizza'. Palla di Neve and Antares are recommended for pasta. Bar Cady, Nico's and the UFO are popular bars. El Bait is quiet and cosy, Antares features live music, and Heaven is equally busy. Other sports include dog-sledding in Ponte di Legno.

TOURIST INFORMATION
Tel 39 0364 903838
Fax 39 0364 903896
Email tonale@valdisole.net
Web site www.valdisole.net

Pila
top 2,750m (9,022ft) bottom 1,750m (5,741ft)

Pila is an old village in a sheltered bowl affording spectacular views. It has undergone a lot of expansion in recent years and is linked to the regional capital, **Aosta**, by an 18-minute gondola ride. It has 70km of mainly intermediate trails served by 12 lifts. Five mountain restaurants are dotted around the slopes. Pila Ski and Snowboard School organises all-day tuition for adults and children, and heli-skiing (see *Heli-skiing*) is available through Interguide. The area has a half-pipe and jumps for snowboarders. Biancaneve is a kindergarten for children from 18 months up to 12 years old. The Wild Surf Pila 2000 ski kindergarten accepts children from three years of age. Hotels include the ski-in ski-out Etoile de Neige, and the Printemps which has a disco. Pila boasts 10 restaurants as well as shops and cafés. Other activities include shopping trips to the ancient Roman town of Aosta.

TOURIST INFORMATION
Tel 39 0165 521148
Fax 39 0165 521437
Email info@pila.it
Web site www.pila.it

San Martino di Castrozza
top 2,385m (7,825ft) bottom 1,450m (4,757ft)

San Martino is on the eastern edge of the Trentino Dolomites, surrounded by wild forest with pink mountain peaks above. In 1700, the violin-maker Stradivari used to go into the same woods to select the spruce for his violins. Due to this historic connection, the area soon became known as the Forest of Violins. Skiing started at San Martino di Castrozza in the early 1930s. It has developed into three separate areas (two of which are linked) with 60km and 26 lifts.

San Martino's two ski schools have now amalgamated to form Nuova Scuola Nazionale di Sci, which takes adults and children from five years old. The mountain guiding companies are Gruppo Guide Alpine and Aquile de San Martino, both of which supply guides for the long off-piste descents of the Pale Highlands. The Rosetta cable-car is open in February and March for ski-touring and snowshoeing expeditions, and the local cross-country skiing takes place on several circuits including one around the lake. Accommodation includes four-star Hotel des Alpes and Hotel Savoia, and the simpler Hotel Colfosco.

TOURIST INFORMATION
Tel 39 0439 768867
Fax 39 0439 768814
Email info@sanmartino.com
Web site www.sanmartino.com

Val di Fassa
top 2,949m (9,676ft) bottom 1,320m (4,330ft)

The main resorts in the valley for tourism are **Canazei** and **Campitello**, which act as gateways to the giant **Sella Ronda** ski area (see separate chapter). These, together with the villages of **Vigo di Fassa, Moena, Pozza di Fassa, Soraga** and **Mazzin**, are all connected by a free ski bus. Each of these little Italian communities has its own tiny ski area. The Val di Fassa and Carezza ski pass covers the separate ski areas in **Alba**, Canazei, Campitello, Pozza di Fassa, **Pera**, Vigo di Fassa and **Carezza**.

Traditional Moena is the principal town of the valley and has 55 hotels including the Hotel Alle Alpi, Belvedere and Rosengarten, and two renowned restaurants: the Malga Panna and Fuchiade (on the Pellegrino Pass). Other accommodation is available in the neighbouring hamlets of Alba, **Forno** and **Passo San Pellegrino**. Mazzin is noted for its attractive architecture. Vigo di Fassa was the administrative centre of the valley during the fourteenth century as well as a transit station for merchants. Today, it is home to 40 tourist hotels including the comfortable Park Hotel Corona, where former Olympic champion Alberto Tomba is often a guest. Pozza di Fassa has a further 55 hotels, including the Hotel Aurora and Garni Patrizia.

Moena is the starting point for the annual cross-country marathon. Floodlit cross-country skiing available at Pozza di Fassa.

TOURIST INFORMATION
Tel 39 0462 602466
Fax 39 0462 602278
Email info@fassa.com
Web site www.fassa.com

Switzerland

Switzerland is once again becoming a popular destination for discerning skiers and snowboarders in search of authentic Alpine atmosphere and challenging, still-unspoilt mountainsides. While it is certainly not true that British holidaymakers introduced the sport here, they did help to promote it in the Parsenn, the Bernese Oberland and the Engadine during the early twentieth century, and their enduring love affair with the 'land of Heidi' continues unabated.

Throughout the 1990s, however, high domestic prices and an unfavourable rate of exchange seriously affected Swiss tourism, both from Britain and other European countries. All but the most ardent and well-heeled winter-sports visitors had little option but to desert some of the most beautiful skiing grounds of the world and turn to more affordable pastures. But now they are returning, in increasing numbers. Prices remain high, but lunch in Zermatt is a less financially painful experience than lunch in Courchevel, as well as being better value for money.

Ecological pressure to preserve the natural mountain environment has largely prevented the overdevelopment of Swiss ski villages. The concept of the giant, linked ski area, so popular in the 1960s and 1970s, was never fully realised here; even the Portes du Soleil only just brushes into Switzerland. Most resorts remain traditional villages, largely unsullied by the demands of mass tourism. Over the past three years, fresh investment in uphill transport has transformed the skiing opportunities in major resorts such as St Moritz, Verbier and Zermatt.

Almost all Swiss resorts can be reached by train from Geneva and Zurich airports. Crossair Saturday flights to Sion in the Rhône Valley give speedy access to Crans Montana, Verbier and Zermatt. Switzerland has two types of rail pass, which can be purchased from the Switzerland Travel Centre in London. These vouchers allow either airport transfers to and from your resort, or 'rover' facilities for the duration of your stay. As might be expected, trains run on time in Switzerland. However, the Swiss themselves rarely travel with more than hand luggage; trolleys are consequently scarce, and there is little provision for suitcases on trains. You are therefore strongly advised to send your luggage separately. You can do this from your departure airport and it should arrive at your destination on the same day.

Crans Montana

ALTITUDE 1,500m (4,920ft)

Beginners ✱✱ Intermediates ✱✱✱ Advanced ✱ Snowboarders ✱✱✱

Crans Montana is the official umbrella name for the agglomerations of **Crans**, **Montana** and **Aminona**. It is a traditional spa resort that cultivates an elite, older clientèle in search of much more than a daily bash down what are incontrovertibly intermediate slopes. This group mixes incongruously with a huge snowboarding crowd who come here for some of the best facilities and tuition in the Alps.

- ✔ Short airport transfer
- ✔ Exceptional sunshine record
- ✔ High standard of hotels
- ✔ Ample non-skiing activities
- ✔ Superb mountain views
- ✔ Glacier skiing
- ✔ Facilities for children
- ✘ Urban landscape
- ✘ Heavy traffic
- ✘ Spread-out resort

The resort has spent an extraordinary amount of money in recent years as the major part of the bid by the nearby town of Sion to host the Winter Olympics in 2006. Its surprising last-minute failure – Sestriere won – has caused considerable local anguish, but skiers and snowboarders can only benefit from the welcome improvements to the lift system.

Crans Montana sits on what is claimed to be the sunniest plateau in the Alps, dotted with larches and lakes. Certainly, the view across the Rhône Valley of 150km of the Alps is the most spectacular of all Alpine panoramas. The resort has evolved from its early days in the 1890s as a centre for tuberculosis clinics into an interlinked skiing complex on the mountainside above. However, it is sometimes hard to believe that the three towns, which grew together over 20 years ago, owe their existence to the once pure mountain air. The urban conglomeration sprawls untidily for over a mile along a busy main road. A funicular takes only 12 minutes to carry snow-users up to Montana from the valley town of Sierre, thus encouraging visitors either to arrive in the region by train or to leave their cars down below.

In 1893, Hotel du Parc, Montana's first hotel, opened its doors. Today smart hotels vie with each other for the number of stars and the quality of their cuisine. Life in Montana revolves around the open-air skating-rink, while the chic shopping at Crans is advertised as the finest in the Alps. Gucci and Valentino are just two of the designer boutiques here. In addition to half-a-dozen cellulite centres and four major medical complexes, an international school and a hotel management school, the resort features a resident astrologer, four reflexologists and three funeral homes. The main lift complexes are a five-minute walk uphill from their respective town centres.

Today some 53 per cent of winter visitors are Swiss. French, Germans and Italians account for most of the rest, but the British are slowly returning in increasing numbers after a price-enforced absence. Crossair runs a weekly direct service on winter Saturdays between Heathrow and Sion, which is only 30 minutes from the resort.

On the snow
top 3,000m (9,840ft) bottom 1,500m (4,920ft)

Crans Montana is an intermediate's resort with good beginner terrain. All the pistes are easier than their ratings suggest. Mountain access is via five points spread from west to east across the base of the mountains between Crans and Aminona. There is free underground parking at the lift stations.

A smart 30-person Funitel gondola gives direct access to the top of the ski area at Plaine-Morte. A modern gondola has replaced the old 'egg' from Crans to Cry d'Err. Queuing is not a serious problem here. The red (intermediate) run from Cry d'Err towards Pas du Loup is, according to reporters, 'the only area that could occasionally be described as congested'. Most visitors are content with making a few casual runs in the sunshine each day on the 160km of groomed piste. Of these, two are modern high-speed quads, but more than half are antiquated drag-lifts.

A single gondola from Montana and the eight-person Cry d'Err gondola at Crans lead up through the woods to Cry d'Err, where a cable-car and chair-lift continue to the 2,600-m summit of that sector. Between Montana and Aminona, the glacier skiing at 3,000m on Plaine-Morte is reached by the Funitel continuing upwards from the Violettes gondolas, which start from the outskirts of Montana at Barzettes. The resort's longest run is the 1,500-vertical-metre drop from the glacier to town-level here. From Crans Montana a bus takes skiers to Aminona, where a gondola rises to Petit Bonvin at 2,400m.

The resort's cross-country tracks include a 12-km loipe set unusually at an altitude of 3,000m on the Plaine-Morte Glacier.

Beginners
Starting at the top, beginners have three short but easy runs on the Plaine-Morte Glacier, where good snow is guaranteed. The nursery slopes down by the golf course in Crans are even easier, but susceptible to sun. Cry d'Err has the most beginner runs, of which a handful are accessible by eight lifts providing skiing all the way down into Crans or Montana. However, it is impossible to ski back to Aminona entirely on blue (easy) runs. The village of **Bluche**, five minutes' drive away, has a free nursery slope lift.

Intermediates
Despite the generally superior standard of piste-grooming everywhere, passages between rock walls, such as on the long red (intermediate) run

from Plaine-Morte, provide an additional thrill. The largest conflux of intermediate pistes is in the Violettes sector, with winding trails through the woods. The Toula chair- and drag-lifts lead to steeper reds. Most exciting are the Nationale World Cup piste and Chetseron, which are well-groomed but have the occasional banked drop-off designed to make the stomach flip when taken at high speed. One reporter describes the Nationale as 'an excellent run with some testing sections'. Two small areas are more difficult; one is the women's downhill racecourse on Chetseron, the other is a seemingly innocuous link between the Violettes mid-station and the long red coming down from the glacier.

Advanced

The only officially graded black (difficult) run in the entire resort is a bumpy fall-line pitch on the ridge under the Toula chair-lift ('no more than a red really'), which is often impeccably groomed on the lower section. The Plaine-Morte run is said to be the most avalanche-prone in Switzerland. Although perfectly safe when officially open, its gunbarrel passages and changes in direction require a high level of concentration.

Off-piste

Crans Montana has no death-defying couloirs, but there are three unmarked itineraries that require guides. From the Plaine-Morte Glacier it is possible to ski across open slopes and through three bands of rock down to the lake at **Zeuzier**. By walking through tunnels (torches required) and skiing a summer roadway you reach the ski lifts in the neighbouring resort of **Anzère**. Another route from the glacier guarantees fresh powder to the Vallon d'Ertenze. The only way out at the bottom is by helicopter.

Snowboarders

Crans Montana is a very active snowboarding centre, with some excellent facilities for freestylers and some of the best snowboarding tuition in the Alps. The funparks are in Aminona and Merignou, and there is a half-pipe at Cry d'Err. The nearby resort of Anzère is highly recommended for advanced freeriding.

Tuition and guiding

There are two branches of the Swiss Ski School (ESS) in Crans and in Montana. Teaching in Montana is said to be 'imaginative, with a lot of emphasis on technique. Most instructors speak good English'. Surf Evasion, affiliated with the Montana Ski School, offers group snowboard lessons during holiday periods, private lessons at other times, and heli-boarding. The Swiss Snowboard School in Crans, part of the ESS, is a highly respected learning centre.

Mountain restaurants

The Crans Montana clientèle prefers to eat in town. Lift station eateries at Cry d'Err, Petit Bonvin ('we were revolted to find horse meat on the menu') and Plaine-Morte are adequate but not inspiring. The Cabane des Violettes is an authentic alpine club touring hut with simple meals. The Café de la Cure alongside the blue run down to Aminona has character, but the best inns with sunny terraces are Merbé for its tortellini and Plumachit for its wild strawberry tart.

Accommodation
The resort that sprawls across its three communities has few pretensions to charm. The tower-block Résidence Vermala, sticking out like a sore thumb on a hill above Montana, is one of the greatest eyesores in the Alps. Traditionally Crans was the smartest of the three towns, followed by mass-market Montana and sleepy Aminona. Today the social divisions have come down as the concrete has gone up, and Crans and Montana have equally impressive four- and five-star establishments as well as more reasonably priced hotels.

The Hostellerie Pas de l'Ours in Crans is one of the most charming hotels in the Alps, a small chalet-style establishment decorated with a bear theme, in keeping with its name. It has oak beams, carved ceilings and painted furniture, while its enormous suites all have spa baths and unusual log fireplaces. This, together with the Crans-Ambassador in Montana, the Royal and the Grand Hotel du Golf, both in Crans, head the luxury cast.

The three-star Mont Blanc, on a hill above the resort, has 'the biggest terrace and best views'. Hotel St George in Montana is 'conveniently placed and has good food and service. However, the rooms are shamefully pokey for a four-star'.

Eating in and out
The modestly priced Diligence in Montana specialises in Middle Eastern cuisine ('the locals eat here as well as regular weekenders, so booking is essential'). Otherwise, the most celebrated non-hotel gourmet dining is at the Cervin, the Rôtisserie de la Reine, and La Poste. The Mont Blanc, in the woods above Crans, has a marmot zoo for children and serves tasty sea bass. Dun Huang is Cantonese, and the Christina has Portuguese specialities. Valais-style raclette and fondue are on offer at the Bergerie du Cervin and Le Chalet. Snowboarders congregate at the pub-style San Nick's.

Après-ski
The Absolut Disco in Crans heads the surprisingly long list of late-night entertainment spots that includes seven discos. The younger crowd, many of whom are riders, gathers immediately after skiing at Amadeus in Montana or Constellation in Crans, where Le Pub is also popular. Teenagers flock to Montana's Number Two Bar for late drinking. In Crans, The Pascha Club has mostly techno music and the Memphis is a comfortable jazz bar. The older set are to be found in the Miedzor, Aida Castel and Crans-Ambassador hotels.

Skiing facts: Crans Montana

TOURIST INFORMATION
CP 372, CH-3962 Crans Montana
Tel 41 27 485 0404
Fax 41 27 485 0460
Email information@crans-montana.ch
Web site www.crans-montana.ch

THE RESORT
By road Calais 901km
By rail Sierre 18km, bus to resort
Airport transfer Geneva 1½hrs,
Sion ½hr
Visitor beds 40,000
Transport free bus service

THE SKIING
Linked or nearby resorts Aminona (l),
Anzère (n), Bluche (n)
Number of lifts 37
Total of trails/pistes 160km (38%
easy, 50% intermediate, 12% difficult)
Nursery slopes 7 lifts
Summer skiing July–Aug, 2 lifts on
Plaine-Morte Glacier

LIFT PASSES
Area Pass SF239 for 6 days
Beginners 1 free lift in Bluche,
2km away
Pensioners women 62yrs and over,
men 65yrs and over SF203 for 6 days
Credit cards yes

TUITION
Adults ESS Crans tel: 27 485 9370,

ESS Montana tel: 27 481 1480, Ski and
Sky tel: 27 485 4250
Snowboarding Stoked tel: 27 481 4160,
Surf Evasion (ESS Montana), Swiss
Snowboard School (ESS Crans)
Other courses Big Foot, carving, cross-
country, extreme skiing, heli-skiing and
heli-boarding, mono-skiing, race camps,
seniors, skiing for the disabled,
snowblading, ski-touring, teen skiing,
telemark
Guiding ESS Crans and Montana

CHILDREN
Lift pass 6–15yrs, SF143
Ski & board school as adults
Kindergarten (ski/non-ski) ESS Crans
and Montana, Jardin des Neiges, Fleurs
des Champs tel: 27 481 2367, Garderie
Zig Zag tel: 27 481 2205

OTHER SPORTS
Alpine flights, curling, dog-sledding on
the frozen lake, horse-riding, hot-air
ballooning, indoor climbing wall, indoor
tennis and squash, luge-ing, night-
skiing, night-snowshoeing, parapente,
skating, sleigh rides, snowbiking,
tobogganing

FOOD AND DRINK PRICES
Coffee SF2.80–3, glass of wine
SF2.30–3, small beer SF2.80–3.20,
soft drink SF3.50,
dish of the day SF15–18

Childcare
Infants from three months old can attend the Fleurs des Champs
kindergarten, next to Hotel Eldorado in Montana. Garderie Zig-Zag,
also in Montana, takes children of between two and six years of age.
The Montana Ski School has its own Jardin des Neiges up on the Grand
Signal mid-station. The Crans Ski School also has a kindergarten.

Davos/Klosters

ALTITUDE Davos 1,560m (5,117ft), Klosters 1,130m (3,706ft)

Beginners ✱ Intermediates ✱✱✱ Advanced ✱✱✱ Snowboarders ✱✱✱

D avos is the European birthplace of downhill skiing. The first pair of skis was brought here from Norway in 1882 by a former patient at the tuberculosis clinic run by Dr Alexander Spengler. Some 20 years earlier the German-born doctor had recognised the beneficial affects of the mountain climate in this corner of Switzerland and begun the transformation of Davos from remote mountain community to international resort. His son Carl tried out the giant Lapp hunting skis, and his abortive flounderings on the slopes above the town created local interest. The following year Robert Paulcke, who owned the Davos pharmacy, gave his teenage son Wilhelm a pair for Christmas. It so happened that one of his teachers, Agnes Duborgh, came from Norway and had a vague idea of what you were meant to do with them. Within weeks, this new 'skiing' was the rage of Davos secondary school.

> ✔ Long runs
> ✔ Large linked ski area
> ✔ Good restaurants at all levels
> ✔ Off-piste for all standards
> ✔ Impressive slope grooming
> ✔ Ski-touring opportunities
> ✔ Tree-level skiing
> ✔ Good-value lift pass
> ✔ Village atmosphere (Klosters)
> ✗ Straggling town (Davos)
> ✗ Lack of skiing convenience

'It has come to our notice that people in Davos this winter are experimenting with the Norwegian sport of skiing', wrote the editor of the town's weekly newspaper in 1883.

Saddle-maker Tobias Branger and his brother Johann had the foresight to realise that this skiing business could be as big as cheese, chocolate and watches. They imported skis from Norway and improved the leather-and-metal bindings. But in order to become the first Swiss ski instructors, they first had to learn to ski. To avoid embarrassment they did this by night. In 1894, accompanied by Dr Arthur Conan Doyle, they crossed the Maienfeld Furka Pass to **Arosa** on skis.

The slopes of the Parsenn, which Davos shares with **Klosters**, its much more attractive neighbour, developed gradually with the introduction of the annual Parsenn Derby race in 1924, the opening of the funicular railway in 1931, and the installation of the first drag-lift in 1934 (said to be the first in the world). In recent years the town has established itself as one of Europe's best-known conference centres, hosting the annual World Economic Forum.

The town – it claims to be the highest in Europe – straggles inconveniently for four miles from the railway station of Davos Dorf to Davos

Platz. It consists largely of giant hotels, built in practical rather than pleasing style, interspersed with expensive boutiques and a good range of other shops. The efficient bus service is included in the lift pass and runs in a loop around the one-way system. Nevertheless, where to stay deserves serious consideration. Davos Dorf is quiet and stately with handsome old hotels, while Davos Platz is the bustling commercial heart. Dorf gives the most direct access to the main Parsenn ski area, but Platz has the lion's share of the nightlife. Enthusiasts will enjoy the renovated Wintersport Museum at Platz, which traces the development of equipment and clothing through the years.

Klosters, by contrast, is a small, rural farming community. It welcomed its first winter sports enthusiasts in 1904, and has prospered from its connection with the British royal family, in particular Prince Charles. Despite its high 'by Royal Appointment' profile, it remains essentially a small and discreet Swiss village.

Again, the resort is divided into two bed bases. Klosters Platz is the main community clustered around the railway station and the Gotschna cable-car. Klosters Dorf is a sleepy outpost at the bottom of the Madrisa lift system. The two are connected by a regular bus service, but only those of a reclusive disposition should consider staying in Dorf. Platz is conveniently compact, with a range of hotels in each category. A new

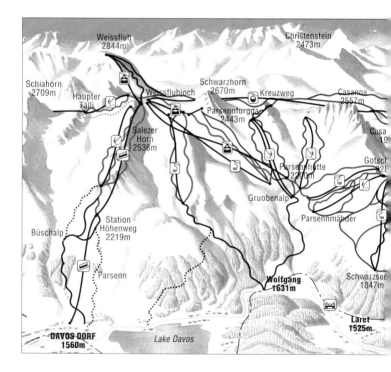

bypass road tunnel has solved the valley's unsightly traffic problem, enabling Klosters to be pedestrianised. This tunnel links to a second and much more ambitious 21-km Chunnel-style rail/road tunnel that provides a direct link to the Engadine Valley, allowing skiers from St Moritz to reach Klosters and Davos in 45 minutes.

On the snow

top 2,844m (9,328ft) bottom 813m (2,667ft)

Much has changed since the Davos English Ski Club built its first mountain refuge on the Parsenn in 1906, only to have it destroyed almost immediately in a fatal avalanche. Where there were once no lifts a sophisticated network of 54 covers five separate areas. The largest of these, which is shared with Klosters, is the Parsenn.

It is dominated by the 2,844-m Weissfluh, the highest point on the piste map and the starting point for a web of wide, sweeping runs that flatter your skiing technique. However, the steeper slopes at the Klosters end of the circuit are sufficiently long and demanding to deter all but truly accomplished skiers. In mid-season snow conditions it is possible to ski 12km through a full 2,000 vertical metres down to the valley villages of **Küblis** and **Serneus**.

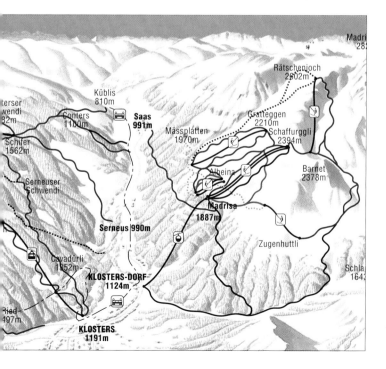

Three of the different lift companies that manage the skiing in the region have now amalgamated, with the result that the slopes are some of the best groomed in Switzerland, and easy access is greatly enhanced by a hands-free electronic lift pass system.

The Parsenn is accessed most directly by the Parsennbahn funicular from Davos Dorf, but it is also reached from Davos Platz via the Schatzalp/Strela lift system. Plans to build a new cable-car and giant gondola to replace the queue-prone Parsennbahn have progressed, and work started in summer 2000. The two-stage Gotschna cable-car provides the only access to the slopes from Klosters, with the second stage carrying fewer people than the first, resulting in a scrum of people. Plans to rectify this situation are on the drawing board, but they are unlikely to be realised in the near future. Once up the mountain, however, the crowds thin out and the Parsenn provides a pleasing combination of undulating intermediate and steeper advanced terrain.

This skiing heartland is supplemented by four further ski areas, three of them on the other side of the Davos Valley, and the fourth beyond Klosters. In the Davos catchment area, the three peaks are Pischa, Jakobshorn and Rinerhorn. They are accessed by bus from Dorf, directly from Platz, and by bus or train from **Glaris**, the next stop on the line down to Chur. Beyond Klosters, the alternative to the Parsenn is the Madrisa, where the slopes stretch up to the Swiss–Austrian border.

In contrast to the Parsenn, these outlying areas are often enticingly empty. The easiest to reach from the Parsenn is Strela, a remote ski area linked by rickety cable-car across the Hauptertälli from the highest point of Weissfluhjoch. Here the slopes are sunny and uncrowded.

Beginners

Like many large, non-purpose-built resorts, Davos is not the place to learn to ski from scratch. If you must, the wide Bolgen nursery slope at the bottom of the Jakobshorn, a short walk from Platz, is the best starting point. In Dorf the equivalent is Bünda, which has a longer but steeper pitch. In Klosters, the sunny, user-friendly nursery slopes are up the mountain on the Madrisa, which means buying a full lift pass and returning by gondola at the end of the day. Once the basics of skiing or snowboarding are mastered, there is no shortage of blue (easy) runs to which you can progress.

Intermediates

Those who profit most from the Davos/Klosters area are intermediates with the energy to ski all the hours the lift company allows. Nearly all the marked runs are blue or red (intermediate), most are invitingly wide, and several are over 10km long. The ones from the top of the Weissfluh to the valley villages of Küblis, **Saas** and Serneus start high above the tree-line, then track down through the woods to the railway line, providing a degree of excitement that is definitely not attainable in more crowded places. Another unmissable cruiser starts at the top of the Madrisa lift system and descends to Klosters Dorf via the Schlappin Valley. All five ski areas offer plenty of easy terrain, so there is no excuse for not ranging far and wide. In terms of variety, the lift pass is good value.

Advanced

Since the mountains in the area become steeper near the bottom, the black (difficult) runs are mostly confined to the lower sections, which means that they can be icy in all but the most favourable snow conditions. The advantage is that they are generally among trees, and therefore the visibility is always good. The best conditions are usually on the north-facing Klosters side; the Gotschnawang, which is no longer marked as a piste and is in any case rarely open, and the Drostobel provide serious challenges. Turn right from the Gotschnagrat and you come to a prime mogul-basher under the Schwarzeealp chair. Further gruelling bump runs on the Standard Ersatz and the Unterer Standard immediately above Davos Dorf offer considerable challenge. The most highly recommended black run starts on the Meierhofer Tälli at the top of the Parsenn and goes down to the hamlet of Wolfgang.

Off-piste

Those who are prepared to don skins and climb a bit can explore the huge potential for deep-snow adventure in one of Switzerland's most extensive ski areas. The longest, but by no means the most exciting, of the runs are the 18-km descents to Fideris and Jenaz, each with short climbing sections along the way. The Madrisa provides excellent opportunities for learning powder technique and is also the starting point for the trans-border loop to the hamlet of **Gargellen** at the head of the Montafon Valley. The best part of the tour is down to the attractive village of **St Antönien**.

   Skiing to Arosa in the tracks of Conan Doyle is a more serious business, with a three- to four-hour climb to the Maienfeld Furka Pass above **Frauenkirch**, followed by a gentle descent through woods to the bottom of the valley and then a 40-minute plod up through the town to the railway station for the three-hour return to Davos.

Snowboarders

Throwing tradition out of the window, the area has embraced snowboarding with enthusiasm and admirable commercial acumen. It is ideal for riders, with lots of trees, a boardercross circuit, and nightriding. Riders who used to range all over the mountain in large numbers now congregate at the Parsenn funpark with its two half-pipes and on the Jakobshorn. They are joined by carving skiers, who can try their hand at the dedicated carving courses beneath the Totalp chair-lift.

Cross-country

Davos offers 75km of prepared cross-country trails on the valley floor and in the Sertigtal and Dischmatal areas. Evening expeditions can be made on the 2.5-km floodlit section, and dogs are allowed on some of the trails. The highlights of the cross-country year are the Davos Nordic World Cup and the 20-km Volks Langlauf.

Tuition and guiding

The Swiss Snowsportschool Davos (SSSD) has ski and snowboard classes for adults and teenagers. Half-day safety classes for off-piste beginners (with a maximum of six per group) are available, covering the use of ABS-rucksacks and avalanche transceivers. Daily or weekly guided ski-tours can be arranged between January and Easter. We have no reports on the Swiss Snowsportschool Klosters (SSSK). Duty Board Prattigau/Bananas is the specialist snowboarding school in both resorts, while Top Secret Snowboarding School in Davos Platz is highly recommended for first-timers.

The Saas Ski and Snowboard School (Saas S&S-S) in Klosters, which in the past has received complimentary reports ('friendly instructors with good English') no longer seems as competitive. Bruno Sprecher, the guiding force behind it, is more often to be found in Canada these days and according to one regular reporter, 'the school appears to have lost direction'. A new school for the 1999–2000 season was Absolutely Klosters.

Mountain restaurants

'Go low' is the recommendation in an area where skiing to lunch should be an integral part of a long adventure run. Intelligent use of the piste map makes it possible to locate the many small establishments in the woods on the way down to the outlying villages. The restaurant at the Teufi on the off-piste descent from the Jakobshorn is recommended, as is the Hotel Kulm (also known as Jakob's) in Wolfgang. Another winner is the pizzeria at the end of the Schlappin run in Klosters Dorf, but in general, enterprise should yield gastronomic dividends. The Erika on Madrisa is recommended. The Conterser Schwendi is renowned for its rösti and other local specialities, as is the Serneuser Schwendi ('popular, but a bit noisy and smoky'). The Gotschna at Serneus serves delicious cheese dishes. The Strela Alp restaurant is frequented by almost as many walkers as skiers.

Accommodation

Davos has two five-star hotels: the Steigenberger Belvédère, up on the hillside above Platz, and the Flüela, opposite the railway station in Dorf. Both offer old-fashioned comfort in the stolid Swiss manner, a style copied by many of their competitors in the four- and three-star brackets. The new four-star Victoria Turmhotel at Dorf is warmly recommended: 'excellent health centre and splendid food'. In Platz, the Waldhotel Bellevue is rich in tradition. The same can be said of the Berghotel Schatzalp.

One of the reasons the Jakobshorn is popular with riders is its proximity to what is said to be the world's first dedicated snowboard hotel, the Bolgenschanze. Kleines Palace für Snowboarder offers low-budget accommodation for riders only.

Skiing facts: Davos

TOURIST INFORMATION
Promenade 67, CH-7270 Davos
Tel 41 81 415 2121
Fax 41 81 415 2100
Email davos@davos.ch
Web site www.davos.ch

THE RESORT
By road Calais 1,010km
By rail Davos Dorf and Davos Platz
stations in resort
Airport transfer Zurich 2½hrs
Visitor beds 24,251
Transport free ski bus with lift pass,
free ski train with Rega Pass

THE SKIING
Linked or nearby resorts Arosa (n),
Gargellen (n), Glaris (l), Klosters (l),
Küblis (l), Saas (l), Serneus (l),
St Moritz (n), Wolfgang (l)
Number of lifts 54 in Davos/Klosters
area
Total of trails/pistes 320km in
Davos/Klosters area (30% easy, 40%
intermediate, 30% difficult)
Nursery slopes 2 lifts

LIFT PASSES
Area pass Rega Pass (covers all Davos
and Klosters lifts, buses and railway),
SF273 for 6 days
Beginners no free lifts
Pensioners 20% reduction for women
62yrs and over, men 65yrs and over
Credit cards yes

TUITION
Adults SSSD tel: 81 416 2454, Top
Secret tel: 81 413 2040
Snowboarding as ski schools, Duty
Board Prattigau/Bananas tel:
81 410 1014
Other courses carving, cross-country,
extreme skiing, moguls, seniors, powder
clinics, race-training, snowblading, teen
skiing, telemark
Guiding SSSD

CHILDREN
Lift pass 6–16yrs, Rega Pass SF164
for 6 days
Ski & board school as adults
Kindergarten (ski/non-ski) SSSD
tel: 41 416 2454

FOOD AND DRINK PRICES
Coffee SF3.80, glass of wine SF8–10,
small beer SF4.50–5, soft drink SF4,
dish of the day SF16–25

In Klosters, the four-stars are headed by the Walserhof which has an excellent reputation. The Chesa Grischuna is rustic and has a popular bar. The modern Hotel Alpina and the Stockhorn hotel are also recommended. The 30-room Wynegg is a resort institution run by the formidable yet charming Ruth Guler, a close friend of Prince Charles. The hotel is run much like a large chalet for its mainly British guests, though the overspill can find a quieter refuge in the Bundnerhof next door. Four-star Hotel Pardenn receives criticism from reporters: 'the bedrooms are horribly decorated, with lumpy beds. The common parts of the hotel smelt, very strongly, of a retirement home. The swimming-pool has an attendant in a white orderly's uniform, and a hair dryer that dates from the 1950s. The restaurant is grim, with inattentive staff'. The ancient Vereina, budget winter home to generations of British families, has been rebuilt as luxurious hotel apartments.

Eating in and out

As in all resorts with a huge choice of restaurants in every category, the main criterion must be price. In Davos, as elsewhere in Switzerland, those who stray outside half-board deals must pay highly for the privilege, unless they are prepared to eat in chains like Burger King or Charly's Bakery. Money is well spent in Hubli's Landhaus, the Magic Mountain restaurant in the Bellevue, and the Stübli in the Flüela hotel. The Montana Sporthotel has very reasonable prices. Try the Zauberberg restaurant in the Hotel Europe or the Goldener Drachen in the Hotel Bahnhof Terminus for Chinese, and the Steinhof for Thai cuisine. Local dining, at correspondingly lower prices, can be found in the outlying villages of Frauenkirch, Wolfgang and **Laret**.

In Klosters, the Chesa Grischuna must be booked three days in advance, and tables at rival establishments require at least one day's notice. This is certainly true of the Wynegg, which capitalises on its royal connections to sell meals that are more rustic than gastronomic. Hotel Walserhof ('the food is excellent, more French in style than pure Swiss') has a Michelin-rated restaurant presided over by renowned Swiss chef, Beat Bolliger. Other favourable eateries are in the hotels Alte Post, Alpina and Rustico.

Après-ski

In the late afternoons, the high-lifers at Davos congregate in the Café Schneider in Platz and the Café Weber in Dorf, both specialists in temptation cakes. The most favoured bar is the rustic Chämi, which is full to bursting with revellers of all ages until closing time. As the resort attracts a lot of non-skiers, the entertainment on offer is extensive. In the pre-dinner hours, major league ice-hockey matches take place in the handsome Sports Centre; other activities include skating on the largest natural ice-rink in Europe. The Montana has a pool bar.

The area's pulsating nightlife can be found in Davos Platz, and especially in the Ex-Bar. The laser show at the Cabanna Club disco attracts the very young, while the Pöstli in the Posthotel Morosani caters for an older crowd. The Cava Grischa has modern techno and disco. The largest casino in the canton of Graubunden, also in the Hotel Europe, is now up and running. The Scala restaurant in the same building stays open until 1.30am. Hotel Bolgenschanze is where riders hang out.

After-skiing activities in Klosters start with a drink at Gaudi's at the foot of the slopes. However, when it comes to nightlife, this resort, with its many private chalets and few bars, is not a major player. The Steinbock Bar attracts locals as well as tourists. Alternative watering holes include the Verruckte Baustellen in the Hotel Kaiser, and the piano bars in the Aldiana Club and the Chesa Grischuna. For late-night dancing and snacks try the Casa Antica, the Kir Royal in the Aldiana Club, the new Fellini's, or Rufinis in Klosters Dorf.

Skiing facts: Klosters

TOURIST INFORMATION
Alte Bahnhofstrasse
CH-7250 Klosters
Tel 41 81 410 2020
Fax 41 81 410 2010
Email info@klosters.ch
Web site www.klosters.ch

THE RESORT
By road Calais 1,000km
By rail Klosters Dorf and Klosters Platz
stations in resort
Airport transfer Zurich 2½hrs
Visitor beds 8,600
Transport free ski bus with lift pass,
free ski train with Rega Pass

THE SKIING
Linked or nearby resorts Arosa (n),
Davos (l), Gargellen (n), Glaris (l) Küblis
(l), Saas (l), Serneus (l), St Moritz (n),
Wolfgang (l)
Number of lifts 54 in Davos/Klosters
area
Total of trails/pistes 320km in
Davos/Klosters area (30% easy, 40%
intermediate, 30% difficult)
Nursery slopes 2 lifts in village,
2 on Madrisa

LIFT PASSES
Area pass Rega Pass (covers all Davos
and Klosters lifts, buses and railway),
SF273 for 6 days
Beginners 1 rope-tow lift to ski school

Pensioners 20% reduction for women
62yrs and over, men 65yrs and over
Credit cards yes

TUITION
Adults Absolutely Klosters tel: 79 487
2346, SSSK tel: 81 410 2028, Saas
S&S-S tel: 81 420 2233
Snowboarding as ski schools, Duty
Board Prattigau/Bananas
tel: 81 422 6660
Other courses carving, cross-country,
race training, telemark
Guiding through ski schools

CHILDREN
Lift pass 6–16yrs, Rega Pass SF164
for 6 days
Ski & board school as adults
Kindergarten (ski/non-ski) Madrisa
Kindergarten tel: 81 410 2333

FOOD AND DRINK PRICES
Coffee SF3.50, glass of wine SF8–10,
small beer SF4.50, soft drink SF4, dish
of the day SF15–25

OTHER SPORTS
Davos/Klosters: climbing wall, curling,
dog-sledding, hang-gliding, horse-riding,
ice-climbing, ice speed-skating, indoor
badminton, indoor tennis and squash,
night-skiing/night-riding, parapente,
skating, sleigh rides, snowshoeing,
swimming

Childcare
The Swiss Snowsportschool Davos offers children's classes for three-year-olds and upwards on Bünda or Bolgen, with supervised lunch and lifts included in the price, and a Bobo Wonderland playground, complete with cartoon characters, in each area.

In Klosters there is a kindergarten on the Madrisa for the over-threes, although the area is somewhat inconvenient.

Jungfrau

ALTITUDE Wengen 1,274m (4,180ft), Grindelwald 1,034m (3,391ft),
Mürren 1,650m (5,412ft)

Beginners (except Mürren) ✱✱✱ Intermediates ✱✱✱ Advanced ✱✱
Snowboarders ✱✱

The Jungfrau region is the most popular in Switzerland with British visitors and one which is again flourishing, thanks to favourable exchange rates and excellent snow-cover for the past two winters. It is recognised as the Edwardian nursery of modern skiing and has always had an edge on quality, which it has some-how managed to maintain over the years. Trains are a crucial part of any holiday to the region's principal resorts of **Wengen**, **Grindelwald** and **Mürren**; the mountain railway, which dates from the 1880s, is still the back-bone of the lift system today, making both Wengen and Grindelwald ideal bases for non-skiers. Wengen and Mürren remain traffic-free and remarkably unspoilt by the passage of a century. The three resorts share a ski pass that covers 45 lifts in the Jungfrau Top Ski region, offering 213km of wonderfully scenic skiing against the awesome backdrop of the Eiger, Mönch and Jungfrau mountains.

- ✔ Beautiful scenery
- ✔ Variety of slopes
- ✔ Car-free villages (Wengen/Mürren)
- ✔ Facilities for non-skiers
- ✘ Poorly linked ski areas
- ✘ Lower slopes can become icy or worn

Henry Lunn, a non-skiing Methodist minister and one-time lawn tennis equipment salesman, is credited with introducing the first-ever ski package holidays here in the winter of 1910–1911. To encourage the class-conscious British to come on his tours he founded the Public Schools Alpine Sports Club and somehow managed to persuade the Swiss to continue to operate their mountain railways during the winter. His more distinguished son, Sir Arnold, went on to found the Kandahar Ski Club in Mürren, where slalom racing was first introduced in 1922.

Ski tourism started in Wengen with the Downhill Only Club, a pioneer band of British skiers formed in February 1925 to race against their Kandahar Club rivals in Mürren. The club name developed from its members' customary train ride up the mountain in order to ski down, a process considered distinctly unsporting by the standards of the day when people thought there should be no gain without pain. Both British ski clubs are alive and functioning in the resorts today.

Wengen, Grindelwald and Mürren are all reached by rail from Interlaken. The track divides at Zweilütschinen, with the left-hand fork veering towards Grindelwald. The right-hand fork goes to

Lauterbrunnen, which is more of a railway halt than a resort, although it does have a number of hotels, and some reporters consider it a convenient and much cheaper base from which to ski the area.

Trains from Lauterbrunnen run steeply up to Mürren on one side of the valley and up to Wengen on the other. The railway climbs as high as the main ski area at Kleine Scheidegg, above Wengen, before descending into Grindelwald. Trains stop at wayside halts throughout the area to pick up and set down skiers. They run as accurately as a Swiss watch to a timetable printed on the back of the piste map. However, this form of transport is painfully slow, and the trains can be as crowded as the London Underground at rush hour, although the network has been augmented by conventional cableways and chairs.

Wengen remains much as it was – a single pedestrian street of unremarkable shops and a cluster of chalets around one of the best nursery slopes in the Alps. There is also a magnificent skating-rink. The presence of Club Med at the northern end of town seems incongruous in this otherwise neo-Edwardian setting. The handful of old hotels have been refurbished and others built.

Grindelwald is the oldest of the three villages – a large and busy year-round resort spread along the valley floor between the soaring peaks of the Wetterhorn and the Eiger on the one side, and the gentler wooded slopes of its First ski area on the other. There are few more cosmopolitan resorts to be found in the world, with every nationality imaginable listed among its guests, not least the Japanese, who come here in numbers to visit the Eiger and the Jungfraujoch, which at 3,454m is the highest station in Europe. However, Grindelwald's low altitude means that snow-cover in the village and on the lower mountain is uncertain.

WHAT'S NEW
Magic carpet lift at Frosty's Schneewelt

Mürren has few rivals as the prettiest and most unspoilt ski village in Switzerland. Old chalets and hotels line the paths between the railway station at one end and the cable-car at the other. The car-free village is on a sunny shelf perched on top of a 500-m rock-face above Lauterbrunnen. The same British families, nearly all of them members of the Kandahar Club, have been returning here for generations and have forged firm links with the villagers.

On the snow
Wengen: top 2,320m (7,610ft) bottom 1,274m (4,180ft)
Grindelwald: top 2,501m (8,206 ft) bottom 1,034m (3,393ft)
Mürren: top 2,970m (9,724ft) bottom 796m (2,611ft)

A circuit of lifts around the Lauberhorn and Tschuggen peaks links the ski areas of Wengen and Grindelwald through the Männlichen and Kleine Scheidegg. Skiers have a choice of taking the train up to Kleine Scheidegg and Eigergletscher or climbing the Männlichen ridge by

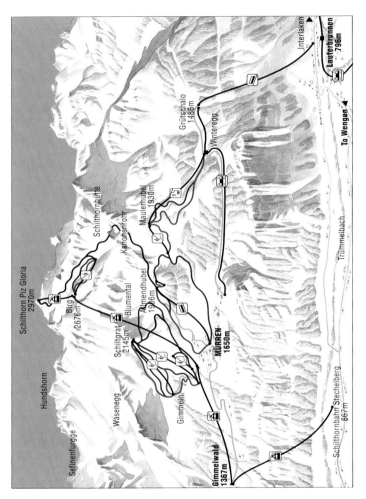

cable-car from Wengen. The bottom station, destroyed in an avalanche in 1999, has now been rebuilt in a safer position. Between Eigergletscher and Kleine Scheidegg are high Alps served by chair-lifts and tows.

From Grindelwald a gondola rises to the Männlichen, while the train also carries on up to Kleine Scheidegg. On the other side of Grindelwald, the First area is easily accessible, even for Wengen-based skiers. The areas complement each other well, and one of the pleasures of visiting any of them is to spend days exploring the others.

Mürren, separated from the other two resorts by the Lauterbrunnen Valley, sits on an east-facing shelf. Its skiing is spread across three parallel ridges – the Schiltgrat, the Allmendhubel and the Maulerhubel

343

– that run roughly north and south above the village. These slopes provide decent skiing conditions whatever the weather: powder on the north slopes, spring snow on the south, high bowls for fine weather, trees for shelter and visibility in blizzards.

Beginners

Wengen has an excellent nursery area in the middle of the village with a baby lift, a magic carpet and an unusual three-person drag-lift, which is surprisingly easy for snowboarders to use. There are also satisfyingly long blue (easy) runs on which even those with little technique can stretch their legs. From Kleine Scheidegg, a broad tree-lined road leads to Brandegg and on to Grindelwald.

Grindelwald also has nursery slopes right by the village and others up on the Hohwald and Bargelegg lifts, although beginners will want to return to base via the First gondola.

Mürren is not an ideal resort for beginners. The small nursery slope is on the upper road behind the Jungfrau Hotel; this is historic ground where the world's first modern slalom was set. Another beginners' area lies at the top of the Allmendhubel lift and is served by a small tow.

Intermediates

Wengen and Grindelwald owe much of their popularity with families to their long, medium-to-difficult runs. You can take the Männlichen cable-car and explore the route under the gondola right down to **Grund**. From there the train goes up to Kleine Scheidegg, which has a similarly well-networked area recently improved by the installation of a detachable quad on the Lauberhorn. The famous World Cup race-course, at two-and-a-half kilometres the longest in the world – forms a fairly testing descent. The Standard run offers an easier way down.

From Grindelwald, the First gondola leads to the Stepfi, a satisfying red (intermediate) run from Oberlager down to the Hotel Wetterhorn. As you pass the hotel you can see the old cable-car cabin, which was built in 1908 to take summer climbers up to the Gleckstein Hut on the Wetterhorn. The lift was closed in 1914 after being damaged by an avalanche, and the cabin was left as a relic. This is a satisfying stop-off before returning by bus to Grindelwald.

At Mürren, some very pretty intermediate skiing can be reached by taking the Allmendhubel railway and then a small T-bar to the Hogs Back area; turn right towards the Maulerhubel T-bar, at the top of which is a wide area of open slopes leading either back to the bottom of Maulerhubel or off to the mid-station on the main railway. You can return to the village from the bottom of the Maulerhubel on the wide Palace Run.

The Muttleren and Kandahar chair-lifts halfway up the Schilthorn give access to plenty of intermediate skiing in a snow-sure bowl. However, the only way out for those unwilling to face the often icy Kanonenrohr piste is by a steep and uncomfortable T-bar. This is one of the very few places where queues form.

Advanced

From Wengen, the train up to Eigergletscher leads to the black (difficult) runs of Blackrock and Oh God. In sunny weather these are best left until late morning, as they can be hard and icy before the sun reaches them. The Aspen run is the steepest way down from the Männlichen towards Grund. Grindelwald's First area has a challenging black piste under the gondola. At Mürren, the extremely steep run from the top of the Schilthorn can be followed by another steep pitch alongside the Muttleren chair-lift, and then the Kanonenrohr, to give an almost continuous black run with plenty of challenge.

Off-piste

All three resorts have a great deal of easily accessible off-piste skiing between the trails. In Mürren, the Blumental is famous for its powder, Tschingelchrachen off the Schilthornbahn should be treated with care as it is very steep and often closed, and Hidden Valley from the summit of the Maulerhubel to Grutsch is a delight. The White Hare, which starts from the foot of the Eigerwand, is a dramatic and exciting powder run; it can be accessed from both Wengen and Grindelwald.

Local mountain guides are essential here, and Grindelwald's Bergsteigerzentrum is one of the most famous guiding establishments in the world; both ski-touring and heli-skiing can be organised through the centre. Day tours over to the **Lötschental** can be arranged.

Snowboarders

Wengen has a new funpark with a half-pipe and boardercross course, which is served by the Bumps lift. Wengen is the best spot for beginners, Grindelwald is a good choice for intermediates, and Mürren has a half-pipe and some challenging freeriding.

Tuition and guiding

The Swiss Ski and Snowboard School (SSS) operates in each village, and the standard of service varies alarmingly. Group lessons are given mornings-only from Sunday to Friday. Most, but by no means all, instructors speak more than adequate English. One reader encountered a class of 14 in Grindelwald: 'our instructor was just interested in skiing madly downhill'. Another reader who went to Wengen complained: 'I did not receive one word of advice about my skiing'.

We have more positive reports of the Privat Ski and Snowboard School run in Wengen by Tino Fuchs. A reporter in Mürren complained that his mountain guide didn't speak English. Grindelwald has two dedicated snowboard schools: Backside and Mad House.

Mountain restaurants

The area is littered with enjoyable eating places. The Hotel Jungfrau at Wengernalp has beautiful views and a friendly atmosphere, not to mention the high standard of cooking. At Grindelwald the Brandegg restaurant is famed for its 'quite extraordinarily delicious' apple fritters.

The Kleine Scheidegg station buffet is more interesting than it looks, and besides its variety of Swiss fare offers its own *Röstizza*, a cross between rösti and pizza. The Eigergletscher restaurant has 'the best rösti and the best views'. The Jagerstübli is a farmhouse below Männlichen, with a 'cosy ambience and delicious home cooking'.

The Aspen above Grund has a loyal clientèle. Mary's Café just above Wengen is recommended for its raclette. The Hotel Victoria-Lauberhorn, near the skating-rink, has a pizzeria/crêperie with quick service. The rösti in the stübli of the Hotel Eiger is recommended.The restaurant at Bort above Grindelwald is 'pleasant and reasonably priced, but the food is not exceptional'. The big self-service at First boasts 'a glorious hamburger'. Hotel Wetterhorn on the way down to Grindelwald has a 'convivial atmosphere and delicious food'.

The Birg restaurant above Mürren is 'nothing to write home about,' but Gimmeln has 'tasty raclette and *Apfelküchen*'. We have a series of complimentary reports of the revolving Piz Gloria on the summit of the Schilthorn ('not expensive and good value'). One reporter had 'an imaginative salad – it took a full revolution to demolish it'. Another claimed it to have 'the best and the cheapest menu to be found in Switzerland'. The Schilthornhütte, on the descent from here, is a mountain refuge serving simple dishes (a 'fun atmosphere and wonderful views').

Accommodation

In **Wengen** the accommodation is split between hotels, apartments and chalets. The attractive resort is quite spread out and distinctly steep. While location is of little importance for the skiing (if staying high up you can ski down to the train, which will take you back to your hotel), a long uphill slog after midnight tends to deter many a holidaymaker from exploring what limited nightlife there is. The Hotel Eiger (Wengen) is central and has long been a favourite among the British. The Falken is variously described as 'delightfully old-fashioned', 'ramshackle' and 'very comfortable'. The ski-in ski-out Hotel Brunner, on the piste, a 10-minute walk above the village centre, is described as 'one of those Alpine secrets that visitors – many of them with children – like to keep to themselves'. Hotel Wengener Hof, five minutes' walk from the station, was strongly criticised by one reporter ('food only just better than my work canteen').

Hotel Silberhorn, once lavishly praised by readers, appears to be going through troubled times. One reporter commented: 'the food was very disappointing and the wine list was unspeakable in choice, quality and expense. Nevertheless, we had an excellent family room, despite unreliable hot water'. The three-star Hotel Belvédère is a seven-minute uphill walk from the station and has 'grand art-deco public rooms'. The four-star Hotel Sunstar has family 'maisonettes', a swimming-pool and is one of the most conveniently placed hotels in town. Club Med here has a fine reputation, although the presence of large, noisy classes of French skiers on crowded pistes can lead to Agincourt-style confrontations with the more conservative British element.

Grindelwald has the five-star Grand Hotel Regina, which is partly decorated with eighteenth-century antiques and is famous for the ice sculptures in its grounds. A host of four-star hotels include the 'excellent' Hotel Spinne. Hotel Jungfrau is praised for 'good and plentiful food; we would have paid twice the price just for the view from our window'. The Hotel Alpenhof, a few minutes' walk from the village, has a sound reputation. Hotel Derby and Hotel Hirschen are both recommended. Hotel Bodmi on the nursery slopes is convenient for families, and Parkhotel Schönegg is warmly acclaimed. Hotel Bernerhof is centrally located close to the station and has 'friendly and attentive service'.

In **Mürren** the Hotel Eiger, across the road from the railway station, has some luxurious suites as well as standard hotel rooms and apartments. Hotel Jungfrau is 'modern, clean, and tidy with efficient service'. However, one 20-something reader complained: 'it lacks alpine character and the management is without warmth or any concept of hospitality'. The Alpenruh at the Schilthornbahn end of the village has an excellent restaurant. The popular Edelweiss is 'convenient, clean and friendly', and the Bellevue-Crystal and Blumental are both recommended, together with the simpler Belmont. The supermarket is said to be adequate and there is also a butcher's shop.

The village of **Lauterbrunnen** in the valley below is well placed for less expensive accommodation and the chance to try a different area each day, but it suffers from being hemmed in by sheer mountains.

Eating in and out

Most restaurants in Wengen are in hotels, but Sina's Italian is warmly recommended ('good value for money in a warm and friendly ambience'). Mary's Café offers cheese fondue accompanied by alpenhorn-blowing contests on Tuesdays. Restaurant Wengen in the Hotel Hirschen specialises in fondue *chinoise*. The Berghaus is known for its fresh fish and the Bernerhof for fondue and raclette. On sunny days, the Hotel Eiger has outdoor tables next to the railway station.

The à la carte Derby Restaurant is one of the best places to dine in Grindelwald. Reporters also speak warmly of the Schweizerhof. The restaurant in the Hotel Alte Post is popular with the locals. The Alpina is good for fondue, and the Cava restaurant in the Hotel Derby has 'the best fondue and pasta in town'.

In Mürren the Hotel Eiger's stübli has an excellent, if somewhat expensive, menu. At the other end of the village, the Alpenruh comes well recommended, and the Belmont offers 'excellent value'.

Après-ski

Wengen's nightlife remains muted in comparison with other Alpine resorts. The last ski trains of the day are full of families with toboggans going up to Wengernalp for the four-kilometre descent back to the village. The TeePee Après Ski Bar at Kleine Scheidegg is busier during

Skiing facts: Wengen

TOURIST INFORMATION
CH-3823 Wengen, Bernese Oberland
Tel 41 33 855 1414
Fax 41 33 855 3060
Email information@wengen.com
Web site www.wengen-muerren.ch

THE RESORT
By road Calais 835km
By rail station in resort
Airport transfer Zurich 3hrs,
Geneva 4hrs
Visitor beds 2,500
Transport taxis, otherwise traffic-free
resort

THE SKIING
Linked or nearby resorts Grindelwald
(l), Grund (l), Lauterbrunnen (n),
Mürren (n)
Number of lifts 35 in linked area, 45 in
Jungfrau Top Ski Region
Total of trails/pistes 213km in Jungfrau
Top Ski Region (28% easy, 57%
intermediate, 15% difficult)
Nursery slopes 3 lifts
Summer skiing 1 lift at Jungfraujoch

LIFT PASSES
Area pass Jungfrau (covers Wengen,
Grindelwald and Mürren), SF254 for 6 days

Beginners points tickets
Pensioners SF229 from 62yrs
Credit cards yes

TUITION
Adults SSS tel: 856 2022,
Privat Ski and Snowboard School
tel: 855 5005
Snowboarding as ski schools
Other courses heli-skiing, racing,
telemark
Guiding through ski schools

CHILDREN
Lift pass under 6yrs (without parent)
SF25, 6–15yrs SF127, 16–19yrs SF203,
both for 6 days
Ski & board school as adults
Kindergarten (non-ski) Little Playhouse
tel: 41 79 465 73 43

OTHER SPORTS
Curling, ice-hockey, indoor climbing
wall, indoor tennis and squash,
parapente, skating, sleigh rides,
snowshoeing, tobogganing

FOOD AND DRINK PRICES
Coffee SF3.20, glass of wine SF5,
small beer SF3.50–5, soft drink SF3.80,
dish of the day SF15–20

the skiing day. Crowds gather in Mary's Café, and the ice-bar outside the Hotel Brunner is lively.

In the village itself the twin skating-rinks at times offer ice-hockey matches on one and curling on the other. In the afternoons it seems that there are almost as many people skating as there are skiing. Reporters complain that Wengen has no real tea-and-cakes places apart from Café Grübi, which is full of atmosphere but rather cramped. The Tanne, Sina's Pub and Hot Chilli are the most popular bars, while Tiffany's in the Silberhorn is the disco.

In Grindelwald the Espresso bar draws a young crowd straight after skiing, while the Gepsi attracts a slightly older clientèle. Later on the

Skiing facts: Grindelwald

TOURIST INFORMATION
CH-3818 Grindelwald, Bernese Oberland
Tel 41 33 854 1212
Fax 41 33 854 1210
Email touristoffice@grindelwald.ch
Web site www.grindelwald.ch

THE RESORT
By road Calais 835km
By rail station in resort
Airport transfer Zurich 2hrs,
Geneva 3hrs
Visitor beds 11,700
Transport ski bus free with lift pass

THE SKIING
Linked or nearby resorts Mürren (n),
Lauterbrunnen (n), Grund (n),
Wengen (l)
Number of lifts 35 in linked area, 45 in
Jungfrau Top Ski Region
Total of trails/pistes 213km in Jungfrau
Top Ski Region (28% easy, 57%
intermediate, 15% difficult)
Nursery slopes 2 lifts

LIFT PASSES
Area pass Jungfrau (covers Wengen,
Grindelwald and Mürren), SF254 for
6 days

Beginners points tickets
Pensioners SF229 from 62yrs
Credit cards yes

TUITION
Adults SSS tel: 853 5200
Snowboarding SSS, Backside tel: 853
3355, Mad House 853 59 69
Other courses carving, cross-country,
heli-skiing, race-training, telemark
Guiding Bergsteigerzentrum Grindelwald
tel: 853 5200

CHILDREN
Lift pass under 6yrs (without parent)
SF25, 6–15yrs SF127, 16–19yrs SF203,
both for 6 days
Ski & board school as adults
Kindergarten (non-ski) Club Bodmi
tel: 853 5200, Children Village Sunshine
tel: 33 853 30 04

OTHER SPORTS
Curling, llama treks, parapente, skating,
snow-karting, snowshoeing

FOOD AND DRINK PRICES
Coffee SF3.20, glass of wine SF5,
small beer SF3.50–4, soft drink SF3.80,
dish of the day SF15–20

Challi bar in the Hotel Kreuz and Post, the Cava in the Derby, and Herby's in the Regina are the most popular. The Plaza Club and the Mescalero rock on into the small hours. Snow-karting (go-karting on snow) and daily llama treks around the First ski area are Grindelwald's original new attractions.

For such a small village, Mürren is surprisingly lively after skiing. The Ballon bar in the Palace Hotel, together with the Grübi in the Jungfrau and the Pub in the Belmont, are all popular. The Tächi bar in the Hotel Eiger is one of the main meeting places. The Bliemlichäller disco in the Blumental and the Inferno disco in the Palace Hotel buzz at weekends and in season. The village boasts an excellent sports centre.

Skiing facts: Mürren

TOURIST INFORMATION
CH-3825 Mürren, Bernese Oberland
Tel 41 33 856 8686
Fax 41 33 856 8696
Email info@muerren.ch
Web site www.wengen-muerren.ch

THE RESORT
By road Calais 835km
By rail station in resort
Airport transfer Zurich 3hrs, Geneva 4hrs
Visitor beds 2,000
Transport traffic-free resort

THE SKIING
Linked or nearby resorts Grindelwald (n), Grund (n), Lauterbrunnen (n), Wengen (n)
Number of lifts 12 in Mürren, 45 in Jungfrau Top Ski region
Total of trails/pistes 213km in Jungfrau Top Ski region (28% easy, 57% intermediate, 15% difficult)
Nursery slopes 2 lifts

LIFT PASSES
Area pass Jungfrau (covers Wengen, Grindelwald and Mürren), SF254 for 6 days

Beginners free lift, points tickets
Pensioners SF229 from 62yrs
Credit cards yes

TUITION
Adults SSS tel: 855 1247
Snowboarding as ski school
Other courses carving, cross-country, heli-skiing/heli-boarding, snowblading, telemark
Guiding through ski school

CHILDREN
Lift pass under 6yrs (without parent) SF25, 6–15yrs SF127, 16–19yrs SF203, both for 6 days
Ski & board school as adults
Kindergarten (non-ski) Guest Kindergarten tel: 856 8686

OTHER SPORTS
Curling, hang-gliding, ice-hockey, climbing wall, indoor tennis and squash, parapente, skating, snowmobiling, swimming

FOOD AND DRINK PRICES
Coffee SF3.20, glass of wine SF5, small beer SF3.50–4, soft drink SF3.80, dish of the day SF15–20

Childcare
We have pleasing reports of high standards of tuition in all three resorts. However, the decision by all three branches of the Swiss Ski School to run group lessons only in the mornings seriously detracts from Jungfrau's erstwhile reputation as an ideal area for families with young children ('some unhappy parents found their skiing day curtailed at lunch-time'). Mürren has little easy skiing and is not suitable for small children. The non-ski Little Playhouse in Wengen takes children from two to seven years old and has a sound reputation. Club Bodmi in Grindelwald caters for pre-ski children in its play area on the nursery slopes. Children's Village Sunshine is the resort crèche.

St Moritz

ALTITUDE 1,800m (5,904ft)

Beginners ✱ Intermediates ✱✱✱ Advanced ✱✱ Snowboarders ✱

St Moritz is an urban resort located on two levels, above and along the shores of a fir-lined lake in the scenic Engadine valley. It is not only a ski area but an all-round winter sports resort situated three to four hours by road from Zurich. Winter Alpine holidays were invented here in 1864 by the British, and while other resorts have long since emulated its seasonal formula of snow fun, few have eclipsed its hedonistic allure. No other ski resort in the world has so many luxury hotels – 63 per cent are four- or five-star. The urban architecture, however, is bland. The beauty of St Moritz lies not in the views of the resort itself, but in the views from it. It is small enough to walk around, though most hotels have shuttle vans, and buses and trains provide adequate public transport to all regions. Designer boutiques are as prevalent as the fur coats worn by the clientèle, which, though German-dominated, is truly international.

✔ Wealth of luxury hotels
✔ Fine dining opportunities
✔ Good snow record
✔ Extensive snowmaking
✔ Facilities for cross-country skiing
✔ Exceptional climate
✔ Choice of winter sports
✘ Lift queues at peak times
✘ Widely dispersed skiing sectors
✘ High prices
✘ Long airport transfer
✘ Lack of architectural charm

Twice host to the Winter Olympics, the resort sets the world standard for luxury and indulgence. Skating, curling, golf, cricket, polo and a number of exotic horse-racing events take place throughout the winter on the frozen lake. The Cresta Run, the origin of the new Olympic sport of skeleton tobogganing, is still closed to women and has been the ultimate demonstration of machismo for more than a hundred years. The bobsleigh also made its debut here.

The Upper Engadine regional ski pass covers 55 lifts and 350km of pistes from one end of the valley to the other. **Celerina**, **Pontresina**, **Silvaplana** and **Sils Maria** are outlying villages with ski lifts. **Dorf** is the name used for St Moritz proper, and **Bad** is down on the lake below.

On the snow
top 3,303m (10,834ft) bottom 1,720m (5,642ft)

Few skiers in St Moritz are fanatics. However, there is a wide range of skiing, with sunny blue (easy) slopes, abundant red (intermediate) runs, and adequate advanced and off-piste routes scattered around the dozen lifts rising from the valley floor. The region divides into the sectors of Corviglia, Corvatsch and Diavolezza–Lagalb. From St Moritz itself the home mountain is Corviglia, accessed by a funicular from the centre of town or from Suvretta, with skiing up to 3,057m at Piz Nair. Celerina and Bad also give access to the mostly red runs of Corviglia. Summer skiing is no longer available on the Diavolezza Glacier.

Corvatsch, on the other side of the valley, has more advanced terrain and is accessed from Sils Maria and **Surlej**. Diavolezza and Lagalb, both at nearly 3,000m, are reached by train or bus.

The steady investment in modern chair-lifts has done much to diminish waiting time, although a bottleneck remains at Piz Nair. Snowmaking ensures skiing on six Corviglia pistes, to the bottom of Corvatsch at Surlej, and from top to bottom of Diavolezza.

The frozen lakes of the Engadine and the forest trails make St Moritz one of the most interesting and beautiful cross-country areas in the Alps, with loipe of every standard. Ideally, serious langlaufers should stay in Bad, as this is where the tracks are based. The 42-km Engadine Marathon is held here each season and attracts thousands of entrants.

Beginners

There are nursery slopes at Corviglia, and guests at the Suvretta House even have their own beginner lift. However, because of the spread-out nature of St Moritz, and its high prices, this is not the ideal resort in which to learn. A long, gentle blue (easy) run goes down from the Marmite restaurant on Corviglia, through the woods back into St Moritz, or all the way across to the cable-car at Bad. Every sector has some blue runs. The Furtschellas drag-lifts go up to blue runs at 2,800m above Sils Maria, but beginners will have to ride the cable-car down.

Intermediates

Corvatsch has the highest skiing and links with even more red (intermediate) runs on Furtschellas. South-facing Corviglia has a number of flattering reds. The run under the Piz Grisch chair always has excellent snow. However, the least crowded skiing is out of St Moritz in the Lagalb sector at nearly 3,000m. The Giandas red under the cable-car has the longest and most direct fall-line skiing in the Engadine.

Advanced

The black (difficult) Hahnensee run from the top of Corvatsch winds over open snowfields and on into the woods at the edge of Bad, providing around 8km of non-stop skiing for 1,600 vertical metres. At Diavolezza, the Schwarzer Hang black piste drops through bands of rock for some excellent steep skiing down the Bernina black run all the way to the bottom. The Diavolezza itinerary is long, steep and very scenic.

Off-piste

The steep face of Piz Nair provides incredible thrills when enough powder snow covers the sheer rock. The long glacier itinerary from the top of

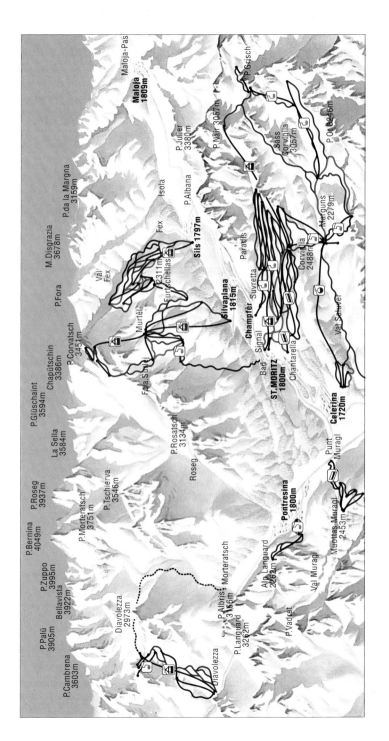

353

Diavolezza, around and over crevasses to Morteratsch, is one of the classic off-piste routes in the Alps. Although off-piste guiding is not widely in demand, it is available through the St Moritz SSS, All Activities Agency (AAA) and The St Moritz Experience. Heli Bernina and Heliswiss offer heli-skiing.

Snowboarders

Although much of the terrain is suitable for riders, the resort's high prices for accommodation and nightlife are off-putting. The Diavolezza area is particularly recommended for freeriding, while the funpark at Corviglia is reached by the Munt da San Murezzan chair-lift and contains a half-pipe and obstacle course.

Tuition and guiding

In 1929 the St Moritz and Suvretta were Switzerland's first ski schools, and today are both branches of the Swiss Ski School (SSS). Together they employ 300 instructors. The Palace Hotel has its own school. Snowboard School St Moritz and The Wave Snowboard School are part of the joint St Moritz and Suvretta ski schools.

Mountain restaurants

Renowned among snow-users and gourmets alike, the Marmite on Corviglia is an essential lunch stop, although reservations are necessary. Owner Reto Mathis, whose father, Hartly, was the first man to bring haute cuisine to the high mountains, counts caviar and truffles by the kilo. Also on the Corviglia, the Skihütte Alpina is great for pasta and rustic charm, as well as being snowboarder-friendly. Cheese specialities are best at the Piz Nair. Isla Pers is on the Diavolezza itinerary. The Suvretta owns three mountain eateries – the intimate Chassellars, the Chamanna which is frequented by riders, and Trutz Lodge, which boasts self-service and a la carte restaurants.

Accommodation

The Palace Hotel, with its grotesque tower, is the most famous of the five-stars and has its own ski school. The pastel blocks of the Kulm are preferred by the Cresta crowd. The Suvretta House is a mini resort within a resort, with its own spa, skating rink, nursery slope and ski-lift. The hotel attracts older, European clients, many of whom have long forsaken skiing. The Carlton has a country-house atmosphere. The four-star Schweizerhof and Steffani hotels, both with active nightlife, are downtown and affordable. The Parkhotel Kurhaus is next to the cross-country track in Bad. A reasonable choice of less exalted accommodation is also available.

Eating in and out

Hanselmann's in the town centre has been around for more than a hundred years and serves coffee, pastries and delectable ice-cream. Lunch at the Chesa Veglia, an architectural museum-piece owned by the Palace Hotel, is not expensive compared with dinner. All the top hotel restaurants have a strict dress code. The Suvretta's Trutz Lodge, reached by a chair-lift that runs at night, is open for evening fondue parties. In Celerina, the Stuvetta Veglia is recommended.

Après-ski

The Palace Hotel's Kings Club is still the place to go. The stübli at the Schweizerhof has late-night dancing on tables, and after 10pm it is so crowded that you could not possibly fall off. The Vivai disco is popular. Muli Bar has country-and-western music. Bobby's Bar is for the under-20s. The newest disco is Prince, opposite the Kulm Hotel. The Cascade Bar and the Cava Bar in the Hotel Steffani are both praised. Hotel Waldhaus am See boasts the world's biggest variety of malt whisky.

Childcare

The kindergarten in the Schweizerhof and Parkhotel Kurhaus both accept children over three years old on a daily basis, with lunch included. The Suvretta's Teddy Bear Club has a kindergarten for children from 12 months old, and a dedicated children's restaurant; both are for residents. The ski schools accept children over four years.

Linked or nearby resorts

Celerina
top 3,057m (10,030ft) bottom 1,720m (5,643ft)

A village atmosphere, old stone houses painted with the local graffito designs, and ski access to Corviglia make Celerina an attractive and quiet alternative. The village has just 1,850 visitor beds and its own ski and snowboard school. Tobyland is the ski kindergarten for children from three and a half years old and Zwergliclub Hotel Cresta Palace offers daycare. Chesa Rosatsch is a 350-year-old inn.

TOURIST OFFICE
Tel 41 81 830 0011
Fax 41 81 830 0019
Email info@celerina.ch
Web site www.celerina.ch

Pontresina
top 2,262m (7,421ft) bottom 1,800m (5,904ft)

With no big lifts of its own, Pontresina is about midway between the outlying Diavolezza sector and Corviglia. It has good indoor sports facilities and a loyal clientèle of Italian and German families. Kochendorfer's Albris is an inexpensive hotel with its own bakery and chocolate shop. The Steinbock and Engadinerhof are comfortable, traditional hotels. The four-star Saratz Hotel is highly praised and has a kindergarten. Allegra Garni is a new hotel for the 2000–1 season. The local Swiss Ski School offers lessons. The Swiss Mountaineering School organises off-piste skiing and Pontresina Events offers heli-skiing. Night-skiing takes place every Friday.

Skiing facts: St Moritz

TOURIST OFFICE
Via Maistra 12,
CH-7500 St Moritz, Graubunden
Tel 41 81 837 3333
Fax 41 81 837 3366
Email information@stmoritz.ch
Web site www.stmoritz.ch

THE RESORT
By road Calais 1,047km
By rail station in resort
Airport transfer Zurich 3–4hrs
Visitor beds 8,689
Transport bus free with ski pass

THE SKIING
Linked or nearby resorts Celerina (l),
Champfèr (n), Pontresina (n), Samedan
(n), Sils Maria (l), Silvaplana (l), Surlej
(l), Zuoz (n)
Number of lifts 23 in St Moritz, 55 in
linked area
Total of trails/pistes 80km in St Moritz
(10% easy, 70% intermediate, 20%
difficult), 350km in linked area
Nursery slopes 3 lifts in St Moritz

LIFT PASSES
Area pass Upper Engadine (covers
St Moritz, Celerina, Silvaplana,
Pontresina, Sils), SF254–282 for 6 days
including a day's skiing in Livigno
Beginners no free lifts
Pensioners 20% reduction for 75yrs
and over
Credit cards yes

TUITION
Adults St Moritz SSS tel: 81 833 8090,
Suvretta Snowsports tel: 81 833 3332
Snowboarding as ski schools
Other courses carving, cross-country,
freestyle, hang-gliding, heli-skiing, race-
training, seniors, skiing for the blind, ski-
jumping, slalom, teen skiing, telemark
Guiding St Moritz SSS, AAA
tel: 81 832 2233, The St Moritz
Experience tel: 81 833 7714,
Heliswiss tel: 81 852 3535,
Heli Bernina tel: 81 852 4677

CHILDREN
Lift pass SF141 for 6–16yrs, SF230 for
16–20yrs
Ski & board school as adults
Kindergarten (ski) St Moritz SSS, (non-
ski) Parkhotel Kurhaus tel: 81 832 2111,
Hotel Schweizerhof tel: 81 837 0707

OTHER SPORTS
Climbing wall, Cresta Run, cricket, curling, dog-sledding, golf and cricket on the
frozen lake, hang-gliding, horse-racing,
hot-air ballooning, ice-driving, indoor
tennis and squash, night skiing, Olympic
bob-run, parapente, polo, skating, ski-
joring, ski-jumping, sleigh rides, snowbiking, snowshoeing, swimming

FOOD AND DRINK PRICES
Coffee SF3.50–4.50, glass of wine
SF6–7, small beer SF4–5, soft drink SF4,
dish of the day SF12–25

TOURIST OFFICE
Tel 41 81 842 6488
Fax 41 81 842 7996
Email pontresina@compunet.ch
Web site www.pontresina.com

Verbier

ALTITUDE 1,500m (4,920ft)

Intermediates ✱✱   Advanced ✱✱✱   Snowboarders ✱✱✱

Verbier is a resort reborn. After a decade in the doldrums it has reclaimed its place among the world class, alongside St Anton, Val d'Isère, Chamonix, Zermatt and Whistler. Not only does it have an enormous range and variety of challenging pistes, but it is also home to some of Europe's most exciting lift-served, off-piste skiing. Nowhere is there a more extensive and diverse menu of glaciers, couloirs and deep powder bowls to tickle the palates of advanced skiers. The Savolèyres and Lac des Vaux sectors provide a much more limited playground for inter-mediates, while beginners here are best described as 'aspiring experts'.

✔ Easy rail and road access
✔ Wealth of off-piste
✔ Excellent sunshine record
✔ Summer glacier skiing
✗ Expensive nightlife
✗ Minimal hotel accommodation
✗ Inadequate mountain restaurants
✗ Traffic and difficult parking

Unlike its pedigree rivals in the Parsenn and the Bernese Oberland, which have a skiing tradition dating from the nineteenth century, brash Verbier is relatively *nouveau riche*. The first lift – a curious petrol-driven cable that pulled a 12-person sledge up 200m – was not built until 1946, and serious skiing here only started to take off 11 years later with the construction of Les Attelas cable-car. International skiers were immediately attracted to the demanding terrain that this opened up, and during the boom years of the 1960s and 1970s Verbier developed into one of the most famous ski resorts in Europe.

However, the mountain path to its present status has been marked by a series of pitfalls. Verbier failed to put back into the mountain a judicious proportion of the money it had taken out in the first place. Consequently, in the late 1980s, it plunged in popularity. Two-hour high-season lift queues, combined with an abysmal rate of exchange, became too much for all but the most dedicated snow-users, and the number of British visitors fell to seven per cent. Only now, thanks to prodigious investment by the lift company, Téléverbier (of which France's Compagnie des Alpes now owns a 22 per cent share), has Verbier climbed back out of the crevasse. The number of British skiers and boarders was over 12 per cent in the 1999–2000 season, and should continue to rise.

Anyone expecting a chocolate-box village of Heidi-style chalets is in for a disappointment. The resort comprises concrete apartment blocks and less severe wooden buildings, thrown up to no apparent design. Only 1,500 of the 15,000 beds are in hotels, and none of these has doorstep skiing. The whole hotch-potch is dominated by a church with a 40-m (130-ft) spire, built in 1962. This, depending on your viewpoint, is seen as a monstrous intrusion on the mountainside or an outstanding example of period architecture. But Verbier's plus points include less than two hours' motorway access from Geneva and more than 300 days of sunshine per year.

However, there are other problems. An essential part of Verbier's appeal is that it links to the so-called Four Valleys, the ski area it shares with its less famous neighbours, comprising 410km of piste served by 96 lifts. Since the introduction of a hands-free, computerised lift ticket, **Thyon**, **Nendaz** and **Veysonnaz** have been arguing bitterly about revenue sharing. In October 1999 the uneasy entente collapsed and for a while it looked as if Verbier must go it alone, reducing the available skiing on its own lift pass by 64 per cent. However, we understand that an agreement has now been brokered that secures the links for a further six seasons. Verbier's skiing also includes the separate family resorts of **Bruson**, **Fouly** and **Vichères**.

On the snow
top 3,330m (10,925ft) bottom 1,500m (4,920ft)

The main reason for Verbier's comeback is its renovated lift system. This began with the introduction in 1994 of the Funispace 30-person giant gondola linking Les Ruinettes to Les Attelas. Then an eight-person gondola was opened at Tortin in 1998–9, giving easy access to one of Verbier's most notoriously steep slopes. Piste grooming has improved enormously and the hands-free,

WHAT'S NEW

Replacement gondola from Le Châble to Medran

electronic lift pass provides significant advantages for users.

Verbier's best skiing is not visible from the resort and almost impossible to decipher from the cramped piste map, which receives universal criticism from readers: 'runs on the map are missing from the mountain'. Lifts passes here are extremely complicated and therefore we have listed only the Four Valleys and Family Pass in the Skiing Facts box towards the end of this entry. You are advised to assess the area you want to cover before parting with any money.

The quickest route from Verbier's Medran base area is up the six-person gondola. From Les Ruinettes mid-station, the Funitel gondola zips up to Attelas at 2,740m. From here skiers can ride a cable-car up to Mont Gelé (3,023m), ski down into the intermediate Lac des Vaux sector for chair-lift access to Tortin and further cable-cars to Mont-Fort (3,330m), or ski over to the south-facing intermediate runs of La Chaux, where the 150-person Jumbo cable-car rises to the glacial slopes of Gentianes and Mont-Fort.

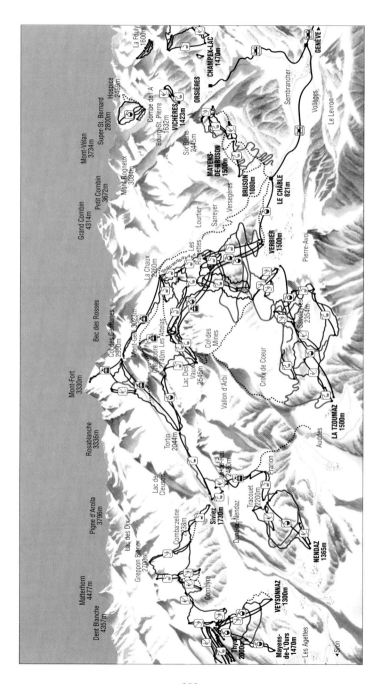

Savolèyres is a separate intermediate mountain, accessed by an old (1970) gondola, with sunny south-facing slopes towards Verbier and longer, better runs down its back side to **Tzoumaz**.

Beginners

Novices should 'go somewhere else, unless your main aim is après-ski', according to one reporter. There is one short nursery slope mid-town on the Moulins golf course, and another crowded area on Esserts. Those certain of their snowploughing technique can ski blue (easy) runs higher up the mountain on the usually excellent snow at Lac des Vaux.

Intermediates

Savolèyres and its north side down to Tzoumaz, along with La Chaux and Lac des Vaux, are about the limit for intermediate skiing. It is impossible to ski all the way down to Les Savolèyres base-station on piste, which is a cause of much complaint as skiers are diverted sideways across the mountain to a dead-end bus stop. Verbier's main arterial highway, the pistes from Attelas to Les Ruinettes, and the inescapable roadway to the main lift station at Medran, are unreasonably overcrowded. The bottom road is made even more dangerous by a profusion of pedestrians, children on sledges, and dogs.

Advanced

Except for the one run down Mont-Fort, all of Verbier's black (difficult) pistes have been reclassified as 'ski itineraries' to avoid legal responsibility in case of accident. Skied by thousands on a daily basis, such itineraries are essentially pistes, albeit not groomed. Most notorious is Tortin, a steep, wide slope usually pounded into bumps and often dangerous to access because of exposed rocks at the top. Gentianes, the run under the eponymous cable-car, offers a huge scope of bumps and ravines. Col des Mines (an open, south-facing slope returning to Verbier), and Vallon d'Arbi (a tremendously scenic, steep-sided valley leading eventually to Tzoumaz), are both accessed by a traverse beginning in Lac des Vaux. It is important to respect warning signs if this traverse is closed, as it is an area where several deaths have occurred. Marked itineraries down to **Le Châble** from Verbier are seldom skiable owing to poor snow cover.

Off-piste

You could devote an entire book to describing the best of Verbier's off-piste. Only a decade ago Creblet, the front face of Mont Gelé, and the back of Mont-Fort down to Cleuson were considered radical descents. These days, like Stairway to Heaven and Hidden Valley, they are skied-out within an hour of a fresh snowfall. Bec des Rosses (3,220m) is now the venue for extreme snowboarding contests, and skiing off the back down into Fionnay wins jealous admiration. The 'North Face' of Mont-Fort, with its B52 and Poubelle variants is routinely skied, despite its 'if-you-fall-you-die' start. The Grand Banana and Paradise are examples of off-piste sectors that are not so much difficult to ski as dangerous to access.

Snowboarders

Although riders are welcomed in Verbier and the freeriding is awesome from Mont Gelé, they still make up only a small proportion of the total snow-users since the resort is prohibitively expensive. It has a funpark with a half-pipe and obstacles at both Mont-Fort and Les Ruinettes.

Tuition and guiding

We have mixed reports of the Swiss Ski School (ESS), which has expanded in recent years. All children and beginner adults gather in the Medran parking lot; other adults meet at Les Ruinettes. La Fantastique and Adrénaline provide healthy competition. No Bounds is the dedicated snowboard school. Off-piste skiers should beware of local ski bums in Pub Mont-Fort offering illegal and uninsured guiding.

Mountain restaurants

Nowhere in the Four Valleys is there a gourmet restaurant to compare with those in Zermatt or St Moritz, except in price. The best are Cabane Mont-Fort, a real Haute Route touring hut with an olde-worlde atmosphere that serves fondue and other typically Swiss fare, and Chez Dany at Clambin which is perennially overcrowded and serves nothing more ambitious than cheese dishes. Worst are the fast-food terraces at Les Attelas and La Chaux with their blaring loud-speakers and indifferent food. Les Ruinettes cafeteria has tempting pastries and an acceptable sit-down restaurant upstairs.

On Savolèyres, the primitive Buvette de la Marlenaz is far off-piste. The station café at Le Châble is warmly recommended by one reporter: 'don't tell anybody, as the seating is limited'. The wooden shacks at Tortin and Gentianes are money-earning gold-mines for their owners and hunting grounds for ski bums scavenging leftovers at the outdoor tables, but offer meagre sustenance.

Accommodation

The vast majority of visitors stay in tour-operator-run chalets or in the wealth of self-catering apartments, which comprise 90 per cent of Verbier's 15,000 beds. Although Verbier can boast 26 hotels, it is the only Swiss resort of note with no five-stars. Even the four-star Rosalp, Verbier's flagship, suffers from cramped rooms and lacks a swimming-pool. The most comfortable, but not very central, is the Trois Rois. The modest Hotel Verbier in the village square is friendly, as is Serge Tacchini's Mazot around the corner. Rois Mages, hidden away near the church, is modern and elegant. Hotel Vanessa is 'wonderfully convenient with good food'. The Montpelier and good-value Les Touristes are both praised. Hotel Bristol is recommended by one reporter ('there is not a more convenient location in Verbier'). However, 'the hotel houses a disco on the first floor, which can provide some noise late into the night'. It has the advantage of a small, free parking area, which is a rarity in the resort.

Eating in and out

The Rosalp remains a true gourmet treat and one of the best restaurants in Switzerland. Of the cheeseries, the best are the unpretentious and homey Les Touristes and the Vieux Valais. Borsalino ('the best'), Chez Martin and Al Capone all serve pizzas. Harold's in the square is famous for burgers. Grotte à Max has an interesting range of *Rösti* dishes, with kangaroo and ostrich. The Hacienda Café ('the worst') features Tex-Mex, with indifferent success. The Bouchon Gourmand wins good reviews for its southwestern French dishes. The Relais des Neiges is recommended for simple home cooking at modest prices, while Verbier Beach is also good value. Hotel Montpelier's restaurant offers outstanding cuisine and is second to the Rosalp as the best eatery in town.

Après-ski

The Hotel Farinet, in the central square, has been bought by the owners of Dick's Tea-Bars. Fer à Cheval, sometimes serving free pizza, is packed out as soon as the lifts close. Harold's Snack is a cybercafé. The most original hangout remains the Offshore, famed for its pink VW. At night chalet girls and ski bums flock to the Pub Mont-Fort. The Farm Club is 'as expensive as ever, with vodka at £100 a bottle, but people still queue to get in'. Ravers prefer the Scotch ('very basic') or Marshall's ('techno'). Crok No Name is Verbier's most sophisticated bar, although the over-50s will find Jacky's piano bar more to their taste. Sub-teens will enjoy the video games and pool tables at the Big Ben. The Nelson is 'crowded and with the décor and atmosphere of a Birmingham pub'.

Childcare

Chez les Schtroumpfs has an excellent reputation for day-long indoor childminding (ages five months to seven years). The Kids Club skiing programme for children over three years is run by the ESS at its Moulins nursery site which has its own lift and restaurant.

Linked or nearby resorts

Bruson
top 2,445m (8,022ft) bottom 1,100m (3,543ft)

Verbier's lift company has plans for a direct gondola from the valley train station in Le Châble to the top of Bruson. But for the moment Bruson remains uncrowded and boasts some of the best steep powder skiing available on the Verbier skipass, especially in its larch forests.

Two chair-lifts and two T-bars make up the lift system, serving only 30km of groomed pistes. But with some hiking, long excursions down to **Sembrancher** and **Orsières** over snow-filled pastures, then a free train-ride back to Châble, are possible. Access is by free bus

Skiing facts: Verbier

TOURIST INFORMATION
CH-1936 Verbier, Val de Bagnes
Tel 41 27 775 3888
Fax 41 27 775 3889
Email verbiertourism@verbier.ch
Web site www.verbier.ch

THE RESORT
By road Calais 998km
By rail Le Châble 15mins
Airport transfer Geneva 2hrs
Visitor beds 15,000
Transport free ski bus

THE SKIING
Linked or nearby resorts Bruson (n),
Champex-Lac (n), La Fouly (n), Nendaz
(l), Super-St-Bernard (n), La Tzoumaz
(l), Thyon (l), Veysonnaz (l), Vichères (n)
Number of lifts 39 in Verbier, 95 in area
Total of trails/pistes 150km in Verbier,
410km in area (33% easy, 42%
intermediate, 6% difficult, 19% very
difficult)
Nursery slopes 4
Summer skiing 2 lifts, end of June
to July

LIFT PASSES
Area pass Four Valleys SF282 for 6
days. Family Pass (covers whole area)
SF282 for 1st adult, 40% reduction for
2nd, 70% reduction for 6–16yrs, 40%
reduction for 17–20yrs, 15% reduction
for 17–20s travelling alone

Beginners no free lifts
Pensioners 40% reduction for six days
for 65yrs and over
Credit cards yes

TUITION
Adults ESS tel: 27 775 3366,
La Fantastique tel: 27 771 4141,
Adrénaline tel: 27 771 7459
Snowboarding as ski schools, and
No Bounds tel: 27 771 5556
Other courses carving, extreme
skiing/boarding, heli-skiing/boarding,
moguls, race-training, telemark
Guiding through ski schools

CHILDREN
Lift pass 6–16yrs 40% reduction
Ski & board school as adults
Kindergarten (ski) ESS Kids Club
tel: 27 771 4469, (non-ski) Chez les
Schtroumpfs tel: 27 771 6585

FOOD AND DRINK PRICES
Coffee SF3, glass of wine SF2.80, small
beer SF3.50–4, soft drink SF3, dish of
the day SF14–20

OTHER SPORTS
Climbing wall, curling, hang-gliding,
horse-riding (Le Châble), ice-climbing,
indoor golf, parapente, skating,
ski-touring, squash, snowbiking,
snowcarting, snowshoeing,
swimming, tubing

from Le Châble, itself connected to Verbier by gondola or another
free bus. Bruson has apartments midway up the mountain, and
a restaurant.

TOURIST INFORMATION
Tel 41 27 776 1682
Fax 41 27 776 1541

Champex-Lac
top 2,188m (7,178ft) bottom 1,470m (4,823ft)

The narrow hairpin road up to Champex guarantees that this delightfully forested family resort, with its scenic frozen lake, never sees a queue. Unfortunately for Verbier-based skiers, the resort has opted out of the Four Valleys lift pass and you must buy a separate ticket. Skiing is limited: two chair-lifts access no more than 10km of pistes, which are very steep if taken off-piste directly under the main chair. Powder on the north face remains good for weeks, and the resort's clientèle rarely ventures into the untracked snow among the trees.

The Belvédère is outstandingly characterful and one of the more unusual hotels in the Alps. Its few bedrooms are panelled in broad Arolla pine and furnished with hand-painted furniture. The food is of a high standard and modestly priced. Champex has a small branch of the Swiss Ski School. The kindergarten has closed down.

TOURIST INFORMATION
Tel 41 27 783 1227
Fax 41 27 783 3527
Email info@champex.ch
Web site www.champex.ch

Nendaz
top 3,330m (10,925ft) bottom 1,365m (4,478ft)

Nendaz offers cheaper accommodation than Verbier but complicated and inefficient access to the best of the Four Valleys skiing, although a free bus does run from Nendaz to **Siviez**. The ESS and Neige Aventure are the two ski schools, while P'tit Bec is a kindergarten for children aged sixteen months to seven years old.

TOURIST INFORMATION
Tel 41 27 289 5589
Fax 41 27 289 5583
Email info@nendaz.ch
Web site www.nendaz.ch

Siviez
top 3,330m (10,925ft) bottom 1,730m (5,676ft)

Skiers desperate to save money and determined to be first up Mont-Fort might consider Siviez. It is sunny and at the hub of the Four Valleys, with a high-speed chair link to the Gentianes–Mont-Fort cable-cars. Accommodation is limited to one hotel, a concrete apartment block and a youth hostel.

TOURIST INFORMATION
Tel 41 27 289 5589
Fax 41 27 289 5583

Zermatt

ALTITUDE 1,620m (5,314ft)

Intermediates ✳✳✳ Advanced ✳✳✳ Snowboarders ✳✳

If you take your skiing with sugar and cream, then Zermatt is the resort in which to stay, provided, of course, you have both the wherewithal and the luck to find a vacant room in a tourist centre that has no low season at all. Arriving off the train from the end-of-the-road hamlet of Täsch is an astonishing experience, regardless of financial status. At the station back-packers mingle with fur-clad socialites surrounded by mounds of Louis Vuitton luggage, but everyone is equally awestruck by the mountain setting that greets them. Zermatt – dominated by the Matterhorn – is Switzerland's southernmost skiing terrain, with 29 summits of over 4,000m. It is one of the most scenically beautiful ski resorts in the world. The announcement that a dynamic new learning academy called The Ski School is to be introduced here for the 2000–1 season to rival the much-criticised branch of the Swiss Ski School can only be greeted with delight.

Zermatt was a settlement from the early Middle Ages and inaugurated its first three tourist beds in 1838. Development has since been constrained by steep valley walls, leaving nothing between the Matterhorn

✔ Superlative scenery
✔ Excellent mountain restaurants
✔ High standard of accommodation
✔ Alpine charm
✔ Lively après-ski
✔ Activities for non-skiers
✔ Long runs
✔ Extensive ski area
✔ Car-free resort
✔ Extensive snowmaking
✔ Glacier skiing
✘ Inadequate ski school
✘ High prices
✘ Spread-out resort
✘ Long airport transfer

and the village edge but open pasture dotted with wooden barns. In Zermatt's narrow lanes, sheep are still shorn outside centuries-old wooden *mazots* (ramshackle barns on stilts fitted with stone discs to keep the rats at bay), but the conflux of overpriced electric taxis and horse-drawn carriages on the main thoroughfare provide a fresh inter-pretation of 'traffic free'. Complimentary but often oversubscribed ski buses link the separate ski areas, but any visitor to Zermatt must be prepared for a considerable amount of walking in ski boots.

The lift system dates from the construction of the Gornergrat cog railway in 1898. A combined lift pass with **Cervinia**, which is linked off the back of the Klein Matterhorn, is available, but it is more sensible to pay the daily supplement for the occasional foray across the border for a lazy lunch on Italian territory.

Cervinia's skiing is bland by comparison, but on a sunny day in good snow conditions the run down to the town or to the linked resort of **Valtournenche** can be sensational and a welcome contrast to Zermatt's more demanding slopes.

On the snow
top 3,899m (12,788ft) bottom 1,620m (5,314ft)

Zermatt is a resort for the adept skier with deep pockets and a taste for good living. No competent skier will find him- or herself outclassed by any groomed slope in Zermatt, but 20-minute queues for the Klein Matterhorn cable-car and longer for the Gornergrat cog railway – not to mention packed crowds coming down to the village at the end of the day on narrow, icy trails – will keep even experts on the edge ('at peak time it took us over two hours to get to the top of the Klein Matterhorn'). A convenient hands-free lift pass was introduced for the 1999–2000 season.

The three once-separate ski areas are now linked – albeit tenuously – and mountain access has been transformed by the addition of the cable-car from Gant to Hohtälli. This effectively links the Sunnegga and Gornergrat areas and dispenses with the necessity of ever having to take the long, slow, but beautiful train journey up the Gornergrat.

An underground funicular runs up to the Sunnegga sector, with sunny slopes continuing up to Blauherd and Rothorn, which are connected by an efficient 150-person cable-car. From here you can either return towards the resort or take the long run down to Gant and the new cable-car to the Hohtälli-Stockhorn-Gornergrat sector.

Zermatt's other ski area, the Klein Matterhorn, stretches up to the Italian frontier. It can be reached from Gornergrat but is more easily accessed from the resort by cable-car or gondola to Furi. From there, lifts branch left for the Trockener Steg and Klein Matterhorn sectors and right for the Schwarzsee area, with Furgg straight up the middle. Zermatt retains 16 antiquated drag-lifts among its impressive cable-cars. Reporters complain of inconsistent piste-grading: 'some blue (easy) runs seemed more like red (intermediate) ones and yet the reds were very straightforward, especially on Trockener Steg'. Reporters complain that piste grading is erratic. Zermatt is now one of Switzerland's leading resorts for artificial snowmaking.

Beginners
Zermatt cannot be recommended for novices, but beginners do have the rare chance to ski at exceptionally high altitude on the Theodul Glacier (Klein Matterhorn sector). The snow never melts here, and skiing continues throughout the year. Normally, the ski school takes beginners to the nursery slope just below Sunnegga, which is reached by a lift inside the top-station of the underground. From here they progress by gondola to Blauherd for the blue run back down to Sunnegga and on down to Patrullarve. Gornergrat offers more beginner

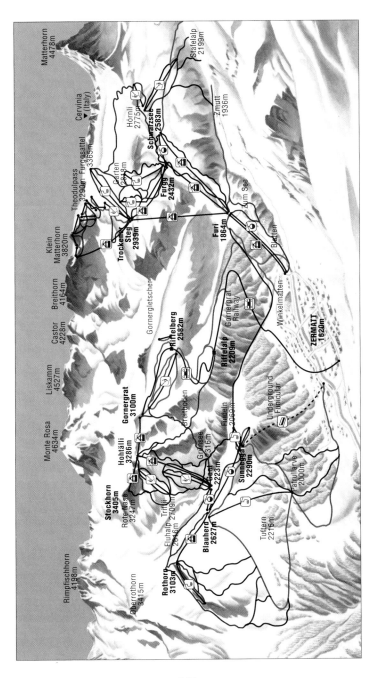

terrain, but it is important to get off the train at Rotenboden, one stop earlier, to avoid a 'nasty bit' at the top.

Intermediates

Zermatt's red runs often become more than ordinarily testing due to icy conditions and extreme overcrowding on the narrow sections down to the village. The highest and easiest intermediate skiing is in the Klein Matterhorn and Trockener Steg sectors. From the Klein Matterhorn, the long KL red flows alongside blue-ice crevasses down past the Plateau Rosa T-bars and over to the Testa T-bar.

Aggressive intermediates will be thrilled by the Kelle run from Gornergrat, passing over a 'scary' ridge to link up at Breitboden with the classic White Hare red, which begins with a narrow, challenging passage up at Hohtälli. Both reds proceed on terrain bordered by woods all the way to Furi – a good 30 minutes on skis without stopping. Intermediate skiing on the Sunnegga–Blauherd sector is sunnier and smoother, making ideal 'ski to lunch' terrain.

Advanced

Triftji is one of the most famous black (difficult) runs in the Alps. Unfortunately, this and the other black trails down under the Hohtälli–Rote Nase sector require so much snow to make them skiable that they are often closed until mid-January. Together, the Stockhorn and Grieschumme blacks make an almost perfect fall-line descent from Rote Nase down to Gant, a bone-jarring bump bonanza that only the most rubber-legged will achieve without stopping.

Further afield, and invisible to spectators, is Zermatt's least crowded, best black-run skiing. Sloping sharply down from the Stafel–Hörnli drag-lift into the tree-line, Tiefbach and Momatt are steep runs that dive towards Zmutt and the borders of the resort. Notorious as an accident black-spot as well as an expert run, the Furgg–Furi stretch is described by one reporter as being 'like the M25' in late afternoon, when it is the main homeward-bound route. But early in the morning, when Furgg–Furi has yet to be scraped clean of snow, it makes an excellent downhill course for more advanced skiers.

Off-piste

The Schwarzsee sector is cold and uncrowded. The Aroleid trail under the cable-car is normally a bump run all the way to Furi. Less skied are the Garten gullies. From the top of the Furgg–Garten drag, and to the left of the Garten red run, the two Garten couloirs offer a choice of narrow chutes, which are very steep for the first 40m but not life-threatening should you fall. At the bottom a favourite 'sky ramp' jump of about 20m has the attractions of a perfect landing and good views for spectators from the Garten lift. Down from Rothorn on the sunny side of the mountain, three itineraries (Chamois, Marmotte and Arbzug) become wide-open powder routes after a good storm.

A day's heli-skiing excursion to **Monterosa** or the Alphubeljoch above Zermatt is a popular way to escape the pistes ('the most amazing experience – we were flown past the Matterhorn and dropped on to a tiny ledge in what seemed the middle of nowhere').

Snowboarders

The funpark and half-pipe above Furgg are served by the Sandigerboden chair. Blauherd also has a beginner funpark. Advanced riders will find a lot of excellent off-piste, as well as heli-boarding. Snowboard school Stoked has its own beginner area with lift at Trockner Stegg.

Tuition and guiding

For a decade we have consistently criticised the Swiss Ski School (SSS) here; it operates as a 'jobs for life' co-operative for those of the resort's adult population not employed in full-time commerce. Once you have the coveted red and white jacket ('actually, you can buy one in the town's sports shops') no one, it seems, can ever take it away. The rules do not include a compulsory retirement age and as a consequence nearly 10 per cent of the 250 teachers who give daily lessons to tourists in Switzerland's premier ski resort are aged over 65.

However, we are assured that a brand new ski school will be in place by December 2000. The Ski School is to be run by Christian Meier and his young team, who are also behind Stoked, the established Zermatt snowboard school. Their policy is '100 per cent quality – we therefore restrict group lessons to between four and eight people at any time'. All the instructors will be aged between 20 and 40. Courses that will be offered include group and private ski lessons, carving, heli-skiing (see *Heli-skiing*) and heli-boarding, full moon skiing, off-piste excursions and snowshoeing. Special pre-season packages that include accommodation, transfers and lift passes will be available. For the present, no specialist children's courses will be offered, although this is expected to change in the future.

Mountain restaurants

Lunching on a wooden terrace comes a close second to gazing at the Matterhorn as the main occupation in Zermatt. This is no place to pack a picnic – not when old wooden barns like Chez Vrony provide crystal glasses, starched napkins, sofas on the terrace and intimate nooks and crannies for serious dining. Also in Findeln, Paradies and the Findlerhof, run by mountain guide Franz Schwery, are warmly recommended. The centuries-old hamlet of Zum See houses an inn of the same name, which is run by Max and Greti and has an established reputation as one of Zermatt's best – it is worth trying the curried noodles and king prawns here. Higher up in the Furi sector, Simi is the rösti headquarters but also serves delicious salads at reasonable prices. Tony's Grotta at Riffelalp has delectable pasta. Fluhalp, at the top of Rothorn, has some of the finest food and certainly the best panorama of the Matterhorn. Stafelalp is 'charmingly situated with unusual views of the Matterhorn'.

Accommodation

Hotel-keepers rule in Zermatt and chalet accommodation is minimal. It is important to choose a hotel close to where you want to ski and spend your evenings. The new Into The Hotel is an exotic all-glass confection perched on top of a rock and reached only by a lift. For indulgent romantics nothing compares with the five-star experience of the venerable Zermatterhof. Its interior was recently overhauled and redecorated in palatial style. The central, five-star Mont Cervin has fewer balconies but has opened sumptuous apartments in a recently built annex. All have private saunas, whirlpools, fireplaces, and most have kitchens. The four-star Alex Schlosshotel Tenne is an Alpine-Byzantine architectural mélange. The Monte Rosa, a favourite of Sir Winston Churchill and the base from which Edward Whymper, the Victorian mountaineer, set off to conquer the Matterhorn, exudes understated opulence ('the service and food were faultless'). Grandhotel Schönegg is a chalet-style establishment close to the river and the Sunnegga lift station.

The chalet-style Malteserhaus has generously sized apartments. The Albana Real is 'modern and comfortable'. Hotel Holiday is a family-run three-star with good food, close to the Sunnegga Express. Nearby Hotel Parnass is said to have 'a quiet and relaxed atmosphere – not wildly luxurious, but good value for money'. Hotel Bijou, two minutes' walk from the Klein Matterhorn lift, is praised by several reporters as 'small and friendly with rooms even better than a four-star; the food was a culinary delight each evening,' and 'spacious, clean and tidy. The staff were very friendly and helpful'. The Excelsior is 'central, next to a bus stop, and caters for vegetarians'. We also have glowing reports of Le Petit Hotel and the Darioli.

Eating in and out

Zermatt's restaurants (there are more than a hundred) have a deserved reputation for high quality and price. As elsewhere in the Alps, world-class cuisine is hard to find. Excepting menus at the Chinese restaurant next to the London Bar and the Fuji Japanese restaurant in the Hotel Albana, meat, cheese and potatoes prevail. Le Mazot and Le Gitan are at the top of most lists for haute cuisine, although the Buffet Royal in the Zermatterhof Hotel is more sumptuous. American-style steaks are grilled at the Viktoria-Centre and Cheminée Steak house. Fish, even in fondue, is good at the Coquille Fischstube. Lamb from the owner's own flock (watch out for the sheepdog in the foyer) is excellent at the Schäferstübli. The Whymperstube in the Hotel Monte Rosa serves traditional fondues in an Edwardian ambience. Chez Gaby is a warm and friendly place and recommended for its fondue Bourguignon.

The Spaghetti Factory has 'food of a consistently high quality and great ambience'. Zermatt has about 15 grocery shops. The best is said

Skiing facts: Zermatt

TOURIST INFORMATION
Bahnhofplatz,
CH-3920 Zermatt
Tel 41 27 967 0181
Fax 41 27 967 0185
Email zermatt@wallis.ch
Web site www.zermatt.ch

THE RESORT
By road Calais 1,076km
By rail station in resort, or Visp 36km
Airport transfer Geneva 4hrs, Milan
3hrs, Sion 90mins, Zurich 5hrs
Visitor beds 13,200
Transport free ski bus with ski pass

THE SKIING
Linked or nearby resorts Cervinia (I),
Crans Montana (n), Grächen (n),
Riederalp (n), Saas-Fee (n)
Number of lifts 39, 70 with Cervinia
Total of trails/pistes Zermatt only
150km, 245km including Cervinia (29%
easy, 42% intermediate, 29% difficult)
Nursery slopes 3 runs
Summer skiing 25km of trails and 10
lifts on Klein Matterhorn Glacier

LIFT PASSES
Area pass SF306 for 6 days
Beginners no free lifts
Pensioners 25% reduction for men
65yrs and over, women 62yrs and over
Credit cards yes

TUITION
Adults SSS tel: 27 966 2466,The Ski
School tel: 27 967 8788
Snowboarding SSS, Stoked
tel: 27 967 8788
Other courses carving, cross-country,
heli-skiing and heli-boarding, teen
snowboarding, telemark
Guiding Alpin Center tel: 27 966 2460,
Air Zermatt tel: 27 966 8686

CHILDREN
Lift pass 50% reduction for 9–16yrs,
free until 9th birthday
Ski & board school as adults
Kindergarten (ski) SSS, (non-ski) Hotel
Nicoletta kindergarten tel: 27 967 0151,
Kinderclub Pumuckel at Hotel La
Ginabelle tel: 27 966 5000,
SSS Pingu-Club tel: 27 966 2466,
Kinderparadies tel: 27 967 7252

OTHER SPORTS
Curling, dog-sledding, gorge-climbing,
helicopter rides, ice-climbing,
ice-diving, indoor tennis and
squash, parapente, rock-climbing,
skating, sleigh rides,
snowshoeing

FOOD AND DRINK
Coffee SF3.30, glass of wine SF3–3.50,
small beer SF4.30, soft drink SF4, dish
of the day SF20–28

to be La Source, but one reader recommends Martin Welschen, opposite the skating-rink, for the lowest prices.

Après-ski
Elsie's Place, by the church, is expensive and crowded, but irresistible for
champagne and oysters or snails. The Post Hotel complex caters for
everybody; the Pink Elephant has a high standard of live jazz; Le Village
is for house music, and Le Broken is a traditional disco that incites danc-

ing – to '70s, '80s and '90s music – on huge beer barrels until 3am. However, the Post's Boathouse bar, not to be confused with the Zermatt Yacht, Golf and Country Club, is a tiny haven of cocktail civilisation decorated like the inside of a sloop. For a whale of a time, Moby Dick's Dancing pub is open until late and has pool tables. The Alex Hotel's nightclub is sedate but it is the only place where 30-somethings and upwards can dance to music that allows conversation. Grampi's Pub is a glass-fronted haunt with the cheapest beer in Zermatt. Z'Alt Hischi is small, atmospheric and in the old part of town. The Papperla has 'good beer and live music'. The North Wall and the Brown Cow are where you find the resort workers. The T-Bar in Hotel Pollux was new in 1998, and the Vernissage cinema/bar/gallery is the coolest après-ski spot in town.

There are a number of expensive jewellery shops and some good sports shops, but few of the chic boutiques one finds in Crans Montana or St Moritz.

Childcare

Zermatt's facilities for families with small children have greatly improved in recent years, and Zermatt now offers a good choice of daycare. The Pingu-Club cares for children aged four to six years all day at its kindergarten up the mountain at Riffelberg. Children meet outside the tourist information office then travel up (and down) by special train. Care includes indoor and outdoor games and ski lessons. 'Well organised and absolutely excellent,' said one reporter. The ski school takes children from six to twelve years with supervised lunch at Blauherd or Riffelberg. Stoked runs snowboarding classes for children and teenagers. Packages are available for six to nine year olds, including lunch, board and boots, knee protectors and helmet.

At Hotel Nicoletta, Seiler's Children's Paradise takes kids from two years old. Childminding, with optional ski lessons (from six years old) on a baby slope by the river, is available at Hotel La Ginabelle's Kinderclub Pumuckel for children from two-and-a-half years old. Kinderparadies cares for children from two years and is also open as a babysitting service in the evenings until 10pm.

Round-up

Adelboden/Lenk
top 2,109m (6,919ft) bottom 1,068m (3,503ft)

Adelboden is an unspoilt village of wooden chalets with the advantage of no through-traffic. Lenk is a traditional spa village with its own sulphur spring, situated at the end of the wide Simmen Valley. The two villages share a 160-km ski area served by 50 lifts. The new six-seater gondola enhances the lift links between the resorts. Lift passes for more than four days give you one day's free skiing in Gstaad.

Adelboden and Lenk ski schools both organise tuition for adults and children from four years old, with carving classes, cross-country, extreme skiing, snowblading and telemark on offer. Lenk also caters for disabled skiers. Crazy Sports is Adelboden's specialist snowboarding school, while Adrenaline is the equivalent in Lenk. Alpine School Adelboden and Hansrüdi Rösli in Lenk provide off-piste guides. Adlis Winterplayground in Adelboden and the Swiss Ski and Snowboard School (SSBS) in Lenk care for non-skiing little ones from two years old and skiers from four years old.

Adelboden's recommended hotels include the Beau Site, the attractively located Parkhotel Bellevue, Grand Hotel Regina and Hotel Steinmattli. Adelboden has 23 restaurants in and around town. Other sports available in both resorts include dog-sledding and night-skiing. Lenk offers the unusual sports of ski-joring and board-joring (where you are pulled along behind a horse and rider on a choice of skis or snowboard).

TOURIST INFORMATION
Tel (Adelboden) 41 33 673 8080/ (Lenk) 41 33 733 3131
Fax (Adelboden) 41 33 673 8092/ (Lenk) 41 33 733 2027
Email (Adelboden) info@adelboden.ch (Lenk) info@lenk.ch
Web site (Adelboden) www.adelboden.ch (Lenk) www.lenk.ch

Andermatt
top 2,965m (9,725ft) bottom 1,445m (4,740ft)

Andermatt is a retreat for a dedicated skiing minority. It boasts enormous off-piste opportunities and a reputation for generous dumps of snow, but at the same time it is one of Switzerland's lesser-known little gems. It is situated at a major Alpine crossroads on the route to the St Gotthard Pass into Italy and was once one of the busiest of Swiss resorts. Now the high Urseren Valley, of which Andermatt is the main village, is underpassed by the Gotthard road and rail tunnels, making it a virtual dead-end in winter.

Four ski areas, with a total of 13 lifts and 56km of piste, run along the sides of the Urseren Valley, between the Furka and Oberalp passes. The two main areas lie at either end of Andermatt; the two smaller and less popular ones lie to the south west, above the villages of **Hospental** and **Realp**. Descents down the shaded face of Gemsstock, which has 800m of severe vertical and treacherous off-piste skiing in the bowl, should not be tackled without a guide; nor should some of the long off-piste alternatives in other directions from the top-station. Beginners tend to ski in the Grossboden area. Andermatt is part of the Gottard-Oberalp area, which links the resort with three further villages of **Disentis**, **Oberalp** and **Sedrun**, making a total ski area of 34 lifts and 166km of piste. Andermatt has a convenient hands-free lift pass.

Andermatt has an SSBS for adults and children from four and a half years old. The off-piste guiding companies are Alpine Sport-school, Bergschool Uri and Montanara.

Andermatt itself has cobbled streets and a traditional character. However, it is one of Switzerland's major centres for the training of alpine troops, and severe barrack buildings are a feature of the architecture. The heart of the old village receives little sun as it is hemmed in by mountains. There is not much traffic and no public transport. Accommodation is in a mixture of hotels and appealing old chalets. Hotel Schweizerhof is a two-star, described as 'a bit old but quite central – the food was satisfactory'. Pension Sternen is reported to have a cosy atmosphere with 'excellent *Rösti* for lunch'.

TOURIST INFORMATION
Tel 41 41 887 1454
Fax 41 41 887 0185
Email info@andermatt.ch
Web site www.andermatt.ch

Arosa
top 2,653m (8,702ft) bottom 1,800m (5,904ft)

In 1883, ski-tourer Dr Otto Herwig-Hold stumbled across the tiny village of Inner Arosa high in the Swiss Graubunden. He climbed to the top of the 2,512-m Hörnli, looked down at the village and realised that it was the perfect site on which to build his new tuberculosis sanatorium. With its wide range of international patients, the hospital soon put Arosa on the Alpine map.

Today the resort is one of the truly all-round ski resorts of the Alps. Arosa's skiers are not here to bash the pistes from dawn until dusk; instead they are in search of the complete winter-sports experience. The ski area consists of wide, sunny slopes, mostly above the tree-line, and covering the three peaks of Hörnli, Weisshorn and Bruggerhorn. It is well linked, and though small with only 15 lifts, boasts a total of 70km of piste. Much of this is made up of blue (easy) and red (intermediate) runs over hilly rather than mountainous terrain. One of the only hazards of Arosa's skiing is the number of pedestrians and tobogganers on the piste; non-skiers can buy hiking passes that allow them to use gondolas and some chair-lifts.

The lift system is modern and efficient by Swiss standards. The top of the Hörnli is the starting point for a variety of ski-tours, involving skins (artificial seal skins that allow you to travel uphill on skis) and public transport, to neighbouring resorts. Arosa has a dramatic half-pipe and is keen to promote snowboarding. The SSBS and the ABC Snowsportschool both offer courses in carving, cross-country, seniors, skiing for the disabled, snowblading and telemark.

Arosa Kulm and the Tschuggen Grand Hotel are the two five-stars, while Waldhotel National is 'convenient, comfortable, but lacking in style'. Every bedroom at Hotel Eden is decorated in an individual style. Carmennahütte is the best of half-a-dozen mountain restaurants, but the choice of resort restaurants and nightlife is limited. Crazy is the only nightclub. Access to the village is tricky, with 244 bends in the scenic 32-km road from the busy, medieval valley town of Chur. Taking the train through stunning scenery is the better option. Once in the village, a toboggan is the essential form of transport.

TOURIST INFORMATION
Tel 41 81 378 7020
Fax 41 81 378 7021
Email arosa@arosa.ch
Web site www.arosa.ch

Brienz-Meiringen-Hasliberg
top 2,433m (7,982ft) bottom 1,061m (3,481ft)

Meiringen-Hasliberg is situated in the Bernese Oberland, halfway between Lucerne and Interlaken. The resorts have now merged with **Brienz-Axalp**, to form the new Alpen Region Brienz-Meiringen-Hasliberg. Although the area has many claims to fame, it is not an obvious ski destination for most people. Meiringen is best known for the Reichenbach Fall where Sir Arthur Conan Doyle's character of Sherlock Holmes fell to his death during his final struggle with arch-villain Moriarty. The sweet-toothed might also be interested to hear that meringues were originally created in Meiringen.

The Meiringen-Hasliberg area has 16 lifts and 60km of slopes ('many interesting runs'), 60 per cent of which are rated intermediate. Mountain access is by cable-car from Meiringen via Hasliberg Reuti and on to the main ski area, or by gondola from Hasliberg Wasserwendi at 1,160m. The terrain here is ideal for snowboarders, with a half-pipe and natural obstacles that form Switzerland's first 'natural snowboard park'. Brienz-Axalp, which is not linked into the main area, has four of its own lifts and 20km of runs.

The resorts do not have a crèche, but the SSBS has a ski kindergarten and is praised as 'excellent, and I find it hard to imagine better facilities for teaching children'. SSBS is the main school, with Team Spirit the alternative. Adults skiing, snowboarding, cross-country and telemark are among the courses on offer. Off-piste guiding is available with the SSBS, Bergsteigerschule Castor, or Team Spirit. Heli-skiing and heli-boarding (see *Heli-skiing*) can be booked through the SSBS.

There are five mountain restaurants in the ski area, including a new one with a scenic lookout tower called the Alpen Tower. Meiringen has 15 hotels, among which are the Alpin Sherpa Hotel, Parkhotel du Sauvage, and three-star Sporthotel Sherlock Holmes. Hasliberg's 16 hotels include the Bären and the Bellevue. Other activities available in the resorts include horse-riding, ice-climbing and indoor tennis. The Sherlock Holmes museum holds mystery weekends and mystery nights.

TOURIST INFORMATION
Tel 41 33 972 5151
Fax 41 33 972 5150
Email info@alpenregion.ch
Web site www.alpenregion.ch

Flims/Laax
top 3,018m (9,902ft) bottom 1,100m (3,609ft)

Flims is a year-round destination that lies in the heart of the Graubunden on the road from Chur to Andermatt. Together with its neighbours, **Laax** and **Falera**, it serves the wide south-facing ski area known as the Alpine Arena. **Flims Dorf** is the livelier and more convenient part of town in which to stay. The hotels in **Flims Waldhaus** are not within easy walking distance of the lifts, but the larger ones have a courtesy minibus service to the base-station in Flims.

The pleasant old village of Laax is 5km to the west, with a modern satellite base-station at **Laax-Murschteg**, and low-cost, on-mountain accommodation at Crap Sogn Gion. In recent years Laax has become a popular snowboarding base. The farming hamlet of Falera offers a rustic alternative.

At Flims/Laax and Falera there is a nursery area called Dreamland, and higher up the mountain some gentle practice slopes are inviting for beginners. Motorway-style pistes give the intermediate snow-user the run of the whole mountain. The longest black (difficult) run is the FIS downhill from Crap Sogn Gion to Laax-Murschteg. The off-piste potential is surprisingly high, with tree-level runs above Laax.

In Flims the SSBS gives lessons at three separate bases. Snowboard Fahrschule in Flims and Laax offers tuition, while Crap Sogn Gion and the Vorab Glacier areas boast two well-maintained half-pipes and funparks each. Extensive cross-country trails along the valley floor are available at Flims, including one loipe that is floodlit at night. Flims SSBS offers classes for children from three years old, and reports of the ski kindergarten are favourable. Both the Park Hotels Waldhaus and the Hotel Adula have crèches.

The best mountain eateries are at the lower levels and not on the skiing trails, although the Runca hut below Startgels and the Tegia Larnags are both worth the detour. Among the higher altitide options, the Segnes-Hütte is welcoming, the Foppa is an old wooden chalet with a sun terrace, and the popular Elephant restaurant at Crap Masegn has delicious food.

The choice of accommodation is wide, ranging from the five-star Park Hotels Waldhaus, which comprises five buildings with opulent rooms, to the well-run three-star Hotel La Siala in Falera. Hotel Adula is praised for its children's facilities. Hotel Sunstar Surselva is said to be 'excellent and central', with a swimming-pool and health centre. The top choice in Laax is the Posta Veglia. Laax is the more 'happening' base for snowboarders, with The Rider's Palace a boarders-only hotel at the base-station of Laax-Murschetg.

Recommended restaurants include Pizzeria Pomodoro, the Barga in Hotel Adula, La Cena in the Park Hotels Waldhaus, and the seafood restaurant in Hotel National. The all-glass Iglu Bar opposite the base-station is the height of Flims chic for après-ski drinks. Later on the action focuses on the Angel Club at the Flims base-station, the Crap Bar and the Casa Veglia at the Laax base-station, or the quieter Segnes Bar in Flims.

TOURIST INFORMATION
Tel 41 81 920 9200
Fax 41 81 920 9201
Email rkonrad@alpenarena.ch
Web site www.alpenarena.ch

Gstaad
top 2,979m (9,744ft) bottom 1,000m (3,280ft)

To serious skiers, the lure of Gstaad is incomprehensible. However, skiing is only a decorative accessory to the charm of this small but smart resort. The village stands at 1,050m, with none of the local skiing above 2,200m, which means that snow cover can be unreliable. The redeeming factor is the nearby presence of Les Diablerets Glacier, where the lifts go up to 2,979m. Regulars argue that the sheer extent of the skiing included in the Ski Gstaad lift pass – 66 lifts covering 250km of piste (nearly half of it rated as easy) and 10 villages – makes up for the lack of challenge.

The local skiing is inconveniently divided into three separate areas. Regular ski buses to the surrounding villages of **Rougemont**, **Saanenmöser** and **Schönried** give access to slopes offering considerably more scope. Schönried itself has a new pedestrianised village centre for the 2000–1 season. The other villages covered on the lift pass are **St Stephan**, **Zweisimmen**, **Lauenen**, **Gsteig**, **Saanen** and **Château d'Oex**.

The Snowboard Schule Gstaad has a good reputation. Gstaad has funparks at Hornberg above Saanenmöser, at Rinderberg above Zweisimmen, on the Glacier des Diablerets, and a new one on the Eggli. Heli-skiing (see *Heli-skiing*) and ski-touring are available, ice-climbing is one of the alternative sports on offer and there are 140km of cross-country loipe. The area's four ski and snowboard schools take children from four years old. Recommended mountain restaurants include Chemihütte above St Stephan, and Cabane de la Sarouche at Château d'Oex. Ruble-Rougemont at the bottom of the Gouilles chair-lift is 'half the price of anywhere else'.

Gstaad is filled with top-quality hotels and a cluster of well-preserved wooden buildings in the traffic-free village centre. The best-known hotel is the Palace, which has fairytale turrets and sits on the hill like a feudal castle dominating the village and its daily life. The opulent Gstaad Hotel Park is downhill but not downmarket. The four-star Bernerhof is conveniently close to the railway station, and the Christiania has individually designed bedrooms. The three-star Olden is family-run and cosy, as is the Posthotel Rössli, while Sporthotel Rutti is the most basic but has a high standard of food and is said to be good value. Most of the cheaper hotels are in the surrounding villages of Schönried and Saanenmöser. Some hotels can arrange babysitting and the Palace Hotel has a nursery.

Recommended restaurants include La Cave in the Hotel Olden and the sixteenth-century Chlösterli. The Bären at Gsteig offers traditional Swiss fare. Café du Cerf in Rougemont is a typical Swiss restaurant with live music at weekends. The Palace's Greengo nightclub is the main late-night venue for those who can afford it. The locals meet at Richi's. Other haunts include Pubbles in the Hotel Boo in Saanen, Club 95 at the Sporthotel Victoria and the Grotte in the Hotel Alpin Nova in Schönried. Down Town is a bar with live jazz in the Hotel Hermitage-Golf, also at Schönried.

TOURIST INFORMATION
Tel 41 33 748 8181
Fax 41 33 748 8183
Email gst@gstaad.ch
Web site www.gstaad.ch

Kandersteg
top 1,920m (6,299ft) bottom 1,200m (3,937ft)

Kandersteg is a delightful village in the Bernese Oberland, much favoured by langlaufers for its 75km of loipe. One trail is floodlit at night. The resort also has attractive alpine skiing for beginners ('the perfect resort for our first-ever skiing holiday') with 7 lifts, 2 of which are free for beginners, 14km of piste, and a ski school with a sound reputation. Mountain access is via a chair-lift to Oeschinen, where a couple of drag-lifts take you on up to the small assortment of blue (easy) and red (intermediate) runs. A cable-car outside the village also gives access to a drag-lift that serves two blue runs, as well as a long and more challenging descent to the valley. Hotels include the four-star Victoria, which has 'wonderful food and lovely indoor swimming-pool'. The Berestübli, the Alfa-Soleil, Au Vieux Chalet and the Bahnhof Buffet are all recommended restaurants. Evening entertainment centres around the High Moon Pub and the hotel bars; Hotel

Alpenblick provides folkloric dance displays. Other activities include curling and skating.

TOURIST INFORMATION
Tel 41 33 675 8080
Fax 41 33 675 8081
Email info@kandersteg.ch
Web site www.kandersteg.ch

Lenzerheide/Valbella
top 2,865m (9,397ft) bottom 1,500m (4,920ft)

Lenzerheide used to attract a fair number of British families, but in recent years it has decreased in popularity. The area has considerable charm, including magnificent cross-country skiing. The villages of Lenzerheide and Valbella lie at either end of a lake in a wide, wooded pass running from **Churwalden** to **Parpan** and **Lantsch/Lenz**, with high mountains on either side. Transport is based on an efficient system of buses travelling clockwise and anti-clockwise.

The skiing is in two separate sectors, Rothorn and Danis/Stätzerhorn, on either side of the inconveniently wide pass. The skiing terrain in both is partly wooded and partly open. None of these pistes is particularly difficult, although the Rothorn cable-car opens up some off-piste skiing. A total of 33 lifts serve 155km of piste, with an additional 4 lifts and 27km of piste at nearby **Tschiertschen**. There are five branches of the SSBS in the area, with three snowboard schools – Primus at Lenzerheide, Snowboard school Valbella, and Exodus at Churwalden. Freeride camps and Skwal are just two of the many courses offered.

The main street of Lenzerheide has some attractive old buildings, and hotels include the four-star Sunstar in the middle of Lenzerheide, with a swimming-pool and piano bar. Valbella has less identity, being no more than a large community of hotels and concrete holiday homes crammed on to a hillside. However, it is less of a roadside strip than Lenzerheide and gives direct access to the eastern and western ski areas. As alternative bases to Lenzerheide, Churwalden is the ideal gateway to the skiing, Parpan is a typical Grison village, while Lantsch/Lenz is the starting point for the cross-country skiing.

TOURIST INFORMATION
Tel 41 81 385 1122
Fax 41 81 385 1121
Email info@lenzerheide.ch
Web site www.lenzerheide.ch

Leysin
top 2,200m (7,218ft) bottom 1,200m (3,937ft)

The south-facing resort of Leysin, above the town of Aigle, is a successful and attractive mix of modern hotels and old chalets. The resort has long been associated with the diverse attractions of finishing schools, health clinics, and cut-price holidays for students and schoolchildren. Today it is also one of the top resorts in Switzerland for snowboarders. The area boasts 60km of piste and 17 lifts. Most of the skiing and riding is in the popular Mayen/Berneuse area, reached by a choice of two cable-cars. There are nursery slopes at the Centre Sportif. Although most of the runs in the ski area are blue (easy), some good off-piste for skiers and freeriders can be found, particularly around Tour d'Ai. Heli-Chablais is the local operation in Leysin (see *Heli-skiing*).

Freestyle riders have a pro quarter-pipe and funpark between Berneuse and Mayen. The SSBS offers morning lessons for adults and all-day ones for children, while the Bureau des Guides organises off-piste excursions. Central Résidence is the local kindergarten, and takes children from two years old.

The all-glass revolving restaurant of Kuklos at Berneuse is said to be 'worth a visit, if only for the views of 29 peaks'. Free buses run regularly throughout the village, but the best-placed accommodation for the skiing is found in the four-star Hotel Classic ('large, comfortable rooms, which are a little overheated') and the simple Bel-Air. La Fromagerie is a cheese restaurant as well as a museum. The town has two sports centres and a handful of bars and nightclubs, including the Top Pub for pool and Club Vagabond which is the cool spot for riders. The resort has an indoor climbing wall, and other activities include ski-joring and go-karting on ice.

TOURIST INFORMATION
Tel 41 24 494 2244
Fax 41 24 494 1616
Email tourism@leysin.ch
Web site www.leysin.ch

Saas-Fee
top 3,600m (11,811ft) bottom 1,800m (5,904ft)

Saas-Fee is a delightfully unspoilt and picturesque resort set against one of the most dramatic glacial backdrops in the Alps. Its narrow streets are lined with some 56 hotels interspersed with ancient barns and chalets of blackened wood. Designer ski shops rub shoulders with working farmhouses where you can buy fresh milk by the pail, even in the centre of the village. Saas-Fee breaks new ground this winter with the introduction of free weekly lift passes for all children under 16, provided both parents buy passes. For 2000–1 this represents a saving of about £186 for a family with three children.

At this high altitude, snow-cover is virtually guaranteed, and the long vertical drop of 1,800m (5,904ft) provides a total of 100km of varied runs. However, these are few in number because the available groomed area is severely limited by the 'active' glaciers. The risk of falling down crevasses is extreme for anyone foolish enough to stray without a local guide: 'the area is so riddled with glacial crevasses that you risk your life if you duck under the rope boundaries'. There are exceptional possibilities for ski-touring, and the local mountain guide association, Bergsteigerschule Saastal, has an impressive programme of ski-tours.

Saas-Fee has been a pioneer in the development of hi-tech ski lifts, and the main mountain access is by the sophisticated Alpin Express cableway and the world's highest underground funicular system, the Metro Alpin. The area boasts 39 lifts, including those at the smaller, separate areas at the nearby villages of **Saas-Almagell**, **Saas-Balen** and **Saas-Grund**.

Five drag-lifts at the bottom of the mountain are part of an excellent nursery-slope complex flanked by a horseshoe of eight of the highest glaciers in Europe. The SSBS in Saas-Fee is run as a co-operative and suffers from poor organisation and overcrowding, especially during peak holiday periods. Inconveniently, weekend and afternoon group lessons are not available.

Snowboarding is big business here, and the SSBS suffers fierce and healthy competition from the refreshingly radical Paradise Snowboard School. The funpark beneath Mittelallalin has a boardercross course, half-pipe and various obstacles. A second, smaller funpark is usually less crowded.

The SSBS Pulvo ski kindergarten takes children from three years old for one and a half hours on weekday afternoons only, and the regular ski school takes children from five years old for weekday mornings only. The Bären-Club in the Hotel Garni Berghof offers all-day care for children from three to six years old.

Saas-Fee is traffic-free. On arrival you must leave your vehicle at the edge of the village in the pay car park, at a cost of SF67 per week. There are no buses, and electric taxis are not readily available. Where you stay is therefore of some importance if you want to avoid a long trek, which could be as much as 2km, to the ski area.

Recommended hotels include the four-star Walliserhof and the Schweizerhof. The four-star Saaserhof is conveniently situated. The extremely comfortable four-star Metropol is one of the oldest and best hotels in town. The Burgener is a small, single-storey family hotel close to the lifts, Hotel Gletschergarten is a cosy chalet-style two-star, and the newly-renovated three-star Hotel Mistral 'deserves high praise'. The Fletschhorn Waldhotel is a remarkable hotel set in the woods above Saas-Fee; it houses an art gallery of modern paintings, sculptures and Persian carpets, all of which are for sale and are on display in every nook and cranny. The Mistral is 'superb and reasonable'. The Allalin is said to be 'very comfortable, very good service, with an excellent restaurant. Worth a visit just to look at the carved chairs in the dining room, some of which have faces, as well as the very imaginative light fittings'.

Recommended mountain restaurants include the rustic Berghaus Plattjen and the Gletschergrotte. The world's highest revolving restaurant at Mittelallalin receives criticism ranging from 'it isn't worth the bother', to 'the worst food at the highest prices'. The Maste 4 Mid-Station has 'the usual cafeteria-style pasta at restaurant prices'.

Village eateries include Hotel La Collina, which has 'sumptuous Mediterranean cuisine'. The Hofsaal in the Schweizerhof is recommended for fish, and the Cheminée for flambées. The Fletschhorn Waldhotel has one of Switzerland's better restaurants. The Crazy Night is the hippest techno venue, with a Chevy on the dance floor and pool tables. Rowdy drinking is frequent at Nesti's Ski Bar. The Go-Inn and the Why-Not pubs are 'essential watering holes'.

TOURIST INFORMATION
Tel 41 27 958 1858
Fax 41 27 958 1860
Email to@saas-fee.ch
Web site www.saas-fee.ch

Villars/Les Diablerets
top 2,979m (9,744ft) bottom 1,128m (3,700ft)

Villars, situated on a sunny balcony above the Ollon Valley, is reached either by a winding road or a quaint Edwardian mountain railway. It has a strong international following as a family resort. The impressive intermediate skiing is linked directly by a quad-chair with the neighbouring resorts of **Gryon** and **Les Diablerets**. Together, the three areas provide 125km of pistes, with four funparks, served by 47 lifts.

Les Diablerets Glacier, reached by a new cable-car, provides high-altitude, snowsure skiing, but can get crowded when conditions are poor in nearby Villars and **Gstaad**. The area is suitable for novices ('the blue runs won't prove intimidating to most beginners') and has mainly intermediate skiing ('the only true black run is Pierres Pointes over at Les Diablerets Glacier'). However, it is especially recommended for its extensive off-piste: 'plenty of easily accessible off-piste, including some good tree skiing'.

The quickest access to the hub of the skiing in Villars is by gondola from the edge of town. A second gondola from the nearby village of **Barboleusaz** also feeds into the system. The nursery slope at Bretaye is gentle, and first-timers quickly graduate to a wide choice of blue runs. A drag-lift connects Bretaye with Roc d'Orsay. A separate ski area, Isenau, offers easy but limited skiing. The resort now has several new lifts: a four-seater chair between Bretaye and Les Chaux offers an easy link between Villars and Gryon, and a six-seater chair runs between Col de Bretaye and Chamossaire.

The SSBS in Villars is commended for its friendly instructors. The Moderne Ski and Snowboard School uses the *ski évolutif* method of teaching beginners. Riderschool is the snowboard specialist. Courses include women's ski clinics and teen skiing. The Villars SSBS children's classes are praised by reporters, and the Pré Fleuri ski kindergarten is said to be 'quite excellent'. La Trotinette is a non-ski kindergarten for children from birth up to six years old. The SSBS has a school in Les

Diablerets, and the New Devil School is for boarding. Bureau des Guides in Les Diablerets is the off-piste guiding company. Hotel Le Chamois in Les Diablerets runs a kindergarten for children aged three to six years old, and the Garderie Les Guignols takes non-skiers from babies to children of 12 years old. Heli-skiing and -boarding (see *Heli-skiing*) is available from both resorts through a choice of three operations: Air Glaciers SA, Heli-Chablais in Leysin, and Flying Devil SA in Lausanne.

The Lac des Chavonnes is one of the great alpine restaurants, in a delightful lakeside setting above Villars; unfortunately it is now only open by reservation outside the busiest weeks. The Col de Soud ('extremely good food') is an attractive chalet with superb views of Les Diablerets Glacier. La Crémaillère in Barboleusaz is a good-value option. Hotel du Lac at Bretaye has 'slow self-service. The table-service is a much better bet and no more expensive'. The self-service at Isenau is rated 'poor – with smelly toilets'.

Hotel Bristol, in the town centre, has a comfortable and modern interior. Hotel du Cerf has 'home-style cooking', and three-star Hotel Elite is convenient for the gondola. The large Eurotel is an eyesore, is criticised for unfriendly staff, but contains 'spacious and clean apartments'. Three-star Hotel du Golf opposite the station is praised by reporters. The Grand Hotel du Parc, which 'easily deserves its five stars; the staff are friendly and helpful and the food is wonderful', contains Le Mazarin, the smartest restaurant in town. Vieux Villars and Café Carnotzet specialise in fondue and raclette.

Les Diablerets is a sprawling village with mainly chalet accommodation. The few hotels seem out of place, but the overall atmosphere is relaxed. The Eurotel, Le Chamois and the Mon Abri hotels are recommended. Dining in Villars takes place in both fine restaurants and informal stüblis, with the Auberge de la Poste and the Buvette du Pillon singled out for praise. Hotel Les Sources is said to be 'incredibly inconveniently located, but clean and friendly'. The nightlife in both Les Diablerets and Villars is quiet and centres around a few bars and discos. Villars has two discos, the Fox and El Gringo; the latter is said to be 'the best club in the Alps'.

TOURIST INFORMATION
Tel (Villars) 41 24 495 3232/ (Les Diablerets) 41 24 492 3358
Fax (Villars) 41 24 495 2794/ (Les Diablerets) 41 24 492 2348
Email (Villars) information@villars.ch (Les Diablerets) info@diablerets.ch
Web site (Villars) www.villars.ch (Les Diablerets) www.diablerets.ch

North America

Canada and the USA provide the main bolt-hole from the frustrations of European skiing and snowboarding that most of us – at times – yearn for, and about 60,000 British snow-users achieve annually. What they find on arrival is a world in which amiable citizens queue peacefully in line for lifts and everyone is intent upon having a good time. North American resorts tend to be owned and operated by a single company. The result is a co-ordinated policy of keeping customers happy.

Prices remain reasonable and it is possible to spend a fortnight staying in luxury accommodation in a resort such as Banff/Lake Louise for less than you would invest in a similar holiday in Zermatt or Courchevel 1850. However, we are frequently told by reporters that their reasons for returning to North America each winter are by no means based on price alone. They point out that after a single visit to North America even the most famous Alpine resorts fail to measure up to their expectations.

Children's facilities are in a different league from those in Europe. Ski instruction places its emphasis on fun, instead of the 'you are here to learn' attitude found particularly in French ski schools. Staff are friendly, and children (we have heard of no exceptions) always want to go back for more. Families tied to taking their skiing holiday during February half-term should seriously consider the transatlantic alternatives to Alpine resorts with their sky-high prices.

Sufficient snow-cover can be expected but by no means guaranteed, except in Canada. Recent winters to the south of the 49th parallel have been blighted by poor early-season cover, with resorts such as Taos and Telluride struggling to open before Christmas and others having to rely almost entirely upon man-made snow until the New Year.

British Airways flights give direct access to Denver for the main US Rocky Mountain resorts such as Breckenridge and Vail. Whistler and Banff/Lake Louise, which still attract the lion's share of business from Britain, are served by direct flights to Vancouver and Calgary. A choice of attractive destinations on the east coast of both countries is reached with a shorter flight time to Boston and Montreal.

In general, the skiing is blander than in Europe, and it is important to note that Americans operate a different colour-coding system: green is easy, blue is intermediate, black is difficult, black-diamond is more difficult or advanced, and double-black-diamond is very difficult.

With the exception of the increasing trend towards chalet holidays, most packages to North America are offered on a room-only basis, and the extra cost of food must be taken into consideration.

Aspen

ALTITUDE 7,945ft (2,422m)

Beginners **✱✱✱** Intermediates **✱✱✱** Advanced **✱✱✱** Snowboarders **✱✱**

Aspen still suffers from its dated image as Hollywood-on-ice, being more of a winter playground for the rich, the famous and the wannabees than a ski resort for serious skiers. Certainly, it continues to attract a handful of big names in showbusiness and sport, some of whom, such as Jack Nicholson, Michael Douglas, Martina Navratilova and Chris Evert-Mill, have made their homes here. What these celebrities have in common is that they are all fanatical skiers. Aspen has some of the best skiing in North America for all standards, from complete beginner to advanced.

> ✔ Excellent children's facilities
> ✔ Attractive Victorian town
> ✔ Wide choice of restaurants
> ✔ Ideal for non-skiers
> ✔ Lively nightlife
> ✔ Shopping opportunities
> ✗ Ski areas not linked
> ✗ High prices

The town's first claim to fame, however, was as a silver-mining centre. The brave and sometimes desperate miners defied vicious weather and marauding Ute indians to set up their first rickety camp in Colorado's Roaring Fork Valley in the late 1870s. During the boom years Aspen's population reached 12,000, and the town was served by two railroads, six newspapers, three schools, ten churches and a notorious red-light district. But by 1893 it was all over; the silver market collapsed, and the town virtually died. It did not start to recover for almost 50 years.

The town of Aspen is situated at the foot of Aspen Mountain – now officially known as Ajax – and today boasts about 200 shops ('I'm sure even platinum card holders could find their credit limits here') and a large variety of restaurants. Planners have managed to conserve the low-rise appeal of the original Victorian mining town; the older buildings have been authentically refurbished, and recent additions are in sympathetic style.

Although considerably larger than most US ski resorts, the centre is relatively compact, and outlying hotels and the ski areas are served by a highly efficient bus service. Celebrity status attracts higher prices, and day-to-day living in Aspen is more expensive than in any of its Colorado counterparts. However, with a little care in your choice of restaurants and nightlife it is still possible to have a moderately-priced holiday.

Snowmass is an alternative and cheaper accommodation base, but having come so far it seems a pity not to partake fully of Aspen's greater facilities. **Aspen Highlands** is currently undergoing significant expansion, making it an important alternative base for those who want to enjoy more off-beat skiing and boarding. It is in the process of developing its own village, with a new restaurant, bars and shops due for completion in time for the 2000–1 season.

Aspen has its own airport, served by flights from Denver, Minneapolis and Phoenix, which must at all times be booked. Eagle County Airport (70 miles away) has direct flights from a number of hub cities.

On the snow
Ajax top 11,212ft (3,418m) bottom 7,945ft (2,422m)
Snowmass top 12,510ft (3,813m) bottom 8,104ft (2,470m)
Aspen Highlands top 11,675ft (3,559m) bottom 8,040ft (2,451m)
Buttermilk top 9,900ft (3,018m) bottom 7,870ft (2,399m)

Aspen has four completely separate mountains: **Ajax**, a name taken from an old mining claim (also known as Aspen Mountain); **Aspen Highlands**; **Buttermilk**; and **Snowmass**, 12 miles (19km) out of town. Ajax is strictly the reserve of good skiers and has no beginner slopes.

Buttermilk is ideal beginners' and children's terrain, with no hidden surprises but plenty of variety for novices. Snowmass, which has skiing for all levels, is the furthest of the separate ski areas from Aspen and is a resort in its own right under the same ownership. Aspen Highlands has the toughest, most radical terrain and greatly adds to Aspen's appeal for advanced skiers.

WHAT'S NEW

New restaurant, bars and shops open for the 2000–1 season at Aspen Highlands

The four mountains are linked by free ski bus. A useful extra is the equipment transfer – at the end of the day you can have your skis or snowboard and boots taken from any of the ski areas to another for a nominal fee, and they will be waiting for you the next morning. As a welcome addition, free coffee, hot (non-alcoholic) cider and biscuits are served at all the information points on the mountain.

Beginners
Buttermilk is one of North America's best mountains for beginners, and Snowmass also has excellent novice slopes. The area below Buttermilk's West Summit is packed with green (easy) runs like Westward Ho and Homestead Road, and more advanced beginners will thrive on a large network of long blue (intermediate) runs. The nursery slopes at Snowmass hug the lower slopes and most are accessed by the Fanny Hill high-speed quad. At Aspen Highlands the main nursery slopes, such as Apple Strudel, Riverside Drive and Nugget, are concentrated mid-mountain and are reached most quickly by the Exhibition quad-chair. The Skiwee lift at the base also serves a small beginner area.

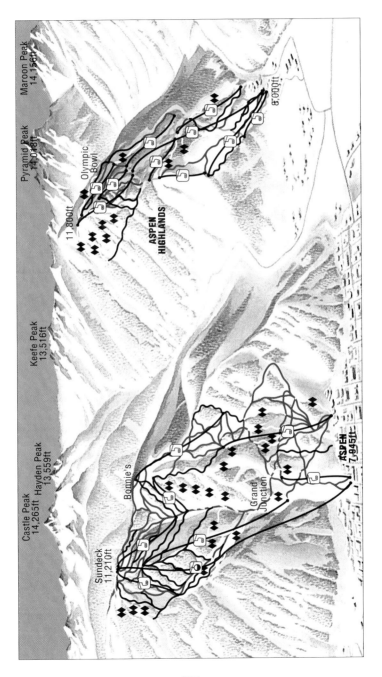

Castle Peak 14,265ft Hayden Peak 13,559ft

Keefe Peak 13,516ft

Pyramid Peak 14,018ft

Maroon Peak 14,156ft

Olympic Bowl

11,800ft

ASPEN HIGHLANDS

8,000ft

Bonnie's

Sundeck 11,210ft

Grand Junction

ASPEN 7,945ft

Intermediates

Among Aspen's four mountains, Snowmass has the largest intermediate appeal. Almost every run mid-mountain and below provides good cruising. Snowmass is famous for its Big Burn area, where a clutch of blue trails separated by a few trees provides almost unlimited scope for cruising. Although the runs have individual names (Whispering Jesse, Timberline, Wineskin, Mick's Gully, etc), the Big Burn is one huge intermediate trail as much as a mile wide in places.

Plenty of strong intermediate skiing with top-to-bottom cruising is found on Ajax ('don't be put off by the tough rating of Ajax. You don't have to ski the bumps'). Straying on to more difficult terrain by mistake is less likely here than at many resorts; most of the black (difficult) runs tend to be hidden away from the main slopes. The best area for middling skiers at Aspen Highlands is near the top of the mountain, where the Cloud Nine lift accesses runs such as Scarlett's, Grand Prix and Gunbarrel. Golden Horn and Thunderbowl offer enjoyable cruising.

Advanced

Ajax is riddled with short, sharp and quite steep double-black-diamond (very difficult) chutes, including the famous 'dump runs' such as Bear Paw, Short Snort and Zaugg Dump, which were created by miners throwing out spoil as they tunnelled their way into the mountain. One reporter warns: 'Watch out for Aztec – it might be groomed but it is pretty steep and can be very hard packed'. Walsh's is considered to be the most challenging. Bell Mountain, a peak that juts out from Ajax, looking as if it has been stuck on, provides excellent opportunities for mogul skiers with its variety of individual faces, including Face of Bell, Shoulder of Bell and Back of Bell.

Much of the skiing at Aspen Highlands falls into the advanced category. The large and challenging gladed area to the left of the Exhibition quad-chair includes Bob's Glade, Upper Stein and Golden Horn Woods, which are all double-black-diamond trails. At Snowmass, real challenges are to be found in the largely gladed chutes in the Hanging Valley Wall and Hanging Valley Glades, and The Cirque has even steeper terrain mainly above the tree-line; access to all of these runs is on the Cirque lift.

Off-piste

Aspen Highlands has some of the most exhilarating off-piste terrain in the valley, much of it accessed by the Loge Peak quad-chair at the top of the ski area. The chair follows a ridge with steep terrain on both sides. As you ride up, a dramatic area known as Steeplechase opens up on your left; this comprises about half-a-dozen steep chutes. On your right is even steeper terrain in Olympic Bowl, although the gradient is not always fully appreciable until you have progressed some way down the slopes. Deception is aptly named; it starts off at a fairly moderate pitch, but the further down you ski, the steeper it becomes. During the past two years new steep areas (called the Y and B Zones) on Highlands

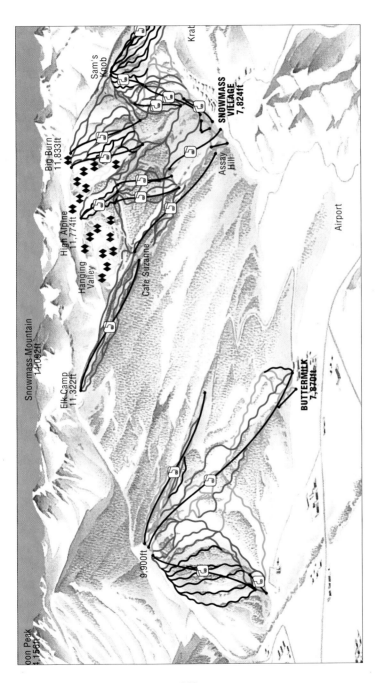

Bowl have been opened, offering some of the most radical terrain of any resort in Colorado.

Snowboarders

Snowboarding is not permitted on the front side of Ajax, but the other three mountains encourage it, especially Buttermilk, which has ideal rolling terrain. All three areas have improved facilities for riders, with additional half-pipes and enlarged terrain parks. Excellent riding – and skiing – can be accessed by snowcat off the back of Ajax through Aspen Mountain Powder Tours.

Tuition and guiding

As well as traditional lessons, the Ski and Snowboard School of Aspen offers biathlon, race-training clinics, skiing for the disabled, women's ski seminars and a variety of other courses. Ski Ambassadors are based on all four mountains to give free mountain tours at 10am and at 1.30pm. Aspen Adventures can organise off-piste tours.

Mountain restaurants

Only in Aspen could you find no less than three mountain restaurants – The Sundeck on Ajax, Bumps at Buttermilk, Gwyn's High Alpine at Snowmass – where you can have a massage along with your lunch at $1 a minute. All of the restaurants are good for eating as well as relaxing. The fourth altitude restaurant at Ajax is Bonnie's ('an intimate place with superb strudel and hot apple dumplings'). Gwyn's, at the bottom of Ruthie's and Roch Run, has table-service. At the base of the Silver Queen gondola the Ajax Tavern serves Mediterranean food.

Snowmass has six restaurants including Up 4 Pizza at the top of the Big Burn lift, which is warmly praised. Ullrhof, at the bottom of the same lift, serves 'a hearty skier's breakfast, and has a wood-burning stove and sun-deck'. Sam's Knob has a new upstairs dining-room called Finestra, complete with white linen tablecloths, which serves North Italian fare. Café Suzanne, at the bottom of the Elk Camp lift, features a southern French menu.

At Aspen Highlands, the Merry Go Round Restaurant at mid-mountain offers home-made soups, chilli and burgers. The Highlands Café is another breakfast and lunch spot at the base. Buttermilk boasts three mountain restaurants: the Café West near the bottom of Lift 3, which is designed in the style of a French café; Bump's, at the base, which includes a rôtisserie and grill; and the Cliffhouse, at the top of the Summit Express, which has some of the best scenery on the mountain. Cloud Nine Café at Highlands serves Austrian specials and offers spectacular views of Pyramid peak.

Accommodation

In Aspen, skiers who can afford to live like celebrities should try the Little Nell and the St Regis, although many people's favourite is the historic Hotel Jerome. Those on limited budgets can try one of the

Skiing facts: Aspen

TOURIST INFORMATION
425 Rio Grande Place, 81611 Aspen, CO 81611
Tel 1 970 925 1220
Fax 1 970 920 0771
Email info@skiaspen.com
Web site www.aspensnowmass.com

THE RESORT
Airport transfer Eagle County Airport 1¼hrs, Aspen Airport 10mins
Visitor beds 17,000 in area
Transport free shuttle bus between all 4 mountains

THE SKIING
Linked or nearby resorts none
Number of lifts 39 in resort
Total of trails/pistes 4,730 acres (1936 hectares) – 16% easy, 40% intermediate, 24% difficult, 20% expert (4 mountains)
Nursery slopes 3 slopes and 2 beginner lifts

LIFT PASSES
Area pass (covers all 4 mountains) $330 for 6 days, $234 for advance bookings by 1 Dec 2000
Beginners free lifts on first day with ski school
Pensioners 65–74yrs 20% reduction, free for 75yrs and over
Credit cards yes

TUITION
Adults Ski and Snowboard School of Aspen tel: 970 925 1227
Snowboarding as regular ski school
Other courses biomechanical alignment, carving, cross-country, moguls, powder clinics, race camps, seniors, skiing for the disabled, snowblading, snowcat skiing and boarding, teen skiing, telemark, women's ski clinics
Guiding Aspen Adventures tel: 970 925 7625

CHILDREN
Lift pass 7–12yrs $198, 13–17yrs $234, both for 6 days, free for 6yrs and under
Ski and board school as adults, and Too Cool For School tel: 970 925 1220
Kindergarten (ski) through ski school, one at each base area tel: 970 925 1227, (non-ski) Kids Room tel: 701 456 7888, Snow Cubs at Snowmass tel: 970 923 1227

OTHER SPORTS
Climbing wall, curling, dog-sledding, hang-gliding, helicopter rides, ice-climbing, indoor tennis and squash, parapente, skating, sleigh rides, snowmobiling, snowshoeing, tubing, swimming

FOOD AND DRINK PRICES
Coffee $2 (free at mountain bases), glass of wine $5, small beer $3.50, soft drink $2, dish of the day $8–15

numerous modestly-priced lodges such as the Limelite. Hotel Durant, St Moritz and the Innsbruck Inn are all recommended. The Aspen Mountain Lodge is a little more expensive but is also praised. The Sardy House is a small Victorian hotel with a friendly atmosphere and excellent cuisine. Top-of-the-range accommodation at Snowmass includes the Silvertree, the Snowmass Club, the Chamonix and Crestwood. More reasonably priced are the Snowmass Mountain Chalet and the Stonebridge Inn. For those counting their cents, the Pokolodi Lodge and the Snowmass Inn are both close to the slopes, as are the Aspenwood and Laurelwood condominiums.

Eating in and out

Aspen has a huge variety of restaurants, with almost every type of cuisine imaginable. Bentley's is a Victorian-style pub and restaurant at the Wheeler Opera House, featuring American food and a selection of 35 beers from around the world.

The Jerome provides excellent fare at its Century Room. The Chart House on East Durant is well known for steaks and seafood. L'Hostaria is an authentic Italian restaurant. Pacifica has a fine selection of seafood and a caviar menu. Aspen has three gourmet Japanese restaurants – Kenichi, Takah Sushi and Matsuhisa, plus a Japanese take-away (Sushi Ya Go-Go). The Hard Rock Café chain has a restaurant here. Sage, in the Snowmass Club, is a bistro serving contemporary Colorado cuisine. La Cucina and The Steak Pit are where you will find lower-priced eating.

Après-ski

Aspen has wall-to-wall après-ski in dozens of nightspots. The Jerome Bar (better known as the J-Bar), where miners once congregated to celebrate when they struck silver, is always lively. The sun-deck at the Ajax Tavern attracts the crowds at the bottom of Ajax when the lifts close. Shooters is a Country-and-Western saloon with live bands. Mezzaluna offers inexpensive beers and pizzas. Aspen Billiards is casually elegant and smoke-free. The Cigar Bar has fine liqueurs and cigars. Club Chelsea attracts a sophisticated clientèle, while the glitterati congregate at the members-only Caribou Club or the 426. The health-conscious can try the Aspen Club's luxurious spa, where the comprehensive range of treatments include acupuncture, yoga, massage and 'body polish'. Going home in The Ultimate Taxi is an après-ski experience in itself. Owner Jon Barnes performs a cabaret act as he drives slowly along telling jokes and playing miniature drums, saxophone or piano while dry ice swirls from the taxi floor. It may sound dangerous, but the town's police give him special dispensation.

Childcare

Aspen has an in-town nursery service (Kids Room) and a kindergarten at each mountain base. At Snowmass, Snow Cubs caters for children aged between six weeks and three years. Older children can join the Big Burn Bears from three-and-a-half or the Grizzlies from five years. At Aspen Highlands, the Snow Puppies occupy skiing children from three-and-a-half years old. The Powder Pandas Ski School at Buttermilk is for kids aged between three and six. Parents can register their children at Ajax for Max the Moose Express to bring them to Buttermilk, where they can take part in The Brave Good Eagle Great Feather Chase and the Max the Moose Challenge race. Older children can join one of the Too Cool For School groups.

Banff/Lake Louise

ALTITUDE 5,350ft (1,631m)

Beginners ✳✳ Intermediates ✳✳✳ Advanced ✳✳ Snowboarders ✳✳

'Banff is an ordinary little tourist resort in mountainous country, with hills and a stream and snow-peaks beyond,' wrote the First World War poet Rupert Brooke a year before his death, 'but Lake Louise – Lake Louise is of another world'. Little has changed. Banff is a small, attractive community with a frontier-town atmosphere, just 10 miles (16km) inside Banff National Park. Apart from the breathtaking scenery, the town is famous for its railway history and wildlife. It is quite common to see elk grazing on vegetation protruding through the snow ('our children saw 120 elk in 10 days').

✔ Spectacular scenery
✔ Reliable snow record
✔ Long skiing season
✔ Extensive children's facilities
✔ Few queues
✘ Distance between ski areas
✘ Extremely low temperatures
✘ Shortage of slopeside lodging

After Canadian Pacific Railways started bringing tourists to Banff to marvel at the scenery, the company built the neo-Gothic Banff Springs Hotel in 1888 and promptly looked for a second site. It found it in a dramatic glacial setting at **Lake Louise**. The magnificent Chateau Lake Louise, Canada's most celebrated hotel, opened its doors in 1890. Lake Louise remains no more than a railway halt; the shopping mall barely constitutes a village. **Sunshine Village** is simply a ski area with nominal accommodation up the mountain and nothing but a snack bar at the bottom.

Today Banff is the most popular destination in North America for British skiers, and no doubt it comes as a surprise to many of them to discover that Banff is not a ski resort at all. Instead it is an attractive little town in the Banff National Park, which each summer plays host to four million tourists, and each winter acts as the main accommodation base for three small (by European standards) ski areas up to 35 miles (56km) apart. Anyone expecting to find hundreds of kilometres of linked skiing on the scale of the Trois Vallées or L'Espace Killy (Val d'Isère/Tignes) is in for a disappointment. However, the region does have sufficient terrain to keep most skiers happy for a 10-day holiday, and even the most jaded of powderhounds could not fail to be impressed by the scenery and the lack of blatant commercialisation.

Charter flights from London and Manchester bring up to 1,000 snow-users a week for bargain-priced skiing amid spectacular scenery. However, the nine-hour flight, two-hour transfer and seven-hour time difference have to be taken into consideration, and it really requires a visit of at least 10 days to adjust and relax fully in such unfamiliar surroundings.

The area has reliable snow conditions, but temperatures on the mountain can be extreme, falling to as low as -40°C for three or four weeks between December and mid-February. 'My wife nearly passed out from the cold on one chair-lift', one reporter commented. The daytime average in the valley at Banff is -7°C in January.

On the snow
top 8,954ft (2,730m) bottom 5,350ft (1,631m)

Lake Louise is the furthest ski area from Banff but is easily the largest and most varied. The skiing begins three miles (5km) from the tiny village of Lake Louise; its 11 lifts attract the majority of daily skiers, who make the bus journey from Banff. Importantly, Lake Louise boasts that every difficult run is matched by an easy one, allowing families and groups of mixed ability to ski together. From the Mount Whitehorn base at Whiskyjack Lodge, the choice of three chair-lifts includes the Friendly Giant Express quad, which takes skiers to mid-mountain at Whitehorn Lodge. From here the Top of The World Express is another high-speed quad, providing the fastest way up and over to the Back Bowls or down to Mount Lipalian's Larch area.

Sunshine Village, 10 miles (16km) from Banff, is the highest of the three resorts and has predominantly medium-length, moderately steep, intermediate terrain above the tree-line. Despite the name, sunshine is not guaranteed and it can be a bleak and cold place on a grey day. Goat's Eye Mountain virtually doubles the size of the ski area and provides more advanced terrain. **Mount Norquay** is four miles (6km) from Banff and is the smallest, mainly beginner, area. However, the development of **Mystic Ridge** has given it more intermediate appeal and it also has its share of steep pitches. A free bus service links Banff with the three resorts ('extremely efficient – one of the drivers provided a detailed description of the wildlife seen along the Trans Canadian Highway, lucidly described all the mountains and told stories about tourist incidents with bear and big-horned sheep').The distances are such that it is not really worth trying to ski more than one area in a day.

Reporters recommend taking time out to visit **Nakiska**, a small ski area situated a one-hour drive from Banff. It was the site of the men's downhill at the Calgary Olympics in 1988: 'beautiful runs planned by computer, immaculately groomed and virtually deserted'. **Fortress Mountain**, a further 30 minutes by bus from Banff, shares a lift pass with Nakiska and is dramatically positioned at the foot of sheer, granite cliffs. Some excellent off-piste can be accessed by snowcat, and Fortress Mountain is particularly popular with snowboarders.

Beginners
Because of Lake Louise's policy of ensuring an easy way down from each major lift, novices can share the pleasure of roaming the mountain

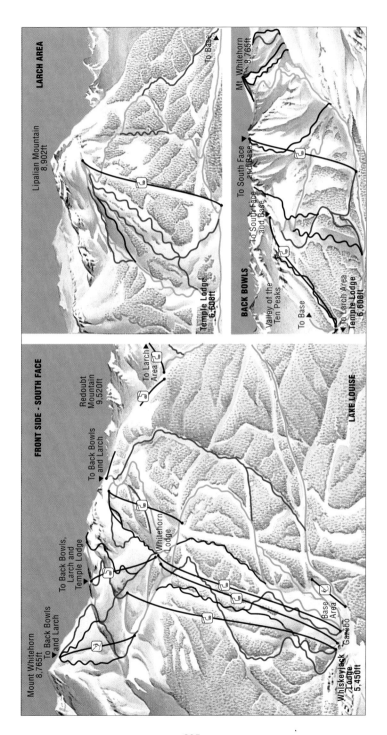

LARCH AREA

Lipalian Mountain
8,902ft

To Base

Temple Lodge
6,608ft

Mt Whitehorn
8,765ft

BACK BOWLS

To South Face
and Base

To South Face
and Base

Valley of the
Ten Peaks

To Base

To Larch Area
Temple Lodge
6,608ft

FRONT SIDE - SOUTH FACE

Mount Whitehorn
8,765ft
To Back Bowls
and Larch

To Back Bowls,
Larch and
Temple Lodge

To Back Bowls
and Larch

Redoubt
Mountain
9,520ft

To Larch
Area

Whitehorn
Lodge

Base
Area

LAKE LOUISE

Whiskeyjack
Lodge
5,450ft

Gondola

almost at will. Although riding high-speed quads could seem daunting in other resorts, here you can board them confidently ('there were loaders to assist who were extremely helpful on the chair-lifts') and meander down the green (easy) Saddleback and Pika trails to the Larch chair. Alternatively, you can warm up on the Sunny T-bar and try skiing the long but gentle Wiwaxy trail, although one reporter warned this can be intimidating when very crowded. Cameron Way is a usually less congested parallel run.

At Sunshine, the best choice of novice runs is served by the Wheeler double chair-lift from the Gondola mid-station. The Strawberry triple-chair and the Standish double-chair also give access to gentle terrain. A long, green trail starts from the top of Lookout Mountain, but in all cases beginners need to take care not to stray accidentally on to neighbouring black (difficult) runs. Beginners at Norquay are recommended to ski the runs off the Cascade quad-chair or the Sundance tow. Norquay has recently spent CDN$1 million on enhancing its beginner terrain.

Intermediates
At Lake Louise, intermediates can clock up huge mileage over all the terrain, with the possible exception of some of the steeper bowls. Skyline is a steepish blue (intermediate) from the high point of the ski area. Larch is a wide, fast-cruising blue. Stronger skiers will want to sample the black-diamond (difficult) Ridge Run and Whitehorn 1 on the Back Bowls side. Most of the runs at Sunshine are within the grasp of intermediates. At Norquay nearly all of Mystic Ridge trails were specifically created for skiers of medium experience.

Advanced
At Lake Louise, the Front Face has challenging men's and women's downhill runs. Other tough black-diamond pistes – Outer Limits, Sunset and the Flight Chutes – start higher up. Ptarmigan and Raven are testing glade runs on the Back Bowls side, and Exhibition has the additional challenge of exposing skiers to the gaze of people riding the Ptarmigan chair. Whitehorn 1 is steep and usually holds the snow; Whitehorn 2 is even steeper. Lynx is the one advanced trail (the others are off-piste) in the Larch area. Fall Line Glades, a 100-acre (40-hectare) area between Exhibition and Ptarmigan provides some of the best tree-skiing in this part of Canada. Lone Pine, which is fiercely steep and mogulled, is the big challenge at Norquay. At Sunshine, runs like Little Angel, Ecstasy and Big Angel offer steep chute skiing from the top of Lookout Mountain and 'stupendous views of the Rockies'. Goat's Eye Mountain has a number of long and tricky runs including Hell's Kitchen and Freefall ('a challenging mogulfield through the trees').

Off-piste
Large areas of the Back Bowls at Lake Louise are permanently closed because of avalanche danger. These are well marked, but sometimes bowls that are normally skiable can be closed too. Paradise Bowl and

East Bowl provide challenging off-piste skiing. Serious powderhounds who do not mind a hike claim Purple Bowl provides the best fresh tracks on the mountain. Some of the most rewarding tree-skiing can be found between the upper parts of the Larch chair and the Bobcat run below. Goat's Eye Mountain has some excellent untracked terrain. After 20 years Delirium Dive has been reopened. The run allows access to a steep bowl with over 600m of vertical with a gradient of up to 40°.

Snowboarders

Riders are catered for with a large funpark, with a quarter-pipe, jumps and table-tops, reached from the Cascade chair-lift at Mount Norquay. Lake Louise has a funpark with a big half-pipe which is reached by the Olympic chair off the Wiwaxy trail. Sunshine is a good freeriding mountain, with plenty of trees. The Club Snowboard programme operates in all three areas. Lake Louise, with its easy runs around the base area, is an excellent place for first-time riders.

Tuition and guiding

All three resorts offer special packages for beginners, which includes equipment rental, a beginner area lift ticket and a half-price pass valid for all areas for the following day, as well as a ski lesson. Instruction at Sunshine is said to be 'friendly and positive'. The Club Ski/Snowboard programme enables skiers to stay with one instructor for three hours a day, visiting all three areas. All the resorts offer a free piste-guiding service, and RK Heli-ski Panorama organises guided trips (see *Heli-skiing*).

Mountain restaurants

Reporters complain that the range and character of mountain eateries do not bear favourable comparison with those in the Alps. Lake Louise's rebuilt Whiskyjack Lodge looks 'better from the outside than the inside'. Another reporter summed up the mountain restaurants as 'utilitarian motorway service station at worst, barn-like at best'. At Lake Louise, The Temple is singled out as the best 'with a nice outdoor terrace, a barbecue, and wait-service upstairs – but the food is nothing special'. Another reporter recommended taking the free bus down to Chateau Lake Louise ('a longer lunch break but the deli is great value').

At Sunshine Village, Mad Trapper's Saloon has 'Tex-Mex, good beer, good atmosphere and unlimited free peanuts'. Norquay's base lodge contains restaurants on both levels as well as a barbecue on the deck outside.

Accommodation

Unfortunately, not everyone has the budget to stay at the two Canadian Pacific hotels. Winter rates are considerably lower than those in summer, but these have inevitably increased because of the rise in resort's global popularity in recent years. However, there is plenty of

Skiing facts: Banff/Lake Louise

TOURIST INFORMATION
Ski Banff/Lake Louise, PO Box 1085, Banff, Alberta
Tel 1 403 762 4561
Fax 1 403 762 8185
Email info@skibanfflakelouise.com
Web site www.skibanfflakelouise.com

THE RESORT
Airport transfer Calgary 1½hrs
Visitor beds 14,846 in Banff/Lake Louise
Transport free ski buses

THE SKIING
Linked or nearby resorts Sunshine Village (n), Mount Norquay (n)
Number of lifts 11 at Lake Louise, 12 at Sunshine Village, 5 at Mount Norquay
Total of trails/pistes 62 miles (100km) at Lake Louise, 52 miles (83km) at Sunshine Village, 10 miles (16km) at Mount Norquay (area: 18% easy, 47% intermediate, 35% difficult)
Nursery slopes 1 lift at Banff, 1 at Lake Louise, 2 at Sunshine Village

LIFT PASSES
Area pass CDN$334 for 6 days
Beginners tow-passes available
Pensioners 65yrs and over, CDN$42 per day
Credit cards yes

TUITION
Adults Banff Mt Norquay tel: 403 762 4421, Club Ski/Snowboard (all areas) tel: 403 762 4561, Lake Louise tel: 403 522 1333, Sunshine Village tel: 403 762 6560
Snowboarding as ski schools
Other courses carving, cross-country, extreme skiing, heli-skiing/heli-boarding, moguls, race-training, seniors, skiing for the disabled, snowblading, telemark, women's clinics
Guiding RK Heli-ski Panorama Inc. tel: 250 342 3889

CHILDREN
Lift pass 6–12yrs, CDN$128 for 6 days, reductions for 13–17yrs
Ski & board schools as adults
Kindergarten (ski/non-ski) as ski schools

OTHER SPORTS
Broomball, canyon ice walks, dog-sledding, ice-fishing, skating, sleigh rides, snowmobiling, snowshoeing, snow volleyball, swimming, tobogganing

FOOD AND DRINK PRICES
Coffee CDN$1.25, glass of wine CDN$4, small beer CDN$3.75, soft drink CDN$1.60—3, dish of the day CDN$9

choice elsewhere. In Lake Louise, the Post Hotel ('an award-winning wine list') and Deer Lodge are both recommended. In Banff, the Mount Royal is conveniently located on Banff Avenue. The King Edward, the town's original hotel, has been completely modernised and is 'surprisingly quiet, with extremely helpful staff'. Caribou Lodge is also recommended. The Inns of Banff ('not within easy walking distance of the town – 20 minutes') has a small indoor swimming-pool and a large hot tub on the roof. Siding 29 Lodge is described as 'a no-frills hotel with large comfortable rooms and a heated underground car park'. Rundle Manor apartments are 'spacious, comfortable, and cheap'. Norquay has opened the Timberline Inn at the base of its access road, and the only on-mountain accommodation at Sunshine is the Sunshine Inn.

Eating in and out

Banff has a surprisingly wide range of restaurants serving cuisine from at least a dozen countries. 'If you haven't been to Bumper's, you haven't been to Banff,' is the motto of Bumper's Beef House. Joe Btfsplk's Diner looks like a misprint but serves 'meals like Mom used to make, including apple pie'. Silver Dragon is Chinese, while Sukiyaki House is one of six Japanese restaurants. El Toro is a Greek restaurant despite its Spanish-sounding name; similarly, the Magpie and Stump is not an English pub but a Mexican cantina. Guido's Spaghetti Factory is long established and has 'good-value Italian food at reasonable prices, so don't be put off by the tatty entrance'. The Barbary Coast has 'plenty of atmosphere and a wide range of dishes including vegetarian options'. Melissa's serves fish steaks and 'potent home-brewed ale'. Caboose Steak and Lobster at the railway depot is 'superb in every way'.

In Lake Louise The Post Hotel and Deer Lodge are warmly recommended for some of the best food in the region: 'pleasant décor and good service – Canadian fine dining at its finest'. In Lake Louise, The Station, which was used as a location for *Dr Zhivago*, is warmly praised: 'absolutely delightful, try to book into the old Victorian Canadian Pacific dining car'. Chateau Lake Louise has a multiple choice of restaurants.

Après-ski

One reader described Banff's nightlife as 'refreshingly unsophisticated, plenty of cowboy bars and line dancing'. Another said it reminded him of Söll in his youth: 'after dinner the streets get busy with Brits and Germans noisily moving from bar to bar'. There is rock 'n' roll at Eddy's Back Alley, country-rock at Wild Bill's, blues at The Barbary Coast, live entertainment at Bumper's, and live bands at the Silver City Beverage Co. The Caboose has karaoke. The Rose and Crown is one of Banff's most popular bars. Constables and the Mount Royal have 'pitchers of beer and lots of atmosphere'. The nightlife at Lake Louise is largely confined to drinking in the Glacier Saloon at the Chateau. Charlie Two's Pub and the Outpost in the Post Hotel are the alternatives, along with the disco at the Lake Louise Inn.

Childcare

This is a great place for children who can stand the low temperatures. At Lake Louise, the nursery takes babies from three weeks old. The Kinderski programme is geared for three to six year olds. There is also a Club Ski programme, where children are guided around the mountain with instruction along the way ('class sizes excellent, the instructors were exceptionally friendly and the attitude was as much about having fun as learning to ski'). At Sunshine Village and Mount Norquay, daycare is for toddlers from 18 months.

Beaver Creek

ALTITUDE Beaver Creek 8,100ft (2,470m)

Beginners ✱✱✱ Intermediates ✱✱✱ Advanced ✱ Snowboarders✱✱

Beaver Creek is an elegant family resort situated at the end of a private road, a 20-minute drive from its sister resort of Vail. The two are under the same giant corporate ownership and share a ski school and other mountain facilities, but there the similarity ends. While Vail is big and brash, Beaver Creek is more compact, with an intimate atmosphere and plenty of slopeside accommodation that enhances its appeal to families.

✔ Favourable snow record
✔ Family-friendly resort
✔ Excellent ski school
✔ Easy introduction to off-piste
✘ Limited choice of mountain restaurants
✘ High prices

Like most other Colorado resorts, Beaver Creek first staked its claim to fame through gold, although it is far more successful now than it ever was as a mining village. James Lyon and Frederick Westlotom first struck pay-dirt here in 1881, but their Aurora mine never produced a decent strike, and the settlers who followed the miners fared little better in their attempts to farm the land. After its rebirth as a ski resort, ex-US president Gerald Ford made his home here and helped to put it on the world map. Today Beaver Creek exudes an air of sophistication and wealth, and the excellent childcare facilities consistently win it awards as one of America's top family resorts. The nearby valley town of Avon houses most of the workforce in the region and has a wider range of shops.

Reporters praise Beaver Creek as 'very smart and friendly – we were offered cookies while waiting in the lift queue, and escalators carry you up from the bus stop to the base of the lifts'. Multi-day lift passes can be used at Vail, and also at **Arapahoe Basin**, **Breckenridge** and **Keystone**. A regular subsidised shuttle service operates between the resorts.

On the snow
top 11,440ft (3,488m) bottom 8,100ft (2,469m)

The substantial ski area of 146 tree-lined trails on undulating scenic terrain is served by a network of 17 lifts on four mountains. The skiing includes the linked villages of Bachelor's Gulch and Arrowhead, in the nearest approximation you will find in the United States to the ubiquitous European ski circuit. Main mountain access from Beaver Creek is by the high-speed Centennial Express chair, which takes you up to Spruce Saddle, the mid-mountain station. From here the Birds of Prey

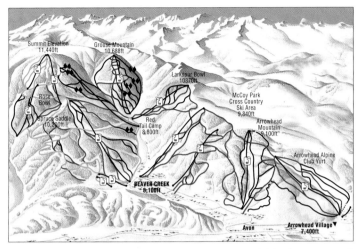

Express chair continues on to Summit Elevation, the highest point of the ski area. A number of green (easy) and double-black-diamond (very difficult) runs lead down to a choice of lifts as you progress further into the ski area. The Strawberry Park Express and Elkhorn lifts also give access from Beaver Creek. You can also take the Bachelor's Gulch Express from Bachelor's Gulch or the Arrow Bahn Express from Arrowhead, and work your way along the adjoining mountains.

Beginners
The beginner areas are at the base of the Centennial Express lift, at the top of the Stump Park lift, and at Arrowhead. Once the basic techniques have been mastered, novices can ascend to Summit Elevation, from where green (easy) runs including Red Buffalo, Jack Rabbit Alley, and Booth Gardens all lead gently down to the Drink of Water lift, providing the easiest introduction to linked-turn skiing amid delightful high mountain scenery. Flat Tops, Powell and Piney all lead on to Cinch, a green run that allows beginners to reach Spruce Saddle and the more low-altitude runs off the Haymeadow lift, before returning to the resort. One reporter recommended setting off from Arrowhead and concentrating turns on the lower half of Smooth Moose.

Intermediates
Long, cruising intermediate trails are the hallmark of Beaver Creek's skiing. The cross-mountain journeys to Bachelor's Gulch and Arrowhead enable you to feel you are going somewhere for the day in the European-style of the Trois Vallées, rather than the more usual American experience of skiing variations of the same terrain over and over again. Grubstake and Gunders (off the Bachelor's Gulch Express) and Golden Bear, reached by the Arrow Bahn Express, are favourites with reporters. Stone Creek Meadows is a wide, fast trail that runs from

Spruce Saddle to the bottom of the Rose Bowl and it is usually uncrowded. Harrier and Centennial are both enjoyable fall-line runs from Spruce Saddle to the resort, but reporters point out that both have black (difficult) sections ('however, neither should pose a problem for anyone who can ski a European red run with even a modicum of confidence'). Raven Ridge on Grouse Mountain, served by the Grouse Mountain Express, is similarly graded on its lower section, 'but the less confident can always cut skier's right and join the easier lower half of Golden Eagle'. The Larkspur lift also accesses some pleasant intermediate runs. From the top you can make your way across to the trails served by the Strawberry Park Express.

Advanced
The most challenging terrain is found on Grouse Mountain. Screech Owl and Osprey are usually heavily mogulled. Royal Elk Glades is a steep double-black-diamond (very difficult) run from the top of the mountain. Golden Eagle, from the top of the Birds of Prey Express, is the upper part of Beaver Creek's World Cup downhill course, which even when not prepared for racing can provide a demanding test of technical skills. One reporter said he spent 'almost my entire holiday' here and on the adjoining Peregrine and Goshawk double-black-diamonds. The Rose Bowl lift also serves a choice of black (difficult) runs including Ripsaw, Spider and Cataract.

Off-piste
Vail, 10 miles (16km) away, is famous for its off-piste opportunities in the ungroomed Back Bowls. Early in the morning on big powder days, the local powder hounds come over to Beaver Creek. They are headed for Grouse Mountain, which provides some truly spectacular runs between the trees and along the edge of the ski area boundary. All runs lead down into the gulch, where a path brings you back to the bottom of the lift. Free mountain tours are run by the resort at weekends.

Tuition and guiding
The Beaver Creek Ski and Snowboard Center is part of the impressive Vail/Beaver Creek Center. Here it is based at Village Hall and on the mountain at Spruce Saddle. We have continuing favourable reports: 'I learned much more in a week than I have ever done in Europe.' However, another reporter complained at the cost: '$95 a day seemed really excessive compared to what I paid in Italy, but I think it was probably worth it.' The Center offers one of the largest skiing for the disabled programmes in North America.

Snowboarders
Beaver Creek is, according to one visiting rider, 'much too quiet and expensive'. Nevertheless, it does boast seven dedicated snowboard trails through chutes and gullies, and two half-pipes on Moonshine. Stickline Park between Harrier and Centennial has a combination of

tabletops, banks and log slides. Mystic Isles is a funpark for beginners situated at the top of the Birds of Prey Express. A separate snowboard map at the resort shows riders how to avoid flat paths.

Mountain restaurants

Due to the well-heeled nature of its clientèle, Beaver Creek takes lunch more seriously than many American resorts – but unfortunately the public are unable to share the best part of it. Beano's Cabin has the pick of the cuisine, but at lunchtime it remains a members-only private club. The same applies to Zach's Cabin and Allie's Cabin. Spruce Saddle Lodge is the main self-service ('great buffalo chilli and a highly acceptable pizza'). Rafters at Spruce Saddle has 'good food at reasonable prices, but you have to book. The service is cheerful but desperately slow'. Redtail Camp, at the finish of the Birds of Prey downhill course, has an indoor and outdoor barbecue. Gundy's Camp in Bachelor's Gulch also has a barbecue. The Broken Arrow Café in Arrowhead has 'home-made soup and enormous club sandwiches'.

Accommodation

The Hyatt Regency, with its impressive lobby complete with vast log fire and enormous elk horn chandelier, is situated on the edge of the piste in the village centre and caters in style for its opulent guests ('staff put my skis on the snow at the start of the day and took them away when I arrived back in the afternoon. The only thing I had to do was the actual skiing'). The Charter is equally luxurious, with condominiums as well as rooms. The Inn at Beaver Creek is adjacent to the Strawberry Park lift ('great comfort and a wonderful outdoor pool'). The Post Montane Lodge is 'small and comfortable'. Trapper's Cabin is an exclusive hideaway in the woods, reached only on skis or by snowmobile.

Eating in and out

Allie's, Beano's and Zach's, which are closed by day to the public, are open by night to all; though you cannot help but wonder whether diners are drawn by the restaurants' daytime exclusivity. In the case of Beano's, dinner involves a sleigh ride behind a diesel-belching snowcat ('the food was at best average'). Splendido at the Chateau is 'the ultimate in fine dining American-style, at a cost you would expect'. The Mirabelle is at the entrance to the resort ('best elk I have ever tasted'). Toscani is Italian and 'an altogether less formal and more tasty option in relaxed surroundings'. The Blue Moose is a budget pizzeria.

Après-ski

The Rendezvous Bar and Grill serves 'wicked Martinis'. The Coyote Café and Dusty Boot Saloon capture the main crowd, along with McCoy's and the Overlook Bar at the Hyatt. Cassidy's at Avon caters to a more culturally and financially diverse clientèle. The Black Family Ice Rink is open until 10pm. All the major hotels have spas, not least Allegria at the Hyatt Regency.

Skiing facts: Beaver Creek

TOURIST INFORMATION
PO Box 7, Vail, CO 81658
Tel 1 970 496 6772
Fax 1 970 479 2905
Email international@vailresorts.com
Web site www.beavercreek.com

THE RESORT
Airport transfer Eagle Country 45mins, Denver 2½hrs
Visitor beds 41,305 in Beaver Creek and Vail
Transport bus between Beaver Creek, Breckenridge, Keystone and Vail (nominal charge)

THE SKIING
Linked or nearby resorts Arapahoe Basin (n), Breckenridge (n), Copper Mountain (n), Keystone (n), Vail (n)
Number of lifts 17
Total of trails/pistes 1,625 acres (658 hectares) – 34% easy, 39% intermediate, 27% difficult
Nursery slopes 3

LIFT PASSES
Area pass $174–210 (tour operator rates), $234–342 (ticket window rates), both for 6 days (covers Arapahoe Basin, Breckenridge, Keystone and Vail)
Beginners no free lifts
Pensioners free for 70yrs and over
Credit cards yes

TUITION
Adults Beaver Creek Ski and Snowboard Center tel: 970 845 5300
Snowboarding as ski school
Other courses bumps, carving, cross-country, powder clinics, race camps, seniors, skiing for the disabled, teen programmes, telemark, women's ski courses

CHILDREN
Lift pass 5–12yrs, $126 (tour operator rate), $114–222 (ticket window rates), both for 6 days. Free for 4yrs and under
Ski & board school Beaver Creek Ski and Snowboard Center tel: 970 845 5464
Kindergarten (ski) Beaver Creek Ski and Snowboard Center (non-ski) Small World Play School tel: 970 845 5325

OTHER SPORTS
Basketball, climbing-wall, dog-sledding, hang-gliding, horse-riding, hot-air ballooning, ice climbing, ice-fishing, ice-hockey, indoor climbing wall, indoor tennis and squash, skating, sleigh rides, snowbiking, snowmobiling, snowshoeing, swimming, tubing

FOOD AND DRINK PRICES
Coffee $2, glass of wine $5, small beer $3.50, soft drink $3, dish of the day $15

Childcare
Beaver Creek ranks as one of the top US resorts for families ('one of the best resorts we've ever been to with our children'). It has a pedestrianised centre and an excellent ski school. The Small World Play School is the non-skiing kindergarten. The Children's Ski and Snowboard Center is for three- to thirteen-year-olds and is based at Village Hall along with the adult classes. Arrowhead has learn-to-ski or -snowboard programmes. Spruce Saddle has a dedicated playpark for children.

Breckenridge

ALTITUDE 9,600ft (2,927m)

Beginners ✱✱✱ Intermediates ✱✱✱ Advanced ✱ Snowboarders ✱✱✱

Breckenridge was the beachhead for the British skiers' invasion of America in the 1980s. In the heart of the Rockies and boasting the infrastructure of a small city as well as the restored charm of an old mining 'boom town', Breckenridge remains a leader in the evolution of American skiing and snowboarding; it was the first resort in Colorado to permit snowboarders. These days Breckenridge is under the same ownership as **Beaver Creek**, **Keystone** and **Vail** – consequently it has benefited from the huge sums of money that Vail Resorts is continuing to invest in its portfolio of resorts.

> ✔ Good base for visiting other resorts
> ✔ Attractive town centre
> ✔ Choice of dining and après-ski
> ✔ Range of ski school courses
> ✔ Reliable snow record
> ✘ Peak period overcrowding
> ✘ High altitude can cause sickness
> ✘ Skiing exposed to weather

The four resorts share a lift pass, along with nearby **Arapahoe Basin** (A-Basin), and are served by a heavily subsidised shuttle bus. Nearby **Copper Mountain** was not included in the buy-out but was soon snapped up by Canadian resort developer Intrawest and provides alternative and enjoyable terrain if you can find the time.

Breckenridge is a bustling town which prides itself on accommodating 24,000 snow-users among its 254 restored structures downtown (which date from 1859) and in its self-contained resort/shopping complexes closer to the slopes. It is the oldest continually occupied community in Colorado and has embraced conservation with a fervour that European visitors might regard as verging on the kitsch or over-cute. However, international visitors, who exceed 10 per cent of all snow-users, are courted ardently.

The extremely low humidity and altitudes in excess of 12,000ft (3,937m) can cause dehydration and headaches – made worse by exercise – which can be avoided by resting, drinking plenty of water and abstaining from alcohol. 'We were constantly out of breath even though two of us are regular gym users and so pretty fit,' was one comment. Reporters also complained of the cold: 'alternative name could be Breckenfridge'.

Skiing began here in 1961, on Peak 8, and expanded a decade later to Peak 9; Peak 10 opened in 1985, and Peak 7 in 1993. A total of 14 chair-lifts and nine drag-lifts carry over 30,000 snow-users per hour to 138 well-manicured pistes and half-a-dozen wilderness bowls spread across 2,043 acres (822 hectares). Complaints about both the early closing of the pistes (the higher lifts as early as 3.30pm) and over-crowding in town and on the mountain are common.

Breckenridge was the first resort in the world to install a high-speed detachable quad chair-lift (it now has six) and in the 1999–2000 season it opened a double-loading six-person chair-lift. However, one reporter complained that two chair-lifts, including one you have to take to reach Peak 7, have no safety bar: 'there was no way I could take my fidgety six-year-old, and I have a slight phobia about heights'.

The resort has responded to demands from American skiers for more 'European-style off-piste terrain' by opening huge, above-tree-line bowl areas to skiers – who must prove their stamina and determination to ski such steeps by first walking uphill, which is not easy at this height. Long criticised for its unchallenging intermediate terrain, the resort now successfully exploits its high altitude and ample natural snow to attract hard-core snowboarders and telemark skiers, as well as the spoilt-for-choice Denver market, who arrive by the thousands with each substantial snowfall.

On the snow
top 12,998ft (3,962m) bottom 9,600ft (2,927m)

Breckenridge's skiing – exceptionally high-altitude by Alpine standards – fans out above the town from left to right across four interconnected mountains, numbered from 7 to 10, in the Ten Mile Range of the Rockies. Most skiing faces roughly north, exposed to weather that gives the resort its nickname 'Breckenwind'.

Skiing is mostly below tree-level, and Peaks 7 and 8 require 30- to 60-minute climbs to reach their summits. Peaks 8 (intermediate to expert) and 9 (beginner to intermediate) account for most of the resort's groomed skiing, sharing about the same lift capacity and number of runs, though Peak 8 has double the amount of skiing terrain. Peak 10 has only one lift, and Peak 7 has none, thus truly proving the original Edwardian dictum that there is no downhill gain without uphill pain.

Actual skiing and snowboarding experiences range from 'wide, well-groomed, relatively easy runs,' through scenically forested, flat slopes at the resort base, to steeps and deeps ('heavily mogulled') in the ample chutes above tree-level – as good as anything in the Alps – on Peaks 7 and 8.

Beginners
Advanced snow-users' dismay is beginner's luck: vast tracts of the lower slopes are as flat as a pancake. At least half of Peak 9 is beginner terrain, with strictly enforced slow-skiing zones. On Peak 8, chairs 5 and 7 access half-a-dozen beginner runs that are effectively barred to faster skiers. All this beginner terrain is beautifully dotted with widely spaced trees.

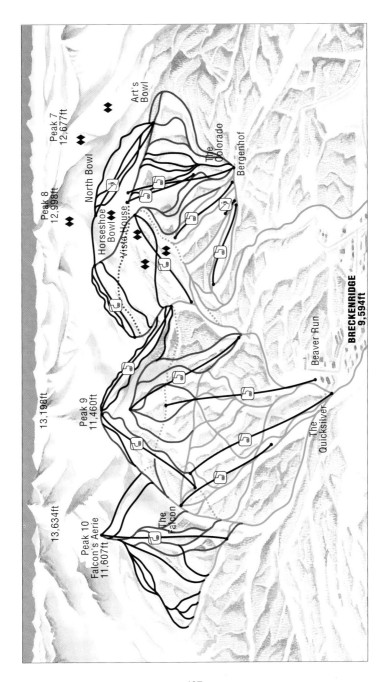

Art's Bowl

Peak 7
12,677ft

The Colorado

Bergenhof

Peak 8
12,998ft

North Bowl

Horseshoe
Bowl

Vista House

13,198ft

BRECKENRIDGE
9,594ft

Beaver Run

Peak 9
11,460ft

The
Quicksilver

13,634ft

Peak 10
Falcon's Aerie
11,607ft

The
Falcon

Intermediates

Peak 9 is medium-standard cruising, marked as blue (intermediate) and green (easy) from top to bottom. There is an intermediate way down from everywhere except for the Peak 8 T-bar. Union connects Peak 10 to Peak 9, and subsequently Peak 8, from the top. Four O'Clock and Lehman are long, easy ways home from Peaks 8 and 9 respectively.

Advanced

The best advanced skiing in Breckenridge is accessed from Chair 6 and the Peak 8 T-bar, both of which offer skiing above 11,480 (3,500m). From the T-bar to the skier's right are six black (difficult) runs in the North Bowl area. To the skier's left, just past the warming hut, are Horseshoe, Contest and Cucumber bowls, all marked double-black-diamond (very difficult) but all wide open and less than threatening. A dozen marked chutes in the Way Out sector below the Lake Chutes feed into the black Psychopath trail under Chair 6 for a ride up Chair E to the longest-lasting powder on the mountain in the 41 acres (17 hectares) of the North Chutes.

Off-piste

Piqued by its reputation for less than adrenaline-inducing skiing, Breckenridge has in the past few years gone to extremes and opened (when safety conditions permit) the Lake Chutes sector, which offers 20 acres (8 hectares) of 656-vertical-feet (200-vertical-metre) pitches of up to 50 degrees. The Lake Chutes can be accessed by climbing some 820 vertical feet (250 vertical metres) to the top of Imperial Bowl on Peak 8 from the top of the Horseshoe Bowl T-bar. Less taxing is the climb of 492 vertical feet (150 vertical metres) from the same spot to the summit of Peak 7 for the open, untracked Whale's Tail, Peak 7 and Art's bowls. It is also possible to cheat on the climb by traversing into the lower sectors of these bowls from the T-bar.

Snowboarders

Freestylers are well served here with two popular funparks and half-pipes; of these the Gold King funpark on Peak 9 has some impressive jumps. Easily accessed bowls and chutes make Breckenridge hugely popular with boarders, who voted the resort's facilities the best in North America. Away from groomed runs, boarders vastly outnumber skiers, especially on powder days.

Tuition and guiding

Breckenridge Ski School is big – 600 instructors – but diversified, with specialised clinics such as the 50-plus seminars (taught by oldies for oldies), women's workshops, and teen-only programmes. Instructors try their hardest, as work is assigned according to reports of client satisfaction ('classes were typically small: three students with a maximum of about eight'). However, not all reports are favourable: 'the instructor knew his stuff and was friendly but confused us by throwing too many ideas into the ring'. The ski school runs an off-piste course for women called Babes in the Backcountry. Snowboarding is big here, and the school teaches everything 'from carving and riding to busting out of the half-pipe'.

Mountain restaurants

Falcon's Aerie on Peak 10 is little more than a warming hut that serves cold fare for skiers on the move. Peak 9's eponymous eatery exhausts the shortlist of high-altitude dining spots, as well as the patience of skiers queuing for cafeteria fodder. Down below, American blueberry muffins, burritos and 'salads by the pound are on offer at Bergenhof at the base of Peak 8. Ten Mile Station restaurant ('has a lovely large deck and does BBQs when weather permits') is at the base of Peak 10.

Accommodation

Nearly all the accommodation in Breckenridge is non-smoking and much of it is within a five-minute walk of the lifts. Most convenient for the lifts are the huge shopping and hotel complexes of the Beaver Run Resort, the Great Divide Lodge (formerly the Hilton) and the Village at Breckenridge, in descending order of altitude. All of these attract large conference groups, as does the Lodge & Spa outside the Breckenridge town limits. Restored 'Victorian' houses featuring bed-and-breakfast accommodation include the romantic Williams House, furnished with American antiques, and the Evans House, which are both downtown. Hunt Placer Inn is a European chalet-style bed-and-breakfast. Aspenglade Cabin is a rustic out-of-town retreat. The Safari Ranch and Muggins Gulch Inn, set in 160 acres (65 hectares) of land, are also out of town. Budget accommodation includes the family-oriented Breckenridge Wayside Inn and the old-fashioned Ridge Street Inn. The town has a free bus service.

Eating in and out

Breckenridge has a lot of places to eat in (more than 50) but beware of local advice, as Americans often confuse kitsch décor – impossible to escape in Breckenridge – with decent cuisine. Reservations are essential and are unlikely to be honoured if you are so much as 15 minutes late. Casual dining favours Mexican cuisine at Mi-Casa ('lively atmosphere, but the service is a bit familiar'). Spicy Louisiana Cajun fare can be found at Poirrier's. Fatty's and the Village Pasta Company offer exotic pizzas. The Bamboo Garden provides respectable Szechwan and Mandarin food.

Café Alpine ('a bit of an event') has won several local gourmet awards, but Pierre's River Walk Café is the sole 'real' French restaurant, eclipsed only by the Top of the World restaurant at the Lodge & Spa, where the red deer carpaccio and buffalo-stuffed pasta are exquisite. Downstairs at Eric's describes itself correctly as 'Breckenridge's most outrageous beer hall and pizza joint'. The Hearthstone is praised for its 'interesting menu'. Bubba Gump's Seafood has 'a lively, busy

Skiing facts: Breckenridge

TOURIST INFORMATION
PO Box 1058, Breckenridge,
CO 80424
Tel 1 970 496 6772
Fax 1 970 479 2905
Email international@vailresorts.com
Web site www.breckenridge.com

THE RESORT
Airport transfer Denver International
2hrs, Eagle County 1hr
Visitor beds 24,000
Transport free bus throughout resort.
Shuttle bus to Beaver Creek, Keystone
and Vail

THE SKIING
Linked or nearby resorts Arapahoe
Basin (n), Beaver Creek (n), Copper
Mountain (n), Keystone (n), Vail (n)
Number of lifts 23
Total of trails/pistes 2,043 acres (822
hectares) – 14% easy, 26%
intermediate, 60% difficult
Nursery slopes children's areas at the
Village Center, Beaver Run and Peak 8
Children's Center

LIFT PASSES
Area pass $174–210 (through tour
operator), $174–276 (ticket window
rates), both for 6 days (covers A-Basin,
Beaver Creek, Keystone and Vail)
Beginners no free lifts
Pensioners no reduction through tour
operator, 65–69yrs, $162–222 (ticket

window rates) for 6 days. Free for
70yrs and over
Credit cards yes

TUITION
Adults Breckenridge Ski and Snowboard
School (3 centres) tel: 888 496 7201
Snowboarding as ski school
Other courses Babes in the
Backcountry, bumps, carving, cross-
country, extreme skiing, family ski clinics,
moguls, race-training, seniors, skiing for
the disabled, teen programmes, telemark,
women's seminars
Guiding through ski school

CHILDREN
Lift pass 5–12yrs, $126 (through tour
operator), $102–126 (ticket window
rates), both for 6 days
Ski & board school as adults
Kindergarten (ski/non-ski)
Breckenridge Children's Centers tel:
970 496 3258

OTHER SPORTS
Climbing wall, dog-sledding, horse-
riding, hot-air ballooning, ice-fishing,
indoor tennis, racquet-ball, skating,
sleigh rides, snowmobiling,
snowshoeing, swimming

FOOD AND DRINK PRICES
Coffee $1.80, glass of wine $6, small
beer $3, soft drink $1.80, dish of the
day $12–18

atmosphere with food ranging from good to nasty', and Ullr's
Sports Grill is described as having 'unpleasant surroundings and poor
food'. Spencer's at Beaver Run is said to be 'good for surf and turf, but
the wine was disappointing'. Sushi Breck ('the best food in
Breckenridge and the cheapest sushi that we have encountered
anywhere') is informal and good value.

Après-ski

Breckenridge is renowned as a 'party town'. 'Really friendly, even by American standards' is a frequent comment on the Breckenridge crowd, the rowdier section of which is to be found in the cheerfully seedy surroundings of Shamus O'Toole's Roadhouse Saloon. The Underworld Club is popular with snowboarders, and the Gold Pan is a typical 'cowboy' bar. Breckenridge Brewery attracts a tumultuous throng. More sophisticated – and pretentious – is Cecilia's Cigar Parlor, which is the only smoking zone in town. The Back Stage Theatre is strictly amateur but entertaining. Tiffany's Nightclub has cheap drinks and techno. The Alligator Lounge presents live reggae, rock and blues acts of some note seven nights a week.

The resort is chock-a-block with boutiques, art galleries and ski shops. Scores of designer discount shops can also be found in the nearby factory outlet centres of Frisco and Silverthorne.

Childcare

Advance reservations are advisable for either of the base-area kindergarten at Peaks 8 and 9. The former accepts infants as young as two months, and the latter children from three years of age. Both have pagers for parents to hire, provide lunches and offer a non-skiing, outdoor snow-play programme. The children's learning area has two 'magic carpet' conveyor belts. Children from three years old can join ski school through the Children's Centers, and five-year-olds attend regular ski school. The children's ski school is praised by reporters: 'the ski school was friendly – always a welcoming party for the children before the lesson, therefore no tears,' and 'I would definitely recommend Breckenridge to families with children who require warm coaxing into having lessons'. The school also runs a teens-only programme.

Jackson Hole

ALTITUDE 6,311ft (1,924m)

Beginners ✱✱   Intermediates ✱✱   Advanced ✱✱✱   Snowboarders ✱✱✱

Jackson Hole is the Jerusalem of skiing and snowboarding, the pilgrimage point to which all true adherents to the faith must finally travel to pay their obeisance to the god of snow. In this remote corner of Wyoming the snow-capped Tetons rise like jagged shark's teeth from the valley floor with no foothills to reduce their visual impact. Grand Teton, the greatest of these, soars towards the heavens – the equivalent of seven Eiffel Towers stacked one on top of the other. This optical feast assails you even before you leave the aircraft at Jackson Hole Airport. What appears to be a toytown landing strip, fringed by 8,000 grazing elk in their winter refuge and the odd moose, is in fact served by jet airliners from Denver, Salt Lake City, Chicago and Los Angeles.

- ✔ Cowboy-town atmosphere
- ✔ Lively nightlife
- ✔ Ideal for non-skiers
- ✔ Beautiful scenery
- ✔ Attractive town
- ✔ Well-run kindergarten
- ✘ Distance from town to slopes
- ✘ Short ski season
- ✘ Remote location

A 15-minute car-ride from the airport takes you into the quaint cowboy town of Jackson. Jet-lagged visitors assume that the steeped groomed trails immediately above it are their ski destination, but this mountain is the small and entirely separate resort of **Snow King**. Jackson Hole Ski Resort is located a further 20-minute drive away at Teton Village on the far side of the Snake River, an enticing trout stream that coils across the valley floor. This leaves you with a dilemma of where to base yourself. Both places have hotels of equal standard, but the convenience of doorstep skiing in Teton Village has to be weighed against the shops, restaurants and nightlife of Jackson. Others have tried, but only Jackson – and Telluride on a smaller scale – has succeeded in welding the dusty gun-slinging charisma of a Western frontier town to the high-tech facilities of a modern ski resort.

In summer Jackson plays host to two million visitors, who arrive by camper van en route to Yellowstone Park and Old Faithful, the world's largest geyser. In the winter it returns to its natural state, a basically authentic cattle town complete with wooden boardwalks and shops selling Western clothing. The central square is crowned by a triumphal arch made from thousands of naturally discarded elk antlers. Late-night revellers returning from the Million Dollar Cowboy Bar with a skinful of bourbon should not be surprised to happen upon the occasional former four-legged owner roaming the streets.

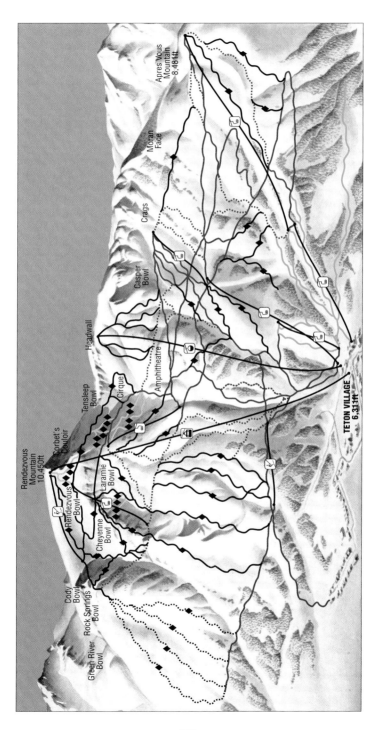

Apres Vous Mountain 8,481ft

Moran Face

Crags

Casper Bowl

Headwall

Tensleep Bowl

Cirque

Amphitheatre

Corbet's Couloir

Rendezvous Mountain 10,450ft

Rendezvous Bowl

Laramie Bowl

Cheyenne Bowl

Cody Bowl

Rock Springs Bowl

Green River Bowl

TETON VILLAGE 6,311ft

Working ranches still surround the town, and horses are the secondary means of transport behind the four-wheel-drive.

Teton Village has doubled in size in recent years, but it still only amounts to a few hotels and a couple of ski shops clustered around a picturesque clock tower and the Bridger Center base lodge. A regular 20-minute bus service connects with Jackson, but a rental car is recommended.

On the snow
top 10,450ft (3,186m) bottom 6,311ft (1,924m)

Jackson Hole has one of the longest continual vertical drops in the USA (the longest is now in Snowmass, Colorado). The skiing takes place on two adjoining mountains, steep Rendezvous and much more benign Apres Vous. In the past you needed to be either an expert or a complete beginner to enjoy the experience. Anyone in between risked having their confidence slaughtered by the daunting steepness of the rugged terrain. However, more intermediate trails have been introduced to satisfy commercial demand.

While other North American resorts make do with three colour codings for the degree of difficulty of their ski trails, Jackson needs five. Its hardcore of devoted fans around the world see Rendezvous as one of the last wild frontiers of macho mountainside, a place where 'a man's gotta ski what a man's gotta ski', and a place where powderhounds compete for the number of vertical feet they can clock up in a day, in a season or indeed, in a lifetime. Its ancient lifts, including an antique tram (cable-car), were all part of the legend.

A change of ownership has brought considerable innovations in recent years. A high-speed gondola up Headwall gives access to 90 per cent of the ski terrain without the necessity of having to queue for the tram that still runs to the top of the mountain. The old fixed double and triple chair-lifts are gradually being replaced by detachable quads. While Jackson may have been tamed to create wider appeal it has by no means lost its bite. Most of Rendezvous is given over to black (difficult) runs, steep chutes and unlimited off-piste, which is a rarity in America. Even some of the blue (intermediate) runs are left ungroomed. The Bridger gondola takes 2,000 snow-users per hour on a seven-and-a-half-minute ride up to Headwall. Planning permission has been granted for a further nine lifts, and snowmaking has been increased to cover 152 acres (62 hectares).

One criticism of Jackson Hole is that for a resort of such international fame the ski area is quite small, and there is little other skiing within driving distance. Snow King, which confusingly is in the town of Jackson Hole, is smaller still. **Grand Targhee**, 47 miles (76km) away, goes some way towards offsetting this disadvantage. The early closure of Jackson's skiing in early April is dictated by the annual elk migration.

Beginners

All the beginner slopes are concentrated at the base of Teton Village, where both the adults' and children's ski schools meet. The nursery slopes are serviced by two short chair-lifts; this allows beginners to start on the easiest slopes and then graduate to steeper gradients. Second-week snow-users can find easier blue runs down Apres Vous Mountain and should tackle these before venturing up Headwall.

Intermediates

As in St Anton and Chamonix, the colour-grading is radical, and you must study carefully the unique colour-coding system, which is explained on the lift map; for most snow-users 'intermediate' means 'difficult', and 'difficult' means 'extreme'. While an acceptable amount of the terrain provides varied skiing for good intermediates, gradients can change suddenly, and in certain conditions unpisted runs are unpredictable and difficult. The friendliest intermediate skiing can be found off Headwall and the Casper Bowl triple-chair. The runs are well-marked, but you must pay attention as several blues turn into black runs on the lower part of the mountain. Only the truly confident should stray up the tram.

Advanced

Most of the truly testing terrain can be reached from the top of the gondola – you make your way down Amphitheater to the foot of the Thunder quad-chair. This lift gives access to a series of short but difficult chutes such as Paint Brush and Tower Three before you ride the lift back up and hop into Laramie Bowl. The steep Alta chutes can then be reached from the Sublette quad-chair. From the top of this, Rendezvous Trail, Jackson's nearest equivalent to a long cruiser, allows you to drop off down Central Chute or Bivouac. The possibilities for frightening yourself are endless.

Off-piste

Jackson Hole is one of the few US resorts with unlimited off-piste skiing. Indeed, as grooming is kept to a minimum, it is hard to define what is piste and what is not. Until recently the best powder was to be found in the Hobacks, on the lower section of Rendezvous Mountain. This enormous open area is reached from Rendezvous trail and is best skied early in the day. However, during the 1999–2000 season Jackson Hole enterprisingly opened up a further 2,500 acres off the back of Rendezvous to experts. Anyone can 'sign out' at various gates of the patrolled ski area, but you are advised to carry avalanche transceivers and to take a guide. The new powder opportunities serve to enhance Jackson's reputation as one of the world's greatest resorts.

For those with sufficient nerve, Corbet's Couloir, off the top of Rendezvous Mountain and only reached by the tram, is a chute so steep it seems inconceivable that anyone could ski it and survive. It is entered by a 12-ft (4-m) jump off a cornice; if you manage to control your skis you will land on a ribbon of snow dropping away at 50 degrees, where you must either turn or fall. Wise skiers and riders wear helmets.

Snowboarders

Riders are catered for by a groomed half-pipe on Apres Vous Mountain, and a natural half-pipe on Dick's Ditch. Nearby Grand Targhee also has a natural half-pipe for freestylers, but it is the freeriders who will really appreciate the area for its untracked snow.

Tuition and guiding

The ski and snowboard school emphasises having fun and being able to tackle simple slopes in a short time. Group, private and three-day courses are offered in alpine, nordic skiing and snowboarding. The ski school uses video evaluation for many of its classes.

Mountain restaurants

A pizzeria is situated at the top of the gondola, but otherwise eating on the mountain is limited. The Casper self-service serves both hot food and salads in a pleasant setting with a roaring log fire and Native American memorabilia on the walls, but it tends to get overcrowded. Two small snack-bars at the base of the Thunder chair-lift and at the top of the tram provide light refreshment. Most skiers and riders head to the Rocky Mountain Oyster Bar downstairs at the Mangy Moose or to the Alpenhof, a Tyrolean-style restaurant with waiter service.

Accommodation

The Wort Hotel in Jackson is the original, rebuilt stagecoach inn and is also the most convenient hotel in town. Other hotels include the Forty Niner, The Lodge at Jackson ('pleasant, but inconveniently located'), and the Parkway Inn for bed and breakfast. The Sundance is central and has a strong following. The Best Western Inn and Best Western Resort at Jackson Hole are two four-star hotels at the base of the lifts in Teton Village. Self-caterers need to go to Jackson for the supermarkets.

The most luxurious place to stay is the new Amangani which clings to a bluff in an isolated position between Jackson and Teton Village. From its 35-m terraced pool and from every sunken bathtub in the building, guests are treated to a dress circle view of the ski area. Inside, its cathedral-sized public rooms cut into the mountainside, exude the naturally tranquil ambience of some fantasy Native American teepee with Oriental overtones. Next door Spring Creek Resort is another comfortable rural option where you can stay in the main lodge or in separate self-catering chalets.

Eating in and out

Breakfast is a serious business in cowboy country. The real McCoy of 'eggs-over-easy', stacks of pancakes, hash browns and grits are on offer at the Mangy Moose in Teton Village. In the evening, the art-deco-style Cadillac Grille in Jackson has hamburgers, seafood and fresh pasta and is one of the few places that accepts children. The Silverdollar Bar and Grille in the Wort Hotel serves breakfast including home-made cereals and pancakes. In the evening it offers ribs in various forms. Sweetwater,

Skiing facts: Jackson Hole

TOURIST INFORMATION
PO Box 290, Teton Village, WY 83025
Tel 1 307 733 2292
Fax 1 307 733 2660
Email info@jacksonhole.com
Web site www.jacksonhole.com

THE RESORT
Airport transfer Jackson Airport 15–20 mins from Jackson and Teton Village
Visitor beds 12,000
Transport bus service between Jackson and Teton Village ($3)

THE SKIING
Linked or nearby resorts Grand Targhee (n), Snow King (n)
Number of lifts 10 in Jackson Hole
Total of trails/pistes 2,500 acres (1,011 hectares) (10% easy, 40% intermediate, 50% difficult)
Nursery slopes 3 lifts

LIFT PASSES
Area pass $258 for 6 days
Beginners reductions on beginner lifts
Pensioners 65yrs and over, $25 per day
Credit cards yes

TUITION
Adults Jackson Hole Ski & Snowboard

School tel: 307 739 2663
Snowboarding as ski school
Other courses cross-country, Explorers' ski course, extreme ski & board, heli-ski & -board, powder clinics, race-training, seniors, skiing for the disabled, steep skiing, teen skiing, telemark, women's ski clinics
Guiding Jackson Hole Alpine Guides tel: 307 739 2663, High Mountain Heli-skiing tel: 307 733 3274

CHILDREN
Lift pass 14yrs and under, $129 for 6 days. Free for 5yrs and under on Eagle's Rest
Ski & board school as adults
Kindergarten (ski and non-ski) Kids' Ranch tel: 307 739 2691

OTHER SPORTS
Climbing wall, dog-sledding, indoor tennis, parapente, night-skiing, skating, sleigh rides, snowcat skiing (Grand Targhee), snowmobiling, snowshoeing, Swimming, tubing

FOOD AND DRINK PRICES
Coffee $1.75, glass of wine $2.75–3.50, small beer $2.75, soft drink $2, dish of the day $6.50–8.50

the Snake River Grill and the Blue Lion all offer the American fine dining experience, but as one reporter commented 'just because you are paying more for the food doesn't mean it is going to taste any better'. Reporters unanimously praised the Snake River Brewery ('better beer and a less touristic approach to good food').

Après-ski
Unless you can prove you are 21 or over, you are not going to enjoy yourself outside skiing hours here. So strict are Wyoming's licensing laws that even young-looking 30-year-olds should carry identification at all times. The Million Dollar Cowboy Bar and the Silverdollar are the

main meeting places along with the Snake River Brewery. The Cowboy Bar has the most atmosphere, with real leather saddles as bar stools and a stuffed grizzly bear in a glass cage silently directing proceedings.

The Mangy Moose at Teton Village is one of the finest après-ski bars in The Rockies. It often has live music in the evenings and a video room for those under age. The Wingback Lounge at the Inn is a quieter option, and the Stockman's Lounge at the Sojourner usually has ski videos and free appetisers.

Teton Village has a skating rink. Other après-ski activities include night-skiing at Snow King resort, sleigh rides through the elk reserve, and snowmobile tours of Yellowstone National Park. Shops sell everything from cowboy boots at Corral West to cut-price ski clothing at Gart Sports, and include Gap and the excellent Broadway Toys & Togs. Teton Sports is recommended for clothing and equipment.

Childcare
Kids' Ranch in the Bridger Center is, in a country of excellent ski kindergartens, one of the best. It has a magic carpet conveyor-belt style and its own building called Cody House. Programmes available at the Kids' Ranch are Rough Riders for skiers aged three to five years old, and Tenderfoots daycare for children aged 2 to 18 months. Wrangler Childcare is the non-ski kindergarten for children aged 19 months to 5 years. Explorers is a ski course for children aged 6 to 14; instruction is combined with scouting for moose, porcupines and eagles.

Linked or nearby resorts

Grand Targhee
top 10,230ft (3,118m) bottom 8,000ft (2,438m)
This small resort just inside the Wyoming border and 42 miles from Jackson Hole is blessed with an excellent snow record, which is why the main attraction is snowcat skiing and boarding in the virgin powder (1,500 acres of it). This is by previous arrangement only, as the cat takes a maximum of 10 passengers, plus the guide and a patrolman. If you can't get a booking, the resort's 1,500 skiable acres (607 hectares) outside the cat skiing are varied, exciting, and are served by four lifts. They trails are often left ungroomed in fresh snow. The resort has one ski and snowboard school, a kindergarten, a small shopping centre, and restaurants are limited. Prices are notably lower than those in Jackson Hole. The Trap has 'friendly table service, ski videos, and a good variety of local beers'. Accommodation includes the Teewinot Lodge.

TOURIST INFORMATION
Tel 1 307 353 2300
Fax 1 307 353 8148
Email info@grandtarghee.com
Web site www.grandtarghee.com

Keystone

ALTITUDE 9,300ft (2,835m)

Beginners ✱✱✱ Intermediates ✱✱✱ Advanced ✱✱ Snowboarders ✱✱✱

Set among forests of pine in the heart of the Rocky Mountains in Colorado, Keystone is a modern purpose-built sprawl of multi-level complexes running west to east along Highway 6; 90 miles (145km) west of Denver Airport. The resort has been almost entirely rebuilt during the past few years, with $700 million spent on new condominiums in the River Run and Ski Tip Ranch sectors of town, together with new shops and restaurants. However, fewer than 50 families are in residence all year round, and consequently there is a lack of atmosphere. Bussing from one sector of the resort to another in search of some nightlife becomes tiresome. The high altitude can have adverse effects for some – altitude sickness or headaches brought on by dehydration can persist for days.

Keystone has won numerous awards for its family facilities. Two of its restaurants rate among the best in American ski resorts, though overall standards are unexceptional. Children under 13 stay for free and children under 5 ski for free. The resort also boasts a superlative range of intermediate terrain and America's most comprehensive snowmaking and night-skiing operations. Keystone's three mountains, with 22 lifts and 116 trails, are owned by the same company as **Vail**, **Beaver Creek** and **Breckenridge**. The four resorts are connected by shuttle bus, and you can now ski all of them on the same lift ticket (if purchased for three or more days), though with various restrictions. Nearby **Arapahoe Basin** provides limited, but exciting, advanced skiing.

- ✔ Two of the top US resort-restaurants
- ✔ Long ski season
- ✔ Whole ski area covered by snow-cannon
- ✔ Major night-skiing centre
- ✔ Recommended for families
- ✔ Excellent grooming and signposting
- ✔ Range of ski school courses
- ✗ Limited nightlife
- ✗ High altitude can cause sickness
- ✗ Weekend and holiday crowds

On the snow
top 11,980ft (3,652m) bottom 9,300ft (2,835m)

Keystone's skiing is laid out on three interlinked mountains, one behind the other; each progressively more challenging. Facing the resort is Keystone Mountain, with 16 lifts and 55 invitingly easy, meticulously groomed, rolling trails through forest. North Peak's three lifts access 19 shorter, more difficult runs, some of which are left ungroomed in sections. The huge Outback area, the size of both other mountains combined, is protected from the wind and is an excellent introduction to advanced skiing, especially in its two wilderness bowls. Queues used to exceed 15 minutes at weekends, especially on the Skyway Gondola, but a new high-speed quad that runs in tandem has considerably eased congestion. However, the ride can be a cold one. Locals warn of the 'Keystone donut' effect: icy slopes whenever nearby Lake Dillon fails to freeze over.

Beginners

Progressing from the Discovery beginner slope, even the most inept snow-user will be flattered by the wealth of ultra-simple green (easy) and blue (intermediate) runs, which comprise almost all of Keystone Mountain's front face. The next step up is Schoolmarm ('extremely long, and narrow in places'), running 3 miles (5km) from top to bottom via a traverse of the resort's western boundary. Ina's Way is a new green run to the village.

Intermediates

Intermediates have the run of all three mountains. The Flying Dutchman blue trail takes the most direct line down Keystone Mountain's front face. North Peak has five gladed blue runs, with Star Fire taking the most direct and challenging line. In the Outback area, Elk Run is the widest, with Wolverine throwing up more trees to dodge, although it is still graded blue.

Advanced

Keystone's cautious grading puts black (difficult) runs within the scope of aggressive intermediates, who may first want to test their skills on the short black sections near Area 51 on Keystone Mountain's west border. North Peak has six fall-line black runs tumbling down to the Santiago chair. But it is the Black Forest in the Outback that is most testing, with four narrow, heavily bumped tree-line runs, particularly adored by snowboarders.

Off-piste

A short hike above the Outback lift at 11,980ft (3,652m) brings you to the North and South bowls, which are within Keystone's boundaries. In powder conditions they provide a good mix of quite steep, untracked terrain leading down into the trees.

Snowboarders

Keystone has one of the biggest and best-designed funparks in America. Area 51 features numerous pipes in a 20-acre (8-hectare) funpark and is lit at night.

Tuition and guiding

Keystone Ski and Snowboard School is rated among America's top five and features a varied menu of special clinics for women,

Skiing facts: Keystone

TOURIST INFORMATION
PO Box 38, Keystone, CO 80435
Tel 1 970 496 6772
Fax 1 970 496 4215
Email international@
vailresorts.com
Web site www.keystoneresort.com

THE RESORT
Airport transfer Vail/Eagle County
1¼hrs, Denver 1½hrs
Visitor beds 5,200
Transport free resort bus service, also
to Breckenridge

THE SKIING
Linked or nearby resorts Arapahoe
Basin (n), Beaver Creek (n),
Breckenridge (l), Vail (n)
Number of lifts 22
Total of trails/pistes 1,861 acres
(753 hectares), 13% easy, 36%
intermediate, 51% difficult
Nursery slopes 3

LIFT PASSES
Area pass $174–210 for 6 days
if booked through tour operator
(also valid at Arapahoe Basin,
Beaver Creek, Breckenridge, Vail)
Beginners no free lifts
Pensioners 65–69yrs, $162–222 for

6 days (at ticket window), free for
70yrs and over
Credit cards yes

TUITION
Adults Keystone Ski and Snowboard
School tel: 970 496 4170
Snowboarding as ski school
Other courses backcountry nature
tours, bumps, carving, cross-country,
freestyle, Mahre race-training camps,
teen programmes, women's clinics
Guiding through ski school

CHILDREN
Lift passes 5–12yrs, $102–126 for
6 days (at ticket window)
Ski & board school as adults
Kindergarten (ski/non-ski) Keystone
Children's Centre tel: 970 496 4181

OTHER SPORTS
Indoor climbing wall, indoor tennis,
dog-sledding, moonlight cross-country
tours, skating, sleigh rides, snowbiking,
snowmobiling, snowshoeing, swimming,
tubing

FOOD AND DRINK
Coffee $1.50, glass of wine $5,
small beer $3, soft drink $1.50,
dish of the day $12–18

bump skiers and those convinced they will 'never ever' be able to ski. Former members of the USA ski team, brothers Phil and Steve Mahre, also run regular race-training clinics, which have an avid following.

Mountain restaurants
The Alpenglow Stube is without question the best and highest – at 11,444ft (3,488m) – haute cuisine in North America. Culinary delicacies served here include tenderloin of wild boar. The Mountain House self-service is reasonably priced.

Accommodation

The most characterful accommodation is at the Ski Tip Ranch, which used to be an old stagecoach inn and retains the intimate and appealing atmosphere. Keystone Lodge is a hotel with swimming-pool, fitness centre and hot tubs. It is a bus ride away from the skiing and is, according to visitors, 'rather spread out with a long walk to the rooms'. The Inn is closer to the lifts and has rooms with private hot tubs. The Pines condominiums are recommended: 'well equipped and spacious'. Nearly 1,000 condo flats and private homes of quite luxurious standards are also available.

Eating in and out

The Edgewater Café and the Bighorn Southwestern Grille at the Keystone Lodge are uninspiring, but reporters praised The Garden Room at the Keystone Lodge for its à la carte menu. Soda Creek Homestead is a rustic cabin reached by horse-drawn sleigh. But truly memorable dining is reserved for two of the best resort-restaurants in America: the Ski Tip Lodge (Colorado's oldest such establishment) and the Keystone Ranch, which is rated by some US publications as the best resort-restaurant on the continent.

Après-ski

Take a stagecoach to dinner, rip through the Arapahoe National Forest on a snowmobile or ski until 9pm. Aside from America's largest outdoor ice-skating lake and excellent indoor tennis courts, really exuberant nightlife is quashed by the preponderance of families with small children. However, Kichapoo Tavern (with live music), The Great Northern Taverne and Inxpot add atmosphere in the River Run sector, and The Snake River Saloon has two pool tables. The nightly bonfires with marshmallow-roasting are popular. Shopping in the resort is limited to a few sports and gift shops, but the factory outlet shopping village at Silverthorne is about 15 minutes' drive from the resort and is well worth a visit.

Childcare

The nursery at Keystone Children's Center takes babies from two months old, and is open from 8am to 5pm. Telephone pagers are available for parents. The Ski and Snowboard School also takes children from the ages of three to fourteen. Fort Saw Whiskers is a children-only ski playground. Babysitting in resort accommodation must be booked 24 hours in advance.

Killington

ALTITUDE 2,200ft (671m)

Beginners ✱✱✱ **Intermediates** ✱✱ **Advanced** ✱ **Snowboarders** ✱✱✱

Killington is the largest East Coast resort of the giant American Skiing Company, which now owns 11 resorts across the USA. The large amount of skiing available, coupled with ease of access and an unusually vibrant nightlife, make it one of the most popular US destinations for British skiers. A choice of direct flights to Boston, a journey that takes only seven hours from Britain, and a three-hour transfer to the resort give Killington an edge over its Colorado rivals in this respect. Alternatively, visitors can fly to New York and take the Amtrack rail service to Rutland, a 30-minute drive away.

> ✔ Easy resort access
> ✔ Excellent facilities for children
> ✔ Extensive snowmaking
> ✔ Modern lift system
> ✔ Lively nightlife
> ✔ Wide choice of restaurants
> ✗ Lack of charm
> ✗ Straggling layout
> ✗ Cold climate

The downside is the New England weather, which is often extremely cold or wet, with low cloud. To combat this all the Vermont resorts invest large amounts of money in snowmaking equipment, and nowhere more so than Killington, where 24 hours a day (temperature permitting), state-of-the-art cannons mounted on 15-foot 'giraffe' pylons power out a white substitute for the snow that nature does not always produce. So sophisticated is the system that the big business of skiing and snowboarding can continue here without weather worries.

For the present, those without a car are tied to the shuttle bus service from their lodging to the mountain or, in many cases, between their lodging and any form of entertainment. Waiting for the bus is a bitterly cold experience, but a whole new slopeside village has been planned, and the newest accommodation will be very convenient. The three-level base-lodge has a cafeteria, a ski rental shop and includes a selection of other retail outlets.

The resort already has more to offer than most of its New England rivals. The après-ski starts early, with hot snacks available from 3pm onwards and heavy competition for complimentary chicken wings. This sets the tone for the varied nightlife, with a choice of bars and clubs and cosmopolitan restaurants. Unlike the Rocky Mountain states, Vermont allows older teenagers into bars – but not clubs – provided they do not drink alcohol.

Killington opened for skiing in 1958, when the first tickets were sold out of a ticket booth made from a converted chicken coop. The resort now has a new gondola to Killington peak, new chair-lifts and a major new hotel, the Killington Grand, at the base area. The lifts are spread across seven mountains, but until the pedestrianised slopeside village is realised the resort will continue to lack a heart, with most of the hotels, condominiums, restaurants and bars lined up on either side of Killington Road, the five-mile (8-km) link between the ski area and the junction to the main highway.

On the snow
top 4,220ft (1,287m) bottom 1,045ft (3,19m)

Killington's seven peaks provide plenty of skiing and riding for all grades, but by European standards the emphasis is on mileage rather than variety. At this low altitude it is inevitable that the runs are glades cut through the all-embracing forest. Although the pitch changes, it is hard to tell one run from the next and piste naming is 'chaotic'. On the plus side, different levels are catered for in separate areas, with beginners safely corralled on their own hill – an arrangement that benefits everyone. The Edge frequent skier card means that skiers and riders can earn points towards free skiing with every lift pass they buy.

WHAT'S NEW
30% additional snowmaking

Beginners
The beginner slopes on Snowshed are served by a quad-chair and two double-chairs and encourage a gentle learning curve. The Perfect Turn Discovery Center, Killington's introductory programme for skiing and snowboarding, is located at the Snowshed Base Lodge. Once confident on the beginner trails, snow-users can graduate to the three easy inter-mediate trails of Timberline, Header and Swirl.

Intermediates
The most comfortable approach to Killington's slopes, especially in hostile weather, is via the two-stage Skyship up to Skye Peak. The eight-person gondola is described as the longest and fastest lift in the east of the USA, but more importantly it has heated cabins. Many of the runs from the top are green (easy), with Great Eastern providing a long, gentle return to the base-station. Those pistes starting from the compli-cated junction at the top are black (difficult), and it is necessary to take care when selecting a route.

The blue (intermediate) trails to look out for are Needle's Eye, Home Stretch and Cruise Control. Halfway down Great Eastern, snow-users come to the Bear Mountain quad, which opens up another zone, again with more black and green runs than blue ones. Snowdon, which is networked with green and blue trails, is recommended for lower inter-mediates, while more confident snow-users can graduate to the black-diamond (more difficult) runs on Skye Peak.

Advanced

The most extensive area of double-black-diamond (very difficult) trails is on Killington Peak, with Double Dipper, Cascade, Escapade and Downdraft among the names to look out for. Big Dipper is a gladed trail, but care should be exercised when conditions are icy. Killington's alternative macho challenge is the Outer Limits double-black-diamond mogul slope ('the steepest mogul slope in the East') on Bear Mountain.

Off-piste

Although there are no powder fields, the resort has created three Fusion Zones in the forest by thinning out the trees and clearing away the undergrowth. Squeeze Play, off Rams Head, is the logical starting point, with Low Rider on Snowdon and Julio, between Killington and Skye Peaks, providing a sterner test.

Snowboarders

Killington has two funparks, a half-pipe and a boardercross racecourse, as well as a special trail map for snowboarders. The permanent boarder-cross course is located on Middle Dream Maker. Beginner snowboard-ers are advised to join a learn-to-ride programme in the enclosed novice area on Snowshed before heading for the beginner-pipe at Highline. The neighbouring resort of **Pico** has its own dedicated snowboard area.

Tuition and guiding

The resort has a Perfect Turn Discovery Center at Snowshed Base Lodge. This incorporates the Graduated Length Method of ski teaching for beginners: 'kind and caring instructors who made it all seem easy and hassle-free. We made surprisingly quick progress in a single week'.

Mountain restaurants

Killington Peak Restaurant offers views of five US states as well as Canada. All six day-lodges have extensive restaurant facilities. The Mahogany Ridge Bar at the Killington base has a typically limited soup, sandwich and salad menu, but a comprehensive drinks list, with foreign beers, including Newcastle Brown. Its selection of hot alcoholic concoctions is welcome after a morning spent combating the wind-chill factor. Max's Place is said to be civilised.

Accommodation

The Killington Lodging and Travel Service is the central booking office for accommodation of all types, including condominiums, country inns, lodges and motor inns. The Trail Creek, Whiffletree, Edgemont and Fall Line condominiums are the most conveniently situated. Cortina Inn, eight miles (13km) from the mountain, offers luxurious accomm-odation. The Inn of the Six Mountains is close to the nightlife and runs its own courtesy bus to the lifts. The Killington Grand Hotel is a slopeside condominium-hotel with a health club. The Red Rob Inn is recommended.

Skiing facts: Killington

TOURIST INFORMATION
4763 Killington Road, VT 05751
Tel 1 802 422 3333
Fax 1 802 422 6118
Email info@killington.com
Web site www.killington.com

THE RESORT
Airport transfer Boston 156 miles,
Burlington 84 miles
Visitor beds 13,000
Transport shuttle bus

THE SKIING
Linked or nearby resorts Pico (l)
Number of lifts 33
Total of trails/pistes 1,260 acres
(32% easy, 32% intermediate,
36% difficult)
Nursery slopes 4 lifts

LIFT PASSES
Area pass $270 for 6 days
Beginners no reductions
Pensioners $168 for 6 days
Credit cards yes

TUITION
Adults Perfect Turn 802 422 3333
Snowboarding as ski school
Other courses carving, cross-country,
moguls, powder clinics, race camps,
skiing for the disabled, snowblading,
teen skiing/boarding, telemark,
women's clinics
Guiding none

CHILDREN
Lift pass 6–12yrs $168, 12–18yrs
$240, both for 6 days
Ski & board school as adults
Kindergarten (ski/non-ski) Perfect Kids
tel: 802 422 3333

OTHER SPORTS
Night-skiing/night-riding, skating, sleigh
rides, snowmobiling, snowshoeing,
tubing

FOOD AND DRINK PRICES
Coffee $1.50, glass of wine $4.75,
small beer $3, soft drink $1.50,
dish of the day $5.95

Eating in and out
Hemingway's, the only four-star restaurant in Vermont, is popular.
Claude's is known for its European cuisine, while Santa Fe and Casey's
Caboose specialise in basic American 'surf and turf'. PPeppers bar and
grill is recommended for breakfast, the Outback for oven pizzas, and
Sushi Yoshi is Japanese. The Killington Market sells everything
required for self-caterers, including fresh meat, groceries, local cheeses
and wines. Cortina Inn is a pleasant eaterie out of town.

Après-ski
The six-mile (10-km) Killington Road is lined with pubs and clubs. The
multi-level Pickle Barrel is the centre of the action, with a season-long
schedule of big-name bands playing every weekend. The Wobbly Barn
attracts a noisy crowd and it combines steakhouse dining with an
accompaniment of live rhythm and blues. The Outback and Mother
Shapiros are local bars with pool tables. Teenagers can dance and listen

to live music at Bumps, in the Killington Dance Club at the Rams Head base lodge, on Friday and Saturday evenings. Racquetball, skating and snowmobiling are the other sports available in the resort.

Childcare

The Rams Head area is the ultimate in luxury for families, with four of its own lifts. At the bottom of the hill the flattest slope is designated as a funpark and is served by a 'magic carpet' conveyor belt and two hand-tows. However, young snow-users soon graduate to a modern high-speed quad, which gives effortless access to wide, sweeping descents.

The Perfect Kids programme is divided into sections according to age and skiing ability, with the Friendly Penguin nursery at the Rams Head Family Center caring for children between six weeks and six years old. The First Tracks programme offers ski tuition for children from two years of age. Four-year-olds are encouraged to join the Ministars and Lowriders programme, which teaches the basics. Seven-year-olds graduate to the Superstars programme, with coaching available for all levels in skiing and snowboarding. Teenage riders can join the SnowZone programme.

Lake Tahoe

Heavenly 6,500ft (1,982m) Squaw Valley 6,200ft (1,890m)

Beginners ✱✱ Intermediates ✱✱✱ Advanced ✱✱✱ Snowboarders ✱✱✱

California is a world unto itself, so it is not surprising that its ski resorts are also unique. The majority of them – 15 alpine and 8 cross-country – are clustered around the shores of Lake Tahoe, a glimmering stretch of cobalt-blue water which lives up to its reputation as the second largest and most magnificent alpine lake in the world after Lake Titicaca in Peru.

- ✔ Spectacular scenery
- ✔ Diverse resorts share lift pass
- ✔ Facilities for children
- ✔ Extensive snowmaking (Heavenly)
- ✔ Recommended for cross-country
- ✔ Plenty of tree-level skiing
- ✔ Lively après-ski (South Lake Tahoe)
- ✘ No resort centre at Heavenly
- ✘ Few non-skiing activities

Heavenly (on the Nevada–California state-line) and **Squaw Valley** (on the far side of the lake) are the main players, but nearly all the others are worth a visit for a day's skiing. Transport is easy, and interchangeable lift tickets can be bought through the North Lake Tahoe Resort Association and used at Heavenly, Squaw Valley, **Kirkwood**, **Northstar-at-Tahoe**, **Alpine Meadows** and **Sierra-at-Tahoe**. Kirkwood is a favourite among locals, and one reader described it as 'the star of the show'. Sierra-at-Tahoe has crowd-free trails and some challenging runs for snowboarders. Alpine Meadows only opened its doors to boarders in 1996 and is now one of the most popular resorts in the area for riders.

Squaw Valley is currently being reconstructed by Canadian developer Intrawest. The new village centre will contain a total of 80 shops and restaurants as well as 640 'designer mountain homes'. Heavenly is part of the American Skiing Company's empire and has consequently also undergone major redevelopment. The Tamarack Express six-person detachable chair-lift was built as the first stage of a 10-year masterplan of on-mountain improvements, followed by two high-speed quads.

Heavenly is a resort of extraordinary contrasts: from the top of the Sky Express chair-lift you can turn left to ski in Nevada, with views of the arid vastness of the Nevada Desert, or turn right to the Californian side overlooking the lush beauty of Lake Tahoe. Off the slopes, in the nearest town of South Lake Tahoe, serenity switches to frenzy amid the clunk of one-arm bandits in the 24-hour casinos. Gambling is legal in South Lake Tahoe on the Nevada side of the state-line. Unfortunately, reporters agree that the view is the best part of Heavenly, which otherwise lacks charm and challenge. The blatant flashing lights, huge neon signs and monstrous casino complexes are such a contrast from the lake front and its simple, single-storey homes that it takes a while to digest the town of South Lake Tahoe.

Alternatively, you can ignore the tacky glitter and find a small restaurant for an intimate dinner. This is easier in Tahoe City, a 15-minute drive (five miles) from Squaw Valley. The small town has considerable atmosphere and several appealing restaurants on the lakeside. The drive to Squaw Valley from the South Shore along the lake past Emerald Bay is spectacular.

Squaw Valley, which hosted the 1960 Winter Olympics, provides the steeper and altogether more demanding terrain in a corner of the Sierra Nevada that has a long skiing tradition. As far back as 1856 John 'Snowshoe' Thompson, a Norwegian immigrant, used to carry the mail on skis between the mining camps in these mountains. Until the railroad was built in 1872, skiing was the miners' only winter link with the outside world.

On the snow

Heavenly top 10,100ft (3,079m) bottom 7,200ft (2,195m)
Squaw Valley top 9,050ft (2,759m) bottom 6,200ft (1,890m)

With 29 lifts, Heavenly is one of America's larger ski areas, and almost all of it is below the tree-line. It also has one of America's most extensive snowmaking programmes: 37 miles (59km) of terrain are covered by snow-cannon (a total of 69 per cent of the resort's trails). The skiing itself is divided between the Nevada and the Californian sides of the mountain.

The Nevada face consists mainly of blue (intermediate) runs; the advanced skiing is in the Mott Canyon area, a north-facing wall with a selection of chutes through the trees, and Killebrew Canyon, which has steep unpisted chutes. The green (easy) trails are mostly on the lower and middle slopes. The upper Californian side is mainly fast, blue, cruising terrain. The most difficult skiing on the Californian side is just above the Base Lodge and on the bowl runs. Higher up the mountain are some black-diamond (very difficult) runs off Skyline Trail.

> **WHAT'S NEW**
>
> New pedestrian village under construction at Squaw Valley

The skiing at Squaw Valley takes place on six peaks: Granite Chief, Snow King, KT-22, Squaw Peak, Emigrant and Broken Arrow. The area is divided into three sectors, but the 30 lifts, rather than the runs, are colour-graded. All the main lifts on KT-22, Squaw Peak and Granite Chief are black, while those on Snow King and Emigrant are blue. Intermediates will find a huge amount of skiing, with the highlight a three-mile (5-km) trail from the High Camp area down to the mountain base. During the 1998–9 season the main access gondola was replaced by the Gold Coast Funitel. It has an hourly capacity of 4,000 snow-users, and its dual cable allows it to operate in winds of up to 75mph. The Funitel includes a VIP cabin with music, heating and upholstered seating.

Beginners

Heavenly has three beginner areas: The Enchanted Forest at the California base, Boulder Base Lodge, and midway up the mountain on the California side. Squaw's main beginner area is located adjacent to the High Camp Bath and Tennis Club at the top of the mountain and accessed by cable-car.

Intermediates

Medium-standard skiers will find they can ski virtually every run on the mountain at Heavenly. Most of the trails are long cruisers bordered by banks of pine trees, with the highlight the stunning view of the lake. You can take the Sky Express chair and try Liz's or Betty's, then head to Nevada for the Big Dipper, Sand Dunes, Perimeter and Galaxy runs. You need to make your way back to the state in which you started by 3.30pm.

Squaw Valley has three main intermediate areas: the runs off the Squaw Creek and Red Dog lifts, which are best tackled later in the day; the area off Squaw One Express; and the bowls off Emigrant Peak and the Shirley Lake express chair-lift.

Advanced

Heavenly's Milky Way Bowl provides challenging skiing, but the most advanced skiing is in Mott Canyon and Killebrew Canyon. Steep chutes are cut through the trees, with runs such as Snake Pit. Heavenly has the odd black run (difficult) – such as Ellie's from the Sky Express and the Face near the California base-lodge – as well as huge areas of tree-level skiing. Gunbarrel is a challenging mogul slope.

Squaw was the birthplace of the American extreme skiing movement and has some seriously steep couloirs as well as open bowl skiing. The most radical terrain is to be found off the KT-22, Headwall, Cornice II and Granite Chief chair-lifts.

Off-piste

Heavenly is known to have the best tree-skiing in the Tahoe area on a powder day. The Milky Way, Mott Canyon and Killebrew Canyon are large expanses of off-piste; you need to arrive early as they are quickly skied-out.

At Squaw Valley, the further away from the lifts you travel the more likely you are to find good powder snow. Many skiers opt for Headwall, Cornice II and KT-22, but some excellent skiing is also found off Granite Chief and Silverado.

Snowboarders

Heavenly has two half-pipes, two funparks, and a boardercross course with huge 'tabletops' and 'rhythm sections' located around the mountain. Central Park at Squaw Valley is a dedicated funpark under the Riviera chair-lift, which overlooks Lake Tahoe and contains rollers, a variety of terrain features including rails, a half-pipe, a boardercross course and a sound system, and is open until 9pm at night. Under the Belmont chair-lift is a funpark with a half-pipe for beginner riders. KT-22 is a particularly good area for freeriders in search of challenge and excitement.

Tuition and guiding

The Perfect Turn ski and snowboard school at Heavenly is identical to the other American Ski Company schools you will find in Killington and Sunday River. It offers courses that include carving, race camps, seniors groups, skiing for the disabled, teen skiing and boarding, Mountain Adventure (off-piste) and women's ski seminars.

The Squaw Valley Ski and Snowboard School has programmes for all ages and abilities. Advanced ski clinics, mogul clinics, seniors, skiing for the disabled, telemark, women's clinics, and beginner's packages are also available, as well as X-Clinics (tuition in extreme skiing).

Mountain restaurants

Heavenly's restaurants can arrange on-mountain catered picnics, which include a 'snow table' complete with linen tablecloth and a vase of flowers together with a private waiter to serve the food and champagne. The Monument Peak restaurant is in the Top of the Tram complex at Heavenly and boasts a sun-deck. You can cook your own food at a barbecue at Sky Meadows on the California side. Boulder Lodge offers a bar, cafeteria and sun-deck, while Stagecoach Lodge has a cafeteria. The Slice of Heaven Pizza Pub at the Stagecoach Base Lodge is warmly recommended.

The Gold Coast, at the top of the Funitel, has a barbecue, restaurants and bars on three levels. High Camp boasts five different restaurants and bars, and the main dining-room is open at night. At the base village, dining options range from a hearty breakfast to pizza, burgers, sandwiches and Mexican food.

Accommodation

The ski area of Heavenly and the town of South Lake Tahoe are separate entities, although the Tahoe Seasons Resort hotel complex is close to the lifts at the California base. Harrah's and the Horizon Casino Resort in South Lake Tahoe are two of the bigger casino-hotels; others include Caesar's Tahoe and Harvey's Resort (all have good spas). The Station House Inn and the Timber Cover Lodge are acceptable motels that have been singled out by reporters. Much of the accommodation is in condominiums.

The Resort at Squaw Creek is a large ski-in ski-out complex near the base of Squaw Valley and has its own restaurants, bars, fitness centre and ice-skating rink ('I can't imagine why anyone would want to stay anywhere else here'). Squaw Valley Lodge and the newly refurbished

Plump Jack at Squaw Valley Inn are also close to the base lifts, and the Olympic Village Inn is nearby. Tahoe City provides an alternative bed base for visiting resorts in the area.

Eating in and out

In South Lake Tahoe the big casino resorts offer a wide choice of restaurants. The Summit in Harrah's is rated one of America's top 100 restaurants, Caesar's has Planet Hollywood – complete with movie paraphernalia. Harvey's Mexican restaurant is recommended, as is Chevy's. Zachery's and Dixie's specialise in Cajun cooking. The Swiss Chalet is recommended for fondue, while Red Hute, Ernie's and Heidi's are all popular for breakfast. The Station House Inn serves reasonably-priced meals, and the Chart House is more expensive but affords great views. The Gourmet Café, on the edge of South Lake Tahoe, is highly rated, while The Dory's Oar, just outside Squaw Valley, serves good seafood.

At Squaw Valley, the Resort at Squaw Creek is warmly praised. Glissandi is a high-priced Italian, and Graham's (in the valley) is cosy. The restaurants in Tahoe City and several in Truckee ('a characterful Wild West town'), half-an-hour away, are more fun. In Tahoe City, Za's is a basic Italian, while Christy Hill's is upmarket and overlooks the lake. The Cal-Neva Lodge in Crystal Bay on the north shore has two restaurants and an oyster bar.

Après-ski

Heavenly base has no après-ski apart from the California Bar, where there is live music from Wednesday to Saturday. Most of the after-skiing activities take place in South Lake Tahoe, with bars in all the hotels and Vegas-style celebrity shows. McP's is a lively Irish pub, Turtle's has dancing, and the Christiania Inn is close to the ski area and has a good atmosphere. The gaming tables attract money, and money attracts the top names in showbusiness. The nightlife includes taking in a show – some excellent cabaret acts and pop concerts are staged here and often feature top artists. Nero's disco may temporarily be stopped for 'The Best Buns' contest, or you can have a flutter at the tables.

At Squaw there is music at Gold Coast on the mountain and at Bar One in the base village. Other post-slope options include Salsa, the Plump Jack at Squaw Valley Inn, and the Red Dog Saloon, which is where you will find the locals. The High Camp Bath and Tennis Club is open until 9pm with tubing and ice-skating in winter, and swimming during the spring. Night-skiing is included in the daily lift ticket.

Childcare

Heavenly has redesigned its Perfect Turn Children's Center along the lines of the other highly successful American Skiing Company resorts. Here, childcare is completely flexible, with children dropped off for either half- or full-days, with or without lunch. Parents can rent a Perfect Kid's pager to keep in touch. The Daycare Center is for non-skiers from two months to four years old, while a ski/snowplay combination is offered for three- to four-year-olds. Ski Clinics are for children from four to twelve years old, and Snowboard Clinics for eight- to twelve-year-olds.

At Squaw, Children's World is a 12,000-sq-ft complex at the base of the mountain and is convenient for families. Parents can deliver their offspring and buy their tickets at the same time. Toddler Care is a kindergarten that takes two- to three-year-olds for snow play and arts and crafts. At Children's World Ski and Snowboard School, instructors teach children between four and twelve years old.

TOURIST INFORMATION
Tel (Heavenly) 1 775 586 7000/(Squaw) 1 530 583 6985
Fax (Heavenly) 1 775 588 5517/(Squaw) 1 530 581 7106
Email (Heavenly): info@skiheavenly.com/(Squaw) squaw@squaw.com
Web site (Heavenly): www.skiheavenly.com/(Squaw) www.squaw.com

Linked or nearby resorts

Public transport is efficient and frequent, but a car is useful for exploring the enormous amount of skiing on offer. Alpine Meadows, next to Squaw, has similar steepish terrain and is rated as one of the top US resorts for backcountry (off-piste) skiing in its open bowls. Kirkwood has some of the best snow in the area and some advanced terrain, ranging from smooth slopes to sheer cliffs. Sierra-at-Tahoe is the third largest resort around the lake and has three high-speed quad-chairs.

Donner Ski Ranch, geared mainly towards good intermediates, was linked in January 2000 to the more gentle area of **Boreal** to give a total of 15 chair-lifts, 86 runs and five funparks. However, at present the link is planned to open only three days a week.

Granlibakken, just outside Tahoe City, is the oldest resort on the lake and is open only at weekends. **Sugar Bowl** has 58 trails and a 1,500-ft (457-m) vertical drop. Locals' favourite **Mount Rose** has 43 trails and is only 22 miles (35km) from Reno. Northstar-at-Tahoe has five lifts and a cross-country centre. **Diamond Peak** calls itself 'Tahoe's premier family ski resort'. **Ski Homewood** on the West Shore has views of the lake on every run and is popular with snowboarders. **Tahoe Donner** and **Soda Springs** are both beginner areas.

TOURIST INFORMATION
(Lake Tahoe resorts)
Email info@tahoe.com
Web site www.tahoe.com

Mammoth

ALTITUDE 7,800ft (2,377m)

Beginners ✹✹ Intermediates ✹✹✹ Advanced ✹✹ Snowboarders ✹✹✹

For the present, Mammoth still has the feel of the family-run resort that it was throughout the second half of the twentieth century. Founder Dave McCoy set up the first rope tow here in 1941, bought the resort in 1953 and has spent most winter days on the mountain ever since. But in 1998 he sold out his majority share-holding to Canadian giant Intrawest, and Mammoth became the latest ski resort victim of giant corporate interests. Size-wise it competes favourably with many Alpine resorts. What it might lack in vertical drop it makes up for in altitude and sheer expanse of terrain. New ownership has resulted in major transformations. The resort, together with the nearest town of Mammoth Lakes, is investing more than $830 million to transform the ski region. This includes the development of The Village on Minaret Road, the approach route to the existing resort. Work started in summer 2000 on what is conceived as a European-style ski community, eventually to be linked to the main ski area by gondola and a return ski trail. Meanwhile, two new luxury lodges, Sierra Star and Eagle Lodge, are being built at the Juniper Springs. The new high-speed Eagle Express six-person chair provides increased mountain access from here.

- ✔ Large ski area
- ✔ Varied terrain including three funparks
- ✔ Exceptionally long season
- ✔ Good sunshine and snow records
- ✘ Remote location
- ✘ Spread-out town and lack of ski village ambience
- ✘ Limited après-ski
- ✘ Shortage of on-mountain restaurants
- ✘ Long airport transfer

First impressions suggest Mammoth was named after the size of its ski area, which is still one of the largest in North America. However, its name dates from the Victorian Gold Rush and refers to the consolidation of small operations into one Mammoth Mining Company. The season here is equally mammoth – it officially runs from November to June and often extends to Independence Day in July. The average snowfall of 383 inches (9.73m) is deposited by major storms rolling in from the Pacific.

Getting to this remote corner of the eastern Sierra Nevada is also a gargantuan task. The resort is situated three hours and 168 miles (270km) from Reno, and six hours and 307 miles (494km) from Los Angeles. You can stay in condominiums or hotels at the foot of the lifts,

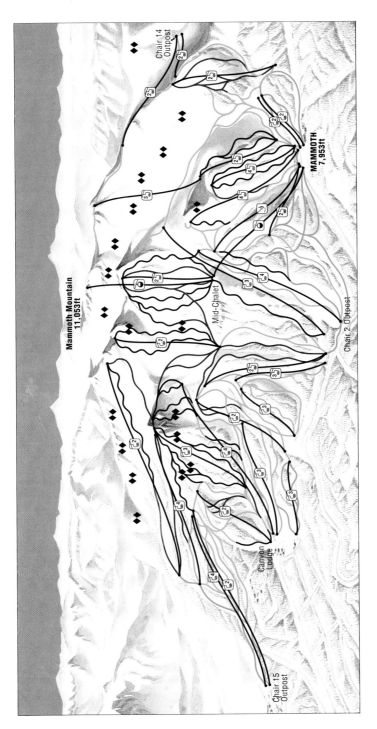

but most accommodation is situated four miles (7km) away in Mammoth Lakes. A frequent, free town shuttle-bus runs to and from the ski area bases at Main Lodge, Canyon Lodge and Juniper Springs. An airport shuttle operates between Reno and Mammoth.

Mammoth Lakes has excellent shopping with numerous sports outlets as well as brand-name factory stores where you can buy clothing and equipment for considerably less than in the UK. The town and the slopes tend to be quiet during the week for much of the winter but become overcrowded at weekends with the influx of Los Angelinos. The town's small airport is being upgraded, and a scheduled air service is expected to resume in time for the 2001–2 season.

Twenty miles away by road to the north lies its baby sister resort of **June Mountain,** which offers more benign terrain and seven lifts in a spectacular craggy mountain setting.

On the snow
top 11,053ft (3,369m), base 7,953ft (2,424m)

Four separate bases provide access to 28 lifts serving 150 trails set in more than 3,500 skiable acres. The two-stage eight-person Panorama gondola from Main Lodge provides the fastest way to the 11,053-ft (3,369-m) summit and some of the best skiing. This top section gives access to some extremely steep bowls but it is not just for experts – the narrow blue (intermediate) Road Runner provides a gentle cruise around the shoulder of the mountain.

This top section is at the mercy of high winds and prone to avalanche risk, but die-hards line up when it reopens in order to cut fresh tracks in deep powder on the steep faces below the cornice.

WHAT'S NEW
Commencement of The Village construction
Eagle Express six-person chair-lift
The Discovery quad-chair replaces two old chairs
Juniper Springs Lodge
Outdoor skating rink
Expanded snowmaking on lower slopes

Canyon is the sunny side of the mountain, where fresh snow can become heavy. In spring, slushy conditions are offset by the beach atmosphere outside the lodge, with sun loungers, BBQ and bar animated by live bands.

At weekends the slopes immediately above the access points are prone to overcrowding. One reporter suggested heading for the older double- or triple-chairs higher up the mountain where trails are 'nearly always deserted'. Snow-cannon cover 25 per cent of the area.

Beginners
Green (easy) runs surround all the access points, and separate ski schools operate from both Main and Canyon Lodge. Students will quickly advance to blue (intermediate) terrain, enabling them to cover the whole mountain.

Intermediates

Mammoth's ski area is littered with intermediate pistes that allow skiers and riders to progress gradually from basic blue to advanced-intermediate terrain (marked blue-black). The familiar black-diamond (more difficult) and double black-diamond (very difficult) signs can be offputting.

Chairs 12, 13 and 14 give access to plenty of cruising terrain with run such as Surprise, Secret Spot and Bristlecone. Broadway at Main Lodge and Stump Alley above The Mill Café are recommended. Gold Rush Express quad gives access to interesting blue runs, such as Lower Dry Creek (a natural half-pipe) and provides liaison with intermediate slopes above Canyon Lodge.

Advanced

The majority of seriously challenging double-black-diamond (very difficult) terrain is reached from the top of the Panorama gondola and Chair 23. Seekers of scary steeps are not disappointed. The upper half of the ski area offers open bowls, gullies and tree-skiing. The bumps here are generally considered to be some of the most demanding in California. Few of the black trails are groomed – Cornice Bowl being a regular exception. Face Lift and Chair 5 lead to some black – diamond (more difficult) terrain, including Dry Creek and West Bowl, which tends to develop friendly bumps. Chair 22 gives access to Lincoln Mountain with steep, ungroomed but sheltered runs through the trees

Off-piste

Skiing and riding is permitted everywhere within the boundary. There are even some out-of-bounds routes, such as Hole in the Wall, which instructors are allowed to take clients down (with permission from the ski patrol). Almost all the expert terrain is left ungroomed, as is enough of the intermediate slopes to allow less accomplished skiers and snowboarders a piece of the action.

Snowboarders

Mammoth is one of the USA's top snowboarding destinations – it now has three funparks. The original (best suited to advanced riders) is reached by Thunder Bound Express from Main Lodge and includes a half-pipe, quarter-pipe, tabletops and other jumps. This area and the adjacent blue ski trail (intermediate) is floodlit until 9pm at weekends and holidays. The two other funparks are at Canyon Lodge and below the Roller Coaster chair. The varied terrain of the mountain offers considerable interest. Boardertown at June Mountain has spines, pipes and rails.

Tuition and guiding

Mammoth Mountain Sports School offers three-hour group lessons each morning for skiers and riders ('good, quality instruction by a teacher who had the ability to explain what he meant'). The High Alpine Freeride Camp is tailored to advanced skiers seeking to improve their performance on steep terrain and in difficult snow conditions.

Skiing facts: Mammoth

TOURIST INFORMATION
PO Box 48, Mammoth Lakes,
CA 93546
Tel 1 760 934 2512
Fax 1 760 934 7066
Email mmthvisit@qnet.com
Web site www.visitmammoth.com

THE RESORT
Airport transfer Mammoth Lakes–June
Lake Airport 15 mins, Los Angeles 6hrs,
Reno 3hrs
Visitor beds 8,200
Transport free shuttle bus links
Mammoth Lakes with ski area

THE SKIING
Linked or nearby resorts June
Mountain (n)
Number of lifts 28
Total of trails/pistes 3,500 acres
(1,400 hectares) – 30% easy, 40%
intermediate, 30% difficult
Nursery slopes 2 lifts

LIFT PASSES
Area pass (covers Mammoth and June
Mountain) $271 for 6 days
Beginners free with ski lessons
Pensioners 65yrs and over, $156 for
6 days
Credit cards yes

TUITION
Adults Mammoth Mountain Sports
School tel: 760 934 2571
Snowboarding as ski school
Other courses carving, cross-country,
extreme skiing/boarding, moguls,
powder clinics, race camps, seniors,
slalom, skiing for the disabled, telemark,
women's ski seminars
Guiding Mammoth Mountaineering
School tel: 760 924 9100

CHILDREN
Lift pass 7–12yrs, $135 for 6 days, free
for 6yrs and under
Ski & board school Mammoth Kids
tel: 760 934 2571
Kindergarten (ski/non-ski) Small World
Child Care tel: 760 934 2571

OTHER SPORTS
Dog-sledding, horse riding, hot-air
ballooning, ice-climbing, indoor climbing
wall, indoor tennis, night-skiing/night-
riding, ski-joring, sleigh rides,
snowmobiling, snowshoeing, swimming,
tubing

FOOD AND DRINK PRICES
Coffee $1.50, glass of wine $4, small
beer $3.50, soft drink $2, dish of the
day $7

Women's Seminars are perennially popular. You can fine-tune your
slalom skills with the former Olympic downhill racer at AJ Kitt's Ski &
Race Camp. Free piste tours are hosted by local volunteers.

Mountain restaurants
Self-service cafeterias are located in both Main and Canyon Lodge and
at the mid-station of the gondola. A quick bite can be taken on the run at
the BBQ snack bars at the bases of Chairs 14 and 15. The Mill Café at the
bottom of Stump Alley is a cosier and more relaxing alternative, with an
open fire, a sunny deck and Californian cuisine. The Mountainside Grill

in the Mammoth Mountain Inn and The Yodler Bar & Pub – a Swiss chalet shipped piecemeal from the Alps – are the other options.

Accommodation

Enthusiasts wanting a head start in the mornings should stay at Mammoth Mountain Inn at the Main Lodge base or the Austria Hof ('good value with good rooms') at Canyon Lodge. Juniper Springs Lodge and the new Eagle Run (opening 2001–2) provide ultimate slopeside self-catering accommodation. The Alpenhof, located in The Village, is within easy access of the skiing and the town, and one reporter described it as 'well above average with friendly staff'. In Mammoth Lakes, the Shilo Inn is warmly recommended. Double Eagle Resort & Spa opened at June in November 1999; it offers a swimming-pool, steam room, whirlpool, fitness classes and a gym. While the Mammoth ski pass covers June Mountain, there is no free bus service.

Eating in and out

Mammoth Lakes has a variety of international cuisine to suit the demanding palates of visiting Los Angelinos. Skadi and Nevados are 'both excellent for a special night out', while Ocean Harvest specializes in seafood. Shogun is the best Japanese restaurant, and Karlotta's and Matsu's both offer an eclectic oriental menu, including Thai and Chinese specialties. The Charthouse and the Mogul are recommended for steaks. Alpenrose provides the inescapable (even here) cheese fondue. Giovanni's is praised for its pizzas, and Roberto's is authentic-ally Mexican. One reporter recommended The Restaurant at Convict Lake, a 20-minute drive away, as 'an absolute must'. Vons supermarket is said to offer the best value. Pioneer Market, situated at North Village, is pricier.

Après-ski

Skiers and riders gather at The Yodler when the lifts close. Canyon Lodge regularly has a live band. Later in the evening, The Clocktower pub at the Alpenhof is a popular resort rendezvous along with nearby Whiskey Creek. In town, Grumpy's Sports Bar attracts a young crowd. Shogun has a separate bar serving sushi and Japanese snacks. Ocean Harvest and neighbouring High Sierra Rock and Grill also have night-clubs with dancing and live entertainment. The outdoor skating rink in town is a welcome addition to après-ski activities.

Childcare

Mammoth Kids at the Woollywood Sports School offers morning and afternoon lessons for children aged four to fourteen years. Small World Child Care (based at Mammoth Mountain Inn) accepts infants from birth to 12 years of age for half or full days, with or without ski school. The new base-station houses the expanded Woollywood Sports School. The new Discovery Chair ensures beginners and little children maxi-mum snow time.

Ski Utah

RESORTS COVERED Park City Mountain Resort, Snowbird, Alta Ski Area, The Canyons, Deer Valley Resort, Snowbasin, Solitude Mountain Resort, Sundance

A group of distinctively different resorts make up Ski Utah, a marketing consortium of destinations clustered around Salt Lake City in the state that boasts the finest, driest powder snow in the world. In 2002 it will be the focus of world attention when the city plays host to the next Winter Olympics. These resorts offer the most accessible skiing and snowboarding from any airport in Europe or North America. You can stay either in Salt Lake City, which offers the greatest variety of accommodation, restaurants and entertainment, and drive 45 minutes to a different resort each day, or base yourself in any one resort. A car is useful for exploring the area and the ski slopes.

PARK CITY MOUNTAIN RESORT
- ✔ Tree-level skiing
- ✔ Excellent snow record
- ✔ Short airport transfer
- ✔ Wide choice of restaurants
- ✔ Activities for non-skiers
- ✘ Spread-out town and resort
- ✘ No children's daycare

Beginners ✱✱ Intermediates ✱✱
Snowboarders ✱✱

The two main resorts are **Park City Mountain Resort** and **Snowbird**. Park City is the most central, and the largest actual ski town. It is situated between **Deer Valley** and **The Canyons**. Snowbird and **Alta**, its smaller neighbour, are an hour's journey away by rail. Other sizeable resorts in the region are **Solitude** and **Sundance**, and **Snowbasin**, where the former Swiss champion Bernhard Russi currently spends much of his time forging the course for the next Olympic Men's Downhill, promised to be the most demanding and dramatic of all time. **Beaver Mountain, Brighton, Elk Meadows, Nordic Valley Ski Mountain** and **Powder Mountain Ski Area** are the smaller centres. The principal cross-country locations are **Brian Head Resort, Homestead, Ruby's Inn, Sherwood Hills** and **White Pine Touring**.

The focus for the Olympic Alpine events is on Park City. However, the best skiing is to be found up Little Cottonwood Canyon at Snowbird and the little 60s-retro resort of Alta. The Canyons is currently being transformed, at a cost of $530 million, into North America's newest international ski resort. There is some suggestion that, at an unspecified date in the future, it could be linked to adjacent Park City and Deer Valley to create the largest and best-equipped single resort in North America. At present the resorts are under rival ownership, but all three have indicated that lift-linking is a viable possibility. Park City and Deer Valley already operate a joint lift pass. Technically, linking would be

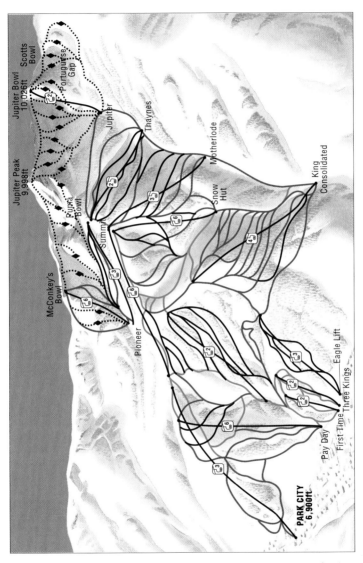

simple, and with a computer-based ticket system revenue-sharing would not present any problems.

Utah's two leading resorts could hardly be more dissimilar. While Snowbird is confined in the steep-sided Little Cottonwood Canyon and trapped in purpose-built glitz, Park City town and its ski area sprawl along a much wider valley with little regard for convenience.

Since mining began here in the mid-nineteenth century, silver to the value of $400 million has been extracted from the hills surrounding Park City, which has artfully converted its mining past into a colourful touristic present. The heart of the town is Main Street, home to the Wasatch Brewery, the Egyptian Theatre and a host of art galleries and boutiques. Among them are numerous bars, coffee shops and restaurants. The centre is a moderately well-designed complex on three levels, with shops and cafés set around an open-air ice-skating rink. Today, Park City has a reputation for being rather more than a ski town. Its cultural aspirations have been enhanced by the emergence of the Sundance Film Festival. This event, which takes place over the last 10 days in January each year, under the patronage of Robert Redford's Sundance Institute, is now recognised as the premier showcase for independent American films.

SNOWBIRD

✔ Impressive scenery
✔ Excellent snow record
✔ Short airport transfer
✔ Variety of off-piste
✔ Late-season skiing
✔ Doorstep skiing
✘ Limited après-ski
✘ Lack of village centre
✘ Few mountain restaurants

Intermediates ✱✱✱ Advanced
✱✱✱ Snowboarders ✱✱

Snowbird is rightly considered to be the home of 'champagne powder', a dream-like substance of talcum-type flakes. These have been freeze-dried in their journey over the desert from the distant ocean before being deposited in copious quantities on the steep slopes surrounding Little Cottonwood Canyon. The skiing terrain is more scenic than in many Utah resorts, but the architecture is considerably less attractive.

When Dick Bass, a Texan oilman, built Snowbird almost 30 years ago, he had apparently fallen under the spell of the latest concrete additions in the French Alps. His argument was that the concrete blends in with the granite walls of the canyon, and that by adopting the tower block option he fulfilled avalanche safety regulations while avoiding the sprawling condominium suburb of so many of his American competitors. Officially, the heart of the resort is Snowbird Center, the departure point for the cable-car, known as the 'tram'. It is the mirrored walls of the Cliff Lodge, however, with its 11-storey atrium, that dominate the long, narrow swathe of contemporary buildings and car-parks. The Snowbird Center comprises the Plaza Deck, an open space surrounded by limited shops on three levels. Outlying buildings house condominiums, and the overall impression is of a single-function resort with few alternatives for non-skiers.

On the snow
Park City Mountain Resort: top 10,000ft (3,049m) bottom 6,900ft (2,104m)
Snowbird: top 11,000ft (3,352m) bottom 7,740ft (2,359m)
As the Winter Olympics 2002 approach, major on-mountain improvements are under way in the region, both for the racers and for the tens

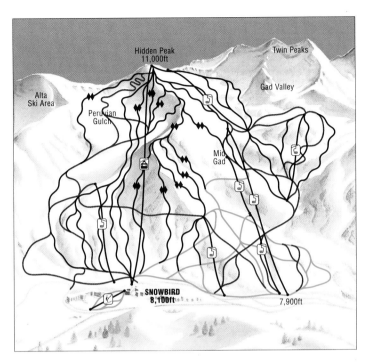

of thousands of skiers and riders who are expected to descend on Salt Lake City. The main skiing at Park City consists of 3,300 acres (1,336 hectares) served by 14 lifts. The terrain ranges from rolling runs to open bowls. Although the US Ski and Snowboard teams are based here, the skiing is much less challenging than at Snowbird.

Access to the top of the main ski area is by two detachable six-person chair-lifts, which take 12 minutes from Park City to the Summit House Restaurant. The highest point is Jupiter Bowl. Snow-users of all standards will find suitable runs from the summit to the bottom of the Silverlode six-person chair. Park City has floodlit skiing.

Snowbird boasts one of America's few cable-cars. The 'tram' carries 125 skiers almost 3,000ft (914m) to the top of Hidden Peak in eight minutes. There is only one relatively easy run down: Chips, a 3-mile (5.5-km) trail back to the base-area. Elsewhere, the higher skiing is dominated by bowls, chutes and gullies – an exciting arena for advanced skiers who enjoy powering through steep slopes on ungroomed snow. Intermediates are well catered for but there is a shortage of novice skiing. The ski area has recently been expanded by 25 per cent with the development of Mineral Basin, a back bowl experience for skiers and boarders of all abilities. Access is via the cable-car and a new detachable quad chair-lift. Together they serve 18 trails covering 500 acres (202 hectares) with a vertical drop of 1,439ft (439m).

Beginners

Park City has two beginner areas, one at the base with two lifts and another centred around the Silverlode chair. Beginners can profit from a 3.5-mile (6-km) green (easy) descent from the Summit Smoke House & Grill to the Park City centre, via the top of Claimjumper, Bonanza and Sidewinder. This is broad, flat territory, which is perfect for discovering the pleasures of the beautifully groomed snow. The less experienced should avoid it late in the afternoon, when it becomes a race-track back to base as the lifts close. Claimjumper is a green boulevard curving round the mountain towards the Snow Hut restaurant.

Snowbird's Baby Thunder lift opens up a network of green runs and the slightly more demanding blue (intermediate) trail, Thunder Alley, which all end up below the village. Novice skiers and riders should stay away from the top of Hidden Peak unless they really feel they can cope with Chips Run, which is a very long blue. If you have the stamina for only part of Chips, the Peruvian lift goes almost halfway. Complete beginners might want to ski off the Chickadee lift down by the Cliff Lodge. Otherwise, the Mid Gad lift (with a midway unloading station) and the Wilbere lift serve some of Snowbird's least intimidating terrain. This includes Big Emma, which is a wide green slope, named after the popular *madame* of a mining camp brothel.

Intermediates

At Park City, 44 per cent of the trails are listed as intermediate and cover every area of the mountain except Jupiter Bowl. Confident skiers and boarders will not find themselves unduly tested by Hidden Splendour, Mel's Alley, Powder Keg and Assessment. However, Prospector, Single Jack, Sunnyside and Parley's Park take more direct routes down the mountain. Favourite trails include 10th Mountain.

The ski area at Snowbird offers a number of well-groomed runs best suited to confident parallel skiers. Bassackwards, Election, Bananas and Lunch Run are all straightforward cruising trails. However, the ski area is littered with black (difficult) slopes and intimidating double-black-diamond (very difficult) runs; considerable care should be taken to avoid embarking on a slope that may be too testing.

Advanced

The highest point of Park City is Jupiter Bowl, which is reached by the Jupiter and McConkey chairs and is recommended for advanced snow-users only. Experienced skiers and boarders have a choice of moderate black (difficult) runs, including The Hoist, Thaynes, Double Jack, Ford Country and Glory Hole, which all lead into Thaynes Canyon, a blue cruiser that marks the eastern boundary of the ski area. Halfway down, the Motherlode chair-lift takes you back to the Summit Smoke House & Grill, or you can continue down to the King Con chair-lift, which is the access point for 10 blue runs into Broadway and Hot Spot.

Snowbird's strong skiers are spoilt for choice, with everything from fairly easy, open-bowl skiing to very difficult bump chutes. With the exception of Chips, all the trails off Hidden Peak are classified as either black or double-black-diamond. Challenging black runs through spruce and lodge-pole pine, such as Gadzooks and Tiger Tail, are reached from the Gad 2 lift. The Road To Provo traverse from Hidden Peak (also reached by the Little Cloud lift) leads to other demanding runs such as Black Forest and Organ Grinder.

Off-piste

Those in search of adventure at Park City should take the Jupiter Access trail from the top of the Pioneer chair-lift to the Jupiter chair-lift. This goes up to the top of the resort, a wind-blown ridge with a variety of ungroomed options. Shadow Ridge and Fortune Teller go straight down under the chair through sparsely wooded snowfields, but a 10-minute walk along the ridge to the east brings skiers to the top of Scott's Bowl. Further along, Portuguese Gap is a narrow, often heavily mogulled, field between the trees. A 20-minute walk along the ridge to the west leads to Jupiter Peak. Here there is a choice between the steep descent into Puma Bowl via the East Face, or back to the chair-lift via the West Face. All these runs are well worth the walk.

The black options to the west of Park City are six parallel descents through aspen trees, though these are prone to closure in poor snow conditions. A guided programme called Ski Utah Interconnect is a full-day off-piste adventure that covers five ski areas. Park City Powder Cats arrange guided snowcat-skiing or -boarding.

Snowbird's off-piste terrain is superb, and the key to it is the Cirque Traverse from Hidden Peak. From this narrow ridge skiers can drop off both sides into a large selection of chutes and gullies. Some are sandwiched between pines which have been twisted and stunted by blizzards; others are guarded by imposing outcrops of granite. Plunges into Silver Fox, Great Scott and Upper Cirque on one side and Wilbere Chute, Wilbere Bowl, Barry Barry, Steep and Gad on the other can be exhilarating in fresh, deep snow and quite frightening in difficult conditions. There is also some awesome back-country (off-piste) skiing below Twin Peaks in Gad Valley.

Snowboarders

At Park City the Jupiter Access trail from the top of the Pioneer chair-lift offers some excellent ungroomed riding. Some of the best freeriding, such as Scott's Bowl and Puma Bowl, is only accessible by first walking uphill for about 10 minutes. The resort does not have a funpark, so freestylers will have to find their own natural hits. Off Payday trail is a half-pipe, which is illuminated at night. Freeriders at Snowbird have a superb choice of terrain that varies from gentle bowls to extreme chutes from Hidden Peak.

Tuition and guiding

The Park City Mountain Resort Ski and Snowboard School uses the American teaching system, as prescribed by the Professional Ski

Instructors of America (PSIA). Full-day and half-day adult group lessons are available for visitors aged 14 years and over. We have enthusiastic reports: 'the ski school is the best we have found anywhere.' The Mountain Experience programme takes good intermediate to advanced snow-users into the high bowls on Jupiter Peak. The other courses available are carving, moguls, race-camps, skiing for the disabled, telemark and women's clinics. Private lessons are also on offer.

Beginners and low intermediate snowploughers meet at the bottom of the mountain; intermediate to advanced at the Summit Ski School area at the top of the Motherlode chair. Special courses include moguls, freestyle, slalom, off-piste, race clinics and women's ski performance workshops. The Utah Winter Sports Park, located beside The Canyons, is one of the few places in the world offering recreational ski-jumping on three days each week during the mid-winter months as well as bobsleigh and luge.

Snowbird Mountain School operates speciality workshops for style. Bumps-and-Diamonds and racing, as well as normal lessons. A Mountain Experience clinic for powder and free guided tours are offered.

Mountain restaurants

The Mid-Mountain restaurant at Park City, a modified version of an old miners' dwelling, offers high-quality fast food ('simply heaven on a sunny day'). Its rivals are the Summit Smoke House & Grill and the Snow Hut at the bottom of the Silverlode lift. The new Legacy Lodge, which opens for the 2000–1 season, features a day-service restaurant and an international food bar. 'Skiosks' are yurt-style shelters on the mountain where guests can stop for a quick snack or drink.

The only real restaurant on the mountain at Snowbird is at Mid Gad. The Snowbird trail-map accurately describes it as a 'fuel stop'. The Peak Express warming hut on Hidden Peak serves coffee and light snacks. Serious lunchers must return to the base area.

Accommodation

Much of the accommodation in Park City is in condominiums. One of the most convenient places to stay is the Silver King Hotel, a complex offering 85 units ranging from studios to penthouses. Most of the hotels are a few miles from Park City on the free bus route, and include The Radisson Inn and Yarrow Hotel. The Chamonix Lodge is at the foot of the slopes, and The Prospector Square Hotel, which is about 15 minutes away by bus, resembles a collection of Nissen huts and is priced accordingly. The hotel also has a superb athletics club with an Olympic-sized indoor swimming-pool, four racket-ball courts and an impressively mechanised gym. At the unusual Angel House each room is modelled on a different member of the heavenly host ('delightful angelic antiques'). The Best Western Landmark Inn at Kimball Junction is good value and has its own sports complex.

At Snowbird most people stay either at the Cliff Lodge or at one of the three other condominium lodges nearby: the Lodge at Snowbird, The Inn and the Iron Blosam Lodge.

Eating in and out

Park City is a strong contender for the 'best dining' accolade in a US ski resort. A traditional start to an evening on Main Street would be dinner at The Claimjumper, an all-American establishment serving 'surf-and-turf'. The Irish Camel is more Mexican than its name suggests ('charismatic ambience, booking essential'). Chimayo is for Mexican and Southwestern cuisine. Kampi Sushi has a wide selection of fresh fish. 'Excellent crab and enormous Pacific mussels' can be found at 350 Main Street. Grappa is classic Tuscan. Zoom, owned by Robert Redford, has Californian cuisine, while Mercato Mediterraneo turns out stylish pizzas. The Riverhorse Café is American and trendy, and Texas Red's is 'cheap and cheerful with great chilli'.

Snowbird has 12 restaurants, including the Aerie at the top of the Cliff Lodge, which is enclosed by glass and offers continental cuisine. Summit Café offers a health-conscious menu as well as sushi. Keyhole Junction, also in the Cliff Lodge, specialises in Southwestern cooking. Pier 49 at Snowbird Center serves gourmet pizzas, and the Steakpit offers an all-American menu that includes king crab. The Wildflower Ristorante at the Iron Blosam Lodge specialises in Italian food.

Après-ski

As the Olympics draw near the stiff stance on alcohol consumption is being visibly relaxed. In actual fact, licensing laws here are no more severe than they were in England and Wales until a few years ago. Any establishment serving food is allowed to sell beer and usually wine. Late-night bars must conform to the strictures of a private club licence, but temporary membership is easily obtained. In Park City, the Alamo Bar displays the local Park City Rugby Club memorabilia on its walls, alongside stuffed moose and elk heads.

Snowbird's bars are few in number and formal enough to deter all but the most enthusiastic nightlifers. Immediately after the lifts close, skiers gravitate towards the Forklift, just across the plaza from the tram (cable-car), and the Wildflower Lodge. The Tram Club at Snowbird Center has live music and dancing. Later on, the Aerie often has a pianist, but sitting here until closing time at 1am is not particularly exciting. If the roads are clear and no storms are imminent you could try a night out in Salt Lake City, 25 miles (40km) away.

Other activities in Park City include a climbing wall, hang-gliding, helicopter rides, hot-air ballooning, ice-driving, indoor tennis and racket-ball, parapente, skating and curling, sleigh rides, snowmobiling, snowshoeing, swimming and tubing at the new adventure park, as well as bob-sledding, ice-rocketing (a one-person sled) and ski-jumping at the Olympic Sports Park. The Factory Stores at Kimball Junction, four miles (6km) drive from Park City, is a large shopping centre selling end-of-the-line designer clothing at cut prices, and is well worth the visit.

Snowbird offers an indoor climbing wall, indoor tennis and squash, luge, racket-ball, skating and tubing.

Childcare

The Park City Mountain Resort Ski and Snowboard School divides its tuition into Youth (7 to 12 years) and Kids' Mountain Adventure School (three to twelve years) for daily programmes. The Kid's package also includes lunch and indoor supervision. There are no crèche facilities for non-skiing children. The Burton Chopper Center, for seven- to twelve-year-olds, allows kids to practise their moves on a training trampoline and balance boards while they are off the snow.

Daycare for children of two months and over at Snowbird is available at the Camp Snowbird Children's Center at the Cliff Lodge. The ski school offers ski instruction with daycare. One reporter described Snowbird as 'the most child-friendly resort I have ever been to'.

TOURIST INFORMATION
Park City Mountain Resort
Tel 1 435 649 8111
Fax 1 435 647 5374
Email pcinfo@pcski.com
Web site www.parkcitymountain.com

TOURIST INFORMATION
Snowbird
Tel 1 801 742 2222
Fax 1 801 742 3344
Web site www.snowbird.com

Linked or nearby resorts

Alta Ski Area
top 10,550ft (3,216m) bottom 8,530ft (2,600m)

This is a stylishly old-fashioned, unpretentious resort revered by powder skiers, ski bums and those in search of a cheap lift ticket and powder that can sometimes better Snowbird's. Alta, just a mile up the hill from Snowbird in Little Cottonwood Canyon, was here some 30 years before Snowbird and is proud of the fact. It has rather more beginner and lower intermediate terrain, and also phenomenal chutes and secret powder caches reached only by back-country (off-piste) hiking. Devotees refuse to accept that Snowbird is in the same class; realists count their blessings that two outstanding powder resorts are so close together. Many believe that eventually the two will be linked; they already form the most challenging section of the back-country Interconnect circuit, which includes Park City Mountain Resort, Solitude and Brighton, in an attempt to reproduce the Alpine concept of skiing from one resort to another.

On piste, Alta has eight chair-lifts and five drag-lifts. The resort limits its uphill capacity to 10,750 skiers per hour in order to make the skiing experience more pleasant. The Alf Engen Ski School was named after its founder, who taught skiing here in 1948; children's lessons are offered as well as adult tuition. The Alta Children's Center is a privately run daycare organisation.

Alpenglow and Watson's Cafés on the mountain are both recommended, along with Chic's place ('proper restaurant with waiter service and free slippers for aching feet'). Albion Grill, Alta Java and Goldminer's Daughter are located at the mountain base. Alta's oldest and most charming lodge is the Alta Pine Lodge, which has been attracting visitors since 1938 and was renovated in 1990. Other accommodation includes the Alta Peruvian Lodge.

TOURIST INFORMATION
Tel 1 801 359 1078
Fax 1 801 799 2340
Email info@altaskiarea.com
Web site www.altaskiarea.com

The Canyons
top 9,990ft (2,986m) bottom 6,800ft (2,071m)

For the past three years The Canyons has been evolving from a local hill into a resort village, with the facilities to attract destination skiers and snowboarders. To date, the bill for on-mountain investment, including a modern lift system and a range of day lodges, is $33 million. Over the next five years, a further $500 million will be spent on a state-of-the-art base area, with hotels, restaurants and malls attractively linked to a central forum by walkways and waterways. Originally called Park City West, the resort opened in 1969, later changing its name to Park West and later still to Wolf Mountain, before being reborn under the patronage of the giant American Skiing Company as The Canyons.

Not much of the 3,300 acres (1,005 hectares) of ski area can be seen from the base, but a short walk takes guests to the Flight of the Canyons gondola and so to the Red Pine Lodge mid-station, and from here its full magnificence is revealed. A total of 12 lifts give access to skiing on seven peaks. Only 14 per cent of the terrain is suitable for beginners; most of it on the Meadows runs immediately above Red Pine. The rest divides fairly evenly between intermediate and advanced, with enough chutes and tree-skiing to satisfy the most adventurous skier or rider.

Red Pine gives rapid access to the Saddleback and Tombstone express quads, the first lifts put in by the new management for the 1998 season. Both offer long cruisers and short chutes in glades cut through forested hillsides. The Ninety-Nine 90 Express opened in 1999 to serve an impressive double-black-diamond zone, with open bowls and spectacular views. Others may prefer Peak 5, a millennium addition that has been nicknamed the Enchanted Forest for its challenging tree runs. Development of an eighth peak, as yet unnamed, is planned for 2001–2, with a new quad serving a further 300 acres (121 hectares) to the south of the existing area – another step towards the final target of 7,000 skiable acres (2,833 hectares), accessed by 22 lifts. Riders and skiers on the new twin-tips (double-ended skis) are served by a funpark on Saddleback and half-a-dozen natural half-pipes.

There are three on-mountain restaurants: Red Pine, Lookout Cabin and Sun Lodge. As befits the central link in the lift system, Red Pine is large and busy, with the full range of Rocky Mountain lunch options: pizza, grill, deli and salad bar. Lookout Cabin, at the top of the Raptor chair, is much quieter, with a more sophisticated menu and table service. Sun Lodge, a new addition in 2000, lives up to its name with a sheltered deck and an open-air grill.

The embryonic Resort Village lacks atmosphere, with bulldozers hard at work by day and a shortage of options by night. Grand Summit is a new slopeside condominium hotel and conference centre, with 358 rooms. The 150-room Sundial Lodge provides accommodation on a rather less grandiose scale. The Cabin, in the Grand Summit Hotel, with its kitchens under the control of master chef Houman Gohary, is the smartest in the region. Alternatives include the Gondola Bar and Lounge and the deli-style Café. Smokey's Smoke House is family-friendly, with a Cajun menu and a barbecue, while Docís is the watering hole of choice for the resort staff. Those who are looking for nightlife may prefer to stay in Park City, served by a free shuttle-bus between the downtown hotels and The Canyons every 20 minutes.

Perfect Kids, conveniently based at the Grand Summit, offers daycare from 18 months to 9 years of age, from 8.30am to 4.30pm, with group ski clinics for four- to twelve-year-olds and group snowboard clinics for children aged seven to twelve. For adult beginners, the Perfect Turn programme has three-day Learn-to-Ski (using gradated ski lengths to build up confidence) and Learn-to-Ride packages.

TOURIST INFORMATION
Tel 1 435 649 5400
Fax 1 435 649 7374
Email info@thecanyons.com
Web site www.thecanyons.com

Deer Valley Resort
top 9,400ft (2,865m) bottom 7,200ft (2,195m)

Unashamedly luxurious, Deer Valley Resort is one mile north-east of Park City, up a winding mountain road lined with multi-million-dollar homes. A free bus service operates from Park City. Deer Valley is a place where grooming counts, both on the meticulously pisted slopes ('like going skiing at Harrods') and with the clientèle, who are a walking advertisement for designer clothing. 'It is worth a visit for two or three days,' said one reporter, 'if only to observe the outfits'.

The resort is the venue for the slalom and freestyle events at the 2002 Winter Olympics and a new day lodge is being built at the bottom of the Empire Express and Ruby chair-lifts.

The 1,745 acres (531 hectares) of skiing takes place on four mountains, served by 19 lifts and is constantly being expanded. Some 15 per cent is rated beginner, 50 per cent intermediate, and 35 per cent difficult. The Deer Valley Ski School offers group and private lessons, and special ski courses including performance clinics, women's courses, and specific courses for teenagers. Snowboarding is not allowed at Deer Valley. Children aged two months to twelve years are looked after by Deer Valley Children's Centre, and Deer Valley Children's Ski School takes children from three and a half to twelve years of age.

The resort does not have a village base as such. Slopeside accommodation is in large, luxurious condominiums and smart hotels. These include the Lodges at Deer Valley, the Chateaux, the Goldener Hirsch Inn and the Stein Eriksen Lodge. Restaurants include the excellent Mariposa and the Snow Park Seafood Buffet. The lounge at Snow Park Lodge is popular for après-ski.

TOURIST INFORMATION
Tel 1 435 645 6503
Fax 1 435 645 6939
Email patti@deervalley.com
Web site www.deervalley.com

Snowbasin
top 9,288ft (2,831m) bottom 6,291ft (1,914m)

Snowbasin is the venue for the Blue Riband events of the 2002 Winter Olympics, the men's and women's downhills and super-Gs, on a course crafted by the veteran Swiss racer Bernhard Russi. Skiing came to the mountain in 1940, when the road from Ogden, a strict Mormon town to the north of Salt Lake City, was constructed. In the early days, facilities were limited to a rope-tow run off a dump truck's engine by a schoolteacher called Ted McGregor, so that his pupils could ski on Saturday mornings. A local entrepreneur bought the little resort in 1984, and in preparation for the Olympics has doubled the ski area from 1,800 to 3,200 acres (589 to 975 hectares), spending $80 million on facilities that include two 8-person gondolas, a high-speed quad, an Olympic tram and a computerised snowmaking system with 40 miles of underground pipes.

The Olympic courses are accessed by the John Paul Express quadchair, named not after the Pope, but after a 20-year-old Ogden boy who died with the 10th Mountain Division in Italy in World War II. John Paul is steep, with an average gradient of 34 per cent compared to the 29–30 per cent that is normal for a men's downhill course – so competitors and regular skiers can be sure of a gruelling workout. Beginner slopes are very limited but the rest of the resort, accessed by the Strawberry Express and the Middle Bowl Express gondolas, is largely intermediate, apart from a small zone of bowls and chutes on De Moisy for experts. The terrain is interestingly varied, with clumps of trees rather than dense forest, so skiers and boarders can choose their line over most of the mountain. The Snowbasin Ski School has daily group lessons for those aged four and over.

The hill is ready for the Olympics, but the access road and proposed day lodge have yet to be built.

TOURIST INFORMATION
Tel 1 801 399 1135
Fax 1 801 399 1138
Email info@snowbasin.com
Web site www.snowbasin.com

Solitude Mountain Resort
top 10,035ft (3,059m) bottom 7,988ft (2,435m)
Just 28 miles (45km) and 45 minutes' drive from Salt Lake City, Solitude Mountain Resort is in the heart of Big Cottonwood Canyon in Utah's Wasatch-Cache National Forest. Solitude is dedicated to creating and maintaining some of the best-groomed slopes you will find anywhere. State-of-the-art machinery ensures that 50 per cent of the mountain is groomed on a rotating basis, including the steeper terrain. Seven lifts serve 1,200 acres (486 hectares), of which 20 per cent is rated beginner standard, 50 per cent intermediate and 30 per cent difficult. Accommodation is available at the Inn or at Creekside. Six restaurants include the Mongolian-style hut, the Yurt, situated a third of a mile from the Inn at Solitude and reached either on snowshoes or cross-country skis through the trees.

TOURIST INFORMATION
Tel 1 801 534 1400
Fax 1 801 649 5276
Email info@skisolitude.com
Web site www.skisolitude.com

Sundance
top 8,250ft (2,515m) bottom 6,100ft (1,859m)
When Sundance was created by the film star Robert Redford in 1969, he visualised a community where the arts, environment and recreation would thrive harmoniously together. The resort is 55 minutes' drive from Salt Lake City, or a 40-minute scenic drive through the Heber Valley from Park City. Lift queues are a rarity here, and a variety of terrain – ranging from wide open trails to bowl skiing – is available. Four chair-lifts serve a choice of 41 trails. The two mountain restaurants, the Tree Room and the Foundry Grill, serve regional dishes. Accommodation is in the Sundance Cottages.

TOURIST INFORMATION
Tel 1 801 225 4107
Fax 1 801 223 4551
Web site www.sundanceresort.com

Smugglers' Notch/Stowe

ALTITUDE Smugglers' Notch 1,030ft (314m), Stowe 1,300ft (396m)

Beginners ✱✱✱ Intermediates ✱✱ Advanced ✱✱ Snowboarders ✱✱

The Smugglers' Notch pass in Vermont was given its name shortly before the American War of Independence, when it was used for the illicit passage of supplies from Canada. Sensibly, given the nature of its mainly gentle pine-clad slopes, the resort of Smugglers' Notch has not tried to compete with its bigger sisters in Colorado and Utah but has carved a niche that no other resort in the world has so far been able to match. 'Smuggs', as the locals call it, has established itself at the cutting edge of the family market and regularly wins awards for its child-friendly facilities. This is not a resort that attracts couples or singles; in fact you would not choose to come to Smuggs if you did not have small chil-

> ✔ Superb children's facilities (Smuggs)
> ✔ Lack of queues
> ✔ Outstanding ski school (Smuggs)
> ✔ Attractive village of Stowe
> ✘ Subzero temperatures

dren. The key is convenience, with the lifts and accommodation within a 350-yd (320-m) radius and apartments designed with the family in mind.

Smuggs is a small, unadorned village consisting mainly of condominiums. A single sports shop in the village provides the necessary balaclavas and neoprene face masks, and one small supermarket sells provisions for self-caterers.

In complete contrast, the eighteenth-century town of Stowe over the mountain has been a sophisticated tourist centre for more than a century and attracts wealthy Bostonians. It is a typical Vermont town of red-and-white weather-boarded houses set around a steepled white church on attractive Main Street, where most of the shops and some of the accommodation are located. Convenience is not a feature here because, as is often the case in US resorts, the village is separated from the skiing base by 5 miles (8km) of winding highway lined with the customary motels, rental shops and restaurants.

On the snow
Smugglers' Notch: top 3,640ft (1,109m) bottom 1,030ft (314m)
Stowe: top 4,393ft (1,339m) bottom 1,300ft (396m)

The skiing at Smugglers' Notch is mainly benign, with 70 trails serviced by nine lifts, although a handful of unpublicised tricky mogul slopes keep competent parents happy. Snow records are excellent, with an average of 98 inches (250 cm) per season, but patches of unpleasant ice on groomed runs, known locally as 'frozen granular patches', are an all-too-common occurrence. The three mountains – Morse, Madonna and Sterling – are interconnected, and Sterling in turn links with Stowe's Spruce Peak via Snuffy's Trail. This requires a lot of poling in both directions. The old fixed double chair-lifts at Smugglers' Notch are in dire need of upgrading, but their low hourly uphill capacity means that the slopes generally remain uncrowded even in high season.

The skiing at Stowe is on two mountains outside the village centre, with 59 per cent of the trails rated intermediate and a possible 73 per cent of the terrain covered by artificial snow. The top of the skiing is Mount Mansfield, Vermont's highest peak, which is reached in comfort by an eight-seater gondola. Although the ForeRunner quad to the Octagon Web Café is considerably more exposed, it opens up a much bigger part of the mountain, with a choice of runs for all standards.

Beginners

Morse is the beginners' mountain, conveniently situated in the village centre of Smugglers' Notch. A new novice area, Morse Highlands, is set halfway up the mountain and is serviced by five trails. From the top of Morse Mountain at 2,250ft (684m) you can ski along a green (easy) trail to the base of Madonna Mountain and back again. From the top of the Mountain Triple and Toll House Double lifts at Stowe are a network of blue (intermediate) trails to the Toll House base.

Intermediates

More adept snow-users quickly move on from Morse Mountain in Smuggs to the other two mountains, which are reached either by bus or on skis. Madonna Mountain has some pleasant trails such as the blue Upper and Lower Drifter, and Upper and Lower Chilcoot. From the top of the ForeRunner lift at Stowe there are some good blue cruisers, one of which – Rimrock – connects across to the second half of the mountain. Here the choice of trails back to base comprises three blues: Perry Merrill, Switchback and Gondolier.

Advanced

Smugglers' Notch has several sharp double-black-diamond (very difficult) trails, as well as The Black Hole, which is billed as 'the only triple-black-diamond in the east'. The trail directly below the Madonna 1 chair-lift is intimidating: 'Looking down from the chair at rocks covered in ice, I could hardly believe they were actually skiable.'

The skiing can also be near perpendicular in places at Stowe. It is said that if you can ski Stowe's celebrated Front Four, you can ski anywhere. Starr, Liftline, National and Goat are ready to test the most proficient of snow-users, especially when the familiar 'boilerplate' ice is in place. Chinchip is the sole black (difficult) trail back to base on Mount Mansfield.

Off-piste

There is some unpatrolled skiing through the trees, but snow-users in search of powder adventures would be better giving these resorts a miss.

Snowboarders

Madonna at Smuggs has a large terrain park for intermediate and advanced skiers and boarders, with a 300-ft-long (90-m-long) half-pipe and music that belts out above your head from speakers that are attached to the lift pylons. A second terrain park is on Morse, which contains 'hips, rolls and spines', and a new park on Sterling is for beginner riders. There are two funparks at Stowe.

Tuition and guiding

Smugglers' Snow Sports University is the impressive ski and snowboard school at Smuggs. Special courses include 'Dad & Me' and 'Mom & Me', where you and your child are taught together, with the emphasis on picking up useful tips to teach your child yourself. A vast range of other options are available, including Terrain Park Tactics for skiers, riders and snowbladers.

Stowe's Ski and Snowboard School has adult workshops, race clinics, women's ski clinics, courses for seniors, snowblading, telemark, and even Quick Fix where you 'take a run with a personal ski trainer'.

Mountain restaurants

At Smuggs the only on-mountain eating place is the small, bleak hut called Hearth & Candle At The Top Of The Notch. Although it still only provides self-service drinks and snacks served during limited hours, on one evening a week it now also offers gourmet dining (see *Eating in and out*). During the day, most snow-users return to the two bases, where at Morse there is a choice of The Village Lodge, which houses the Green Mountain Café & Bakery, and Rigabello's Pizzeria. At Madonna base you can lunch at the Green Peppers Pub, the Black Bear Lounge, which serves foot-long sandwiches, or the cafeteria with 'boring old hamburger and uninspired pasta'.

The Cliff House Restaurant on Mount Mansfield at Stowe serves a Skiers' Express Lunch for $11.95. Other eating places include HH Bingham's for pasta and seafood, the Midway Café for pizzas and soup, and José's Cantina at Midway for Mexican cuisine. The most unusual place to eat is the Octagon Web Café at the top of Stowe's ForeRunner quad, where computer terminals are set up for guests' use and free email postcards can be sent. The restaurant serves good food and has a new cappuccino bar.

Accommodation

The Village at Smugglers' Notch offers a variety of self-catering apartments. The resort's condominiums are highly recommended for families: 'The best two-bedroomed apartment we have ever seen, with a separate 30-ft sitting room and a television in every room, including one angled above the family-sized whirlpool.'

Staying in Stowe is civilised rather than riotous, especially at the Trapp Family Lodge 4 miles (2.5km) out of town. The tone is opulent Austrian-staid, and afternoon tea is a major attraction. Ye Olde

England Inne plays heavily on its name, with Laura Ashley fabrics in the bedrooms and a red telephone box outside the door; its architecture is Fawlty Towers-Tudor. The Green Mountain Inn is a no-smoking establishment boasting a health club and heated outdoor swimming-pool. The 1860 House is a small bed and breakfast inn. The expensive Inn at the Mountain is the only slope-side accommodation. Altogether Stowe musters 32 three- and four-diamond lodges and restaurants, which is more than any other New England town including Boston.

Eating in and out

All the restaurants in and around Smugglers' Notch are child-friendly. Breakfast is at The Mountain Grille where children under 12 years old are charged half their age in dollars for all they can eat. The Hearth & Candle restaurant is the only eatery that has a separate upstairs section – for adults without children. Hearth & Candle At The Top Of The Notch offers gourmet dining on one evening a week, reached by snow-cat, and is lit solely by candles. Café Bandito's is recommended: 'My children voted it their favourite après-ski spot, they loved the Mexican food and played pool while they waited for their food to arrive'. Three Mountain Lodge has an authentic Vermont atmosphere.

In Stowe, a hearty breakfast is served at The Colonial Coffee Shop from 7am. In the evening, Winfield's in the Stoweflake Resort is recommended for fish, as is The Golden Eagle which specialises in fresh Cape Cod seafood. The Fireside Tavern serves lunch and dinner. Copperfields at Ye Olde England Inne serves game and seafood. The gondola at Mount Mansfield runs in the evening so that visitors can dine in the gastronomic Cliff House Restaurant. La Toscana and Trattoria La Festa both serve Italian cuisine. The pizzas from The Pie in the Sky in Stowe are recommended.

Après-ski

Nightlife in Smuggs is geared to family entertainment, with tobogganing and karaoke evenings, torchlight parades, fireworks and dance parties designed to provide fun for children of all ages. The atmosphere is more Butlins-on-snow than Beaver Creek. After skiing, hot chocolate awaits you as you gather around a camp fire at the foot of Morse Mountain, while a man in a Disney-style mouse suit and another dressed as a bear hand out sweets to children and pose for photos with them.

Floodlit snowboarding and tubing down Sir Henry's Sliding Hill provide the later evening entertainment. Snowshoeing on Sterling Pond is another popular après-ski adventure. There is also a family-friendly swimming-pool under one inflated dome and The Fun Zone 'family play center' under another. The Tub Club has outdoor whirlpools, saunas and steam rooms. Art and craft sessions are available in the resort, along with Tai Chi classes and shows performed by Marko the Magician.

The Family Snowmaking Center is an educational experience you can ski to on your way home on the Meadowlark green trail. A $50 self-drive snowmobile tour of the mountain by night and a skating-rink are the other evening activities.

At Stowe, Mr Pickwick's Polo Pub serves international ales, including Youngs and Morland Old Speckled Hen. Next door, the Fox and Hounds provides further evidence that Stowe is an aspiring home from home for visiting Brits. Bars to look out for include the Backyard Café, which has pool tables, the Shed, which has its own micro-brewery, the Rusty Nail, which often has live music and dancing, and the Broken Ski. However, the resort verdict from a dedicated snowboarder from Pennsylvania was succinct: 'it's even quieter than back home.'

Other activities at Stowe include night-skiing, sleigh rides, snowmobiling, snowshoeing, squash and swimming.

Childcare

Children are what Smuggs is all about, and everything centres around them. The only disadvantage is the numbingly low temperatures. Little ones from just six weeks of age spend their days at Alice's Wonderland Child Care Center, which includes a children's zoo and an outdoor pirate ship playground in the warmer weather. The ski school ('outstanding and put anything in Europe that we had experienced to shame') takes children to and from the slopes in a tractor-drawn trailer, and in the cold weather classes frequently return to base for hot chocolate, videos and snacks. The timed carving course provides endless on-slope entertainment for more proficient children.

The amenities at Stowe's base include Cub's Daycare for children aged between six weeks and six years, and the Children's Adventure Center.

TOURIST INFORMATION
Smugglers' Notch
Tel (0800) 196 8219 (*freephone*)
Fax 1 862 644 2713
Email smuggs@smuggs.com
Web site www.smuggs.com

Stowe
Tel 1 802 253 3000
Fax 1 802 253 3439
Email info@stowe.com
Web site www.stowe.com

Tremblant

ALTITUDE 870ft (265m)

Beginners ✱ Intermediates ✱✱ Advanced ✱✱ Snowboarders ✱✱✱

Located in the Laurentian Mountains, 75 miles (120km) northwest of Montreal, Tremblant offers skiing in a cold climate, combined with a chance to appreciate Quebec culture and cuisine. A massive investment of CD$1 billion over a 10-year period by the owner, Intrawest, has transformed – and is continuing to transform – the traditional ski village into a state-of-the-art resort. Intensive piste-grooming and Canada's largest snowmaking system do much to combat the prevailing icy conditions. The old part of Tremblant has been meticulously restored, and the new section artfully designed to create steeply terraced main streets with painted wooden buildings which are modelled on the old quarter of Montreal. The numerous boutiques in the Place St-Bernard are enticing; the resort has a total of 80 shops and restaurants.

- ✔ State-of-the-art lift system
- ✔ Recommended for families
- ✔ Extensive snowmaking
- ✔ Atmospheric village
- ✔ Wide choice of restaurants
- ✔ Car-free centre
- ✔ Short airport transfer
- ✘ Extremely low temperatures
- ✘ Peak-season overcrowding

On the snow
top 3,001ft (914m) bottom 870ft (265m)

Tremblant opened its first chair-lift in February 1939. Today, it has 50 miles (80km) of varied pistes and 12 lifts, and these figures are still growing. The eight-person heated gondola is a welcome addition to the chair-lifts ('pretty uncomfortable in bad weather'). The lifts on both sides of Tremblant – Versant Sud and Versant Nord – meet at Le Grand Manitou Lodge at the top. Versant Soleil is a new area on the south side of the mountain, which is reached by the new Le Soleil high-speed quad-chair.

Tremblant claims to have Canada's most powerful snow-making system, with 620 snow-cannon that guarantee season-long snow cover. However, reporters agree that the snowmaking is 'excessive', and 'on most days up to two-thirds of the runs were impassable and the noise of these infernal machines was deafening. Both views and sunshine were blocked out by the cloud of vapour rising into the sky'. Peak-week queuing is a problem: 'the resort was very, very busy over Easter, with too many skiers for the size of the ski area'.

The piste map indicates a designated 'mogul zone' and a 'blade zone'. Tremblant boasts 50 miles (80km) of cross-country trails. The small neighbouring ski area of **Gray Rocks** at St Jovite makes an interesting day out when high winds shut the lifts at Tremblant.

Beginners

As much as 16 per cent of the runs are for beginners, so second-weekers and early intermediates are able to go almost anywhere: 'skiing as a family with two small children, we were able to go all over the mountain'. Enchanted Forest is a special beginners' and children's trail on the mountain, which is graded green (easy), and you can also travel from top to bottom of the south face on green trails. However, the downside of the resort is the extreme cold, which can make the first few days in a beginners' class – traditionally spent falling and standing around waiting for others who have fallen – not a lot of fun.

Intermediates

Those keen to bash the pistes will find plenty of scope on both sides of the mountain. Intermediate snow-users have 12 blue (intermediate) trails on the generally easier south face, while over the top the skiing is more challenging.

Advanced

The ski area on both sides of the mountain is surprisingly demanding, with over half designated as advanced terrain. Dynamite is a double-black-diamond (very difficult) trail located on the north side of the mountain; it has a 42° pitch, making it one of the steepest trails in eastern Canada. Beside it, the legendary Expo piste is for lovers of tricky moguls, and Cossack has been the site of three world freestyle championships.

> ## WHAT'S NEW
>
> Le Soleil high-speed quad to Versant Soleil area
> Tremblant Westin Resort four-star hotel
> Increased snowmaking

The Edge is a corner of the mountain that has been set aside for advanced skiers and riders and is served by its own quad-chair. It has three demanding trails – Emotion, Action and Haute Tension – the difficulty of which is accentuated by the icy hardpacked snow conditions which prevail in East Coast resorts.

Off-piste

Three intermediate runs among frozen spruces provide a dramatic introduction to tree-skiing. The Edge sector has some difficult gladed skiing at the sides of its trails.

Snowboarders

The resort is excellent for snowboarders, with two funparks. These include the large floodlit Xzone on the front (south) face of the mountain, which boasts a half-pipe, jumps and obstacles.

Skiing facts: Tremblant

TOURIST INFORMATION
3005 ch. Principal, Mont-Tremblant, QC
JOT 1Z0
Tel 1 819 681 2000
Fax 1 819 681 5996
Email info_tremblant@intrawest.com
Web site www.tremblant.com

THE RESORT
Airport transfer Montreal 1½hrs
Visitor beds 1,400
Transport free bus service

THE SKIING
Linked or nearby resorts Gray Rocks
at St Jovite (n)
Number of lifts 12
Total of trails/pistes 50 miles (80km),
16% easy, 32% intermediate,
41% difficult, 11% very difficult
Nursery slopes magic carpet lift

LIFT PASSES
Area pass CDN$288 for 6 days
Beginners 1 free lift
Pensioners CDN$38 per day for 65yrs
and over
Credit cards yes

TUITION
Adults Tremblant Snowschool
tel: 1 819 681 2000
Snowboarding as ski school
Other courses carving, cross-country,
cybercamps, Discovery Program
(for beginners), moguls, Parallel
Perfection, race camps, seniors,
skiing for the disabled, snowblading,
teen skiing/boarding, telemark,
women's clinics
Guiding no

CHILDREN
Lift pass 6–12yrs CDN$126 for 5 days
Ski & board school as adults
Kindergarten Kidz Club at ski school

OTHER SPORTS
Dog-sledding, horse-riding, ice-climbing,
night-skiing/night-riding, skating,
sleigh rides, snowmobiling, snowshoeing,
swimming, tobogganing, tubing

FOOD AND DRINK PRICES
Coffee CDN$2.50, glass of wine CDN$4,
small beer CDN$4.50, soft drink
CDN$2.50, dish of the day CDN$18

Tuition and guiding
The Tremblant Snowschool organises lessons between 10am and midday
and between 1.30 and 3pm. The school also offers a choice of courses ('a
bewildering variety'). Ladies Love Wednesdays is a crèche- and lunch-
inclusive midweek package bookable through the ski school for women
skiers with children. We have received criticism about the ski school
during high season: 'the queues for ski lessons were awful. After a long
wait we were told that all the classes were full and the next available group
lessons would be in a week's time. Even private lessons were scarce'.

Mountain restaurants
Mountain eating opportunities are disappointing; Le Grand Manitou at
the summit is the only restaurant. It houses a self-service restaurant and
La Légende, a table-service restaurant that promotes its 'fine dining

experience'. Restaurants near the base are easily accessible at lunchtime and provide more variety. These include Le Shack in the square ('a good atmosphere at lunch-time and a view of the slopes').

Accommodation
Six hotels have been built so far, including Château Mont Tremblant, which is undeniably the smartest and most comfortable place to stay on the slopeside. The Lodge de la Montagne and La Tour des Voyageurs are two of the newer hotels, and brand new in April 2000 was the Tremblant Westin Resort four-star hotel containing a bistro, a Japanese restaurant and a spa. Those who prefer self-catering can choose from a variety of condominiums.

Eating in and out
In contrast to the better-known Canadian resorts, such as Banff and Lake Louise, restaurant prices in Tremblant are high – indeed they are equivalent to those in any medium-sized French resort. However, the choice of eating places is wide, ranging from pizzerias to atmospheric establishments serving *cuisine québécois*. Le Gascon, a brasserie transported from the foothills of the Pyrenees, boasts 'outstanding cassoulet and robust bottles of *vin rouge*'. Pizzateria is lively and busy, and Mexicali Rosa's is recommended for its food and service. Coco Pazzo is an elegant Italian restaurant. La Grappe à Vin calls itself a 'resto-bar', specialising in 'rare liquors' and wild game.

Après-ski
The nightlife is concentrated at Vieux Tremblant, which has a growing number of bars and clubs. Le Cirque Blanc is a no-go area for adults, where children up to 18 years of age can play pool and video games, listen to music and enjoy non-alcoholic drinks at the bar. La Source Aquaclub, which has a swimming-pool modelled on a lake with an island in the middle and has a 9-ft deep diving area with rocks to jump from, makes good early evening entertainment. Other activities include deer observation outings.

Childcare
Low temperatures aside, this is an ideal resort for families. At the base of the slopes is the Kidz Club, which is served by a 'magic carpet' conveyor belt lift. The club organises ski lessons for three- to twelve-year-olds and snowboarding from seven years of age, as well as twice weekly après-ski for children (between 5.30 and 9.30pm) including a hot meal. Also in the evening is 'sliding fun for tots' at the base of the mountain.

Vail

ALTITUDE 8,120ft (2,475m)

Beginners ✱✱✱ Intermediates ✱✱✱ Advanced ✱✱✱ Snowboarders ✱✱✱

Vail is the showcase of American skiing. Other resorts, from Vermont to California, look in the window of this Colorado super-store and then race home to emulate what they have seen. Through massive investment in recent years Vail has wooed both domestic and international skiers to its immaculately groomed slopes, and now delivers the largest ski area of any US resort, unbeatable service and guaranteed snow. The primping and pampering of an otherwise mediocre stretch of mountainside signals the danger of homogenising the skiing and snowboarding experience to the level of a Disney-style theme park. However, this cynicism is completely lost on the resort's big-buck owners and its flock of devotees, who heartily concur with Vail's worldwide advertising slogan: 'Once Is Never Enough'. As one reader put it: 'Vail is pure escapism, but then so too is all skiing. Vail may not be Chamonix, but it is still enormous fun'.

- ✔ Favourable snow record
- ✔ Large ski area
- ✔ Separate children's ski area
- ✔ Excellent ski school
- ✔ Easy introduction to off-piste
- ✔ Wide choice of resort restaurants
- ✘ Limited steep terrain
- ✘ Homogenised skiing
- ✘ Limited choice of mountain restaurants
- ✘ High prices

Anyone expecting a classic Rocky Mountain settlement at their journey's end is in for a disappointment. The pedestrianised village centre is built in neo-Tyrolean style with chalets clustered around a central clock tower. Vail's suburbs sprawl for 7 miles (11km) along the busy I-70 freeway. It shares a lift pass with its sister resort **Beaver Creek**, 10 miles (16km) to the west, as well as **Arapahoe Basin**, **Breckenridge** and **Keystone**, and there is a regular subsidised shuttle service between them.

Queuing is not a problem except at the main access points during peak-season rush hour. In the words of one reporter: 'Vail does everything right. It overwhelms you with service and courtesy. Indeed, if you feel it does not, then they want to know about it'.

On the snow
top 11,450ft (3,491m) bottom 8,150ft (2,485m)

Vail's main skiing takes place on the north-facing side of the mountain above the resort and is reached from three main access points along the

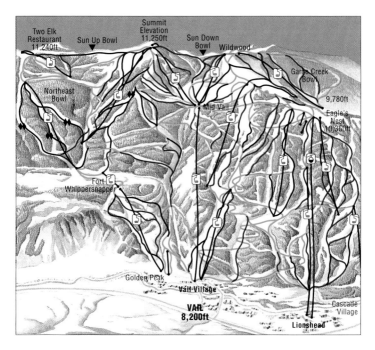

valley floor: the Vista Bahn in Vail Village, a gondola and high-speed quad in Lionshead, and the Riva Bahn Express at Golden Peak. There is also a slow quad chair-lift at Cascade Village. All these lifts are served by an efficient ski bus system. The backside of the mountain is devoted to the largely unpisted Back Bowls area, renowned for its powder. When the resort is busy you can take the new and much under-used detachable quad-chair at Golden Peak, which connects with the Northwoods Express lift and provides direct access to the Back Bowls.

Typical Colorado conditions are on a par with exceptional days in Europe. Ice, crud, bare patches or uncovered rocks are a rarity. Ample fluffy snow and top-to-bottom skiing from mid-November to the end of April is usual. Vail has state-of-the-art snowmaking. A battalion of snowcats manicure the slopes at the end of each day, all the pistes are well signposted, and any obstacles are marked. One criticism, however, is lack of variety. While many of the runs on the front face are indistinguishable apart from their names, some of the steeper trails are heavily mogulled and there is some exciting tree-skiing and plenty of long cruising runs.

Beginners

The two beginner areas in Vail are at Golden Peak and Eagle's Nest. The former, at the east end of the mountain, has a number of easy runs and short lifts at the base area. Fort Whippersnapper, at the mid-station of the Riva Bahn lifts, is an extensive ski-in ski-out playground for children. At Eagle's Nest, reached directly by the gondola from Lionshead, are several easy runs and an activity centre that includes tubing, skating and a funpark. Advanced beginners can find suitable runs on all areas of the mountain by following the green (easy) runs on the piste map.

Intermediates

Vail is essentially an intermediate's mountain. If you want to perfect your turns, the wide open pistes are a perfect training ground. Most skiers head to the top of the mountain via the Vista Bahn to mid-Vail ('worst queues of anywhere in the region'), where two high-speed quads let you explore the central west side of the mountain. The Back Bowls can be reached from the Mountaintop Express or Wildwood Express lifts. Intermediates favour the long, cruising runs from the Northwoods Express or the easier trails off Game Creek Express lift. For fast and smooth cruising you can take the runs off Eagle's Nest Ridge, such as Lodgepole, Berries and Ledges, down to the Avanti chair or all the way to the base. Although the Back Bowls are well-known off-piste areas, they are not at all steep, with the easier runs offering a gentle introduction to powder skiing. A few runs such as Poppyfields are groomed.

> **WHAT'S NEW**
>
> Continued expansion of Blue Sky Basin ski area
> Additional high-speed quad-chair

Advanced

Highline and Roger's Run are both double-black-diamond (very difficult) trails, which are steep and heavily mogulled. Skipper, off the Windows Road catwalk, is little skied and can provide considerable challenge. Ouzo Woods off Faro, Ouzo and Ouzo Glade all offer excellent tree-skiing. Look Ma and Challenge under the Wildwood Express chair are testing in good snow. Kangaroo Cornice, and North Rim under the Northwoods Express are also well worth skiing. Most advanced skiers and riders congregate in the Back Bowls, which provide superb skiing and boarding in true powder conditions. However, they can be closed in bad weather or when snow cover is insufficient.

Off-piste

The Back Bowls provide Vail's off-piste skiing and snowboarding, and it is rewarding to make fresh tracks here on a powder day. Chutes, drop-offs and fine tree-skiing are available in the Mongolia Bowls. Vail's newest bowl, Blue Sky Bowl, which is the next peak across from the Back Bowls, is expanding to add another 125 acres of terrain along with a new high-speed quad. The Minturn Mile takes you down through some scenic and challenging terrain to the small town of **Minturn**; margaritas or pitchers of beer at The Saloon here provide a pleasant end to the outing.

Snowboarders

Vail has enthusiastically embraced snowboarding and prides itself on the variety and challenge of its riding terrain, which includes dedicated pistes cut through the trees. These are marked on a separate snowboarding map. Vail has three half-pipes, one of which – the Tag Heuer – is said to be the largest in the US. The funpark is spread over 12 trails, with a combination of natural and man-made features.

Tuition and guiding

The Vail/Beaver Creek Ski and Snowboard Center, with a total of 1,300 instructors, is one of the largest in the world. In Vail it has six separate locations: at the base of Golden Peak, Lionshead and in Vail Village, and at Two Elk, Mid-Vail and Eagle's Nest. Reporters continue to comment on the high quality of instruction and the friendly attitude of the teachers: 'what a change from Europe. Our instructor became a real pal, and we learned more from her in a week than in the previous three seasons in France'. The school has 150 snowboard teachers with dedicated classes in high season for teenagers. Vail Sno Tours is the off-piste guiding company.

Mountain restaurants

Size rather than intimacy seems to be the priority at most of the mountain restaurants here. The Two Elk self-service reopened in December 1999, built on an even grander scale than previously. The smaller Wildwood Smokehouse is renowned for its tuna sandwiches. Buffalo's at Chair 4 is good for snacks. All the mountain restaurants are owned by the resort and are geared towards high turnover rather than the leisurely lunching enjoyed by most Europeans. Larkspur at Golden Peak is an exception. Garfinkels, or Bart and Yeti's at Lionshead are recommended, as are Pepi's and Los Amigos in Vail Village. The Lodge at Vail has 'a wonderful value lunchtime buffet'.

Accommodation

The Lodge at Vail and the Sonnenalp are the most luxurious hotels. Vail Village Inn and Holiday Inn's Chateau Vail head the second rank. Marriott's Mountain Resort at Vail has spent $10 million upgrading its rooms and is warmly praised. Cheaper are the Roost, in West Vail, and West Vail Lodge.

Eating in and out

The Vail Valley has an enormous choice of restaurants, serving food of every nationality from Mexican to Thai and Japanese. Terra Bistro, in the Vail Athletic Club, and Sweet Basil are praised for their Californian cuisine. The Wildflower in The Lodge, La Tour and the Left Bank are also strongly recommended for a special night out, as are The Tyrolean Inn and Lancelot. Vendetta's is Italian. Montauk in Lionshead is excellent for seafood. The Half Moon Saloon in West Vail is worth a visit, as

Skiing facts: Vail

TOURIST INFORMATION
PO Box 7, Vail, CO 81658
Tel 1 970 496 6772
Fax 1 970 479 2905
Email international@vailresorts.com
Web site www.vail.com

THE RESORT
Airport transfer Eagle County 45mins, Denver 2½hrs
Visitor beds 41,305 in Vail and Beaver Creek
Transport bus between Beaver Creek, Breckenridge, Keystone and Vail (nominal charge)

THE SKIING
Linked or nearby resorts Arapahoe Basin (n), Beaver Creek (n), Breckenridge (n), Keystone (n)
Number of lifts 33
Total of trails/pistes 5,289 acres (2,140 hectares) 28% easy, 32% intermediate, 40% difficult
Nursery slopes 2 areas at Golden Peak and top of Eagle's Nest

LIFT PASSES
Area pass $174–210 (through tour operator), $234–342 (ticket window rates), both for 6 days (covers Arapahoe Basin, Beaver Creek, Breckenridge and Keystone)
Beginners no free lifts
Pensioners free for 70yrs and over
Credit cards yes

TUITION
Adults Vail Ski and Snowboard Center tel: 970 476 3239
Snowboarding Vail Ski and Snowboard Center tel: 970 479 4350
Other courses bumps, carving, cross-country, extreme skiing, powder clinics, race-camps, seniors, skiing for the disabled, teen programmes, telemark, women's ski courses
Guiding Vail Sno Tours tel: 970 476 9090

CHILDREN
Lift pass 5–12yrs, $126 (tour operator rate), $114–222 (ticket window rates), both for 6 days. Free for 4yrs and under
Ski & board school Vail Ski and Snowboard Center tel: 970 476 3239
Kindergarten (ski) Vail Ski and Snowboard Center, (non-ski) Small World Play School tel: 970 479 3290

OTHER SPORTS
Climbing-wall, dog-sledding, hang-gliding, horse-riding, hot-air ballooning, ice-climbing, ice-fishing, ice-hockey, indoor climbing wall, indoor tennis and squash, skating, sleigh rides, snowbiking, snowmobiling, snowshoeing, swimming, thrill sledding, tubing

FOOD AND DRINK PRICES
Coffee $2, glass of wine $5, small beer $3.50, soft drink $3, dish of the day $15

is The Saloon at Minturn ('try their quail speciality'). Up The Creek is praised for its 'excellent duck'. May Palace in the West Vail Mall is a recommended Chinese restaurant. Cassidy's in Avon is 'unique and truly wonderful'. For cheaper food, try the Hubcap Brewery, Kitchen and Pazzo's Pizzeria. Higher up the mountain, the luxurious members-only Game Creek Club is now open to the public at night.

Après-ski

Check out the sunset at the Blue Moon bar at Eagle's Nest, or sip a margarita at Los Amigos at the bottom of the Vista Bahn lift. Mickey's Piano Bar at the Lodge is the place in which to spot celebrities. Other favourite post-ski hang-outs are the deck at Pepi's Bar and the Red Lion. In Lionshead go to Garfinkels, Trail's End or Bart and Yeti's. The Ore House has après-ski happy-hour prices. For coffee go to the Daily Grind, and for tea the Alpenrose. Later on, Garton's has rock'n'roll and sometimes country and western. Club Chelsea has a disco. The Platz'l is one of Vail's hotspots. Locals hang out at The George, and riders at Shieka's and Nick's. Silverthorne, 40 minutes away, has factory outlets such as Nike, Osh-Kosh, DKNY, Gap and Levis, all of which offer some great bargains.

Childcare

The Small World Play School at Golden Peak and at Lionshead is a non-ski kindergarten. The Children's Ski and Snowboard School at both locations is for kids from three to thirteen years of age. After-skiing children's and family programmes include Kid's Night Out Goes Western, for children aged five to thirteen, with music, pizza and a Wild West show. Kids can ski with the Buckaroo Bonanza Bunch, a group of Western characters who tell stories about the Wild West.

Whistler

ALTITUDE 2,214ft (675m)

Beginners ✱✱✱ Intermediates ✱✱✱ Advanced ✱✱✱ Snowboarders ✱✱✱

In the past, less than a dozen resorts (Sun Valley, Cortina d'Ampezzo, Megève, Kitzbühel, Davos, Aspen, St Moritz, St Anton, Chamonix and Val d'Isère) have taken a brief turn as being the acknowledged snow capital of the world, the anvil on which innovation is forged and the seat of learning to which all serious skiers and snowboarders must aspire. However, for the present and for the foreseeable future the baton of honour is firmly grasped by Whistler.

✔ Long vertical drop
✔ Attractive village centre
✔ Modern lift system
✔ Long ski season
✔ Extensive off-piste
✗ Harsh maritime climate
✗ Short skiing days
✗ Weekend lift queues

Whistler in British Columbia provides the most challenging skiing and the most cosmopolitan atmosphere of any ski resort in North America. Here you can ski or snowboard your heart out on two adjoining peaks that offer skiing for all standards, with plunging powder bowls, sheer couloirs and gladed skiing. Down below, the once unconnected villages of Whistler and Blackcomb have been skilfully melded into one charismatic resort by the owners, Intrawest, and Blackcomb has been renamed Upper Village.

It is reached from Vancouver airport by a visually intoxicating drive northwards along the Sea-to-Sky highway 'sandwiched between soaring hemlocks on one side and open vistas of the Pacific on the other'. Whistler is prime evidence that a purpose-built resort can be attractive. It is a mixture of chalet-style apartments, inns, lodges and condominiums, with weatherboarding more in evidence than concrete. Its steep rooflines and pastel colours are an alluring contrast against the snow-capped mountains. There are few large buildings, and the biggest hotel, the Chateau Whistler Resort, is built in a neo-Gothic style. The centre of Whistler is car-free, and getting from Village Square to Mountain Square at the base of the two gondolas involves a two-minute walk. A third area, Market Place, is the cheaper base, where many of the resort staff shop and stay.

Such has been the scale of development that anyone who has not visited Whistler during the past few years would fail to recognise it. With the addition of new condominiums, hotels, shops and restaurants, the resort has virtually doubled in size. The increased number of tourist beds has encouraged mass-market British tour operators to compete with each other, and the immediate effect has been to lower holiday costs dramatically. Purists argue that the character of the resort has already changed irrevocably.

Whistler Mountain stands at only 7,160ft (2,182m) but affords over 5,020ft (1,530m) of vertical – one of the longest continuous drops in North America. Its more rugged neighbour, Blackcomb Mountain, was originally developed in 1980 by a breakaway consortium. The contrastingly different, and often more demanding, terrain includes two glaciers and a set of truly awesome couloirs.

Since Whistler and Blackcomb merged in 1997 some CDN$68 million has been spent on improvements to the lift system and mountain facilities in addition to the CDN$500 million investment in the base area. The final construction stage commenced in summer 2000 – the development of a completely new village in the satellite of Whistler Creek, along with sufficient parking and swift mountain access to absorb the day-visitors from Vancouver, who clog the main resort at weekends. The

> **WHAT'S NEW**
>
> Development has begun on Whistler Creek Village
> Four Seasons Lodge on the piste near Chateau Whistler
> Westin Resort and Spa at base of Whistler Mountain opens in April 2000

continued development has met with opposition from permanent residents, who argue that the focus on increased tourism is too intense and that insufficient funds have been set aside for schools and other social structures needed by such a burgeoning community.

Whistler may indeed be a winter sports colossus, but it has one major problem which no amount of investment can solve. Its maritime position means that much of the heavy winter precipitation falls as rain in the village and only as powder snow higher up. As one reporter put it: 'there is no denying the damp weather and dreary temperamental skies that are the colour of crude oil. Plan to get wet. When it rains, bring an umbrella or kiss your new hair-do goodbye'. A common fact of life in these high mountains is that you never know until you get up there what awaits you at the top. Days go by without one ray of sunshine, but you don't need to pick sunny days to enjoy the skiing. Occasionally the skies clear, and the locals run like startled moles up the mountain. Sunshine days are statistically scarce in comparison with the weather enjoyed by Whistler's Rocky Mountain cousins in the USA. Changes in temperature between village and summit can be frost-bitingly dramatic, although not as extreme as in **Banff/Lake Louise**.

High-season queues – particularly at weekends, when the number of snow-users on both mountains is augmented by day-visitors from Vancouver – are a problem. President's weekend in February (which often coincides with British schools' half-term) should be avoided. However the new Fitzsimmons Express chair-lift from Whistler base as well as a couple more up the mountain have considerably eased congestion. Whistler's position on the edge of the Pacific Rim means it attracts visitors from Japan as well as Europe. As a consequence its shops and restaurants have an international ambience that is unusual in a North

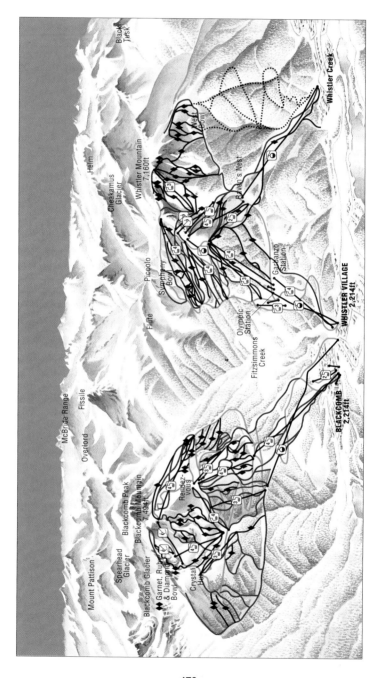

American ski resort. During February the Japanese can account for nearly as high a percentage of the clientèle as the British, when both seek to escape the rigours of their own respective winters. Australians and New Zealanders inevitably complete the equation by providing a fair proportion of the resort workforce.

Whistler's appeal is multi-faceted. The world's top skiers and riders congregate here, and a hardcore have made it their home. As a consequence, equipment and clothing manufacturers see Whistler as the world's premier testing ground for their products.

On the snow
top 7,492ft (2,284m) bottom 2,214ft (675m)

'The variety of skiing is nothing short of startling,' said one reader, 'Whistler stands in a class alone. Be surprised at nothing.' The two mountains of Whistler and Blackcomb stand side by side and share a lift pass, but they are divided by Fitzsimmons Creek and are at present linked only at the foot. Plans to create a mid-mountain gondola link should be realised within five years. For the present, snow-users wanting to cross over from Blackcomb to Whistler have to travel all the way down to the bottom and take a green trail to catch the revamped Whistler Village Gondola or the Fitzsimmons Express chair up the other side. Similarly, Whistler snow-users have to return to the village to take the Excalibur Gondola up Blackcomb. During the 1999–2000 season the resort added two additional high-speed quads to give extra access to Whistler Mountain from the village.

Superficially, the two mountains are not dissimilar: each claims more than a hundred runs and each has long cruising trails. But whereas Whistler is known for its bowls, Blackcomb prides itself on its two glaciers and some dramatic couloirs.

Beginners

Both areas have easy trails high on the mountain, so novices can enjoy the wide-open spaces and a vertical drop usually associated with intermediate ambitions. At Whistler, you can ride all the way up to the Roundhouse on the gondola and also access ski trails such as Upper Whiskeyjack and Pony Trail (where packhorses once helped transport lift equipment). Papoose, Bear Cub and Expressway are other options lower down.

On Blackcomb Mountain take the Wizard Express quad-chair and switch to the Solar Coaster Express, which takes you to the easy Expressway link with the Seventh Heaven Express quad and Xhiggy's Meadow – a black-diamond (very difficult) run that is also the top of the easy Green Line trail. From here beginners can also ski from the top of Crystal Traverse, which leads to the Jersey Cream and Glacier Express quads, both of which access some easy learner trails. Nursery slopes are also situated around the Olympic Station of the Whistler gondola and at the Blackcomb base area.

Intermediates

Whistler and Blackcomb mountains both offer exhilarating top-to-bottom skiing, much of it below the tree-line. Half of the runs on the two mountains are graded intermediate. Easier access routes to Whistler Bowl and West Bowl have opened up this huge area to less experienced snow-users. Franz's run is a 'good high velocity cruiser' that drops from the tree-line all the way to Whistler Creek, where a gondola takes you back up to the mid-station in just seven minutes.

On Blackcomb, the Seventh Heaven Express quad-chair and Showcase T-bar to the Blackcomb Glacier serve mainly intermediate terrain at the top of the mountain. The mid-mountain area beneath the Solar Coaster Express quad-chair is dominated by a large number of medium-standard runs, including the long Springboard trail. Zig Zag and Cruiser are also popular pistes. Rock 'n' Roll on Blackcomb is 'a three-mile screamer with relaxing sections punctuated with steeper plunges'.

Advanced

At Whistler, much depends on whether the Peak chair or Harmony Express quad are open. If not, good advanced terrain can be found around Chunky's Choice and GS. Lower down, Seppo's and Raven off the Black chair-lift provide black-diamond skiing, and the Orange chair accesses the long Dave Murray Downhill and two expert cut-offs: Bear Paw and Tokum. Some of Blackcomb's most difficult runs are among the trees in a broad triangle between the lower sections of the Glacier Express and Crystal Chair, which means you can inspect them before you ski. Trapline, Straight Shot, Rock'n Roll and Overbite are Crystal Chair's featured runs, and The Bite, Staircase and Blowdown are on your right as you board the Glacier Express.

Off-piste

Blackcomb's couloirs and Whistler's bowls are the main areas of interest for off-piste snow-users. Couloir Extreme separates the advanced skier from the expert ('nerves of steel are a distinct advantage'). It is the location for an annual extreme ski-race in which more than a hundred competitors, both professional and amateur, compete in a contest described as '2,500ft of thigh-burning hell'. Pakalolo is another couloir that attracts experienced snow-users. It has a fearsome reputation but is not in the same league as Couloir Extreme. A short hike from the top of the Showcase T-bar on Blackcomb gives access to a delightful intermediate off-piste run down the Blackcomb Glacier. Whistler's five bowls – Symphony, Glacier, Whistler, Harmony and West Bowls – offer a wide spectrum of off-piste challenges. For those prepared to don skins, the touring possibilities are endless. However, it should be noted that couloirs and bowls in the immediate vicinity of the resort that are marked as 'permanently closed' should be avoided. Anyone caught skiing here by the ski patrol is liable to forfeit his or her lift ticket. One local company, Whistler Heli-skiing (see *Heli-skiing*), runs daily excursions.

Snowboarders

Whistler is the best snowboarding resort in Canada and arguably in the whole of North America. The terrain on both mountains is exceptionally well-suited to riding, and both have funparks: 16 acres with two half-pipes on Blackcomb, 26 acres and one half-pipe on Whistler. Blackcomb gives riders the choice of an intermediate or expert run. Whistler is less challenging and offers more of a freeride experience. The best free-riding and off-piste snowboarding is accessed by the new Peak quad-chair. Expect to find a considerable number of skiers and snowbladers in both parks. Some ski-patrol members use boards rather than skis to make riders feel they have equal status on the mountain.

Tuition and guiding

Whistler/Blackcomb Ski and Snowboard School (SSS) has an excellent reputation — 'the tuition was so illuminating, with smooth and rapid progress, that I wondered how we had ever skied without it. We never felt rushed and the instructor answered any questions that we had. Any weak areas were pinpointed with the accuracy of a laser'. The resort's regular free tours of the pistes with some of Canada's greatest skiers are strongly recommended: 'it was an extraordinary experience to ski with someone of world class, and one that I will never forget'. The ski-patrol's Avalanche Awareness Course is described as 'a must for all advanced skiers, but you don't need to be an expert to do it'. Extremely Canadian gives lessons in extreme skiing and snowboarding.

Mountain restaurants

On Whistler Mountain, the totally revamped Roundhouse Lodge promises 'everything from burgers and fries to fresh pasta and Asian cuisine'. However, one reporter described it as 'unappetising and with poor service'. Early birds are recommended to start the day here with the Fresh Tracks programme. You board the Whistler gondola at 7.15 for an all-you-can-eat breakfast before setting off down the mountain as soon as the ski patrol declares it open. However, reporters in high season found the queues 'intolerable – not just for the gondola but also for the self-service breakfast once we were in the restaurant'. The Raven's Nest at the top of the Creekside gondola specialises in pasta and home-made soup. The Chick Pea at the top of the Garbanzo chair-lift opened in the 1999–2000 season and serves soup and snacks.

At Blackcomb, Christine's Restaurant in the Rendezvous Lodge, winner of the Mountain Restaurant of the Year 2000, was described as 'a sad disappointment' by one disgruntled family, 'maybe we got a bad day, but lunch was as dismal and the service as chilly as the weather outside. We booked early and waited forever for food so poorly microwaved that it was still partly frozen. To be fair, the management had the good grace to completely waive the bill, but it was a long way to go for such a poor lunch'. The Rendezvous offers more casual but faster service. The River Rock Grill, upstairs at the Glacier Creek, is praised for 'a cosmopolitan choice of cuisine with wonderful glacier views'. Béla's in the Excalibur Base II Day Lodge serves all-day breakfast. At Excalibur Village Station, Essentially Blackcomb has an outdoor barbecue. Crystal Hut at the top of the Crystal chair-lift is 'just like an atmospheric Swiss or Italian alpine hut with the same primitive toilets'.

Accommodation

The 13-storey Chateau Whistler Resort sits on the edge of the piste at Blackcomb and dominates the skyline as you ski down to the resort. It remains one of the truly great ski hotels of the world, although prices have risen in proportion to demand. We also have good reports of the Delta Whistler Resort ('next to the mountain and very convenient'). The Pan Pacific Lodge is another convenient and centrally placed hotel for both the skiing and the village with all of its shops and restaurants; it also has a swimming-pool. Timberline Lodge is 'comfortable, well-situated and friendly'. The Crystal Lodge and the Listel Whistler Hotel are both popular.

The Town Plaza apartments are 'comfortable and well-located – or rather would have been if our bedroom window had not overlooked the entrance to Garfinkel's night club which made any sleep difficult.' Westin Resort and Spa at the base of Whistler Mountain opened in April 2000. Work has started on the new Four Seasons Lodge on the piste near Chateau Whistler Resort. Condominiums at the Blackcomb Lodge and Mountainside Lodge are both recommended. Carney's Cottage is 'the best bed-and-breakfast in, or rather on the edge of, town'. Haus Stephanie is 'a friendly little bed-and-breakfast'. Travel firms operate a growing number of catered chalets. It is worth checking the exact position before booking as many are situated an inconvenient distance from the lifts and village centre.

Eating in and out

You can tell a remarkable amount about a ski resort by its restaurants – in this case 87 of a dozen nationalities. As one reporter put it: 'eating out in Whistler is nothing short of sensational. We ate Japanese, Chinese, Thai, Italian, Greek, French, American and pub food. We did not have one bad or even mediocre meal'. Trattoria di Umberto and Il Caminetto di Umberto are both recommended along with La Rua. The Wildflower Restaurant in the Chateau Whistler Resort is warmly praised: 'smart dining, not too expensive and very worthwhile'. Zeuski's Taverna is said to have 'soundly priced and tasty meals'. Sushi Village ('excellent but expensive – so popular that we booked before we even left home') is one of eight Asian restaurants. Ristorante Araxi has Mediterranean cuisine and is 'absolutely delightful'. Monks Grill, Thai On One and the Garibaldi Lift Co. are all warmly praised. Ingrid's Café

Skiing facts: Whistler

TOURIST INFORMATION
4010 Whistler Way, Whistler,
BC V0N 1B4
Tel 1 604 664 5625
Fax 1 604 932 5758
Email reservations@tourismwhistler.com
Web site www.tourismwhistler.com

THE RESORT
Airport transfer Vancouver Airport 2hrs,
frequent coach service to resort
Visitor beds 20,000
Transport free shuttle bus within the
village loop

THE SKIING
Linked or nearby resorts Whistler
Creek (l)
Number of lifts 33
Total of trails/pistes 7,050 acres
(2,853 hectares), (20% easy,
55% intermediate, 25% difficult)
Nursery slopes 5 baby lifts
Summer skiing mid-June to mid-August
on Horstman Glacier at Blackcomb
Mountain

LIFT PASSES
Area pass CDN$324 for 6 days
Beginners no free lifts
Pensioners 65yrs and over, CDN$275 for
6 out of 7 days, 75yrs and over ski free
Credit cards yes

TUITION
Adults Whistler/Blackcomb SSS
tel: 604 932 3434,
Extremely Canadian: 604 932 4105
Snowboarding as ski school, Extremely
Canadian tel: 604 938 9656
Other courses avalanche awareness,
cross-country, heli-skiing and -boarding,
race camps, slalom, teenagers' courses,
women's clinics
Guiding Whistler Alpine Guides Bureau
tel: 604 932 4040, Whistler Heli-skiing
tel: 604 932 4105

CHILDREN
Lift pass 7–12yrs, CDN$162, 13–18yrs,
CDN$275, both for 6 out of 7 days
Ski & board school Ski Scamps at
Whistler and Blackcomb
tel: 604 932 3434
Kindergarten (ski) as ski school, (non-ski)
The Nanny Network tel: 1 604 938 2823

OTHER SPORTS
Dog-sledding, indoor climbing wall,
indoor tennis and squash, parapente,
skating, sleigh rides, snowmobiling,
snowshoeing, swimming

FOOD AND DRINK PRICES
Coffee CDN$1.50, glass of wine CDN$7,
small beer CDN$5, soft drink CDN$1.50,
dish of the day CDN$10–22

is 'cheap, cheerful and wholesome'. Queues for the Hard Rock Café
are 'tiresome, but it is worth the wait'. Nester's is said to be the
best-priced supermarket.

Après-ski
Whistler's nightlife is highly praised by reporters: 'the bars and nightlife
were wonderful – no drunks and hooligans, just loads of friendly, happy
people telling you their escapades of the day's skiing'. Dubh Linn Gate
is an Irish pub described by one reporter as ' a great place to step out of

your wet clothes and into a dry Martini'. The Longhorn Saloon at the foot of the slopes catches skiers and snowboarders as they come off the mountain ('beers gush from the tap like oil from a pipeline, a great place for anyone slightly deaf and with a cast-iron liver'). Merlin's at Blackcomb base is lively. Tapley's Pub is 'friendly, cheap and used by the locals'. Garfinkel's, Tommy Africa's and the Savage Beagle are all extremely popular nightclubs. One of the newer 'in' places for riders is the Maxx Fish disco. Shops stay open until 10pm, and shopping is a core part of the evening entertainment either before or after dinner, with ski clothing such as North Face at approximately half British prices, plus a Helly-Hansen outlet. Other shops worth visiting include a Guess Jeans shop and a large Gap. Lush 'sells unusual unguents for the bath,' and Skitch Knicknacks & Paddywacks is for original gifts.

Childcare

Whistler Kids caters for children aged three months to twelve years on both mountains with all-day care and lessons for appropriate ages – 'my four-year-old daughter learned more in a week than she had done in two previous weeks in France. She enjoyed every minute of it and cried when she had to leave'. Whistler/Blackcomb SSS also runs special classes for teenagers. Parents with small children at the kindergarten are given optional pagers so they can be called anywhere on the mountain if their child needs them. Ski Scamps ski and snowboard school is based at Whistler and Blackcomb mountains. The Nanny Network provides babysitters who will come to your lodging during the day or evening ('we booked in the morning during the busiest week of the year and childcare was instantly arranged for that evening').

Round-up

RESORTS COVERED Alberta: Jasper. British Columbia: Big White, Fernie, Panorama, Red Mountain, Silver Star, Sun Peaks. Colorado: Arapahoe Basin, Copper Mountain, Crested Butte, Purgatory, Steamboat, Telluride, Winter Park. Idaho: Sun Valley. Maine: Sunday River. Montana: Big Sky. New Mexico: Taos. Quebec: Mont Sainte-Anne

ALBERTA

Jasper
top 8,533ft (2,601m) bottom 5,640ft (1,719m)

The most northerly and arguably the most beautiful of Canadian resorts is set among the glaciers, forests, frozen lakes and waterfalls of Jasper National Park. The ski area at **Marmot Basin**, a 20-minute drive from the town, is not large but the terrain is extremely varied, with open bowls, steep chutes and glades cut through the trees. The 53 trails are split evenly between green (easy), blue (intermediate) and black (difficult), and are serviced by seven lifts. The longest run is three and a half miles (5.6km) long. Plans are at an advanced stage for a new quad chair-lift for the 2001–2 season to provide easy access to extensive terrain on Eagle East, Chalet Slope, and part of Thunder Bowl

Founded by fur traders in 1811, Jasper has developed into a typical Canadian railroad town, with a wide choice of restaurants and bars. In spite of the long transfer time (Calgary International Airport is a five-hour drive to the south) visitors say that the resort is an exceptionally good place in which to unwind.

Alpine Sports Training Center organises skiing, snowboarding and telemark classes. Children can take private tuition from three years old and group lessons from four.

A dozen hotels are headed by the Jasper Park Lodge, a huge Canadian Pacific hotel at Lac Beauvert on the outskirts of the town. It has 442 rooms spread out in bungalows and two-storey buildings in the extensive grounds, plus four restaurants, a nightclub, shopping mall and an outdoor heated swimming-pool, and is a resort in its own right.

Its main rival, Chateau Jasper, is a quarter of the size and much closer to the action, with friendly staff and fine food. The Whistler Inn, a budget hotel named after a local mountain, is smaller still and even more central, with its own Italian restaurant, pub, and wildlife museum. Other entertainment includes ice-climbing, sleigh rides, snowmobiling and skating on the lake. The ice-covered Maligne Canyon is unique, and heli-skiing (see *Heli-skiing*) is possible at **Valemount**, an hour's drive away.

TOURIST INFORMATION
Tel 1 780 852 3816
Fax 1 780 852 3533
Email info@skimarmot.com
Web site www.skimarmot.com

BRITISH COLUMBIA

Big White
top 7,606ft (2,319m) bottom 4,950ft (1,508m)

The recipient of lavish funding that many resorts would envy, this Australian-owned mountain is in the process of transforming itself into a major player in the Okanagan Highlands, to the east of the huge Lake Okanagan. Local lore has it that Big White is named after the cloud that often conceals it. The resulting humidity creates a phantom forest of snow-ghosts: trees frozen into eerie formations reminiscent of the dinosaurs in *Jurassic Park*. The extensive, but predominantly gentle, ski area is better suited to families than radical adventurers but, given sunshine and powder, Big White is a magical place. The snowboarding is spectacular, with two funparks, a half-pipe, an illuminated quarter-pipe (for night-riding) and some large powder bowls.

The nine-lift system provides high-speed access to 2,150 acres (870 hectares) of terrain, of which only 750 acres (304 hectares) are groomed. A wide variety of green and blue trails can be reached via Ridge Rocket Express, Bullet Express and Black Forest Express, while the much shorter Plaza quad-chair gives access to a first-timer's area and children's park below the main village. Advanced skiers must head for less speedy lifts: the Alpine T-bar for steep, open slopes, or the Powder Chair for glade-skiing.

Big White's Ski and Snowboard School has 60 instructors who teach kids and adults. Tot Town Daycare caters for children aged eighteen months to six years old, and Ski Cubs looks after children aged three to six years.

All the accommodation is ski-in ski-out. Coast Resort is smart and comfortable. The White Crystal Inn has rooms as big as football pitches and is just about as chilly, but its Grizzly Bear lounge is popular for après-ski. Snowshoe Sam's is a particularly good example of the one-stop nightlife that is typical of the British Columbian interior: rough-hewn and friendly, with pool tables, a dance area and a restaurant – it is all things to all visitors, which is fortunate because the alternatives are few. Seven eating places range from cafés to establishments offering fine dining.

TOURIST INFORMATION
Tel 1 250 765 3101
Fax 1 250 765 8200
Email bigwhite@bigwhite.com
Web site www.bigwhite.com

Fernie
top 6,316ft (1,925m) bottom 3,500ft (1,067m)

Until 1998 Fernie was a little-known and unfashionable resort in the southeast corner of the British Columbian Rockies with unexpectedly good terrain and an exceptional snow record. It is in the midst of a major $100-million expansion – doubling its terrain – having been acquired in 1998 by Charlie Locke, the owner of a portfolio of Canadian resorts including Lake Louise. It now has nine lifts serving some 2,504 acres (1,013 hectares) of skiing and claims to be the fourth largest ski resort in Canada. With an extensive array of steeper-than-average terrain, impressive off-piste opportunities in five bowls and challenging snowcat-skiing, it is 'reminiscent of Argentière before it got too busy – some of the best terrain I have every skied anywhere'.

The two main peaks tower above the base area of Timberline Villages, giving evocatively named black-diamond runs such as Stag Leap, Sky Dive and even blue trails the appearance of being so steep as to be scarcely skiable. Fortunately, this transpires to be something of an illusion. Conversely, a few of the many green trails are quite steep for novices. Fernie is a good resort for learning to snowboard, with plenty of suitable trails.

Snowcat-skiers and -boarders will be in their element. Several companies will arrange trips, including Island Lake Lodge, with 7,000 acres (2,833 hectares) of terrain six miles (10km) further along the valley, and Fernie Wilderness Adventures.

The children's programme is extensive: Ski Bunnies for three-year-olds, Ski Wizards And Surfers for children between five and twelve years of age and a Freeriders Programme for experienced children up to the age of 17. Resort Kid's Daycare looks after children from 35 months from 8.30am to 4.30pm.

The somewhat drab town of Fernie, three miles and five minutes' drive to the east, has the potential but as yet little of the glitz of such Rocky Mountain mining-towns-turned-ski-resorts as Telluride or Crested Butte. However, one reporter says it is preferable to stay here rather than at the resort.

Accommodation at the rapidly expanding base area includes condominiums and an assortment of brand new chalets and town houses. Cornerstone Lodge is 'the best location on the mountain'. Three new lodges opened in the 1999–2000 season. In town, the Regal Hotel is said to be 'hugely characterful'. Park Place Lodge is 'spacious and modern' but has 'disappointingly impersonal service'. The Ginger Beef Restaurant is 'to be avoided, greasy platefuls of food pretending to be Chinese'. Gabriella's Restaurant at the base area is recommended: 'Italian food with Canadian *bonhomie*'.

TOURIST INFORMATION
Tel 1 250 423 4655
Fax 1 250 423 6644
Email info@skifernie.com
Web site www.skifernie.com

Panorama
top 7,800ft (2,360m) bottom 3,800ft (1,158m)

Panorama lies a two-hour drive to the southwest of Banff and is on the edge of the Bugaboos mountain range, best known for its heli-skiing (see *Heli-skiing*). The lift system also gives Panorama 4,000ft (1,220m) of vertical, one of the longest in North America.

Ten lifts serve 80 runs. More than half of the 2,000 acres (809 hectares) of terrain is intermediate, with long, sweeping runs making the most of the impressive vertical. Beginners can gain confidence on easy and magnificently groomed runs. The Panorama heli-skiing operation, based in the village, involves an exhaustive instructional preamble, followed by three to four runs and a picnic lunch. Other activities include night-skiing and night-boarding, skating, sleigh rides, snowmobiling and tubing. Wee Wascals Childcare looks after children aged 18 months to five years.

This is a small family resort, which until recently has consisted of a single ski-in ski-out hotel and a few condominiums. However, in summer 2000 a new 82-condominium hotel in the upper village – close to the Ski Tip and Tamarack Lodges – opened. Panorama's condominiums at Ski Tip, Tamarack, Horsethief, Toby Creek, Hearthstone and Panorama Springs are all equipped with kitchenettes and fireplaces. The Pine Inn is functional, and breakfast may be included in the price. The Kicking Horse is the liveliest bar, the Jackpine pub is great for a pint and darts, Heliplex offers 'fun food', and Toby Creek leads the way for fine dining.

The owner, Intrawest, has invested CDN$70 million to date in the resort. New for the 1999–2000 season was a condo-hotel, a waterpark, a people-mover in the village, as well as more ski trails. *Ski Canada* magazine rates Panorama as having the Best Ski School, Best New Terrain and Best New Base Area. Panorama is part of the Canadian Rockies Super Pass, enabling you to ski at eight other resorts, including **Banff/Lake Louise**, Fernie, **Nakiska**, **Kimberley**, and **Fortress Mountain**. The latter has some excellent tree skiing and is particularly recommended for snowboarders.

TOURIST INFORMATION
Tel 1 250 342 6941
Fax 1 250 342 3395
Email paninfo@intrawest.com
Web site www.panoramaresort.com

Red Mountain
top 6, 800ft (2,072m) bottom 3,888ft (1,185m)

Rossland, the distressed mining town that serves Red Mountain, had its heyday in the 1890s when the discovery of gold and copper attracted fortune hunters including immigrant Scandinavians, who established the first local ski club in 1896. Their rugged, macho view of skiing has been carefully conserved by Eric Skat Petersen, who has been running

Red Mountain in his own ebullient image since 1989. By refusing to invest in state-of-the-art lifts, he has kept the pioneering spirit intact, and the terrain has done the rest. The resort has 83 trails, four chair-lifts and a T-bar, and the longest run is four and a half miles (7.5km).

Located in the Kootenay Mountains, very close to the US border, Rossland enjoys a microclimate with higher temperatures and clearer skies than elsewhere in the Canadian Rockies. It is most readily reached via Spokane in Washington State, a two- to three-hour drive away, although it is also possible to fly into Castelgar via Calgary. Red's hard core is made up of ski bums, many of whom have small incomes and enjoy the machismo that goes with the territory throughout the winter. Most of the passing strangers see their visit as a rites-of-passage pilgrimage to a resort with a reputation for testing the best. Snowboarders view the resort as one of the top two in Canada (the other is Whistler), with especially good riding for experienced freeriders.

Beginners and intermediates have limited prospects in Red Mountain. However, the old slow double chair-lift has been replaced by two triple chair-lifts, which have greatly improved access to some of the less formidable runs. Because everyone who skis Red skis trees, all the pistes have sizeable moguls to add to the general sense of hazard. Most of the runs have open bowls interspersed with gladed sections of varying degrees of difficulty. Beer Belly, Short Squaw and Powder Fields are skiable one way or another, but the trees tighten up on Roots and Paleface, while Cambodia, with its 15-ft (4.5-m) drops over frozen waterfalls, is a stretch too far for most people.

The main hotel in Rossland is the Uplander, which has simple rooms but serves unexpectedly good meals in the Louis Blue Dining Room. The hotel also has the Powder Keg Pub, the town's hotspot, with pool tables and a video ski game. Ramada is opening a new base-area hotel for the 2000–1 season. The Ram's Head Inn, a comfortable bed-and-breakfast establishment, is close enough to the slopes to ski back to, but the most convenient place to stay is the family-run Red Shutter, right next to the car park; it is so small that it is often fully booked by groups of up to 12.

The Swiss Alps Inn serves the best *Rösti* breakfast in town. The only on-mountain restaurant is at Paradise Lodge, but Rafters, on the third floor of the base lodge, has a simple but substantial lunch menu, a well-stocked bar and a cheerful ambience.

TOURIST INFORMATION
Tel 1 250 362 7384
Fax 1 250 362 5833
Email redmtn@ski-red.com
Web site www.ski-red.com

Silver Star
top 6,280ft (1,915m) bottom 3,780ft (1,152m)
The design of Silver Star is a law unto itself – a colourful ski-in ski-out village, which is said to be modelled on a typical British Columbian

mining town of the 1890s and painted in unexpectedly bright colours. However, the cheerful paint is welcome in a place where temperatures may dip to uncomfortable levels – even though it is said to have the best weather of any Canadian Rocky Mountain ski resort. It is currently undergoing a CDN$150-million expansion. Improvements for 2000–1 include a new 10,000 square foot day lodge and a 130-bed slope-side youth hostel.

The most challenging skiing is to be found on the north-facing Putnam Creek side of the mountain, reached by a long high-speed quad-chair. This area has a 'hike-in adventure skiing area' called Valhalla as well as a network of the highest number of double-black-diamond (expert) trails in British Columbia.

The south-facing Vance Creek area overlooking the village has long cruises recommended for intermediates: Sundance, Whiskey Jack and Interloper. The Yellow Chair serves a funpark, and the Silver Queen Chair a beginners' area. In all, Silver Star has nine lifts serving 2,600 acres (1,012 hectares), and a proposed new quad-chair would give access to a further 4,000 acres (1,619 hectares).

The Craigellachie Room at Putnam Station Inn features beef, salmon and trout. The Wine Cellar, also at the inn, serves a good selection of wines. Paradise Camp, at mid-mountain, offers a varied menu that includes buffalo burgers.

The heart of the village resembles a pedestrianised film set, with horse-drawn sleighs adding a further touch of theatricality. The Delta Silver Star Club Resort is the most prominent hotel. The recently-modernised Vance Creek has two acceptable restaurants – Lucciano's Trattoria and Clementine's Dining Room. Even better is the Silver Lode Restaurant, a genuine Swiss outpost serving *Apfelstrudel* and *Bratwurst*. The town of Vernon is 20km away and offers a bigger choice of facilities. Star Kids Centre takes children from 18 months of age with optional ski lessons for those aged over three years.

TOURIST INFORMATION
Tel 1 250 542 0224
Fax 1 250 558 6090
Email reserv@junction.net
Web site www.skisilverstar.com

Sun Peaks
top 6,814ft (2,077m) bottom 3,970ft (1,210m)

Nancy Greene, who became the *grande dame* of Canadian ski-racing after winning the Olympic gold at Grenoble in 1968, came to Sun Peaks via Red Mountain, where she was born and raised, and Whistler, where she played a key role in developing the resort. Now she and her husband, Al Raine, are aiding the transformation of Tod Mountain – the local hill for the logging town of Kamloops for the past 30 years – into Sun Peaks, a modern five-lift resort funded with CDN$150 million of Japanese money. Sun Peaks is the newest resort in British Columbia and is considered to be one of the most beautiful villages in Canada – with a 3,000-ft (1,000-m) vertical drop.

Sun Peaks lies deep in the British Columbian heartland, a four-hour drive east of Whistler. Alternatively, it can be reached by plane to Kamloops, via Vancouver or Calgary. Sun Peak has picked up a number of national accolades including *Ski Canada* magazine's award for Best Grooming, Best Hotel Service and Best Family Features.

The change of resort name was prompted by the need for an international image – Tod means 'death' in German – but the best skiing is still on Mount Tod. The Top of the World area is a steep-sided dome above the tree-line, with advanced skiing in chutes and bowls. The toughest terrain is on the lower half of the Burfield quad chair-lift. Challenger is one of the steepest marked trails in Canada. Other demanding runs are on the Headwalls, a wide face of short, double-black-diamond shots above the main on-mountain pit stop, the Sunburst Lodge. However, a five-mile (8-km) green trail leads from the top of the skiing back to the resort, making it user-friendly for all standards.

Below the tree-line, the mountain flattens out progressively, with the easiest slopes just above the resort. This is an excellent arrangement for beginners and lower intermediates, who have their own zone served by the Sundance Express quad. This is an ideal resort for beginner snowboarders, but the more experienced are also well catered for by a vast funpark boasting half-pipes and its own access lift. The ski area between the tree-line and the village, served by the Sunburst Quad, offers excellent moguls and some of the best advanced cruising terrain in this part of Canada.

The Village Day Lodge, a study in elegant design in local timber and glass, has a gastronomic restaurant and an excellent ski rental shop. Nancy Greene's Cahilty Lodge, in a sheltered position overlooking the valley, offers four-star comfort. Sun Peaks Village is ski-in ski-out and now has six slopeside hotels. An array of two dozen shops is set in a pedestrian mall, and the new eateries range from steakhouses to a Japanese restaurant. Sun Peaks has two outdoor skating rinks and an outdoor swimming-pool.

TOURIST INFORMATION
Tel 1 250 578 7842
Fax 1 250 578 7843
Email info@sunpeaksresort.com
Web site www.sunpeaksresort.com

COLORADO

Arapahoe Basin
top 13,050ft (3,967m) bottom 10,780ft (3,283m)

Arapahoe Basin (or A-Basin as it is usually known) is a small, steep ski area that first opened its lift-served skiing in 1948. Its high altitude means that skiing is assured here until June, when Keystone and other neighbouring resorts have closed. A-Basin can be skied on the Vail lift pass, which also includes Beaver Creek, Breckenridge and Keystone. From the top of the Lenawee and Norway lifts almost every run down the middle is intermediate or beginner terrain, and Dercum's Gulch gives access to the long easy runs of Wrangler, Sundance and Chisholm. At the top of the ski area, Palavicinni is one of the longest and steepest bump runs in North America, and the Alleys and East Wall provide some exciting off-piste. Five lifts serve 490 acres (198 hectares) of terrain.

A-Basin has a ski and snowboarding school for adults and children but does not have any of its own accommodation. The nearest is six miles (10km) away at **Keystone**. The Legends Café and the 6th Alley Bar is a popular après-ski venue. Kids Room takes children from four months to seven years with optional one-to-one lessons for older children. Children's Centre Nursery caters for children from one to three years old.

TOURIST INFORMATION
Tel 1 888 272 7246
Fax 1 970 496 4546
Email abasin@colorado.net
Web site www.arapahoebasin.com

Copper Mountain
top 12,313ft (3,767m) bottom 9,712ft (2,926m)

Copper Mountain, situated on the Denver side of the Vail Pass, has been the subject of a complete $400-million makeover since it was acquired in 1998 by Canadian resort developer Intrawest. The new resort base is slowly emerging from the initial building-site phase, and contractors promise to complete the second construction phase before the start of the 2000–1 season. The car-free village is set around four new lodges and plazas with shops and restaurants. This should be a major improvement on the original village which was constructed in a style reminiscent of a French purpose-built resort – which may explain the presence of Club Med. One reporter described the resort as 'having all the aesthetic appeal of a North American Les Menuires'. However, the actual skiing is well worth the visit. Copper likes to describe its ski area as one of the best-designed in North America.

There is a natural tendency for the tree-lined trails to become more difficult as you move east (left on the piste map). Thus, advanced skiers and boarders tend to stick to the main face of Copper Peak, and beginners will find little beyond their capabilities on the west side of the resort. In between, the terrain is mainly intermediate. Copper Bowl and Spaulding Bowl provide some of the best off-piste skiing in Colorado, with the latter full of natural jumps and lips for riders. Copper has a total of 21 lifts serving 118 groomed trails. The mountain summit is reached in eight minutes by the six-person detachable Super Bee chair-lift.

Copper Mountain Ski and Snowboard School offers group and private lessons, as well as bumps and powder workshops and beginner packages. Most of the accommodation is in apartments. Copper's nightlife is fairly quiet, with the exception of the popular O'Shea's restaurant. The Double Diamond Grill and good-value Farley's Prime Chop House are recommended. Imperial Palace is an oriental restaurant which 'does a first-class take-away'. Molly B's is new and serves burgers and pasta.

The Copper Mountain Racquet and Athletic Club has excellent facilities, including a swimming-pool, indoor tennis and racquet-ball courts. Belly Button Babies kindergarten accepts children from two months to two years old, and its stablemate, the Belly Button Bakery, caters for children over two and skiers over three years of age. Copper Mountain has Junior and Senior ski programmes for children.

TOURIST INFORMATION
Tel 1 970 968 2882
Fax 1 970 968 6142
Email copper-marketing@ski-copper.com
Web site www.ski-copper.com

Crested Butte
top 12,162ft (3,707m) bottom 9,100ft (2,774m)
This small, historic town is one of the most attractive ski resorts in Colorado. In the old town's Main Street, 40 of the original nineteenth-century buildings, with their colourful wooden façades, have been converted into shops and restaurants, giving the place a Wild West atmosphere. The town is overlooked by the Butte (pronounced as in 'beaut-iful'), which is a mountain that stands alone. Hotels and guesthouses scattered around the town include the Nordic Inn, a family-run ski lodge which is firmly recommended. The other option is to stay at either the Sheraton Resort or at the new Club Med (it takes children from four years old), which has opened a village where the Marriott used to be. Both are at the base of the ski slopes three miles (5km) away from the town. Crested Butte's nightlife has a cowboy atmosphere and is mainly good value. The Idle Spur has live music, steaks and beer, and Talk of the Town is another busy place to hang out.

Crested Butte is renowned for its steep skiing and each year hosts ski-extreme championships. At the opposite end of the scale, it also has some of the easiest skiing in Colorado. The resort's 14 lifts serve 1,434 acres (580 hectares) of ski terrain. A high 58 per cent of the runs are classed as difficult, 29 per cent intermediate and 13 per cent easy. The Extreme Limits area comprises some 550 acres (223 hectares) of ungroomed extreme skiing and snowboarding, which locals claim is some of the most challenging in Colorado. Off-piste enthusiasts would be wise to hire the services of a local mountain guide or at the very least buy *The Extreme Limits Guide*, which is a lift and trail guide telling you where it is safe to ride and ski. Crested Butte's funpark is designated for riders only.

Children under two years old ski free, children under 16 years pay their age in dollars per day. The Baby Bears kindergarten takes potty-trained toddlers.

TOURIST INFORMATION
Tel *freephone* (0800) 894085/ 970 349 2222
Fax 1 970 349 2397
Email info@cbmr.com
Web site www.crestedbutteresort.com

Purgatory
top 10,822ft (3,299m) bottom 8,793ft (2,680m)

Purgatory is a purpose-built, alpine-style resort 25 miles from Durango Airport and receives enthusiastic praise from reporters: 'it has an old town feel in an unspoilt forest area of the Rockies. We felt very welcome and shall be endeavouring to make a return visit soon'. The ski area has 10 lifts and 1,200 acres (486 hectares) of trails.

Purgatory Ski and Snowboard School offers group and private lessons to adults and children. The kindergarten accepts non-skiing children from two months old, and from three years for skiing. Snowboarders are well catered for with the Pitchfork Snowboard Park. The Adaptive Sports Association provides lessons for disabled skiers and is ranked as one of the best ski schools of its type in the USA.

Powderhouse, which serves pizzas, pasta and salads, and Dante's ('downstairs self-service, upstairs sit-down service') are the only two on-mountain restaurants, while Columbine Station is at the base of the slopes of the same name. Farquahrt's in the village centre serves pizzas to live music. Powdermonkey Grill is a 10-minute free shuttle-bus ride from the centre and receives rave reports: 'the very pleasant owner welcomes his guests personally, and the atmosphere and quality of the food is of an extremely high standard'. Purgatory and Durango together have over 50 eateries including Mexican, oriental and Mediterranean restaurants.

Mountain area hotels include the Purgatory Village Hotel and Sheraton Tamarron Resort. The Twilight View Condos are recommended ('huge picture windows and balconies overlooking the ski slopes'). Of the nine bed-and-breakfasts, Apple Orchard Inn, Blue Lake Ranch, Country Sunshine and River House all boast fireplaces and hot tubs.

Other activities in the resort include cross-country, sleigh rides, snowmobiling, tubing and visits to the local hot springs.

TOURIST INFORMATION
Tel 1 970 247 9000
Fax 1 970 385 2107
Email dweltz@frontier.net
Web site www.ski-purg.com/snow

Steamboat
top 10,568ft (3,221m) bottom 6,900ft (2,103m)

Steamboat lies at the foot of Rabbit Ears Pass in northwest Colorado, a 3½-hour drive from downtown Denver. Winter sports started here as long ago as 1912, when a Norwegian, Carl Howelsen, introduced ski-jumping lessons. Downhill skiing took off in the 1960s, triggered by the opening of the first double chair-lift on Storm Mountain. Snowboarders are particularly welcome and account for one in three of the lift tickets sold. The resort is part of the empire of the American Skiing Company and has 20 lifts serving 2,939 acres (1,189 hectares) of skiing.

Each January Steamboat hosts The Cowboy Downhill, a unique slalom with roping and saddling elements contested by more than 100 professional rodeo riders in full costume. While Steamboat trades heavily on this cowboy motif in its marketing strategy, the reality is that it has less of a Wild West atmosphere than Colorado rivals Crested Butte and Telluride.

The skiing covers three interlinked mountains: Sunshine Peak, Storm Peak and Mount Werner. Although the area is served by a modern lift system backed up by extensive snowmaking, the terrain is of limited variety and challenge. The Silver Bullet gondola takes snow-users up to the Thunderhead mid-station, and two high-speed quads allow them to fan out rapidly over the upper slopes.

The development of the Morningside Park bowl off the back of Storm Peak provides gentle terrain and better access to the rugged skiing off the face of Mount Werner. The Pioneer Ridge sector opens up 12 trails mainly for advanced skiers.

The wide, flat area at the base of the gondola is an ideal place to learn to ski or board and is served by six beginner lifts. Steamboat Ski School offers lessons for adults, children and teenagers. The Billy Kidd Center provides more advanced training in bumps, racing and other disciplines. The Kids Vacation Center takes skiing children from two to six years old. Babies and non-skiing children are looked after at Kiddie Corrall Child Care.

In tune with the current trend in the Rockies, Steamboat provides gourmet lunches as a supplement to cafeteria fare. The most sophisticated option is Hazie's at the Thunderhead mid-station. The alternative sit-down choice, Ragnar's at Rendezvous Saddle, specialises in Scandinavian dishes. Both the Thunderhead and Rendezvous self-services have sun-deck barbecues.

Visitors stay either at the purpose-built Steamboat base area or four miles (6km) away in the town of Steamboat Springs. The Steamboat Grand Resort and Conference Center – the resort's first venture into the hotel business – opens for the 2000–1 season. The Sheraton and the Ptarmigan Inn close to the lifts at Steamboat are both recommended. But the real action is in the Old Town area of Steamboat Springs, which houses shops that go far beyond the normal range of ski-related goods as well as the best restaurants. The Harbor Hotel and the Alpiner Lodge are among the most popular hotels.

When the lifts close, beer lovers gather at Slopeside in Ski Time Square and the Steamboat Brewery and Tavern on Lincoln Avenue in Steamboat Springs. Watering-holes include the Hilltop Bar, the Tugboat and Dos Amigos, which are all near the mountain base. In the downtown area, Tap House is for live music, and the Old Town Pub has pool tables. Cellar Lounge is lively until late, as is Harwigs.

For a resort of this size, the range and quality of the restaurants are impressive. Sevens at the Sheraton represents hotel-chain grandeur and expense, but finer dining can be found at L'Apogee, Antares, Giovanni's and the Steamboat Yacht Club. Riggio's has cheaper Italian fare, and the Chart House has the best salad bar in town. There is Chinese food at the Panda Garden and the Canton, sushi at Yama Chan's and Mexican at La Montana. Another option is a snowcat-ride to Ragnar's for a five-course dinner and live music.

Steamboat offers an interesting variety of other sports ranging from bobsleigh and bungee jumping to dog-sledding, hot-air ballooning, ice-driving, night-skiing, skating, ski-jumping, sleigh rides, snowmobiling, swimming and winter fly-fishing. Steamboat Powder Cats runs day snowcat-skiing trips to Buffalo Pass in the Routt National Park, a few miles out of town. The natural springs at Strawberry Park Hot Springs, also a few miles out of town, provide a less stressful alternative.

TOURIST INFORMATION
Tel 1 970 879 6111
Fax 1 970 879 7844
Email info@steamboat-ski.com
Web site www.steamboat-ski.com

Telluride
top 12,247ft (3,734m) bottom 8,725ft (2,660m)

A colourful history surrounds Telluride, an old mining town in a beautiful box-canyon in the San Juan Mountains. At the height of the gold rush, 5,000 prospectors crowded into the town, the name of which derives either from tellurium, a non-metallic element in gold and silver ore, or less probably from 'to hell you ride' – a sobriquet that could apply to Butch Cassidy, who robbed his first bank on Main Street in 1889 before escaping on horseback. In keeping with the rollicking climate of those times, Main Street divided the town, with a residential district on one side and a flourishing red light district on the other.

The wide street, dominated by the New Sheridan Hotel (it was new in the Victorian times) and the original court house, is architecturally little changed today, but over the last decade the nature of the resort has been radically altered by the construction of the Mountain Village Resort. Four miles away by road, it is connected to the town by gondola between 7am and 11pm on weekdays and between 7am and midnight at weekends. The development of condominiums, shops and a golf course triggered a real-estate boom and attracted a number of Hollywood investors. However, they have now mainly gone again, although Tom

Cruise and Nicole Kidman remain regular visitors. Both town and mountain village are equally convenient for the skiing, although the delightful town is one of the prime reasons for visiting this remote corner of Colorado.

The backbone of the area is the appropriately named See Forever, a long, rolling blue run from the top of the skiing to the mountain village; it provides encouragement or speed, according to ability and taste. The Galloping Goose area, isolated to one side of the mountain village, is perfect for beginners. Aggressive skiers head for the double-black-diamond Spiral Stairs or hike up the ridge towards Gold Hill to the short, off-piste glades. Three new high-speed quads replaced four older chair-lifts for the 1999–2000 season. The giant funpark with a half-pipe is the largest in Colorado and was built to the same specifications as the one used in the Nagano Winter Olympics. At the same time, Telluride is also one of the best places in the state to learn to snowboard.

A new restaurant, Club St Sophia, opens for the 2000–1 season to offer fine on-mountain dining reached by gondola. The choice of where to stay is dictated by the nightlife, which is much better in the downtown area. The New Sheridan is central and traditional, with a handsome mahogany bar, while the restaurant serves fashionable dishes of elk, venison and ostrich. The Ice House is modern, central, smart and convenient for the Oak Street base-station. The best placed hotel in town is Camel's Garden, right next to the gondola station. Skyline Guest Ranch on the outskirts of town is run as a home from home by the hospitable Farney family. The Peaks Resort at Mountain Village is 'the ultimate in luxury spa hotels'. Telluride Sports has an excellent range of ski clothing and equipment.

TOURIST INFORMATION
Tel 1 970 728 3041
Fax 1 970 728 6475
Email skitelluride@telski.com
Web site www.telski.com

Winter Park
top 12,057ft (3,676m) bottom 8,973ft (2,735m)

As it is the nearest recreation ground for the people of Denver, only 67 miles (108km) away, Winter Park has a high number of weekend skiers, who commute here by snowtrain on Saturdays and Sundays. In the past, one of the resort's biggest disadvantages has been the lack of slopeside accommodation. Future plans include a gondola link directly from the town to the ski area, and land has already been purchased to this aim, but for the present visitors must stay at the new base village at the foot of the skiing. The village has been under construction for two seasons but should be fully operational for 2000–1. It is built around the Zephyr Mountain Lodge, which comprises a restaurant, pub and ski shop as well as 230 condominiums. A second block, Winter Park Mountain Lodge, also opens for the 2000–1 season.

The skiing here is excellent, with long, wide runs, challenging mogul fields, few midweek queues, efficient lifts and perfectly manicured slopes. The area is divided into two main sections – Winter Park and Vasquez Ridge, which have mostly intermediate trails, and Mary Jane, which has hard bump-skiing as well as tree-level runs and long blues from the Parsenn Bowl. At present there are 22 lifts, including 7 detachable quads, which serve 2,886 acres (1,168 hectares).

Winter Park has three funparks and a half-pipe for snowboarders. The children's area has a 'magic carpet' lift where the ski school takes beginners.

Mountain restaurants include the Dining Room at the Lodge at Sunspot, which is on the summit of Winter Park Mountain, as well as several cafeterias and a pizza parlour mid-mountain.

Winter Park's wild neighbour is **Berthoud Pass**, named after a Victorian surveyor. The resort first opened in the 1930s and has since had a chequered history of openings and closures. What you will find is just two chair-lifts, but these open up 1,000 acres (406 hectares) of some of Colorado's most exciting skiing terrain. For the present, the unsophisticated town of Winter Park (two miles from the ski area) has the main accommodation, with private homes attractively set in the woods above.

Winter Park boasts a separate après-ski piste map dedicated to pubs and eateries. The Black Diamond Nightlife Tour takes in 23 restaurants and bars, kicking off at The Club Car at the base of Mary Jane and ending up at The Crooked Creek Saloon.

TOURIST INFORMATION
Tel 1 970 726 5514
Fax 1 970 726 5823
Email kate_mullany@mail.skiwinterpark.com
Web site www.winterparkresort.com

IDAHO

Sun Valley
top 9,150ft (2,789m) bottom 5,750ft (1,753m)

America's oldest ski resort has been a magnet for the Hollywood élite since it opened in 1936. As with so much of the USA, Sun Valley's rise to prominence was railroad-led. Averell Harriman, then the chairman of the Union Pacific Railway, commissioned Count Felix Schaffgotsch to find a place to build a ski resort near a Union Pacific railhead. His choice, the mountainside near the dilapidated mining town of Ketchum, was inspired – both for its terrain and its sunshine records. In August 1936, the world's first chair-lift, adapted from a system for moving stems of bananas in Panama, was installed. However, no allowance was made for the snowfall – by the winter, it was completely stuck.

Today, the skiing is divided between Dollar/Elkhorn, the site of the original lift, and the much more demanding slopes of Bald Mountain, which has earned a reputation as one of the best single ski mountains in the United States. It provides a 3,400-ft (1,034-m) vertical drop, and the whole ski area is served by a network of 17 lifts. The upmarket clientèle has encouraged the establishment of some excellent restaurants, on and off the mountain. The Soupçon and the Evergreen Bistro offer gourmet dining. The Pioneer Steakhouse, Clint Eastwood's favourite, is cheerful and much cheaper.

TOURIST INFORMATION
Tel 1 208 726 3423
Fax 1 208 726 4533
Email svmkting@micron.net
Web site www.visitsunvalley.com

MAINE

Sunday River
top 3,140ft (957m) bottom 800ft (244m)

Sunday River is one of the largest resorts in the east of the USA. It belongs to The American Skiing Company, whose portfolio also includes Steamboat in Colorado, Heavenly in California, and The Canyons in Utah. The picturesque state of Maine suffers at times from sparse natural snow, but given low temperatures this is of little consequence thanks to an arsenal of custom-built cannons – increased to 1,450 for 2000–1 – that blast out man-made crystals throughout the winter. Unlike European artificial snow, which is harder and more difficult to ski on than the real thing, their recipe feels remarkably natural and can cover up to 92 per cent of the total terrain.

The range and quality of the skiing compares favourably with that of a medium-sized resort in Italy or France. Fortunately, Sunday River is situated in a rural area sufficiently far from New York not to suffer from the overcrowding to which the Vermont resorts are prone. The slopes are uncrowded even during high season ('we had the steeper runs almost entirely to ourselves').

The resort is flanked at one end by the Grand Summit Hotel and at the other by the Jordan Grand Resort. In between lies the main base area beneath a ridge of eight peaks offering a variety of terrain, ranging from beginner trails to Chutzpah, one of the 10 most extreme runs in eastern USA. A total of 654 acres (265 hectares) of skiing is served by a substantial network of 18 lifts. The two main base areas are also linked by an efficient bus service.

Perfect Turn is the name of the ski and snowboard school as well as being The American Skiing Company's revolutionary method of tuition for adults and children. Beginner skiers are wooed with the Graduated Length Method, an easy method of learning where you start on short skis and progress daily in length as you increase in confidence and ability. Other courses include cross-country, skiing for disabled people, and women's ski clinics.

Sunday River is an ideal resort for families with children of all ages and for all standards of snow-user. It is also popular with British school groups. Tiny Turns Childcare intersperses play with one-hour private ski lessons until your child is ready for his or her first group ski class. Children aged four to six can join all-day Mogul Munchkins classes and seven- to twelve-year olds join the Mogul Meisters.

The resort is rider-friendly ('lift operators slowed down for boarders'), with two major funparks, a separate mini-pipe for beginners, a floodlit half-pipe and a boardercross course. Yet another half-pipe and a top-to-bottom terrain park are opening for the 2000–1 season. Floodlit tubing at the White Cap Fun Center is a popular evening activity, along with skating and night-snowboarding. The nearby small town of Bethel is the quintessential Maine community, complete with a plethora of craft shops and restaurants.

TOURIST INFORMATION
Tel 1 207 824 3000
Fax 1 207 824 5110
Email snowtalk@sundayriver.com
Web site www.sundayriver.com

MONTANA

Big Sky
top 11,150ft (3,399m) bottom 6,970ft (2,125m)
In Montana, big is good but bigger is better, which provides the rationale behind the Lone Peak Tram – a tiny cable-car cabin that briefly and slightly dubiously gave Big Sky the right to claim the longest vertical drop in the USA from previous holder Jackson Hole. Both resorts have now been upstaged by Snowmass. Nevertheless, Big Sky's skiing is worthwhile with an impressive 17 lifts and 3,700 skiable acres (1,497 hectares), and its extensive slopes are among the least crowded in the northern hemisphere. This is not surprising, as it is an hour's drive from Bozeman, the nearest airport, and seven hours from Salt Lake City, the nearest major city. However, the wide, open snowscape is attractive, especially to Europeans accustomed to crowds. The runs are on two well-linked mountains: Lone Peak, which has the bulk of the serious skiing, and Andesite, where beginners and intermediates will find plenty to occupy them. Skiers have to hike to reach the A–Z chutes, but all except the most extreme skiers will prefer the bowl off the triple-chair and the glades off the slow, 'experts only' Challenger chair. Further new runs served by the triple chair in the new Lone Moose ski sector will open for the 2000–1 season.

Big Sky was created by Chet Huntley, the late NBC newscaster of the 1960s and a Montana man who wanted to give something back to the state in which he was born. The Huntley Lodge and the Shoshone Condominium Hotel provide comfortable ski-in ski-out accommodation, but the nightlife is limited to a poker game in Chet's Gaming Parlor and a small assortment of bars. These include Dante's Inferno, Scissorbills, Lolo's Saloon and the Black Bear Bar and Grill. At lunch-time, Mountain Top Pizza, the Lone Peak Café and the Sun Dog Café are the main sources of sustenance.

The road from Bozeman winds along the River Gallatin, where Robert Redford directed *A River Runs Through It*, a taster for the magnificent scenery that makes Montana a favoured hideaway for contemporary Hollywood. Andie MacDowell rates the acreage of her ranch as 'too big to count'. There is a sense of history too, with Little Bighorn, the location of Custer's last stand, a mere two-hour drive away. As Montana has abolished the speed limit, that may well be quite a distance.

TOURIST INFORMATION
Tel 1 406 995 5000
Fax 1 406 995 5001
Email info@bigskyresort.com
Web site www.bigskyresort.com

NEW MEXICO

Taos
top 11,819ft (3,603m) bottom 9,207ft (2,807m)
Taos likes to describe itself as 'the last bastion of pure skiing – a lot of sun, snow, mountains … and no snowboarders'. Provided you prefer two planks rather than one, the Taos Valley has a charm that is all its own. Although it is at the same latitude as Rome, the snow in a north-facing bowl in the Carson National Forest is surprisingly good. A few miles down the road, the cacti and sagebrushes that characterise the New Mexican desert stretch as far as the eye can see. The town of Taos, an art-led, cosmopolitan melting pot with a dominant Native American culture, is 20 miles (32km) away.

The Taos Ski Valley was created by the legendary Ernie Blake, a Swiss-born German who discovered what he recognised as perfect skiing terrain while flying over the Rockies in the early 1950s. In 1956 Blake was joined by the French racer Jean Mayer in an enterprise that still combines Teutonic efficiency with Gallic flair. Blake was a firm believer in ski classes, even for cocky Americans who thought that they could ski, and he created the best ski school in the country in his own image. Mayer's interest was gastronomic, and he indulged it at the slopeside Hotel St Bernard, which is usually booked out for the next season by early June.

Blake died in 1989, but Taos continues in the same distinguished tradition under the stewardship of his son Mickey and son-in-law Chris

Stagg. The mountain is imposing, especially from the village perspective. Al's Run, the tough mogul field under the lift line, makes such an impression that a notice reassures visitors of easier skiing further up the hill. While this is true, there is also even more difficult skiing, especially off the high traverse, where runs like Oster, Blitz and Stauffenberg testify to the founder's anti-Nazi stance during the Second World War. Sir Arnold Lunn, the father of modern European skiing, is also commemorated on the piste map. The key run in the beginner's area is Honeysuckle, while intermediates should head for Porcupine and Powderhorn, both ego-boosting cruisers. Taos has a total of 72 trails served by 12 chair-lifts.

The town of Taos is extremely compact, and hotel accommodation is limited. The St Bernard was one of the first hotels to be built here, while the Thunderbird Lodge is comfortable and has live jazz. The Sagebrush Inn was built in 1929 and is in Taos town. The other hotels are the Edelweiss, the Inn at Snakedance and the Hondo Lodge. The choice of condominiums is wider, with the Kandahar at the top of the list of recommendations. Four miles (6km) down the valley, the adobe Quail Ridge Inn has a desert ambience, indoor and outdoor tennis and an outdoor swimming-pool.

TOURIST INFORMATION
Tel 1 505 776 2291
Fax 1 505 776 8596
Email tsv@skitaos.org
Web site www.skitaos.org

QUEBEC

Mont-Sainte-Anne
top 2,625ft (800m) bottom 575ft (175m)

With a vertical drop of more than 2,000 feet (610m), 56 trails covering 40 miles (64km), 13 lifts (including an eight-person gondola) and skiing on three sides of the mountain, Mont Sainte-Anne is one of the most significant ski and snowboarding areas in eastern Canada. The resort has magnificent views across the drifting ice-pack of the St Lawrence and Quebec City 25 miles (40km) away. Like all destinations in Quebec, Mont Sainte-Anne – nicknamed *La Belle et La Bête* (Beauty and The Beast) – can be very cold in the depths of winter. In spite of this, 15 runs are open for night skiing on what is claimed to be the biggest illuminated vertical drop in Canada.

The modern base-area, with electronic ticketing, has four restaurants, with three more on the mountain itself. There is a 282,500 square-foot (86,106 sq-m) funpark as well as half-pipes. Eighty per cent of the mountain has snowmaking capabilities. The Children Centre welcomes children from six months to ten years, and Kinderski and Kindersnow programmes mix games with ski or snowboard lessons for children of four and over. Children under seven ski free. A tubing centre has now been opened at the base area, and off-piste skiing and riding are allowed on the previously restricted west side of the mountain.

For convenience, most people stay at the Chateau Mont Sainte-Anne at the base area, or the Chalets Mont Sainte-Anne, a condominium complex close by. The Hotel Val des Neiges is also at the base area. Dog-sledding, parapente, skating, snowmobiling and snowshoeing are also available. Mont Sainte-Anne also claims to have the largest cross-country trail network in Canada. A new Carte-Blanche multipass allows skiers and boarders to visit the nearby resorts of **Stoneham**, **Le Massif** and **Le Relais**. Le Massif, right on the banks of the St Lawrence river has a vertical drop of 2,645 feet (806m) – the biggest in eastern Canada.

TOURIST INFORMATION
Tel 1 418 827 4561
Fax 1 418 827 3121
E-mail info@mont-sainte-anne.com
Web site www.mont-sainte-anne.com

Andorra

RESORTS COVERED Arcalis, Arinsal, Pal, Pas de la Casa/Grau Roig, Soldeu/El Tarter

Beginners ✱✱✱ Intermediates ✱✱ Snowboarders ✱✱

With the steady decline in popularity of eastern Europe as a value-for-money ski destination, Andorra has consolidated its position as the favoured country for those on a tight budget. Unlike Bulgaria and Romania in recent seasons, the tiny Pyrenean principality has been blessed with abundant snow-cover. Even more importantly, while the former Communist states rely on archaic lift systems that date from the Khrushchev era, Andorra has invested £47 million to create a sophisticated network of gondolas and detachable chairs to rival many Alpine resorts.

- ✔ Low prices
- ✔ Facilities for children
- ✔ Excellent skiing tuition
- ✔ Lively nightlife
- ✘ Few mountain restaurants
- ✘ Lift queues
- ✘ Lack of resort ambience
- ✘ Heavy traffic (Pas de la Casa)

Somehow (and certainly not through its own moribund marketing efforts in Britain), Andorra has gained the youthful allure of indecent Ibiza and combined it with the comfortable family reliability of opulent Obergurgl, to create the 'in' snow destination for Euro-youth. At the same time, a blossoming sense of national identity has led to a cultural renaissance. The 1960s concrete apartment blocks have given way to attractive new buildings of natural stone that are in keeping with the beauty of their mountain surroundings.

Catalan, once banned by General Franco, is taught in schools along with Spanish and French, and has emerged once again as the national language. Despite their considerable differences, Soldeu and Pas de la Casa offer by far the best skiing in the country. Prices are similar, but Soldeu is actively creating a smarter image in contrast to the 'yoof' culture that thrives in Pas de la Casa and to a lesser extent in Arinsal. The standard of ski school tuition (particularly in Soldeu/El Tarter) is high, and most of it is provided by native English-speakers.

The new Andorra is anxious to portray an image that goes beyond wall-to-wall perfume shops, supermarkets, and boutiques selling cosmetics, booze, clothing and ski equipment at knockdown prices. Anyone looking for ski bargains should consider the fact that resort shops are allegedly used as dumping grounds by manufacturers for last year's products. On display are entire ranges of models in a profusion of colourful but confusing graphics that never find their way to the Alps. However, with branded vodka selling at £6 per litre and genuine Armani jeans at £45, it is hard to complain. Holiday bargains as well as low prices for basics such as mountain lunches and après-ski entertainment also help to explain Andorra's current crest of success. The peseta is the official currency but the French franc is also accepted.

The choice of where to stay is expanding each year. The valley town of **Encamp** now has a giant gondola financed by Pas de la Casa that rises to the top of Grau Roig. Visitors who choose to base themselves here or in more cosmopolitan **Andorra la Vella** can now bypass the winding, and usually congested, arterial road to reach the heart of the best skiing in Andorra without staying in Soldeu/El Tarter. This has added fuel to a centuries-old quarrel between Pas de la Casa and Soldeu. The latter promptly responded by building another giant gondola from the neighbouring community of **Canillo** to the top of their territory.

Arcalis
top 2,600m (8,530ft) bottom 1,940m (6,363ft)
Arcalis is a ski area without a village, situated at the end of a remote and beautiful valley. It has five chair-lifts and eight drag-lifts serving 26km of piste. In early 2000 the sunny Creussans area was incorporated, with a new quad chair-lift taking you up to the ridge at 2,624m for a winding 2km blue (easy) run down past the lake to the new La Coma restaurant. A timed slalom course has also been introduced. The kindergarten cares for children from 12 months old while the Snow Garden looks after children from four to nine years old. Visitors are almost exclusively Spanish, and the resort offers some of the most challenging terrain in Andorra. It is a 20-minute drive from the villages of **Ordino** and **La Massana**, both of which offer a reasonable choice of hotels. Hotel Rutllan in La Massana is described as 'the perfect jumping-off point for Pal, Arinsal and Arcalis'.

> ## WHAT'S NEW
>
> Arcalis: new Creussans ski area and quad-chair
> Arinsal: enlarged half-pipe and funpark
> Pal: ski area enlarged with quad-chair
> Pas de la Casa: new six-person chair-lift and two drag-lifts. Nursery slope at the Encamp gondola mid-station. Parking area at Encamp.
> Soldeu/ El Tarter: eight-seater gondola from Canillo to El Forn and new nursery area. Six chair-lifts and major expansion of ski area

TOURIST INFORMATION
Tel 376 737 080
Fax 376 839 225
Email ito@andorra.ad
Web site www.andorra.ad/comuns.ordino

Arinsal
top 2,573m (8,442ft) bottom 1,550m (5,084ft)
Arinsal provides extremely limited beginner terrain in a pleasant mountain setting. The resort has been greatly enhanced by the construction

of a six-person access gondola from the heart of the village. This takes you directly up the mountain in four minutes to the start of the main skiing at 1,950m, avoiding the previous options of a steep mountain road or an ancient chair-lift that follows the path of a bubbling stream.

The skiing itself takes place in a bleak and treeless area enclosed between two ridges that funnel back to the large reception centre above the gondola station. This houses restaurants, bars, the ski school and sports shops. The resort now has a total of 18 lifts serving 28km of groomed runs, which collectively provide the least variety of all Andorra's skiing. The funpark and half-pipe were enlarged last year to cater for the high percentage of riders among the resort's clientèle. The two main pistes – the black (difficult) La Devesa and the blue (easy) Les Marrades 1 – drop from the top of the main Arinsal lift down to the resort and are sometimes closed due to lack of snow. This limits the remainder of the area to beginner and lower-intermediate terrain. As all the runs are channelled into a V shape that ends on the nursery slopes, even beginners will feel the pressure of the limited runs ('crowded nursery slopes with resultant long queues'). One reporter complained of 'hordes of un-controlled Spanish youngsters whose behaviour appeared to be condoned by their instructors'. The kindergarten caters for children aged one to four, and the Snow Garden looks after three- to seven-year-olds.

The mountain restaurants serve 'ubiquitous burgers 'n' beer in surroundings that make up for in price what they lack in charm'. Quo Vadis is a popular bar with videos. Surf Bar, Cisco's and Bar El Derbi are the alternatives. Much of the accommodation is cheap and primi-tive. The Poblado apartments are recommended, while Hotel Rossell has 'basic food'. Attitude and service at the Hotel Font came under fire from reporters. The Hotel Daina, 15 minutes' walk from the centre, is a newer addition, while Hotel Janet is a small, family-run establishment on the outskirts of town. Recommended restaurants include El Rusc ('excellent food in amicable surroundings') and Borda ('authentic Catalan cuisine and a great night out'). We have good reports of the children's ski school, and the resort also operates a crèche.

TOURIST INFORMATION
Tel 376 737 020
Fax 376 836 242
Email emap@andornet.ad
Web site www.arinsal.ad

Pal
top 2,358m (7,736ft) bottom 1,780m (5,840ft)
Pal is a small village down the road from Arinsal, with a separate ski area further up a winding road. It shares a lift pass with its neighbour, and the skiing has considerably greater variety. The 14 lifts and 32km of piste are accessed from four different points. Of its 24 runs, half are graded red (intermediate), and 80 per cent of the skiing terrain is covered by artificial snow. The ski area has been widened for the

2000–1 season with the addition of two new red (intermediate) runs
and a quad chair-lift. From the top of the ski area at the Pic del Cubil
you can either descend to Coll de la Botella via two red runs or ski over
towards Refugi Pla de la Cot on a choice of four red runs. Off to one
side is Edifici La Caubella, where most of the shorter and easier runs are
situated. The crèche takes children from 12 months and the kindergarten from three to eight years.

TOURIST INFORMATION
Tel 376 827 117
Fax 376 835 904
Email emap@andornet.ad
Web site www.pal.ad

Pas de la Casa/Grau Roig
top 2,580m (8,465ft) bottom 2,095m (6,872ft)

Pas de la Casa is a border town that divides not only countries but
cultures; a tawdry small-time Tijuana that promises (but not necessarily
delivers) rock-bottom prices along with a heady release from the strictures of bourgeois existence across the frontier in provincial France.
Every weekend the youth of Toulouse come over the border in search of
daytime snow and night-time action in a town where the pub crawl has
been raised to an art form. They are joined, in coaches from Carcassone,
Toulouse and Barcelona airports, by hordes of Brits in search of holiday
debauchery. 'One of the cheapest places in the world to be sick in', says
one reporter. Snow-users aged between 16 and 25 years of age might
find a holiday here off – and even on – the slopes an enjoyable experience. If you are older, you might do well to look elsewhere.

The fundamental impression of Pas de la Casa is of a brash city of
giant advertising hoardings, scores of tacky shops, crowds of shoppers
and choking traffic fumes. The architecture is both higgledy-piggledy
and ugly. The town feels like a resort that owes its existence to bargain
basements rather than skiing. Supermarket shelves are piled high with
cut-price alcohol, much of it produced locally.

The skiing is linked to the neighbouring ski area of Grau Roig and
jointly they offer 33 lifts and 100km of the pick of Andorra's skiing.
This in turn should be connected to the 29 lifts and 86km of Soldeu/El
Tarter on the far side of the pass. The lift links are in position and
usually operating, but because the two bitter neighbours have failed to
agree upon a joint lift pass, you must buy a second pass if you stray into
foreign territory. The rivals originally fell out over common land grazing rights in the eighteenth century – and relationships remain almost
comically volatile. Pas de la Casa's brochure and lift map fail to show
any lifts at all in Soldeu.

The short lift-link from the top of Soldeu was first established in
1998, but was closed again for the first half of winter 1999 when each
resort accused the other of spying on its development plans. Both sides
are entrenched, so don't count on any definite progress for 2000–1.

Pas de la Casa's skiing takes place mainly in two bowls on either side of the 2,600-m pass, making it the highest resort in Andorra. Recent winters have been blessed with abundant snow-cover until the end of April, and the main slopes are well covered by snow-cannon. The Font Negra piste above the village is floodlit for night-skiing.

The main access to the pass is via an efficient but usually over-subscribed quad chair-lift. From the top you can return to the resort via a choice of runs, which can be crowded and icy. Alternatively, you can ski on down the gentler but more rewarding pistes to Grau Roig, which is little more than a car park and a hotel on the floor of the adjoining valley. A new six-seater chair-lift now takes you up from the bottom of the Serrat Pinos red (intermediate) run to the top of the Encamp cable-car. A new parking area at the bottom of the cable-car is a huge improvement for skiers and snowboarders staying in the Encamp region or visiting from other parts of Andorra.

One major complaint is that beginners are forced to buy a full area lift pass just to use the two short drag-lifts on the nursery slopes. Indeed, none of the ten beginner lifts are free. One reporter griped: 'during February half-term the resort was overcrowded, the ski school overloaded and the lift queues enormous'. Here, as in other Andorran resorts, the standard of English spoken by instructors is high, and many have BASI or similar qualifications.

Pas de la Casa's snowboarders congregate at the half-pipe at La Coma III in the Grau Roig area. Both Pas de la Casa and Grau Roig have ski kindergarten for children aged three to six years. Both also have crèches that care for one- to three-year-olds.

The five mountain eating-places in the Pas de la Casa/Grau Roig ski area are little more than cheap and functional snack-bars. The Bar El Piolet at the bottom of the Del Clot drag-lift is recommended. Refugi de Pessons has 'a log fire, pleasant food and service'.

While Pas de la Casa cannot in any way be called attractive, it does have a large variety of accommodation ranging from the comfortable to the very basic. Two of the more expensive hotels, which receive favourable comments from reporters, are the Sporting and the Central, both at the lower end of the resort. The budget hotel Llac Negre has a varied local menu and friendly staff.

Much of the resort accommodation is in apartments. 'Many of the younger people choose the apartments close to the slopes, while families and those seeking a quieter life choose the hotels.' Of the many self-catering apartments, neither Paradis Blanc nor Lake Placid seem to have many admirers; reporters complain about their small size and lack of sound-proofing.

The restaurants are cheap and cheerful. The food is mainly Spanish, with fresh seafood and the ubiquitous paella, although some concessions have been made to the French. Nightlife is frenetic and cheap, and even bars with dancing seem to have resisted the urge to charge for entry. The Marseilles 'is the place for a quiet drink and has great lasagne'. The Discoteca Bilboard is popular and is split into two with 'general nightclub music played in one half and house/garage music in the other; there is no entry fee and you are able to roam between the two halves'. Other favourite nightspots include Milwaukee's and KYU. Le Pub has a happy hour each evening and holds weekly theme nights.

There are two crèches, one in town and the other on the piste. The Jardi di Neu kindergarten is set in a small wooden hut with its own fenced-off ski and play area; it has a button-lift close to a smelly, diesel-driven drag-lift and the busy car park. Grau Roig also has a children's snow garden with its own drag-lift.

TOURIST INFORMATION
Tel 376 80 10 60
Fax 376 80 10 70
Email pasgrau_reserves@andornet.ad
Web site www.pasdelacasa.ad

Soldeu/El Tarter
top 2,560m (8,399ft) bottom 1,800m (5,904ft)

Soldeu and linked El Tarter together provide the best combination of skiing, accommodation, architecture, scenery and ambience of any resort in Andorra. Readers are unanimous in their praise: 'I would recommend Soldeu to anyone. It is especially great for beginners, and the ski school is excellent for all levels. The nightlife is cheap and suitable for anyone of any age.' The ski school has an enduring reputation as one of the best in Europe and is a contributory reason for Andorra's new-found success, based not only on sound technique but also on language ('top marks for organisation, friendliness, and teaching'). A startling 110 of its 170 instructors are native English speakers. Andorra, where the population is outnumbered six-to-one by seasonal guest-workers, welcomes foreign ski teachers.

An eight-person gondola spearheaded a host of new and mainly high-speed lifts and a major expansion of the area, which now has 29 lifts and 86km of groomed pistes. The gondola emerges from beneath yet another four-star hotel to whisk skiers across the gorge of the river Valira – formerly negotiated via a rickety Indiana Jones-style bridge – and up to the mid-mountain ski school meeting area at Els Espiolets. At the end of the run a new piste bridge across the river takes you swiftly back up to the gondola station. An alternative route is by chair-lift from El Tarter, 2km down the road.

In the winter of 1999–2000 an eight-person gondola from the village of Canillo to El Forn was constructed, thus creating what is effectively a new ski resort. A ski school, kindergarten, restaurant and cafeteria have been built at El Forn, and the new beginner area here is served by a four-seater chair-lift. A high-speed quad forms the link to El Tarter, and a drag-lift serves 4km extra of red and blue runs. Elsewhere, three new detachable six-seater chairs and a fixed quad have transformed uphill transport and given access to 11km of new red and blue runs. Snow-cannon now cover 25 per cent of the entire ski area.

Sadly, the link to neighbouring Pas de la Casa remains unviable while the two resorts fail to agree on a joint lift pass. The ski area of Soldeu/El Tarter is made up of mainly long cruising runs, with open terrain at the top of the area and forest from the mid-mountain downwards. The 21 lifts serve 74km of principally intermediate skiing. There is little here to attract advanced skiers used to the Alps, but low-cost heli-skiing is available. The area is otherwise highly suited to beginners and second-weekers, although one reporter commented that 'some of the greens are like cross-country runs'. Soldeu is the best resort in Andorra for snowboarding, especially for first-timers, although the slopes can be crowded. It has an ungroomed snowboard zone. The Club dels Pinguins kindergarten cares for children aged three to ten, with ski lessons for older children.

Architecturally, Soldeu and El Tarter provide a marked contrast to Pas de la Casa, consisting of little more than a ribbon of stone-and-wood buildings alongside the main road. Environmentally sympathetic regulations mean that even the recent constructions are much more attractive than those of their neighbour.

The Esqui Calbo restaurant is recommended for its service and good value. Xalet Sol I Neu, at the bottom of the mountain at Soldeu, serves 'tasty chicken curry made with better cuts of chicken breast than I have ever experienced in an English curry house'. Both mountain cafeterias are usually overcrowded between 11am and 4pm.

The best hotels include the four-star Piolets and the Sport, which has its own fitness centre. Aparthotel Edelweiss and the Cabo apartments both share the Sport Hotel's facilities. The newly refurbished Hotel Soldeu is said to be 'very comfortable and has reasonable food'. At the foot of the slopes in El Tarter is the conveniently placed Hotel Llop Gris, which has a swimming-pool and squash courts. Further down the road is Parador Canaro, which offers an even higher standard of comfort. The Deu Sol apartments are situated midway between Soldeu and El Tarter ('a 15-minute walk along a busy unlit road with no pavement'). Reporters say they are 'poorly equipped and maintained', while inadequate cooking facilities and a lack of local food shops 'made a mockery of any notion of self-catering'.

Nightlife thrives at seething discos such as Fat Albert's and the Irish Pub, while Aspen's features live music with a band called The Dog's Bollocks. The Esquirol and the Hard Rock Café are also popular, but the nightlife does not try to compete with the fleshpots of Pas de la Casa. We have good reports of the nursery slopes in Soldeu, which are 'well prepared and fenced off from the rest of the pistes'. The ski school has a long tradition of teaching British children, while non-skiing children are cared for at a choice of two crèches.

TOURIST INFORMATION
Tel 376 89 05 00
Fax 376 89 05 09
Email soldeu@andornet.ad
Web site www.soldeu.ad

Eastern Europe

RESORTS COVERED Bulgaria: Bansko, Borovets, Pamporovo, Vitosha
Romania: Poiana Brasov, Sinaia
Slovenia: Bled, Kranjska Gora

Beginners ✻✻ Intermediates ✻

M ost of the mountainous countries of eastern Europe offer skiing in some shape or form and have done so for 40 years, regardless of political orientation. For a while, when the Berlin wall came down and the Iron Curtain was raised, it looked as if a few of them – led by Bulgaria and Romania – would realise their potential and become serious destinations. However, this was not to be.

> ✔ Low prices
> ✔ Fascinating cultural experience
> ✘ Poor-quality food
> ✘ Lack of alpine charm
> ✘ Few consumer goods

The transition to a market economy has so far failed to provide the kind of national or international investment needed to build a serious infrastructure for any of the undeveloped resorts in these countries. This, coupled with intermittent hostilities in the Balkans, has limited their potential. Furthermore, while most of the Alps have been blessed with ample cover in recent seasons, the snowfall here is by no means reliable.

The most persuasive reason for choosing this part of the continent remains its value for money. Although we have continuing reports that bars and restaurants in Bulgaria have been hiking up their prices from week to week, depending on the level of demand, it is still true to say that, in general, eastern Europe represents excellent holiday value for visitors on a budget. However, the strength of sterling continues to make Andorra and the rest of the Pyrenees almost as financially attractive – and with far better skiing. The downside of the 'bargain basement' of eastern Europe is the severely limited nature of the slopes.

Eastern European countries that offer skiing include the Czech Republic, Poland, Romania, Serbia, Slovakia and Slovenia, as well as Russia, Georgia and a number of smaller states of the former USSR. Here we concentrate on the principal ones. We have not given the telephone numbers of the local tourist information offices because we recommend that you travel through a bonded tour operator or via a country's own state travel agency (see *Skiing by numbers*).

BULGARIA

Bulgaria has been a favourite eastern European destination with British skiers for 20 years, with **Borovets** and **Pamporovo** the most popular resorts, and **Vitosha** and **Bansko** the smaller, less sophisticated options. Bulgarian skiing is, by Alpine standards, extremely limited. The largest ski area is not much bigger than a relatively unknown resort in the French Jura. The number of visiting skiers has declined significantly in recent years and will no doubt continue to do so until the local authorities appreciate the inadequacies of their lift systems. Lengthy queues for single-seater chair-lifts, followed by deeply rutted and ill-prepared slopes, may still attract first-time skiers on a budget – but the amount of repeat business will inevitably be small. However, we must point out that a hard core of our readers are unstinting in their praise. They shrug off the deprivations, swallow the indifferent food, smile in the endless lift queues and return for more year after year.

Reports of Bulgarian hospitality are mixed, with opinion split fairly evenly between those who found their hosts brusque and unhelpful, and more positive assessments of an affable people who are keen to please. A turbulent history of occupation by neighbouring powers has left the Bulgarian people unsure of how to deal with foreigners. The political changes of the early 1990s may have led to a progressive thaw in attitudes towards visitors, but there is still some way to go before the country will be fully geared to a tourist industry.

Visitors will find badly maintained roads, sub-standard accommodation and inadequate facilities for exchanging currency. Credit cards are rarely accepted except in the major hotels, and worn foreign banknotes are often refused, even by banks. Journeys by taxi can be unnerving, and public transport is unpredictable

On the positive side, Bulgaria is a country with a fascinating cultural heritage. The ski resorts are located in areas of considerable natural beauty, close to places of great historical significance. The Rila Monastery, midway between Borovets and Bansko, is one of the most perfectly preserved medieval structures of its type in the world. Equally, the ancient town of Plovdiv has much to recommend it. Shoppers will find a range of unusual goods, from hand-carved music-boxes to pirate CDs, on street-corner stalls and even at the base of the Borovets ski lifts.

Mountain restaurants tend to be temporary-looking – indeed, some are just caravans on the hill. Few serve more than toasted cheese, chicken and chips, and soup, and even fewer have WCs. Those that do are in such a sorry state of hygiene that they are to be avoided in all but the direst necessity ('when I asked for directions to the lav, I was pointed to a little hut amongst the trees with no door'). The quality and blandness of hotel food is the main complaint, but reporters say that you can eat well at little cost in simple restaurants and bars. The quality of rental equipment is improving, but it is not uncommon to see skis and bindings that are 10 to 15 years old. However, if you are a competent skier and insist on a higher grade of rental gear, superior skis and boots usually materialise from a back room of the hire shop.

Bansko
top 2,000m (8,202ft) bottom 936m (3,079ft)

A little over 160km south from Sofia and about an hour's drive beyond Borovets, Bansko is a largely unspoilt – and undeveloped – resort. The town lies in the shadow of the 2,915-m peak of Vihren, the highest mountain in the spectacularly beautiful Pirin range close to the borders with Macedonia and Greece. There are few shops and no supermarkets, but what the town lacks in retail facilities it more than compensates for in extensive cultural diversions: three museums and a magnificent old church that is unlikely to have altered much in 500 years.

The main focus of the skiing is located out of town at Shiligarnika, the largest of three ski areas at the foot of the 2,746-m peak of Todorin. This is reached by a free, half-hour ski-bus ride along a narrow, picturesque mountain road through dense forest. The base-station at Shiligarnika is little more than a couple of new hotels in the midst of a forest clearing. The area offers about 20km of mainly wide, tree-lined slopes reached by a fast, modern three-seater chair-lift and two drags. The Chalin Valog area, a little further down the mountain, offers the most difficult piste skiing. In good snow conditions off-piste opportunities are plentiful and by Alpine standards the cost of a local guide is remarkably low.

The Dado Pene, a converted eighteenth-century town house, and the equally atmospheric Mexana Rumen Baryakov are highly recommended restaurants. The Torino cabaret bar is unexpectedly upmarket and popular with prosperous-looking Sofians. The Pension Sema and the central Hotel Alpin, are both recommended as places to stay in town. Up the mountain, the Hotel Todorka is impressive if somewhat isolated. However, it does offer free transfers to the town centre three nights a week.

Borovets
top 2,540m (8,333ft) bottom 1,323m (4,339ft)

What started as a hunting lodge for the Bulgarian royal family in the nineteenth century developed in the 1970s into an international ski resort set in the pine forest at the foot of Mount Moussala, the highest peak in the Balkans. Bulgaria's oldest and most sophisticated ski resort is attractively located amid a dense pine forest in the southern Rila Mountains, but like much of eastern Europe it has squandered the natural beauty of its setting by erecting buildings of dubious architectural merit.

The extent of the skiing surpasses anything found elsewhere in the country, but the ancient lift system and lack of adequate piste-grooming are a constant source of irritation. The skiing is divided into two annoyingly separate sectors linked by a long walk on an ice-rutted road, or more comfortably – if you don't mind the farmyard odour – by a £2 ride in a horse-drawn taxi.

Principal access to the main area is by a 20-year-old six-person gondola ('the queue went around the block'). The Markoudjik sector above it offers what is arguably the best of the resort's 40km of marked skiing, which is mainly above the tree-line with a highest ski point of 2,540m. The separate Martinovi Baraki area has a quad chair-lift and four drag-lifts, but the top section can be reached only by an ancient single chair-lift, which is prone to enormous queues. All the nursery slopes are located at the base of this area.

Both ski schools are well regarded, and English is widely spoken. Don't be surprised if you come across instructors touting for business in the main street, and ski classes do not have priority on the lifts. The ski kindergarten is praised, and additional daycare is available for three-to seven-year-olds in the Rila Hotel.

Accommodation is almost exclusively hotel-based, with the conveniently located Samokov standing out as by far the best example, offering a range of modern facilities including a swimming-pool, sauna, bowling alley and fitness room. It also has a nightclub and 'American' bar, both of which appear to be magnets for what one reporter described as 'young single women of entrepreneurial disposition'. The giant Rila Hotel is more basic but of reasonable standard. Hotel Breza is 'quiet, comfortable, and rooms have adequate showers and WCs'. The Hotel Mura has also earned good reports. Hotel food followed by the state of the on-mountain toilets (these defy description) are guests' biggest subjects of complaint.

Borovets is situated in the heart of Bulgaria's potato-growing region. The approach road to the resort is lined with the cars and carts of hopeful farmers selling souvenir spuds at 10p a pound. These, served boiled or re-presented as salads, form the core of hotel restaurant fare along with greasy soups and stews. Consequently, the motley collection of bars and private restaurants in the surrounding woods do a healthy trade in hamburgers and chicken-and-chips.

Pamporovo
top 1,925m (6,316ft) bottom 1,450m (4,757ft)

Pamporovo is a small resort with the majority of its accommodation in hotels strung out between the centre and the lift station, about a ten-minute journey by free ski-bus. Most of the hotels face the area's only ski mountain, Snezhanka, the summit of which is crowned by the Bulgarian equivalent of the British Telecom Tower.

There is one black (difficult) run (optimistically called 'The Wall'), which is immediately beneath the summit, and a couple of good-quality red (intermediate) runs on either flank. One of these provides the resort's longest run of 4km. Otherwise, the whole place is mostly geared to novices and lower intermediates and could easily be skied in a morning. However, the 25km of marked skiing, most of which is on tree-lined runs, is undeniably pretty. One relatively modern three-seater chair links the base and summit, but the remaining lifts comprise a double chair, three archaic single-seaters, and an assortment of four equally ancient drag-lifts. Lift queues are rare, except for a 15-minute spell in the morning when all the ski school classes set off simultaneously.

The locals claim that the Pamporovo Ski School is internationally renowned, although one reporter queried whether this might be for 'the grumpiness of its instructors'. Another, who chose the resort for a week's snowboarding course, reported that her instructor was 'charming, helpful, could board like a dream but, alas, wasn't all that gifted at passing on his undoubted talent'.

Of the resort's hotels, the Perelik was described as 'basic but comfortable – unless your room is above the disco that closes at 3am'. The hotel also houses Pamporovo's only swimming-pool and the main shopping centre. Among the competition, the Chevermeto restaurant is recommended for its 'folk' nights, when whole sheep are roasted over open fires, and dancers in traditional dress provide a colourful floor show.

Vitosha
top 2,295m (7,530ft) bottom 1,650m (5,413ft)

Bulgaria's highest resort is on Mount Vitosha, overlooking Sofia, which is 20km away and can be reached by a cheap bus service. The resort consists of a couple of comfortable hotels, old hunting lodges, a hire shop and lift station. A total of 22km of north-facing slopes above the tree-line are served by a small network of lifts. Vitosha is an ideal resort for beginners and early intermediates. The ski school is said to be excellent. Vitosha's proximity to the capital means that it is inundated with weekenders, and lift queues can be a problem.

Hotels include the Hunting Lodge, a unique residence set in its own grounds, 700m from the nearest ski lift. The Proster is the largest hotel, with facilities including a swimming-pool and the resort's only disco. One reporter commented: 'the view was fabulous, but the maintenance appalling; it was very noisy, and the food was poor'. Hotel Moreni is 'basic, with no frills'.

ROMANIA

Prices in Romania are even lower than in Bulgaria. For example, bus and taxi fares can be measured in pence rather than pounds, a three-course dinner with wine costs £6 and a bottle of beer or a soft drink as little as 30p – but this is Romania's only appeal as a ski destination. While other former eastern-bloc countries have steadily improved facilities for tourists, Romania seems stuck in a time warp from which it shows no signs of freeing itself. Consumer goods are scarce. Ski lifts are dilapidated, prone to lengthy delays, and the safety of some of them must be seriously questioned. We are promised that major refurbishment – particularly at **Sinaia** – is in hand, but we see no sign of it. English is spoken everywhere and the standard of ski tuition is generally high, although classes can be oversized.

Poiana Brasov
top 1,775m (5,823ft) bottom 1,021m (3,350ft)

This is the best-known resort in Romania, located three hours' drive north of Bucharest in the attractive Carpathian Mountains. It is purpose-built, founded by the Ceauşescu administration in the 1950s to promote tourism, and resembles an enormous holiday camp rather than a village. A few hotels, restaurants and a large sports centre are set back from the base of the ski area; the furthest hotels are about 2km away.

The 14-km ski area is reached either by gondola, an antiquated open-air affair 'like a series of mop buckets on a string'. or by two cable-cars ('do not expect them both to be running at the same time') to the summit. Piste-marking, grooming and artificial snow are non-existent. The nursery slopes are at the bottom of the mountain, but when there is a lack of snow, beginners are taken to a gentle slope at the top of the gondola. Most of the skiing is intermediate, with runs roughly following the line of the lifts. There are two black (difficult) runs, one of which circumnavigates the mountain and ends at the base.

The ski school is unanimously recommended: 'Exceptionally good value'. There is no shortage of ski-school instructors who speak fluent English and are keen to show you a good time. One reporter warned that medical facilities are poor, and Brasov hospital 'is a sight to behold'. There are a couple of simple mountain restaurants, the best of which is a wooden chalet at the top of the gondola. The food is cheap and basic: 'expect to pay less than £2 for lunch with a couple of beers'. One reporter found the resort 'full of British yobbos on cheap drunken sprees', but at the same time described his holiday as 'a culturally fascinating experience'. The Sport is the best-situated hotel. The Bradul has a faded air. The Alpin is of a slightly higher standard, but one reporter complained that 'the public rooms were full of surprisingly pretty prostitutes haggling with fat old Turks'.

Non-skiing activities are limited; other sports include skating, bowling and swimming. The après-ski takes place in the hotels, nearly all of which have discos or floor shows. The centre of activity is Vicky's Bar. Dinner at The Outlaws Hut is lively, starting with musicians playing around a log fire ('it is OK if you can cope with eating roast bear'). Alternatively, you can take part in a wine tasting and folklore dinner at the Carpathian Stag in Brasov. The Dacia restaurant specialises in wild boar. There are excursions to Dracula's Castle, and cheap buses and taxis that can take you into the town of Brasov for limited shopping. It is worth spending a day in Bucharest.

Sinaia
top 2,219m (7,280ft) bottom 855m (2,805ft)

Sinaia is where the Romanian royal family used to spend their summers. Each monarch built a summer residence and, while some of these are now run-down, the beautiful Peles Castle should not be missed. The old Royal Palace is now a hotel and is a short walk from the cable-car.

A two-stage cable-car from the town, its top section duplicated by a chair-lift, serves long intermediate runs down the front of the mountain. These runs are poorly marked and are consequently challenging in uncertain visibility. The main area is on exposed, treeless slopes behind the mountain and on subsidiary peaks beyond. It consists of short inter-mediate runs with some variety and plenty of scope for off-piste. Snowboarding is not encouraged. Hotel Palace is a traditional place overlooking a park and is a short walk from the lifts. Hotel Mara Holiday Inn resort is less convenient. The town is quiet and has just a few bars and restaurants.

SLOVENIA

'A poor man's Austria with less skiing and less alpine charm' is how one reporter described Slovenia. Like other eastern European countries, it is reasonably priced – food, drink and internal travel are about one-third of British prices. Reports of the ski schools are generally favourable, with English widely spoken and the video analysis helpful.

Bled
top 1,275m (4,183ft) bottom 880m (2,657ft)

The attractive old spa town of Bled looks on to a seventeenth-century church on an island in the middle of a lake. Its main, simple ski area is 8km away at Zatrnik, where a total of five lifts serve 18km of easy wooded slopes in a bowl; these are ideal for beginners in good snow conditions but provide little challenge for intermediates. Another even smaller area is Straza, which has just two lifts; both areas have artificial snowmaking. The Golf, a quiet hotel set slightly away from the main centre, is recommended, while the Lovec is an older, wood-panelled hotel. Hotel Vila Bled is an elegant residence set in its own grounds on the shore of Lake Bled. It has 10 rooms and 20 suites.

Kranjska Gora
top 1,630m (5,348ft) bottom 810m (2,667ft)

This is one of the best-known resorts in the region. Set in a pretty flat-bottomed valley between craggy wooded mountains, it is close to the Italian and Austrian borders and is Austrian in ambience, even down to its domed church. Hotels are improving, although are still not compar-able in standard to cosy Austrian gasthofs. The four nursery runs are short, wide and gentle and set right on the edge of the village; the tran-sition to real pistes is rather abrupt, with the mountains rising steeply from the valley floor. A total of 30km of pistes, the majority of which are blue (easy), are served by 20 lifts of which 16 are T-bars. The longest run, Vitranc, is reached by chair-lift to the top of the ski area and is graded red (intermediate). The other lifts go only halfway up the small mountain, which means limited skiing and the risk of poor snow cover.

The Alpine Ski Club offers both group and private lessons, though with only private lessons for snowboarding and cross-country available. Children are catered for in the ski school but there is no kindergarten. The Kompass, one of the resort's best hotels, has a swimming-pool and disco. The modern Hotel Larix is recommended for its location and facilities, and Hotel Prisank has a friendly atmosphere.

Scandinavia

RESORTS COVERED Finnish Lapland: Levi
Norway: Geilo, Hemsedal, Lillehammer, Oppdal, Trysil, Voss
Sweden: Åre, Sälen

Beginners ✱✱✱   Intermediates ✱✱   Snowboarders ✱✱

English is widely spoken in all the Scandinavian resorts, and both Norway and Sweden are particularly welcoming to the British.

- ✔ **Ideal for small children**
- ✔ **Extensive cross-country skiing**
- ✔ **Few lift queues**
- ✔ **Relaxed atmosphere**
- ✔ **Reliable snow cover**
- ✔ **Good-value lift passes**
- ✔ **English widely spoken**
- ✘ **Low altitude**
- ✘ **Few long runs**
- ✘ **High-priced alcohol**
- ✘ **Extremely low temperatures**

Finnish Lapland is now also beginning to attract an international market, with flights to Rovaniemi, the capital of the Lappi province, via Helsinki. Visitors are guaranteed their fill of reindeer – both on the hoof and on the plate – and there's always the hope of glimpsing a familiar old man with a long white beard and a red coat bombing down the piste.

Traditionally, skiers travelling to **Norway** tend to be beginners, intermediates and cross-country enthusiasts – it is fair to say that this is not the best destination for advanced skiers. Although the country has almost 200 locations where skiing is possible, including scores of cross-country centres and some very small ski hills, Norway's mountains have vertical drops of only 300 to 750m, and less than a dozen ski areas can truly be called downhill resorts. Alpine skiing is treated as part of an all-round winter holiday.

The Norwegians are justly proud of their ski schools, which are well-organised with English-speaking instructors who are described as 'friendly and helpful'. Telemarking is making a big comeback to this, its country of origin. Norway is highly recommended for families, and a keen emphasis is placed on safety. Hemsedal and **Geilo** even provide free lift passes along with free helmets for children of up to seven years of age, provided the helmets are worn. Free lift passes and helmets are also given to children up to the age of eleven in **Åre** in Sweden, and up to age seven in **Levi** in Finnish Lapland. Children's ski areas in Norway are often roped off with netting to stop adult snow-users hurtling into them at the end of a downhill run. For children of three months and over, the resorts have Trollia (Troll Club) kindergarten for skiing with indoor and outdoor play, which are usually open seven days a week.

Norwegians on holiday are late risers, and the slopes here are almost deserted until midday. This means that there are no morning lift queues, even in high season, although the slopes are busier in the afternoon. Travelling by train in Norway is particularly comfortable, with exemplary restaurant cars and wonderful facilities for small children, including a 'crèche-carriage' on inter-city trains, containing baby-changing and feeding rooms and an indoor play area, complete with climbing frame and Wendy house. Some of the Norwegian resorts offer a Winterlandet card, which allows you to ski other resorts that share a lift pass. For example, Geilo, **Hallingskarvet**, Hemsedal, **Gol** and **Al** offer a total of 74 runs and 45 lifts.

Skiing in **Sweden** is an altogether more serious affair and is much more comparable to mainstream Europe. Daylight hours are limited in mid-winter, and temperatures can be extreme. The skiing season is a long one in Scandinavia, but nowhere more so than in the resort of **Riksgränsen** in Swedish Lapland on the Arctic Circle. In the late spring the pistes here stay open for night-skiing under the 'midnight sun'.

Throughout Scandinavia alcohol remains expensive – even more in Sweden than in Norway. Expect to pay about £3 for a bottle of beer and a minimum £20 for a bottle of imported wine whether from Bulgaria or Bordeaux. Prices for spirits are off the scale. However, ski rental and lift passes are now about one-third of the price of their Alpine counterparts. Most important of all is that Scandinavia's snow record is not subject to the peaks and troughs experienced in more southerly latitudes. The Scandinavian buffet is the staple dinner diet, and visitors are pleasantly surprised by the range and quality of dishes on offer, although fresh, smoked and marinated fish does predominate. Reindeer features strongly in the meat section of any menu.

Other activities available in Scandinavia include dog-sledding, go-karting on ice, hang-gliding, heli-skiing, snow-biking (Sweden), ice-climbing, ice-fishing, sleigh-rides, snowmobiling, snowshoeing, snow rafting, telemark, tyre-racing and waterfall-climbing.

FINNISH LAPLAND

Levi
top 725m (2,378ft) bottom 400m (1,312ft)

This small and unusual resort lies in the Arctic Circle, 161km (100 miles) by road north of Rovaniemi. It has a total of 18 lifts and is at the centre of 270km of cross-country trails. Snow is guaranteed here from mid-October until early June. When we visited at the end of November it was mainly dark and the sun never actually rose. 'Daylight' (you still needed to use car headlights) was restricted to a couple of late-morning hours, but the main runs were floodlit and the ski area remained open until 7.45pm. The Lapps use soft, low-wattage bulbs to light their homes, and the day – whether indoors or outdoors – passes in a gentle twilight. By night, if you are lucky, the Northern Lights provide nature's supreme fireworks display, adding to the surreal atmosphere of the place. The hours of daylight increase each month until the late spring, when the Arctic becomes the 'land of the midnight sun'.

It is worth visiting a traditional Lapp farm for a reindeer sleigh ride, and Santapark – an underground theme park with Disney-style rides at Rovaniemi – should not be missed by families with young children.

Recommended hotels include Hullu Poro (Crazy Reindeer), with 'enormous, comfortable apartment rooms with private saunas', and the even more luxurious Levitunturi. The resort has a ski- and non-ski kindergarten. Children under seven years ski free and borrow free equipment if they wear the free helmets supplied by the rental shops. Most restaurants are in hotels, and the nightlife is limited to a few bars.

TOURIST INFORMATION
Tel 358 166 43466
Fax 358 166 43469
Email levi.info@levi.fi
Web site www.levi.fi

NORWAY

Geilo
top 1,178m (3,864ft) bottom 800m (2,624ft)

This is a traditional resort midway between Bergen and Oslo and only 30 minutes' drive from Geilo Airport Dagali. It is especially recommended for cross-country skiers as one of the centres on the famous Hardangevidda Plateau. The downhill skiing, which comprises 35 pistes served by 18 lifts, is relaxed and uncomplicated, with several reporters describing the terrain as 'perfect for novice and intermediate skiers'. Although there are seven nominal black (difficult) runs, advanced skiers will quickly run out of steam here. Plans for a major mountain development have so far failed to materialise.

The skiing is made up of two areas inconveniently situated on either side of a wide valley, with the resort beside the lake in the middle. However, a free ski bus service now links the two throughout the day.

The Vestlia area, with a vertical drop of 244m, has the easiest skiing and is where the excellent ski- and non-ski kindergarten, the Troll Club, is based. The highlight of this area is Bjornloypa, a popular long green (beginner) run. The main ski area, on the other side of the valley on the slopes of the Geilohovda, has a much wider selection of pistes than Vestlia, including some steeper terrain and a vertical drop of 378m. Apart from its three ski schools, Geilo also has Aktivitets Guiding for off-piste skiing; snowboarding lessons are available, and there is a funpark. Norway is famous as the home of cross-country skiing and nowhere more so than Geilo. This is a traditional cross-country resort, boasting 220km of loipe, both on the valley floor and on the Hardangevidda Plateau at 1,312m, and floodlit cross-country skiing.

Six restaurants are scattered around the two ski areas: most of them are rather soulless cafeterias. The fast-food restaurant at the top of the main area at Geilohovda is popular, and sun-lovers congregate on the terrace of the stately Dr Holms Hotel, one the most famous hotels in Norway ('stylishly furnished and patronised by sleek Scandinavian families exuding wealth and health'). You can ski to the three-star Solli Sportell Hotel, and the Highland Hotel is also recommended. The Vestlia Hotel is 'warm and comfortable, the food was excellent, and we were two minutes' walk from the lifts'. The Usterdalen Hotel received favourable comments: 'friendly owners, an excellent buffet, a crafts club for children, and after-dinner live entertainment'. Norwegian resorts also have an abundance of usually expensive cabins and apartments. Bars include the Hos Josn, and the Laven at the Vestlia Hotel.

Geilo's Trollia kindergarten is the Troll Inn, where children under three can take part in indoor and outdoor activities, and which is warmly praised. The downside is that lunch is not provided. The children's ski school receives high acclaim: 'the children were very well looked after', and 'the lessons were fun'.

TOURIST INFORMATION
Tel 47 320 95900
Fax 47 320 95901
Email skiheiser@geilo
Web site www.geilo.no

Hemsedal
top 1,497m (4,911ft) bottom 675m (2,214ft)

Although only an hour's drive from Geilo, in the heart of Norway's Winterland region between Oslo and Bergen, Hemsedal's peaks look a lot more mountainous than Geilo's rounded ski hill, giving a much stronger impression of a serious ski resort. Despite the fact that Hemsedal has fewer runs than Geilo, and **Oppdal** has a larger ski area and more off-piste, Hemsedal has some of the best skiing in Norway, with a long season stretching from mid-November to May.

In a country where ski resorts are dominated by the T-bar, Hemsedal also has the most modern lift system, with one quad chair-lift and five triple-chairs among its 14 lifts serving 36km of piste.

The resort has a couple of genuinely steep black (difficult) runs and some entertaining tree-level skiing. One snag is that the village is about 3km from the ski area, and the free ski bus service is infrequent (two go from the village in the morning and two return in the afternoon). This means, for example, that guests staying at the Skogstad Hotel (which serves dinner between 6 and 8pm) who wish to take advantage of the much-advertised night-skiing, run the risk of missing dinner. Hemsedal has some good off-piste skiing through the trees – known as 'taxi skiing', because you will need to organise transport to get you back to the slopes or to your base. It also has a severe off-piste run called Reidarskaret, which starts with a steep, narrow couloir that is usually too dangerous to attempt unless weather and snow conditions are perfect.

Hemsedal Aktiv is the ski and snowboard school, and Norske Opplevelser As organises off-piste guiding. Snowboarding is popular in Norway, particularly in Hemsedal where there is a floodlit funpark and a self-timing course. In Hemsedal the excellent slope-side babysitting service, Trollia Childrenpark, comes free with a lift pass of at least three days.

Two mountain restaurants are near the top of the Hollvinheisen triple-chair. A third, Skistua, is at the base area and has the option of self- or table-service. Hotels include the Fossheim ('small, family-run and very comfortable'). Hemsedal has some packed, noisy bars during the busy weekends. The Garasjen (the old bus garage) can become so crowded that skiers overflow on to the street and those left inside have to come to a tacit agreement as to the moment when snatching a quick sip of beer – in unison – is possible. The Skogstad Piano Bar and Hemsedal Café are almost as crowded. You may have more room to breathe at the Kro Bar in the Fanitullen apartment block.

TOURIST INFORMATION
Tel 47 320 55300
Fax 47 320 55301
Email hemsedalskisenter@skiinfo.no
Web site www.hemsedal.com

Lillehammer
top 1,050m (3,444ft) bottom 200m (656ft)

Lillehammer resembles an American frontier town, with its clapboard houses and single main street. The nearest skiing is based 15km away at **Hafjell**, which has 25km of prepared trails served by 11 lifts. The best pistes are from Hafjelltoppen (1,050m) down either the Kringelas or Hafjell runs. Both are graded black (difficult), and formed part of the 1994 Winter Olympic slalom courses. Night-skiing is also available once a week. **Kvitfjell**, 50km from Lillehammer, was created as the downhill course for the 1994 Winter Olympics. Its 4km of skiing is limited but provides a steeper challenge than anywhere else in the region. The Sas Radisson and the Lillehammer are reported to be the best hotels in town; both have indoor and outdoor swimming-pools.

TOURIST INFORMATION
Tel 47 612 59299
Fax 47 612 56585
Email post@lillehammerturist.no
Web site www.lillehammerturist.no

Oppdal
Top 1,300m (4,265ft) bottom 545m (1,788ft)

Oppdal lies 120km south of Trondheim and is one of Norway's most northerly downhill resorts. It is also technically the biggest. Although it has only 28 runs and a vertical drop a little lower than that at Hemsedal, it has extensive areas of off-piste terrain spread between its four ski areas. It offers 78km of pistes served by 17 lifts. The most challenging marked trails are Bjorndalsloypa, Hovdenloypa and Bjerkeloypa on the front face of Hovden, the central ski area.

The Vangslia area also offers a mixture of terrain, while Stolen at the other end of the resort is made up entirely of beginner and intermediate pistes. The fourth area, Adalen, is set in a huge bowl behind Hovden and is dominated by long, mainly blue (easy) cruising runs. At 1pm, for a fee, snowcats will take up to 50 skiers at a time to the top of the mountain at Blaoret for sightseeing and an additional 240 vertical metres of off-piste skiing.

Oppdal has a specialist guiding service called Opplev Oppdal; guides escort skiers around the area and carry a full kit of safety equipment, including avalanche transceivers (rarely used in Norway), shovels and avalanche probes. On Wednesdays at the Sletvold Park slope, the resort offers night-riding with special floodlit courses, complete with rental equipment and a buffet. Oppdal also has 60km of cross-country trails covering a variety of terrain; five of its tracks are floodlit.

The resort has six mountain restaurants: one at the bottom of each base area, and two more at the top of the Hovden and Stolen lift complexes. Only the Vangslia lifts are without a mid-mountain restaurant. The semicircular restaurant at the top of Hovden was originally part of a water-storage structure. The restaurant at the bottom of Stolen, where most of the easiest family skiing takes place, is usually the busiest on the mountain.

The recently refurbished Hotel Nor Alpine is a sound choice, and guests at the 75-room Hotel Oppdal, right by the quiet railway station, describe it as cosy and quaint, despite its size. Reporters speak favourably of the 'Viking evening' (a misnomer) at a timbered round-house in the woods, where local stews, pâtés and sausages are served in front of a roaring fire to an accordion accompaniment. Although Oppdal is a fair-sized town, nightlife is limited to a few bars and restaurants.

TOURIST INFORMATION
Tel 47 724 00470
Fax 47 724 00480
Email post@oppdal.com
Web site www.oppdal.com

Trysil
top 1,132m (3,714ft) bottom 600m (1,969ft)
Situated three hours' drive from Oslo, Trysil is said to have the most reliable snow cover anywhere in the country. Its 85km of piste, served by 26 lifts, are spread across the wooded slopes of Trysilfjellet with a 685-m vertical drop. An additional chair-lift has been added for the 2000–1 season. As with many Norwegian resorts, the lifts are several kilometres from the resort centre. The skiing varies from easy green (beginner) trails to some more challenging red

(intermediate) runs, but is criticised for having too many runs graded green – 'cross-country tracks in disguise'. Ninety kilometres of cross-country trails (of which 3km are floodlit for night skiing) wind through the woods on the lower half of the mountain. Accommodation in Trysil is mainly hotel- and apartment-based, although mountain cabins make a pleasant change for hardy self-caterers. Hotel Trysil Gjestegard Panorama, situated 1km to the south of Trysil, is favoured by reporters. The Norlandia Trysil Hotel and Trysil-Knut are in the centre, while the Trysilfjell aparthotel is on the slopes.

TOURIST INFORMATION
Tel 47 624 50511
Fax 47 624 51164
Email info@trysil.com
Web site www.trysil.com

Voss
top 945m (3,100ft) bottom 91m (300ft)

Despite its low altitude, Voss has a reasonable ski area for beginners and lower intermediates. The 40km of prepared pistes includes three black (difficult) runs, two of which are reasonably challenging, and some off-piste. The 10 lifts (almost one for each run) include a cable-car, and the longest descent is 3km. Enthusiasts of cross-country skiing will certainly not be disappointed with the 60km of prepared loipe that is close to the centre, although more is available in the valleys around the area. The resort's historic hotel is the Fleischer, which is wood-built in traditional style.

TOURIST INFORMATION
Tel 47 565 20800
Fax 47 565 20801
Email vossn@online.no
Web site www.voss-promotion.no

SWEDEN

Åre
top 1,274m (4,180ft) bottom 380m (1,312ft)

Åre, or Årefjallen Resort, in the north of Sweden, offers some of the most challenging skiing in Scandinavia – 96km of piste served by 49 lifts, stretched across four ski areas beside a scenic fjord. The skiing here is certainly comparable to a medium-sized Alpine resort, with enough challenging runs, including the Salombacken and the World Cup downhill, to keep accomplished skiers happy. Beginners are served by a choice of six lifts. The transfer time is about 90 minutes from Östersund Airport. The ski school at Åre has a sound reputation, and all instructors speak fluent English. Cross-country is also popular here, with the Södra Årefjallen area on the south side of the lake offering extensive trails, and long, scenic tracks on the north side. Some 6km out of the total of 84km are floodlit for night-skiing. Children are well catered for, with a free lift pass and free – compulsory – helmets provided for children up to the age of 11. There is a crèche for three- to five-year-olds, and a ski kindergarten with up to five per group.

We have positive reports of both the four-star Åregarden and Renen hotels. The Backpackers' Inn ('cheerful') is the budget option. Restaurants include Grill Hörnan and Tännsforsen, which welcomes children. The resort has an English pub called the White Hart. The Skier's Bar at the Diplomat Ski Lodge, Sunwing and Broken Dreams are all lively bars which are busy when the lifts close. Other buzzing nightspots include the Bygget and the Country Club.

TOURIST INFORMATION
Tel 46 647 17700
Fax 46 647 17710
Email bokning@areresort.se
Web site www.areresort.se

Sälen
top 950m (3,135ft) bottom 550m (1,815ft)
Sälen is Scandinavia's largest ski area. It is made up of four resort bases and two separate ski areas, Lindvallen-Högfjället and Tandådalen-Hundfjället, which are linked by ski bus. Together they offer a total of over 97 lifts and 152 pistes with a maximum vertical drop of 303m. The skiing is best suited to beginners and intermediates, although there are also a few testing black (difficult) runs. The Wall area at Hundfjället is used for speed-skiing.

Ski school instructors in Sälen are fluent English speakers. For snowboarders there are funparks at both Lindvallen and Hundfjället and a half-pipe at Högfjället. Skiing is free for children under seven years old, and a children's ski school as well as ski- and non-ski kindergartens are available. A total of 45 restaurants are divided between Sälen's two ski areas. You can ski to and from the Högfjälls Hotel.

After skiing Sälen buzzes with live music in a whole range of bars, including Grandfather's Corner and the Piano Bar at the Högfjällshotellet. Recommended hotels include the Tandådalen Fjäll and the Högfjällshotellet. Onkel Jean restaurant is praised for its 'delicious elk steaks'. McSki is the world's first and only ski-thru McDonalds. Late-night action centres on the HC night club at the Högfjällshotellet and Fjällis in the Tandådalen Fjäll hotel.

TOURIST INFORMATION
Tel 46 280 20250
Fax 46 280 20580
Email turist.saelen@malung.se
Web site www.salen.nu

Scotland

RESORTS COVERED Cairngorm (Aviemore), Glencoe, Glenshee, The Lecht, Nevis Range

Beginners ✱✱✱ Intermediates ✱✱ Advanced ✱ Snowboarding ✱

The quality of Scotland's ski areas is entirely dependent on the weather and on the type of snow that falls. On the one hand, a sudden temperature rise can bring a rapid thaw, or rain and gale-force winds can make conditions on the mountain extremely unpleasant as well as closing vital access lifts. On the other, you can experience beautiful sunshine and no wind, with temperatures low enough to keep the snow crisp. When this happens, swarms of enthusiastic Scottish skiers clog up the car parks, rental shops and ticket counters. Scotland is keen to update its old skiing image of wind-blown slopes, obsolete lifts, nasty cafeterias and even nastier WCs. Much has been done to improve facilities, but the unkind winter climate remains unchanged. However, the 1999–2000 season was a good one, and Nevis Range had enough snow for five lifts to continue to run over the May Bank Holiday.

✔ Friendly atmosphere
✔ Wide range of non-ski activities
✔ Late-season skiing
✔ BASI tuition
✘ Unpredictable weather conditions
✘ Lift queues at peak periods
✘ Limited skiing

Because of the weather, it is a constant battle for the resort operators to groom the slopes effectively, and they have to erect chestnut paling fences everywhere in an attempt to catch and contain drifting snow. Rapid temperature fluctuations make the manufacture of artificial snow difficult. The positive side of all this is summed up in one reader's comments on Cairngorm: 'although the weather and snow conditions can be disappointing, to me they just make an otherwise limited mountain more challenging'.

The five ski centres in the Scottish Highlands are often marketed together. **Nevis Range** is on the west coast, 33 miles (55km) from **Glencoe**. **Cairngorm (Aviemore)** is in Strathspey, in the Central Highlands, and **The Lecht** and **Glenshee** lie to the east.

The achievements of the resort operators and their staff cannot be overstated. That they manage to build and maintain their operations against this background of meteorological unpredictability, while persuading public and private institutions to invest the capital needed to expand and improve the centres, is a testimony to the dedication of the Scottish skiing fraternity. While some critics may moan about Britain's standing in competitive world skiing, it is Scotland that provides most of the national team members.

Scotland boasts an exceptional number of ski schools, many of them based at or near Cairngorm. Most offer a high standard of tuition under the auspices of the British Association of Snowsport Instructors (BASI), the teaching methods of which are internationally accepted. The Nevis Range Ski School runs various courses, including 'over the back' guided trips, clinics for steep skiing and bumps, over-50s and women's workshops.

British interest in snowboarding was pioneered in Scotland in the late 1980s, and riders are now a common sight at all the centres. Cairngorm and Nevis Range both have funparks and competition-standard jumps, with more funparks planned for 2001. The downside is a distinct lack of bowls or trees, making the area boring for riders. Glencoe and Nevis Range have the superior terrain, with a natural half-pipe at the latter.

Scotland offers plenty of opportunities for cross-country skiing and ski-mountaineering. However, because of the cold winds, clothing needs to be extra-protective. Most of Scotland's cross-country skiing is along forest trails, which hold the snow better than the more open terrain. The season runs from early January to mid-March on the lower, wooded trails and sometimes until early May higher up the mountain. The most challenging ski-mountaineering routes are on the rounded mountains of the Central and Eastern Highlands.

> ## WHAT'S NEW
>
> **Cairngorm:** construction has commenced for the £14.7 million funicular
> **Nevis Range:** expansion of funparks Year-round mountain bike downhill course

The changeable snow and weather conditions mean that a Scottish skiing holiday is not suitable for those who like to plan ahead. It also makes sense to be based where you have access to more than one centre, and not invest in a week's lift ticket for just one resort. Glenshee and Glencoe offer a joint ticket, as do Nevis Range and Glencoe.

It is unrealistic to expect to enjoy the same sort of skiing holiday here as you would in the Alps, but it is possible to have an excellent time simply by keeping an open mind and being flexible. The Highlands are so used to uncertain weather that the range of alternative outdoor pursuits available puts even the world's top ski resorts to shame: these include canoeing, climbing, gliding, gorge walking, hang-gliding, skating, off-road vehicles, shooting, squash, swimming and tennis – and Nevis Range even has a new year-round mountain bike downhill course from the base of the ski area. Readers consistently comment on the warmth of the welcome. As one reader put it: 'Highland service and general friendliness were positively disarming, sharply contrasting with so many experiences in mainland Europe'.

Cairngorm (Aviemore)
top 3,608ft (1,100m) bottom 1,804ft (550m)

Aviemore is located about 120 miles (192km) north of Edinburgh and Glasgow on the A9 and is the nearest town to the Cairngorm ski area, which lies 10 miles (16km) to the east. It is served by rail direct from Inverness and the south. Daily flights operate from Heathrow, Stansted and Luton. In the 1980s Aviemore suffered from having its facilities based around the Aviemore Centre, a hideous 20-year-old concrete development, which has been in a serious state of decay for the last 10 years. Planners have optimistically renamed the area Aviemore Mountain Resort and hope to invest £15 million in it. New base and middle stations and a new restaurant are in the pipeline, with completion scheduled for autumn 2002.

Until now, the Centre itself has been left behind by developments on Aviemore's main street and on the outskirts of the town ('a modern sprawl with large hotels'), where high-quality accommodation and leisure attractions have emerged, helping to make the region more of an appealing outdoor holiday destination. At present, parts of the medium-sized ski area are often shut because of poor weather or snow shortage: 'when the top chair-lifts are closed due to high winds, it can be infuriating if the snow conditions are good on the runs that are affected'.

This will change when the long-promised funicular is finally built. After years of objections by environmentalist groups, construction has now started on the £14.7 million mountain railway. It follows the line of the existing White Lady chairs that it will replace. For much of its length the track will be carried on a viaduct to keep it clear of drifting snow, and the final 250m of the funicular will go through a tunnel. The first trains should be running in time for the start of the 2001–2 season. Meanwhile, the 17 lifts serve two distinct sectors that are accessed from separate bases at Coire Na Ciste and Coire Cas, meeting below the 4,084-ft (1,245-m) Cairngorm peak. Head Wall offers challenging skiing, and White Lady has some excellent moguls. West Wall and Ciste Gully are recommended first thing in the morning.

The Cairngorm Snowsports School has a snowboard section, with an excellent reputation, and the area also boasts a funpark. Other courses include carving, cross-country, snowblading and telemark. The Uphill Ski Club runs classes for disabled skiers in the resort.

Trail-marking is not one of the region's strong points, and you need to keep an eye out for half-buried snow fences. Off-piste routes (with a guide) include the East Wall gullies and Coire Laogh Mor; these are reached by a long traverse, which often has wind-broken snow.

The Fun House crèche is for children from birth to 12 years, and the ski schools arrange children's tuition on demand ('in good weather', according to the local tourist board).

Cairngorm has four snack bars: two at the base lodges, Shieling at the mid-station, and the fourth at the panoramic Ptarmigan. The Shieling is one of the only restaurants in Scotland that allows skiers to eat packed lunches at the table. The funicular scheme will allow for a new 250-seat restaurant at Ptarmigan.

Between Aviemore and the Cairngorm slopes is the Stakis Coylumbridge Resort, which has plenty of facilities, including a swimming-pool, and a wide range of children's activities. In nearby

Carrbridge, the An Airidh Ski Lodge re-creates the cosy atmosphere of an alpine ski chalet, and the Mercury in Aviemore itself offers good-value accommodation.

Scotland is still saddled with an unfair reputation for a limited choice of eating places. Littlejohns restaurant in Aviemore has a friendly atmosphere, with 1930s paraphernalia and copious quantities of American and Mexican food. The Gallery is at Inverdruie, a mile outside Aviemore; readers praise its food and recommend booking in advance as it has few tables. The Taverna Bistro has reasonable prices.

Aviemore used to be known for its rowdy and sleazy nightlife, but most of the bars have been refurbished, and there is now less of the tough, hard-drinking Scottish pub atmosphere. Crofters is one of the most popular of Aviemore's clubs, and the bar at the Highland Hotel is also recommended. Non-ski activities include a theatre, cinema, swimming, skating, and off-road driving courses. Reporters generally found the nightlife 'disappointing', with the disco stopping at 11pm. Prices for drinks are 'at the usual pub rates but somewhat inflated in the more expensive hotels'.

TOURIST INFORMATION
Tel (01479) 810363
Fax (01479) 811063
Email cairngorm@sol.co.uk
Web site www.aviemore.com/cairngorm

Glencoe
top 3,637ft (1,109m) bottom 2,001ft (610m)

Glencoe Ski Centre, 74 miles (118km) north of Glasgow, has attracted a dedicated following for four decades (Britain's first chair-lift opened here in 1961), and during the past few seasons there has been considerable investment in infrastructure here.

There are six miles (10km) of piste and seven lifts with an uphill capacity of 4,300 people per hour. Beginners are catered for on the gentle nursery areas of the Plateau, and intermediates can progress to the long, sweeping descents of Coire Glades. Glencoe boasts the longest single descent and steepest black run in Scotland. It has no special facilities for snowboarders but the resort claims that 'Glencoe's diversity of natural terrain featuring jumps, drop-ins and wide open runs means that there is no need to construct a man-made park'. The Glencoe Ski Centre Ski & Snowboard School offers courses for adults and children.

The Plateau Mountain Café has been upgraded and the Log Cabin Restaurant at the foot of the slopes is 'hugely welcoming in bad weather'. The Centre is open seven days a week and has a ski and snowboard school as well as a rental shop. Glencoe has no childminding facilities, but the ski school can arrange lessons. The resort shares a Monday-to-Friday lift pass with the Nevis Range. Recommended accommodation nearby includes the Kingshouse Hotel, the Clachaig Inn and The Isles of Glencoe Hotel.

TOURIST INFORMATION
Tel (01855) 851226
Fax (01855) 851233
Email glencoe@sol.co.uk
Web site www.ski.scotland.net

Glenshee
top 3,504ft (1,068m) bottom 2,000ft (610m)

Glenshee operates 'Britain's largest network of ski lifts and tows, covering four mountains and three valleys'. Its 26 lifts have an uphill capacity of 18,500 people per hour and give access to 25 miles (40km) of piste. The centre is on a rather desolate pass on the A93, with the lifts located on both sides of the road. The skiing has considerable variety and in fine weather it offers plenty of scope for strong intermediate and advanced skiers. A number of reporters rate Glenshee as having the best skiing in Scotland. For the past two seasons it has hosted a successful telemark festival. Tuition can be taken with the Glenshee Ski Centre Ski & Snowboarding School, which organises courses that include cross-country, race-training, and skiing for disabled people. The resort has a funpark at Meall Odhar and a dedicated snowboard rental shop with 200 boards and pairs of soft boots. There is a modest licensed café at the base and a better high-altitude restaurant, the Cairnwell. Also on the slopes, Meall Odhar Mountain Café offers a cosy alternative. The Invercauld Arms Thistle Hotel, seven miles (11km) away in Braemar, is warmly recommended. Others include the Old Stables at Alyth, Rosemount Golf and the Victoria Hotel at Blairgowrie.

TOURIST INFORMATION
Tel (013397) 41320
Fax (013397) 41665
Email glenshee@sol.co.uk
Web site www.ski.scotland.net

The Lecht
top 2,600ft (793m) bottom 2,109ft (643m)

The Lecht is Scotland's smallest ski area, a network of a dozen short button-lifts on both sides of the A939 Cockbridge to Tomintoul, 56 miles (89km) west of Aberdeen and about 45 miles (72km) from both Glenshee and Cairngorm. One reader said 'it is hardly mountainous and you could mistake it for a winter scene at various locations in England, but it is friendly and unpretentious'. The area is best suited to beginners and intermediates living within reasonable driving distance – The Lecht could not be described as a destination resort. The longest run is 900m. Extensive snowmaking and a 200-m artificial slope are a precaution against the vagaries of Scottish weather and The Lecht has now introduced a tubing slope and a small funpark. The rental shop has skis and snowboards with soft boots. Parking is free and the single café is licensed. The nearest accommodation is the Allargue Arms, three miles (5km) away at Corgarff; a choice of hotels and bed and breakfast options six miles (10km) away at Tomintoul includes the 'comfortable and welcoming' Gordon Hotel, the Glen Avon and the Richard Hotel.

TOURIST INFORMATION
Tel (019756) 51440
Fax (019756) 51426
Email thelecht@sol.co.uk

Nevis Range
top 4,006ft (1,221m) bottom 2,148ft (655m)

Nevis Range is Scotland's nearest equivalent to an alpine resort. It is located seven miles (11km) north of Fort William and close to Ben Nevis, Britain's highest mountain. Its own mountain, Aonach Mor, has 11 lifts and 35 runs, reached from the car park by a modern six-seater gondola. This takes you up to the Snowgoose Restaurant, from where a quad-chair and a series of tow lifts fan out ('the views are stunning, with mouth-watering scenery in every direction'). The longest run is 2km. The Braveheart chair-lift gives easy access to the back bowls of the Coire Dubh. This provides excellent off-piste terrain after a fresh snowfall for skiers and snowboarders alike. Queues for the return gondola journey back down the mountain can be huge when the weather is good in high season. Nevis Range has a ski and snowboard school with off-piste clinics when conditions are favourable, as well as junior race-training, women's ski clinics, and telemark. It has a funpark served by the Quad chair-lift. The kindergarten accepts children from three years old. There is a restaurant, the Snowgoose, at the top of the gondola as well as snack bars at the foot of the Goose and Rob Roy T-bars.

The delightful hamlet of Torlundy offers bed and breakfast, but most of the accommodation is in Fort William, an old lochside town with strong tourist appeal. It has a wide choice of hotels and restaurants, and a leisure centre. Nearby hotels include Inverlochy Castle, which is frequented by Hollywood stars and the occasional US president. The nineteenth-century castle is set in 500 acres (202 hectares) of grounds, and has sumptuous bedrooms. One reader praised The Moorings Hotel: 'a friendly three-star'. The Milton Hotel has a health club, and the Crannog restaurant a good reputation for its seafood.

TOURIST INFORMATION
Tel (01397) 705825
Fax (01397) 705854
Email nevisrange@sol.co.uk
Web site www.ski.scotland.net

Further information about accommodation near some of these resorts can be found in the *Which? Hotel Guide 2001* and *The Good Bed and Breakfast Guide*, available from Which? Books.

Spain

Beginners✱✱ Intermediates ✱✱ Snowboarders ✱

Spain does not have a historical connection with skiing, and indeed, it may seem surprising that a country associated with beaches and sunshine should have any skiing at all. However, in recent years the popularity of skiing, and particularly snowboarding, within Spain has greatly increased. As a consequence, its main resorts have undergone substantial improvements. Prices were always considerably lower than in the French Alps, and the fact that sterling has gained 30 per cent against the peseta since 1995 makes it a financially enticing ski destination.

✔ Efficient lift system
✔ Typically Spanish nightlife
✔ Reasonable prices
✗ Lack of resort charm
✗ Short runs

Spain has two quite separate mountain ranges: the Pyrenees in the northeast and the Sierra Nevada in the south. Both normally receive adequate winter snowfalls, regardless of what is happening in the main Alpine countries. Avid Spanish snow-users forsake the cities for both major ski areas at weekends and holiday times – led by the sport's prominent champion, King Juan Carlos, and other members of the royal family.

Foreigners on the slopes are few, and the Spanish enjoy their skiing and nightlife vociferously, with the same passion they dedicate to other sports. We have generally poor reports of the Spanish ski schools, largely because not many instructors speak English in comparison with those at Alpine schools, and few British speak Spanish.

In Spain partying is an even more serious business than skiing or snowboarding. Anglo-Saxons who stray into this unfamiliar ski-resort environment either adopt local hours or suffer from what quickly develops into a severe Latin mutation of jet-lag. Local skiers hit the slopes at a leisurely 10am and ski furiously until lunch at 2pm. They grab a final hour on the piste before the lifts close at 5pm and then head for the tapas bars before an evening snooze. The length of the 7pm ski siesta is largely dependent on the amount of energy expended on skiing, the size of the paella you ate for lunch, and your intake of *calamares* and Rioja at tea-time. Nobody (not even families with young children) sits down to dinner before 9pm, and restaurants begin to get busy at 11pm. Dancing does not begin before 1pm and can carry on into daylight hours. As one reporter put it: 'if your aim here is to après-ski enthusiastically, then it would be a good idea to book an additional week's holiday on return to recover'.

The high and usually snow-sure resort of **Sierra Nevada** lies in the far south of the country in the mountains of the same name. However, most of the skiing takes place hundreds of kilometres to the northeast in the Pyrenees, which also usually provide reliable snow cover between Christmas and April. **Baqueira-Beret** remains the most important of the Pyrenean resorts – a small but smart development that attracts wealthy skiers from Madrid and Barcelona.

Baqueira-Beret
top 2,510m (8,235ft) bottom 1,500m (4,920ft)

Baqueira-Beret is Spain's answer to Megève; a smart and fashionable resort where not all the designer ski suits you see parading down the main street ever make it on to the snow. It lies at the head of the beautiful Val d'Aran, near Viella on the northern side of the Pyrenees; access from France is easy, and the drive from Toulouse airport takes less than two hours. In keeping with its chic status, prices are higher than you might expect in Spain.

The skiing takes place on four wide, well-linked mountains with a vertical drop of about 1,000m over varied, often exciting terrain. Most of it is suited to intermediates, but one icy couloir, evocatively named Where Goats Tumble, is a real challenge. The opening up of the Bonaigua area has greatly enhanced its appeal to good skiers. Reporters widely praise the standard of piste-grooming and the amount of snowmaking.

Considerable investment in recent years means that Baqueira-Beret now has a total of 23 mainly modern lifts, covering 77km of piste. The main mountain access is by quad-chair from the top of the village, which 'goes up the mountain like the proverbial scalded cat'. The largely modern lift system includes two detachable six-person chair-lifts. There is a half-pipe at Bonaigua, and the lower slopes are well covered by snow-cannon. In the past, the Spanish

> ### WHAT'S NEW
> Baqueira-Beret: six person chair-lift
> Increased snowmaking

ski school has been severely criticised: reporters complained that the instruction was mainly of the 'follow-my-leader' type and that little English was spoken. However, Ski Miquel, the sole British tour operator here, now employs its own BASI instructor. The kindergarten takes children from three months at three piste-side locations as well as at a crèche in the resort itself.

Baqueira's mountain eating-places serve good food at reasonable prices but lack atmosphere. One exception is Restaurant 1800 ('wonderful *paella* for eight, but you must order a day in advance'). The restaurant at Bonaigua 'resembles a Gothic castle and is cheaper and better than anywhere else'.

The terrain, right down to the scrubby Engelmann spruce which grows here at the lower altitudes, is strongly reminiscent of Squaw Valley in California – although here the resemblance ends. Baqueira is purpose-built in an aesthetically adequate style. The village lies beside the road that leads up to the very high Bonaigua Pass, which is often closed in winter. Recent, more attractive development has increased its appeal as a base, with some good shops, hotels, restaurants and a leisure centre. The atmosphere is relaxed and friendly.

Beret is the second base-area rather than a separate resort, and consists of little more than a car park and a cafeteria. The veteran Olympic skier José Moga, who taught King Juan Carlos to ski and who also runs the main ski shop in town, described it as 'the best-value skiing in a less pretentious atmosphere than you can find anywhere in Europe'.

Baqueira is still largely unknown outside Spain, mainly because of the limited rental accommodation available in the resort. Many of its 12,000 beds are owned or rented for the season by Spaniards, who make the journey here every weekend from Barcelona and other cities. The four-star Hotel Montarto is widely recommended, although one reporter commented 'the décor is in need of being revitalised'. The less expensive Hotel Tuc Blanc has a strong following. Hotel Val de Ruda is said to be 'a pleasant three-star in a good position'. Chalet-hotel Salana is warmly praised. Many regular visitors prefer to stay in the more traditional hotels further down the valley. There are good *paradors* (inns) in nearby Viella.

The menus in Baqueira are truly international and come in three versions: Spanish, Catalan and Aranes (a language peculiar to this corner of the Pyrenees). Fortunately, the resort's proximity to the border means that French is also widely understood, if not spoken. This is not a place for vegetarians or the culinary squeamish; Borda Lobato is a lavishly converted cow shed which is considered to be the best restaurant in town ('barbecued rabbit was followed on my second evening by a choice of roast suckling pig or whole baby lamb carved with garden shears'). Other recommended restaurants include La Perdiu Blanca, La Ticolet for pierrade and Tamarro's for tapas. Tiffany's is the busiest nightclub.

Baqueira has three good ski- and non-ski kindergarten which cater for children from three months to eight years old.

TOURIST INFORMATION
Tel 34 973 64 44 55
Fax 34 973 64 44 88
Email viajes@baqueira.es
Web site www.baqueira@baqueira.es

Sierra Nevada
top 3,470m (11,385ft) bottom 2,100m (6,888ft)

Sierra Nevada lies in Andalucia, 32km from the ancient Moorish city of Granada, and offers mainland Europe's most southerly skiing. The presence of a ski resort here seems at complete odds with the nearby resorts of Marbella and Malaga, with their yacht clubs and golf courses. The resort used to be marketed under the name of Sol y Nieve (Sun and Snow), and the purpose-built village in which most skiers stay (at 2,100m) is known as **Pradollano**.

The village is short on alpine charm but now has a square, Plaza Andalucia, which gives it the focal point it previously lacked. ('It is certainly nowhere near as ugly as the Andorran resorts.') The ski area is extremely vulnerable to bad weather and the mountain range as a whole is exposed to high winds. One reporter commented that 'too much snow and too wintry conditions are almost as likely to stop you skiing as too little snow'. When the weather here is bad everything stops, but when conditions are good the skiing can be excellent and the views striking; on a clear day you can even see Morocco. However, because of its proximity to Granada and the Costa del Sol, the resort suffers from extreme crowds at weekends and on public holidays ('on a high season Monday we queued 50 minutes for the main gondola, but once you know the lift system, you can avoid this').

The resort now has 19 lifts serving 34 mainly intermediate pistes totalling 61km. Access to the main skiing area is by a choice of three lifts, including a gondola, from the edge of the village. Sierra Nevada has a choice of three ski schools. In keeping with the Spanish fondness for lunch, the main bowl houses a wide choice of mountain eateries.

The accommodation is mainly in hotels. The Melia Sol y Nieve and the four-star Melia Sierra Nevada, both near the main square, are convenient and pleasant. The Melia Sol y Nieve has a mini-club for children between five and eleven years of age. Melia Sierra Nevada has a swimming-pool, disco, and its own shops, and was described by one reporter as 'the best hotel we have been to in 28 years of skiing'. The Kenia Nevada is quiet. 'Most guests were Spanish, the service was generally friendly and attentive and the bedrooms comfortable and clean.' The chalet-style *parador*, set on its own above Pradollano (accessible by chair-lift and piste), is fairly functional but has exceptional views. The Albergue Universitani is said to be excellent value and clean.

A small range of restaurants serve local, French, Turkish and Italian cuisine. The Borreguiles is one of the most popular eating-places. A kindergarten operates at Pradollano for children aged three months to four years.

Most of Pradollano's buildings date from the 1960s and 1970s. It is not an attractive place ('just like Torremolinos with snow and litter'), but the atmosphere is 'quiet, with quite a Spanish feel to the resort'. The late-nightspot is Sierra Nevada 53. Early-evening entertainment centres on the Crescendo bar. Others recommended include Chimay, Sticky Fingers, Soho and Golbe. Though as one reporter warned: 'Nightlife only begins after 1am and carries on until 6am. The taxi service doesn't run at night and so you are in for a long walk home unless you are staying in the village centre'.

TOURIST INFORMATION
Tel 34 958 24 91 00
Fax 34 958 24 91 31
Email cetursa@globalnet.es
Web site www.cetursa.es

Offbeat resorts

If **Australia's** mountains were transported without their flora and fauna to Europe, they would probably attract fewer skiers than France's Jura range. However, in their rightful place in New South Wales and Victoria, with the ubiquitous eucalyptus trees and abundant semi-tropical bird life, they have a charm of their own. If the snow is reasonably good, skiing in Australia is not to be sneered at. It should be noted that regardless of conditions – even on a hot day with no snow on the approach roads – the authorities insist that you carry chains. Chain rental stores are en route to the slopes.

The skiing in **New Zealand** is of a higher quality than that in Australia, with some moderately impressive resorts in the Southern Alps, together with numerous 'club fields' (these are less sophisticated than ski resorts, with rope-tows, no grooming, but cheap lift tickets) and some formidable slopes at **Whakapapa** on the North Island. Prepare yourself for some hair-raising mountain roads, which, in the absence of on-mountain accommodation, must be negotiated twice a day. It is important to realise that weather conditions in the Southern Alps can be even more changeable than in other mountain ranges, and that conditions here at up to 2,400m (8,000ft) can be as severe as they sometimes are at much higher altitudes in the European Alps, the Rockies and the Andes. As often as not, a blue-sky day will be followed by a day of unsettled weather, and vice versa.

The South American Andes are closer to Europe than the New Zealand and Australian mountain ranges, with excellent skiing to be found in both **Chile** and **Argentina** – although snow cover of any description was markedly absent throughout the winter of 1998. The mountains are mystically beautiful, and in good conditions the skiing is unusually varied. Unfortunately, the most breathtaking scenery and the best slopes do not always go together; the further south down the Cordillera you travel, the more entrancing the scenery is, but the less challenging and extensive the skiing tends to be.

Australia, New Zealand and South America have their winters, and therefore skiing seasons, during our summer. The ski season in **Japan**, however, corresponds to those in the Alps and North America. Japan has 105 resorts, with the Nagano region covering 26 different ski areas and Niigata 23. Although there are so many ski areas here, they are mostly small. Notable exceptions are the resorts in the Hakuba Valley, where the 1998 Nagano Winter Olympics downhill took place at **Happo'one**.

We have given web sites addresses rather than telephone numbers for obtaining further information. Alternatively, you can contact the countries' tourist information offices. Their telephone numbers are given in *Skiing by numbers*.

ARGENTINA

Gran Catedral (Bariloche)
top 2,050m (6,725ft) bottom 1,050m (3,445ft)

Gran Catedral is the name given to the ski resort on Catedral Mountain, which used to be called **Bariloche**. Confusingly, as with many resorts that change their name, it is still generally known as Bariloche. This is Argentina's most celebrated ski area and was the first in the country to install mechanised lifts, during the late 1930s. It is a large, attractive and vigorous region in the southwest of this vast country, near the Chilean border, on the northern end of a range that extends from Lake Nahuel Huapi to Lake Mascardi in the south.

However, the resort has two serious flaws: its snow record is unpredictable, and, owing to a history of fragmented ownership, it lacks organisation and direction. One typical shortcoming is inadequate trail-marking – often it is difficult to tell whether the sticks at the side of a slope are to give warning of rocks or to mark the piste. Bariloche is perched above beautiful Lake Nahuel Huapi and attracts considerable precipitation, much of it falling as rain. Fortunately there are good beginner slopes at the top of the mountain as well as the bottom, so in the event of heavy rain at the base, beginners can be taken higher. Only when the rain is accompanied by strong winds do the vital lifts to the higher nursery slopes close, leaving beginners with nowhere to ski. With 29 lifts and 50 runs, however, Bariloche can still justify its claim to be South America's biggest single resort. Recent improvements are the 'Superbubble' – a six-person, high-speed covered chair-lift – and a computerised 'chip pass' lift ticket, which makes the lift system more convenient. Hotels in Bariloche include the five-star Panamericano and the four-star Hotel Nevada.

Web site www.worldski.com.ar/resorts/bariloch/bariloch.htm

Las Leñas
top 3,340m (11,243ft) bottom 2,240m (7,349ft)

Ski purists would almost certainly rank the terrain at Argentina's most recently built resort above that at its oldest, Bariloche. Las Leñas is also highly rated by riders who are prepared to hike up to the sheer cliff faces. Constructed almost entirely from a brick-red, wood-lookalike material, the resort was built in 1983, with the tourist board of Les Arcs in France acting as consultant. Hotels, pistes and lifts are named after signs of the zodiac; runs have names such as Venus, Apolo, Neptuno and Mercurio.

Although it is not the easiest of resorts to get to (1,027km from Buenos Aires) the powder is some of the best in the entire continent. However, the skiing is almost all above the treeline, making it very exposed and windy. The Marte chair-lift feeds what amounts to a separate ski area, with 40 challenging chutes, but when the lift is closed because of high winds, only the less demanding main ski area of ten lifts is accessible.

The ski school has been managed by an Austrian since 1993 and employs 100 instructors, many of whom are from North America and Europe. Beginners have a free drag-lift at the base-station. Piscis, at the foot of the Venus trail, is a five-star hotel offering the best accommodation in town. Cheaper lodging is available in the valley at Malargue.

Web site www.laslenas.com

AUSTRALIA

Falls Creek/Mount Hotham
Falls Creek: top 1,842m (6,043ft) bottom 1,500m (4,921ft)
Mount Hotham: top 1,850m (6,070ft) bottom 1,450m (4,757ft)

While the major resort of **Thredbo**, in New South Wales, was recovering from a mudslide disaster in 1997, the main focus of Australian skiing shifted to the state of Victoria. Its two major resorts, Falls Creek and Mount Hotham, are owned by the same company, share a lift pass and are linked by a helicopter service. The six-minute flight is almost two and a half hours quicker than by road. The new commercial airport at Horsehair Plain, 20km from both resorts, opened in June 2000.

Falls Creek, which is 30km from Mount Beauty on the edge of the Bogong High Plains, brings a flavour of the Alps to Australia. It has a European-style ski-in ski-out village atmosphere with a difference – accommodation among gum trees. Parking is at the base of the village, and luggage is transported to your lodge by snowcat. You can ski directly to eight different lifts from every lodge.

Altogether there are more than 20 lifts spread across four distinct areas: Village Bowl (with the principal slopes and some long challenging runs), Sun Valley (beginner to intermediate), the Maze Area (narrow tree skiing) and the Snowboard Terrain Park. Falls Creek is famous for the bumps under the Summit quad-chair, particularly on Exhibition run, and provides the venue for many of Australia's mogul competitions. One reporter describes Falls Creek as 'the flattest mountain I have ever seen'. The resort is four hours' drive from Melbourne.

Mount Hotham is the highest alpine resort in Victoria, and it really does have a down-under flavour. It is divided by a road that effectively separates the beginner slopes at the top of the area from the intermediate and more advanced slopes lower down, although these are now linked by a bridge. A special tunnel was built under the road to allow the pygmy possum, a threatened species, to reach its feeding and breeding grounds.

Runs such as Mary's Slide, the Chute and Gotcha are quite challenging. The three lifts at Mary's Slide above Swindler Valley have doubled the lift-served ski area and opened up new off-piste opportunities. The best pistes are in the Heavenly Valley region. Good nursery slopes are served by the Summit quad-chair and T-bar, and the Big D quad at Mount Higginbotham. In all, the area has 13 lifts. **Dinner Plain**, Mount Hotham's new architect-designed sister village, provides reasonably priced accommodation and is situated 10km from the mountain, linked by an efficient free bus service.

Web sites www.fallscreek.net
www.hotham.net.au

Mount Buller
top 1,804m (5,917ft) bottom 1,390m (4,559ft)
The principal area for Melbourne-based skiers, Mount Buller has the largest lift capacity in Australia. The 27 lifts include 8 quads. The resort is a three-and-a-half-hour (200-km) drive north-east from Melbourne, through Ned Kelly country, and has some of the most impressive scenery in the Victorian Alps, with extensive views across the gum forests. There is substantial snowmaking and 80km of trails, including one that is 2.5km long. Night-skiing takes place two evenings each week. The Schuss Lodge is a small hotel with 27 beds and some magnificent views.

Web site www.mt-buller-accom.com.au

Perisher-Blue
top 2,034m (6,672ft) bottom 1,605m (5,264ft)
What were originally the three separate resorts of **Perisher/Smiggins**, **Blue Cow** and **Guthega** in New South Wales have combined to form the largest ski area in Australia. Perisher alone has 20 lifts, and the combined area has 50. The only way to reach the main complex is by train: the modern Ski Tube takes skiers through 10km of tunnels on a 20-minute journey to Perisher and Blue Cow from Bullocks Flat. The name Smiggins refers to the 'smiggin holes' formed by cattle gouging the soil for salt licks. Blue Cow prides itself on its testing terrain and the high proportion of black-diamond (difficult) runs. However, 60 per cent of the terrain is graded intermediate.

The resort's best accommodation is in the Perisher Valley Hotel, which is on the slopes and has 31 rooms and suites. Also at Perisher is the Perisher Manor, a family-run, ski-in ski-out establishment. The Lodge at Smiggins is a no-smoking, Austrian-style hotel with a swimming-pool. Heidi's Chalet is opposite the lifts at Smiggins.

Web site www.perisherblue.com.au

Thredbo
top 2,037m (6,683ft) bottom 1,365m (4,478ft)

This New South Wales resort, 450km (280 miles) from Sydney, has arguably the best skiing in the country, plus extensive and sophisticated snowmaking and an attractive Alpine-style village. It has been extensively remodelled since the tragic mudslide of July 1997, in which 18 people died. In the 1950s a large number of Austrians came here to work on the Snowy Mountain hydro-electric scheme, stayed on to take an active part in the skiing business, and have left their cultural imprint on the town. The 40 runs are served by 13 lifts.

The resort's leading hotel is the Thredbo Alpine Hotel, which adjoins Village Square with its range of shops and cafés. Other accommodation includes the recently renovated Snowgoose Lodge. Bursills Lodge boasts an indoor swimming-pool, and House of Ullr has a Scandinavian theme.

Web site www.thredbo.com.au

CHILE

El Colorado/La Parva/Valle Nevado
El Colorado: top 3,333m (10,935ft) bottom 2,430m (7,972ft)
La Parva: top 3,630m (11,909ft) bottom 2,670m (8,760ft)
Valle Nevado: top 3,670m (12,040ft) bottom 2,880m (9,450ft)

These three resorts, which are more or less linked, comprise the best conventional skiing in Chile and are the closest major slopes to any capital city in the world. At less than 64km north of Santiago, the city is so close that its pollution causes magnificent sunsets on the slopes. The ski areas are served by 42 lifts and offer some excellent off-piste. You are strongly advised to employ the services of a guide.

El Colorado is made up of two villages – traditional Villa Farellones and the more modern Villa Colorado. The resort tends to serve skiers from Santiago and is therefore busy at weekends but quiet during the week. La Parva, which has the most varied skiing, has no real hotels at present and remains a second- or third-home resort for affluent Chileans. Valle Nevado is the only true destination resort of the three, and attracts an international clientèle. It was purpose-built by the French in the 1980s, and is twinned with both Courchevel and Vail. Hotel Valle Nevado, Hotel Puerta del Sol and Hotel Tres Puntas provide the accommodation. Restaurants range from La Fourchette d'Or, serving fine French cuisine, to Café de la Plaza, which offers traditional Chilean dishes.

Web sites (El Colorado) www.andesweb.com/colorado.html
(La Parva) www.andesweb.com/parva.html
(Valle Nevado) www.andesweb.com/valle.html

Portillo
top 3,348m (10,984ft) bottom 2,512m (8,241ft)

This picturesque but slightly quirky ski area, situated in a steep-sided valley next to the breathtakingly beautiful Laguna (lake) del Inca, celebrated its 50th birthday in 1999. To mark the occasion the resort opened a new quad chair called Laguna, with striking views of the lake and a new intermediate trail, David's Run. Portillo is in the heart of the Southern Andes, close to the Argentinian border and just under 160km north of Santiago – a two and a half hour drive. Access is via the awe-inspiring Uspallata Pass, one of only two passes between Chile and Argentina accessible during the winter. Aconcagua, the highest mountain in the western hemisphere, is nearby. Most visitors to Portillo stay at the bright yellow Hotel Portillo, which dominates the resort. A quaint colonial atmosphere still pervades, with the red-and-white jacketed waiters hurrying around the vast lakeside dining-room. The resort is run by a veteran American, Henry Purcell, and the grooming and signposting on the 23 runs, served by 12 lifts, are as efficient as you would expect to find in any North American resort. Nearly half the slopes are rated as difficult, and the resort has its own heli-ski operation which departs from the door of Hotel Portillo.

Portillo also has the only serious snowmaking programme in Chile. This has proved crucial in recent drought years, particularly the disastrous winter of 1998, and snow-making facilities have been further extended for the 2000–1 season. The strong North American influence is reinforced by a large number of US ski instructors from Aspen and Vail. There are two bizarre but exhilarating *va et vient* lifts at Portillo, specially designed for accessing the steep chutes in avalanche-prone areas. The larger, Roca Jack, hauls five skiers at a time on linked platters at considerable speed to the top of the chute before suddenly coming to a halt; skiers must disengage backwards. These lifts are unique to Portillo and were designed by the Pomagalski lift company, which was also responsible for the invention of the 'Poma' lift. *Va et vient* lifts are a combination of a conventional cableway and a towerless cable tow. Should an avalanche hit the lift, the cable drops and is buried until it can be located once again. It can then be repaired or replaced then reinstalled.

Web site www.interknowledge.com/chile/portillo

Termas de Chillán
top 2,500m (8,200ft) bottom 1,800m (5,900ft)

For skiers and riders in search of the more offbeat face of the Chilean Andes without sacrificing quality, this spa resort best combines the two. Beware, however – the more exotic the location, the more treacherous the access route is likely to be. Do not attempt to reach Termas de Chillán without a four-wheel-drive vehicle or at least chains; the final 29km of the journey is on an icy, rocky and potholed road.

The resort itself is 480km south of Santiago and 80km east of

Chillán, the birthplace of Chile's first president, Bernardo O'Higgins. There are 28 groomed runs spread across 10,118 hectares (25,000 acres) of unusually varied terrain. A vertical drop of 1,100m (3,600ft) is possible for those prepared to hike above the lifts. There are eight lifts, of which the Don Otto chair-lift is reputedly the longest on the continent. The excellent off-piste includes the 14-km Shangri-La run, with its volcanic scenery, and Pirigallo – one of the resort's most celebrated itineraries, which comes complete with fumaroles belching sulphur fumes. It also suffers from avalanche danger after a storm. Extreme skiers can reach either of the two summits from the top of the chair-lift, with the Volcán offering the largest variety of steep chutes.

Termas de Chillán is popular with snowboarders, who are attracted to the long vertical drop. The resort also contains Chile's first snowboarder funpark and pipe. There is good cross-country touring to the west of the ski area and below the tree-line.

The Gran Hotel has expensive ski-in ski-out accommodation. If you are on a lower budget, then the place to head for is Las Tranoas, 10km away, where there are some more reasonably priced apartments. Another option is the Villa del Bosque Nevado condominiums; these are next to the Pirigallo Hotel and share its restaurant and spring water swimming-pool.

Web site www.andesweb.com/termas.html

JAPAN

Happo'one/Hakuba Valley
top 1,831m (6,007ft) bottom 760m (2,493ft)

Happo'one was the site for the men's downhill and Super G at the Nagano Winter Olympics in 1998. Nagano is 200km from Tokyo, with high-speed rail links that are making the area increasingly popular. As well as offering splendid mountain scenery, some challenging terrain and longer-than-average runs for Japan, Happo'one is one of the prettiest ski villages in the country. Another plus is the quick access to other ski areas in the same valley, including **Hakuba 47**, **Iwatake**, **Goryu-Toomi** and **Sunalpina Sanosaka**. All are about four hours' drive from Tokyo's Ueno railway station. Accommodation includes the Omoshiro Hasshinichi hotel at the base of Happo'one. It has four restaurants, a nightclub and indoor and outdoor swimming-pools. Seemingly endless tannoy messages and musical refrains are broadcast around the resort.

Web site www.skijapanguide.com/skiskiareaguidenagano.htm

Naeba
top 1,800m (5,905ft) bottom 900m (2,953ft)

This bustling ski area in Niigata Prefecture is one of the most frenetic resorts in the northern Japanese Alps. It is dominated by the Naeba

Prince, said to be the largest ski hotel in the world, with a shopping arcade, a Sega amusement area, a health centre and more than 40 restaurants, including one that stays open all night. This enables skiers and riders who are anxious to pack in as many hours on the slopes as possible to take breakfast at 3.30am and ski under floodlights at 4am. There is no need to stop skiing until 11pm, which means that die-hard snow-users can keep going for 19 hours. At weekends, when packed bullet trains and buses bring their human cargo, an almost absurd number of skiers floods the slopes – the record stands at 40,000 in one weekend – so at least at 4.30am there is some chance of finding a little space. The resort has 28 trails and a funpark. The lifts are open from early November until early May.

Web site www.pref.niigata.jp/en/index.html

Shiga Kogen
top 2,305m (7,562ft) bottom 1,228m (4,028ft)

Nagano's largest ski area, Shiga Kogen, was the venue for the majority of the 1998 Winter Olympic events. It is an extraordinary patchwork of 21 different 'resorts', served by more than 80 lifts, dotting six inter-linked mountains. None of the sectors are big or particularly difficult; in Alpine terms the whole area would make up just two or three linked resorts of reasonable size. A competent skier or rider could cover all the terrain in a couple of days. Apart from the skiing, another major tourist attraction is the hot sulphur baths, into which monkeys sometimes leap from the surrounding trees. Accommodation includes Villa Alpen (which has its own ski school and equipment rental shop) in the Sun Valley resort, with easy access to the other 20 areas.

Web site www.jinjapan.org/atlas/nature/nat25.html

NEW ZEALAND

Craigieburn
top 1,811m (5,942ft) bottom 1,570m (5,151ft)

New Zealand's club fields offer cheap, but not necessarily cheerful, skiing. Try battling to get up the slopes on a primitive 'nutcracker' rope-tow, then fighting to get down them in crusty, ungroomed snow. Unlike almost all commercial resorts, club fields usually have on-mountain accommodation, albeit fairly basic. One and a half hours' drive from Christchurch, in the South Island, Craigieburn deserves special mention because of the unusually challenging and spectacular terrain. Its 725-m vertical drop – which you have to walk up – is one of the longest in Australasia. However, because of its primitive facilities the resort attracts only hard-core skiers.

Web site www.craigieburn.co.nz

Mount Hutt
top 2,075m (6,808ft) bottom 1,585m (5,200ft)

The most famous of New Zealand's resorts is often patronised by north-ern hemisphere race teams for training out of season. Located on the South Island, a 35-minute drive from Methven and 70 minutes from Christchurch, Mount Hutt has magnificent views across the Canterbury Plains. It is also renowned for its access route: 12km of unsurfaced road at the mercy of strong winds, with somewhat alarming drops. The skiing can be excellent, although unpredictable weather has given the resort the rather unfair sobriquet 'Mount Shut'. A more flattering one is 'Ski field in the sky'. Mount Hutt has one of the most extensive snow-making systems in the southern hemisphere. The 672-m vertical drop is helped by the South Face runs that end up below the base area. The choice of accommodation is between hotels in Christchurch, farm cottages or 'homestays' where you live and eat with a local family.

Web site www.canterburypages.co.nz/ski/hutt.html

Porter Heights
top 1,980m (6,495ft) bottom 1,280m (4,200ft)

The closest commercial ski field to Christchurch (one hour's drive), this is a rather underrated resort which has evolved from club-field status. Apart from a couple of beginner 'platter' lifts at the base area, it has just three T-bars, but these serve a considerable area of interesting and quite steep terrain. Much depends on whether high winds and/or avalanche danger close the all-important Number 3 T-bar, which gives skiers access to the ridge. From here you can reach Big Mama, one of the country's greatest off-piste runs, which is a steep descent with a vertical drop of 720m. There is further fine off-piste skiing and snowboarding on the other flank of this fairly steep valley, down McNulty's Basin and Stellar Bowl. Number 1 T-bar provides some good mid-valley intermediate terrain. The Porter Heights Ski Club Alpine Lodge is ski-in ski-out.

Web site www.snow.co.nz/porterheights

Queenstown (Coronet Peak/The Remarkables)
Coronet Peak: top 1,620m (5,315ft) bottom 1,200m (3,937ft)
The Remarkables: top 1,957m (6,421ft) bottom 1,600m (5,315ft)

Situated in the south-west of the South Island, this is a lively and picturesque lakeside town with two separate resorts, the old and the new, which have interchangeable lift passes. The traditional resort at Coronet Peak, with a vertical drop of 420m, has been modernised and enlarged and now provides a wide variety of good all-round skiing and a much-improved lift system. The Remarkables, which opened for skiing in 1985, is visually exciting but has fewer options than Coronet Peak. From Queenstown the range seems impossibly steep, with the peaks resembling a set of sharp, pearly-white teeth, dominating the shoreline of Lake Wakatipu. Fortunately, the ski area is on the other side, where gentle bowls belie the severity of the mountains.

Although The Remarkables provides predominantly intermediate terrain for skiers and riders, some short, sharp couloirs, including Escalator and Elevator, add challenge. Among the steep off-piste sections, for those who are prepared to walk up, are the Homeward Runs. These emerge at the access road to the resort from where a truck takes skiers back up to the base area. Toilet Bowl, which also ends at the road below, is great for freeriders.

Web sites (Coronet Peak) www.nzski.com/coronet_peak
(The Remarkables) www.nzski.com/remarkables

Treble Cone
top 1,860m (6,102ft) bottom 1,200m (3,936ft)
The atmosphere at Lake Wanaka is as tranquil as that at Lake Wakatipu is vibrant. This is the idyllic gateway to Treble Cone. Although it ranks as one of the country's top three resorts (the others being Mount Hutt and Queenstown), Treble Cone is not well known outside New Zealand. It once had a reputation for favouring advanced snow-users, but in recent years some good beginner terrain has been developed. Advanced skiers and freeriders can hike for 20 minutes to the 2,100-m summit to enjoy some of the best off-piste in the area. Challenging heli-skiing can be found nearby.

Web site www.new-zealand.com/treblecone

Turoa
top 2,322m (7,618ft) bottom 1,600m (5,249ft)
Turoa, on the southwestern face of Mount Ruapehu, offers the biggest vertical drop (720m) in Australasia, even exceeding that of **Whakapapa**, its better-known neighbour. The upper slopes, like Whakapapa's, include some of the exotic qualities associated with volcanic terrain. Because Mount Ruapehu and other nearby volcanoes attract sudden storms and high winds, conditions in the off-piste areas above the lifts can be extreme. A climb to the summit affords breathtaking views of the Tasman Sea. It is possible to ski down, but check with the ski patrol first as the uppermost slopes can be dangerous. Apart from an unusual and exhilarating terraced effect – steep little sections followed by long, flatter sections – the lift-served slopes provide rolling, wide-open and largely uneventful cruising, with a few runs of up to almost 4km. The Turoa Ski Lodge is a comfortable place to stay, with a restaurant, a bar and roaring log fires.

Web site www.snow.co.nz/turoa

Whakapapa
top 2,300m (7,546ft) bottom 1,625m (5,331ft)

Whakapapa is the country's largest developed ski area. It has a vertical drop of 675m, 30 trails including a wide selection of cruising runs, exciting off-piste in its Black Magic area, and some severe terrain below the magnificent, snow-encrusted Pinnacles – which resemble a scaled-down version of the jagged Teton Mountains of Jackson Hole in Wyoming. The area is wonderful but the unpredictable weather is frustrating. In good conditions the skiing is some of the best in the southern hemisphere.

The resort is built on the flanks of the Mount Ruapehu volcano, which attracts some of the more inclement weather on the North Island, with storms moving in fast and furiously. Until 1995, when a series of spectacular volcanic eruptions brought the ski season to a premature close, it was possible to make the three-hour climb to the Ruapehu crater lake and then ski down. Whakapapa is great for riders, with its varied terrain of cliffs and gullies, as well as a well-maintained half-pipe.

Web site www.laketaupo.co.nz/skiing/skiopen.htm

Heli-skiing and heli-boarding
New Zealand claims to have more helicopter skiing and boarding than anywhere apart from Canada, and the South Island has a bewildering number of options. (See *Heli-skiing*).

Useful web sites
Argentinian resorts *www.worldski.com.ar/resorts/resorts.htm*
Australian and New Zealand resorts *www.ciau.com.au/snow/*
Japanese resorts *www.skijapanguide.com*
New Zealand resorts *www.snow.co.nz*
South American resorts *www.andesweb.com*

Heli-skiing and heli-boarding

Many non-skiers and even some skiers have the erroneous impression, doubtless culled from a James Bond film, that heli-skiing involves jumping out of a helicopter while it is in mid-air. In reality, however, it is no more than a luxurious form of taxi service . . . and the helicopter does land before you get out.

Helicopter skiing is an exotic, expensive but very rewarding way for accomplished skiers and riders to reach untracked snow in high mountain regions far beyond the scope of ski-lifts. It is now possible to heli-ski and heli-board in a variety of countries, including Canada, the USA, Italy, Switzerland, Sweden, New Zealand, India and even Georgia in the USSR.

Heli-skiers and heli-boarders expect powder snow, and fresh tracks are taken for granted, but inevitably there are frustrating days when, because of bad visibility or howling winds, it is not possible to fly. If you are staying at a remote wilderness lodge, this also means no skiing or riding. Canadian Mountain Holidays (CMH), which has ten bases in British Columbia, stresses the dangers to its clients: 'There are no guarantees as to what you will encounter during your week. It could be the best skiing of your life, but it could also be poor and very demanding. We want to make it absolutely clear that there are risks beyond our control that you must share with us'.

Basics

The helicopters used to transport skiers and boarders to the mountain tops include the Bell 210 and 212 that seat up to 12 passengers, including a guide. The smaller Aerospatiale Squirrel (known in North America as the A Star), which takes up to five passengers and a guide, is also popular. The most important person in a heli-skiing operation – even outranking the highly trained guide – is the pilot. Mountain pilots will fly in almost all weathers, including lightly falling snow, as long as there is adequate visibility and low to moderate wind speeds.

The heli-ski experience can range from an introductory run or a single-day package in Europe or North America, to a full week in British Columbia or even the Himalayas, with the number of 'drops' per group running into double figures on most days. A 'drop' is equivalent to one long 'run' in a ski resort. A group of skiers or boarders is deposited on the snow by the helicopter in order to ski or ride down. This group is then collected at the bottom of the run by the helicopter.

In Canada, for example, up to 44 clients will spend a week in a ski lodge in the British Columbian mountain wilderness where they are divided into groups according to ability or who they want to ski with.

How good do you have to be?

Generally you should be reasonably fit and of high intermediate standard (i.e. you should be able to do parallel turns on a red run and to manage a black run with confidence). The introduction of wide-bodied or 'fat' skis that allow you to 'float' over all types of snow has made skiing less tiring and has made heli-skiing more accessible and easier. Snowboarders should be of a similar standard. There are no age restrictions, but common sense dictates that the experience is too physically demanding for all but the most accomplished of sub-teenage children as well as skiers in the twilight of their sporting prowess.

For skiers or riders wishing to sample the sport before committing themselves to a lodge in the middle of nowhere for an entire week, heli-skiing or heli-boarding for a single day is easily available in Italy and Switzerland.

Safety

Before you even get into the helicopter, you will be given a safety briefing and required to learn some basic procedures for avalanche rescue using transceivers, as well as how to move safely in and around the helicopter. There are several vital points to remember:

- Do not ski or ride past your guide. He or she may have stopped because of changing snow conditions, a tricky cliff area, or even a crevasse.
- Do not ski or ride near the helicopter, regardless of whether or not the rotor-blade is moving.
- Never go round the back of the helicopter
- Do not chase loose items of clothing if they blow away.

What to wear

One-piece suits are better than two pieces for skiing through very deep powder. However, any warm and waterproof outfit will be suitable. The weather can change rapidly, so wear goggles rather than sunglasses and always take a hat.

Heli-skiing around the world

EUROPE

Most European heli-skiing companies are based in **Italy** and **Switzerland**. Italy's best-known operations are in the Aosta Valley within easy reach of Courmayeur and Cervinia. In the Monterosa Ski region there are huge 1,500-m vertical drops, with descents to Champoluc (Italy) or down the stunningly beautiful Gornergletscher to Zermatt. On the Swiss side of the border heli-skiing and heli-boarding opportunities are available at Aeschhorn (3,500m) and from the Alphubeljoch (3,600m). You can also heli-ski around Verbier on the Petit Combin, Rosablanche and the awe-inspiring Trient Glacier. World-class drops can be made at Grindelwald at Rosenegg and Sustenalp, with descents in excess of 2,000 metres.

Heli-skiing is banned in France for environmental reasons, although companies based in France can arrange trips to the Italian Alps. In **Austria**, it is very restricted, with the exception of a few designated 'drop' points around Lech and Zürs.

In Sweden you can try heli-skiing in Åre, and in April and May in the far north of the country at Riksgränsen.

CANADA
In Canada first-timers can sample the sport in Whistler and Panorama, before moving on to major heli-ski areas such as the Bugaboos, Monashees and Cariboos in British Columbia.

INDIA
You can also try heli-skiing in the Himalayas in Manali in the north Indian province of Himachal Pradesh. The Himachal Helicopter Skiing company employs Swiss pilots, who fly state-of-the-art helicopters, and guides from New Zealand, North America and Australia.

NEW ZEALAND
New Zealand claims to have more heli-skiing opportunities than anywhere apart from Canada. Most companies offer one-day packages from the South Island, with between three and five drops a day, although seven or more are possible.

The striking scenery on Mount Cook resembles the glacial terrain of the Vallée Blanche, and both the snow quality and the weather conditions are unpredictable. Your guide will almost certainly take you to explore one or two cavernous crevasses with domed ceilings of ice, which are known to be completely safe.

How much will it cost?
A single drop at Valgrisenche in the Italian Aosta Valley costs approximately £80; for a full day of three descents of 1,000 vertical metres the cost is £200. A more adventurous single descent from the Ruitor Glacier in Italy down into France near Sainte-Foy costs £100. Unless you are based in France, you will then need to take a taxi back to La Rosière for the return journey by chair-lift to La Thuile in Italy.

At Grindelwald, depending on the number of passengers, the cost per drop ranges from £86 to £145. At Åre in Sweden it costs around £92 per drop. One descent off the Monterosa range in Italy, not including the guide's fee, costs about £65 per person. At Zermatt one descent costs about £50 per person, not including the guide's fee.

In the Himalayas both the cost and the altitude at which you ski (up to 5,000 metres) are high – around £650 per day.

Staying in a Canadian heli-ski lodge costs around £420 per day. You will also have to pay an extra £9 for every extra 1,000 vertical metres (3,280 vertical feet) you ski above a guaranteed 100,000 vertical feet (30,488 vertical metres) for a week. Conversely, if bad weather prevents you skiing your minimum weekly 'ration' you should qualify for a refund. Three- and five-day packages are also an option in some locations. RK Heli-ski at Panorama in British Columbia specialises in beginner packages: a day's package of three drops and lunch is just over £200, with additional runs at £25 each. Mike Wiegele, based at Blue

River in British Columbia, routinely uses two guides per drop – one to lead the group and one to 'sweep' (check for any skiers or boarders who have fallen) – which is a unique selling-point and an additional safety asset.

In New Zealand, a three-run day will cost £240, or seven runs £325. A week-long package will cost from £1,370.

(The costs listed here are per passenger and include a heli-ski guide but not intercontinental flights, unless stated otherwise. Prices were correct at time of writing.)

What will you get for your money?

On a week-long package picnic lunches are normally flown in and served on the slopes unless the weather is bad, and dinner is usually a substantial affair in a location where there is little else to do but ski, absorb the scenery and enjoy the camaraderie. You can expect to ski or board 100,000 vertical feet in a week, but some groups manage more.

Heli-ski companies

Listed below are a selection of heli-ski companies from around the world. It must be emphasised that we only have personal experience of some of them. You are strongly advised to check safety standards with your chosen company before booking.

ASIA
Gudauri Heli-skiing
Tel 41 81 720 2121
Email at@alpintravel.ch
Web site www.alpintravel.ch
European agent Alpin Travel

Himachal Heli-skiing (*India*)
Tel 020-7681 2032 (UK) or
1 250 336 2501 (Canada)
Email roddy@himachal.com
Web site www.himachal.com
UK agent Ski Club of Great Britain
(020-8410 2000)

AUSTRIA
Wucher Heli-skiing (*Lech, St Anton, Zürs*)
Tel 43 5583 2950 **Fax** 43 3880 306
Email helicopter@wucher.at

CANADA
Canadian Mountain Holidays
Tel 020-7736 8191 **Fax** 020-7384 2592
Web site www.cmhski.com
UK agent Powder Skiing in North America

Crescent Spur
Tel 1 250 553 2300 **Fax** 1 250 553 2301
Email regina@crescentspurheliski.com
Web site www.crescentspurheliski.com
UK agent James Orr Heli-skiing
(020-7483 0300)

Great Canadian Heli-skiing
Tel/Fax 1 604 344 2326

Klondike Heli-skiing
Tel 1 867 634 2224
Email khmi@yknet.yk.ca
UK agent Ski Club of Great Britain

Last Frontier Heli-skiing
Tel 1 250 558 7980
Fax 1 250 558 7981
Email info@lastfrontierheli.com
Web site www. lastfrontierheli.com
UK agent James Orr Heli-skiing

Mike Wiegele Helicopter Skiing
Tel 1 250 673 8381
Fax 1 250 673 8464
Email mail@wiegele.com
Web site: www.wiegele.com

UK agent Ski Scott Dunn
(020-8767 0202)

Purcell Helicopter Skiing Ltd
Tel 1 604 344 5410
Fax 1 604 344 6076

RK Heli-ski Panorama Inc.
Tel 1 250 342 3889 **Fax** 1 250 342 3466
Email info@rkheliski.com
Web site www. rkheliski.com

Selkirk Tangiers Helicopter Skiing Ltd
Tel 1 403 762 5627 **Fax** 1 403 762 2708
Email selkirktangiers@revelstoke.net
Web site www.selkirk-tangiers.com

TLH Heli-skiing
Tel 1 250 558 5379 **Fax** 1 250 558 5379
Email info@tlhheliskiing.com
Web site www.tlhheliskiing.com
UK agents James Orr, Ski Club of
Great Britain

Whistler Heli-skiing
Tel 1 604 932 4105 **Fax** 1 604 938 1225
Email heliski@direct.ca
Web site www.heliskiwhistler.com

FRANCE
ESI Pra-Loup (*over the border in
Italian Alps*)
Tel 33 492 84 05 99

Pros-Neige (*based in Val Thorens, to
Le Chaud and Ruitor Glacier*)
Tel 33 479 01 07 00 **Fax** 33 479 01 07 01
Email prosneige@club-internet.fr
Web site www.cosa-mental.fr/prosneige

Ski Safari Pepi Prager (*based in Val
Thorens, to Valgrisenche*)
Tel 33 479 00 01 23
Fax 33 479 07 59 48

Top Ski (*based in Val d'Isère, to
Valgrisenche, Val Veny, Monte Rosa*)
Tel 33 479 06 14 80
Fax 33 479 06 28 42
Email top.ski.val.isere@wanadoo.fr
Web site www.perso.wanadoo.fr/topski

ITALY
Air Vallée (*Val Veny near Courmayeur*)

Tel 39 0165 869814
Fax 39 0165 236669

Elisusa Heli-skiing (*Sauze d'Oulx*)
Tel 39 0122 623162 **Fax** 39 0122 31920
Email elisusa2000@hotmail.com
Web site www.members.xoom.com/elisusa

ETI 2000 (*Cervinia, Courmayeur,
Valgrisenche*)
Tel 39 0165 765 417
Fax 39 0165 765 418
Email eti2000@netvallee.it
Web site www.eti2000.pointer.it

Giana Helicopter (*Macugnaga,
Domodossola*)
Tel 39 0324 35395 **Fax** 0324 35283
Email gianaheli @tin.it

Heli-ski Europe
Tel 020-7584 6287 (UK)
Fax 020-7581 9422
Email emma@aquiver.co.uk

Interguide (*Pila*)
Tel 39 0165 40939
Fax 39 1065 44448
Email guidealpine@netvallee.ip
Web site www. guidealpine.com

Team Nature (*Bormio, Cervinia, Isola
2000, Val d'Aosta, Zermatt*)
Tel 33 493 58 77 24
Fax 33 493 58 77 77
Web site www.teamnature.com

NEW ZEALAND
Harris Mountains Heli-ski (*The
Remarkables, Coronet Peak,
Treble Cone and Cardrona,
The Doolans, Tyndall Glaciers,
and The Buchanans*)
Tel 64 3 443 7930

Methven Heli-ski (*Arrowsmith and
Ragged Ranges*)
Tel 64 3 302 8909

Mount Cook Heli-ski
Tel 64 181 741 5652

SWEDEN
Åre Ski School
Tel 46 647 130 50

Riksgränsen Ski School *(April and May)*
Tel 46 980 400 80

Ramundberget Ski School
Tel 46 684 290 00

SWITZERLAND
Air Glaciers *(Saanen near Gstaad)*
Tel 41 33 744 5550 Fax 41 33 744 0141
Email gstaad@airglaciers.ch
Web site www.airglaciers.ch

Bohag *(Bernese Oberland)*
Tel 41 33 828 9000 Fax 41 33 828 9010
Email info@bohag.ch
Web site www.bohag.ch

Bergsteigerzentrum Grindelwald
Tel 41 33 853 5200
Email bergsteigerzentrum@grindelwald.ch

Flying Devil *(Lausanne)*
Tel 41 21 340 0304 Fax 41 21 323 9922

Heli Bernina *(Engadine area)*
Tel 41 21 340 0304 Fax 41 21 323 9922
Email helibernia@bluewin.ch
Web site www.helibernia.ch

Heli Chablais *(Leysin)*
Tel 41 24 494 3434 Fax 41 24 494 3030
Web site www.heli-chablais.com

Heliswiss *(Gstaad)*
Tel 41 33 755 1321 Fax 41 26 921 1330

Heliswiss *(Samedan near St Moritz)*
Tel 41 81 852 3535 F
ax 41 81 852 3272

Air Zermatt
Tel 41 27 966 8686 Fax 41 27 966 8685
Email zermatt@air-zermatt.ch

Mountain Guides Verbier
Tel 41 27 775 3363
Fax 41 27 775 3369
Email info@verbier-sportcenter.ch

Trans-Heli SA – Air Glaciers SA
Tel 41 24 473 7070 Fax 41 24 473 7071

USA
Helitrax *(Telluride, Colorado)*
Tel 1 970 728 3895 Fax 1 970 728 4904
Email powder@helitrax.com
Web site www.helitrax.com

High Mountain Heli-skiing
(Jackson Hole, Wyoming)
Tel 1 307 733 3274
Web site www.heliskijackson.com

North Cascade Heli-skiing *(Seattle)*
Tel 1 800 494 HELI (contactable from
USA only)

Ruby Mountain Helicopter Skiing
(Nevada)
Tel 1 775 753 6867
Email rubyski@sierra.net
Web site www.helicopterskiing.com

Sun Valley Heli-ski *(Idaho)*
Tel 1 208 622 3108
Email svheli@sunvalley.net
Web site www.svheli-ski.com

Valdez Heli-Ski Guides *(Alaska)*
Tel 1 307 733 6331
Email valdezheli@blissnet.com
Web site dougcoombs.com

Wasatch Powder Guides
(Snowbird, Utah)
Tel 1 801 742 2800
Web site www.heliskiwasatch.com

UK COMPANIES THAT CAN ORGANISE HELI-SKIING
Momentum Travel
Tel 020-7371 9111

The Ski Company
Tel 020-7730 9600

Safety on the slopes

The mountains, like the sea, are enormously enjoyable but can also be dangerous and should be treated with the utmost respect at all times. Only when you find yourself in a potentially dangerous situation, or witness an accident at first hand, do you fully appreciate what the risks are.

Occasionally the combination of exceptionally heavy snowfalls and high winds in parts of the Alps means that the ever-present threat of avalanches spreads from the off-piste slopes to the villages. Snow-users have to make decisions on whether it is even safe to travel to their holiday destinations, let alone to ski when they get there. In such unusual circumstances it is advisable to check not only with your tour operator but also with the resort tourist information office and the appropriate avalanche control authority (see *Skiing by numbers*). All the information below applies to both skiers and snowboarders.

Weather and exposure

Mountain weather can change at a moment's notice and varies dramatically at different altitudes. Always dress with this in mind and be prepared for all conditions. Several layers of clothing are best, and it is always preferable to be too hot rather than too cold. More heat escapes through the head than any other part of the body, and you should never set off without a hat, as well as sunglasses or goggles. In the event of an accident, a 'space blanket' (a metallic sheet that folds to handkerchief-size and can be bought from any reputable ski or mountaineering shop) can save a life.

Exposure to bad weather can result in frostbite or hypothermia. Frostbite is the excessive cooling of small areas of the body, usually the fingers, toes, nose, cheeks or ears. The affected tissue turns white and numb. This is called first-degree frostbite and can be dealt with by immediate, gentle rewarming. In cold conditions, watch out for signs of frostbite in your companions. Hypothermia results from a drop in the body's temperature. It is difficult to diagnose; some of the more obvious symptoms are physical or mental lethargy, sluggishness, slurring of speech, spurts of energy and abnormal vision.

All young children should wear safety helmets, preferably with chin guards. These can be worn on their own, or over a thin balaclava or hat on extremely cold days. Unfortunately, apart from in a few Scandinavian resorts, helmets are not yet compulsory. In the United States, more adults now wear helmets for recreational skiing, and we applaud this trend. Never ski with a baby or small child in a backpack; anyone, however competent, can catch an edge and fall, or someone could crash into you.

Rules of the slopes

The FIS (International Ski Federation) has established rules of conduct for skiers and snowboarders. This is a summary:

Respect Do not endanger others.

Control Adapt the manner and speed of your skiing to your ability and to the general conditions on the mountain.

Choice of route The skier in front has priority – leave enough space between you and the preceding skier or snowboarder.

Overtaking Leave plenty of space when overtaking a slower skier.

Entering and starting a run Look up and down the mountain each time before starting on or entering a marked run.

Stopping Only stop at the edge of a piste or where you can be seen easily.

Climbing When climbing up or down, always keep to the side of the piste.

Signs Obey all signs and markers – they are there for your safety.

Assistance In case of accidents, provide help if you can or alert the rescue service.

Identification All those involved in an accident, including witnesses, should exchange names and addresses.

All the above rules are legally binding and apply to both skiers and snowboarders. You could be in serious trouble if you are to blame for an accident while in breach of these rules.

Important guidelines for skiers and snowboarders

- Consider fitness sessions and taking lessons on a dry slope before going on holiday.
- You ski at your own risk.
- Ski on marked runs – these are protected from unexpected mountain dangers.
- Watch out for piste machines.
- Respect nature – take care not to ski in areas where young trees or wildlife will be disturbed and do not drop litter.

Special rules for snowboarders

- Do not attempt the sport without instruction.
- The ability to ski does not automatically mean you have the ability to snowboard.
- Your front foot must be firmly tethered to the board by a safety strap.
- It is essential to look carefully to the right and left when changing direction. When starting a turn heelside, look backwards as well.

Off-piste

Outside the marked pistes and itineraries are areas that are NOT protected from mountain dangers.

Signs and flags around the ski area may warn you when avalanche danger is present, but do not rely on these alone. Take local professional advice. Even when there is no warning of avalanches there could be localised snow slides.

Both the unified European and the North American avalanche risk scales are numbered 1 to 5 and colour-coded. However, not all countries use colours and the colours are not the same on both sides of the

Atlantic. Critics argue that the weight of the descriptions varies from language to language.

1 Low (*Europe*: green *North America*: green)
Europe: release of avalanches is only possible on very few and very steep slopes. Only small spontaneous avalanches are to be expected. Off-piste generally good.
North America: avalanches very unlikely. Isolated areas of instability.

2 Moderate (*Europe*: yellow *North America*: yellow)
Europe: larger additional loads (e.g. a group of skiers) may release avalanches, especially on indicated steep slopes. Larger spontaneous avalanches are not to be expected. Off-piste is only moderately stabilised on some steeper slopes, but otherwise generally well-stabilised.
North America: natural avalanches are unlikely. Human-triggered avalanches are possible. Slab avalanches are possible on steep terrain.

3 Considerable (*Europe*: dark yellow *North America*: orange)
Europe: release of avalanches are likely by moderate additional loads (e.g. a jumping skier or a pedestrian) on the steepest slopes. Occasional medium-sized avalanches and also large spontaneous avalanches have to be expected. The snowpack is only weakly to moderately stabilised on many steep slopes.
North America: natural avalanches possible. Human-triggered avalanches probable. Slabs probable on steep terrain.

4 High (*Europe*: orange *North America*: red)
Europe: avalanches are likely to occur even in the case of low additional loads on most steep slopes. In some cases many medium-sized and sometimes also large natural releases are to be expected. Off-piste is weakly stabilised on the steepest slopes.
North America: Widespread natural or human-triggered avalanches certain. Unstable slabs likely on a variety of aspects and slope angles.

5 Very high (*Europe*: red *North America*: black)
Europe: numerous large natural releases are to be expected even in moderately steep terrain. Off-piste generally not possible.
North America: travel in avalanche terrain is not recommended. Extremely unstable slabs certain on most aspects and slope angles. Large, destructive avalanches possible.

Only venture off-piste with a fully qualified guide. This rule applies particularly to glacial terrain, where the risk of crevasses is added to that of avalanches. Always wear a recognised avalanche bleeper and take the time to learn how to use it by making a practice grid search before you set off.

Listen to your guide, learn basic snowcraft and how to read a slope. However, it is important to remember that guides can be fallible and that you alone must take responsibility for decisions concerning your safety. In the event of an avalanche, try to ski to the side. If you fall, try to get rid of your skis, poles and backpack. The chances of survival after an avalanche deteriorate rapidly after the first five minutes beneath the surface of the snow. Make swimming motions with your arms and legs and fight to stay on the surface.

Tips to remember when skiing or snowboarding off-piste

- Always ski in a group, never alone.
- Always ski in control behind the guide.
- Always stop behind the guide (there may be cliffs or other hazards ahead).
- Carry a map of the area and a compass. Know how to use both.
- Be wary of slopes where the run-out is not clearly obvious from the start. Following other skiers' or snowboarders' tracks does not necessarily mean the route is safe.

Accident procedure

Speed is essential when an accident has occurred:

- **Secure the accident area** Protect the casualty by planting crossed skis in the snow a little way above the accident. If necessary post someone above the accident site to give warning to other skiers.
- **First aid** Assess the general condition of the casualty:
  Airway – Check it is clear. Make sure nothing is obstructing the mouth or throat.
  Breathing – If the casualty is not breathing, administer artificial respiration (mouth-to-mouth resuscitation). If the casualty is breathing but unconscious, turn him/her on to his/her side to minimise the risk of choking.
  Limbs – Protect any fractured limb from movement. Do not remove the ski boot if there is injury to the lower leg as it acts as a splint.
  Circulation – Check for pulse. Cover any wound using a clean handkerchief or scarf and **keep the casualty warm**. Give nothing to eat or drink, especially alcohol. If the accident victim appears to be in shock (going pale, cold and faint), he/she should be encouraged to lie with his/her head lower than his/her feet.
- **Alert the rescue service** Contact the ski patroller, ski teacher or lift attendant. Give the place of accident (piste name and nearest piste-marker), the number of people injured and the types of injury.
- **Establish the facts of the accident** Take names and addresses of the people involved and of witnesses. Note the place, time and circumstances of the accident; the terrain, snow conditions, visibility, markings and signs.
- **Report to the police as soon as possible**.

Which tour operator?

Below is a list of ski and snowboard operators that offer inclusive holiday packages. All but a handful fully satisfy the government requirements for bonding. Those that do not have been included because their main client-base is not in the United Kingdom. A large number of other companies and individuals offer accommodation-only holidays or have limited bonding (often through 'borrowed' ATOL licences), which we feel is insufficient. Many of these firms are well-established and have sound reputations. Our decision to exclude them does not necessarily mean they should be avoided. Before parting with any money, however, it would be wise to satisfy yourself with what would happen in the event of sudden company closure. Payment by major credit card may act as a secure secondary insurance on your investment.

ABERCOMBIE & KENT
Sloane Square House, Holbein Place,
London SW1W 8NS
Tel 020-7371 8659
Fax 020-7730 9376
Email info@abercrombiekent.co.uk
Web site www.abercrombiekent.co.uk
Luxury hotels in the Alps and North America

ACTION VACANCES/UCPA
30 Brackley Road, Stockport SK4 2RE
Tel/Fax 0161-442 6130
Email av4ucpa@btinternet.com
Web site www.ucpa.co.uk
18–40s budget skiing and snowboarding holidays

AIRTOURS
Wavell House, Holcombe Road,
Helmshore, Rossendale BB4 4NB
Tel (0870) 157 7775
Fax 0161-819 2044
Web site www.airtours.com
Major tour operator

ALL CANADA SKI
Sunway House, Lowestoft NR32 2LW
Tel (01502) 565176
Fax (01502) 500681
Email ski@all-canada.com
Web site www.all-canada.com
Ski holidays in Canada

ALPINE ACTION
3 Old Salts Farm Road, Lancing BN15 8JE
Tel (01903) 761986
Fax (01903) 766007
Email alpineaction@mistral.co.uk

Web site www.alpine-action.co.uk
Small operator to the Trois Vallées

ALPINE ANSWERS SELECT
The Business Village, 3–9 Broomhill
Road, London SW18 4JQ
Tel 020-8871 4656
Fax 020-8871 9676
Email select@alpineanswers.co.uk
Web site www.alpineanswers.co.uk
Tailor-made hotel holidays worldwide

ALPINE TOURS
54 Northgate, Canterbury, CT1 1BE
Tel (01227) 454777
Fax (01227) 451177
Email alpinetoursltd@btinternet.com
Schools and groups

ALPINE TRACKS
40 High Street, Menai Bridge,
Anglesey LL59 5EF
Tel (01248) 717440
Fax (01248) 717441
Email alpinetrac@cs.com
Web site www.alpine-tracks.co.uk
Holidays in Lech, Morzine and Whistler

A.P.T. HOLIDAYS
PO Box 125, Rayleigh SS6 9SX
Tel (01268) 783878
Fax (01268) 782656
Email apt.holidays@virgin.net
www.apt-holidays.co.uk
Weekend coach holidays to Austria

BALKAN HOLIDAYS
Sofia House, 19 Conduit Street,
London W1R 9TD

Tel 020-7543 5555
Fax 020-7543 5577
Email reservations@balkanholidays.co.uk
Web site www.balkanholidays.co.uk
Holidays in Bulgaria

BALKAN TOURS
61 Ann Street, Belfast BT1 4EE
Tel 028-9024 6795
Fax 028-9023 4581
Email mail@balkan.co.uk
Holidays in Bulgaria and Romania

BEAUMONT HOLIDAYS
Pinnacle House, 17–25 Hartfield Road,
London SW19 3SE
Tel/Fax 020-8544 0404
Email stay@beau-mont.com
Web site www.beau-mont.com
Holidays in Chamonix and Cervinia

BELVEDERE CHALETS
Peach House, Gangbridge Lane,
St Mary Bourne SP11 6EW
Tel (01264) 738257
Fax (01264) 738533
Web site www.belvedere.chalets.co.uk
Luxury chalets in Méribel

BIG COUNTRY
Llanmaes, St Fagans, Cardiff CF5 6DU
Tel (02920) 675205
Fax (02920) 675201
Email enquiries@big-country.co.uk
Web site www.big-country.co.uk
Holidays in North America and Canada

BIGFOOT TRAVEL
186 Greys Road, Henley-on-Thames
RG9 1QU
Tel (01491) 579601
Fax (01491) 576568
Email ann@bigfoot-travel.co.uk
Web site www.bigfoot-travel.co.uk
*Holidays in Chamonix, Argentière
and Les Houches*

BORDERLINE
Les Sorbiers, F-65120 Barèges, France
Tel 00 33 562 92 68 95
Fax 00 33 562 92 83 43
Email sorbiers@sudfr.com
Web site www.borderlinehols.com
Skiing and snowboarding in Barèges

CHALET SNOWBOARD
31 Aldworth Avenue, Wantage OX12 7EJ
Tel (01235) 767575
Fax (01235) 767576
Email info@chalet-snowboard.co.uk
Web site www.chalet-snowboard.co.uk
Snowboarding in France

CHALET WORLD
PO Box 260, Shrewsbury SY1 1WX
Tel (01952) 840462
Fax (01952) 840463
Email sales@chaletworld.co.uk
Web site www.chaletworld.co.uk
Alpine chalet holidays

CLASSIC SKI
Ober Road, Brockenhurst SO42 7ST
Tel (01590) 623400
Fax (01590) 624387
Email info@classicski.co.uk
Holidays in France for mature skiers

CLUB EUROPE
Fairway House, 53 Dartmouth Road,
London SE23 3HN
Tel (0800) 4964996
Fax 020-8699 7770
Email ski@club-europe.co.uk
Web site www.club-europe.co.uk
Schools and groups

CLUB MED
Kennedy House, 115 Hammersmith
Road, London W14 0QH
Tel 020-7348 3333
Fax 020-7348 3336
Email cmmarketing@compuserve.com
Web site www.clubmed.com
*All-inclusive holiday villages,
with childcare*

COLLINEIGE SKI
30–32 High Street, Frimley GU16 5JD
Tel (01276) 24262
Fax (01276) 27282
Email info@collineige.com
Web site www.collineige.com
*Chalets in Chamonix Valley, with
childcare and mountain guides*

CONTIKI
Wells House, 15 Elmfield Road,
Bromley BR1 1LS

Tel 020-8290 6422
Fax 020-8225 4246
Email contiki@contiki.com
Web site www.contiki.com
18–35s holidays in Hopfgarten

THE CORPORATE SKI COMPANY
Spectrum House, Bromells Road,
London SW4 0BN
Tel 020-7627 5500
Fax 020-7622 6701
Email john@vantagepoint.co.uk
Corporate ski events

CRESTA HOLIDAYS
Tadley Court, Victoria Street, Altrincham
WA14 1EZ
Tel 0161-385 4100
Fax 0161-385 4059
Email lroberts@crestaholidays.co.uk
Family holidays in France, with ski-drive

CRYSTAL HOLIDAYS
King's Place, Wood Street, Kingston
KT1 1JY
Tel (0870) 848 7000
Fax (0870) 848 7032
Email travel@crystalholidays.co.uk
Web site www.crystalholidays.co.uk
Major tour operator

DESCENT INTERNATIONAL
Laverstoke Mill, Laverstoke, Whitchurch
RG28 7NR
Tel 020-7989 8989
Fax 020-7989 8990
Email ski@descent.co.uk
Luxury chalet in Méribel

ELEGANT RESORTS
The Old Palace, Little St. John's Street,
Chester CH1 1RB
Tel (0870) 333 3336
Fax (0870) 333 3331
Email enquiries@elegantresorts.co.uk
Web site www.elegantresorts.co.uk
Luxury hotels in major resorts

EQUITY TOTAL SKI
Dukes Lane House, 47 Middle Street,
Brighton BN1 1AL
Tel (01273) 298298
Fax (01273) 203212
Email ski@equity.co.uk

Web site www.equity.co.uk
*All-inclusive holidays in Europe and
North America*

ERNA LOW
9 Reece Mews, London SW7 3HE
Tel 020-7584 2841
Fax 020-7589 9531
Email info@ernalow.co.uk
Web site www.ernalow.co.uk
Apartments and hotels in France

FAIRHAND HOLIDAYS/SKISARUS
216–218 Main Road, Biggin Hill
TN16 3BD
Tel (01959) 540796
Fax (01959) 540797
Email ian.porter@skisarus.com
Web site www.skisarus.com
*Tailor-made holidays in France
(Fairhand) and North America (Skisarus)*

FANTISKI
The Oast, Warmlake Estate, Maidstone
Road, Sutton Valence ME17 3LR
Tel (01622) 844302
Fax (01622) 842458
Email fctravel@dircon.co.uk
Web site www.fantiski.co.uk
*Family-run operator to France and
Colorado, with childcare*

FINLAYS SKIING
The Barn, Ancrum, Jedburgh TD8 6XH
Tel (01835) 830562
Fax (01835) 830550
Email finlayski@aol.com
Web site www.finlayski.com
*Chalets in Courchevel and Val d'Isère,
also short breaks*

FIRST CHOICE
Olivier House,18 Marine Parade,
Brighton BN2 1TL
Tel (0870) 754 3477
Fax (01273) 676410
Email fcski@lineone.net
Web site www.first-choice.com
Major tour operator

FLEXISKI
Olivier House, 18 Marine Parade,
Brighton BN2 1TL
Tel (0870) 909 0754

Fax (0870) 909 0329
Email flexi@btinternet.com
Web site www.flexiski.co.uk
*Holidays of variable length in Austria,
France and Switzerland*

FREEDOM HOLIDAYS
Solar House, Market Square, Petworth
GU28 OAS
Tel (01798) 342034
Fax (01798) 343320
*Holidays of variable length in
Châtel and Portes du Soleil*

FRONTIER SKI
6 Sydenham Avenue, London
SE26 6UH
Tel 020-8776 8709
Fax 020-8778 0149
Email info@frontier-travel.co.uk
Web site www.frontier-ski.co.uk
Holidays in Canada

HANDMADE HOLIDAYS
The Old Barn, Yew Tree Farm, Stroud
GL5 2EF
Tel (01453) 885599
Fax (01453) 883768
Email travel@handmade-holidays.co.uk
*Specialist operator to Europe and
North America*

HANNIBALS
Farriers, Little Olantigh Road, Wye,
Ashford TN25 5DQ
Tel (01233) 813105
Fax (01233) 813432
Email sales@hannibals.co.uk
Web site www.hannibals.co.uk
Specialist operator to France

HEADWATER HOLIDAYS
146 London Road, Northwich CW9 5HH
Tel (01606) 813333
Fax (01606) 813334
Email info@headwater.com
Web site www.headwater.com
Ski and cross-country holidays

HF HOLIDAYS
Imperial House, Edgware Road, London
NW9 5AL
Tel 020-8905 9558
Fax 020-8205 0506

Email info@hfholidays.co.uk
Web site www.hfholidays.co.uk
Alpine and cross-country holidays

HUSKI CHALET HOLIDAYS
63a Kensington Church Street, London
W8 4BA
Tel 020-7938 4844
Fax 020-7938 2312
Email sales@huski.com
Web site www.huski.com
Specialist chalet operator to Chamonix

INDEPENDENT SKI LINKS
Little Arram Farm, Bewholme Lane,
Seaton, Hull HU11 5SX
Tel (01964) 533905
Fax (01964) 536006
Email david@ski-links.com
Web site www.ski-links.com
Holidays in the Alps and North America

INGHAMS
Gemini House, 10–18 Putney Hill,
London SW15 6AX
Tel 020-8780 4433
Fax 020-8780 4405
Email travel@inghams.co.uk
Web site www.inghams.co.uk
Major tour operator

INNTRAVEL
Hovingham, York YO62 4JZ
Tel (01653) 628811
Fax (01653) 628741
Email inntravel@inntravel.co.uk
Specialist cross-country operator

INTERHOME
383 Richmond Road, Twickenham
TW1 2EF
Tel 020-8891 1294
Fax 020-8891 5331
Email interhome.uk@ibm.net
Web site www.interhome.co.uk
Chalets and apartments in the Alps

INTERSKI
Acorn Park, St Peter's Way, Mansfield
NG18 1EX
Tel (01623) 456333
Fax (01623) 456353
Email email@interski.co.uk
Web site www.interski.co.uk

Holidays in Italy, with own ski school and equipment hire

KUONI
Kuoni House, Deepdene Avenue, Dorking RH5 4AZ
Tel (01306) 742500
Fax (01306) 744222
Email switzerland.sales@kuoni.co.uk
Web site www.kuoni.co.uk
Operator to 20 Swiss resorts

LAGRANGE
168 Shepherds Bush Road, London W6 7PB
Tel 020-7371 6111
Fax 020-7371 2990
Email lagrange@globalnet.co.uk
Web site www.lagrange-holidays.com
Self-catering holidays in 118 French resorts

LEISURE DIRECTION SKI
Image House, Station Road, London N17 9LR
Tel 020-8324 4042
Fax 020-8324 4030
Email richard@ldl.u-net.com
Web site www.leisuredirection.co.uk
Ski-drive to 25 French resorts

LE SKI
25 Holly Terrace, Huddersfield HD1 6JW
Tel (01484) 548996
Fax (01484) 451909
Email mail@leski.co.uk
Web site www.leski.co.uk
Chalets in French Alps, with own ski school and childcare

LOTUS SUPERTRAVEL
Sandpiper House, 39 Queen Elizabeth Street, London SE1 2BT
Tel 020-7962 9933
Fax 020-7962 9965
Email donald@lotusgroup.co.uk
Holidays in the Alps and North America, with childcare

MADE TO MEASURE HOLIDAYS
57 East Street, Chichester PO19 1HL
Tel (01243) 533333
Fax (01243) 778431
Email madetomeasure.holidays@which.net
Web site www.madetomeasureholidays.com
Tailor-made holidays in Europe and North America

MARK WARNER
10 Old Court Place, London W8 4PL
Tel (08708) 480482
Fax (08708) 480481
Web site www.markwarner.co.uk
Chalet-hotels with childcare

MASTERSKI
Thames House, 63–67 Kingston Road, New Malden KT3 3PB
Tel 020-8942 9442
Fax 020-8949 4396
Email holidays@mastersun.co.uk
Web site www.mastersun.co.uk
Christian holidays in France

MCGARRY THE SKI SYSTEM
5 Barnhill Road, Dalkey, County Dublin
Tel 00 353 1 28 591 39
Fax 00 353 1 28 499 32
Holidays and specialist courses in Châtel

MERISKI
The Old School, Great Barrington, Burford OX18 4UR
Tel (01451) 843100
Fax (01451) 844799
Email sales@meriski.co.uk
Web site www.meriski.co.uk
Chalets with childcare in Méribel

MGS SKI
109 Castle Street, Saffron Walden CB10 1BQ
Tel/Fax (01799) 525984
Email skimajor@aol.com
Web site www.mgsski.com
Holidays in Val Cenis, France

MOMENTUM TRAVEL
The Studio, 179c New Kings Road, London SW6 4SW
Tel 020-7371 9111
Fax 020-7610 6287
Email sales@momentum.uk.com
Web site www.momentum.uk.com

Tailor-made holidays worldwide, and weekend breaks

MOSWIN TOURS
Moswin House, 21 Church Street, Oadby, Leicester LE2 5DB
Tel (0116) 271 9922
Fax (0116) 271 6016
Email germany@moswin.com
Web site www.moswin.com
Holidays in Germany

MOTOURS
Buckingham House, Longfield Road, Tunbridge Wells TN2 3DQ
Tel (01892) 677770
Fax (01892) 677677
Email admin@motours.co.uk
Web site www.motours.co.uk
Ski-drive to France

NEILSON
2–4 Godwin Street, Bradford BD1 1SD
Tel (08705) 141414
Fax (01274) 387740
Email sales@neilson.co.uk
Web site www.neilson.co.uk
Major tour operator

OAK HALL SKIING
Oak Hall, Otford TN15 6XF
Tel (01732) 763131
Fax (01732) 763136
Email oakhall@clara.net
Web site www.oakhall.co.uk
Christian holidays in the Alps and North America

THE OXFORD SKI COMPANY
PO Box 357, Banbury, OX15 5XT
Tel (07000) 785349
Fax (07000) 785340
Email info@theoxfordskico.demon.co.uk
Web site
www.theoxfordskico.demon.co.uk
Chalets in Crans Montana, Switzerland

PANORAMA
Vale House, Vale Road, Portslade BN41 1HG
Tel (01273) 427777
Fax (01273) 427111
Email panorama@pavilion.co.uk

Web site www.phg.co.uk
Value holidays in the Alps and the Pyrenees

PASSAGE TO SOUTH AMERICA
Fovant Mews, 12 Noyna Road, London SW17 7PH
Tel 020-8767 8989
Fax 020-8767 2026
Email psa@scottdunn.com
Holidays in South America

PAVILION TOURS
Lynnem House, 1 Victoria Way, Burgess Hill RH15 9NF
Tel (0870) 2410427
Fax (0870) 2410426
Email sales@paviliontours.co.uk
Web site www.paviliontours.co.uk
Holidays in Europe and North America

PEAK SKI
White Lilacs House, Water Lane, Bovington HP3 0NA
Tel (01442) 832629
Fax (01442) 834303
Email peakski@which.net
Web site www.peak-ski.co.uk
Holidays in Verbier

PGL SKI EUROPE
Alton Court, Penyard Lane, Ross-on-Wye HR9 5GL
Tel (01989) 768168
Fax (01989) 768376
Email ski@pgl.co.uk
Web site www.pgl.co.uk
Schools and groups

PISTE ARTISTE
1874 Champéry, Switzerland
Tel 020-7436 0100
Fax 00 41 24 479 3344
Email ski@pisteartiste.com
Web site www.pisteartiste.com
Chalets and variable length holidays in Champéry

PLUS TRAVEL
52 Ebury Street, London SW1W 0LU
Tel 020-7259 0199
Fax 020-7259 0190
Email sales@plustravel.freeserve.co.uk
Holidays in Switzerland

POWDER BYRNE
250 Upper Richmond Road, London
SW15 6TG
Tel 020-8246 5300
Fax 020-8246 5322
Email enquiries@powderbyrne.co.uk
Web site www.powderbyrne.com
Luxury holidays in the Alps,
with childcare

PYRENEAN MOUNTAIN TOURS
2 Rectory Cottages, Wolverton, Tadley
RG26 5RS
Tel/Fax (01635) 297209
Email Pmtuk@aol.com
Web site www.pyrenees.co.uk
Ski-touring, snowshoeing and
ice-climbing

RAMBLERS
PO Box 43, Welwyn Garden City
AL1 3XT
Tel (01707) 331133
Fax (01707) 333276
Email info@ramblersholidays.co.uk
Web site www.ramblersholidays.co.uk
Group cross-country holidays

ROCKY MOUNTAIN SNOWBOARD
TOURS
Hills House, Wellington Road, Wavertree,
Liverpool L15 4JN
Tel 0151-733 7593
Fax 0151-734 4300
Email
snowboarding@rockymountain.co.uk
Web site www.rockymountain.co.uk
Snowboarding in Colorado

SAVOIE SKI
5 Woodbine Cottages, Shalford Common,
Guildford GU4 8JF
Tel (01483) 452500
Fax (01483) 452001
Email faith@fmta.freeserve.co.uk
Web site www.fmtaski.freeserve.co.uk
Holidays in Valloire and Valmeinier

SCOTT DUNN SKI
Fovant Mews, 12 Noyna Road, London
SW17 7PH
Tel 020-8767 0202
Fax 020-8767 2026
Email ski@scottdunn.com

Luxury chalet operator, with childcare

SEASONS IN STYLE
Telegraph House, 246 Telegraph Road,
Heswall, Wirral CH60 7SG
Tel 0151-342 0505
Fax 0151-342 0516
Email sales@seasonsinstyle.co.uk
Web site www.seasonsinstyle.co.uk
Luxury hotels in Europe and
North America

SILVER SKI HOLIDAYS
Conifers House, Grove Green Lane,
Maidstone ME14 5JW
Tel (01622) 735544
Fax (01622) 738550
Email hazal@silverski.co.uk
Web site www.silverski.co.uk
Catered chalets in France, with childcare

SIMPLY SKI
Kings House, Wood Street, Kingston-
upon-Thames KT1 1UG
Tel 020-8541 2209
Fax 020-8541 2280
Email ski@simply-travel.com
Web site www.simplyski.co.uk
Catered chalets in the Alps, with childcare

SKI ACTIVITY
Lawmuir House, Methven PH1 3SZ
Tel (01738) 840888
Fax (01738) 840079
Email sales@skiactivity.com
Web site www.skiactivity.com
Operator to France, Switzerland
and North America

SKI THE AMERICAN DREAM
1–7 Station Chambers, High Street North,
London E6 1JE
Tel 020-8552 1201
Fax 020-8552 7726
Email holidays@skidream.com
Web site www.skidream.com
Specialist operator to North America

SKI AMIS
Alanda, Hornash Lane, Shadoxhurst,
Ashford TN26 1HT
Tel (01233) 732187
Fax (01233) 732769
Email skiamis@compuserve.com

Web site www.skiamis.com
Holidays in the French Alps

SKI ASTONS
Clerkenleap, Broomhall, Worcester
WR5 3HR
Tel (01905) 829200
Fax (01905) 820850
Email ski@astons-coaches.co.uk
Web site www.astons-coaches.co.uk
Coach holidays for schools and groups

SKI BARRETT-BOYCE
Unit 16, Westmead House, 123
Westmead Road, Sutton SM1 4JH
Tel 020-8288 0042
Fax 020-8288 0761
Email skibb@atlas.co.uk
Web site
www.holidaybank.co.uk/skibarrettboyce
*Chalet in Megève, with tuition
and childcare*

SKI BEAT
Metro House, Northgate, Chichester
PO19 1BE
Tel (01243) 780405
Fax (01243) 533748
Email ski@skibeat.co.uk
Web site www.skibeat.co.uk
Chalets in the French Alps, with childcare

SKIBOUND
Olivier House, 18 Marine Parade,
Brighton BN2 1TL
Tel (0870) 900 3200
Fax (0870) 333 2329
Email info@skibound.co.uk
Web site www.skibound.co.uk
Specialist schools operator

SKI CHAMOIS
18 Lawn Road, Doncaster DN1 2JF
Tel (01302) 369006
Fax (01302) 326640
Email skichamois@morzine1550.
freeserve.co.uk
Web site
www.ski-chamois.freeserve.com
Chalets in Morzine

SKI CHOICE
27 High Street, Benson, Wallingford
OX10 6RP

Tel (01491) 837607
Fax (01491) 833836
Email info@choicetravel.co.uk
Web site www.choicetravel.co.uk
Tailor-made holidays in the Alps

**SKI CLUB OF GREAT
BRITAIN/FRESH TRACKS**
The White House, 57–63 Church Road,
Wimbledon, London SW19 5SB
Tel 020-8410 2022
Fax 020-8410 2001
Email holidays@skiclub.co.uk
Web site www.skiclub.co.uk
*Specialist holidays, weekends
and instruction courses*

THE SKI COMPANY
The Old School, Great Barrington,
Burford OX18 4UR
Tel (01451) 843123
Fax (01451) 844799
Email sales@skicompany.co.uk
Web site www.skicompany.co.uk
*Luxury chalets in the Alps,
with childcare*

SKI EQUIPE
27 Bramhall Lane South, Bramhall,
Stockport SK7 2DN
Tel 0161-440 0010
Fax 0161-440 0080
Email ski@skiequipe.fsbusiness.co.uk
Web site www.ski-equipe.com
Chalets in the Alps and North America

SKIERS WORLD
6 Cwrt-Y-Parc, Earlswood Road,
Llanishen, Cardiff CF4 5GH
Tel 029-2076 4477
Fax 029-2076 4455
Email info@skiersworld.com
Web site www.skiersworld.com
Schools operator

SKI ESPRIT
Oaklands, Reading Road North,
Fleet GU13 8AA
Tel (01252) 618300
Fax (01252) 618328
Email travel@skiesprit.co.uk
Web site www.ski-esprit.co.uk
Specialist family operator to the Alps

SKI EXPECTATIONS
Jasmine Cottage, Manor Lane,
Great Chesterford CB10 1PJ
Tel (01799) 531888
Fax (01799) 531887
Email ski.expectations@virgin.net
*Tailor-made holidays in Europe
and North America*

SKI FAMILLE
Unit 9, Chesterton Mill, French's Road,
Cambridge CB4 3NP
Tel (01223) 363777/568224
Fax (01223) 519314
Email info@skifamille.co.uk
Web site www.skifamille.co.uk
*Specialist operator to Les Gets,
with childcare*

SKI FRANCE
Unit 3 & 4 Marco Works, Pembroke
Road, Bromley BR1 2RY
Tel 020-8313 0690
Fax 020-8466 0653
Email ski@skifrance.co.uk
Web site www.skifrance.co.uk
Holidays in France

SKI FREEDOM
PO Box 377, Bromley BR1 1LY
Tel 020-8313 0999
Fax 020-8313 3547
Email uv.uk@unitedvacations.com
Web site www.unitedvacations.co.uk
Holidays in North America

SKI GOWER
2 High Street, Studley B80 7HJ
Tel (01527) 851411
Fax (01527) 851417
Email louise@gowstrav.demon.co.uk
*Tailor-made holidays in Poland
and Switzerland, for schools
and groups*

SKI HILLWOOD
Lavender Lodge, Dunny Lane,
Chipperfield WD4 9DD
Tel (01923) 290700
Fax (01923) 290340
Email sales@hillwood-holidays.co.uk
*Specialist operator to Austria
and France, with childcare*

SKI HIVER
119a London Road, Waterlooville
PO7 7DZ
Tel (02392) 428586
Fax (02392) 428904
Email skihiver@aol.com
Web site
www.holidaybank.co.uk/skihiver
*Specialist operator to Peisey-
Nancroix, France*

SKI INDEPENDENCE
Broughton Market, Edinburgh EH3 6NU
Tel (0870) 600 1462
Fax (0870) 550 2020
Email ski@ski-independence.co.uk
Web site www.ski-independence.co.uk
*Holidays in North America and
ski-drive to Europe*

SKI MIQUEL
73 High Street, Uppermill, Oldham
OL3 6AP
Tel (01457) 821200
Fax (01457) 821209
Email ski@miquelhols.co.uk
Web site www.miquelhols.co.uk
Operator to the Alps, Spain and Canada

SKI MORGINS HOLIDAYS
The Barn, 1 Bury Court Barns,
Wigmore HR6 9US
Email info@skimorgins.co.uk
Web site www.skimorgins.co.uk
Small specialist operator to Morgins

SKI NORWEST
8 Foxholes Cottages, Foxholes Road,
Horwich, Bolton BL6 6AL
Tel (01204) 668468
Fax (01204) 668568
Email skinorwest@compuserve.com
Web site www.skinorwest.com
*Ski weekends and coach trips
to Scotland*

SKI OLYMPIC
PO Box 396, Doncaster DN5 7YS
Tel (01709) 579999
Fax (01709) 579898
Email gavin@skiolympic.freeserve.co.uk
Web site www.skiolympic.co.uk
*Chalets and hotels in France,
with childcare*

SKI PARTNERS
Friary House, Colston Street, Bristol
BS1 5AP
Tel 0117-925 3545
Fax 0117-929 3697
*Schools operator to the Alps and
North America*

SKI PEAK
Campbell Park, Milland, Nr Liphook
GU30 7LU
Tel (01428) 741144
Fax (01428) 741155
Email ski@ski-peak.ltd.uk
Web site www.ski-peak.ltd.uk
*Specialist operator to Vaujany,
with childcare*

SKI SAFARI
41 Canada Wharf, 255 Rotherhithe
Street, London SE16 5ES
Tel 020-7740 1221
Fax 020-7740 1223
Email info@skisafari.com
Web site www.skisafari.com
Specialist operator to Canada and USA

SKISAFE TRAVEL
Unit 4, Braehead Estate, Old Govan
Road, Renfrew PA4 8XJ
Tel 0141-812 0925
Fax 0141-812 1544
Operator to Scotland and Flaine

SKI SOLUTIONS A LA CARTE
84 Pembroke Road, London W8 6NX
Tel 020-7471 7777
Fax 020-7471 7771
Email alc@skisolutions.com
Web site www.skisolutions.com
Hotels and luxury apartments worldwide

SKI SUPREME
26 Brodick Drive, Stewartfield,
East Kilbride G74 4BQ
Tel (01355) 260547
Fax (01355) 229232
Email info@skisupreme.demon.co.uk
Web site www.skisupreme.demon.co.uk
Self-drive and coach operator to France

SKI TOTAL
3 The Square, Richmond TW9 1DY
Tel 020-8948 3535

Fax 020-8332 1268
Email ski@skitotal.com
Web site www.skitotal.com
*Chalet operator to the Alps and
Canada, with childcare*

SKI VAL
Shortlands, Middlemoor, Tavistock
PL19 9DY
Tel (01822) 611200
Fax (01822) 611400
Email post@skival.co.uk
Web site www.skival.co.uk
*Chalets and chalet-hotels in the
French Alps*

SKI VERBIER
26 Chesson Road, London W14 9QX
Tel 020-7385 8050
Fax 020-7385 8002
Email info@skiverbier.com
Web site www.skiverbier.com
Holidays in Verbier

SKI WEEKEND
2 The Old Barn, Wicklesham Lodge
Farm, Faringdon SN7 7PN
Tel (01367) 241636
Fax (01367) 243833
Email info@skiweekend.com
Web site www.skiweekend.com
Weekend breaks with specialist courses

SKI WORLD
41 North End Road, London W14 8SZ
Tel 020-7602 4826
Fax 020-7371 1463
Email sales@skiworld.ltd.uk
Holidays in the Alps and the Rockies

SKI YOGI
Jasmine Cottage, Manor Lane, Great
Chesterford CB10 1PJ
Tel (01799) 531886
Fax (01799) 531887
Email ski.expectations@virgin.net
Holidays in the Italian Dolomites

SLOPING OFF
31 High Street, Handley, Salisbury
SP5 5NR
Tel (01725) 552247
Fax (01725) 552489
Email victorytours@dial.pipex.com

Web site www.victorytours.co.uk
Coach holidays for schools and groups

SNOWBIZZ VACANCES
69 High Street, Maxey PE6 9EE
Tel (01778) 341455
Fax (01778) 347422
Email snowbizz@snowbizz.co.uk
Holidays in Puy-St-Vincent,
with childcare

SNOWBOARD LODGE
The Yellow Room, Unit 1a, Franchise
Street, Kidderminster DY11 6RE
Tel (01562) 743888
Fax (0870) 0548543
Email info@snowboardlodge.co.uk
Web site www.snowboardlodge.co.uk
Chalets for snowboarders in Morzine and
Avoriaz

SNOWCOACH/CLUB CANTABRICA
146–148 London Road, St Albans
AL1 1PQ
Tel (01727) 866177
Fax (01727) 843766
Email info@snowcoach.co.uk
Web site www.snowcoach.co.uk
Value holidays in the Alps and
the Pyrenees

SNOWLINE
Collingbourne House, 140–142
Wandsworth High Street, London
SW18 4JJ
Tel (07000) 101110
Fax (07000) 404140
Email ski@snowline.co.uk
Web site www.snowline.co.uk
Small operator to the French Alps

SNOWPLUS
19 Craigielaw Park, Aberlady, East
Lothian EH32 0PR
Tel (0704) 145 0100
Fax (0797) 008 2534
Email scottfree@compuserve.com
Web site www.snowplus.co.uk
Holidays in Nendaz, Switzerland

SNOWSCAPE
108 Wylds Lane, Worcester WR5 1DJ
Tel (01905) 357760
Fax (01905) 357825

Email skiandboard@snowscape.co.uk
Web site www.snowscape.co.uk
Holidays in Austria

SOLO'S
54–58 High Street, Edgware HA8 7ED
Tel 020-8951 2800
Fax 020-8951 1051
Email travel@solosholidays.co.uk
Web site www.solosholidays.co.uk
Singles holidays in the Alps and
the Rockies

STANFORD SKIING
3 Genoa Avenue, London SW15 6DY
Tel 020-8789 2929
Fax 020-8576 7670
Email stanskiing@aol.com
Web site www.lattimore.co.uk/stanford
Specialist operator to Megève

SWISS TRAVEL SERVICE
Bridge House, 55–59 High Road,
Broxbourne EN10 7DT
Tel (01992) 456123
Fax (01992) 448855
Email swiss@bridge-travel.co.uk
Web site www.swisstravel.co.uk
Quality holidays in 18 Swiss resorts

THOMSON SKI & SNOWBOARDING
King's Place, 12–42 Wood Street,
Kingston-upon-Thames KT1 1UG
Tel (0870) 606 1470
Email reservations@thomson-ski.com
Web site www.thomson-ski.co.uk
Major tour operator

TOPS TRAVEL
Lees House, 21 Dyke Road, Brighton
BN1 3GD
Tel (01273) 774666
Fax (01273) 734042
Email sales@topstravel.co.uk
Club-hotels and chalets in France,
with childcare

TOP DECK SKI
131–135 Earls Court Road, London
SW5 9RH
Tel 020-7370 4555
Fax 020-7373 6201
Email res@topdecktravel.co.uk

Web site www.topdeckski.com
Holidays in the Alps and the Pyrenees

TT SKI TANGNEY TOURS
Pilgrim House, Station Court,
Borough Green TN15 8AF
Tel (01732) 886666
Fax (01732) 886885
Email ttours@cix.co.uk
Group operator to the Pyrenees

VACATION CANADA
Cambridge House, 8 Cambridge Street,
Glasgow G2 3DZ
Tel (0870) 707 0444
Fax 0141-353 0135
Email vacationcanada@btinternet.com
Web site www.Vacationcanada.com
Holidays in Canada

VIP
Collingbourne House, 140–142
Wandsworth High Street, London
SW18 4JJ
Tel 020-8875 1957
Fax 020-8875 9236
Email ski@valdisere.co.uk
Web site www.valdisere.co.uk
Specialist operator to Val d'Isère

VIRGIN SKI
The Galleria, Station Road,
Crawley RH10 1WW
Tel (01293) 617181
Fax (01293) 536957
Email brochure.requests@fly.virgin.com
Web site www.virginholidays.co.uk
Hotel holidays in North America

WASTELAND
21 Jerdan Place, Fulham Broadway,
London SW6 1BE
Tel 020-738 65544
Fax 020-738 65533

Email mail@wasteland.co.uk
Web site www.wasteland.co.uk
Holidays in the Trois Vallées, France

WAYMARK HOLIDAYS
44 Windsor Road, Slough SL1 2EJ
Tel (01753) 516477
Fax (01753) 517016
Cross-country skiing holidays

WEEKENDS IN VAL D'ISERE
96 Dora Road, London SW19 7JT
Tel/Fax 020-8944 9762
Email valweekends@btinternet.com
Web site www.val-disere-ski.com
Small specialist operator

WHITE ROC SKI
69 Westbourne Grove, London W2 4UJ
Tel 020-7792 1188
Fax 020-7792 1956
Email ski@whiteroc.co.uk
Web site www.whiteroc.co.uk
*Weekends and tailor-made holidays
in the Alps*

WINETRAILS/SKI GOURMET
Greenways, Vann Lake, Ockley,
Dorking RH5 5NT
Tel (01306) 712111
Fax (01306) 713504
Email sales@winetrails.co.uk
Web site www.winetrails.co.uk
Gourmet catered chalet in Filzmoos

YSE
The Business Village, Broomhill Road,
London SW18 4JQ
Tel 020-8871 5117
Fax 020-8871 5229
Email sales@yseski.co.uk
Web site www.yseski.co.uk
Specialist chalet operator to Val d'Isère

Who goes where?

ANDORRA
Arcalis Snowcoach
Arinsal Airtours, Crystal, First Choice, Independent Ski Links, Inghams, Neilson, Panorama, Ski Norwest, Ski Partners, Snowcoach, Thomson
Encamp First Choice, Thomson
Grau Roig Inghams
La Massana Inghams
Pal Panorama, Snowcoach, Ski Norwest
Pas de la Casa Airtours, Crystal, First Choice, Independent Ski Links, Lagrange, Neilson, Panorama, Thomson, Top Deck
Soldeu/El Tarter Airtours, Crystal, First Choice, Independent Ski Links, Inghams, Lagrange, Neilson, Panorama, Pavilion, SCGB/Fresh Tracks, Ski Partners, Thomson, Top Deck

ARGENTINA
Gran Catedral (Bariloche) Passage to South America
Las Leñas Passage to South America

AUSTRALIA
No current tour operator. We advise you to contact the Australian Tourist Commission (see *Skiing by numbers*) for a list of tour operators to Australia and to contact resorts direct.

AUSTRIA
Alpbach Crystal, First Choice, Independent Ski Links, Inghams, Interhome, Thomson
Altenmarkt Sloping Off
Axamer Lizum Lagrange, Ski Partners, Sloping Off
Bad Gastein Club Europe, Crystal, First Choice, Independent Ski Links, Inghams, Made to Measure, PGL Ski Europe, SkiBound, Ski Miquel, Ski Partners
Bad Hofgastein Crystal, Inghams
Bad Kleinkirchheim Alpine Tours, Crystal, Ski Partners, Sloping Off
Brand Crystal, Interhome
Brixen Alpine Tours
Ellmau Airtours, Crystal, Independent Ski Links, Inghams, Interhome, Motours, Neilson

Fieberbrunn First Choice, Ski Astons, Snowscape
Filzmoos Inghams, Neilson, Winetrails
Finkenberg Crystal, First Choice
Flachau Ski Partners, Thomson
Fulpmes Crystal
Galtür Made to Measure
Gargellen Interhome, Made to Measure
Gerlos Interhome
Going Solo's
Hintertux Alpine Tours, Lagrange
Hopfgarten Contiki, First Choice
Igls First Choice, Inghams, Lagrange
Innsbruck First Choice, Made to Measure
Ischgl Inghams, Made to Measure, Ski Solutions, Thomson
Itter Neilson
Jenbach Ski Astons
Kaprun Club Europe, Crystal, Made to Measure, Neilson
Kirchberg Equity Total Ski, Interhome, Lagrange, Ski Partners, Top Deck
Kirchdorf Crystal, Snowcoach
Kitzbühel Airtours, Crystal, Elegant Resorts, First Choice, Independent Ski Links, Inghams, Interhome, Lagrange, Made to Measure, Neilson, Panorama, PGL Ski Europe, SCGB/Fresh Tracks, Ski Astons, SkiBound, Ski Partners, Ski Solutions, Thomson
Kühtai Inghams
Lech Abercrombie & Kent, Alpine Tracks, Elegant Resorts, Flexiski, Independent Ski Links, Inghams, Momentum Travel, Seasons in Style, Simply Ski, Ski Choice, Ski Solutions, Ski Total, White Roc
Leogang Equity Total Ski
Lofer Ski Partners
Maria Alm PGL Ski Europe, Ski Astons
Mayrhofen Airtours, Crystal, Equity Total Ski, First Choice, HF Holidays, Independent Ski Links, Inghams, Neilson, Ski Astons, Snowcoach, Thomson
Mühlbach PGL Ski Europe, SkiBound,
Nassfeld Sloping Off
Neustift Crystal, Interhome, Made to Measure
Niederau/Oberau First Choice, Inghams, Neilson, Ski Partners, Thomson

Obergurgl/Hochgurgl Airtours, Crystal, First Choice, Independent Ski Links, Inghams, SCGB/Fresh Tracks, Thomson
Obertauern Club Europe, Inghams, Seasons in Style, Skiers World, Ski Partners, Ski Solutions, Thomson
Rauris APT Holidays
Saalbach-Hinterglemm Airtours, Club Europe, Crystal, First Choice, Independent Ski Links, Inghams, Interhome, Neilson, Panorama, PGL Ski Europe, SkiBound, Skiers World, Ski Partners, Thomson
Scheffau Crystal, First Choice, Ski Astons, Ski Partners, Thomson
Schladming Crystal, Equity Total Ski, Independent Ski Links, Interhome, Oak Hall Skiing, PGL Ski Europe, SkiBound, Ski Partners
Schruns Interhome
Seefeld Crystal, Headwater, Inghams, Interhome, Lagrange, Neilson, Thomson
Serfaus Alpine Tours, Interhome, Made to Measure
Sölden/Hochsölden Made to Measure
Söll Airtours, Crystal, First Choice, Independent Ski Links, Inghams, Interhome, Motours, Neilson, Panorama, Ski Astons, Skiers World, Ski Hillwood, Thomson
St Anton Abercrombie & Kent, Airtours, Alpine Tours, Chalet World, Crystal, Elegant Resorts, First Choice, Flexiski, Independent Ski Links, Inghams, Lotus Supertravel, Mark Warner, Momentum Travel, PGL Ski Europe, SCGB/Fresh Tracks, Simply Ski, Ski Activity, Ski Equipe, Ski Solutions, Ski Total, Ski Val, Skiworld, Thomson, White Roc
St Christoph Abercrombie & Kent, Elegant Resorts
St Johann in Tirol Crystal, Panorama, SkiBound, Ski Partners, Thomson
St Johann im Pongau Ski Astons, Ski Partners
St Michael Alpine Tours, Equity Total Ski, Ski Partners
St Wolfgang Airtours, Crystal, Inghams, Neilson, PGL Ski Europe, Thomson
Tulfes Ski Partners
Wagrain Club Europe, Thomson
Waidring Thomson
Westendorf Inghams, Neilson, Thomson
Wildschönau PGL Ski Europe

Zell am See Airtours, APT Holidays, Crystal, First Choice, Independent Ski Links, Inghams, Interhome, Neilson, Panorama, PGL Ski Europe, SkiBound, Skiers World, Ski Astons, Ski Partners, Thomson
Zell am Ziller Club Europe, Oak Hall Skiing, PGL Ski Europe, Skiers World, Ski Partners, Sloping Off, Thomson
Zauchensee Sloping Off
Zürs Elegant Resorts, Made to Measure, Seasons in Style

BULGARIA
Borovets Balkan Holidays, Balkan Tours, Crystal, First Choice, Inghams, Neilson, SkiBound, Ski Partners, Solo's, Thomson
Pamporovo Balkan Holidays, Balkan Tours, Crystal, First Choice, Neilson, Skiers World
Bansko Balkan Holidays

CHILE
La Parva/Valle Nevado/Portillo Passage to South America
Termas de Chillán Passage to South America

FINNISH LAPLAND
Levi Inghams

FRANCE
Abondance Interhome
Alpe d'Huez Airtours, Club Med, Crystal, Erna Low, Eurotunnel Motoring Holidays, Fairhand, First Choice, Independent Ski Links, Inghams, Interhome, Lagrange, Leisure Direction, Motours, Neilson, Panorama, SCGB/Fresh Tracks, Ski Activity, Ski Astons, SkiBound, Ski Independence, Skiers World, Ski Miquel, Ski Partners, Skiworld, Thomson, Tops Travel
Les Arcs Action Vacances/UPCA, Airtours, Chalet Snowboard, Club Med, Crystal, Erna Low, Eurotunnel Motoring Holidays, Fairhand, First Choice, Independent Ski Links, Inghams, Interhome, Lagrange, Leisure Direction, Motours, Neilson, PGL Ski Europe, SCGB/Fresh Tracks, Ski Activity, Ski France, Ski Hiver, Ski Independence, Ski Supreme, Skiers World, Thomson

Argentière Bigfoot, Collineige, Crystal, Erna Low, Independent Ski Links, Interhome, Lagrange, Motours, Ski Hillwood, Ski Weekend, Snowline, White Roc

Avoriaz Airtours, Chalet Snowboard, Club Med, Crystal, Erna Low, Eurotunnel Motoring Holidays, First Choice, Independent Ski Links, Lagrange, Leisure Direction, Motours, Neilson, Ski France, Ski Independence, Snowboard Lodge, Thomson

Barèges Borderline, HF Holidays, Lagrange, Pyrenean Mountain Tours, Thomson, TT Ski

Le Bettex HF Holidays

Brides-les-Bains Crystal, Erna Low, Eurotunnel Motoring Holidays, First Choice, Leisure Direction, Inghams, Motours, Snowcoach

Les Carroz Erna Low, Fairhand, Motours, Ski Choice

Cauterets Lagrange, TT Ski

Chamonix Abercrombie & Kent, Airtours, Beaumont, Bigfoot, Club Med, Collineige, Crystal, Elegant Resorts, Erna Low, Eurotunnel Motoring Holidays, Fairhand, Finlays, First Choice, Fresh Tracks, Handmade Holidays, HuSki, Independent Ski Links, Inghams, Interhome, Lagrange, Leisure Direction, Momentum Travel, Motours, Neilson, SCGB/Fresh Tracks, Simply Ski, Ski Activity, Ski Choice, Ski Esprit, Ski France, Ski Independence, Ski Solutions, Ski Weekend, Sloping Off, Solo's, Thomson, White Roc

Champagny-en-Vanoise Erna Low, Fairhand, Independent Ski Links, Lagrange, Leisure Direction, Made to Measure, Motours

Chamrousse Lagrange

Châtel First Choice, Freedom Holidays, Interhome, Lagrange, Leisure Direction, Motours, SkiBound, Ski Independence, Ski Partners, McGarry The Ski System, Tops Travel

La Clusaz Classic Ski, Eurotunnel Motoring Holidays, Fairhand, First Choice, Interhome, Lagrange, Leisure Direction, Motours, PGL Ski Europe, Ski Activity, Ski Amis, SkiBound, Ski Partners

Les Coches Crystal, Erna Low, Lagrange, Leisure Direction, Made to Measure, Motours, Ski Olympic

Les Contamines-Montjoie Classic Ski, Club Europe, Fairhand, First Choice, Interhome, Lagrange, SkiBound, Ski Total, Ski Weekend, Skiworld

Le Corbier Equity Total Ski, Interhome, Lagrange, Motours

Courchevel Abercrombie & Kent, Airtours, Alpine Action, Chalet World, Crystal, Elegant Resorts, Erna Low, Eurotunnel Motoring Holidays, Flexiski, Finlays, First Choice, Independent Ski Links, Inghams, Lagrange, Leisure Direction, Le Ski, Lotus Supertravel, Mark Warner, Momentum Travel, Motours, Neilson, PGL Ski Europe, Powder Byrne, SCGB/Fresh Tracks, Seasons in Style, Scott Dunn Ski, Silver Ski, Simply Ski, Ski Activity, Ski Amis, Ski Esprit, Ski France, Ski Independence, Ski Olympic, Ski Solutions, Ski Val, Ski Weekend, Skiworld, Thomson, Tops Travel, White Roc

Les Deux Alpes Action Vacances/UCPA, Airtours, Club Med, Crystal, Equity Total Ski, Fairhand, First Choice, Handmade Holidays, Independent Ski Links, Inghams, Interhome, Lagrange, Leisure Direction, Motours, Neilson, Oak Hall Skiing, Panorama, Ski Activity, Ski Astons, Sloping Off, SkiBound, Skitrek, Skiers World, Ski Independence, Ski Partners, Ski Supreme, Skiworld, Thomson, Tops Travel

Flaine Action Vacances/UCPA, Airtours, Classic Ski, Club Med, Crystal, Erna Low, Eurotunnel Motoring Holidays, Fairhand, First Choice, Independent Ski Links, Inghams, Lagrange, Leisure Direction, Motours, Neilson, SCGB/Fresh Tracks, Ski Choice, Ski France, Ski Independence, Thomson

Les Gets Fairhand, Fantiski, Lagrange, Made to Measure, Motours, Ski Activity, Ski Famille, Ski Hillwood, Ski Independence, Ski Total, Tops Travel

La Grave SCGB/Fresh Tracks

Le Grand-Bornand Motours

Les Houches Bigfoot, Erna Low, Leisure Direction, Motours, PGL Ski Europe, Ski Independence

Isola 2000 Erna Low, Fairhand, Lagrange, Pavilion

Megève Abercrombie & Kent, Elegant Resorts, Fairhand, Finlays, Independent Ski Links, Interhome, Lagrange, Motours, Powder Byrne, Seasons in Style, Simon

Butler Skiing, Ski Barrett-Boyce, Ski Choice, Ski Independence, Ski Solutions, Ski Weekend, Stanford Skiing, Thomson, White Roc

Les Menuires Club Med, Crystal, Erna Low, First Choice, Independent Ski Links, Interhome, Lagrange, Leisure Direction, Motours, Ski Astons, SkiBound, Skiers World, Ski Independence, Ski Partners, Ski Supreme, Ski Total

Méribel Airtours, Alpine Action, Belvedere Chalets, Chalet World, Club Med, Crystal, Descent International, Erna Low, Eurotunnel Motoring Holidays, Fairhand, First Choice, Independent Ski Links, Inghams, Interhome, Lagrange, Leisure Direction, Lotus Supertravel, Mark Warner, Masterski, Meriski, Momentum Travel, Motours, Neilson, Panorama, SCGB/Fresh Tracks, Silver Ski, Simply Ski, Ski Activity, Ski France, Ski Independence, Ski Olympic, Scott Dunn Ski, Ski Solutions, Ski Total, Ski Val, Skiworld, Snowline, Solo's, The Ski Company, Thomson, Tops Travel, Wasteland, White Roc

La Mongie Lagrange

Montalbert Crystal, Erna Low, Interhome, Ski Amis

Montchavin Crystal, Erna Low, Fairhand, Lagrange, Simply Ski

Montgenèvre Airtours, Crystal, Equity Total Ski, Fairhand, First Choice, Independent Ski Links, Lagrange, Neilson, SkiBound, Ski France, Thomson

Morillon Lagrange, Motours

Morzine Alpine Tracks, Chalet Snowboard, Crystal, Fairhand, First Choice, Independent Ski Links, Inghams, Lagrange, Motours, SkiBound, Ski Chamois, Ski Esprit, Ski France, Ski Partners, Ski Weekend, Sloping Off, Snowboard Lodge, Snowline, Thomson, White Roc

Nôtre Dame de Bellecombe SkiBound

Orcières Merlette Club Europe, Motours

La Norma Fairhand, Interhome

La Plagne Action Vacances/UCPA, Airtours, Chalet World, Club Med, Crystal, Erna Low, Eurotunnel Motoring Holidays, First Choice, Independent Ski Links, Inghams, Interhome, Lagrange, Leisure Direction, Mark Warner, Motours, Neilson, PGL Ski Europe, SCGB/Fresh

Tracks, Silver Ski, Simply Ski, Ski Activity, Ski Amis, Ski Beat, Skiers World, Ski Esprit, Ski France, Ski Independence, Ski Olympic, Ski Supreme, Skiworld, Solo's, Thomson, Tops Travel

Plan-Peisey Erna Low

Pra Loup Club Europe, Equity Total Ski, First Choice, Independent Ski Links, Lagrange, SkiBound, Thomson

Puy-St-Vincent Club Europe, Fairhand, Interhome, Lagrange, Snowbizz Vacances, Thomson

Risoul/Vars Crystal, Erna Low, Fairhand, First Choice, Interhome, Lagrange, Leisure Direction, Made to Measure, Motours, Neilson, Ski Astons, SkiBound, Ski Independence, Thomson

La Rosière Erna Low, Fairhand, Interhome, Lagrange, Ski Esprit, Ski Olympic

Sainte-Foy Independent Ski Links, Motours

Les Saisies Classic Ski, Inntravel, Motours

Samoëns Fairhand, Interhome, Inntravel, Motours

Serre Chevalier/Briançon Airtours, Crystal, Equity Total Ski, Erna Low, Fairhand, Handmade Holidays, Hannibals, Independent Ski Links, Inghams, Lagrange, Leisure Direction, Neilson, PGL Ski Europe, SkiBound, Skiers World, Ski Activity, Ski Astons, Ski Independence, Ski Miquel, Sloping Off, Thomson, Tops Travel

St-Gervais Fairhand, Finlays, Interhome, Lagrange, PGL Ski Europe, Ski Barrett-Boyce, Snowcoach

St-Martin-de-Belleville Independent Ski Links, Made to Measure, Motours, Ski Miquel

Superdevoluy Lagrange, Motours

La Tania Airtours, Crystal, Erna Low, Eurotunnel Motoring Holidays, Fairhand, Independent Ski Links, Lagrange, Leisure Direction, Le Ski, Neilson, Silver Ski, Simply Ski, Ski Amis, Ski Beat, Ski France, Ski Independence, Snowline, Thomson

Tignes Action Vacances/UCPA, Airtours, Club Med, Crystal, Erna Low, Fairhand, Independent Ski Links, Inghams, Interhome, Lagrange, Leisure Direction, Masterski, Momentum Travel, Motours, Neilson, Silver Ski, SCGB/Fresh Tracks, Ski Activity, Ski Beat, SkiBound, Ski

Choice, Ski France, Ski Independence, Ski Olympic, Ski Supreme, Skiworld, Thomson
Val Cenis Lagrange, MGS Ski, Motours,
Val d'Isère Abercrombie & Kent, Action Vacances/UCPA, Airtours, Chalet World, Club Med, Crystal, Elegant Resorts, Erna Low, Eurotunnel Motoring Holidays, Fairhand, Fantiski, Finlays, Independent Ski Links, Inghams, Interhome, Lagrange, Leisure Direction, Le Ski, Lotus Supertravel, Mark Warner, Momentum Travel, Motours, Neilson, SCGB/Fresh Tracks, Scott Dunn Ski, SkiBound, Silver Ski, Ski Activity, Ski France, Ski Independence, Ski Solutions, Ski Supreme, Ski Total, Trek, Ski Val, Ski Weekend, Skiworld, The Ski Company, Thomson, VIP, Wasteland, Weekends in Val d'Isère, White Roc, YSE
Valfréjus Lagrange, Made to Measure, SkiBound
Vallandry Erna Low, Independent Ski Links
Valloire/Valmeinier Club Europe, Club Med, Erna Low, Fairhand, Lagrange, Leisure Direction, Motours, Savoie Ski, Snowcoach, SkiBound
Valmorel/St-François-Longchamp Crystal, Erna Low, Fairhand, Independent Ski Links, Lagrange, Leisure Direction, Motours, Neilson, PGL Ski Europe, Skiers World, Ski Independence, Ski Partners, Ski Supreme, Thomson
Val Thorens Action Vacances/UCPA, Alpine Action, Club Med, Crystal, Erna Low, Eurotunnel Motoring Holidays, Independent Ski Links, Inghams, Interhome, Lagrange, Leisure Direction, Motours, Neilson, Panorama, SCGB/Fresh Tracks, Ski Activity, Ski Choice, Ski France, Ski Independence, Ski Olympic, Ski Supreme, Skiworld, Solo's, Thomson
Vars Lagrange, Tops Travel
Vaujany Erna Low, Lagrange, Ski Peak
Villard-de-Lans Inntravel, Lagrange

GERMANY
Garmisch Partenkirchen Moswin Tours

ITALY
Abatone Alpine Tours, Ski Partners
Alagna SCGB/Fresh Tracks, Ski Weekend

Alba Crystal, Independent Ski Links
Alleghe Crystal
Andalo Airtours, Equity Total Ski, PGL Ski Europe, Skiers World, Ski Partners
Aprica Interhome, PGL Ski Europe, Ski Partners, Winterski
Arabba Crystal, Independent Ski Links, Neilson, Ski Yogi
Bardonecchia Airtours, Crystal, Equity Total Ski, Neilson, PGL Ski Europe, Ski Astons, Sloping Off, Thomson
Bormio Airtours, Inghams, Interhome, Neilson, PGL Ski Europe, Ski Astons, Ski Partners, Thomson
Campitello Airtours, Crystal, Inghams, Neilson, Thomson
Canazei Airtours, Crystal, Equity Total Ski, Inghams, Neilson, Ski Partners, Thomson
Cavalese Airtours, Alpine Tours, First Choice
Cervinia Airtours, Beaumont, Crystal, Elegant Resorts, Equity Total Ski, First Choice, Handmade Holidays, Independent Ski Links, Inghams, Momentum Travel, Neilson, Ski Solutions, Thomson
Cesana Torinese First Choice, SkiBound
Champoluc Crystal, Handmade Holidays, Thomson
Clavière Crystal, Equity Total Ski, First Choice, Neilson, SkiBound
Cortina d'Ampezzo Crystal, Independent Ski Links, Momentum Travel, SCGB/Fresh Tracks, Ski Equipe, Ski Solutions, Ski Yogi, White Roc
Courmayeur Airtours, Crystal, First Choice, Independent Ski Links, Inghams, Interski, Lagrange, Mark Warner, Momentum Travel, Neilson, Ski France, Ski Solutions, Ski Weekend, Thomson, White Roc, Winterski
Corvara Crystal
Folgaria Alpine Tours, SkiBound,
Folgarida Alpine Tours, Club Europe, Equity Total Ski, PGL Skiers World, Ski Europe
Foppolo Equity Total Ski, First Choice, PGL Ski Europe, SkiBound, Ski Partners
Gressoney Crystal, Motours, Winterski
Jouvenceaux Ski Partners
Kronplatz Equity Total Ski
Livigno Airtours, Crystal, First Choice, Independent Ski Links, Neilson, Panorama, Thomson

Macugnaga First Choice, Interhome, Neilson, Thomson
Madesimo Inghams
Madonna di Campiglio Airtours, Alpine Tours, Crystal, Equity Total Ski, Inghams, Interhome, SCGB/Fresh Tracks, Solo's, Thomson
Marilleva Equity Total Ski
Moena Thomson
Monte Campione Equity Total Ski
Passo Tonale Airtours, Alpine Tours, Club Europe, Crystal, Equity Total Ski, First Choice, PGL Ski Europe, Ski Astons, SkiBound, Skiers World, Ski Partners, Thomson
Pila Crystal, Equity Total Ski, Independent Ski Links, Interski
San Cassiano First Choice
San Martino di Castrozza Interhome
Sansicario Equity Total Ski
Santa Caterina Airtours, First Choice, Thomson
Sauze d'Oulx Airtours, Crystal, Equity Total Ski, First Choice, Independent Ski Links, Inghams, Neilson, Panorama, Ski Partners, Thomson
Selva/Val Gardena Crystal, First Choice, Independent Ski Links, Inghams, Thomson, Waymark
Sestriere Airtours, Club Med, Crystal, Equity Total Ski, Independent Ski Links, Interhome, Motours, Neilson, Thomson, Winterski
La Thuile Crystal, First Choice, Independent Ski Links, Inghams, Interski, Neilson, Thomson
Val di Fassa Independent Ski Links

JAPAN
Sahoro Club Med

LAPLAND (FINNISH)
Levi Inghams

NEW ZEALAND
No current tour operator. We advise you to contact the New Zealand Tourism Board (see *Skiing by numbers*) for a list of tour operators to New Zealand and to contact resorts direct.

NORTH AMERICA
Alaska Frontier Ski
Alta Pavilion, Ski the American Dream

Alpine Meadows Virgin Ski
Apex Frontier Ski, Ski Safari
Aspen/Snowmass Crystal, Elegant Resorts, Fantiski, Independent Ski Links, Lotus Supertravel, Made to Measure, SCGB/Fresh Tracks, Seasons in Style, Ski Activity, Ski the American Dream, Ski Freedom, Ski Independence, Ski Safari, Skisarus, Skiworld, Solo's, Thomson
Attitash Bear Peak Big Country, Neilson, Skiers World, Virgin Ski
Banff/Lake Louise Airtours, Crystal, Elegant Resorts, Equity Total Ski, First Choice, Frontier Ski, Handmade Holidays, Independent Ski Links, Inghams, Kuoni, Lotus Supertravel, Neilson, SCGB/Fresh Tracks, Seasons in Style, Ski Activity, SkiBound, Ski the American Dream, Ski Equipe, Ski Freedom, Ski Independence, Ski Safari, Skisarus, Skiworld, Thomson, Vacation Canada
Beaver Creek (see Vail)
Big Mountain Ski Independence
Big Sky Ski Activity, Ski The American Dream, Ski Independence, Skisarus
Big White All Canada Ski, Frontier Ski, Independent Ski Links, Made to Measure, Ski Activity, Ski Independence, Ski Safari, Skisarus
Blue River Scott Dunn Ski
Breckenridge Big Country, Crystal, Elegant Resorts, Handmade Holidays, Independent Ski Links, Inghams, Neilson, Ski Activity, Ski the American Dream, Ski Freedom, Ski Independence, Ski Safari, Ski Val, Skiworld, Thomson
Canmore Neilson
The Canyons Ski Freedom, Ski Independence, Ski the American Dream
Copper Mountain Club Med, Independent Ski Links, Ski the American Dream, Ski Freedom, Ski Independence
Crested Butte Club Med, Fresh Tracks, Made to Measure, Ski Activity, Ski the American Dream, Ski Equipe, Ski Freedom, Ski Independence, Ski Safari, Skisarus
Deer Valley Made to Measure, Seasons in Style, Ski the American Dream, Ski Freedom, Ski Independence, Ski Safari, Skisarus
Fernie Airtours, Frontier Ski, Independent Ski Links, Inghams, Ski Activity, Ski

Independence, Ski the American Dream, Ski Safari, Skisarus, Vacation Canada

Grand Targhee Lotus Supertravel, Skisarus, Ski the American Dream

Heavenly (see Lake Tahoe) Crystal, Independent Ski Links, Inghams, Neilson, Thomson, Virgin Ski

Jackson Hole Abercrombie & Kent, Crystal, Elegant Resorts, Handmade Holidays, Independent Ski Links, Inghams, Lotus Supertravel, Made to Measure, Neilson, Seasons in Style, Ski Activity, Skisarus, Ski the American Dream, Ski Freedom, Ski Independence, Ski Safari, Skiworld

Jasper All Canada Ski, Crystal, First Choice, Frontier Ski, Independent Ski Links, Inghams, Neilson, Ski the American Dream, Ski Independence, Ski Safari, Thomson, Vacation Canada

Keystone Big Country, Crystal, Ski the American Dream, Ski Freedom, Ski Independence, Ski Activity, Skisarus

Killington Big Country, Crystal, Equity Total Ski, First Choice, Independent Ski Links, Inghams, Neilson, Ski Activity, Ski the American Dream, Ski Freedom, Skiers World, SkiBound, Ski Independence, Ski Partners, Ski Safari, Solo's, Top Deck, Thomson, Virgin Ski

Kimberley Frontier Ski, Inghams, Ski Safari

Kirkwood Virgin Ski

Lake Tahoe (see Heavenly and Squaw Valley) Big Country, Crystal, Equity Total Ski, Inghams, Ski Activity, Ski the American Dream, Skiers World, Ski Freedom, Ski Independence, Ski Safari, Skisarus, Skiworld, Thomson, Virgin Ski

Loon/Bretton Woods PGL Ski Europe, Virgin Ski

Mammoth Mountain Big Country, Crystal, Independent Ski Links, Ski Activity, Ski the American Dream, Skiers World, Ski Freedom, Ski Independence, Ski Safari, Virgin Ski

Mont Sainte-Anne First Choice, Frontier Ski, Inghams, Skiers World, SkiBound, Ski Partners, Ski Safari, Vacation Canada

Panorama Frontier Ski, Inghams, Oak Hall Skiing, Ski Activity, Ski Safari

Park City Crystal, Independent Ski Links, Pavilion, Ski Activity, Ski the American Dream, Ski Freedom, Ski Independence, Ski Safari, Skisarus, Skiworld

Pico Virgin Ski

Purgatory Ski Independence

Red Mountain Frontier Ski, Ski Safari

Silver Star Frontier Ski, Made to Measure, Ski Activity, Ski Independence, Ski the American Dream, Ski Safari, Skisarus, Vacation Canada

Smuggler's Notch Ski the American Dream

Snowbird Crystal, Made to Measure, Pavilion, Ski the American Dream, Ski Freedom, Ski Independence

Squaw Valley (see Lake Tahoe) Crystal, Ski the American Dream, Ski Independence, Ski Safari, Virgin Ski

Steamboat Big Country, Crystal, Independent Ski Links, Inghams, Lotus Supertravel, Neilson, Ski Activity, Ski the American Dream, Skiers World, Ski Freedom, Ski Independence, Ski Safari, Skisarus, Skiworld, Thomson

Stoneham Inghams, SkiBound, Skiers World, Ski Partners, Ski Safari

Stowe Crystal, First Choice, Independent Ski Links, Inghams, Made to Measure, Neilson, Ski the American Dream, SkiBound, Skiers World, Ski Freedom, Ski Independence, Ski Partners, Thomson, Virgin Ski

Sugarbush Big Country, First Choice, Made to Measure, Ski the American Dream, SkiBound, Skiers World, Virgin Ski

Sugarloaf Big Country, SkiBound, Skiers World, Ski Partners

Sunday River Big Country, Crystal, First Choice, Neilson, Ski the American Dream, SkiBound, Skiers World, Ski Independence, Ski Partners

Sun Peaks All Canada Ski, Frontier Ski, Made to Measure, Ski Activity, Ski the American Dream, Ski Independence, Ski Safari, Skisarus, Vacation Canada

Sun Valley Ski Activity, Ski the American Dream, Ski Independence, Skisarus

Telluride Elegant Resorts, Seasons in Style, Ski Activity, Ski the American Dream, Ski Freedom, Ski Safari, Skisarus, Skiworld

Tremblant All Canada Ski, Crystal, First Choice, Frontier Ski, Independent Ski Links, Inghams, Made to Measure, Neilson, Pavilion, Ski the American Dream, Skiers World, Ski Independence, Ski Safari, Thomson, Vacation Canada

Vail Abercrombie & Kent, Big Country, Crystal, Elegant Resorts, Handmade

Holidays, Independent Ski Links, Inghams, Lotus Supertravel, SCGB/Fresh Tracks, Seasons in Style, Ski Activity, Ski the American Dream, Ski Equipe, Ski Freedom, Ski Independence, Ski Safari, Skisarus, Skiworld, Thomson

Whistler Abercrombie & Kent, All Canada Ski, Alpine Tracks, American Connections, Crystal, Elegant Resorts, First Choice, Flexiski, Frontier Ski, Handmade Holidays, Inghams, Kuoni, Lotus Supertravel, Made to Measure, Neilson, Pavilion, SCGB/Fresh Tracks, Seasons in Style, Simply Ski, Ski Activity, Ski the American Dream, Ski Equipe, Ski Hillwood, Ski Independence, Ski Freedom, Ski Miquel, Ski Safari, Skisarus, Ski Total, Skiworld, Solo's, Thomson, Top Deck

Winter Park Crystal, First Choice, Made to Measure, Neilson, Oak Hall Skiing, Ski Activity, Ski the American Dream, Ski Freedom, Ski Safari, Skisarus, Skiworld, Thomson

NORWAY

Geilo Crystal, Independent Ski Links, Inntravel, Neilson, Thomson, Waymark

Hemsedal Crystal, Independent Ski Links, Neilson

Lillehammer Neilson

ROMANIA

Poiana Brasov Balkan Holidays, Balkan Tours, First Choice, Inghams, Neilson

SCOTLAND

Cairngorm (Aviemore) Ski Norwest, Ski Supreme, SkiSafe Travel

Glencoe HF Holidays, Ski Supreme, SkiSafe Travel

Glenshee Ski Norwest, Ski Supreme, SkiSafe Travel

Nevis Range Ski Norwest, Ski Supreme, SkiSafe Travel

The Lecht Ski Supreme, SkiSafe Travel

SLOVENIA

Bled Alpine Tours, Crystal, Thomson

Bohinj Alpine Tours, Crystal, First Choice

Kranjska Gora Alpine Tours, Balkan Holidays, Crystal, First Choice, Thomson

SPAIN

Baqueira-Beret Ski Miquel

Formigal Inghams, Thomson

Masella Pavilion

La Molina Pavilion

Sierra Nevada First Choice, Neilson, Thomson

SWEDEN

Åre Crystal, Independent Ski Links

SWITZERLAND

Adelboden Interhome, Kuoni, Plus Travel, Swiss Travel Service

Andermatt Made to Measure, Ski Weekend

Anzère Interhome, Lagrange, Made to Measure

Arosa Inghams, Interhome, Kuoni, Plus Travel, Powder Byrne, Ski Choice, Swiss Travel Service

Celerina Made to Measure

Champéry Piste Artiste, Plus Travel, White Roc

Château d'Oex Alpine Tours, Crystal, Erna Low, Skiers World, Ski Independence

Crans Montana Crystal, Elegant Resorts, Erna Low, Independent Ski Links, Inghams, Interhome, Kuoni, Lagrange, Motours, Oak Hall Skiing, Oxford Ski Company, PGL Ski Europe, Plus Travel, SCGB/Fresh Tracks, Swiss Travel Service

Davos Crystal, Elegant Resorts, Finlays, Independent Ski Links, Inghams, Interhome, Kuoni, Momentum Travel, Plus Travel, SCGB/Fresh Tracks, Ski Choice, Ski Gower, Ski Weekend, Swiss Travel Service, White Roc

Les Diablerets Crystal, Interhome, Lagrange, Made to Measure, Momentum Travel, Plus Travel, Ski Gower, Solo's

Engelberg Crystal, Finlays, Interhome, Kuoni, Made to Measure, Ski Gower, Swiss Travel Service

Flims/Laax Finlays, Interhome, Kuoni, Momentum Travel, Plus Travel, Powder Byrne, Ski Choice, Ski Weekend, Swiss Travel Service, White Roc

Grächen Interhome

Grindelwald Crystal, Elegant Resorts, Independent Ski Links, Inghams, Interhome, Kuoni, Plus Travel, Powder

Byrne, Swiss Travel Service, Thomson, White Roc

Gstaad Crystal, Elegant Resorts, Interhome, Momentum Travel, Seasons in Style, Ski Gower, Ski Independence, White Roc

Interlaken Kuoni, Ski Astons

Kandersteg Headwater, Inntravel, Kuoni, Waymark

Klosters Elegant Resorts, Finlays, Inghams, Kuoni, Made to Measure, Momentum Travel, Plus Travel, Powder Byrne, SCGB/Fresh Tracks, Ski Gower, Ski Solutions, Ski Weekend, The Ski Company, White Roc

Lauterbrunnen Oak Hall Skiing, Ski Miquel, Top Deck

Lenk Made to Measure, Swiss Travel Service

Lenzerheide/Valbella Interhome, Plus Travel, Ski Choice

Leysin Club Med, Skiers World, Erna Low, Plus Travel

Meiringen Hasliberg PGL Ski Europe

Morgins Ski Morgins

Mürren Inghams, Kuoni, Oak Hall Skiing, Plus Travel, SCGB/Fresh Tracks, Ski Solutions, Swiss Travel Service, Thomson

Nendaz/Siviez Interhome, Snowplus

Pontresina Club Med, Made to Measure

Saas-Fee Crystal, Erna Low, Independent Ski Links, Inghams, Interhome, Kuoni, Made to Measure, Momentum Travel, Oak Hall Skiing, PGL Ski Europe, Plus Travel, SCGB/Fresh Tracks, Ski Choice, Ski Gower, Ski Independence, Ski Solutions, Swiss Travel Service, Thomson

Saas-Grund Ski Gower

Schönried Interhome

Sils Maria/Silvaplana Interhome

St-Luc Inntravel

St Moritz Club Med, Crystal, Elegant

Resorts, Independent Ski Links, Inghams, Flexiski, Interhome, Kuoni, Made to Measure, Momentum Travel, Oak Hall Skiing, Plus Travel, SCGB/Fresh Tracks, Seasons in Style, Ski Gower, Ski Solutions, Swiss Travel Service

Torgon Interhome

Valbella Club Med

Verbier Abercrombie & Kent, Airtours, Chalet World, Crystal, Elegant Resorts, Erna Low, Flexiski, Fresh Tracks, Independent Ski Links, Inghams, Interhome, Made to Measure, Mark Warner, Momentum Travel, Motours, Neilson, Peak Ski, Plus Travel, SCGB/Fresh Tracks, Simply Ski, Ski Activity, Ski Astons, Ski Esprit, Ski Les Alpes, Ski Verbier, Ski Solutions, Ski Weekend, Skiworld, Swiss Travel Service, The Ski Company, Thomson, White Roc

Villars Club Med, Crystal, Erna Low, Interhome, Kuoni, Lagrange, Made to Measure, Ski Independence, Swiss Travel Service

Wengen Club Med, Crystal, Independent Ski Links, Inghams, Kuoni, Made to Measure, Oak Hall Skiing, PGL Ski Europe, Plus Travel, SCGB/Fresh Tracks, Ski Astons, Ski Gower, Ski Solutions, Swiss Travel Service, Thomson

Zermatt Abercrombie & Kent, Crystal, Elegant Resorts, Erna Low, Independent Ski Links, Inghams, Interhome, Kuoni, Lotus Supertravel, Lagrange, Made to Measure, Momentum Travel, Plus Travel, Powder Byrne, Scott Dunn Ski, Seasons in Style, SCGB/Fresh Tracks, Ski Choice, Ski Gower, Ski Independence, Ski Solutions, Ski Total, Swiss Travel Service, Thomson, Trail Alpine, White Roc

Zinal Interhome

Skiing by numbers

CONTENTS

NATIONAL TOURIST OFFICES

American Travel & Tourism Service
Tel (09065) 508972 (recorded message)

Andorran Delegation
63 Westover Road, London SW18 2RF
Tel/Fax 020-8874 4806
Web site www.andorraonline.ad

Argentinian Consulate
27 Three Kings Yard, London W1Y 1FL
Tel 020-7318 1340 **Fax** 020-7318 1349

Australian Tourist Commission
Gemini House, 10–18 Putney Hill,
London SW15 6AA
Tel 020-8780 2229 **Fax** 020-8780 1496
Email Europe_helpline@atc.gov.au
Web site www.australia.com

Austrian National Tourist Office
PO Box 2363, London W1A 2QB
Tel 020-7629 0461 **Fax** 020-7499 6038
Email info@anto.co.uk
Web site www.austria-tourism.at

Bulgaria, Embassy of the Republic of
186–188 Queensgate, London SW7 5HL
Tel 020-7589 8402 **Fax** 020-7589 4875

Canada, Visit
PO Box 5396, Northampton NN1 2FA
Tel (0906) 871 5000 (premium rates
at all times)
Email visitcanada@dialpipex.com
Web site www.travelcanada.ca

Chile, Consulate of
Tourist Information, 12 Devonshire
Street, London W1N 2DS
Tel 020-7580 1023 **Fax** 020-7323 4294
Email cglonduk@congechileuk.
demon.co.uk
Web site www.chile-travel.com

Czech Tourist Authority
95 Great Portland Street, London
W1N 5RA
Tel 020-7291 9920
Fax 020-7436 8300
Email cta@inform.demon.co.uk
Web site www.tourist-offices.org.uk

Finnish Tourist Board
30–35 Pall Mall, London SW1Y 5LP
Tel 020-7930 5871
Fax 020-7321 0696
Email mek.lon@mek.fi
Web site www.finland-tourism.com

French Government Tourist Office
178 Piccadilly, London W1V OAL
Tel (0891) 244123 **Fax** 020-7493 6594
Email info@mdlf.co.uk
Web site www.franceguide.com

German National Tourist Office
PO Box 2695, London W1A 3TN
Tel 020-7317 0908 **Fax** 020-7495 6129
Email german-national-tourist-
office@compuserve.com
Web site www.germany-tourism.de

Italian State Tourist Office
1 Princes Street, London W1R 8AY
Tel 020-7408 1254 **Fax** 020-7493 6695
Email enitlond@globalnet.co.uk
Web site www.piuitalia2000.it

Japanese National Tourist Organisation
Heathcoat House, 20 Savile Row,
London W1X 2BD
Tel 020-7734 9638 **Fax** 020-7734 4290
Email jntolon@dircon.co.uk
Web site www.jnto.go.jp

New Zealand Tourism Board
New Zealand House, Haymarket,
London SW1Y 4TQ
Tel (09063) 640650
Fax 020-7839 8929
Email enquiries@nztb.govt.nz
Web site www.new.zealand.co.uk

Norwegian Tourist Board
5th Floor, Charles House, 5 Lower
Regent Street, London SW1Y 4LR
Tel 020-7839 6255 **Fax** 020-7839 6014
Email infouk@ntr.no
Web site www.visitnorway.com

Romanian National Tourist Office
22 New Cavendish Street, London
W1M 7LH
Tel 020-7224 3692 **Fax** 020-7935 6435
Email uktouroff@romania.freeserve.co.uk
Web site www.romaniatravel.com

Scottish Tourist Board
23 Ravelston Terrace, Edinburgh
EH4 3EU
Tel 0131-332 2433 **Fax** 0131-343 1513
Email info@stb.gov.uk
Web site www.visitscotland.com

Slovenian Tourist Office
49 Conduit Street, London W1 9FB
Tel 020-7287 7133 **Fax** 020-7287 5476
Web site www.slovenia-tourism.si

Spanish Tourist Office
22–23 Manchester Square, London
W1M 5AP
Tel 020-7486 8077 **Fax** 020-7486 8034
Email info.londres@tourspain.es
Web site www.tourspain.co.uk

Swedish Travel & Tourism Council
11 Montagu Place, London W1H 2AL
Tel 020-7724 5600 **Fax** 020-7724 5872
Email info@swetourism.org.uk
Web site www.visit-sweden.com

Switzerland Travel Centre
Swiss Centre, Swiss Court, London
W1V 8EE
Tel (00800) 100 200 30
Fax (00800) 100 200 31
Email stc@stlondon.com
Web site www.MySwitzerland.com

SKI TRAVEL AGENTS

Alpine Answers
The Business Village, 3–9 Broomhill
Road, London SW18 4JQ
Tel 020-8871 4656 **Fax** 020-8871 9676
Email ski@alpineanswers.co.uk
Web site www.alpineanswers.co.uk

Erna Low
9 Reece Mews, London SW7 3HE
Tel 020-7584 2841 **Fax** 020-7589 9531
Email info@ernalow.co.uk
Web site www.ernalow.co.uk

Ski Solutions
84 Pembroke Road, London W8 6NX
Tel 020-7471 7700 **Fax** 020-7471 7701
Email skihols@skisolutions.com

Ski & Surf
37 Priory Field Drive, Edgware HA8 9PT
Tel 020-8958 2418 **Fax** 020-8905 4146
Email janm@skisurf.com
Web site www.ski-surf.dircon.co.uk

Ski Travel Centre
1100 Pollokshaws Road, Shawlands,
Glasgow G41 3NJ

Tel 0141-649 9696 **Fax** 0141-649 2273
Email anngus@skitravelcentre.com
Web site www.ski-travel-centre.co.uk

Skiers Travel Bureau
Fountain Court, High Street, Market
Harborough LE16 7AF
Tel (01858) 468858 **Fax** (01858) 828130
Email sales@skiers-travel.co.uk
Web site www.skiers-travel.co.uk

Snow Line
1 Angel Court, High Street, Market
Harborough LE16 7NL
Tel (01858) 828000
Fax (01858) 828020
Email sales@snow-line.co.uk
Web site www.snow-line.co.uk

AIRLINES

The main airlines listed below offer
international scheduled flights to airports
close to ski areas

Air Canada
Tel (0990) 247226
Air Engiadina
Tel (08705) 074074
Air France
Tel (0845) 0845 111
Air New Zealand
Tel 020-8741 2299
Alitalia
Tel (08705) 448259
American Airlines
Tel 020-8572 5555
Austrian Airlines
Tel 020-7434 7300
Braathens/Malmo
Tel 091-214 0991
British Airways
Tel (0345) 222111
buzz
Tel (0870) 2407070
Canadian Airlines
Tel (0345) 616767
Continental Airlines
Tel (01293) 776464
Crossair
Tel (0845) 607 3000
Delta Airlines
Tel (0800) 414767
easyJet
Tel (0870) 6000 000

Finnair
Tel 020-8759 1258
go
Tel (0845) 6054321
Iberia Airlines
Tel 020-7830 0011
KLM
Tel (08705) 074074
Lauda Air
Tel 020-7630 5924
Lufthansa
Tel (0345) 737747
Monarch Airlines
Tel (01582) 400000
Northwest Airlines
Tel (08705) 074074
Qantas Airways
Tel (0345) 747767
Ryanair
Tel (0541) 569569
SAS
Tel (0845) 607 2772
Swissair
Tel 020-7434 7300
United Airlines
Tel (0845) 844 4777
Virgin Atlantic Airways
Tel (01293) 747747

UK AIRPORTS

Aberdeen
Tel (01224) 722331
Belfast
Tel (01849) 422888
Birmingham
Tel 0121-767 5511
Bournmouth
Tel (01202) 364235
Bristol
Tel (01275) 474444
Cardiff
Tel (01446) 711111
Dublin
Tel 00 353 1 814 1111
East Midlands
Tel (01332) 852852
Edinburgh
Tel 0131-333 1000
Exeter
Tel (01392) 367433
Glasgow
Tel 0141-887 1111
Leeds Bradford
Tel (0113) 250 9696

London City
Tel 020-7646 0000
London Gatwick
Tel (01293) 535353
London Heathrow
Tel (0870) 0000 123
London Luton
Tel (01582) 405100
London Stansted
Tel (01279) 680500
Manchester
Tel 0161-489 3000
Newcastle
Tel 0191-286 0966
Teeside
Tel (01325) 332811

CAR HIRE
Alamo
Tel (01273) 223300
Avis
Tel (0990) 900500
Budget
Tel (0800) 181181
Europcar
Tel (0113) 2422233
Hertz
Tel (0990) 996699
Holiday Autos
Tel (0990) 300400

AVALANCHE WARNINGS
Austria
Tel 00 43 5522 1588
Web site: www.lawine.at
France
Web site www.skifrance.fr
Italy
Tel 00 39 0461 230 030
Web site www.aineva.it
Scotland
Tel (0800) 096 0007
Web site www.sais.gov.uk
Spain
Tel 00 34 934 232 967/572
Web site www.icc.es/allaus
Switzerland
Tel 00 41 81187
Web site www.MySwitzerland.com

SKI-TOURING
The Alpine Ski Club
Tel (01753) 886665 **Fax** (01753) 880305
Email whmann@btinternet.com

Web site www.alpineskiclub.org.uk
Ski-mountaineering – avalanche transceivers available for hire

The Eagle Ski Club
Tel 020-8959 2214
Email info@eagleskiclub.org.uk
Web site www.eagleskiclub.org.uk
Europe's largest ski-touring club

Eclipse Mountain Guiding
Tel (01539) 444033 **Fax** (01539) 442145
Email philip@eclipse-outdoor.co.uk
Web site www.eclipse-outdoor.co.uk/ mountainguiding
Ski-tours in France and Switzerland with qualified guides

Mountain Experience
Tel/Fax (01663) 750160
Email BrianPHall@email.msn.com
Web site www.mountainexperience.co.uk
Guiding and ski-touring in France, Italy and Switzerland

SKI COURSES
The organisations listed below specialise in ski clinic holidays. Note that several of the companies in *Which tour operator?* also offer ski clinics

Ali Ross (through Ski Solutions)
Tel 020-7471 7777 **Fax** 020-7471 7771
Email alc@skisolutions.com
Specialist ski courses in Tignes

Lauralee Bowie Ski Adventures
Tel 00 1 604 689 7444
Fax 00 1 604 689 7489
Email llbski@canuck.com
Web site www.skiadventures.net
Personalised ski instruction in Lake Louise and Whistler

McGarry The Ski System
5 Barnhill Road, Dalkey, County Dublin
Tel 00 353 1 285 9139
Fax 00 353 1 284 9932
Specialist courses in Châtel

Optimum Ski Courses
Tel (01992) 561085 **Fax** 00 33 479 069356
Email info@optimumski.com
Web site www.optimumski.com

Ski clinics in Les Arcs and Tignes with BASI trainer

Ski Club of Great Britain
Tel 020-8410 2000 **Fax** 020-8410 2001
Email info@skiclub.co.uk
Web site www.skiclub.co.uk
Ski courses for all standards

The International Academy
Tel (02920) 489484 **Fax** (02920) 489555
Email info@international-academy.com
Web site www.international-academy.com
Professional ski and snowboard instructors' courses in USA and New Zealand

The Ski Company
Tel (01279) 653746 **Fax** (01279) 654705
Email theskicompany@compuserve.com
Web site www.theskicompany.co.uk
Year-round ski courses in Canada and France

Top Ski
Tel 00 33 479 061480
Fax 00 33 479 062842
Email top.ski.val.isere@wanadoo.fr
Web site www.perso.wanadoo.fr/topski
Ski clinics in Val d'Isère

SKI RECRUITMENT AGENCY
Fresh Tracks Recruitment Ltd
Tel 020-8785 2626 **Fax** (0870) 1215436
Email efremleigh@yahoo.com
Web site www.fresh-tracks.com

TRADE ORGANISATIONS
Artificial Slope Ski Instructors (ASSI)
Tel 0121-501 2314 **Fax** 0121-585 6448
Email esc@tesco.net
Web site www.englishski.org

Association of British Travel Agents (ABTA)
Tel 020-7637 2444 **Fax** 020-7637 5626
Email abta@abta.co.uk
Web site www.abtanet.com

Association of British Tour Operators to France (ABTOF)
Tel (01989) 769140 **Fax** (01989) 769066
Email abtof@aol.com

Web site www.holidayfrance.org.uk

Association of Independent Tour Operators (AITO)
Tel 020-8744 9280
Brochure line 020-8607 9080
Fax 020-8744 3187
Email aito@aito.co.uk
Web site www.aito.co.uk

British Association of Snowsport Instructors (BASI)
Tel (01479) 861717 **Fax** (01479) 861718
Email basi@basi.org.uk
Web site www.basi.org.uk

British Association of Ski Patrollers
Tel/Fax (01855) 811443
Email skipatrol@basp.org.uk
Web site www.basp.org.uk

British Bobsleigh Association
Tel/Fax (01722) 340014
Email bba@dial.pipex.com
Web site www.british-bobsleigh.com

British Mountain Guides
Tel (01690) 720386
Fax (01690) 720248
Email futurmedia@infinet.u-net.com
Web site www.bmg.org.uk

British Mountaineering Council
Tel 0161-445 4747 **Fax** 0161-445 4500
Email office@thebmc.co.uk
Web site www.thebmc.co.uk

British Ski Slope Operators' Association
Tel/Fax 01928 710009
Web site www.bssoa.co.uk

British Ski and Snowboard Federation
Tel (0131) 445 7676
Fax (0131) 445 7722
Email britski@easynet.co.uk
Web site www.complete-skier.com

British Snowboard Association
Tel (07000) 360540 **Fax** (07000) 720540
Web site www.snowboardbritain.com

Snowsport Industries of Great Britain
Tel 0131-557 3012 **Fax** 0131-557 9466

Email sigb@raremanagement.co.uk
Web site www.snowlife.org.uk

INDOOR SLOPES WITH ARTIFICIAL SNOW

Healthland Snozone
Milton Keynes
Tel (01908) 230260 Fax (01908) 230270

Tamworth SnowDome
Tamworth, Staffordshire B79 7ND
Tel 090 00 00 11 Fax (01827) 62549

SKI COUNCILS

These bodies govern the sport as a whole, taking responsibility for promoting and developing snowsports with the aid of grants from the Sports Council

English Ski Council
Tel 0121-501 2314 Fax 0121-585 6448
Email esc@tesco.net
Web site www.englishski.org

Snowsport Scotland
Tel 0131-445 4151 Fax 0131-339 8602
Email snowsport@snsc.demon.co.uk
Web site www.snsc.demon.co.uk

Ski Council of Wales
Tel (02920) 561904 Fax (02920) 561924
Web site www.snowsportwales.net

SKI CLUBS

Alpbach Visitors Ski Club
Tel 00 43 5336 5282
Fax 00 43 5336 5073
Individual and package holidays

Bearsden Ski Club
Tel 0141-943 1500 Fax 0141-942 4705
Email info@skibearsden.co.uk
Web site www.snowsport.co.uk
Ski club with artificial slope

British Ski Club for the Disabled
Tel/Fax (01747) 828515
Email edski@bscd.org.uk
Web site www.bscd.org.uk

Downhill Only Club
Tel (01305) 848721
Web site www.ukonline.co.uk/dho/
Ski club with junior racing, based in Wengen, Switzerland

Kandahar Ski Club
Tel 020-8878 3445
Email annette.hughes@fdn.co.uk
Ski club with junior racing, based in Mürren, Switzerland

Ladies Ski Club
Tel (01787) 313923 Fax (01787) 375497
Ski racing club

Marden's Club
Tel (01223) 893063 Fax (01223) 890846
Ski club based in Klosters, Switzerland

Scottish Ski Club
Tel 0131-477 1055
Email info@scotski.org.uk
Web site www.scotski.org.uk

Ski Club of Great Britain
Tel 020-8410 2000 Fax 020-8410 2001
Email info@skiclub.co.uk
Web site www.skiclub.co.uk
*The leading club for British skiers
(see Page 11 for details)*

The Uphill Ski Club of Great Britain
Tel/Fax (01799) 525 406
Email Isabel@uphill-ski-club.demon.co.uk
Web site www.ccksb.freeserve.co.uk
Organisation for disabled skiers

World Ski & Snowboard Association
Tel (0114) 279 7300
Fax (0114) 276 2348
Email info@worldski.co.uk
Web site www.worldski.co.uk
Wide range of discounts for members

RETAIL OUTLETS

The following outlets supply skiwear and equipment

Ellis Brigham
Web site www.ellis-brigham.com
UK clothing and equipment brochure

Finches
Web site www.finches-ski.com
UK clothing brochure

Mountain Equipment Co-op
Web site www.mec.ca

Canadian outdoor gear, can be ordered
by phone

REI
Web site www.rei.com
*American co-operative that will ship
orders to the UK*

REI Outlet
Web site www.rei-outlet.com
Separate discount site

Snow + Rock
Web site www.snowandrock.com
UK clothing and equipment brochure

ON-LINE RESOURCES
**Complete-skier.com/Complete-
snowboarder.com**
Web site www.complete-
skier.com/www.complete-
snowboarder.com
*Comprehensive information for
snow-users*

Iglu.com
Web site www.iglu.com
All-round ski information

Liveski.com
Web site www.liveski.com
All-inclusive ski magazine

Ski Hotline
Web sites www.born2ski.com
Snow reports

Ski McNeill
Web site www.skimcneill.com
Specialist ski travel agency

Terradat
Web site www.snow-forecast.com
Worldwide snow data

The First Report
Web site www.thefirstresort.com
*On-line holiday booking and information
for snow-users*

By car or train

Anyone who has experienced Gatwick and Geneva Airports on a Saturday in February will understand why some 25 per cent of British skiers and snowboarders will go by car to the Alps this winter. Apart from avoiding check-in chaos, the rigidity of charter travel and the weekend lottery of air-traffic control in the skies over Europe, driving to the snow offers greater flexibility of destination as well as the freedom to travel with as many pairs of skis and as much luggage as you can fit in.

Limited holiday time and the desire to spend as much of it on the snow as possible have largely confined ski-drive destinations to the French Alps as well as to a handful of Swiss and Italian resorts easily accessible from Lake Geneva or – during the continued closure period of the Mont Blanc Tunnel – via the Grand St Bernard Tunnel. Work has now started on the £120-million restructuring of the Mont Blanc Tunnel and it is expected to open in March 2001. Given fair weather and a co-driver, you can comfortably travel from Calais to Courchevel in under ten hours without breaking the speed limit.

Route planning

Finding your way to the French Alps is simple. Take the A26 autoroute from Calais and carry on past Reims and Dijon. At Mâcon, branch off on to the A40 towards Geneva, or carry on past Lyon for Albertville and Grenoble. The autoroute ends at Albertville but, thanks to the 1992 Winter Olympics, the road to Moûtiers is a fast dual-carriageway. The final stretch to Val d'Isère/Tignes beyond Bourg-St-Maurice takes 40 minutes in good weather conditions provided you miss the weekend change-over traffic.

The AA now provides free detailed routes on its web site (*www.theaa.com*) to destinations that include most major ski resorts all over Europe. It also supplies on-line reports on current road/weather conditions. French-speakers with touch-tone telephones can hear a detailed and usually reliable forecast for snow conditions in the French Alps from Metéo-France tel: 00 33 836680273*2.

Be prepared

It is essential to have your car fully serviced before encountering what may be seriously cold conditions in the Alps. Check the battery and replace it if you are in any doubt. The anti-freeze should be topped up to the level recommended in the manufacturer's handbook for temperatures as low as -30°C. (Remember that anti-freeze may not be effective if it is more than two years old.) You will need a stronger solution of winter screenwash. Carry a windscreen scraper and a can of de-icer.

It continues to be a legal requirement to attach a GB sticker in a vertical or near vertical position at the rear of your car. You must also carry a warning triangle and attach headlamp-beam converters to avoid dazzling other drivers. Take with you a torch, a shovel, an old pair of gloves and a tow-rope.

Motorway tolls

You can calculate in advance the exact cost of French motorway tolls to and from your destination on the French Motorways web site (*www.autoroutes.fr*). It gives details of current tolls and roadworks to avoid. Once en route it is easier (and surprisingly quicker) to pay by credit card rather than carrying small change.

From December 2000 the cost of a windscreen sticker that allows you to use all motorways in Austria is increasing to ATS105 for ten days, ATS300 for two months or ATS1,000 for one year. You can buy these at the border or from service stations close to the border. Switzerland has a similar system which costs SF40 for one year. Stickers are available from the Switzerland Travel Centre in London, or at the frontier. In both countries, ignorance of the law is no excuse.

Breakdown insurance

The AA estimates that about half of those people who drive to ski resorts do not have vehicle breakdown cover, yet as many as one in five has some sort of trouble with their car. The approximate cost of having a car recovered to the UK from France is £2,300. An out-of-hours local tow in France costs between £40 and £70.

Green Cards

The international motor insurance card or Green Card – a standardised proof of insurance – is no longer compulsory. Some companies continue to issue Green Cards, either free of charge or for an administration fee. Others, including the AA, no longer do so. However, you must carry your insurance certificate, original vehicle registration document and a current tax disc.

Before driving abroad you must inform your car insurance company of the dates of departure and return. If you have a comprehensive policy it is important to confirm that your cover abroad is the same as at home.

Driving regulations

In France, the speed limit on non-motorways is 90kph (56mph), on urban motorways 110kph (68mph), on autoroutes 130kph (81mph). In built-up areas the limit is 50kph (31mph) or 70kph (44mph). You can be fined up to 2,500FF on the spot for speeding. You must carry with you at all times a full UK driving licence and your passport.

If you have held a licence for less than two years you are subject to set speed limits: 80kph (50mph) on non-motorways, 100kph (62mph) on urban motorways, and 110kph (68mph) on autoroutes. The drink/drive limit is 50mg in France as opposed to 80mg in Britain. This is rigidly enforced. However, you do not necessarily lose your licence for a first offence.

Snow tyres and chains

Most cars in Britain are fitted with standard summer tyres, which provide insufficient grip in serious winter conditions. The legal requirement in Britain (the requirement varies from country to country) is for the tread of all tyres to be over 2mm. If you travel regularly to the mountains or plan an extended stay, it is worth investing in a set of high-profile snow tyres that can also be used (with some increase in noise and wear) on motorways and other 'dry' roads. Studded tyres are for resort use only and are neither advisable nor necessary.

Even though you may not need to use snow chains during much of the winter, it is a legal requirement to carry them when driving on mountain roads in all European countries. Failure to do so can result in on-the-spot fines of up to £250, and there is evidence to suggest that police forces in both France and Switzerland in particular are increasingly enforcing the law.

Do not wait until you need snow chains before buying them. The price at garages in the mountains is as high as their quality is low. Modern chains come in three basic types – the greater the traction and the easier they are to fit, the more expensive the chains. At the bottom end of the range is the Cable Grip, which is laced around the wheel. The more sophisticated Euromatic is mounted on a flexible steel hoop. The Centrax-Steg is the easiest of all and leaves you with clean hands. You attach an adapter to one wheelnut, throw as much of the chain as you can over the tyre, and it fits and tightens automatically as you drive off.

Snow chains can be bought – but not hired – from both the AA and the RAC at Dover and at the Eurotunnel at Folkestone. Snowchains of Borough Green, Rudd Chains of Whitstable and Brindley Chains of Warrington also sell chains. Prices range from £34 to £250, depending on the type of car and chain. Snowchains of Borough Green is the only major company that continues to hire them from £29.50 for 16 days and it also hires roof boxes at £49.50 for 16 days.

Fitting for the more sophisticated types of chain should not take more than a minute per wheel, but we strongly recommend you practise before you leave home.

Cost of driving

The cost of driving the 2,010km (1,400 miles) from London to Val d'Isère and back in an 1800cc family saloon works out at approximately £400. This price includes tickets through the Channel Tunnel, petrol, tolls, chains, insurance, and wear-and-tear. It does not include refreshments or accommodation en route.

Trains

Eurostar, in partnership with French Railways (SNCF), operates an overnight service (but, alas, with no couchettes) from Waterloo and Ashford on Fridays, as well as a direct daytime service. Both run from December to mid-April. Since the Channel Tunnel was built, this route has proved to be one of the most hassle-free methods of getting to the

Alps, although for a family of four it is more expensive than flying or driving. The overnight train arrives in the Alps early on Saturday morning and the return service leaves the Alps after the lifts close the following Saturday, thus allowing almost two days' extra skiing on the standard 'week'. Reporters complain that the disadvantage of the overnight service is the discomfort of having nowhere to lie down. An alternative is to take Eurostar to Lille or Paris, change stations, and catch an SNCF train equipped with couchettes for the onward journey to the Alps.

You also have to vacate your accommodation on Saturday morning, so before the return journey you will need somewhere to store your luggage, shower and change out of ski clothes.

The daytime service leaves Waterloo each Saturday at around 0900 and arrives in Moûtiers at around 17.45 local time. The return journey is from Moûtiers at around 10.45 on Saturday morning.

Motorail also runs an overnight weekend service to Moûtiers. This leaves Calais on Friday evening and arrives in the French Alps at 09.00 on Saturday. The advantage of this service is that you can stretch out in a couchette. The cost for four people is comparable to Eurostar and you have the additional freedom of a car at your holiday destination.

The weekly Snowtrain, chartered by a group of tour operators, continues to rattle slowly on at a considerably lower price and lower standard of comfort. Passengers leave Calais at about 21.20 on Friday and arrive in Moûtiers 12 hours later. The train continues on to Bourg-St-Maurice. Again, the return journey is on Saturday evening (about 20.00 from Moûtiers) arriving in Calais at 08.45 on Sunday, thus allowing you nearly two extra days of skiing. The Snowtrain is inconvenient, uncomfortable, crowded but praised by almost every reporter who has tried it.

USEFUL NUMBERS

GOING BY CAR

Breakdown insurance
AA Five Star Services
Tel (0800) 444500
Autohome Ltd
Tel (01604) 232334
Britannia Rescue
Tel (01484) 514848
Europ Assistance
Tel (01444) 442211
First Assist
Tel 020-8763 1550
Green Flag National Breakdown
Tel (0345) 670345
Leisurecare Insurance Services
Tel (01793) 750150

Mondial Assistance
Tel 020-8681 2525
RAC Travel Services
Tel (0800) 550055

Channel crossings
Brittany Ferries
(Portsmouth–Caen)
Tel (0990) 360360
Eurotunnel *(Folkestone–Calais)*
Tel (0990) 353535
Hoverspeed *(Dover–Calais,*
Folkestone–Boulogne,
Dover–Ostend,
Newhaven–Dieppe)
Tel (0990) 240241

P & O European Ferries *(Portsmouth–Le Havre, Portsmouth–Cherbourg)*
Tel (0870) 2424999
P & O North Sea Ferries *(Hull–Zeebrugge, Hull–Rotterdam)*
Tel (01482) 377177
P & O Stena Line *(Dover–Calais, Newhaven–Dieppe)*
Tel (0870) 600 0600
Seafrance *(Dover–Calais)*
Tel (0990) 711711
Stena Line *(Harwich–Hook)*
Tel (0990) 707070

Weather and snow
Austrian snow conditions
Tel 00 43 11585 *(Tyrol and Vorarlberg)*
Tel 00 43 11584 *(Salzburgerland)*
Tel 00 43 11590 *(road conditions)*
Met-Call Ski Scotland
Tel (0336) 405 400
Information on Scottish ski resorts
Metéo-France (Savoie)
Tel 00 33 836 68 02 73 *2
*Detailed forecast for French Alps
(in French only)*
Ski Club Snowline
Tel (0906) 951 9191
*24-hr snow and weather information on
over 200 resorts in 10 countries, Europe
and North America*
Swiss Automobile Club
Tel 00 41 31 311 7722 *(road conditions)*
Swiss Touring Club
Tel 00 41 22 417 2727 *(road conditions)*

Ski roof boxes
Kar Rite Europe
Tel (01440) 760000

The Roof Box Company
Tel (01539) 621884
Thule
Tel (01275) 340404

Snow chains
AA
Tel (0990) 500600
Brindley Chains
Tel 01925 825555
RAC
Tel (0800) 550055
Rudd Chains
Tel (01227) 276611
Snowchains
Tel (01732) 884408

GOING BY RAIL

Rail companies (for Alps)
Austrian Federal Railways
Tel 0906 851 7175
Eurostar
Tel (0990) 186 186
German Rail
Tel 0870 243 5363
Motorail
Tel (08702) 415415
Rail Europe *(for European rail bookings)*
Tel (0990) 848 848
Swiss Federal Railways
Tel 020-7734 1921
Gatwick Express *(from Victoria)*
Stansted Sky Train *(from Liverpool Street)*
Heathrow Express *(from Paddington)*
Tel (08457) 484950 (all)

Winter sports insurance

Buying travel insurance is the boring part of planning any kind of holiday. Therefore, it is tempting to just take the insurance offered as part of your holiday package or – if you are making your own arrangements – pick up a policy from a well-known high-street name. But if you would rather not waste money that could be better spent on a slap-up lunch in a mountain restaurant or several well-deserved glasses of *vin chaud*, you would be better off contacting a ski insurance specialist.

As well as saving money, buying from a specialist means that you get better cover with fewer skier-unfriendly exclusions – largely because many policies are designed by people who are keen skiers themselves. Another good reason for avoiding the high street is that – particularly in the case of travel agents – you are likely to be offered insurance for only a single trip. Since many winter sports enthusiasts try to fit in more than one visit to the slopes and will also take a summer holiday, an annual policy that provides cover for a whole year makes economic sense. Annual policies can be particularly good value for couples and families. To avoid unpleasant and expensive surprises when you make a claim, you need to make sure that the limits imposed by the policy cover the activities you plan to indulge in and the value of your ski or snowboard equipment – whether your own or hired.

If you are heading for the mountains you should ensure that your policy covers:

- at least £1 million in medical expenses
- all mountain rescue expenses
- the cost of an air ambulance back to the UK
- at least £1 million (£2 million in the USA) for your personal liability in case you accidentally injure someone or damage their property
- the reimbursement of costs involved in cancelling or cutting short your holiday
- the cost of pre-paid ski or snowboard lessons, lift passes and equipment hire you are unable to use because of illness or injury (if appropriate)
- the costs of travelling to another resort if lack of snow makes this necessary (although you won't need this cover if you have your own transport).

What are you going to get up to?

While it shouldn't be too hard to find a policy that will provide these essential levels of cover (especially if you use any of the companies we have listed), it may take a little more time to find a policy that suits your personal circumstances. You need to be aware that insurers may refuse to pay out if you hurt yourself in any way other than while skiing recreationally on piste.

SNOWBOARDING

Quite surprisingly, a handful of insurance companies do not provide cover for snowboarding. Several others demonstrate their ignorance of the subject by agreeing to cover boarders only if they do not venture away from marked runs.

OFF-PISTE

The off-piste question affects riders and skiers alike. Some insurers take the view that anyone wanting to go off-piste has a death wish, so will not pay out if you have an accident while skiing (or boarding) off-piste. Others cover off-piste only if you are accompanied by a mountain guide. This definition is so vague that it may or may not cover you if you go accompanied by a qualified ski instructor if he or she does not have a separate mountain guide qualification. Most certainly it will not cover you if you are accompanied only by a gung-ho chalet host. If you go to a resort where the dividing line between what is and what is not considered off-piste is rather blurred, you may find yourself skiing off-piste without realising it. For example, in the Arlberg region and in parts of Switzerland, what were once black (difficult) runs have been regraded as unpatrolled 'ski itineraries'. Although they appear on the piste map they could technically be defined as off-piste. Choose a policy that allows you to go off-piste without a guide – and check the insurer's definition of terms.

Skiers planning more intrepid expeditions away from the confines of a resort's ski area need to check cover carefully. Heli-skiing may be covered as standard, but it is unlikely there will be automatic cover for ski-touring with skins (whether it involves climbing or not) unless you pay an extra premium.

OTHER ACTIVITIES

Do not assume that it is only expert skiers and riders who need to worry about their insurance cover. Even beginners will find it worthwhile to quiz a prospective insurer before handing over any money. The insurance world is divided over whether the end-of-week race organised by most ski schools is a bit of harmless fun (and so covered) or whether it is as risky as the racing shown on *Ski Sunday* (and so excluded). The same confusion applies to the popular timed public slalom courses in many resorts where you can compete against friends.

The more cautious insurers will also refuse to pay a claim if you have an accident while taking part in popular après-ski activities such as tobogganing, ice-skating, parapente, dog-sledding or snowmobiling.

INACTIVITY

Most insurers pay a fixed daily allowance of about £20 to £30 if lack of snow or severe weather conditions keep you off the slopes. However, what constitutes 'lack of snow' or 'piste closure' is very carefully defined. The insurer is unlikely to pay out if you can be transported to a neighbouring resort or if a minimal number of lifts are kept open.

Cover for equipment

Many people wrongly assume that, if their skis are damaged or stolen, their insurer will pay to replace them as new. This will happen only if they are insured under your house contents policy (which can be worth doing if your equipment is particularly expensive). Travel insurers take age and wear-and-tear into account when assessing a claim and so will pay out only as much as the equipment would cost to buy second-hand – provided this figure does not exceed the maximum limit given in the policy, which is typically about £500 (although it can be a lot less). It is very unlikely that equipment over five years old will be covered at all.

THEFT OF EQUIPMENT

Unless you are prepared to buy – and use – special ski locks, most insurers will not pay a claim if your skis are stolen while you are having lunch or stopping for a quick drink at a mountain restaurant. These insurers may be prepared to be more lenient if you can show that you took other precautions to prevent theft – such as leaving your skis in mixed pairs. But if you don't want the hassle of proving this, look for one of the handful of insurers who will not penalise you for leaving your skis or board unlocked while on the slopes.

Leaving skis and boards unlocked and unattended *away* from the slopes is a different matter. You are very likely to have a claim refused if equipment is stolen because you failed to lock it away securely. This applies to leaving equipment locked to a car roof rack overnight – although some insurers may cover theft from a car if it happens on your way to and from the slopes.

REPLACEMENT EQUIPMENT

Although you are unlikely to recover the cost of buying new equipment if you are unfortunate enough to lose or damage it, most insurers *will* pay from £100 to £500 (depending on the insurer) towards the cost of hiring replacement kit. You are also likely to find that, within similar limits, your insurer will reimburse you for having to hire equipment if yours failed to arrive at the resort at the same time as you did.

INSURANCE FOR HIRED EQUIPMENT

Check what a policy will pay out if you lose or completely trash hired skis or a board. If nothing else, it will help you to answer the vexed question of whether or not you should take the usually iniquitously expensive insurance that the hire shop will inevitably offer you.

SKI INSURANCE COMPANIES

The following organisations specialise in winter sports cover

American Express
Tel (0800) 700737 **Fax** (01273) 668453
Web site www.americanexpress.com

BIBA
Tel 020-7623 9043 **Fax** 020-7626 9676
Email enquiries@biba.org.uk
Web site www.biba.org.uk

Columbus Direct
Tel 020-7375 0011 **Fax** 020-7375 0274
Email sales@columbusdirect.demon.co.uk
Web site www.columbusdirect.co.uk

Direct Travel Insurance
Tel (01903) 812345 **Fax** (01903) 813555
Email info@direct-travel.com
Web site www.direct-travel.com

Douglas Cox Tyrie Insurance Brokers
Tel (01708) 385500 **Fax** (0870) 2412361

Eagle Star
Tel (0800) 333800
Web site www.eaglestar.co.uk

Endsleigh Insurance Services
Tel 020-7436 4451 **Fax** 020-7637 3132
Web site www.endsleigh.co.uk

Europ Assistance
Tel (01444) 442211 **Fax** (01444) 416799
Web site www.europ-assistance.co.uk

Fogg Travel Insurance
Tel (01623) 631331 **Fax** (01623) 420450
Email col@fogginsure.co.uk
Web site www.fogginsure.co.uk

Hamilton Barr
Tel (01483) 255666
Fax (01483) 255660
Email hamiltonbarr@compuserve.com
Web site www.hamiltonbarr.com

James Hampden
Tel (01530) 416369 **Fax** (01530) 412424

Email infor@jhampden.co.uk
Web site www.jameshampden.co.uk

PJ Hayman
Tel (0800) 614216 **Fax** (023) 9241 3416
Email travel.insurance.@pjhayman.com
Web site www.pjhayman.com

Liverpool Victoria
Tel (0800) 373905
Fax (01202) 502287
Web site www.liverpool/victoria.co.uk

Options
Tel (0870) 848 0870
Fax (01420) 566120
Web site www.optionsinsurance.co.uk

Primary Direct
Tel (0870) 444 3434
Fax (0870) 444 3436
Email info@primarydirect.com

Snowcard Insurance Services
Tel (01327) 262805 **Fax** (01327) 263227
Email enquiries@snowcard.co.uk
Web site www.snowcard.co.uk

Sportscover Direct
Tel (0117) 922 6222
Fax (0117) 922 1666
Email infor@sportscover.co.uk
Web site www.sportscover.co.uk

Touchline Travel Insurance
Tel (0800) 777143
Fax 020-8680 2769
Web site www.touchline.co.uk

Whiteley Insurance Consultants
Tel (01422) 348411
Fax (01422) 33035
Web site www.whiteley-insurance.co.uk

Worldwide Travel Insurance
Tel (01892) 833338 **Fax** (01892) 837744
Web site www.worldwideinsure.com

Reporting on the resorts

Use the structure set out below and send your reports to: Dept CD, Consumers' Association, FREEPOST, 2 Marylebone Road, London NW1 1YN. No stamp is needed. Please write, or preferably type, your reports clearly. A separate sheet must be used for each resort, however short the report. To use your reports we must have them by **30 April 2001**.

Keep sending us your reports; they are an invaluable contribution to the essence of the book. You can also contact us via electronic mail. Email address: goodskiandsnowguide@which.net

Writers of the most informative resort reports win a free copy of the next edition of the Guide.

Resort report checklist:

BASICS
Your name
Your address
Your skiing background (experience, competence)
Resort name/country
Date of visit
Tour operator
Hotel/chalet/apartment block in which you stayed

VERDICTS
Your reaction to our 'ticks' and 'crosses' verdicts on the resort

ACCESS
Remarks on airport transfer by coach or car to your resort, parking, rail connections if used

OPERATION OF LIFTS
New lifts, upgraded lifts, lift queues, lift passes (and where they cover) and other payment systems

OPERATION OF RUNS
Remarks on piste-marking, piste-grooming, piste closure, artificial snow, accuracy of resort piste-map, lift system. Name any favourite runs and interesting off-piste descents

MOUNTAIN RESTAURANTS
Specific named recommendations, comments on type and quality of food, prices

SKI SCHOOLS

Name the school on which you are commenting. Remarks on organisation, tuition, language, use of time, allocation of pupils to classes, group size, etc. Cover private lessons, guiding and special courses (including cost)

SNOWBOARDING

How user-friendly is the resort for snowboarders? Tuition, terrain, facilities, funparks

CHILDREN'S FACILITIES

Name the school, ski- and/or non-ski kindergarten on which you are commenting. Remarks on facilities, staff competence and attitude, language, approach to tuition, meals, hours and cost

LOCAL TRANSPORT

Transport within the resort: where you can and cannot get to, frequency, reliability, convenience, cost, crowding. Parking, value of having a car

SHOPPING

Food shops and supermarkets, including quality, service and prices. Range of other shops

NON-SKIING FACILITIES

Range, quality, convenience and price of non-skiing facilities; excursion possibilities

EATING OUT

Range and type of restaurant; specific recommendations with type of food, prices, atmosphere

APRÈS-SKI

Range, style and prices in bars, restaurants, discos; what happens in the resort after skiing until the small hours (recommendations essential)

ACCOMMODATION

Apartments, chalets or hotels (must be named). Advice on choice of location within the resort

PRICES

General observations on the cost of meals and drinks. Examples should include a beer, soft drink, house wine, cup of coffee, dish of the day

SUMMARY

What did you particularly like or dislike about the resort? What aspect of the resort came as a surprise (pleasant or otherwise)? Who does the resort suit? And who does it not suit? On the whole, do you regret choosing this resort, or would you go back there? If so, why?

Resort index